Stephen Parker
Peter Davies
Matthew Philpotts

The Modern Restoration

Re-thinking German Literary History 1930–1960

Walter de Gruyter · Berlin · New York

♾ Printed on acid-free paper which falls within the guidelines
of the ANSI to ensure permanence and durability.

Library of Congress Cataloging-in-Publication Data

Parker, Stephen (Stephen R.)
   The modern restoration : re-thinking German literary history
1930–1960 / by Stephen Parker, Peter Davies, Matthew Philpotts.
   p.   cm.
Includes bibliographical references and index.
ISBN 3-11-018113-4 (alk. paper)
   1. German literature – 20th century – History and criticism.
2. German literature – 20th century – Periodicals.   I. Davies,
Peter (Peter J.)   II. Philpotts, Matthew, 1973–   III. Title.
PT405.P3395 2003
830.9'0091–dc22
                                                    2004012558

ISBN 3-11-018113-4

Bibliographic information published by Die Deutsche Bibliothek

Die Deutsche Bibliothek lists this publication in the Deutsche Nationalbibliografie;
detailed bibliographic data is available in the Internet at <http://dnb.ddb.de>.

© Copyright 2004 by Walter de Gruyter GmbH & Co. KG, 10785 Berlin, Germany.
Printed in Germany
Printing and binding: Hubert & Co. GmbH & Co. KG, Göttingen
Cover design: Christopher Schneider, Berlin

Stephen Parker / Peter Davies / Matthew Philpotts
The Modern Restoration

W DE G

Foreword

This study is the product of a three-year, collaborative research project undertaken by colleagues from the University of Manchester and the University of Edinburgh with the generous support of the Arts and Humanities Research Board (AHRB). The origins of the project go back to my work as a doctoral student, when, following publications in the 1970s by Frank Trommler and Hans Dieter Schäfer, the issue of continuities in German literature across the political caesurae of 1933 and 1945 was, for the first time, the subject of serious debate. Throughout the 1980s and 1990s, the questions these issues were never far from my own research and from the projects undertaken by my research students at Manchester. Following the establishment of the AHRB, the opportunity arose to conceive projects on the scale that those questions demanded. I was fortunate to be working in the mid- to late 1990s with such talented young researchers as Peter Davies and Matthew Philpotts. It was a relatively easy task to form with them a team to tackle those issues afresh. And it has been a rare pleasure to develop our discussions in the manner that such a project requires and the AHRB's support has permitted. We should like to acknowledge the excellent support that we have received from librarians and archivists at the Academy of Arts and *Staatsbibliothek* in Berlin, and at the libraries of the Universities of Edinburgh, Manchester, Liverpool and Leeds. Research for the chapter on Johannes R. Becher was carried out under the terms of a Leverhulme Trust Special Research Fellowship. The chapter on Huchel benefited from a fellowship awarded by the John Rylands Research Institute, and the section on *Sinn und Form* from a fellowship awarded by the Alexander von Humboldt Foundation. We have tested our ideas in a number of forums. Our thanks go to colleagues whose stimulating suggestions have helped to shape our thinking. We are, however, particularly indebted to our good friend in Berlin, Justus Fetscher, who read our drafts and provided expert comment on them.

Stephen Parker, Manchester, March 2004.

Abbreviations

The following abbreviations are used throughout in the main body of the text:

Aufbau	*Aufbau: Kulturpolitische Monatsschrift*
DiR	*Das innere Reich: Zeitschrift für Dichtung, Kunst und deutsches Leben*
DlW	*Die literarische Welt: Unabhängiges Organ für das deutsche Schrifttum*
Kolonne	*Die Kolonne: Zeitschrift für Dichtung*
Lkv	*Die Linkskurve*
Merkur	*Merkur: Deutsche Zeitschrift für europäisches Denken*
MuW	*Maß und Wert: Zweimonatsschrift für freie deutsche Kultur*
Ruf (Munich)	*Der Ruf: Unabhängige Blätter der jungen Generation*
Ruf (US)	*Der Ruf: Zeitung der Deutschen Kriegsgefangenen in den USA*
SuF	*Sinn und Form: Beiträge zur Literatur*
Wort	*Das Wort: Literarische Monatsschrift*

BB Bertolt Brecht, *Werke: Große kommentierte Berliner und Frankfurter Ausgabe*, ed. by Werner Hecht, Jan Knopf, Werner Mittenzwei, and Klaus-Detlef Müller, 30 vols (Berlin and Weimar: Aufbau; Frankfurt a.M: Suhrkamp, 1988–1998)

GB Gottfried Benn, *Gesammelte Werke in der Fassung der Erstdrucke*, ed. by Bruno Hillebrand, 4 vols (Frankfurt a.M.: Fischer, 1982)

GE Günter Eich, *Gesammelte Werke in vier Bänden*, ed. by Karl Karst and Axel Vieregg, 4 vols (Frankfurt a.M.: Suhrkamp, 1991)

JRB Johannes R.Becher, *Gesammelte Werke*, 18 vols (Berlin and Weimar: Johannes-R.-Becher-Archiv der Akademie der Künste, 1966–1981)

PH Peter Huchel, *Gesammelte Werke*, ed. by Axel Vieregg, 2 vols (Frankfurt a.M.: Suhrkamp, 1984)

Contents

Introduction

This study was born out of a dissatisfaction with the capacity of existing accounts of twentieth-century German literature to provide an adequate underpinning for research and teaching. For decades, the reliance on the emotional force of key political date brackets, rather than on aesthetic criteria, has hampered the conceptualisation of German literary historiography. The latter have been subsumed within a political paradigm which, despite a measure of re-appraisal, not only continues to stress rupture at the expense of continuity but also to some extent replicates the ideological antagonisms and crass binary oppositions in the official discourse of the Nazi and Cold War years. The result has been that the developmental dynamics of German literature across the twentieth century, the mechanisms underlying these developments and, not least, the literariness of this literature has suffered some significant neglect. The present study has been undertaken with a view to initiating a corrective to conventional historiography. Without losing sight of political contexts, it pursues the investigation of literary continuities that cut across the political boundaries of 1933 and 1945.

That it is still necessary to undertake such a corrective is surprising given the research impetus which developed in German studies in the 1970s. The landmark *Germanistentag* in Munich in 1966, at which Eberhard Lämmert and Karl Otto Conrady called for a serious engagement with National Socialism, gave rise to concerted efforts to re-align the terms of German literary history in the mid-twentieth century.[1] The renewed emphasis on socio-political approaches to literary study helped to overcome the evasiveness of much post-war *Germanistik* on the subject of National Socialism: the construction of the 'Weimar Republic' as a literary-historical period, resting on the firm foundation of political and sociological models, provided a renewed impetus to the discussion of German literary culture in the mid-century. The 1933–1945 periodisation that emerged from this serious engagement with National Socialism proved immensely fruitful in the development of 'exile literature', 'inner emigration' and 'post-war literature' as key literary-historical categories, but the same engagement also gave rise to doubts about the usefulness of such political date-boundaries in accounts of literary culture. Two scholars in particular, Hans Dieter Schäfer and Frank

---

1   See Eberhard Lämmert, 'Germanistik: Eine deutsche Wissenschaft' and Carl Otto Conrady, 'Deutsche Literaturwissenschaft und Drittes Reich', in Benno von Wiese and Rudolf Henß (eds), *Nationalismus in Germanistik und Dichtung: Dokumentation des Germanistentages in München vom 17.–22. Oktober 1966* (Berlin: Schmidt, 1967), pp. 15–36 and pp. 37–60.

Trommler, who had worked on exile and 'inner emigrant' literature, sought in a number of essays to relativise the significance attributed to the political caesurae of 1933 and 1945 in accounts of German literary development, shifting the emphasis instead to 1930 and 1960 as the start and end points of a stylistically distinct literary period.[2] In Schäfer's words:

> Die z.T. emotionale, aber stets moralisierende Fixierung auf den Nationalsozialismus hatte bis dahin zu einer Überbetonung der Zäsuren von 1933 und 1945 geführt und eine literaturgeschichtlich differenzierte Darstellung der verschiedenen Zeitstile sowie die Bestimmung der wirklichen Epocheneinheit über diese Daten hinaus verhindert.[3]

Schäfer in particular, drawing on the methodologies developed by the social historians of the Bavaria Project around Martin Broszat and on the re-evaluation of the literary styles and genres of the period 1815–1848 undertaken by Friedrich Sengle, marked out the territory for a fundamental re-appraisal of the literary production of the 'restorative' middle decades of the twentieth century.[4] And yet, despite repeated acknowledgements of the significance of this work and no little constructive, and often provocative, criticism, no full-scale development of this field of study has been forthcoming in the intervening 25 years.

As such, the approach we are proposing retains its potential to challenge our assumptions about the literary production of the mid-twentieth century. Even today, it is difficult to escape the convenient and reassuring boundaries provided by political date brackets. In the periodisations which underpin literary histories and academic conferences, text books and university courses, it is the political paradigm which continues to hold sway; we continue to refer to the literature of the Weimar Republic or of the GDR, to exile literature and to the literature of inner emigration.[5] Alternatively, many accounts of twentieth-century German literary history remain wedded to a narrative which has cast avant-gardism as its hero and which is constructed around a dichotomy between modernist and anti-modernist forms of representation. Here, the 1930s, 1940s, and 1950s have a marginalised role to play, the 'dark decades' during which the privileged centre of modernism was smashed and suppressed by totalitarian ideology. Our aim in this book is to build on and develop the insights offered by the pioneering work of Schäfer and others, as a starting-point for a re-appraisal of these mid-decades of the twentieth century which is able to shed light on this perceived darkness. As

---

2   See Hans Dieter Schäfer, 'Zur Periodisierung der deutschen Literatur seit 1930' and Frank Trommler, 'Nachkriegsliteratur: Eine neue deutsche Literatur?', in Nicolas Born and Jürgen Manthey (eds), *Literaturmagazin 7: Nachkriegsliteratur* (Reinbek: Rowohlt, 1977), pp. 95–115 and pp. 167–86.

3   Schäfer, 'Periodisierung', p. 96.

4   See Martin Broszat, Elke Fröhlich, A. Grossmann (eds), *Bayern in der NS-Zeit*, 6 vols (Munich: Oldenbourg, 1977–1983) and Friedrich Sengle, *Biedermeierzeit: Deutsche Literatur im Spannungsfeld von Restauration und Revolution 1815–1848*, 3 vols (Stuttgart: Metzler, 1971–1980).

5   See, for example, Neil H. Donahue and Doris Kirchner (eds), *Flight of Fantasy: New perspectives on inner emigration in German literature 1933–1945* (New York: Berghahn, 2003).

we shall see, considering this period in its own right – in terms of a characteristic and shared set of aesthetic practices, assumptions, and discourses employed by writers, editors, and critics – illuminates processes of literary continuity and change which run across the twentieth century as a whole and which build up a more complete and differentiated picture of long-term cultural and literary development than has been permitted thus far. Before we are able to set out the precise nature of these defining characteristics, a more detailed consideration is necessary of the research put forward by Schäfer and Trommler, which we subsume under the label 'the 1930 paradigm' and in dialogue with which we have developed our own position.

The 1930 paradigm

A number of key arguments shape the 1930 paradigm as it is enunciated by Schäfer and Trommler. First and foremost, the posited 'restorative' period depends on a loosening of the causal ties between aesthetic and political developments, so that the apparent triumph of more conservative aesthetic tendencies in the German literature of the 1930s is not merely a reflection of the triumph of conservative political forces. As Schäfer writes in his periodisation essay:

> Unsere Zeit vergißt meistens, daß eines der Hauptziele der faschistischen Kultur-politik, nämlich die Identifikation der extremen Formzertrümmerung mit der Krise der Gesellschaft, damals in zahlreichen nichtnationalsozialistischen Kreisen erstaun-lich populär war. Die historischen Stile wie Romantik und Biedermeier, der Realismus des 19. Jahrhunderts und vor allem der Klassizismus gewannen auch als Ordnungs-faktoren überall an Boden, denn die Tendenz, in der Kunst Altes und Bewährtes wiederherzustellen, ist kein Ergebnis der Kulturpolitik Hitlers, sondern Produkt ein und derselben geschichtlichen Krise, die auch den Nationalsozialismus zum Sieg geführt hatte.[6]

As a consequence, the significance of the political date-boundaries of 1933 and 1945 is substantially relativised. Or as Trommler writes with reference to the post-1945 situation:

> Festzuhalten ist jedoch, daß die jungen Nachkriegsschriftsteller wie selbstverständlich einer Poetik folgten, die der überwiegende Teil des Bürgertums nicht erst 1945 und nicht erst 1933 als verbindlich akzeptiert hatte, sondern bereits vor 1933, als die Emigranten in Deutschland selbst noch hatten kämpfen können. Wo Hitler die physische Verfolgung einsetzen ließ, standen bereits vor 1933 Verbotstafeln der

---

6   Schäfer, 'Periodisierung', p. 98.

Republik gegen linksbürgerliche Publizisten und sozial engagierte Autoren. […] Die meisten Entscheidungen über diese Literatur [fielen] bereits vor 1933.[7]

In these accounts, the erosion of these political caesurae shifts attention away from 1933 and on to what Trommler terms 'jene Restauration, die sich Ende der zwanziger Jahre in vielen Bereichen anbahnte' and, in turn, to 'die Kontinuitäten im Zeitraum zwischen 1930 und 1960'.[8] In particular, Schäfer identifies a widespread sense of chaos, confusion, and impotence engendered by the economic and political crises of 1929–1932.[9] These crises are seen, against the backcloth of (post-)Expressionist experimentation which had run out of steam, to have been the catalysts for 'den Durchbruch einer breiten Revision der modernen Stile seit der Jahrhundertwende'. Characterised by 'einem Siegeszug metaphysicher Wertvorstellungen', and 'einer rasch anwachsenden Distanz zu geistigen und künstlerischen Experimenten', this cultural climate is seen to be confirmed or radicalised by the Nazi seizure of power in 1933. Significantly, however, it is not initiated by the horrors of the Third Reich. In Schäfer's words: 'Zweifellos verstärkten die Schrecken der Diktatur, die Not der Ausbürgerung und des Krieges die Restauration, doch die Krise von 1930 ist – übrigens auch international – das entscheidende Ereignis, das der antimodernen Bewegung die Bahn öffnete.'

Significantly, Schäfer and Trommler draw on comparable contemporary sources as attestations of the literary developments to which they refer. In particular, both make much of the nature poetry and literary programmatics of the *Kolonne* Circle of young writers in the journal of the same name between 1929 and 1932, such writers as Martin Raschke, Günter Eich and Peter Huchel providing an important strand of continuity across 1933 and/or 1945 as manifestations of an aesthetic approach which crosses conventional political and geographical boundaries. This approach is perceptible at 1930 amongst the politically committed writers of Left and Right, is manifested after 1933 amongst those who went into exile as well as those who remained in Germany, and persists into the Federal Republic and the GDR in the 1950s. As Trommler puts it, for example: 'Diese Wende – das sei hier vorweggenommen – blieb angesichts der kommunistischen Politik unter Stalin keineswegs ein bürgerliches Phänomen.'[10] Only after 1960 does Schäfer see renewed prosperity and optimism lifting the crisis consciousness of the mid-decades, a change represented in cultural terms by the rise of pop-art, by a re-appraisal of Dada and *Neue Sachlichkeit*, and by the arrival of a new literary generation. To quote Trommler

---

7   Frank Trommler, 'Emigration und Nachkriegsliteratur: Zum Problem der geschichtlichen Kontinuität', in Reinhold Grimm and Jost Hermand (eds), *Exil und innere Emigration: Third Wisconsin Workshop* (Frankfurt a.M.: Athenäum, 1972), pp. 173–97 (pp. 191–92).
8   Trommler, 'Emigration und Nachkriegsliteratur', p. 184 and p. 185.
9   Schäfer, 'Periodisierung', pp. 95–97.
10   Trommler, 'Emigration und Nachkriegsliteratur', p. 183.

again: 'Seit etwa 1960 bezieht sich die Literatur immer deutlicher auf eine Welt, in der der Zweite Weltkrieg nicht mehr alles überschattet. Die Wohlstandsgesellschaft ist etabliert [...]. Ausgedehnte Sprachexperimente laufen mit strengem ideologischem Engagement parallel, und beiden Tendenzen entspricht neuer Zweifel an den Aussagemöglichkeiten von Literatur.'[11]

The Trommler thesis: from *Sachlichkeit* to *Innerlichkeit*

If the Schäfer and Trommler accounts of the 1930 paradigm can be bracketed together in their broad outlines, and much critical literature has tended to conflate the two, a slightly more differentiated picture emerges if we seek to define the precise nature of the '1930 shift' which they seek to describe. Above all, we need to ask ourselves in what particular respects this development can be considered aesthetically 'conservative' or 'restorative'. As far as Trommler is concerned, the answer to this question lies in Herbert Ihering's 1930 essay, *Die getarnte Reaktion*, in which Trommler identifies the description of a common aesthetic approach which bridges differences in theme, form, and political views for a whole generation of writers:

> Sie haben Anteil an der Reaktion gegen die Literatur der Dokumentation, des Parteiengagements und der Massenagitation, jener Reaktion, die der Theaterkritiker Herbert Jhering 1930 ausführlich in ihrer Tendenz zum Individualismus, zur Idylle, zum Mythos diagnostizierte. Sie haben Anteil an einer zunehmend mythisch orientierten Konzeption der Wirklichkeit, einer Rückkehr zum Platonismus, wie er sich um die Jahrhundertwende bei Hofmannsthal, Rilke und anderen Dichtern manifestierte, die mit ihrer Literatur zu den Urbildern des Seins, zum Eigentlichen der Wirklichkeit vorzudringen suchten gegen Naturalismus und 'Oberflächen-Dokumentation' gewandt, im Bestreben, die Entfremdung des Ich von den Dingen zu erfassen und zu überwinden.[12]

Writing elsewhere of the absence of a new literary beginning at 1945, Trommler further clarifies his view of what the 1930 shift represents:

> Dazu gehörte, was die Literatur betraf, die Wiederaufnahme und teilweise Fortführung des um 1930 aufgehenden Rilke- und späteren Benn-Kults, die Weiterführung der um dieselbe Zeit von der Zeitschrift *Die Kolonne* geförderten Naturlyrik und der im *Inneren Reich* gefestigten Vorliebe für Gedicht und Metapher, sowie die Ablehnung einer der Neuen Sachlichkeit entsprechenden Reportageliteratur.[13]

Described explicitly as the 'Abkehr von Sachlichkeitsdichtung und sozialem Engagement' and manifested above all in the Benn and Rilke cults and in the literary journals *Die Kolonne* and *Das innere Reich*, the dynamic at the centre of

---

11 Frank Trommler, 'Der "Nullpunkt 1945" und seine Verbindlichkeit für die Literaturgeschichte', *Basis: Jahrbuch für deutsche Gegenwartsliteratur*, 1 (1970), 9–25 (p. 24).
12 Trommler, 'Nachkriegsliteratur: Eine neue deutsche Literatur?', p. 171.
13 Trommler, 'Emigration und Nachkriegsliteratur', p. 174. Subsequent reference, p. 185.

Trommler's version of the 1930 paradigm allows itself to be summarised in relatively straightforward fashion: it is in essence a shift in the dominant aesthetic category away from *Sachlichkeit* and towards *Innerlichkeit*.

This core conceptualisation runs through not only Trommler's own contributions to the field but also those of a trio of scholars working with Trommler in the United States in the late 1970s and early 1980s. Anton Kaes's documentation of Weimar literary manifestos, for example, clearly bears the hallmarks of Trommler's approach, both in the organisation and selection of material and in the methodology underpinning the editorial introduction. The contemporary essays cited by Trommler as the justification of his thesis all appear, as do programmatic statements published in *Die Kolonne*. As Kaes summarises: 'Im Literarischen setzte sich um 1930 ein im Formalen wie Thematischen rückwärtsgewandter Traditionalismus durch, der vor allem der Lyrik zugute kam.'[14] Two doctoral projects supervised by Trommler at the University of Pennsylvania in the 1970s confirm the fruitfulness of this approach. In his 1976 doctoral thesis and an essay of the following year, Joseph Dolan details the theory and practice of the avowedly apolitical stance of lyric inwardness maintained by the contributors to *Die Kolonne*.[15] The wider significance of this work lies in its capacity to reveal what is conventionally seen as a direct, post-1933 response to the Nazi dictatorship as a tendency with its roots located before that key political date: 'As a response to history [...] such inward leave-taking was not the original creation of the Third Reich but was already a well-defined phenomenon even in the decade preceding 1933.'[16] In Trommler's words:

> Spricht man von der inneren Emigration, sollte man demnach die Entwicklung um 1930 nicht übergehen. [...] Sowenig das literarische Phänomen der inneren Emigration an das Jahr 1933 gebunden ist, so wenig löste es sich 1945 abrupt auf, und man muß auch hinzufügen, daß es auch mit den geographischen Grenzen des Dritten Reiches nicht allein bestimmbar ist.[17]

In a similar vein, Jeanette Atkinson's 1978 dissertation focuses on the predominance of traditional forms and language in German poetry between 1930 and 1945, seeking to break down the boundaries between exile and inner-German literature by comparing for example, the work of Johannes R. Becher and Joseph Weinheber: 'The simple fact that both exiles and the writers who remained in Germany after the establishment of the Nazi regime wrote poetry in traditonal

---

14 Anton Kaes, *Weimarer Republik: Manifeste und Dokumente zur deutschen Literatur 1918–1933* (Stuttgart: Metzler, 1983), p. xlv.

15 Joseph P. Dolan, *Die Rolle der 'Kolonne' in der Entwicklung der modernen deutschen Naturlyrik* (Ann Arbor: Xerox University Microfilms, 1976); Joseph P. Dolan, 'The Theory and Practice of Apolitical Literature: *Die Kolonne* 1929–1932', *Studies in Twentieth-Century Literature*, 1 (1977), 157–71.

16 Dolan, 'The Theory and Practice of Apolitical Literature', p. 157.

17 Trommler, 'Nachkriegsliteratur: Eine neue deutsche Literatur?', p. 173.

forms indicates that the roots of this conservative, at times regressive, style lie farther back than 1933.'[18]

Re-thinking 1930: *Innerlichkeit* and *Sachlichkeit*

Clearly Schäfer's notion of an aesthetic 'restoration' initiated around 1930 is readily compatible with these approaches, and the essays collected in 1981 in *Das gespaltene Bewußtsein* serve to reinforce the point. In particular, the juxtaposition of essays on Oskar Loerke and Johannes R. Becher alongside a slightly amended version of his periodisation essay is a telling indicator of Schäfer's approach and of the proximity of that approach to that developed by Trommler, Dolan, and Atkinson.[19] Indeed, Schäfer's essay on Becher, first published in 1973, clearly anticipates Atkinson: 'Bechers Interesse am Sonett entspricht den Versuchen von Weinheber, Britting und vielen anderen, diese Form während der NS-Zeit zu beleben. Die feste Form erschien den Daheimgebliebenen als zuverlässiger Kordon vor dem anstürmenden Gefühl.'[20] As such, Schäfer founds his thesis on a comparable, widespread retreat into the security of aesthetic introspection. At the same time, Schäfer's more direct, detailed, and systematic account of the 1930 periodisation opens up a more complex conceptualisation of what constitutes the aesthetic conservatism of the period. Consider, for example, the aesthetic features which Schäfer lists as characteristic of the 1930s and 1940s:

1. Krisenbewußtsein.
2. Metaphysische Grundeinstellung; allgemeines Ordnungsdenken.
3. Leserorientierung.
4. Kritik an der Aufklärungstradition des Weimarer Staates.
5. Distanz zu aktuellen Stoffen; Bevorzugung historischer, mythischer oder landschaftlicher Themen.
6. Wiederaufleben von vormodernen Stilen (Realismus des 19. Jahrhunderts, Romantik, Klassik u.s.w.).
7. Rückgriff auf ältere Gattungsarten (Sonett, Ode, Elegie, Hymnus, Lied; Novellistik; historischer Roman, Dorfgeschichte u.s.w.).
8. Dominanz der Gebrauchsliteratur (Kriegsbericht, Reisebeschreibung, Tagebuch, Essay; Predigt, Legende; Rede, Tendenzdichtung).

---

18 Jeanette Atkinson, *Traditional Forms in German Poetry 1930–1945* (Ann Arbor: University Microfilms International, 1983), p. 3.
19 Hans Dieter Schäfer, 'Zur Periodisierung der deutschen Literatur seit 1930'; 'Oskar Loerke, "Winterliches Vogelfüttern"'; 'Johannes R. Becher im Exil', in Hans Dieter Schäfer, *Das gespaltene Bewußtsein: Über deutsche Kultur und Lebenswirklichkeit 1933–1945* (Munich: Hanser, 1981), pp. 55–71; pp. 91–95; pp. 96–106.
20 Schäfer, 'Becher im Exil', p. 101, first published as 'Stilgeschichtlicher Ort und historische Zeit in Johannes R. Bechers Exildichtungen', in Manfred Durzak (ed.), *Die deutsche Exilliteratur 1933–1945* (Stuttgart: Reclam, 1973), pp. 358–72.

9.   Erneuerung dualistischer Darbietungsweisen, wie z.B. Allegorie und Parabel.
10. Vordringen klassizistischer Stilnormen.[21]

The 1930 shift which Schäfer seeks to define is most accurately described as a dual turn: thematically a turn away from social and political engagement towards more metaphysical, historical and mythological concerns (points 2, 4, 5); and stylistically a turn away from experimentation towards traditional, conventional, and classical styles and forms (points 6, 7, 9). Both are undertaken against the background of a profound and consistent mood of crisis (point 1) which helps to define the period.

And yet, if these elements remain readily compatible with Trommler's thesis, Schäfer's eighth characteristic, 'Dominanz der Gebrauchsliteratur', sits rather less comfortably in a paradigm which is essentially defined as a turn towards *Innerlichkeit*. Expressly functional forms of literature and, above all, politically committed *Tendenzdichtung* are precisely the kind of *sachlich* writing, the rejection of which defines Trommler's thesis. Indeed, Schäfer too considers the programmatic rejection by the *Kolonne* Circle of *Neue Sachlichkeit* in the first issue of their journal as a paradigmatic manifestation of the 1930 shift. Clearly this generates a troubling tension, particularly for a thesis which seeks to account for a literary-historical period which, through the Third Reich and GDR, encompasses the unparalleled political instrumentalisation of German literature. For this reason, room must be made to accommodate functional writing of this nature, and in this respect an alternative perspective is offered by Schäfer's own 1974 essay, 'Naturdichtung und Neue Sachlichkeit'.[22] Here, away from the rhetorical excesses of the periodisation debates, Schäfer presents nature poetry and *Neue Sachlichkeit* not as the two elements which are so starkly contrasted in Trommler's model and, to a lesser degree, in his own periodisation essay, but rather as complementary developments of the mid- to late 1920s. Following this logic, the turn towards nature poetry symbolised by *Die Kolonne* at 1930 is less an abrupt rupture with *Neue Sachlichkeit* than an incremental development out of the documentary literature of the 1920s, and this insight provides us with a much more sophisticated means of conceptualising the 1930 paradigm. Indeed, if we ask ourselves what it is that the two apparent poles of nature poetry and documentary literature share, then we find ourselves an important step closer to understanding precisely what it is that characterises the prevailing literary mood of the mid-decades. Again, it is Schäfer's 1974 essay, we would argue, which provides the key here:

> Im Laufe der zwanziger Jahre kam es zu einer deutlichen Aufwertung der Zweckformen wie Lehrstück, Dokumentartheater, Reportage, historischer Roman,

21 Schäfer, 'Periodisierung', p. 103.
22 Hans Dieter Schäfer, 'Naturdichtung und Neue Sachlichkeit', in Wolfgang Rothe (ed.), *Die deutsche Literatur in der Weimarer Republik* (Stuttgart: Reclam, 1974), pp. 359–81. Subsequent reference, p. 359.

Satire, Feuilleton, Biographie, Memoiren usw. Der Zug zum Authentischen war bei
Konservativen wie Fortschrittlichen allgemein. Das empirisch gesammelte Wissen
erschien als das verläßlichste.

Both forms of writing provide in their different ways a much-needed source of
authenticity, reliability, and stability. In contrast to the formal and stylistic
experimentation of Expressionism, both forms of writing no longer seek to
problematise the relationships between reality and text and between text and
reader. Although profoundly different in terms of approach and in terms of
conventional notions of literary genre and creativity, the documentary writing of
Neue Sachlichkeit and the conventional lyric poetry of the post-1930 climate share
substantial common ground in terms of what we might call the 'stability of
meaning', and this is an insight which is central to our own conceptualisation of
the 1930 paradigm.

Reactions and responses

Schäfer's work has proved enormously influential, in particular in relation to the
Third Reich where it has begun to open up the sudy of literature and culture to
the kind of methodological approaches pioneered by the social historians of the
period.[23] In terms of the periodisation thesis itself, response has been rather more
mixed. On the one hand, some form of 1930–1960 periodisation continues to be
advanced as an antidote to the conventional political periodisation for twentieth-
century German lyric poetry. Both Leonard Olschner and Hermann Korte, for
example, deploy many of the same examples as Trommler and Schäfer in support
of a thesis which views the middle decades of the twentieth century as a
disatinctive period during which traditional forms of lyric poetry enjoyed a
notable resurgence.[24] On the other hand, a number of scholars addressing issues
of literary and cultural change at 1945 have expressed considerable doubts about
the value of the 1930 paradigm as it was defined by Schäfer in his 1977 essay. In
essence, these doubts surround two key elements. Firstly, the empirical basis of
the periodisation is perceived to be too narrow and Schäfer over-reliant on the
strand of continuity provided by his young 'non-Nazi' generation of writers.
Christoph Kleßmann, for instance, does not consider continuities in personnel to
be sufficient to constitute genuine literary-historical continuity:

---

23 See, for example, Wolfram Wessels, *Hörspiele im Dritten Reich: Zur Institutionen-, Theorie- und
    Literaturgeschichte* (Bonn: Bouvier, 1985), p. 12.
24 Leonard Olschner, 'Fractured Continuities: Pressures on lyrical tradition at mid-century', *German
    Studies Review*, 13 (1990), 417–40; Hermann Korte, 'Lyrik am Ende der Weimarer Republik', in
    Rolf Grimminger (ed.), *Hansers Sozialgeschichte der deutschen Literatur vom 16. Jahrhundert bis zur
    Gegenwart*, 12 vols, VIII: *Literatur der Weimarer Republik 1918–1933*, ed. by Bernhard Weyergraf
    (Munich: Hanser, 1995), pp. 601–35.

Auf diese Weise wird auch ein Bogen der Kontinuität über die Brüche von 1933 und
1945 hinweg geschlagen. So interessant die Befunde über Schriftsteller sein mögen,
die bereits im 'Dritten Reich' veröffentlichten, so wenig zwingend sind sie als
Argument für eine literaturgeschichtliche Kontinuität. [25]

Wiegand Lange is similarly sceptical: 'Das Verfahren überzeugt, solange es auf
bestimmte Stoffe, Autoren, Stile, Formen und genau abgegrenzte Zeiträume
beschränkt bleibt.' [26] Secondly, for all the importance of emphasising continuities
across moments of political rupture, Schäfer is seen to have gone too far in
erasing altogether the significance of 1933 and 1945. Consider once more
Kleßmann's observations:

> Bei aller Berechtigung, Kontinuitäten zu betonen, sollte daher nicht das tatsächliche
> Gewicht der Zäsur von 1945 verschoben werden. Der Maßstab können nicht die
> hochgespannten Erwartungen der kulturellen Elite der ersten Nachkriegsjahre sein,
> sondern das, was möglich war. [...] Insofern könnte man für eine 'Historisierung' der
> Kontinuitätsdiskussion plädieren, die zwar auf die zeitgenössische Metapher der
> 'Stunde Null' verzichtet, aber auch auf Kontinuitätsthesen, die kaum noch erkennen
> lassen, daß 1945 eine Epochenzäsur war, die in Deutschland vieles schlagartig
> veränderte.

In the polemical drive to counteract the ingrained reliance on 1933 and 1945, it
might be argued that Schäfer is guilty of having somewhat over-stated the case for
1930 and 1960.

Both of these principal objections to the 1930 thesis are also raised by Bernd
Hüppauf in what amounts to the most detailed and methodologically
sophisticated criticism of Schäfer's periodisation thesis. Indeed, in some respects
Hüppauf's verdict is damning:

> Der Versuch, die 'faschistische' von einer 'nicht-faschistischen', zwar während der
> Herrschaft des Faschismus produzierten, aber von ihm weitgehend unberührt
> gebliebenen Literatur zu trennen, und allein auf ihr die Epocheneinheit aufzubauen,
> ist wenig überzeugend. [27]

Above all, Hüppauf queries the inter-relationship between literary and political
criteria in determining that restorative epoch and the mechanisms of cultural
change which such an approach presupposes but fails to thematise explicitly:

> Das Staunen über eine Literatur, die den Zusammenbruch der sie tragenden
> Gesellschaft übersteht kann, läßt sich jedoch nicht durch die überzeugendste

---

25 Christoph Kleßmann, '"Das Haus wurde gebaut aus den Steinen, die vorhanden waren": Zur
    kulturgeschichtlichen Kontinuität nach 1945', *Tel Aviver Jahrbuch für deutsche Zeitgeschichte*, 29 (1990),
    159–77 (p. 171). Subsequent reference, p. 176.

26 Wiegand Lange, 'Die Schaubühne als politische Umerziehungsanstalt betrachtet: Theater in den
    Westzonen', in Jost Hermand, Helmut Peitsch, Klaus R. Scherpe (eds), *Nachkriegsliteratur in
    Westdeutschland 1945–49: Schreibweisen, Gattungen, Institutionen* (Berlin: Argument, 1983), pp. 6–35
    (pp. 8–9).

27 Bernd Hüppauf, 'Krise ohne Wandel: Die kulturelle Situation 1945–1949', in Bernd Hüppauf
    (ed.), *'Die Mühen der Ebenen': Kontinuität und Wandel in der deutschen Literatur und Gesellschaft 1945–
    1949* (Heidelberg: Winter, 1981), pp. 47–112 (p. 56). Subsequent reference, pp. 50–51.

Aufzählung personeller Identitäten oder programmatischer und formaler Kontinuitäten beruhigen. Wie läßt sich die Behauptung verstehen, daß die literarische
'Epocheneinheit' über den Zusammenbruch des gesellschaftlichen Kommunikations-
sytems, der Medien, aller Institutionen der Kulturpolitik, des Erziehungsystems, des
dominierenden Wertsystems hinwegreiche, da die Literatur doch Teil dieser
Strukturen und Institutionen ist?

In marking out 1930–1960 as a stylistically distinct literary period, Schäfer is seen
to assume an extreme autonomy of literary development as compared to political
development. From the over-privileging of political discontinuity at the expense
of the aesthetic continuity, Schäfer runs the risk of moving to the opposite
extreme where aesthetic and stylistic continuities are sufficient to constitute a
period irrespective of political ruptures, what Hüppauf refers to in the
introduction to his volume as the 'leicht kritisierbare[n] Rückzug auf rein
stilistisch literarische Kategorien'.[28] While Hüppaufs criticism overlooks Schäfer's
own explicit disclaimer – 'Um Mißverständnissen vorzubeugen: Es geht um keine
Beschreibung eines autonomen Stilwandels, sondern um die politisch-
ökonomische und geistesgeschichtliche Begründung einer neuen Literatur-
periode'[29] – Schäfer serves only to highlight here the tension in his work between
a periodisation seemingly founded on purely aesthetic criteria (at the expense of
the political) and his explicit recourse to socio-economic explanations for these
aesthetic manifestations of change. Leaving aside this explicit tension in the
conceptualisation of cause and effect, the revised emphasis on 1930 and 1960 as
turning-points, even as a perhaps understandable reaction against the perceived
over-emphasis on 1933 and 1945, risks itself substituting one fixed periodisation
for another.[30] In this sense, it can be argued with some justification that Schäfer's
periodisation obscures both the dynamics of cultural change within the posited
period of restoration and any continuities across the boundary dates of 1930 and
1960, much as a political periodisation obscures both continuities across 1933 and
1945 and cultural heterogeneity between those dates.

It is here that the value of Hüppaufs critique lies, since he is able to move
Schäfer's periodisation forward by proposing a model of cultural change which
seeks to overcome the conventional dichotomy between continuity and change,
thereby shifting the emphasis away from sudden ruptures in development, be they
related to literary (1930) or political (1933) factors:

> Will man die Periodisierung von der Gefahr des unfruchtbaren literarischen Kästchen-
> systems ebenso fernhalten wie von der, kulturelle Strukturen auf abhängige Variable
> der politischen, sozialen, ökonomischen Verhältnisse zu reduzieren, so wird sich die

---

28 Bernd Hüppauf, 'Einleitung: Schwierigkeiten mit der Nachkriegszeit', in Bernd Hüppauf (ed.) *Die
    Mühen der Ebenen': Kontinuität und Wandel in der deutschen Literatur und Gesellschaft 1945–1949*
    (Heidelberg: Winter, 1981), pp. 7–20 (p. 10).
29 Schäfer, 'Periodisierung', p. 96.
30 As do, for example, Wulf Koepke and Michael Winkler, *Deutschsprachige Exilliteratur: Studien zu
    ihrer Bestimmung im Kontext der Epoche 1930 bis 1960* (Bonn: Bouvier, 1984).

Untersuchung eher auf die komplexen Strukturen von Veränderungsprozessen als auf die Bestimmung von Periodenhomogenitäten richten. Die im konkreten Geschichtsprozeß sich aufbauenden Ansätze von Alternativen zum Bestehenden, deren Konstellationen, Veränderungen und Funktionen in der gesamt-gesellschaftlichen Entwicklung, können dabei von zentraler Bedeutung sein. Periodisierung wird dann eher zu einer Frage der Übergänge als der Abgrenzungen.[31]

Here, cultural development is perceived as an on-going process, analogous to social modernisation, where the on-going change only becomes perceptible at particular moments of accelerated development. Hüppauf introduces the notion of 'Kulturkrise' to describe those moments of accelerated cultural development where a shift in the on-going tendency may come about.[32] Hüppauf's notion of *Kulturkrise* serves two useful purposes. Firstly, Hüppauf provides a typology of these threshold moments which allows for their empirical study through a process of what Hüppauf terms 'reconstruction'. In particular, he highlights the active role played by participants in shaping cultural change at these moments through an intensification of debate in cultural journals, and lays down a series of factors which play a role in determining the outcome of these threshold moments. Secondly, the emphasis on a number of threshold moments, where cultural change may or may not be effected, relativises the significance of any one perceived moment of rupture. In this analysis, the period around 1930, the political break of 1933, the immediate post-war situation, and the mid-1960s all acquire an equal status on a continuum of cultural change, as threshold moments of accelerated cultural activity where at least the potential for change existed. As we intend to set out in the following section, Hüppauf's reconstruction method and his view of cultural change which seeks to escape the arbitrariness and artificiality of hard date boundaries are central planks of our own methodology.

The Modern Restoration

Our principal aim in this study is to demonstrate that during the 1930s, 1940s, and 1950s, for all its political dislocations, the German literary sphere is characterised by a common set of aesthetic concerns which, notwithstanding significant continuities both back into the 1920s and forward into the 1960s, are sufficient to distinguish these decades in their own right as a recognisable, discrete, and significant phase in the development of twentieth-century German literary history. More specifically, we have formulated our thesis as follows:

> The prevailing literary mood in the middle three decades of the twentieth century is characterised by a re-assertion of the conventional bourgeois institution of literature,

---

31   Hüppauf, 'Einleitung', pp. 15–16.
32   See Hüppauf, 'Krise ohne Wandel', pp. 59–82.

allied to a search for stability of meaning, against the background of successive and on-going crisis.

Deriving in part from the work of Schäfer and Trommler and synthesising the insights developed in the course of our own research, this concise definition does not seek to rigidly prescribe the nature of literary production in a homogenous period between 1930 and 1960. Rather, it seeks to distil at an ideal-typical level a common core of which the literary culture of these mid-decades, in all its plurality, is the concrete manifestation. Or, to put it another way, this definition seeks to specify the dominant aesthetic climate which shaped individual literary production and against which individual writers had to define themselves even if that self-definition entailed substantial negotiation and partial rejection. In this respect, we have identified three key elements – the conventional bourgeois institution of literature; stability of meaning; and crisis – the last of which also occupies a central position in Schäfer's thesis. Indeed, the very tangible sense of crisis which emerges above all from the literary journals of the period seems to transcend the successive crises of the Wall Street Crash, the Nazi seizure of power, exile and dictatorship, and the catastrophe of 1945. Often it is a longer-term narrative of crisis, a crisis of modernity, into which intellectuals position these individual crises in an attempt to come to terms with them. This sense of crisis is clearly not a new phenomenon at 1930, although thereafter it acquires a remarkable new intensity, but what is new and distinctive in the period we are analysing is the prevailing response to this crisis.

Our definition of this response as at once a re-assertion of the conventional bourgeois institution of literature and a search for stability of meaning seeks to escape the often unhelpful terminology of 'modernism' and 'anti-modernism'. Instead, and with a loosely conceived debt to structuralist literary history, we conceptualise the literary sphere in terms of contrasting poles of 'innovation' and 'conservation' operating along two tightly defined parameters.[33] The first of these is the institution of literature which entails particular notions of authorship, of the writing process, of literary product and genre. What we are seeking to describe in the mid-decades of the twentieth century is a re-assertion of conservation, rather than innovation, in these notions, so that the author begins to be perceived again as an inspired *Dichter*, an elitist, creative genius, rather than a mere *Schriftsteller* or *Journalist*. The conventional writing process which is re-asserted is the spontaneous, creative process of *Schöpfung* or *Gestaltung*, deriving from the inner self, rather than willed and functional writing which derives from superficial external factors. The book is re-asserted as the dominant literary product, re-establishing itself against new, mass-orientated media; quality and prestige emerge again as the dominant categories associated with this literary product. In genre terms, 1930 witnesses a retreat inside conventional, clearly demarcated genre

---

33 See Yuri Tynyanov, 'On Literary Evolution', in Ladislav Matejka and Krystyna Pomorska (eds), *Readings in Russian Poetics* (Cambridge, Mass.: MIT, 1971), pp. 66–81.

boundaries, typified above all by a resurgence in lyric poetry as the epitome of *Dichtung*. This conservation of conventional bourgeois notions of literature also extends to theme, so that the *innerlich*, *zeitfremd*, anti-modern, rural, and apolitical are typically favoured over the *sachlich*, *zeitnah*, pro-modern, urban, and political. Finally, the notion of the literary tradition has a key role to play here too, so that the importance of the German bourgeois tradition, epitomised of course by such figures as Goethe, Schiller, and Hölderlin is also re-asserted. A useful notion which informs our discussion in this regard is that of the 'Bildungsdialekt' deployed by Wolfgang Frühwald to describe the codification of this bourgeois tradition in the nineteenth century.[34] Against the background of crisis, this *Bildungsdialekt* is re-invoked as a source of authority and stability.

This in turn highlights the second parameter along which conservation comes to dominate after 1930, that is a stability of meaning, the search for which comes to constitute an overwhelmingly common gesture amongst German intellectuals. This stability typically assumes a clarity and certainty in the relationship between the writer and the real world depicted in the text and accessed by the reader. Rather than innovating in this relationship, seeking to disrupt and problematise meaning, the characteristic procedure after 1930 is an attempt, not always realised or realisable, to re-secure author-text and text-reader relationships. Of course, this is the procedure which we noted as the connection between *Neue Sachlichkeit* and *Naturdichtung*, and the framework which we have constructed here provides us with a means of conceptualising both the similarity and difference between these two forms of literature. Although both are manifestations of conservation along the parameter of meaning, *Neue Sachlichkeit* clearly constitutes radical innovation along our first parameter, the institution of literature, seeking to redefine conventional notions of authorship, creativity and the literary work, whereas nature poetry typically reinforces these notions. Through this contrast, it becomes clear that it is this *dual* 'conservation', both of the institution of literature and of a stability of meaning, which is the defining feature of the prevailing climate after 1930. This dual conservation is specifically what we mean when we describe the mid-decades of the twentieth century as aesthetically 'conservative' or 'restorative'.

Methodology

This identification of a common stability of meaning between *Neue Sachlichkeit* and the paradigmatic manifestations of our 1930 paradigm clearly points up the need to soften the initial date boundary of 1930, so that the mid-1920s become an

---

34 Wolfgang Frühwald, 'Büchmann und die Folgen: Zur sozialen Funktion des Bildungszitates in der deutschen Literatur des 19. Jahrhunderts', in Reinhart Koselleck (ed.), *Bildungsbürgertum im 19. Jahrhundert, Teil II: Bildungsgüter und Bildungswissen* (Stuttgart: Klett–Cotta, 1990), pp. 197–219.

important transitional phase in the development of the restorative dominant. It is here that Hüppauf's model of cultural change reinforces our conceptualisation of the literary developments we are describing. An understanding of literary-historical change predicated not on abrupt rupture, but on long-term continuities, on *Übergänge* rather than *Abgrenzungen*, opens up the date-boundaries 1930 and 1960, so that these dates can only ever be thought of as a convenient shorthand for on-going processes stretching back into the 1920s and forward into the 1960s. Equally, we do not seek to erase the importance of key political dates within the decades of modern restoration, but view them rather as threshold moments of potential cultural change. Around 1930, after 1933, and then in the years of occupation between 1945 and 1949, existing cultural assumptions were questioned and debated, typically through the forum of literary journals, with an intensity characteristic of what Hüppauf terms the *Kulturkrise*. As such, these threshold moments are susceptible to analysis by a method of synchronic 'reconstruction' through a corpus of literary journals which offers a snapshot of the prevailing literary and cultural climate and of the assumptions which were being contested and confirmed by intellectuals in these debates.[35]

For these reasons, the first part of this study is made up of a 'synchronic' analysis of three sets of literary journals as follows: (i) at 1930: *Die Kolonne*; *Die Linkskurve*; *Die literarische Welt*; (ii) 1933–1945: *Das innere Reich*; *Maß und Wert*; *Das Wort*; (iii) post-1945: *Der Ruf*; *Merkur*; *Sinn und Form*; *Aufbau*. Bound by the institutional circumstances of their foundation to precisely those political and social ruptures which shape the conventional writing of twentieth-century German literary history, these journals function at the same time as purveyors of cultural continuity, sometimes through shared personnel, but more often, and more importantly, through common aesthetic assumptions. In each case, the editors of these journals act as key figures, seeking to position the journals strategically within the public literary sphere through programmatic essays and editorials, while at the same time reflecting contemporary German literary life in the selection of contributions and reviews, albeit through the lens of a specific ideological and/or literary standpoint. The editorial programme and practice of these journals is analysed in the first three chapters of this study which provide a compelling picture of the establishment and persistence of the restorative mood from the late 1920s to the late 1950s, and of the manner in which literary journals not only reflect the prevailing literary climate but also act as agents in shaping that climate. In this way, we seek to avoid the methodological criticisms justifiably levelled at Schäfer and others. We do not seek to replace a politically determined periodisation with an analysis founded only on literary-immanent factors; nor do

---

35 This synchronic methodology finds notable parallels in a number of recent publications looking at these key years in the late 1920s: Ernest Wichner and Herbert Wiesner (eds), *1929 – Ein Jahr im Fokus der Zeit: Ausstellung des Literaturhauses Berlin* (Berlin: Literaturhaus Berlin, 2001); Hans Ulrich Gumbrecht, *1926: Ein Jahr am Rande der Zeit* (Frankfurt a.M.: Suhrkamp, 2001).

we seek to justify a thesis of continuity on a single literary grouping. Instead, the journal corpus provides sound empirical foundations across a range of ideological positions for an analysis which finds room for both socio-political and 'discourse-internal' factors, for both continuity and change between 1930 and 1960.

A diachronic dimension begins to emerge from these first three chapters through the inter-relationships between the historically specific sections of the journal corpus. This dimension is formalised in the second part of the sudy through the investigation of five writers – Gottfried Benn; Johannes R. Becher; Bertolt Brecht; Günter Eich; and Peter Huchel – all of whom were active from 1930 until at least the mid-1950s and who represent a band of stylistic orientations, from Expressionist to post-Expressionist, which undergo change within the restorative climate that prevailed from the late 1920s. As we have seen, Benn and Becher stand as central figures in the exisiting literature which advocates some form of 1930–1960 periodisation: Benn both as an authority for the young *Kolonne* writers and as a figure whose rehabilitation in the early 1950s is representative of cultural restoration in the West; Becher as a poet who undertook a turn towards traditional forms, as a founder of *Die Linkskurve* and *Sinn und Form*, and as one of the leading cultural politicians of German communism. Brecht, on the other hand, acts primarily as a counter-example in existing accounts of the 1930 paradigm, his reception dominated by an anti-restorative narrative which stretches all the way from his early interventions in Weimar literary culture to his unorthodox position within GDR cultural debates. Huchel and Eich, meanwhile, feature as representatives of Schäfer's young generation of post-Expressionist, 'non-Nazi' writers who made their mark in *Die Kolonne* at the key turning-point of 1930, remained active in the Third Reich, and who helped to shape the prevailing literary climate of the 1950s. These five writers represent a range of ideological and political trajectories too, from the Weimar Republic into the Third Reich or exile and then into the Federal Republic or the GDR.

Clearly, each methodological approach brings with it its own dangers, and, in a literary-historical study of this type which seeks to describe a common literary mood across historically, geographically, and ideologically disparate circum-stances, these dangers are particularly acute.[36] Any literary-historical corpus is necessarily selective, any claims to representativity necessarily subjective. In particular, attempts to generalise findings from the individual trajectories of a relatively small group of writers must remain fraught with difficulty. Can the very particular path of Brecht's intellectual and cultural development in the 1930s, 1940s, and 1950s, for example, really tell us anything about the development of other German writers in these decades? How can the fate of five male bourgeois writers, known principally for their lyric poetry, help our understanding of the

---

36 For an illuminating discussion of the methodological issues involved, see David Perkins, *Is Literary History Possible?* (Baltimore: Johns Hopkins University Press, 1992).

plurality of German literary production in the mid-twentieth century? These are legitimate concerns, but we seek to write with an awareness of the difficulties of an undertaking of this nature, seeking to do justice to the individual trajectories – personal, aesthetic and ideological – of our writers, rather than distorting them to fit a single, rigid pattern. For these reasons, we have not sought to impose a restrictive and uniform approach to the chapters on individual authors in the second part of the book. In each case, we have focused primarily on those aspects of the individual writer which most benefit from the fresh perspective provided by our overarching thesis concerning literary continuities in the mid-twentieth century. The first two author chapters focus on Benn and Becher, the two writers whose literary development furthest pre-dates the restorative turn of 1930: for Benn we offer a close reading of his poetry and prose with, and against, the restorative reception which has often dominated that literary practice; for Becher we trace his aesthetic development out of avant-gardism alongside his attempts to position his own fragile and fragmented self-image in a stable autobiographical narrative. In the next chapter, we examine Brecht's complex position in relation to our restorative thesis, looking forward at his poetry from the perspective of the radical positions he adopted in the 1920s and back at his use of literary institutions from the perspective of his increasingly prestigious institutional status in the 1950s. In the final two chapters we consider Eich and Huchel, the two writers whose initiation into the literary public sphere coincides most closely with the onset of our restorative mood. For both Eich and Huchel, the notion of the *Dichter* re-asserted so strongly at 1930 acts as a point of reference with which they seek to reconcile their literary output in the face of the compromises forced upon them by the political and social upheavals of these mid-decades of the twentieth century.

As such, we hope that these individual chapters, together with the sections on individual journals, will be of value to readers in isolation, as well as in the context of the study as a whole. It is in the same spirit that we have indicated the identity of the authors of each of these sections in the table of contents, in order to alert readers to differences in style and approach and also to highlight connections between sections written by the same individual. At the same time, this book remains a single, multi-authored volume, rather than a collection of individual essays. Each chapter derives from a closely collaborative research process, the insights offered inconceivable without those joint, and often divergent, perspectives. And ultimately, it is the coherence and persuasiveness of our central thesis, consistently challenged and re-formulated in that process, which lends this study its importance, we believe, in re-thinking the terms of twentieth-century German literary history.

Part One: Literary Journals

Literary Journals at 1930
Die Kolonne, Die Linkskurve, Die literarische Welt

Introduction

This first section of the journal corpus is conceived as a means of gauging the literary climate in Germany around 1930 through the examination of three contemporary literary journals. Two of these journals − *Die Kolonne: Zeitschrift für Dichtung*, the periodical of the *Kolonne* Circle of young nature poets published by Jess in Dresden; and *Die Linkskurve*, the Berlin-based official organ of the *Bund proletarisch-revolutionärer Schriftsteller* (BPRS) − feature prominently and consistently in existing accounts of the 1930 paradigm. As we have seen, in the approach first proposed by Frank Trommler and taken up by Anton Kaes, *Die Kolonne* functions as a paradigmatic example of the widespread shift towards *Innerlichkeit* perceptible in the final years of the Weimar Republic.[1] The journal plays a similar role in the more recent accounts provided by Olschner and Korte of the predominantly conservative direction of German lyric output in the late 1920s.[2] In both cases, the thesis of aesthetic conservatism is supported primarily through reference to programmatic essays published by Martin Raschke and Günter Eich. A connection between this *Kolonne* position and that of *Die Linkskurve* begins to be established by Atkinson and Korte, both of whom invoke the lyric production of Johannes R. Becher − president of the BPRS and editor of, and prominent contributor to, *Die Linkskurve* − as further evidence of the aesthetic conservatism of the German lyric across the middle decades of the twentieth century.[3] More

---

1   See Frank Trommler, 'Emigration und Nachkriegsliteratur: Zum Problem der geschichtlichen Kontinuität', in Reinhold Grimm and Jost Hermand (eds), *Exil und innere Emigration: Third Wisconsin Workshop* (Frankfurt a.M.: Athenäum, 1972), pp. 173–97; Anton Kaes, *Weimarer Republik: Manifeste und Dokumente zur deutschen Literatur 1918–1933* (Stuttgart: Metzler, 1983).

2   See Leonard Olschner, 'Fractured Continuities: Pressures on lyrical tradition at mid-century', *German Studies Review*, 13 (1990), 417−40; Hermann Korte, 'Lyrik am Ende der Weimarer Republik', in Rolf Grimminger (ed.), *Hansers Sozialgeschichte der deutschen Literatur vom 16. Jahrhundert bis zur Gegenwart*, 12 vols, VIII: *Literatur der Weimarer Republik 1918–1933*, ed. by Bernhard Weyergraf (Munich: Hanser, 1995), pp. 601−35.

3   Korte, pp. 617–18. See also Jeanette Atkinson, *Traditional Forms in German Poetry 1930–1945* (Ann Arbor: University Microfilms International, 1983).

directly, Helmut Kreuzer cites both Lukács in *Die Linkskurve* and Raschke in *Die Kolonne* as evidence of a final phase in Weimar culture between 1929 and 1933 whose dominant characteristic he identifies as 'ein Anwachsen des Traditionalismus im kulturellen Leben'.[4] Schäfer too makes explicit reference to *Die Kolonne* and *Die Linkskurve* in his periodisation essay. Writing of the influence *Die Kolonne* would exercise on German literary culture, for example, Schäfer writes as follows:

> Die Rolle der *Kolonne* kann dabei nicht hoch genug eingeschätzt werden. Auf das Bemühen des Kreises, moderne Stile abzumildern und eine metaphysich-meditative Literatur einzuschmelzen, ist schon vereinzelt hingewiesen worden, übersehen wurde bisher, daß auch nach Einstellung der Zeitschrift Ende 1932 der Freundeskreis erhalten blieb und daß einzelne Mitglieder wie Eich, Huchel, Lange und Elisabeth Langgässer unter der Diktatur ihre Konzeptionen konsequent weiterentwickelten.[5]

As far as *Die Linkskurve* is concerned, Schäfer maintains that the conservative aesthetic programme of the German Left, consolidated in the mid-1930s through the *Volksfront* initiatives and the Expressionism Debate, had already succeeded in asserting itself as dominant by 1932: 'Kennzeichnend für diese Entwicklung ist, daß Georg Lukács in der *Linkskurve* heftig die Reportageromane von Bredel und Ottwald [sic] angriff und nicht minder scharf mit Brechts Theorie des epischen Theaters ins Gericht ging.' In this way, establishing a substantial degree of congruence between the aesthetic programmes of *Die Kolonne* and *Die Linkskurve* proves to be central to existing accounts of the 1930 paradigm.

As such, the first task of this chapter must be to test these claims, made only on the basis of a small number of programmatic pieces, against the make-up of these journals as a whole. For this reason, a detailed examination of the editorial programme and practice of these two journals across their full publication run will constitute the first two sections of this chapter. These analyses will draw on the full range of contributions, from editorial statements to contemporary poetry and prose, from review articles to special editions, from the award of literary prizes to the selection of works from the tradition. The central question here is whether the explicit programme set out in editorials matches the implicit programme constituted by the selection and arrangement of other contributions. For *Die Kolonne*, important questions surround the way in which Raschke and his colleagues sought, in Schäfer's words, 'moderne Stile abzumildern' and the manner in which remnants of modernism lingered in their literary practice. Two aspects are of significance here in relation to what we have termed the search for stability of meaning: firstly the extent to which elements of *Neue Sachlichkeit*, notwithstanding its programmatic rejection by Raschke, continued to provide a

---

4   Helmut Kreuzer, 'Kultur und Gesellschaft in der Weimarer Republik: Ein Vortrag', in Helmut Kreuzer, *Aufklärung über Literatur: Ausgewählte Aufsätze*, 2 vols, I: *Epochen, Probleme, Tendenzen*, ed. by Peter Siebert, Rolf Bäumer, Georg Bollenbeck (Winter: Heidelberg, 1992), pp. 100–17 (p. 115).

5   Hans Dieter Schäfer, 'Zur Periodisierung der deutschen Literatur seit 1930', in Nicolas Born and Jürgen Manthey (eds), *Literaturmagazin 7: Nachkriegsliteratur* (Reinbek: Rowohlt, 1977), pp. 95–115 (p. 99). Subsequent reference, pp. 97–98.

source of that stability; and secondly the extent to which the more troubled nature of meaning exploited by the Expressionist poets continued to make its disruptive presence felt. As far as *Die Linkskurve* is concerned, attention must be focused on the emergence of Lukács's aesthetic position as dominant in the final phase of the journal's existence and above all the location of this aesthetic within the contradictory impulses which informed factional conflict in the BPRS. The Lukács pieces, published only in the last few months of the journal's existence, stand in direct opposition to the kind of proletarian writing the promotion of which had, at least in theory, been the journal's raison d'être since its foundation three years earlier. As such the *Linkskurve* programme picked out by proponents of a 1930 periodisation constitutes a shift from the editorial programme which held for the majority of the journal's existence. Disentangling the parameters on which this shift took place – ideological, factional, or aesthetic – in relation to contested definitions of proletarian writing and Marxist aesthetics is the central task in this context.

These observations highlight the importance of the differing institutional positions of these two journals, the influence of which suggests the aesthetic congruence constructed between *Die Kolonne* and *Die Linkskurve* to be potentially very fragile in nature. As the official organ of the BPRS, *Die Linkskurve* rested on institutional links to the KPD and also to Soviet cultural institutions such as the Russian Association of Proletarian Writers (RAPP). This self-definition of the journal, through not only its overt ideological function but also its very narrow party-political constituency, seems impossible to reconcile with the institutional context of *Die Kolonne*, the purely literary enterprise of an informal group of bourgeois nature poets supported by a small Dresden publishing house. Indeed, the political and social function of literature advocated by *Die Linkskurve*, together with its promotion of documentary and reportage literature from figures such as Egon Erwin Kisch and Hans Marchwitza, often set the journal in direct opposition to *Die Kolonne*. Symptomatic in this respect is the opening issue of *Die Kolonne* in which Raschke rejected a 'Sachlichkeit [...], die den Dichter zum Reporter erniedrigte und die Umgebung des proletarischen Menschen als Gefühlsstandard modernen Dichtens propagierte' (*Kolonne*, 1, 1) and in which Eich's pointedly refused 'auf mein "soziales Empfinden" hinzuweisen, selbst auf die Gefahr hin, die Sympathie von *Linksblättern* nicht zu erringen' (*Kolonne*, 1, 7). While Becher in the opening issue of *Die Linkskurve* was polemically rejecting the failure of bourgeois writers to engage with society – 'Wir umgeben uns nicht mit einem Dunst von Ewigkeit wie die bürgerlichen Literaten, die ausschließlich damit beschäftigt sind, die vorhandenen Tatsachen geistreich als Schicksal zu beschwatzen' (*Lkv*, 1.1, 1) – in *Die Kolonne* Eich was polemically rejecting any notion of social responsibility for the writer: 'Und Verantwortung vor der Zeit? Nicht im geringsten. Nur vor mir selber' (*Kolonne*, 1, 7). This direct antagonism between the journals within the ever radicalising political climate of the Weimar

Republic also finds its expression in the public controversies which surrounded
the figure of Gottfried Benn. Whereas Raschke attached an iconic status to Benn
on behalf of the *Kolonne* writers – 'Gottfried Benn sind auch wir' (*Kolonne*, 1, 35) –
it was an article in which Benn had been held up as 'das Beispiel des
unabhängigen und überlegenen Weltdichters' and Kisch and Becher written off as
'literarische Lieferanten politischer Propagandamaterialien' which earlier in 1929
had ended the collaboration of *Bund* members with Conrad Pohl on the editorial
board of *Die neue Bücherschau* and which continued to inform the content of *Die
Linkskurve* in its early issues.[6] As the radio discussion held between Benn and
Becher in 1930 makes clear, Becher's approach to literature, and by extension that
of *Die Linkskurve*, appears to have been diametrically opposed to that of Benn,
and by extension that of *Die Kolonne*.[7]

In this sense, there is a convincing logic to starting our examination of the
synchronic journal corpus with analyses of *Die Kolonne* and *Die Linkskurve*. On the
one hand, both journals have already been positioned within a restorative 1930
paradigm. Schäfer and others have identified specific contributions to the two
journals which act as evidence for their role in that shift. Furthermore, as small-
circulation, monthly journals representing narrow-interest literary groupings, the
two journals lend themselves to ready comparison. Even the publication runs of
the two journals coincide pointedly, not only with one another but also with the
crisis period 1929–1932 which Schäfer highlights as the catalyst for his shift. On
the other hand, attempts to find common ground between two such divergent
journals offer a rigorous test of Schäfer's thesis. In particular, it remains to be
seen how far the journals, and in particular *Die Linkskurve*, conform to the 1930
paradigm beyond the specific programmatic essays already picked out by Schäfer
and others. If evidence of restorative aesthetic programmes and practice can be
identified in these narrow-interest journals, further questions surround the
significance of that evidence within the context of what is posited to be a much
more wide-ranging cultural shift. Central here will be the possible causal factors in
the emergence of restorative aesthetics evinced by *Die Kolonne* and *Die Linkskurve*.
How far are these the product of narrow, journal-specific factors? How far the
product of more generalised factors which may have applicability to other literary
groupings? How far do the journals demonstrate evidence of a broader threshold
moment of cultural change, triggered either by socio-contextual factors – namely
the political and economic crises of 1929–1932 – or by what we have termed
discourse-internal factors?

It is here that the significance of the third journal in the corpus becomes
apparent. Willy Haas's Berlin literary weekly, *Die literarische Welt: Unabhängiges*

6   Max Herrmann-Neiße, 'Über Gottfried Benns Prosa', *Die Neue Bücherschau*, 7 (1929), 376.
7   See Johannes R. Becher and Gottfried Benn, 'Rundfunk-Gespräch', in Deutsche Akademie der
     Künste (ed.), *Zur Tradition der sozialistischen Literatur in Deutschland: Eine Auswahl von Dokumenten*
     (Aufbau: Berlin, 1967), pp. 148–52.

Organ für das deutsche Schrifttum, initially owned and published by Ernst Rowohlt, differs starkly from *Die Kolonne* and *Die Linkskurve* in terms of institutional factors such as circulation, frequency of publication, and breadth of contributions and contributors. While circulation of *Die Linkskurve* seems to have been somewhere between 3,500 and 5,000 copies per month and that of *Die Kolonne* smaller still, *Die literarische Welt* could claim a weekly circulation of around 20,000.[8] Similarly, while *Die Kolonne* and *Die Linkskurve* each drew on a relatively narrow and discrete base of largely unknown contributors, *Die literarische Welt*, confined neither by self-imposed ideological nor poetological restrictions, was able to call on a remarkable breadth of contributors, both German and international, both established names and emerging talents. As Haas himself stressed in retrospect, ideological diversity characterised his editorial practice: 'Die Vertreter aller geistigen Weltanschauungen veröffentlichten gelegentlich Artikel bei uns, von Ernst Jünger und den hervorragenden Jesuitenvätern Przywara und Muckermann bis zu dem führenden kommunistischen Dichter Johannes R. Becher.'[9] By the same token, Valentini identifies a breadth of opinion as the hallmark of Haas's editorial staff:

> Die Redaktion der Zeitschrift bestand aus einer Gruppe, um die größtmögliche Objektivität der Aussagen über die aktuellen Probleme voll und ganz zu wahren, um ein möglichst breit gefächertes Panorama zu erzielen, die verschiedenen Alternativen zur Diskussion zu stellen und das Urteil dem Leser selbst zu überlassen.[10]

Conceived as a weekly literary newspaper, *Die literarische Welt* sought to reflect contemporary literary life in Berlin, as Haas pursued what he later termed his 'Plan des Universalismus und, soweit es menschenmöglich war, völliger Objektivität'.[11] The journal functioned, in Valentini's words, as 'ein "objektiver" Zeuge (zumindest ihren Absichten nach) des kulturellen Lebens jener Epoche', and in this, its 'unbezweifelbaren repräsentativen Wert', *Die literarische Welt* contrasts starkly with *Die Kolonne* and *Die Linkskurve*.[12]

In this way, Willy Haas's journal is provides a representativity absent from *Die Kolonne* and *Die Linkskurve*, and this clear distinction from the narrow ideological agenda of the BPRS – Becher notably criticised Haas's editorial practice as a 'Standpunkt der Standpunktlosigkeit'[13] – and also from the narrow poetological agenda of the *Kolonne* Circle enables us to assign to *Die literarische Welt* a specific function within the 1930 journal corpus. As a relatively more objective

---

8   See Helga Gallas, *Marxistische Literaturtheorie: Kontroversen im Bund proletarisch-revolutionärer Schriftsteller* (Neuwied: Luchterhand, 1971), and Fritz Schlawe, *Literarische Zeitschriften 1910–1933* (Stuttgart: Metzler, 1962), p. 19.
9   Willy Haas, 'Nachwort', in Willy Haas (ed.), *Zeitgemäßes aus 'Der literarischen Welt'* (Stuttgart: Cotta, 1963), pp. 477–90 (p. 485).
10 Luisa Valentini, *Willy Haas: Der Zeuge einer Epoche* (Frankfurt a.M.: Lang, 1986), pp. 102–03.
11 Haas, 'Nachwort', p. 487.
12 Valentini, p. 12. Haas, 'Nachwort', p. 483.
13 Johannes R. Becher, 'Der tote Punkt: Ein Beitrag zur deutschen Literatur der Gegenwart', *Die rote Fahne*, 28 August 1926.

and wide-ranging reflection of German literary life, *Die literarische Welt* offers an invaluable source of empirical evidence to test the findings of the analyses of *Die Kolonne* and *Die Linkskurve*. Haas's journal is further set apart from the two other journals by the length of its publication run, from 1925–1933. While *Die Kolonne* and *Die Linksurve* were both founded in the immediate context of the crisis identified by Schäfer as the primary causal factor in his posited shift, the founding of Haas's journal in 1925 offers the opportunity to trace literary and cultural developments in Germany in the years in advance of the shocks of 1929–1930. Here, the possibility exists to study the effects of these shocks on what was an already established editorial practice and to construct a broader cultural context for the specific aesthetic programmes of *Die Kolonne* and *Die Linkskurve*. For these reasons, the third section of this chapter will submit *Die literarische Welt* to the same kind of detailed examination undertaken on *Die Linkskurve* and *Die Kolonne*. In this case, it will not only be the specific aesthetic programme promoted prescriptively by Haas through his journal which will be of interest, but also the capacity of the journal to reflect descriptively the dominant mood and trends in German literary life around 1930. Significantly, Haas's journal will also offer the opportunity to examine the development of restorative aesthetic strands in advance of 1930, so that developments around that key date can be considered as a question of continuity as much as one of change.

Die Kolonne

Opening programme

Following its launch in December 1929, *Die Kolonne* rapidly attracted a number of talented young authors, among whom Günter Eich and Peter Huchel would in the coming decades achieve the greatest prominence. In the final years of the Weimar Republic, they helped the journal to gain recognition for its contribution to intellectual life, particularly as a forum for new nature poetry.[14] The journal's title, certainly not directly militaristic, suggests solidarity amongst a group of individuals forming a united front against opposing forces. Martin Raschke was markedly more vigorous than his co-editor A. Artur Kuhnert in promoting a distinctive agenda that struck a chord with like-minded individuals. He positioned *Die Kolonne* as the arbiter of a new mood in the arts, restating the claims of tradition and drawing together intellectual currents of a broadly Romantic revival in order to challenge the, as he saw it, artistic orthodoxy of political 'progressives'

---

14   See Joseph P. Dolan, *Die Rolle der 'Kolonne' in der Entwicklung der modernen deutschen Naturlyrik* (Ann Arbor: Xerox University Microfilms, 1976). Dolan notes (p. 64) that of some 200 poems published in *Die Kolonne*, 150 are by contemporary poets and of those 80 are nature poems.

in the 1920s. The opening editorial sets out a number of programmatic concerns. Raschke and his collaborators amplify upon them throughout the journal's three-year existence by means of editorial comment and literary practice.[15] While indisputably a distinctive *Kolonne* programme emerges, it is, as would be expected, not without its tensions both as programme and in the relationship between programme and literary practice. Principal amongst the journal's concerns is the following view:

> Aber noch immer leben wir von Acker und Meer, und die Himmel, sie reichen auch über die Stadt. Noch immer lebt ein großer Teil der Menschen in ländlichen Verhältnissen, und es entspringt nicht müssiger Traditionsfreude, wenn ihm Regen und Kälte wichtiger sind als ein Dynamo, der nie das Korn reifte. (*Kolonne*, 1, 1)

This insistence on the continuing primacy of nature over the city as a site for the formation and regeneration of a human sensibility attuned to the eternal cycle of birth and death, reverses the hierarchy of values found in the two most significant artistic trends of recent decades within German modernism, Expressionism and *Neue Sachlichkeit*. If nature figures in Expressionism, it is, in Kurt Pinthus's words, 'ganz vermenscht'.[16] Expressionism is a soft target for Raschke's satire, stylistic gymnastics having fuelled its descent into self-parody. Gottfried Benn is judged one of the few not to have succumbed to 'billigen Expressionismen [...], für die ein Schornstein nicht stand, sondern steilte' (*Kolonne*, 1, 36).

The principal target for the journal's sustained polemic is, however, the immediately contemporary trend of *Neue Sachlichkeit*. From there, the attack is broadened out against 'progressive' forces in recent German literature, including not only writing of the Marxist Left, but also the socially critical depiction of the working-class urban milieu. The opening editorial attacks left-wing documentary writing and reportage about urban, working-class life promoted by journals such as *Die Linkskurve*, edited by Johannes R. Becher. Such publications are satirised on account of their ideology-driven aesthetic which claims to be 'im Besitz eines sauber ausgearbeiteten Zukunftsschemas' and which takes the 'proletarischen Menschen als Gefühlsstandard modernen Dichtens' (*Kolonne*, 1, 1). Raschke's mockery of a 'Sachlichkeit [...], die den Dichter zum Reporter erniedrigte' is echoed in subsequent issues, for example, in his laudatory review of Benn's prose: 'Mit einem Kniefall vor der Reportage schreien Pseudodichter allerorten das Dichten als leicht erlernbaren Beruf aus' (*Kolonne*, 1, 35). Under the pseudonym Otto Merz, Raschke attacks Ernst Glaeser's Marxist assumptions (*Kolonne*, 2, 46;

---

15 *Kolonne*, 1, 1. The opening editorial statement is unsigned but has generally been ascribed to Raschke in the light of the fact that the text draws heavily on his piece 'Dank eines Jungen an den alten Hamsun', which appeared in *Die literarische Welt* in August 1929 (*DlW*, 5.31, 5).

16 See Kurt Pinthus, 'Zuvor (Einleitung zur *Menschheitsdämmerung*) 1920', in Thomas Anz and Michael Stark (eds), *Expressionismus: Manifeste und Dokumente zur deutschen Literatur 1910–1920* (Stuttgart: Metzler, 1982), pp. 55–60 (p. 58).

3, 65). Eich, who under his own name and the pseudonym Georg Winter is the most frequent contributor after Raschke, curtly rejects left-wing assumptions:

> Ich […] werde immer darauf verzichten, auf mein 'soziales Empfinden' hinzuweisen, selbst auf die Gefahr hin, die Sympathie von Linksblättern nicht zu erringen und selbst auf die noch furchtbarere Gefahr hin, nicht für 'heutig' gehalten zu werden. Und Verantwortung vor der Zeit? Nicht im geringsten. Nur vor mir selber. (*Kolonne*, 1, 7)

Similarly, Raschke gives short shrift to poetry about working-class life as 'gereimte Reportagen zumeist […]. Die Berichte des Instituts für Konjunkturforschung übertreffen an politischer Wirksamkeit die gesamte proletarische Literatur, soweit sie auf eine politische Wirkung rechnet' (*Kolonne*, 2, 47–48).

Exceptionally, an early issue includes a piece of *neusachlich* theatre which treats illegal abortion, Willi Schäferdiek's *Das Wartezimmer*. However, it prompts decidedly mixed editorial feelings over the 'sentimental' treatment of a topic perceived to be of limited artistic value: 'Viel dienlicher der sozialen Entwicklung, viel mutiger wäre die bescheidene Mitteilung, wie man eine solche Tragik wie die Dargestellte vermeiden kann. Der beste Kampf gegen dieses Gesetz ist noch immer der: es überflüssig zu machen' (*Kolonne*, 1, 21–22). The editorial comment stops short of proposing measures to curb the masses' sexual excesses. In the second issue, a reader suggests that the journal's language indicates 'wohin der Kurs geht und wie weit Sie schon, bewußt oder unbewußt, korrumpiert sind. Solche "sozialbewußten" Dichter braucht die deutsche Bourgeoisie' (*Kolonne*, 1, 14). Where that reader senses a corrupt vision of the relationship between the artist and society, Raschke would see unflinching clarity of purpose in ensuring that art is not corrupted by political *Tendenz* in the representation of a social situation.

Essays and reviews of contemporary works flesh out the emerging pattern of the editor's aesthetic and political preferences. Like his political enemy, Georg Lukács, Raschke employs established categories of literary criticism rooted in psychological realism. He praises Rilke's 'Gestaltung' of 'das ganze Paris der Jahrhundertwende' through the inner life of his protagonist in *Malte Laurids Brigge* (*Kolonne*, 2, 34). For Raschke, *Malte* is the work of a true 'Dichter'. On the other hand, he derides the gimmickry of formal experimentation rife in the contemporary novel. He cites Döblin's *Berlin Alexanderplatz* in order to argue that it was 'keine revolutionäre Tat, Franz Biberkopf aus der Requisitenkammer des Naturalismus zu holen, ein wenig abzustauben und mit einer Balladenmoral auf der Stirne um den Alexanderplatz herum erneut in Marsch zu setzen' (*Kolonne*, 2, 33). Raschke and Eich see dangers of amoral relativism in Brecht, commenting sceptically on his achievement in an issue in which Brecht's nihilistic 'Großer Dankchoral' is juxtaposed with Christian Fürchtegott Gellert's 'Choral' in praise of God (*Kolonne*, 1, 65). Similarly, verses 7 and 8 from 'Vom armen B.B.' are juxtaposed with Gryphius's 'Es ist alles eitel', the former ending 'nach uns wird kommen: nichts Nennenswertes' and the latter 'Noch will, was ewig ist, kein einig Mensch betrachten' (*Kolonne*, 3, 25).

An essential point for Raschke is that even though Christian values have lost their power to bind together individual and society, the search for universal truths should not be abandoned. Eich and Raschke follow Benn and many others at that time in their belief that a biological teleology provides the bridge between the individual and the social whole, between the immediate present and the universal, a view clearly not shared by Brecht. Eich questions Brecht's capacity to emulate the achievements, in their time, of the great anarchic individualists Villon and Rimbaud: 'Denn die Lockung der Zivilisation scheint stärker zu sein, als die Stimme des Bluts' (*Kolonne*, 1, 65). Viewed in these terms, *Die Dreigroschenoper* is simply not a serious work of art (*Kolonne*, 2, 62). Brecht is too wedded to the trappings of contemporary civilisation to grasp the fundamental challenges that Raschke sees ahead: 'Die Gestalt der Zukunft wird davon abhängen, welchen Sinn (Sinn, sage ich) man dem entwurzelten Einzelleben wieder zu geben vermag. Hier kann kein Einzelner antworten. Hier muß ein Volk antworten' (*Kolonne*, 1, 60).

References to 'Blut' and 'Volk' have an ominous ring in the light of National Socialism. Yet Raschke and Eich's use of such terms does not warrant placing them in the *völkisch* literary camp. Indeed, there is ample evidence of Raschke's opposition to that camp. In the opening editorial, Raschke expresses his dissatisfaction with another contemporary fashion, the peasant novel predominantly cultivated by *völkisch* authors. His discussion of them demonstrates that, like many middle-class intellectuals at the time who draw their values from the established canon, he objects to the overtly political in art *per se*. The language that he uses about the peasant novel echoes his criticism of Schäferdiek's 'sentimental' *neusachlich* drama. In similar vein, he identifies an inauthentic strain in the peasant novel: 'Niemand will einer literarischen Mode das Wort reden, die sich mitten in einer Stadt ländlich gebärdet und nicht genug von einer Rückkehr zum Geheimnis sprechen kann' (*Kolonne*, 1, 1). Raschke develops his criticism of *völkisch* fashion in his essay 'Man trägt wieder Erde' (*Kolonne*, 2, 47–48), while in another, 'Die verratene Dichtung' (*Kolonne*, 2, 73), he claims, as Otto Merz, 'nichts [...] ist peinlicher als die Literarisierung des völkischen Fühlens'. And he continues: 'Ach, diese heute so beliebte Stimme der Landschaft, auch die wird von vielen Dichtern schon vom Blatt gesungen, von den Blättern des vorigen Jahrhunderts nach leicht angejahrten Melodien.' Like the politicised works of the Left, those of the *völkisch* Right are manifestations of an inauthentic plebeian culture, manufactured to woo the masses, in this case through pale imitations of familiar classics. Engaging quite unusually in direct political comment, Raschke argues that the calls from writers on the Right, among them Hanns Johst, for the dissolution of the Prussian *Landtag* show that there is no real difference between Nazi and Communist writers. Although those on the Right claim to preserve a traditional image of the poet, in reality it has been reduced to the mechanical and functional one of serving a political agenda.

Raschke's biological metaphysics: *Sachlichkeit* plus *Wunder*

Raschke constructs his intellectual position through reference not only to the biological but also to the metaphysical, forming what has been persuasively termed a 'biological metaphysics'.[17] This was not such a strange hybrid for those intellectuals who were seeking a renewal of meaning through an amalgam of ideas other than the economic materialism of Marxism or the Nazis' *völkisch* populism. Indeed, in the 1920s the search for a greater stability of meaning was manifesting itself in virtually all new artistic and intellectual groupings, however fraught that undertaking. Raschke and his fellow contributors, for the most part born between 1895 and 1905, whose seminal years of development coincided with the up-heavals in German life around the First World War, belong to a generation without the security of the Wilhelmine middle classes that had spawned the Expressionist rebellion. The artistic and intellectual nostrums of Expressionist aesthetic and political revolt are without appeal for Raschke and those of his generation who join him.

That is not to say that Raschke and his collaborators can be simply dismissed as 'anti-modernist' opponents to political and aesthetic modernists and avant-gardists. Rather, he questions some of the premises of modernism with arguments inconceivable without modernism, which has become a historical phenomenon with its own crises. In his search for a renewal of meaning, Raschke cites two contemporaries, Friedrich Markus Huebner and Edgar Dacqué (*Kolonne*, 1, 60). In the mid- to-late 1920s, both contributed to the revival of an essentially Romantic conception of the world, which sought to synthesise biology and metaphysics, science and aesthetics, through the observation of matter and the appreciation of form that, in the German tradition, ultimately draws upon Goethe. Huebner was the author of, among other things, works of popular astrophysics. In 1929 he published the neo-Romantic work *Zugang zur Welt: Magische Deutungen*, which at the very least parallels the articulation of a *Naturmagie* in the renewal of nature poetry in *Die Kolonne*. The paleontologist Dacqué's revival of Romantic natural philosophy in *Urwelt, Sage und Menschheit* of 1924 was accompanied by a rejection of Darwin's theory of evolution. In *Das Leben als Symbol: Metaphysik einer Entwicklungslehre* of 1928, Dacqué proposed a teleological theory of evolution, according to which human beings contain the ideal prototype

---

17 See Walther Killy, 'Martin Raschke', in Walther Killy (ed.), *Deutsche Biographische Enzyklopädie*, 12 vols (Munich: Saur, 1995–2000), VIII, p. 145: 'In mehreren Essays propagierte er eine an neoromantischen Idealen orientierte "biologische Metaphysik".'

and are simultaneously the end of all biological evolution. Dacqué's work prompts the following reflection from Raschke:

> Nur dann, wenn der Einzelne sich als Gleichnis des Ganzen begreifen lernt und sich derart rettet aus seiner erdrückenden Isolierung in das Allgemeine, wenn der Mensch im Sinne Dacqués sein Leben als Symbol zu verstehen sucht und damit alle Unterschiede innerhalb der Welt nur zu Unterschieden zwischen Intensitäten werden, kann es gelingen, die Stagnation in einer gültigen Form zu überwinden. (*Kolonne*, 1, 60)

With its insistence on the continuing relevance of metaphysics, the opening editorial reveals Raschke's indebtedness to the Romantic revival. But it also shows that his search for universal truths was by no means divorced from the 1920s' emphasis on 'Sachlichkeit', if not the predominantly anti-metaphysical attitude of *Neue Sachlichkeit*:

> Wer nur einmal in der Zeitlupe sich entfaltende Blumen sehen durfte, wird hinfort hinterlassen, Wunder und Sachlichkeit deutlich gegeneinander abzugrenzen. So kann auch im Bereich der Dichtung ein Wille zur Sachlichkeit nur dann Berechtigung erlangen, wenn er nicht von Unvermögen, sondern durch die Furcht bedingt wurde, mit allzuviel Worten das Wunderbare zu verdecken. (*Kolonne*, 1, 1)

The emphasis on *Sachlichkeit* and conciseness is further evidence of a post-Expressionist sensibility mistrustful not only of rhetorical excess but also of the ritualised disruption of subject-object relations in Expressionism and Dadaism. Rilke's subtle probing of the world of objects through refined subjectivity in poems such as 'Wendung' (*Kolonne*, 1, 60) is much more congenial.

Sachlichkeit thus remains a key category, when in 1929 Raschke articulates his programme for like-minded young artists. The shift from the urban to the natural world makes perfect sense for those who had experienced the cult of nature in the *Jugendbewegung*, nature providing a more attractive and seemingly more stable alternative to the chaos of social and economic life. Raschke, the follower of Benn and also of Nietzsche, undertakes a revalorisation of *Sachlichkeit*. Not only does he remove the term from the urban and social context and align it with the precise observation of the natural world, a phenomenon that can be observed in the works of other authors from the late 1920s not directly associated with *Die Kolonne*.[18] What is more, in his combination of 'Sachlichkeit' with 'Wunder', he follows the synthesising vision of Dacqué and Huebner, who seek to overcome the conventional opposition between the rational and the non-rational. Raschke was by no means isolated in his espousal of a 'biological metaphysics', which he buttressed through the discussion of further scientific material. *Die Kolonne* reproduces photographs from Robert Henseling's *Der neu entdeckte Himmel*, a work

---

18 For a discussion of scientific work in *Die Kolonne* see Dolan, pp. 106–17. For a discussion of literary works that in the late 1920s deviated from the norms of *Neue Sachlichkeit* in their treatment of nature, including work by Döblin, Jahnn, Lehmann and Loerke, see Hans Dieter Schäfer, 'Naturdichtung und Neue Sachlichkeit', in Wolfgang Rothe (ed.), *Die deutsche Literatur in der Weimarer Republik* (Stuttgart: Reclam, 1974), pp. 359–81 (p. 375). None of these writers figure in *Die Kolonne*, although Lehmann and Loerke were both admired by contributors to the journal.

of astrophysics, and from Ernst Fuhrmann's *Die Pflanze als Lebewesen*. The latter work is reviewed by Peter Anders, who follows Fuhrmann and Dacqué in viewing all material things as analogous: 'Steine, Pflanzen und Tiere stehen unter dem gleichen Gesetze des Lebens, dessen Gleichnisse wir alle sind. Alles ist sich im Fernen einig, wenn es sich auch vor unseren Augen trennt zu verschiedenen Erscheinungen' (*Kolonne*, 2, 42). Anders cites Goethe's 'Die Metamorphose der Pflanzen' to demonstrate the fundamental compatibility between Fuhrmann's project and the work of the figure in the German tradition who, beyond all others, embodies the synthesis of science and poetry through his observation of nature.

Goethe: Raschke's *Bildungsdialekt*

For Raschke, like so many other German intellectuals schooled in the traditions of German culture, Goethe is the key figure the *Bildungsdialekt* by means of which Raschke articulates his value system. The holistic view of all organic life is developed by Raschke with quite deliberate echoes of Goethe. In his essay 'Reisen des Auges', for example, Raschke calls for a detailed, alert and empathetic perception of botanical phenomena in order to recover the sense of wonder that nature can awaken in the beholder:

> Wer nicht die Schönheit eines Baumes liebend begreift, nicht mit wachen Augen die dunklere oder hellere Tönung der Ansatzstellen von Blütenblättern, wer nicht gespannt das Wässrigwerden und langsame Umsinken einer Hyazinthe verfolgen kann, […] wer diese Aufmerksamkeit gegenüber dem Kleinen nicht besitzt, wird auch im Großen nicht zu erleben vermögen. (*Kolonne*, 2, 13)

Goethe is prominent as the journal substantiates its synthesis of science and nature poetry through the reproduction of further works from the tradition. Goethe's 'Über die Natur' opens the double issue 4/5 in year one that establishes *Die Kolonne* as more than a mere *Flugblatt*. 'Über den Granit' follows (*Kolonne*, 2, 29). Goethe is joined by a number of canonical poets whose treatment of nature is accorded a strategic position. They include Eichendorff, Mörike and Hölderlin. Issue six in 1931 contains a selection of Brockes's *Vornehmste Gedichte aus dem irdischen Vergnügen in Gott*. Brockes's significance for *Die Kolonne* is underscored in the editorial comment: 'Ein unerschöpfbares Wunder ist ihm die Welt, und dem Dichter bleibt nichts, als in möglichst genauen Beschreibungen ihren Reichtum zu erfassen' (*Kolonne*, 2, 65).

Brockes provides a point of reference for the discussion in that same issue of two contemporary works, Johannes R. Becher's Marxist epic, *Der Große Plan*, and Benn's response, *Das Unaufhörliche*, composed for Paul Hindemith. The confront-ations between Becher and Benn, representative figures of the Left and the Right, fuelled some of the most explosive debates in literary journals during the final years of the Weimar Republic. Becher's work is the target for a familiar polemic. Goethe's authority is invoked – 'es bildet | nur das Leben den Mann, und wenig bedeuten die Worte' – to introduce the discussion. A section of the epic, 'Gesang der Kommune "Internationale"', is reproduced, which includes lines such as the following: 'Gebt dem Wind den Befehl, | Kräftig die Bäume zu schütteln – | Großes Äpfelfallen' and 'Als der Mensch die Knechtschaft abtat, | Wurde frei | Auch die Erde' (*Kolonne*, 2, 69). The determinist claims of Becher's 'scientific' Marxism are called into question through a typical editorial juxtaposition with a short newspaper report that, again typically, presents contemporary scientific theory, namely Heisenberg's Uncertainty Principle of 1927. Fuelling that strong trend towards metaphysical speculation among the scientific community that, as we have seen, impacted more widely on intellectual life, Heisenberg maintains that either the position or the momentum of a particle in motion can be determined with precision, but not both at once. For Raschke, who is joined in his criticism of Becher by his friends Horst Lange and Eich, Marxist economics has drained the relationship between the individual and the people of its earlier, binding, metaphysical quality. Raschke's position is that it is the task of the intellectual is to address the need to re-establish that relationship, the first step towards repairing the cracks that had opened so alarmingly in contemporary life.

Benn is seen as virtually alone amongst contemporary artists in understanding the nature of the task. His iconic status for *Die Kolonne* is spelt out in Raschke's essay on *Das Unaufhörliche*. In contrast to the ready optimism that flows from Becher's ideological premiss, *Das Unaufhörliche* depicts a universal human condition of suffering that is defined through the eternal cycle of birth and death, with particular emphasis on the problem of death. Benn's penetrating and wholly unsentimental analysis of the human condition devoid of religious consolation is placed by Raschke in a lineage of writers and artists, including Villon, Brueghel, Hofmannswaldau, Savonarola, Brockes, Goethe, and, now, Elisabeth Langgässer, who have struggled with the problem of death in exemplary fashion. This emerges as the major theme for the whole issue and the platform for quite rare, direct comment on the journal's stance towards the crisis gripping German life:

> Als die Aufklärung unsere Welt die beste aller möglichen Welten nannte, schrieb Voltaire seinen *Candide*, eine Attacke gegen diese logisch erschlichenen Glücksgefühle, Schopenhauer antwortete Hegel, und der billige Optimismus marxistischer Utopisten endete im Gelächter Nietzsches. War es nicht immer der Weg des europäischen Geistes, in stetem Wandel auf Optimismus tragisch zu antworten, und selbst die heiteren Gefühle Griechenlands, spielten sie nicht über einem tragischen Grund? Und nun die Jetztzeit und ihre Sehnsucht nach dem happy end, gläubig an die Hygiene, an die Segnungen der Technik und an die unbegrenzten Möglichkeiten einer individual-psychologischen Pädagogik; fast drohte es wiederum, daß wir für immer aus einem tieferen Wissen entwurzelt wurden, und wieder hören wir Stimmen der Umkehr, wie sie immer laut wurden, wenn sich das europäische Denken in einer billigen Wohnung genügsam einrichten wollte. (*Kolonne*, 2, 63)

Becher and Brecht are the heirs to such naive optimism, which it falls to Benn to refute. Raschke's language, like Benn's own, reveals familiar anxieties amongst early twetieth-century European elites in the face of what they viewed as the decadence spawned by 'progress': 'Die weißen Völker scheinen sich in den Gebirgen ihrer Wünsche verstiegen zu haben, und sie erinnern sich nun in ihren Besten an die Kindheit, wo sie noch angstlos im Schoße der Mythen ruhten' (*Kolonne*, 2, 62). In the German tradition, it is again Goethe who stands out for his capacity to confront the problems of existence, synthesising life and death within a vision that lends them equal weighting: 'Gestrost! Das Unvergängliche, | es ist das ewige Gesetz, | wonach die Ros' und Lilie blüht' (*Kolonne*, 2, 63). In the present circumstances, Benn cannot muster that Goethean balance and Goethe's emphasis on creativity, since he is responding to 'Gegner im abschätzigen Sinne, [...] alberne Optimisten, Taschenspieler des Werdens, [...] Verfasser von Dreigroschenopern, [...] pathetische Ingenieure aus expressionistischen Dramen' (*Kolonne*, 2, 62). His recovery of feelings that are lost on such contemporaries occasions his pre-occupation with death. Mildly critical of Benn's over-estimation of the strength of his opponents' position, Raschke nonetheless welcomes the corrective that Benn provides through his insistence that human existence is at bottom tragic and his insight that reaction is a necessary and inevitable corrective to a naive belief in social progress.

In Raschke's eyes, the liberal democracy of the Weimar Republic is a prime example of such naive optimism that triggers an inevitable political reaction. In September 1930, immediately after the Nazis' dramatic electoral success, Raschke, using the pseudonym Otto Merz, sarcastically dismisses Thomas Mann's plea for liberal, republican values: 'Wer wünschte nicht, wie Thomas Mann in seiner Rede an die Jugend, daß der Liberalismus der Retter der Welt sein würde, das große Verstehen und nicht der Terror einer gewillten Minderheit!' (*Kolonne*, 1, 48) For Raschke, the evidence stacks up overwhelmingly against a liberalism that has bred mass unemployment and a culture rotten to the core. The army of the poor would have nothing to say to Mann's dictums such as, 'ich glaube, daß der Liberalismus der Retter der Welt sein wird und nicht die Entschlossenheit'. Resolute action by a minority that does not hold back from terror will allow essential cultural values to re-emerge:

> Mag es auch so sein, wie es Thomas Mann ausspricht, daß in Deutschland allmählich sich zwei Parteien bilden, die des Geistes, ewig in der Minderheit, und die der Geistesfeindlichkeit. Wie wollen deshalb nicht um die Dauer unserer abendländischen Kultur bangen. Wir wollen glauben, daß das Dasein aller Werte, soweit sie solche sind, tiefer verankert ist als in dem vagen Geschehen der Tage. Was verloren gehen kann, soll verloren gehen. Es hat kein Recht auf Dasein.

Raschke articulates an understanding of the crisis besetting Germany which shows a clear affinity with fascism, for all his criticisms of popular, *völkisch* literary fashion: 'Es sind heute Fragen gestellt, die man nicht mehr mit Klugheit und Logik beantworten kann. Wir sollen nicht zu antworten versuchen, wo nur die

Zeit, ein Volk oder ein Messias antworten kann.' Even, or perhaps better, especially at this juncture, Raschke invokes the authority of Goethe in the struggle against Mann and his liberal friends: 'Im Innersten ist uns Goethe, der Kleist unerbittlich ablehnte und so dessen Schicksal mitbereiten half, sympathischer als euer grenzenloses Verstehen. Er war Stein, an ihm konnte man wenigstens zerbrechen.' The uses of Goethe are manifold within Raschke's *Bildungsdialekt*.

Notions of poetry: bourgeois traditions vs the authentic peasant voice

Similarly, while Raschke dismisses the sentimentality and inauthenticity of *völkisch* literary fashion, he admires the robust masculinity of a number of authors who treat rural life in a popular, stylistically conservative manner. In particular, he exempts from his criticisms the Austrian contributors to *Die Kolonne*, Richard Billinger, Karl-Heinz Waggerl and Guido Zernatto. All three figure prominently in the first, predominantly Austrian, issue in 1931, Waggerl with 'Die Entfesselten', an awe-struck piece on drunken violence in village life. Zernatto is promoted strongly through the award of the first *Kolonne* prize for poetry. Raschke acknowledges that Billinger is 'eine jedem Experiment verschlossene Erscheinung', yet his veneration of the earth embraces 'panische und kirchliche Elemente' and 'es muß darum für zukünftig erachtet werden, daß jemand wieder so einfach zu dichten wagt, mag er dabei auch oft in die Nähe schon bekannter Melodien geraten' (*Kolonne*, 1, 22). While the combination of such melodies with an overtly political message warrants the dismissal of *völkisch* authors, Billinger's new simplicity, blended with a metaphysical dimension, earns Raschke's admiration by virtue of the muscular authenticity and independence that this kindred spirit exudes: 'Man spürt Atem und Faust eines Kerls; das macht uns dankbar.' Similarly, Zernatto stands out as a 'character' whose affinity is with Billinger rather than Werfel and whose independent creativity distinguishes him from others vying for the *Kolonne* prize. These include a number of women, who are said to be much more reliant on existing literary models, and countless Rilke epigones, as well as peddlers of Marxist 'Tendenz' and of false religiosity. Echoing Raschke's praise of Billinger, Hermann Kasack stresses Zernatto's intimate understanding of nature and peasant life conveyed simply, though not wholly conventionally, in a 'Milieugestaltung, die etwas Einmaliges und Unwiderholbares [sic] festhalten will' (*Kolonne*, 1, 39). One poem chosen for publication is 'Erste Schlachtung', in which the 'I' is initiated into the life and customs of peasant farming through slaughtering his first sow. The poem includes the following lines characteristic of Zernatto's verse:

Fester mußten alle halten,
denn das Tier riß wild um sich.
Nocheinmal nahm ich das Messer

zielte schnell und traf es besser
und der Vater lobte mich. (*Kolonne*, 1, 40)

Eich, too, lends his support, claiming, not wholly convincingly: 'Zernatto ist kein
so begrenztes Talent, wie es zunächst scheint [...] schon spürt man das in
manchen Gedichten, die aus der ländlichen Begrenzung in die Weite des eigenen
Ichs vorstoßen' (*Kolonne*, 2, 11). This defensiveness can be readily attributed to the
fact that quite a lot of material published in *Die Kolonne* does not in fact differ
significantly from Zernatto's work. Eberhard Meckel's Alemannic dialect poetry,
included in the 'Austrian' issue, is a case in point. 'Das Erbe', for example, begins:

Do isch en Acher
Und do isch e Pflueg.
Nimm nochne Sech vor d' Schor,
Wenns nüt dur de Bode goht,
Spann nochne Roß davor,
Wenns ain nüt cha un stoht. (*Kolonne*, 2, 8)

The dialect colour apparently guarantees authenticity. There is another side to
Meckel's poetry, the reverential imitation of Goethe. It can be seen in the
publication of Meckel's 'Die große Wolke' immediately after Goethe's 'Über den
Granit' in issue 3 of year 2.

Meckel's work illustrates two variations on the problem of 'fogeyism' facing a
conservative undertaking like *Die Kolonne*. Firstly, the return to tradition proves
overpowering for the less gifted, whose work is nonetheless a welcome
contribution to the re-establishment of traditional forms after avant-gardist
excess. In addition, what sophisticated urban intellectuals like Raschke, Eich and
Kasack view as unadorned authenticity and simplicity in the treatment of nature
and peasant life is welcomed by them as a contribution on a popular level to the
conservative renewal of literary culture, but this accomplishment can only be
lauded if – notwithstanding comments on the inauthenticity of *völkisch* authors
and those of the Left – a blind eye is turned to concerns about conventional style.

Raschke is otherwise quick to voice such concerns in his literary judgements
that reveal a fastidious elitism, in which the lone artist figure assumes the mantle
of the Messiah. The editorial 'Über die Aufgabe der *Kolonne*' is perhaps the
clearest articulation of such a position built around the notion of stylistic self-
consciousness and the allegorical significance of the great artist for the people.
The piece, echoing Raschke on Dacqué, spells out that the desired sophistication
can only be achieved through the consciousness of 'der schöpferische Einzelne
als ein Gleichnis seiner Zeit und der Zukunft in ihr [...], der scheinbar ein-
siedlerhaft in der Wüste lebt' (*Kolonne*, 3, 32). The Nietzschean imagery of the
heroic individual engaged in his lonely quest to the ultimate benefit of his people
points to an affinity with writers who seek solutions to the collapse of traditional
social and religious values through aesthetic experience. For Raschke, amongst
contemporary artists, only Rilke and Benn have fully understood their situation.
Three poems by Rilke appear, 'Wendung' (*Kolonne*, 1, 60), an extract from the

ninth Duino Elegy (*Kolonne*, 2, 25) and 'Einheit des Lebens' (*Kolonne*, 3, 22). All are statements of Rilkean wisdom produced by a figure who commends himself by virtue of his search for the visionary in the world of objects. Only one of Benn's poems, 'Immer schweigender', is reproduced, following Raschke's admiring characterisation of him as a figure whose acute, Nietzschean awareness enables him to overcome the constraints that inhibit others and to penetrate thereby the realm of eternal truths: 'Raum- und zeitenthoben, wie nur im Traum, bricht sein Blick durch jeden Anblick in zeitlich entlegenere Epochen: ein Röntgenblick, der hinter allen Gesichtern Gewesenes erspürt, uralte Wiederkehr' (*Kolonne*, 1, 59). In this way, the true artist figure mediates between the individual and the universal, showing the people the difficult, if not impossible, path to the remote regions that he inhabits.

Benn, the austere intellectual and master of form confronting the end of Christian faith, is the masculine model for the *Kolonne* generation: 'Gottfried Benn sind auch wir' (*Kolonne*, 1, 35). Raschke elaborates upon his achievement: 'Selten wurde so deutlich, daß Kunst und Formungstrieb heidnische Überwindungs-formen des Todes darstellen; nur die Möglichkeit der Form gestattet dem Dichter in seiner isolierten Stellung auszuharren' (*Kolonne*, 1, 36). For all the praise, the image of Benn in *Die Kolonne* is not wholly uncritical, as we have seen in the discussion of *Das Unaufhörliche*. He is taken to task by Eich under his pseudonym Georg Winter in the review of Benn's *Fazit der Perspektiven*, a collection of prose and poetry. In Eich's view, Benn has made the mistake of pandering to fashionable demands for new forms: 'So hat er sich halb zum Gedicht, halb zur logischen Darstellung entschieden, zur [sic] einer Mischform, in der die beiden Elemente sich nicht zur doppelten Wirkung addieren, sondern sich aufheben' (*Kolonne*, 2, 23). Like Raschke, Eich maintains that art is at its most compelling within established formal constraints. He shares Raschke's claims for formal simplicity, commenting 'daß die Versuche zu neuen Formen [...] wieder münden in die reine ursprüngliche Beschränkung'.

In heralding Benn and Rilke, Raschke the sophisticated urban intellectual demonstrates his identification with the discourse of modernist aesthetics, appreciating their struggle to authenticate and universalise subjective experience through art. Raschke's own writing, like that of Eich, has its place here. For example, both have short modernist prose in the double issue 4/5 in the first year, Eich's a typical, introspective piece. (Kuhnert, the co-editor, who places his own less sophisticated 'Nordic' prose in the journal with some frequency, offers a point of contrast.) And for all Eich's categorisation as a nature poet and for the cultivation of nature poetry in *Die Kolonne*, his poetry in the journal does not quite fit. Three poems in issue 7/8 in year one treat perception and memory with Eich's distinctive, dark humour mixed with echoes of Benn, possibly also Brecht. 'Gegen vier Uhr nachmittags' ends:

Nur das Nichts, das mit unlösbaren Krallen
sich ins Gedächtnis hängt
und jeden neuen Tag mit allen
andern Tagen vermengt. (*Kolonne*, 1, 52)

Similarly, Eich's two dramas in *Die Kolonne*, the radio piece 'Ein Traum am Edsin-Gol' and an extract from *Der Präsident*, a piece for the stage, are concerned with issues of individual identity in extreme situations.

The strategic juxtaposition of contemporary work with works from the tradition is progressively refined. The journal's motivation is the subject of comment on two occasions. On the first, editorial practice is defended against the attack that the arrangement of contemporary work, including that of the editors, alongside the great voices from the tradition is designed to flatter contemporary figures by association:

> Sehen wir davon ab, daß es uns immer wertvoll erschien und erscheinen wird, an die wesentlichen Leistungen der Vergangenen zu erinnern. Die Redaktion weiß sehr wohl, welcher Zwischenraum zumeist die Arbeiten der jungen Mitarbeiter dieser Zeitschrift von denen der 'Vorbilder' trennt. Aber ihre Arbeiten sollen beieinander stehen: um bescheiden zu machen, bescheiden vor den Werten des Gestern, und um an verwandte Stimmen aus gewesenen Zeiten zu erinnern. Keiner soll sich anmaßen, einen Weg zu gehen, den vor ihm niemand ging, mag er ihn auch mit seinen eigenen Schritten gehen und manches am Wege bemerken, das vor ihm niemand in diesem Lichte wahrnahm. (*Kolonne*, 2, 48)

It is only consistent that *Die Kolonne* should set itself against what it regards as the avant-gardists' arrogant dismissal of tradition, acknowledging instead both the worth of the tradition and the creative insight of the contemporary artist working through it. Indeed, it is within these parameters and beneath the paradigm of nature that the journal undertakes what Dolan refers to as the reconciliation of things seemingly opposed, be they science and art, social classes, or the generations.[19] Reconciliation, of course, pre-supposes acceptance of the proposed paradigm and parameters, which, as we have seen, run counter to recent trends in German modernism.

The second statement underscores the journal's view of literature as suited to the treatment of humanist ideas, in the traditional rather than the Marxist sense, and of universal or final questions:

> [Es] sollen nach Möglichkeit immer Dichtungen des Vergangenen neben Dichtungen des Heute stehen, zum Beweise: daß die Dichtung aller Zeiten immer den Menschen als Gleichnis des Lebens, nie das Kostüm seiner zeitlichen Erscheinung meinte, zum Beweise: daß die Dichtung immer von neuem den Menschen ihrer jeweiligen Zeit in jenen Tiefen einzuwurzeln versuchte, wo Leben und Tod ungemindert regieren. (*Kolonne*, 3, 32)

---

19   See Dolan, p. 32.

It would appear that it is such a statement, coupled with similar sentiments expressed in works by figures such as Benn, that prompts Schäfer to identify *Die Kolonne* and kindred spirits as 'existentialists'.[20] This can only be maintained in general terms. There is, for example, no publication of existentialist texts or discussion of existentialist ideas by figures such as Heidegger or Jaspers. As we have seen, though, Raschke's programmatic statements can be readily understood as an attempt to overcome the contemporary crisis of meaning by re-directing attention towards final questions and by revalorising key concepts in a new synthesis, designed to re-establish the metaphysical quality of the relationship between man and nature threatened by contemporary urban civilisation. Indeed, the programmatic distinctiveness of *Die Kolonne* is to be located in this revalorisation that blends the *Sachlichkeit* of the intellectual climate of the 1920s with nature within the tradition represented by Goethe and in this way seeks to point beyond the insufficiencies of the present. This, the *Kolonne* programme, is maintained in its essentials and refined during the three years of the journal's publication. The juxtaposition of contemporary poetry with work from the tradition is undertaken in a highly conscious manner, inviting the reader's reflection on the undiminished centrality of final questions in an age without faith and plagued by social dislocation.

The mature journal: unity in editorial practice

The first issue which achieves such a thematic unity in editorial composition is the fourth in the journal's second year. This is the second issue for which Raschke is named as editorially responsible. It treats the problem of death and opens with Jean Paul's 'Rede des toten Christus vom Weltgebäude herab, daß kein Gott sei', followed by Hölderlin's hymnic praise of the four seasons, which ends on a note of renewal and rebirth: 'Alsdann erscheint des Frühlings neues Werden, | So glänzt die Natur mit ihrer Pracht auf Erden' (*Kolonne*, 2, 41). Jean Paul's Christ emerges from his despair, his faith re-affirmed and experiencing an epiphany:

> Und als ich aufstand, glimmte die Sonne tief hinter den vollen purpurnen Kornähren und warf friedlich den Widerschein ihres Abendrotes dem kleinen Mond zu, der ohne eine Aurora im Morgen aufstieg, und zwischen dem Himmel und der Erde streckte eine frohe, vergängliche Welt ihre kurzen Flügel aus und lebte, wie ich, vor dem unendlichen Vater; und von der ganzen Natur um mich flossen friedliche Töne aus, wie von fernen Abendglocken. (*Kolonne*, 2, 38)

---

20 Hans Dieter Schäfer, 'Die nichtnationalsozialistische Literatur der jungen Generation im Dritten Reich', in Hans Dieter Schäfer, *Das gespaltene Bewußtsein: Über deutsche Kultur und Lebenswirklichkeit 1933–1945* (Munich: Hanser, 1981), pp. 7–54 (p. 25).

The Christian celebration of creation is further undertaken in Grimmelshausen's 'Komm, Trost der Nacht, o Nachtigall!', while Hoffmannswaldau's 'Vergänglichkeit der Schönheit' strikes a less confident note. Raschke's own poetry, for instance in 'An den Tod', treats the problem of death in the light of the loss of faith, a theme pursued by other contemporaries, Gustav Schenk and Horst Lange. Meanwhile, the renewed confidence placed in the modern scientific method is expressed in Anders's essay on Fuhrmann's *Die Pflanze als Lebewesen*.

By year three (1932), editorial principles and practice are sufficiently established for each issue to exhibit the unity achieved above. It is striking that the polemic against left-wing literature has all but ceased. Issue one in the third year is constructed as a celebration of lyric poetry around the award of the second *Kolonne* poetry prize to Peter Huchel. The issue includes Hölderlin's words of encouragement 'An die jungen Dichter' with the advice 'Fragt die große Natur um Rat!' (*Kolonne*, 3, 3). It includes too Eichendorff's meditations upon lyric poetry as the most subjective of genres akin to song and as 'wesentlich die Poesie der Gegenwart und folglich unruhig und wandelbar wie diese' (*Kolonne*, 3, 2). The issue contains an exchange about the language of poetry between Bernhard Diebold and Eich. Diebold attacks the unworldliness of contemporary poets who continue to write in the idiom of the tradition of nature poetry even though the world has changed out of all recognition through industrialisation and urbanisation. Eich rejects the linkage between poetic language and a particular view of the age. Echoing Eichendorff, Eich argues for the primacy of the poet's subjectivity and for the distinction between lyric poetry and the other genres: 'Der Lyriker entscheidet sich für nichts, ihn interessiert nur sein Ich, er schafft keine Du- und Er-Welt wie der Epiker und der Dramatiker, für ihn existiert nur das gemeinschaftslose vereinzelte Ich' (*Kolonne*, 3, 3).

Though Raschke expresses concern about the artifice of some of Huchel's verse, he is won over by the manner in which Huchel evokes rural childhood memories, universalising experience through *Naturmagie*. The selection of Huchel's poetry includes two such poems about childhood, 'Der glückliche Garten' and 'Die Magd', which contain a magical strain alongside exact description of the natural world. Huchel's poetry thus achieves Raschke's programmatic linkage between 'Sachlichkeit' and 'Wunder' in nature, which is, moreover, articulated within the formal constraint of the *Volkslied*. Huchel himself would later resist the association with *Die Kolonne* in general and Raschke in particular.[21] Yet 'Die Magd', for example, evokes popular magic in an everyday rural setting that is mythologically heightened:

Sie wärmt mein Hemd, küßt mein Gesicht
und strickt weiß im Petroleumlicht.

---

21 For a discussion of this matter see Stephen Parker, *Peter Huchel: A literary life in twentieth-century Germany* (Bern: Lang, 1998), pp. 150–54.

Ihr Strickzeug klirrt und blitzt dabei,
sie murmelt leis Wahrsagerei. (*Kolonne*, 3, 5)

In an exhaustive analysis of 'Der Knabenteich', another Huchel poem about childhood that was selected for the next issue, Dolan develops the view that Huchel's work is the consummate expression of the *Kolonne* programme, in that it involves a complex process of reflection by a sophisticated consciousness, observing the minutiae of the natural world within a universalising vision.[22] He contrasts the *Naturmagie* of Huchel's achievement with a number of other contemporary poets in the journal, who articulate a much less sophisticated identification of the self with nature, though they contribute towards the *Kolonne* programme to some extent through their renewal of the ballad and *Volkslied* forms. These poets include Zernatto and Theodor Kramer, Lange, Meckel and Georg von der Vring. Dolan rightly observes the limitations of von der Vring, who deploys traditional forms and metaphors without regard for changed circumstances.[23] Eich, in the guise of Georg Winter, sees it a little differently in his short review of von der Vring's *Verse*. He identifies von der Vring not with contemporary modernists such as George, Benn, Rilke or Loerke, but with Mörike, concluding: 'Es sind Lieder, es ist die Melodie eines reinen und einfachen Herzens, und das schöne Erlebnis dieses Buches ist, zu wissen, daß jemand diese Melodie in unserer Zeit bewahren konnte, daß etwas wieder lebendig geworden ist, was für immer verloren schien' (*Kolonne*, 3, 31). The establishment of such a continuity across generations apparently far removed was achievement enough for Eich and other like-minded individuals. Yet continuity achieved on that basis did not have sufficient regard for irreversible changes through time to poetic sensibility, not to mention, more crudely, the language of urbanisation and industrialisation. That general criticism affects much of the verse published in the journal.

Dolan singles out Elisabeth Langgässer's work alongside that of Huchel as a consummate expression of the *Kolonne* programme. Her novella *Mars* appears in issue 1 of year 3 and her poetry forms the centrepiece of issue 2, year 3. The issue opens with Langgässer's 'April', a re-working of the Greek myth of Europa, who is seduced by Zeus in the form of a bull. The poem is accompanied by a short commentary on the myth and by Raschke's essay on Langgässer's verse, which precedes a selection of five more of her poems. Raschke presents Langgässer's work in terms of the Jungian collective unconscious, which Benn's poetry, too, is seen to encapsulate with its timeless vision. Whilst Huchel draws on his memories of rural Brandenburg, Langgässer undertakes the return to ancient Greece, the cradle of Western civilisation, 'wo die Völker noch im Schoße der Mythe zu ruhen schienen', in order to refresh 'unser erschöpftes Denken' (*Kolonne*, 3, 20).

---

22   See Dolan, pp. 64–74.
23   See Dolan, p. 138.

Langgässer's 'Leda' celebrates the magical moment when ancient myth is renewed:

Dort, wo das schmächtige Schilfgras der Ufer
Klirrend erschauert im herbstlichen Wind,
Weil sich des Wassers beweglicher Rufer
An die vereinsamten Schwäne entsinnt –
Öffnet sich weit
Eine Bucht in der Zeit,
Und die erneuerte Sage beginnt. (*Kolonne*, 3, 21)

Langgässer's work hovers between magical renewal and the sense that our relationship with the gods has become distant and our power to forge the link with them has diminished. She thus displays the familiar early twentieth-century attitude that Western civilisation finds itself in a state of decline. This is expressed in 'Weges Ende' as follows: 'Wir fühlen schon: | Es läßt die Zeugung nach' (*Kolonne*, 3, 21). Langgässer's belief in the authority of the past and her questioning of our capacity to determine our own fate clearly have their place in *Die Kolonne* and within German culture in the early 1930s, shaken as it had been through the collapse of economic and social structures. Raschke brackets Langgässer with Benn, with whom she shares a mythologising imagination, which provides the narrative for the acceptance of humans' circumscribed powers: 'Wie die stärksten Stimmen unserer Zeit, allen voran Gottfried Benn, müht sich Elisabeth Langgässer, zu zeigen, daß der Mensch nicht sich gehört, sondern nur eines der vielen Worte ist, mit denen größere Mächte sich verständigen' (*Kolonne*, 3, 20).

Only two more issues of the journal appeared, both with the characteristic blend of contemporary poetry and work from the tradition, including Mörike and Eichendorff. There is no indication that issue 4 is to be the final issue. During its short existence, due largely to the intellectual energy of Raschke, but supported by figures such as Eich, *Die Kolonne* made a distinctive contribution to the creation of a new climate in German literary life, acting as an outlet for figures from a young generation who, at their best, in their search for a renewal of meaning sought to combine a modern sensibility with a fresh openness to the potential of tradition. This yielded the difficult idiom practised by Langgässer and the complex web of associations found in Huchel. As we have seen, Raschke also pursued a popular literary agenda, promoting aesthetically less demanding work on the grounds of its authenticity. The achievement of figures such as Meckel, von der Vring and Kuhnert, as well as the Austrians Billinger and Zernatto, who predominate in terms of the volume of poems and stories published, was to re-habilitate traditional forms in a diction that differed little from their illustrious predecessors. With few exceptions – Kramer is one – all these figures remained in Germany and Austria, where they continued their literary careers during the years of the Third Reich. Following the foundation of *Das innere Reich* in 1934, virtually all the *Kolonne* circle gravitated towards that outlet. Whilst Raschke died in the war and Langgässer in 1950, Eich and Huchel emerged as highly regarded writers during the early decades of the Federal Republic and the GDR. In that way, the influence of *Die Kolonne* and its programme can be traced through German literary life from the late 1920s and well into the Germany of post-war division.

Die Linkskurve

Schäfer picks out Georg Lukács's attacks in *Die Linkskurve* on Bredel, Ottwalt, and Brecht as symptomatic of his posited restorative shift amongst the Marxist Left. As such, and notwithstanding the fact that Schäfer refers only to the July 1932 and November/December 1932 issues, four specific contributions made by Lukács to *Die Linkskurve* must come under immediate consideration in our investigation of the journal. The first two of these essays deal directly with Willi Bredel's novels, *Maschinenfabrik N & K* and *Die Rosenhofstraße*. An initial review of the texts was published in November 1931 under the heading 'Willi Bredels Romane' (*Lkv*, 3.11, 23–27), while a follow-up essay, 'Gegen die Spontaneitäts-theorie in der Literatur' (*Lkv*, 4.4, 30–33), appeared in the April 1932 issue in response to Otto Gotsche's vigorous rejection of what he termed Lukács's 'zersetzende Methode der Kritik'.[24] The second two essays take as their starting-point Ernst Ottwalt's novelistic treatment of the Weimar justice system, *Denn sie wissen, was sie tun: Ein deutscher Justizroman*. The first of these essays, entitled 'Reportage oder Gestaltung: Kritische Bemerkungen anläßlich des Romans von Ernst Ottwalt' (*Lkv*, 4.7, 23–30; 4.8, 26–31), appeared in two parts in the July and August issues of 1932. Then, in what was to be the final issue of the journal in November/December 1932, Lukács countered Ottwalt's own response to that original critique, broadening the terms of the debate in an article entitled 'Aus der Not eine Tugend' (*Lkv*, 4.11/12, 15–24) to encompass Brecht's recently published theory of epic theatre.[25] The initial set of questions for our analysis of *Die Linkskurve* must surround these four articles, each of which sets out a position opposed to the documentary-style, fact-based approach to literature which underpinned the Bredel and Ottwalt novels. How the position expressed by Lukács might be brought into harmony with the 1930 paradigm, and by extension with the editorial standpoint of *Die Kolonne*, will constitute the starting-point of this section.

---

24 Otto Gotsche 'Kritik der Anderen: Einige Bemerkungen zur Frage der Qualifikation unserer Literatur', *Lkv*, 4.4, 28–30 (p. 28). For Bredel's own response, see Willi Bredel, 'Einen Schritt weiter: Ein Diskussionsbeitrag über unsere Wendung an der Literaturfront', *Lkv*, 4.1, 20–22.
25 For Ottwalt's response, see Ernst Ottwalt, '"Tatsachenroman" und Formexperiment: Eine Entgegnung an Georg Lukács', *Lkv*, 4.10, 21–26.

The assertion of Lukács's Marxist aesthetic

The common thread running through these Lukács essays is a constructed opposition between a factual style of narrative, 'Reportage', and a more conventional form of literary fiction, 'Gestaltung'. Lukács's principal objection to Bredel's two novels, which give barely fictionalised accounts of a KPD-inspired strike in a Hamburg factory and of everyday life in a working-class housing estate, is that they straddle these two forms of narrative. As he asserts in the first of the Bredel essays (*Lkv*, 3.11, 23–27), there exists 'ein künstlerisch ungelöster Widerspruch zwischen dem breiten, alles wesentliche umfassenden epischen Rahmen seiner Fabel und zwischen seiner Erzählungsweise, die teils eine Art von *Reportage*, teils eine Art *Versammlungsbericht* ist'. Praise for the broad scale of Bredel's narrative, as 'ein inhaltlich richtig gedachter und darum in seinen Umrissen wiederum epischer Entwurf' which offers the opportunity 'die ganze klassenmäßig bedeutsame Entwicklung im Betrieb [...] in eine künstlerische Komposition einzufügen und diese – echt episch – geschlossen [...] also wirklich als Prozeß, als ein Teil des Gesamtprozesses zu gestalten', is counter-balanced by criticism of the superficial and formulaic characterisation and dialogue: 'Was es lebendig machen könnte: lebende Menschen und lebendige, wechselnde, sich im Prozeß befindliche Beziehungen zwischen den Menschen fehlen so gut wie vollständig.' In simple terms, 'ein Roman erfordert eben andere Gestaltungsmittel als eine Reportage', and these methods are for Lukács the more heavily fictionalised dialogue and characterisation of the conventional epic novel.

Although in the second Bredel essay (*Lkv*, 4.4, 30–33), Lukács concerns himself principally with the nature of literary criticism rather than with the nature of Bredel's narrative, the innate traditionalism of his aesthetic standpoint becomes further apparent. In his dismissal of what he perceives to be Gotsche's naive view of literary criticism, for instance, it becomes clear that Lukács's principal point of reference is the bourgeois literary tradition: 'Die bürgerliche Literatur hat diese Kinderkrankheit auch durchgemacht (in Deutschland vor Lessing).' Further, in his elitist defence of the specialist skills of the Marxist literary critic, Lukács starts to reveal the same assumptions which underpin his very conventional view of the specialist literary creativity of the writer. It is this specialist creativity which ensures that a work of literature may derive from a documentary report 'ebensowenig wie aus einer Photographie ein malerisches Kunstwerk wird'. Here, Lukács also begins to develop the distinction between *Reportage* and *Gestaltung.*

> Worüber diskutiert werden müßte, ist dies: kann Bericht oder Reportage die Gestaltung ersetzen? Ist etwa Reportage, wie sowohl in der Sowjetunion, wie bei uns einige proletarische Schriftsteller behaupten, die richtige 'zeitgemäße' Methode unserer Literatur? Oder ist sie eine niedrigere, (in der Sowjetunion überholte, bei uns) zu überwindende schöpferische Methode?

If at this stage Lukács at least claimed to be encouraging debate rather than offering resolution on these questions, three months later he provided an unequivocal answer in the first of the Ottwalt essays, 'Reportage oder Gestaltung' (*Lkv*, 4.7, 23–30; 4.8, 26–31). Here, Lukács drew at its starkest the distinction between *Reportage*, categorised as 'Wissenschaft', and *Gestaltung*, categorised as 'Kunst': 'Die grundlegenden Darstellungsmethoden von Wissenschaft und Kunst schließen sich gegenseitig aus.' Self-consciously founded on genuine events and reports, Ottwalt's attempts to forge literary narrative out of documentary material were bound, on Lukács's terms, to fail as a pseudo-art, as 'Tatsachenfetischismus', incapable of depicting the 'Gesamtprozeß' in society with all its 'wesentlichen und wirklichen treibenden Kräfte'. Ottwalt thereby failed to fulfil the requirements of a successful novel: 'Die Gestaltung des Gesamtprozesses ist die Voraussetzung für eine richtige Komposition des Romans.' Not only did Lukács seek here to ground his rejection of reportage in more theoretical terms, he also outlined the positive model of literary representation he proposed in its place. Instead of being based on the contemporary preference for the objective, the genuine, and the factual, Lukács's notion of what was 'typical' and 'realistic' were founded on the aesthetic principles of the nineteenth-century novelists Balzac and Tolstoy. Only in the fully-rounded, psychological and fictional characterisation of 'typical', and therefore 'realistic', figures could the totality of social reality be depicted in a novel. Indeed, Lukács went as far as to make unfavourable comparison between Ottwalt's depiction of the Weimar justice system and the representation of the Tsarist justice system in Tolstoy's *Resurrection*. What made the latter more effective was its psychological method of characterisation and the emotional involvement which that inspired in the reader.

That this criticism of Ottwalt and Bredel went beyond merely these two individuals had already been made explicit by Lukács. Of Bredel, for instance, he had asserted: 'Seine Fehler sind weniger individuelle Fehler als allgemeine Fehler der ganzen literarischen Bewegung' (*Lkv*, 3.11, 26). Equally, he had begun his attack on Ottwalt as follows:

> Der neue Roman Ottwalts ist repräsentativ für eine ganze Literaturrichtung, für eine ganz bestimmte Art *der schöpferischen Methode*. Er arbeitet mit den Mitteln der Reportage, an der Stelle der 'überkommenen', 'veralteten', 'bürgerlichen' Mitteln der 'erfundenen' Handlung und der 'gestalteten' Menschen. Diese Richtung ist heute international verbreitet: von Upton Sinclair und Tretjakow bis Ilja Ehrenburg arbeiten die verschiedensten Schriftsteller mit dieser Methode. (*Lkv*, 4.7, 23)

In the second of the Ottwalt essays, 'Aus der Not eine Tugend' (*Lkv*, 4.11/12, 15–24), Lukács broadened the scope of his attack still further by expanding the 'Reportage' category into an 'Antigestaltungstheorie' where Ottwalt's aesthetic procedures were equated with those of Brecht. In ascribing to Ottwalt and Brecht a rejection of the notion of *Kunstgenuss* and an opposition to any notion of the cultural tradition, Lukács demonstrated that their aesthetic principles 'sich *im diametralen Gegensatz zu den Anschauungen von Marx, Engels und Lenin befinden*'. In effect reduced to the slogan '*einen radikalen Bruch* mit allem Alten', the aesthetics of Ottwalt and Brecht were set up in fundamental opposition to Lukács's notion of 'Gestaltung'. The latter's emphasis on the importance of the *Erbe* and on more conventional principles of narrative fiction can leave little doubt that what Lukács was promoting in the Ottwalt and Bredel essays was a more conservative, restorative cultural direction, broadly compatible with the existing 1930 paradigm and by extension with the aesthetic programme advanced in *Die Kolonne*.

This observation is confirmed by Helga Gallas, for whom Lukács's sudden productivity in the final six months of the journal's existence, and in particular the Ottwalt essays, forms the basis of a fourth and final phase in the development of *Die Linkskurve*. Given the heading 'Zurückweisung neuer literarischer Techniken und Betonung der Kontinuität der klassischen Literatur-Tradition' and described as a period in which 'ein traditionalistisches Literaturkonzept durchgesetzt wurde, das an klassischen Vorbildern orientierte', this final phase is easily brought into line with Schäfer's restorative shift.[26] Characteristic of this phase for Gallas is not only the positive assertion of Lukács's aesthetic standpoint, but also the rejection of Brecht's, or perhaps more accurately what Brecht was perceived to represent. As Gallas summarises:

> Resumierend läßt sich sagen: Die Entwicklung im Bund proletarisch-revolutionärer Schriftsteller und in der *Linkskurve* führte zur Konfontation zweier sich marxistisch verstehender Theorien, für die die Namen Brecht und Lukács gesetzt werden können. Der verdeckt geführte Streit um eine marxistische Literaturtheorie war bereits Ende 1932 zugunsten von Lukács entschieden, ohne daß Brecht selbst in der *Linkskurve* jemals zu Wort gekommen wäre.

Of central importance in this phase, in addition to the Ottwalt essays, is Lukács's 'Tendenz oder Parteilichkeit' (*Lkv*, 4.6, 13–21), published in June 1932. Here Lukács argues for a replacement of the term 'Tendenz' with the term 'Parteilichkeit' in order to denote proletarian-revolutionary literature. As Gallas points out, Lukács's definition of this latter term – 'die Erkenntnis und Gestaltung des *Gesamtprozesses* als zusammengefaßte Totalität seiner wahren treibenden Kräfte, als ständige, erhöhte Reproduktion der ihm zugrunde liegenden dialektischen Widersprüche' – matches strikingly the aesthetic principles outlined above in the Bredel and Ottwalt essays, so that this essay buttresses, on a still more abstract-theoretical level, the promotion of the aesthetic identified with Tolstoy's literary practice and the rejection of that identified in the practice of Bredel, Ottwalt, and Brecht.[27]

It was not only Lukács who played a prominent role in this final phase in the journal's development. For Gallas, the assertion of this traditionalist aesthetic constitutes a victory for the leadership faction in the *Bund*, consisting principally of Becher, Lukács, Wittfogel, and Gábor, in combating internal opposition from

26 Gallas, pp. 64–65. Subsequent reference, p. 69.
27 Gallas, p. 150.

more radical left-wing factions. In particular Andor Gábor seems to have become an increasingly significant figure in the assertion of the Lukács aesthetic. Indeed, it is the publication in the final issue of the journal of Gábor's review article, 'Zwei Bühnenereignisse' (*Lkv*, 4.11/12, 27–32), together with Lukács's 'Aus der Not eine Tugend', which leads Gallas to describe that final issue as the 'Anti-Brecht-Heft'.[28] As with Lukács's essay, Gábor's review does not deal directly with Brecht's work. Instead he reviews an *Agitprop* production by Gustav von Wangenheim and H. W. Hiller's stage version of Becher's *Der große Plan*. However, in an echo of Lukács, it is not in their subject-matter or in the talent of their directors that the shortcomings of these productions lie, but rather 'in der schöpferischen Methode': 'In beiden Werken, wie in den meisten Versuchen unserer jungen Bühnengeneration, [...] spukt das "epische Theater", das "Lehrstück".' Here, Gábor quotes in full Brecht's schematic opposition between 'dramatic' and 'epic' forms of theatre and explicitly bemoans the latter's emphasis on 'Weltbild', 'Argument', 'Montage', and 'Ratio' in place of 'Erlebnis', 'Suggestion', 'Wachstum', and 'Gefühl'. As he concludes:

> In beiden Darbietungen geraten die Verfasser durch ihre, bewußt durchgeführte, schöpferische Methode, welche die Grundsätze des Marxismus-Leninismus [...] durch neue 'Erfindungen' zu ersetzen versucht, in eine Sackgasse, aus der weder ihr Stoff, noch ihre Begabung, noch die antizipierte Zuneigung einer ideologisch schon vorbereiteten Zuhörerschaft heraushelfen kann.

Striking also is the way in which Gábor, in a review of Hans Marchwitza's *Schlacht vor Kohle* published in the May 1932 issue (*Lkv*, 4.5, 31–36), adopts precisely the method of criticism first employed by Lukács on Bredel and attacked by Gotsche in the previous issue. Flat, schematic characterisation is again the principal object of criticism – 'die Menschen sind Schemen; statt aus Fleisch, Blut, Farbe und Geruch geknetet zu sein, sind sie aus dürftigen, verbrauchten Worten zusammengestellt' – and this failing stems from 'der mangelhaften Beherrschung unserer schöpferischen, dialektisch-materialistischen Methode, die im Durchleuchten und Bewußtmachen des Gesamtzusammenhanges besteht'. For Gábor, as for Lukács, it is the totality of society, 'mit dem total gestalteten Kumpel', and the portrayal of the hero's life as a process which constitutes the appropriate creative method for a Marxist narrative.

The Goethe-year and the turn to the tradition

As the leading literary theoretician in the BPRS before Lukács's arrival in Berlin in the summer of 1931, Karl August Wittfogel had enjoyed prominence in *Die Linkskurve* in the second half of 1930 through an essay-series entitled 'Zur Frage

---

28 Gallas, p. 69.

einer marxistischen Ästhetik', published in consecutive issues between May and November 1930.[29] In the aim to re-evaluate Hegel as a foundation for a Marxist aesthetic, this series of articles is seen by Gallas as an early, initially abortive attempt, 'das bürgerliche Erbe kritisch zu verarbeiten'.[30] It was this same procedure which lay at the heart of Wittfogel's literary-critical activities in the first half of 1932 when he published essays on Goethe in a number of Marxist periodicals, including the *Linkskurve Goethe-Sonderheft*, published in June 1932 as a contribution to the Goethe-year celebrations.[31] Tellingly described by Dieter Schiller as 'die zentrale Würdigung Goethes in der kommunistischen Presse', these essays established for the *Bund* a public position on the question of Goethe's contemporary relevance for proletarian writing.[32] While Wittfogel's approach to Goethe could scarcely be described as uncritical – in the *Linkskurve* essay he did not seek to deny 'die lakaienhaften, spießigen, gegenrevolutionären Züge in Goethe' – his central concern was to define how Goethe's legacy could be productively employed in the development of proletarian-revolutionary literature. Here, he singled out a highpoint in the bourgeois literary revolution which 'in Lessing, Klopstock, Lenz, Klinger, dem jungen Goethe und dem jungen Schiller breit und verheißungsvoll einsetzte'. Given the public scepticism of much of the Marxist avant-garde towards Goethe, the mere fact of the publication of the special issue, let alone Wittfogel's successful attempts to identify productive points of contact for proletarian-revolutionary literature, marks a significant shift towards a more conservative, backward-looking aesthetic direction. In effect, Wittfogel's contributions sought to establish, paradoxically, a Marxist *Bildungs-dialekt.*

It is also noteworthy that the *Linkskurve Sonderheft* was monopolised by the BPRS's two bourgeois literary theoreticians, the only other contemporary contribution coming from Lukács himself.[33] Gallas makes only brief mention of the *Sonderheft*, but as Dieter Schiller suggests the special edition must be viewed within the context of programmatic discussions within the *Bund* concerning the

---

29 K.A. Wittfogel, 'Zur Frage der marxistischen Ästhetik', *Lku*, 2.5, 6–8; 'Zur Frage einer marxistischen Ästhetik (Fortsetzung)', *Lku*, 2.6, 8–12; 'Weiteres zur Frage einer marxistischen Ästhetik', *Lku*, 2.7, 20–24; 'Weiteres zur Frage einer marxistischen Ästhetik', *Lku*, 2.8, 15–18; 'Nochmals zur Frage einer marxistischen Ästhetik', *Lku*, 2.9, 22–27; 'Noch einmal zur Frage einer marxistischen Ästhetik', *Lku*, 2.10, 20–24; 'Noch einmal zur Frage einer marxistischen Ästhetik', *Lku*, 2.11, 8–13.

30 Gallas, p. 54.

31 See K. A. Wittfogel, 'Goethe-"Feier"?', *Die Linkskurve: Goethe-Sonderheft* (1932), 1–10; Karl August Wittfogel, 'Zum 100. Todestag Goethes', *Internationale Presse-Korrespondenz*, 12 (1932), 673–75; Karl August Wittfogel, 'Goethe: Deutschlands größter Dichter – ein Opfer der deutschen Misere', *Die rote Fahne*, 22 March 1932, supplement.

32 Dieter Schiller, 'Goethe in den geistigen Kämpfen um 1932: Über die Goethe-Nummern der Zeitschriften *Die neue Rundschau* und *Die Linkskurve* im April 1932', *Goethe-Jahrbuch*, 103 (1986), 54–72 (p. 66).

33 Georg Lukács, 'Der faschisierte Goethe', *Die Linkskurve: Goethe-Sonderheft* (1932), 33–40.

role of the literary tradition. Indeed, Schiller ties the Goethe edition both to a statement made by Becher in a programmatic essay in the May 1932 issue of the journal (*Lkv*, 4.5, 1–11) and to factional disputes with left-wing radicals in the *Bund*:

> Tatsächlich sollte Goethe hier nicht gefeiert werden; das Goethe-Heft der *Linkskurve* stand im Zusammenhang mit der Programmdebatte des Bundes proletarisch-revolutionärer Schriftsteller und war Bestandteil der – vor allem von Georg Lukács und K. A. Wittfogel betriebenen – Bemühungen um literaturtheoretische ästhetische Grundlagen der Bundesarbeit. Die Aufgabe, 'kritisch an das Erbe heranzugehen und es für unsere Arbeit auszuwerten' – wie Becher einmal formulierte –, konnte und sollte im Goethe-Jahr modellhaft erprobt werden. [...] Nicht um ein Jubiläums-Feuilleton ging es, sondern um die Erarbeitung einer kultur- und kunstpolitischen Position des Bundes. Nicht mehr und nicht weniger sollte erreicht werden, als [...] linksradikalen Vorstellungen über das literarische Erbe entgegenzuarbeiten.[34]

Of course, 'Ablehnung des Erbes' (*Lkv*, 4.11/12, 21) would be one of the accusations subsequently levelled at Ottwalt and Brecht by Lukács, and Schiller sees in the *Sonderheft* a forerunner of the Ottwalt essays:

> Es ist unverkennbar der Anfang einer ebenso folgenreichen wie einseitigen Orientierung der proletarisch-revolutionären Literatur auf das epische Realismus-Modell des 19. Jahrhunderts, auf den 'großen Realismus'. Doch das ist ein Thema, das weit über den Zusammenhang des Goethe-Jahres hinausweist. An dieser Stelle sei nur angemerkt, daß Lukács' Polemiken gegen Bredel und Ottwalt in der *Linkskurve* nur wenige Wochen später veröffentlicht wurden.[35]

Striking here are the parallels in the composition of the *Sonderheft* and the Ottwalt essays in the way that statements by Marx or Engels are invoked as authorities to support the aesthetic position promoted by Lukács and Wittfogel. As we have seen, this procedure was central to Lukács's attempts to discredit the aesthetics of Ottwalt and Brecht. Similarly, the March 1932 edition of *Die Linkskurve* included the full text of Engels's letter to Miss Harkness from 1882 in which he formulated a definition of realism founded on the work of Balzac (*Lkv*, 4.3, 11–14). It was this source which was in turn invoked by Lukács in 'Reportage oder Gestaltung' as the foundation for his theory of realism, much as an Engels text from 1847 on the reception of Goethe acted as a source of authority in the *Sonderheft* for the Wittfogel and Lukács essays alongside it.[36]

In this way, it is not difficult to demonstrate a concerted drive towards an aesthetically restorative position in the pages of *Die Linkskurve* in 1932, spearheaded above all by Georg Lukács and supported by Wittfogel and Gábor. Furthermore, it is significant that for Gallas this position represents a shift from that adopted by prominent *Bund* members in advance of 1930. Gallas highlights,

---

34 Schiller, p. 64.
35 Schiller, p. 67.
36 'Marx und Engels über Goethe: Eine unbekannte Abhandlung aus dem Jahr 1847', *Die Linkskurve: Goethe-Sonderheft* (1932), 11–33.

for example, the theoretical positions of Berta Lask and Erwin Piscator, both members of the *Bund* whose approach to characterisation is summarised by Gallas in such a way as to stand in direct opposition to that subsequently promoted by Lukács: 'Die traditionellen Formen der psychologischen Charakterdarstellung, der individuellen Helden wurden als überholt, als ablösungsbedürftig erkannt.'[37] Similarly, Gallas cites the aesthetic positions of Becher, notably in the foreword to *Levisite*, and of Kisch as strong evidence that highly influential voices in the BPRS favoured an aesthetic position which opposed that asserted in the final phase of the journal's development. To summarise the position immediately in advance of the founding of *Die Linkskurve*:

> Es bleibt also festzuhalten: Die von den Bundesmitgliedern vor der eigentlichen Gründung des BPRS 1928 und noch im darauffolgenden Jahr intendierte Literatur und Theorie zielte auf die Sprengung der traditionellen Gattungsformen, auf antipsychologisierende, dokumentierende Darstellungsweisen, auf die Verwendung kleiner, offener Formen, auf die Verdrängung der herkömmlichen literarischen Konstruktionsprinzipien wie individueller Held, erfundene Fabel, individueller Konflikt, dramatische Spannung usw.

In particular on three key aesthetic parameters – the nature of the literary hero (mass or individual); the nature of literary narrative (documentary or fictional); and literary form (small-scale and open or large-scale and closed) – Gallas portrays a shift from the dominant position in the *Bund* pre-1929 to that which gained ascendancy in *Die Linkskurve* in 1932.[38]

Aesthetic or political shift?

The history of *Die Linkskurve*, that is in effect the process by which this shift took place, is divided by Gallas into four phases: '1. Phase: Distanzierung von linksbürgerlichen Schriftstellern zugunsten Arbeiterkorrespondenten (August 1929 bis Mitte 1930)'; '2. Phase: Kritik der bisherigen Auffassungen und Ausarbeitung einer an Hegel orientierten Literaturtheorie (Mitte 1930 bis Herbst 1931)'; '3. Phase: Opposition von links und Harmonisierung der Gegensätze (Sommer 1932 bis Mitte 1932); '4. Phase: Zurückweisung neuer literarischer Techniken und Betonung der Kontinuität der klassischen Literatur-Tradition (Mitte 1932 bis Dezember 1932)'.[39] For Gallas, the development of these phases is most accurately portrayed as a factional dispute within the BPRS between the radical proletarian 'left' and the more conservative, bourgeois 'right'. While phases two and four witness a pre-eminence for the intellectual theoreticians of bourgeois origin, Wittfogel (phase two) and Lukács (phase four), and by

---

37 Gallas, p. 90. Subsequent reference, p. 96.
38 See Gallas, pp. 86–96.
39 See Gallas, p. 47, p. 51, p. 56, and p. 64.

extension for their traditionalist aesthetic programme outlined above, phases one and three are periods of ascendancy for the proletarian *Arbeiterschriftsteller* and their programme of radical sectarianism and isolationism against bourgeois sympathisers. This view of the development of the journal becomes particularly apparent in phase three, where factional disputes seem to have reached their height. During Becher's absence from Berlin in the early summer of 1931, Gallas sees left-wingers, led by the editor of *Die rote Fahne*, Karl Biro-Rosinger, and the Hungarian writer, Aladár Komját, and supported by the *Arbeiterschriftsteller* and *Arbeiterkorrespondenten*, such as Hans Marchwitza, putting forward their own programme for the development of proletarian-revolutionary literature which advocated a renewed emphasis on writing by and for the proletariat and a rejection of the heavily theoretical position being developed by Wittfogel from within the bourgeois intellectual tradition. Only then through tactical compromise and counter-attack are the Lukács faction, with whom Becher is now aligned, seen to succeed in asserting their own programme in the final phase of the journal's existence. As such, and through considerable to-ing and fro-ing, much of which never found public expression in the journal itself, the history of *Die Linkskurve* from its foundation in 1929 to its final issue in 1932 is portrayed by Gallas *both* as a shift in influence from the left wing of the *Bund* to the right, that is from the proletarian *Arbeiterkorrespondenten* to the bourgeois theoreticians, *and* as an aesthetic shift from the promotion of the open forms of epic theatre to a promotion of the closed forms of the epic novel, in effect from Brecht to Lukács. Such a shift clearly matches what Schäfer describes with reference to the Marxist left as 'diese Öffnung nach rechts'.[40]

And yet, such a schematic overview of developments within the *Bund* and its literary journal inevitably disguises a rather more complex and problematic reality which may start to raise questions concerning the applicability of the 1930 paradigm to *Die Linkskurve*. In particular, by employing the factional positions 'left' and 'right', we run the risk of conflating political standpoints, class origins, and aesthetic standpoints, in such a way that 'left-wing' equates to 'proletarian' equates to 'open aesthetics', while 'right-wing' equates to 'bourgeois' equates to 'closed aesthetics'. If we consider phase one, for instance, it becomes clear that the central question which determined factional positions was not to do with aesthetic form, but to do with the class nature of proletarian-revolutionary literature – about whom was it to be written, for whom was it to be written, and by whom was it to be written? The attacks on bourgeois writers and dramatists, such as Piscator, Vallentin, Toller, and Tucholsky,[41] and editors, such as Barbusse

40 Schäfer, 'Periodisierung', p. 97.
41 See 'Die Piscator-Bühne', *Lkv*, 1.2, 4–5; A. G., 'Zwei Theaterabende', *Lkv*, 1.3, 17–18; Berta Lask, 'Erwin Piscator, *Das politische Theater*', *Lkv*, 2.1, 19–20; M. Vallentin, '"Rotes Sprachrohr": Agitproptruppen', *Lkv*, 2.3, 18–19; Maxim Vallentin, 'Agitpropspiel und Kampfwert', *Lkv*, 2.4,

and Pohl,[42] which characterised this initial phase were self-evidently not attacks on traditionalist aesthetics. Indeed, many of these writers were the most prominent advocates of experimental, open forms. Repeated attacks on Döblin's recently-published *Berlin Alexanderplatz* make it clear that ascendancy for the radical left in this initial phase did not equate to an ascendancy for open aesthetics.[43] Indeed, as we have seen, attacks on Döblin's novel formed part of the restorative aesthetic programme advanced in *Die Kolonne*. Furthermore, the shift from phase one to phase two took place primarily along this class-based parameter, rather than along an aesthetic parameter. The primary distinction between, on the one hand, Steffen's 'Die Urzelle proletarischer Literatur' (*Lkv*, 2.2, 8–9) and Gábor's advocacy of the so-called *Geburtshelferthese* (*Lkv*, 1.3, 3–6), for Gallas characteristic of phase one, and, on the other, Lenz's 'Gegen den Ökonomismus in der Literaturfrage' (*Lkv*, 2.3, 10–12), identified by Gallas as the turning-point towards phase two, concerns the nature of the role to be played by revolutionary writers of bourgeois origins, not aesthetic form. By the same token, Wittfogel's theoretical essays failed to find any resonance in the journal and failed to provoke any theoretical response from the radical left.[44] The suspicion and resentment engendered amongst the radical left by these articles was not inspired by the nature of that aesthetic theory, against which they then sought to advocate an alternative aesthetic programme. The left-wing faction were interested primarily in literary practice, and it was rather the fact of Wittfogel's intellectual theorising in the first place and his implied agenda of inclusion towards the bourgeois factions and exclusion of the proletariat which inspired their objections. Standpoints on aesthetic questions and class questions may have often coincided, and the labels 'left' and 'right' may act as a convenient shorthand for those composite standpoints, but no necessary connection can be assumed between the two.

If phases one and two suggest that the shift from left to right through the publication run of *Die Linkskurve* was not necessarily identical with a shift from open to closed aesthetics, further analysis of Lukács's contributions in phase four raises similar questions. Specifically, two moves by Lukács cast doubt on the apparently aesthetic nature of his programme. Firstly, Lukács's attempts to establish an identity in aesthetic practice between Brecht and the *Arbeiter-schriftsteller* must be considered highly questionable. Indeed, Gallas asserts that

---

15–16; Die Redaktion der *Linkskurve*, 'Antwort auf Vallentin', *Lkv*, 2.4, 16–17; A. G., 'Drei Berichtigungen, die berichtigt werden', *Lkv*, 2.2, 19–20.

42   Kurt Kersten, 'Der Jahrtausendputsch der Literatur-Nihilisten', *Lkv*, 1.1, 19–21; 'Gerhart Pohl: Ein Schriftsteller dieser Zeit', *Lkv*, 1.3, 28–29; Andor Gábor, 'Die bunte Welt des Genossen Barbusse', *Lkv*, 1.5, 5–6; 'Henri Barbusse an *Die Linkskurve*', *Lkv*, 2.2, 5–6; Andor Gábor, 'Antwort an Barbusse', *Lkv*, 2.2, 6–7.

43   See Klaus Neukrantz, '*Berlin Alexanderplatz*', *Lkv*, 1.5, 31; Otto Biha, 'Herr Döblin verunglückt in einer Linkskurve', *Lkv*, 2.6, 21–24; 'Herr Döblin wird gestrichen', *Lkv*, 2.10, 36.

44   Gallas, p. 56.

Lukács himself later conceded that 'es sei "ungerecht" gewesen, Brecht mit der linkssektiererischen Gruppe im BPRS zu identifizieren'.[45] Thus, Lukács admits to having consciously conflated Brecht's aesthetic position with the internal political standpoint of the radical left. Secondly, Lukács's assertion of a more bourgeois-centred aesthetic rested paradoxically not on a discrediting of the *Arbeiterschriftsteller*, but on attacks on writers of bourgeois origin. This focus of Lukács's later attacks on bourgeois writers – that is, the shift in target from Bredel, a proletarian writer, to Ottwalt, Brecht, Sinclair, and Tretyakov, all bourgeois writers – is also revealed by Gallas to have been a tactical manoeuvre on Lukács's part, primarily as a self-protective response to the attacks from the proletarian left embodied by Gotsche.[46] After all, Lukács and other bourgeois intellectuals in the *Bund* held by definition a precarious and insecure position within an association devoted to proletarian literature. As Russell Berman points out, Lukács 'simply moved to the more vulnerable bourgeois allies of revolutionary literature'.[47]

What these observations suggest is that it would be naive to take Lukács's Bredel and Ottwalt essays at face value as expressions of a purely aesthetic viewpoint, and this ties in with other analyses of the Lukács-Ottwalt debate which raise inconsistencies in the Lukács essays. Both Berman and Robert Cohen, for instance, focus on Lukács's analysis of Tolstoy's *Resurrection* where the Russian novelist's living and breathing narrative is contrasted positively with Ottwalt's supposedly flat and schematic portrayal. However, Cohen demonstrates that greater similarity exists between the two texts than Lukács is prepared to admit. Indeed:

> [Die Wanzengeschichte] zeigt, daß gerade jene Mittel des großen bürgerlichen Romans, welche Lukács an Tolstoi so lobt, auch in Ottwalts Tatsachenroman fruchtbar gemacht werden. Und daß dieser Tatsachenroman, beeinflußt von Fontane, Heinrich Mann und wohl auch Tolstoi, sich dem von Lukács geforderten Anknüpfen bei den großen Meistern keineswegs 'radikal' widersetzt.[48]

Berman too undermines Lukács's analysis of the Tolstoy novel as a positive counter-example, concluding that 'the contrasts between the realist novel and the documentary novel which Lukács emphasises are either nonexistent or politically misrepresented', while Simone Barck is another who has raised inconsistencies and contradictions in the Lukács analysis of Ottwalt's novel, arguing that in his

---

45 Gallas, p. 221, note 8.
46 Gallas, p. 123.
47 Russell Berman, 'Lukács' Critique of Bredel and Ottwalt: A political account of an aesthetic debate of 1931–32', *New German Critique*, 10 (1977), 155–78 (p. 173).
48 Robert Cohen, 'Die gefährliche Ästhetik Ernst Ottwalts', *The German Quarterly*, 61 (1988), 229–48 (p. 240).

abstract-philosophical analysis Lukács 'an dem Roman vorbeitheoretisiert'.[49] If Lukács's aim was to repel experimental, open aesthetics, the selection of Bredel and Ottwalt as targets of criticism is difficult to justify. As Cohen suggests, the reportage of a writer such as Egon Erwin Kisch would have made for a more appropriate object of analysis.[50]

Cohen and Berman agree that the resolution to these contradictions lies in a more political interpretation of Lukács's aesthetic essays. Cohen chooses to stress the importance of internal Communist party politics and direct instructions from Moscow in determining Lukács's interventions. As Cohen suggests, the additional dimension provided by internal Communist Party politics is central to understanding the selection of Lukács's targets: 'In Lukács' Kritik an [Brecht] wird deutlich, daß es hier, über die Literatur hinaus, um das Durchsetzen einer Linie ging, von der aus Brecht, ebenso wie Ottwalt und Tretjakov, als "Linksabweichler" erschienen.'[51] Drawing on recent research, Cohen also claims that Lukács had 'den "konkreten Parteiauftrag" gehabt, die in der Russischen Assoziation proletarischer Schriftsteller (RAPP) ausgearbeiteten Richtlinien sowjetischer Literatur auch im deutschen Verband durchzusetzen'. Thus, Ottwalt's novel was not itself the object of Lukács's attack, merely the most convenient piece of evidence he could find, the choice motivated not by genuine aesthetic objections but by tactical, political criteria. This, for Cohen, explains the internal contradictions in Lukács's aesthetic critique. Berman goes one step further, invoking not a Moscow-based cultural-political explanation, but attributing more purely political and ideological motivations for Lukács's attacks on Ottwalt and Bredel. Hence, '[Lukács's] criticism instead must be understood as an ultimately political attempt to subordinate the revolutionary cultural consciousness from below to the Party structure from above'.[52] Particularly revealing in this context are Lukács's responses to Gotsche concerning the nature of literary criticism. Here, Berman sees Lukács 'provoked into revealing his political leaning with embarrassing clarity':

> Wer etwa meint, die marxistische, führende, leitende, falsche Wege der schöpferischen Methode zergliedernde, für richtige schöpferische Methode kämpfende Kritik durch Massenkritik zu ersetzen, der steht literatur-politisch so, wie ein Parteigenosse, der meinen würde, die Arbeit der zentralen ideologischen und strategischen Leitung ließe sich durch spontane Betriebsdiskussionen 'ersetzen'. (*Lkv*, 4.4, 31)

For Berman a political and ideological standpoint of Stalinist authoritarianism lies at the heart of Lukács's aesthetic theory: '[Lukács's] aesthetic theories are the

---

49 Berman, p. 175; Simone Barck, 'Achtung vor dem Material: Zur dokumentarischen Schreibweise bei Ernst Ottwalt', in Silvia Schlenstedt (ed.), *Wer schreibt, handelt: Strategien und Verfahren literarischer Arbeit vor und nach 1933* (Berlin: Aufbau, 1986), pp. 84–118 (p. 98).
50 Cohen, p. 241.
51 Cohen, p. 243. Subsequent reference, pp. 239–40.
52 Berman, p. 156. Subsequent reference, p. 172.

consequence of a thorough rejection of any syndicalist, council communist tendencies. The authoritarian relationship of the critic to the artists, which Lukács represents, equals the relationship of the Party to Lukács's class, of the Party leader to the Party and of theory to practice.'[53] For Berman, Gallas's treatment of the Ottwalt and Bredel debate as an aesthetic debate is inadequate since that debate 'takes on meaning only within the socio-political context of the development of Stalinism'.

Clearly, these non-aesthetic factors are significant in determining the outcome of the aesthetic debates in the *Bund* and *Die Linkskurve*. Textual evidence from the Ottwalt and Bredel debates points to the importance of the Moscow connection. In his response to Gotsche (*Lkv*, 4.4, 30–33), for instance, Lukács makes explicit reference to the leading theoretician of the RAPP, Leopold Averbakh, while in his own response to Lukács Ottwalt pointedly makes it clear 'daß wir nicht blindlings die literaturpolitischen Probleme der Sowjet-Union in unsere literaturpolitische Situation übernehmen können' (*Lkv*, 4.10, 23). Gallas too highlights the importance of the RAPP in determining the aesthetic direction of the BPRS in Germany. Referring, for instance, to the tendency amongst prominent *Bund* members to advocate experimental aesthetics in advance of 1929, Gallas comments as follows: 'Daß der [BPRS] und seine Zeitschrift *Die Linkskurve* schließlich doch nicht zum Träger und Befürworter dieser Entwicklung wurden, verweist zunächst auf die [RAPP] und die Abhängigkeit, in der sich der deutsche Bund ihr gegenüber befand.'[54] Furthermore, it is difficult not to attribute the failure to attack Kisch – a broadly favourable review which entirely overlooked aesthetic questions appears noticeably alongside Gábor's attack on Brecht in the final issue of the journal (*Lkv*, 4.11/12, 32–35) – to factional, internal-political reasons, rather than to any aesthetic criteria.

However, it may also be that a distinction needs to be drawn between Lukács's Bredel and Ottwalt essays, which are so often seen as components in a single debate, not least of course by Schäfer himself. A comparison of the initial Bredel and Ottwalt essays, 'Willi Bredels Romane' and 'Reportage oder Gestaltung', reveals the former to be a much more concrete piece of literary criticism. Of course, the titles given to the essays already indicate that their aims differ: the former tackles Bredel's novels directly, noticeably under the generic heading 'Neue Bücher'; the latter considers much broader theoretical categories. It is also worth noting here that critiques of Lukács's essays centre principally on his Ottwalt analyses and on his response to Gotsche, rather than his initial Bredel essay, and that Bredel himself accepted Lukács's criticism with equanimity. It may be that this first Bredel essay is best read not in conjunction with those later tactically influenced contributions, but with Becher's programmatic essay 'Unsere Wendung' which appeared in October 1931 (*Lkv*, 3.10, 1–8), in the issue

---

53 Berman, p. 172. Subsequent reference, p. 178.
54 Gallas, p. 96.

preceding Lukács's first Bredel essay. In this essay, Becher describes the achievements of proletarian-revolutionary literature to date, but he also devotes much space to a newly found necessity for criticism and self-criticism:

> Die Existenz unserer Literatur können wir aber nur sichern, wenn wir weitergehen und unsere Literatur zur Entwicklung treiben. Wie die revolutionäre Bewegung allein den Mut anbringen kann, vertrauend auf ihre Gesundheit und Stärke, eine schonungslose Kritik zu üben an ihren Schwächen und Fehlern, so kann auch die proletarisch-revolutionäre Literatur allein in aller Offenheit und vor aller Öffentlichkeit sich selbst kritisieren und diese Kritik ertragen. [...] Die Führung des Bundes proletarisch-revolutionärer Schriftsteller ist der Ansicht, daß heute in der Phase der Entwicklung unserer Literatur eine solche Kritik nicht mehr hemmend, sondern weitertreibend wirkt.

This passage seems to find a strong echo in Lukács's Bredel essay:

> Unsere proletarisch-revolutionäre Literatur hat ihre Existenz erkämpft und in harten Kämpfen ihre Existenzberechtigung erwiesen. Unsere proletarisch-revolutionäre Schriftsteller [...] müssen [...] durch unerbittliche Selbstkritik, durch schonungsloses Aufdecken des Zurückbleibens und seiner Ursachen [...] diesen Abstand erkennen und ihn [...] so rasch wie möglich liquidieren. Diese Kritik der Arbeiten Bredels ist im vollsten Sinne des Wortes eine Selbstkritik. (*Lkv*, 3.11, 26)

Behind the formulaic rhetoric lies a genuine and fundamental tension in the advocacy of proletarian-revolutionary literature by Becher and Lukács. To put matters bluntly, much of what was produced under the banner of the BPRS and even within the pages of *Die Linkskurve* continued to be of poor quality. In their own assessment of entries to the journal's poetry prize, for example, the editors had been forced to adopt a consolatory line: 'Und so sind auch deine Gedichte meist noch Versuche. [...] Schadet nichts. Denn gute Gedichte zu machen, ist besonders schwer' (*Lkv*, 2.6, 12–13). If it is difficult to see how the kind of fact-based prose produced by *Arbeiterkorrespondenten* such as Bredel could have been considered too aesthetically experimental, it may rather have been its crudeness and lack of sophistication which attracted the criticism of Lukács and Becher, who after all had their own credibility to uphold.

Crisis and the Marxist Left

What all these observations have in common is that they establish journal-specific motivations for the assertion of a restorative aesthetic in *Die Linkskurve*. In particular, it is clear how internal factional politics can acquire their own strong dynamic, independent of the broader context. As such, although the surface aesthetics match, it becomes increasingly difficult to position the journal within the 1930 paradigm, and increasing distance is established between *Die Linkskurve* and *Die Kolonne*. And yet, we cannot ignore the principal factor which offers an area of potential commonality beyond any superficial manifestation of aesthetic similarities, namely the burgeoning economic and social crises of 1929–1932 which for Schäfer act as a catalyst for his restorative shift. Gallas for one makes little or no mention of the crisis and certainly does not attribute to it any role as a causal factor in the journal's ultimate assertion of a conservative aesthetic programme. Indeed, Gallas even suggests that it was the relative stability of the Weimar Republic, and the resulting absence of enthusiasm for a radical left-wing message, which persuaded the *Bund* to pursue a more inclusive, less sectarian line in mid-1930:

> Als mit der Stabilisierung der Weimarer Republik die Aussicht auf einen baldigen Sieg der proletarischen Revolution schwand, galt es für die KPD [...] vielmehr Parteilose, SPD-Anhänger, Kleinbürger usw. für die Politik der Partei zu gewinnen.[55]

This is certainly a notable oversight on Gallas's part, for what emerges most clearly as a constant throughout the publication run of *Die Linkskurve* is the precarious existence of communist writers in the final years of Weimar. Betraying the status of *Die Linkskurve* as a political organ as much as a literary one, explicit reference to the political turmoil of the times and above all to the reality of censorship and the suppression of KPD publishing activities, can be traced from the opening issue of the journal all the way through to the final issue, in particular on the front page and in the concluding *Glossen-Mitteilungen-Berichte*. In that first issue, for instance, Becher's opening programmatic essay describes the nature of the times as 'eine Zwangstellung', 'die Zeit der großen Schmelze' and 'die Neuschaffung der Welt' (*Lkv*, 1.1, 1–3), Kurt Kersten writes of workers' unrest and of the violent May Day clashes of 1929 (*Lkv*, 1.1, 19–21), while numerous articles deal with censorship and the necessity of armed struggle.[56] In the very final issue of the journal, alongside the anti-Brecht polemics, a palpable sense of crisis remains. The front-page essay is devoted to the crisis caused by unemployment amongst academics and intellectuals, Theodor Balk reports on industrial unrest in the small town of Torgau, while the final brief item appeals for book donations for the 8,000 proletarians already sentenced to imprisonment and the 45,000 awaiting trial.[57] Confirmation, if such were needed, that this mood of crisis impacted on the members of the BPRS, as on others across the political spectrum, is provided by Silvia Schlenstedt: 'Daß eine Kulturkrise bislang ungekannten Ausmaßes die Gesellschaft erschüttert – dieser Tatbestand wird um

---

55 Gallas, p. 83.
56 See Josef Lenz, 'Warum sind wir keine Pazifisten', *Lkv*, 1.1, 3–7; Erich Weinert, 'Niederträchtige Zwischenrufe in dem Antikriegs-Aufruf der SPD', *Lkv*, 1.1, 29–30; Emil Ginkel, 'Fitschgetau oder Ein neuer Zensurskandal', *Lkv*, 1.1, 22–24; Paul Körner, 'Der Ziehhund vor dem Reichsgericht', *Lkv*, 1.1, 35–36.
57 See 'Seele und Brotaufstrich', *Lkv*, 4.11/12, 1–3; Theodor Balk, 'Streik in der Kleinstadt', *Lkv*, 4.11/12, 11–15; 'Bücher für unsere Gefangenen', *Lkv*, 4.11/12, 40.

1930 in Deutschland vielfach benannt. Von ihr sprechen die Marxisten in der *Linkskurve*, die Liberalen im *Tagebuch*, die Konservativen in der *Neuen Rundschau*.'[58]

Nonetheless, there is no explicit evidence that Lukács, Wittfogel and others connected the on-going mood of crisis with their aesthetic programme. Certainly no mention is made in the central essays discussed above, and one could argue, with a certain degree of plausibility, that Lukács, arriving only in the summer of 1931, was insulated from the particularly savage effects wrought by the Wall Street Crash on the German economy and society and that, in any case, the impending collapse of bourgeois capitalist society constituted not a crisis for the Marxist intellectual, but a political opportunity. It is here that Schlenstedt is able to provide a potentially very significant piece of evidence. As a document of the prevailing social mood, the September 1930 issue of *Die Linkskurve* is as persuasive as any. Published in the run-up to the *Reichstag* elections of 14 September 1930, the first three pages of the journal are occupied by a party-political appeal on behalf of the KPD, 'An alle Schriftsteller, Künstler, Gelehrten, Ärzte, Juristen, Lehrer und Studenten Deutschlands!', the opening sentence of which makes clear the single most significant issue to face the readers of *Die Linkskurve*: 'eine wirtschaftliche Krise von größten Ausmaßen rast durch Deutschland' (*Lkv*, 2.9, 1). The following ten pages are devoted to a questionnaire eliciting the views of prominent intellectuals on 'den Kernproblemen der Gegenwart: Wirtschaftskrise, politischer und Kulturfaschismus, Gefahr eines Krieges gegen die Sowjetunion [...]'. As much as anyone else the Marxist intellectual classes found themselves 'im Wirbel der gegenwärtigen Krise' (*Lkv*, 2.9, 4). Closely related to the content of this issue of *Die Linkskurve* is an election pamphlet published by the BPRS for the same Reichstag elections which posed the question in its title 'Kulturkrise und kein Ausweg?'. It is this document which Schlenstedt highlights, and two factors in her analysis mark it out as significant in the context of the 1930 paradigm. Firstly, in its explicit reference to Heidegger – 'wir schweben in Angst' – Schlenstedt sees in the pamphlet an acknowledgement of this anxiety as 'eine Grundstimmung der Zeit und dahinter die verzweifelte Frage nach dem Ausweg'.[59] Or in the words of the pamphlet itself:

> Die persönliche Unsicherheit der Existenz der geistigen Arbeiter, die Unmöglichkeit, ihre Kräfte und Fähigkeiten voll zu entfalten, die Aussichtslosigkeit der Versuche, ihre Leistungen an den Mann zu bringen [...] – alles das kennzeichnet den Umfang der Kulturkrise, in der wir leben.[60]

---

58 Silvia Schlenstedt, 'Schnittpunkt 1930: Standort und Funktion des Schriftstellers in der großen Krise', in Silvia Schlenstedt (ed.), *Wer schreibt, handelt: Strategien und Verfahren literarischer Arbeit vor und nach 1933* (Berlin: Aufbau, 1986), pp. 11–52 (p. 11).

59 Schlenstedt, p. 12.

60 Quoted by Schlenstedt, p. 12.

Secondly, Schlenstedt identifies the writers of the pamphlet as Otto Biha, Alfred Kurella, and Karl August Wittfogel.[61] In this pamphlet and in the figure of Wittfogel, there exists at least a circumstantial connection between the on-going socio-economic crisis, a fundamental mood of anxiety informing intellectual thought around 1930, and the restorative aesthetic programme advanced in the final phase of *Die Linkskurve*.

The reference in the election pamphlet to Heidegger's existential philosophy offers a further point of contact between *Die Linkskurve* and Schäfer's period-isation essay, and through that essay to *Die Kolonne*. In simplified terms, Schäfer presents three possible responses by writers to the crisis of 1930 – commitment to the Marxist left; commitment to the *völkisch* right; and a form of apolitical withdrawal – and it is *Die Kolonne* which Schäfer identifies as the programmatic document for this final 'existentialistische Gruppe'.[62] While we have questioned the applicability of this label in narrow terms to *Die Kolonne* itself, the dissemination of the work of Heidegger and Jaspers is seen by Schäfer to act as an important background to the Third Reich poetry of *Kolonne* writers, such as Eich and Huchel.[63] Furthermore German existential philosophy also figures prominently for other proponents of a 1930 paradigm, including Frank Trommler.[64] Against the background of the successive crises of National Socialism, exile, and war and the on-going crisis of modernisation, this is a strand of thought which offers a significant element of continuity across 1933 and 1945, above all as another possible source of intellectual stability. As we shall see, this is manifested in our corpus in the exile journal *Maß und Wert* and in the post-war journal *Der Ruf*.

Hence, for all their political and ideological divergence, the leading figures in *Die Kolonne* and *Die Linkskurve* clearly shared a common intellectual climate, and if we seek to look beyond their superficially antagonistic positions a broad commonality of purpose may emerge. After all, both Raschke and the *Linkskurve* intellectuals seem to have been seeking sources of authority and authenticity against a background of anxiety and uncertainty. For Lukács and Becher, it was the voices of the proletariat which provided authenticity of experience, and the voices of Marx, Engels, Hegel, and Balzac which offered intellectual authority. If specific tactical and political factors influenced the development of Lukács's aesthetic programme, the prevailing mood of crisis undoubtedly aided its propagation, and it is noteworthy that Lukács, like Raschke, perceived amidst this crisis an opportunity to shape the future direction of German literary culture. In

---

61 Schlenstedt, p. 560, note 1.
62 Schäfer, 'Periodisierung', p. 98.
63 Schäfer, 'Periodisierung', p. 100.
64 See Frank Trommler, 'Nachkriegsliteratur: Eine neue deutsche Literatur?', in Nicolas Born and Jürgen Manthey (eds), *Literaturmagazin 7: Nachkriegsliteratur* (Reinbek: Rowohlt, 1977), pp. 167–86 (pp. 171–72).

this context, one further point might be made in relation to the aesthetics of Bredel and Ottwalt and their relationship to the 1930 paradigm. Robert Cohen compares Ottwalt's mixture of documentary and fictional styles to Döblin's *Berlin Alexanderplatz*, identifying a fundamental difference in the way the two authors handle documentary material.[65] While Döblin unsettles the reader by questioning and undermining the status of 'factual' information, for Ottwalt factual material serves a purely functional purpose as documentary evidence in his critique of Weimar justice. In this sense, factual material acts as a guarantor of authenticity, as a source of stability, where instability of meaning, both aesthetically and socially, prevails. In this way, the Bredel and Ottwalt texts, the rejection of which Schäfer views as paradigmatic for his restorative shift, actually emerge as hybrid, transitional texts in terms of the 1930 paradigm. Pre-1930 in terms of the institution of literature and the conception of the author, these texts with a functional reader-orientation exhibit post-1930 characteristics in terms of the search for a stability of meaning. In this way, 1930 represents not so much a sudden shift to aesthetic conservatism as an accumulation of conservative features.

Die literarische Welt

Haas and Becher: quality or equality?

Amongst the contributions to the opening issue of *Die Linkskurve* which set out its sectarian left-wing agenda was an essay by Kurt Kläber addressed directly 'An die Leser der *Literarischen Welt*' (*Lkv*, 1.1, 24–28). Responding to a special issue of *Die literarische Welt* from July 1929 devoted to *Arbeiterdichtung* (*DlW*, 5.28), the tone of Kläber's essay was throughout scornful of readers of Willy Haas's literary weekly, expressing surprise and sympathy, for instance, that their bath-time reading should be disturbed by 'diese[n] Halbwilden aus der Unterwelt, die sogar schon dichten können', and reserving particular ire for Alice Rühle-Gerstel who in her contribution to the *Sondernummer* (*DlW*, 5.28, 1–2) had questioned how proletarian art might be defined and indeed whether it existed at all. In turn, that first issue of *Die Linkskurve* provoked a caustic response from Haas himself who addressed a mock *Ferienbrief* to his colleagues on *Die literarische Welt* (*DlW*, 5.35, 7–8), in which he savagely satirised the attempts by *Die Linkskurve* to brand non-committed left-leaning intellectuals as contributors to social reaction:

> Vor dem Schlafengehen werden noch, zur besonderen Belustigung des Herausgebers, hungernde Proletarierkinder aus der Belegschaft der *Literarischen Welt* nach 14-

---

65 Cohen, p. 237.

stündiger harter Arbeit ein bißchen mit Rindlederpeitschen gepeitscht, worauf ich befriedigt in meinem Seidenbett entschlummere. [...] Zwischendurch konferiere ich in meinem luxuriösen Rolls Royce mit Mr Morgan und Briand, wie mit Hilfe der *L.W.* ein Blutbad in Sowjetrußland angerichtet werden könnte.

This was not the first clash between Haas and members of the BPRS to find its way into the pages of *Die literarische Welt*. Less than a year earlier in October 1928, Haas had published a front-page editorial entitled 'Wir und die "Radikalen"' (*DlW*, 4.43, 1), in which he condemned bourgeois writers of the radical Left as mere followers of literary fashion. Haas claimed to be responding to criticism from 'ein paar linksradikalen Literaten' that, despite his openly declared sympathy, he had failed to publicly approve the political goals of communism. Principal amongst the left-wing literati attacked by Haas, and named explicitly in the editorial, was the future editor of *Die Linkskurve* Johannes R. Becher. On this occasion it was Becher who was provoked into a response, his letter 'Antwort eines Radikalen' (*DlW*, 4.46, 11) being published in *Die literarische Welt* three weeks later on 16 November 1928.

A number of points of significance emerge from these confrontations between *Die literarische Welt* and the BPRS. Firstly, in the assertion of literature as a weapon in the class struggle – 'Die Kunst ist eine Waffe der Klassen im Klassenkampf' – in the criticism of contemporary bourgeois literature – 'Wir sind aber der Ansicht, daß die heutige bürgerliche Literatur in ihrer Gesamtheit unfähig ist, Wesentliches zur Lösung der großen Fragen der Gegenwart bei-zutragen' – and in the attempt to isolate themselves – 'Trennen wir uns, grenzen wir ab, das ist die einzige Möglichkeit, um vielleicht einmal zusammenzukommen' (*DlW*, 4.46, 11) – Becher's response to Haas again highlights the nature of the founding programme of *Die Linkskurve*. This starkly drawn opposition between the *Linkskurve* programme of party-political engagement and that of *Die literarische Welt* also throws into sharp relief the distinctiveness of Haas's own editorial policy. As Becher had maintained in another attack on Haas's journal as early as August 1926:

'Jeden Standpunkt zu Wort kommen lassen!' Ein derartiger Standpunkt der Stand-punktlosigkeit ist das Programm der besten literarischen Revuen der Gegenwart (zum Beispiel der *literarischen Welt*). Ein interessanter, mit allerlei amüsantem Klatsch zubereiteter Mischmasch, in dem jeder Ansatz von Ernst mit wahren Orgien von Plattheit, frivolstem Zynismus, hohlster Pathetik kombiniert wird; das nennt sich (und kann sich mit Recht nennen) eine repräsentative Vertretung der deutschen Literatur. [...] Diese Literaten sind bestenfalls noch Arrangeure, geistige Schau-fensterdekorateure. Die Welt ist ihnen ein Potpourri, ein sensationelles Ragout von Dingen, Menschen und Meinungen, zu weiter nichts da, als einem ein wenig die eigene Langeweile, Gehirnöde und Herzensarmut zu vertreiben. Zu feige, das offen auszusprechen, wird diese Tatsache dekorativ umschrieben. Unsere Aufgabe aber ist es, das offen auszusprechen, was unausgesprochen in den Äußerungen dieser Literaturcliquen enthalten liegt. Daß es 'auch' eine Aufgabe des Menschen ist, die

Welt zu verändern, das Leben des Menschen bewußt zu gestalten – ach, das hat man längst vergessen.[66]

Of course, symptomatic of the breadth of views published in *Die literarische Welt* is the fact that Becher himself, such a staunch critic of the journal, was given room not only to publish his response to Haas's editorial, but also some of his own literary output. This is a point made by Haas looking back on his editorship:

> Die Tatsache, daß Johannes R. Becher mich ziemlich regelmäßig und sehr scharf in seinem eigenen literarischen Parteiorgan *Die Linkskurve* als 'Sozialfaschisten' angriff, hinderte weder ihn noch mich, von Zeit zu Zeit Erörterungen und dichterische Werke von ihm in der *Literarischen Welt* zu veröffentlichen.[67]

Following his reply to Haas in November 1928, Becher made five further contributions to *Die literarische Welt*, amongst them four poems published in the first half of 1929. Here we find a point of contact between Becher and the *Kolonne* poets, as he looked back to childhood experience as a source of literary inspiration. The publication of his poem 'Meine Kindheit' in March 1929, as a contribution to an article entitled 'Die Krise' (*DlW*, 5.9, 3), also establishes a connection between these shared literary developments, which cut across ideological standpoints, and the on-going mood of social crisis.

The clashes between *Die literarische Welt* and the BPRS are also noteworthy for the way in which they illustrate the scepticism with which many writers and critics regarded the proletarian writing promoted by *Die Linkskurve*. As Gábor was to complain in his review of Marchwitza's *Schlacht vor Kohle* in *Die Linkskurve* in May 1932: 'Der bürgerliche Kritiker und sein Kollege, der Literat, sehen hier [...] nur einen neuen, primitiven Roman, den wieder einer, der nicht schreiben kann, geschrieben hat' (*Lkv*, 4.5, 31). It was this kind of scepticism about the quality of workers' writing which informed Haas's editorial attack on the 'radicals', since Haas saw political engagement being substituted for genuine literary quality. As is clear from this article, it was the maintenance of this notion of quality which underpinned Haas's editorial programme:

> Dieser Qualitätsbegriff hat nichts verschwommen Metaphysisches an sich. Er existiert überall – warum nicht in der Literatur? Ein Motor von Rolls Royce, aus dem konservativen England, ist eben besser als jeder russische Benzinmotor, da läßt sich nichts machen. Welches verdächtige Interesse also haben diese Herren, den objektiven Qualitätsbegriff gerade *aus der Literatur* zu eskamotieren und jeden als Verräter am Proletariat zu brandmarken, der ihn erhalten will? Glaubten wir nicht an diese *objektive* literarische Qualität – dann dürften wir eben keine kritische Literaturzeitschrift herausgeben. Indem wir es tun, bekennen wir unseren Glauben, Qualitäten messen zu können; unseren Glauben *an die Qualität überhaupt*. (*DlW*, 4.43, 1)

By the same token what Gábor and above all Lukács were seeking to achieve in the final phase of *Die Linkskurve* was precisely to apply these kinds of

---

66   Johannes R. Becher, 'Der tote Punkt', p. 18.

67   Willy Haas, 'Nachwort', p. 485.

conventional bourgeois notions of literary quality to proletarian-revolutionary writing. Although Gábor would scarcely have conceded as much, his comments in the Marchwitza review were to some extent as applicable to Lukács, a bourgeois literary critic in all but name, as they were to Haas.

In this respect, all three of the literary journals under consideration here share some degree of commonality of approach. Through Raschke and Eich *Die Kolonne* had been particularly strident in rejecting what it perceived to be the essentially non-literary writing of socialist engagement. That these views were not restricted to the minority-interest pages of *Die Kolonne* is demonstrated by that same special issue of *Die literarische Welt* which prompted Kläber's essay in the opening issue of *Die Linkskurve*. Alongside Rühle-Gerstel's essay on the front page was an essay by a young Martin Raschke entitled 'Eine Kultur wird gestartet' (*DlW*, 5.28, 1–2), in which he surveyed the development of working-class literature since 1914. While perhaps more measured in tone than the polemical stance adopted subsequently in his own journal, Raschke nonetheless encapsulates the scepticism of bourgeois critics alluded to by Gábor, and in fact pre-empts the kind of judgement made by the *Linkskurve* editorial team itself on the journal's own poetry prize:

> Wenn aber diese ewig wiederkehrenden Reime Tot, Not, Brot, Schlacht, Nacht, wenn jedes an romantischem Vorbild geschulte Gedicht Schnittmuster der kommenden Kultur darstellt, wenn es schon genügt, mit dialektischer Färbung bewährten Volksliedton zu wiederholen oder durch billige Vokalmalerei Maschinenbewegung zu imitieren, wenn es wirklich hinreicht, einige Jahre im Bergwerk zu gastieren, um als Dichter des Zukünftigen zu gelten: dann laßt uns diese Kulissenwelt unbekümmert zusammenrennen.

Raschke was far from an infrequent contributor to *Die literarische Welt*, making a total of 49 contributions in the four years between 1929 and 1932, at an average of more than one per month. All but ten of those contributions were short review articles, normally tucked away on page five or six under the regular heading 'Buch-Chronik der Woche', and on only one other occasion did Raschke appear on the front page (*DlW*, 7.43, 1–2). The suspicion that Raschke enjoyed noteworthy prominence on this occasion as a critic of *Arbeiterdichtung* for *Die literarische Welt*, and that he expressed a position with which the editor was sympathetic, is reinforced by the presence of a further Raschke contribution to that special issue surveying workers' literature (*DlW*, 5.28, 5–6). More tellingly perhaps, Haas's satirical *Ferienbrief* appears alongside a rather more earnest open letter from Raschke to Kurt Kläber (*DlW*, 5.35, 8), defending his own contributions to the special issue. At least on this occasion, Haas and Raschke seem to have shared a common purpose, even if that common purpose was expressed in markedly different styles.

Founding programme

We have already noted the claims made for the representativity and objectivity of Haas's journal. As 'eine Zeitung der offensten Diskussion', Haas consciously set his journal against the kind of party-political organ of which *Die Linkskurve* is an example: 'Wer Wert darauf legt, sich schnell und mühelos zu entscheiden, mag sein Parteiblatt lesen, das ihm die Schwierigkeit jeder großen Entscheidung hinlänglich vertuscht und verschweigt; nicht unser Blatt' (*DlW*, 1.1, 2). This objectivity was most readily apparent in Haas's favourite editorial tactic, the *Rundfrage* in which a range of prominent intellectuals were invited to comment on a particular issue. In his memoirs, Haas made clear how his editorial policy operated in relation to such contributions: 'Die Voraussetzung einer solchen Rundfrage ist, daß man alle Antworten unredigiert abdruckt, sonst ist die Pointe der Rundfrage ganz verloren.'[68] Nonetheless, for all this apparent objectivity, it would be incorrect to underestimate Haas's role in steering his journal in a very particular cultural direction. Haas's editorial practice was far from the arbitrary pot-pourri identified by Becher, and as he himself pointed out in the afterword to his subsequent anthology of contributions to the journal: '*Die literarische Welt* wurde redaktionell so gut wie nie improvisiert, es wurde fast immer nach festen Plänen gearbeitet.'[69] As the exchanges with Becher demonstrate, Haas's principal editorial criterion was one of quality and this selectivity is confirmed by his objections to simply imitating the editorial method of *Les Nouvelles Littéraires*: 'Jedenfalls war ich wild entschlossen, etwas anderes als die *Nouvelles Littéraires* zu machen, die zwar international Geltung hatten, mir aber gar nicht gefielen, weil sie Gutes, Mittelmäßiges und Schlechtes ziemlich wahllos zusammenkochten.' Already within the first six months of the journal's existence, Haas went back on an earlier assertion that it needed no explicit programme. In the sixth edition of 1926, he again stressed the necessity for tolerance and the need to present a wide selection of literature to the readers. In addition, he sought to justify another of his common editorial practices, namely the celebration of anniversaries and memorials for prominent writers of the past:

> [Unser Organ] muß versuchen, eine gemeinsame Basis zu schaffen, [...] durch den festen Entschluß, der menschlichen, persönlichen Qualität in der Literatur, mehr als der bloß literarischen, Ansehen und Respekt zu verschaffen. Das deutsche Volk hat einen ungeheuren, unerschöpflichen Schatz solcher menschlichen Werte in den großen Männern seiner Vergangenheit. [...] *Deshalb feiern wir Gedenktage. (DlW*, 2.6, 1)

In this way, the premium placed by Haas on literary quality was allied to a second guiding principle, a respect for the timeless values of the literary tradition. As a special issue (*DlW*, 4.36) devoted to Tolstoy's centenary makes clear, there was the potential for overlap here between Haas's celebration of the tradition and that

---

68   Haas, *Erinnerungen*, p. 180.
69   Haas, 'Nachwort', p. 482. Subsequent reference, p. 477.

subsequently promoted in the final phase of *Die Linkskurve*. However, Haas's maintenance of the tradition, shaped by his own *Bildungsdialekt*, was not restricted by a narrow stylistic or ideologised perspective, but rather encompassed tremendous breadth. Hence, any overlap with the Lukács tradition is indicative not so much of convergence on the particular aesthetic value of nineteenth-century Russian Realism as of a more broadly shared cultural attitude to tradition.

The clearest expression of Haas's attitude to tradition in this founding phase of the journal comes in an essay published in the third edition of 1926, suggestively entitled 'Wege in die Vergangenheit' (*DlW*, 2.3, 6). In this article, Haas considers a number of recent literary phenomena which seek to bring works from various traditions to contemporary attention, namely: an anthology of Japanese literature edited by Paul Adler; reprint editions of the literary journals of German Romanticism; an edition of *Gespräche mit Heine*; and a collection of German prose texts extending from Lessing to Bismarck, edited by Hugo von Hofmannsthal. Significantly, these publications are viewed not as isolated phenomena, but as part of an important literary trend:

> Die nächsten Jahren werden, soweit es überhaupt noch eine geistig gerichtete deutsche Jugend gibt, sehr stark der Durchackerung und Fruchtbarmachung traditioneller Werte gelten; und wer die phantastischen, haltlosen und zum Teil sehr gefährlichen Deutungsversuche solcher Werte bei manchen wertvollen jungen Menschen von heute beobachtet, wird mit dem Verfasser einig sein, daß das Problem der *fruchtbaren Bindung an geistige Traditionen* sehr wichtig und sehr aktuell ist.

What Haas means by a fruitful connection to the tradition becomes clear when he considers recent attempts to create revolutionary art without any such awareness of the past:

> Der Fehler auf geistigem Gebiet war zweifellos die furchtbare Zusammenhang-losigkeit mit der Vergangenheit. Nicht nur, aber vor allem mit der eigenen. Auch das Neue entsteht nicht aus dem Nichts; es ist nur die Neukristallisation nach einem neuen Achsensystem dessen, was immer da war.

It was this dialectic between tradition and revolution, between past and future, which underpinned Haas's advocacy of the tradition. His interest in the 'paths into the past' which he reviewed here was not that of an antiquarian, but as a believer in new art as a synthesis between tradition and revolution: 'So möchten diese "Wege in die Vergangenheit" gewertet werden: als Wege in die Zukunft.'

As Valentini makes clear, the source of this dualism can be traced back to the influence of Hofmannsthal during his long-running correspondence with the young Haas.[70] At the same time, Haas demonstrates in this founding phase an acute sense of the significance of the times which seems to go beyond his own formative influences. For Haas, the value of 'Wege in die Vergangenheit' lies above all in its timing, since it was clear to him that the attempts of the previous seven years (1918–1925) to achieve cultural renewal or revolution had failed:

---

70 Valentini, pp. 71–74.

'Diese Epoche ist vorüber. Alle konsequent Denkenden, die von Rechts wie die von Links, sind sich einig, daß keine Revolution, keine Erneuerung stattgefunden hat.' In this essay Haas expresses a strong intolerance to the culture of the early years of the Weimar Republic:

> Die Zeiten der literarischen Gourmandise sind vorbei. Aber auch die Zeiten des frechen Analphabetentums, des angeblich 'revolutionären' Stotterers, der aufgeblasenen Ignoranz. Wer umstürzen will, muß kennen, was er umstürzt; wer erhalten will, muß es noch besser kennen. Das ist die Lehre, die das Gestern über das Heute hinweg dem Morgen gibt, damit dieses Morgen der Morgen einer besseren Zukunft sei.

In a similar vein, in one of his regular 'Meine Meinung' columns from early 1926, Haas considers an Expressionist theatre review:

> A propos Expressionismus; was macht denn dieser Expressionismus? Immer Wohlauf? Letzthin hat er eine Revue gemacht. Das muß eine Sache sein! – denkt man vorher. Die Revue ist ja eigentlich die logische letzte Konsequenz des Bühnen-Expressionismus. (*DlW*, 2.10, 2)

In so doing, Haas was enunciating a widely-held feeling that Expressionism had run its course, a sentiment which had been current since at least 1920, most notably expressed perhaps by Kurt Pinthus in the 1922 edition of his Expressionist anthology *Menschheitsdämmerung*.[71]

Looking back from the 1960s, Haas emphasised further the significance of the timing of the journal's foundation. For Haas, 1925 'war genau der richtige Zeitpunkt', and 'Berlin genau der richtige Ort und ein Organ wie *Die literarische Welt* genau das richtige Organ'. Retrospectively, Haas saw 1925 marking the initiation of a new literary period: 'Eine Epoche des Hellenismus und Alexadrinismus, der herbstlichen Ernte, war allmählich hereingebrochen.'[72] Two significant features of this Hellenistic or Alexandrine period emerge from Haas's comments. Firstly, it is a transitional period of relative stability bounded by Expressionist revolution at one end and the upheavals around 1930 at the other:

> Der große Sturm dichterischer und künstlerischer Erneuerung, der etwa 1910 begonnen hatte [...] – der vulkanische Ausbruch neuer geistiger Feuer- und glühender Lavaströme – war nun, 1925, abgebbt [...]. Um 1930 bis 1931 schon war fast alles wieder verflogen.

Secondly, its productivity is born out of a reworking of pre-existing literary currents, both Expressionist and pre-Expressionist:

> Übrigens würde man eine solche alexandrinische Epoche tief unterschätzen, wenn man annehmen würde, sie sei schlechtweg unproduktiv. Sie hat nur eben ihre eigene Produktivität. Typisch dafür ist zum Beispiel der ungeheure Erfolg von Brecht-Weills *Dreigroschenoper* 1928. Dieses Werk entspringt gewiß echter Produktivität, aber sie ist gestützt durch viele und vielerlei literarische Traditionen, von François Villon über

---

71 See Anz and Stark, pp. 98–112.
72 Haas, 'Nachwort', p. 483. Subsequent references, pp. 482–83 and p. 483.

Gays *The Beggar's Opera* bis Kipling und Rimbaud. Das eben nenne ich *alexandrinisch.* Ja, wir möchten das zweite, größere Kunstwerk jener Epoche, Alfred Döblins monumentalen Roman *Berlin Alexanderplatz* in diesem Sinne noch *alexandrinisch* nennen: so originell er sich gibt und in der Tat ist, so ist es doch die Ernte aus vielerlei großen Versuchen expressionistischer erzählender Prosa, von Leonhard Franks Frühwerken bis zu James Joyces *Ulysses.*

Of course, in this regard Haas's aesthetic standpoint deviated substantially from that put forward in *Die Linkskurve* and *Die Kolonne.* As we have seen, Haas's enthusiasm for Brecht, Joyce, and Döblin was hardly shared by the *Linkskurve* theoreticians in its final phase, even if much of the antipathy towards Brecht and Döblin derived from factional political concerns, rather than purely aesthetic factors. Very clearly Haas exhibits in his own *Bildungsdialekt* an openness to canonical elements of 1920s modernism not reflected in the other two journals founded at the very end of the decade.

The connection between Haas's turn towards tradition and the specific context of 1925 is not only a literary-immanent phenomenon. As Valentini suggests it is also possible to ascribe to Haas's advocacy of the tradition a stabilising function amidst an on-going sense of social instability and political radicalisation:

> Gegenüber der radikalen Haltung erwies es sich als immer notwendiger, alle kulturellen Faktoren der Tradition zu erhalten, die Konzepte der Freiheit, der Nationalität und der Menschlichkeit, die vielleicht dem deutschen Volke das Bewußtsein seiner selbst hätten wiedergeben können. Das war die letzte Mission des deutschen Bürgertums. Wenn alle Werte in Zweifel gezogen werden, inklusive Dichtung und Literatur, haben Schriftsteller und Literaturkritiker eine klare und verantwortungsvolle Position einzunehmen. Willy Haas, mit der Redaktion der Zeitschrift betraut, war sich seiner Verantwortung als *homme de lettres* dem Publikum gegenüber bewußt und arbeitete auf eine informative Funktion auf zwei Ebenen hin: er wollte die Literatur der neuen Generation bekannt machen, gleichzeitig aber auf die Werte der Tradition und der Vergangenheit hinweisen in einer ununterbrochenen fruchtbaren Gegenüberstellung der Resultate beider Seiten.[73]

In particular in the literary sphere, Haas seems to perceive an on-going sense of crisis well in advance of the shocks of 1929–1932, perhaps what Schäfer refers to as 'das in den zwanziger Jahren latent vorhandene Krisenbewußtsein',[74] to which his advocacy of tradition may be connected. Already in the final three editions of 1925, Haas had published a long article by Walter von Molo entitled 'Die Lage unserer Literatur' (*DlW*, 1.11, 1–2; 1.12, 6; 1.13, 2–3). Von Molo's assessment was a depressing one: 'Was ist "unsere Literatur"? [...] Kurz und hart gesagt: ich finde die Lage unserer Literatur zum Ekeln!' (*DlW*, 1.11, 1) More explicit in terms of socio-historical factors is reference made by Haas to the crippling effects of inflation in an article relating a visit to the Insel publishing house in mid-1926. In

---

73 Valentini, p. 101.
74 Schäfer, 'Periodisierung', p. 96.

this same article, Haas advocates as an antidote the kind of sophisticated
publishing policy favoured by Insel:

> Es ist ein Komplex, der heute kaum noch zu überblicken ist; und doch ein höchst
> harmonisches und organisches Gebilde aus geistiger Vergangenheit und geistiger
> Zukunft, über dem der Goethesche Leitspruch stehen könnte: 'Ältestes bewahrt mit
> Treue, freundlich aufgefaßtes Neue' – also in dieser zerrissenen, orientierungslosen,
> innerlich ganz und gar unsicheren deutschen Gegenwart eine wirklich bildende,
> formende, schöpferische Kulturtat. (*DlW*, 2.29, 5)

Not only does this policy accord strikingly with the sentiments expressed by Haas
in 'Wege in die Vergangenheit', invoking the dialectic of past and future, it is also
seen to acquire its value against a specific background of uncertainty and loss of
orientation in contemporary society.

Beyond 1930: Haas, Raschke and the young generation

This explicit editorial emphasis on tradition and crisis in the literary sphere seems
to fade somewhat from view after the founding phase of the journal in
1925/1926, although Haas's programme of representativity and literary quality is
maintained in the day-to-day editorial practice of the journal. However, from
1930 onwards *Die literarische Welt* is characterised by a re-emergence of the
editorial concerns first expressed in its founding phase. In particular, a scepticism
concerning the cultural values of Germany's youth seems to have lain at the
centre of both the sense of perceived cultural crisis expressed by Haas in
1925/1926 and the accompanying dualism of past and future. Already in 'Wege in
die Vergangenheit' (*DlW*, 2.3, 6), for instance, Haas had questioned whether there
was such a thing as 'eine geistig gerichtete deutsche Jugend', while early in 1926,
he had used another of his 'Meine Meinung' (*DlW*, 2.13, 2) columns as an
opportunity to bemoan the loss of popularity for reading amongst the young and
the accompanying increase in the popularity of sport. The inclusion of this
column in Haas's essay collection *Gestalten der Zeit*, first published in 1930, under
the heading 'Die deutsche Situation um 1930' is indicative of the importance
attached by Haas to the question of the young generation, and the dualism of
youth and age would be taken up by Haas again in a long essay in the Christmas
issue of 1932 (*DlW*, 8.53, 1 and 7–8).[75] Haas's concern with the young generation
re-emerged in the spring of 1932 in the form of two special issues of the journal
entitled 'Die Situation der Jugend' (*DlW*, 8.8/9) and 'Junge Dichtung' (*DlW*,
8.14/15), and it is here, as a representative of the young generation, that Martin
Raschke, and the *Kolonne* circle more generally, played an important role for Haas.
As we have seen, one of the rare occasions on which Raschke stepped outside his
role as a reviewer on *Die literarische Welt* was to make essay contributions to the

---

75   See 'Was ist Jugend?' in Willy Haas, *Gestalten* (Frankfurt a.M.: Ullstein, 1963), pp. 263–67.

special issue on *Arbeiterdichtung*. Another such occasion was the *Sondernummer* 'Die Situation der Jugend' for which Raschke provided an essay, 'Zur jungen Literatur'. Here, Raschke consciously set a new generation of writers against the Expressionist generation:

> Wir haben in den vergangenen Jahrzehnten eine Unzahl literarischer Richtungen erlebt […]. Täglich fast kündigte man eine neue Kunstrevolution an […]. Es ist aus dieser Zeit nicht viel geblieben […]. Geblieben ist aber bei manchen der Glaube, daß jede neue literarische 'Generation' sich mit ähnlichen formalen Überraschungen einführen müsse, sonst sei sie eben keine Generation und ihre Literatur keine Literatur. […] Man wird sich jetzt daran gewöhnen müssen, daß es eine junge Literatur gibt, aus deren Reihen keine so plakatmäßige Kollektiväußerung kommt, wie sie die Anthologie *Menschheitsdämmerung* darstellte. (*DlW*, 8.8/9, 7)

Although explicit reference to their journal was rare, the prominence of young writers in *Die literarische Welt* in the first half of 1932 equated in large measure to a prominence for the *Kolonne* nature poets. The special issue devoted to 'Junge Dichtung' (*DlW*, 8.15/16), for instance, contained verse by Peter Huchel and Elisabeth Langgässer, including Huchel's 'Der Knabenteich' which we have seen to be representative of the mature editorial practice of *Die Kolonne* itself. The front-page editorial to this special issue highlighted above all the poetry of this young generation – 'Unsere großen Hoffnungen werden vor allem gestützt durch die Gedichte junger Menschen' – and singled out above all Huchel – 'eine Figur von Rang' – and Georg Britting – responsible for 'eine runde Leistung'. The editorial made clear where the value of this young writing was seen to lie:

> Es wird hier noch sehr viel von alten Literatur- und Dichtungsvorstellungen zu konservieren versucht. […] Man kann sogar, wenn man will, in der relativ konventionellen Wahl der Themen einen Vorzug finden: es ist der erste Ansatz zu einer mittleren Traditionsgebundenheit über Generationen hinweg, den wir in der deutschen Literatur seit Jahrzehnten erlebt haben. Eine feste Konvention, eine feste Disziplin und Schulung, und damit ein allgemeines annehmbares handwerkliches Niveau unserer Literatur zu erreichen, das wir eigentlich nie hatten, wäre durchaus wünschenswert. Wir glauben nicht, daß man, um Genies hervorzubringen, den literarischen Analphabetismus systematisch züchten müsse.

Huchel, acknowledged on the front page of that special issue as winner of the *Kolonne* prize, had fourteen of his nature poems published by Haas between 1930 and 1932, making him by far the most prolific contributor of poetry to the journal in that period. Over the whole publication run of the *Die literarische Welt* only one poet was more frequently represented, and that was another nature poet who figured in *Die Kolonne*, Georg von der Vring. As if to reinforce the turn to nature, Haas published a further special issue in 1932 entitled 'Die deutsche Landschaft' (*DlW*, 8.29/30), in which Huchel was again prominent. Noteworthy in addition to Haas's promotion of the young Huchel was his advocacy of Wilhelm Lehmann. Between December 1931 and March 1932, Haas published nine poems by Lehmann, including five in the third issue of 1932 which amounted in effect to a special issue devoted to Haas's re-discovery of the 50-year-old writer: 'Es ist eine unglaubliche, aber nichtsdestoweniger unumstößliche Wahrheit, daß ein großer Dichter, einer der größten deutschen Epiker der Natur und des Kosmos, des irdischen Maßes und des über- und unterirdischen Übermaßes unter uns lebt [...] und daß er einfach keinen Verleger [...] findet. [...] Sein Name ist *Wilhelm Lehmann*' (*DlW*, 8.3, 1).

It was above all in the figure of Martin Raschke that the programme promoted in *Die Kolonne* found its most consistent outlet in *Die literarische Welt*, his many review articles providing him with a platform for the propagation of that programme to a wider readership. Hence, a review in September 1929 of Erich Ebermayer's *Deutscher Almanach für das Jahr 1930* emphasises 'Nation, Gnade, Götter, Zeit, Ewigkeit' as 'Themen [...], um die wir ringen und deren Bedeutung wir weder von durchschnittlichen Vernünftlern geleugnet noch von messian-ischen Coiffeuren verkitscht sehen möchten' (*DlW*, 5.37, 6), while advocating the young generation of poets such as Billinger and Eich. In February 1930, Raschke reviewed Eich's 'Die Flüsse entlang' (*DlW*, 6.6, 5), stressing his melancholic depiction of man's eternal location between life and death and evaluating his verse 'als schönste lyrische Leistung der Jüngsten'. Similarly, a subsequent review praises the older Ernst Wiechert as 'einer der größten deutschen jungen Dichter' (*DlW*, 6.27, 5). Two works reviewed programmatically in *Die Kolonne* are also reviewed by Raschke in *Die literarische Welt* in 1931, namely Benn's *Fazit der Perspektiven* (*DlW*, 7.8, 5–6) and Becher's *Der große Plan* (*DlW*, 7.44, 5). In the Benn review, Raschke's pseudo-Nietzschean description of the human condition echoes that repeatedly presented in *Die Kolonne*: 'Auf fremdem Strome, in fremdem Winde treibt der einzelne dahin, Zuschauer seines dauernd entwachsenden Körpers, in dem sich Lust und Vernichtung grausam mischen.' Equally, Benn's text is seen to reveal the inadequacies of the Marxist 'system' as a response to what is perceived to be an elemental crisis: 'Doch ist nicht überall die Angst noch wach, ein furchtbares Urwissen in der Zivilisation, selbst in dem nüchternsten kommunistischen Systematiker, der ein Netz über die Erde wirft, wie um sie tiefer zu fangen?'

It is notable also that across a range of literary reviews, stretching from Aldous Huxley to his *Kolonne* co-editor A. A. Kuhnert, from Anna Seghers to Jean Giono, Raschke's judgements hinge on conventional notions of *Gestaltung* and *Dichtung*. In prose works, it is consistently 'realistic', 'living' characterisation and dialogue, where the author/narrator remains largely unobtrusive, which mark out the true *Dichter*, and here Raschke's literary criticism shares much with that of Lukács in *Die Linkskurve*. As illustration, one example may stand for many, namely Raschke's review of Gunnar Gunnarsson's *Der unerfahrene Reisende*:

> [Die Gestalten] bleiben eine Einheit. [...] Niemals zeigt Gunnarsson mit den Fingern auf sie. Er hat nicht die Unarten moderner Erzähler, die zwischen ihren Fingern wie in einem Wachsfigurenkabinett als Erklärer herumgehen, ängstlich, die Figuren könnten sich durch ihr Handeln nicht genügend verdeutlichen. Das vollzieht sich in

einer Sprache, die nichts von der Blutlosigkeit eines absichtlichen Stiles hat, der sich zwischen uns und die Gestalten wie ein Vorhang senkt. Sie paßt genau zu diesen Menschen [...]. Man könnte auch denken, daß viele Menschen so reden wie dieser Gunnarsson, daß eine Landschaft aus ihm spricht. (*DlW*, 7.35/36, 11)

This attempt to equate character with countryside which Raschke made elsewhere – 'Die Gestalt der Katrin löst sich vom Papier, gewinnt Leben. Sie ist [...] ein Stück Landschaft' (*DlW*, 6.36, 6) – highlights the distinction between the different aesthetic and ideological contexts of *Die Kolonne* and *Die Linkskurve* within which Raschke and Lukács composed their reviews. Nonetheless in his preference for 'rein geformte Gestalt' over caricature, his praise for conventional *Entwicklungsroman* narrative, and his maintenance of the *Dichter* as a superior category of writer, Raschke's critical method in *Die literarische Welt* clearly starts to dismantle that same distinction.[76]

Similarities between Raschke's contributions to *Die literarische Welt* and the programme advanced in *Die Kolonne* go beyond broad thematic parallels. Raschke's attack on the literary fashion for rural sentimentality, 'Man trägt wieder Erde', which would soon appear in *Die Kolonne*, first appeared in *Die literarische Welt* in June 1931 (*DlW*, 7.25, 5). Similarly, in one of his earliest contributions in May 1929, Raschke reviewed Richard Billinger's *Gedichte*. Here, in the description of Billinger as 'eine jedem Experiment verschlossene Erscheinung' and in the praise for the strength of Billinger's verse – 'man spürt Atem und Faust eines Kerls; das macht uns danken' (*DlW*, 5.22, 5–6) – Raschke employed precisely the words he would subsequently use of Billinger in *Die Kolonne*. Not only that, but the Billinger review is one of two contributions made by Raschke to *Die literarische Welt* in advance of the foundation of *Die Kolonne*, in which it is possible to locate, almost word-for-word, extracts from the anonymous opening statement of the *Kolonne* programme. Hence in that review, still six months before the opening issue of *Die Kolonne*: 'Noch lebt ein großer Teil der Deutschen in ländlichen Verhältnissen, und es entspringt nicht müßiger Traditionsfreude, wenn ihnen Regen und Kälte wichtiger sind als ein Dynamo, der noch nie das Korn reifte.' Two months later, Haas devoted the front page of the journal to a celebration of Knut Hamsun's 70th birthday. Such literary luminaries as Gerhart Hauptmann, Gottfried Benn, Ernst Toller, and Alfred Döblin wrote short tributes. On page three, Raschke wrote a more lengthy tribute, 'Dank eines Jungen an den alten Hamsun' (*DlW*, 5.31, 5). This piece, in which Raschke again seems to have been called upon to act as the spokesperson of his generation, includes lines to be repeated almost exactly in the first sentence of that subsequent *Kolonne* statement: 'Die Zeit, sie ist nichts, das vor den Fenstern der Geistigen sich abspielte, Flieger, Telegraph, Gewerkschaft, wie Literaten uns verschiedentlich glauben machen

---

76 See Martin Raschke, 'Arnold Ulitz, *Worbs*', *DlW*, 6.26, 8; Martin Raschke, 'Kurt Hauser, *Die Reise ins Innere*', *DlW*, 7.29, 5; Martin Raschke, 'Anna Seghers, *Auf dem Weg zur amerikanischen Botschaft*', *DlW*, 7.14/15, 7–8.

wollen, die im Besitz eines sauber ausgearbeiteten Zukunftsschemas nur die seiner Verwirklichung dienenden Schritte uns gemäß nannten.'

This direct interface between Raschke's contributions to *Die literarische Welt* and the *Kolonne* programme continued after the foundation of the latter journal in December 1929. Just over a year later in February 1931 (*DlW*, 7.5, 5–6), for example, Raschke reviewed Robert Henseling's *Der neu entdeckte Himmel*, photographs from which he had already had reproduced in *Die Kolonne*. This particular review is exemplary in uniting the distinctive elements of Raschke's *Kolonne* programme, as insights from Benn's aesthetic philosophy are set alongside those drawn from Huebner and Dacqué. Above all, it is the troubled role of the individual within a rapidly modernising and de-individualised society which concerns Raschke. In a repeat of a statement made in *Die Kolonne*: 'Die Gestalt der Zukunft, auch einer kommunistischen, wird davon abhängen, welchen Sinn (Sinn, sage ich) man dem entwurzelten Einzelleben zu geben vermag.' Further, through his appreciation, awe even, of Henseling's study of cosmology, Raschke finds cause to re-state the synthesis between *Sachlichkeit* and *Wunder* first set out in the *Kolonne* programme:

> Es ist gut, daß am Ende der ungeheuren technischen Entwicklung der letzten Jahrzehnte (wie viele Hymnen galten ihr) nur Bescheidenheit und Demut steht. Alle sollten das Buch von Robert Henseling lesen und wieder und wieder anschauen. Wer nur einmal in dem Zeitraffer sich entfaltende Blumen sah, wie diese Aufnahmen von Sternnebeln und Welten hier, wird es hinfort unterlassen, Wunder und Sachlichkeit deutlich gegeneinander abzugrenzen.

For all Raschke's scepticism towards the on-going process of social modernisation, his reviews of *Schaubücher* (*DlW*, 7.46, 8) and of works on modern architecture (*DlW*, 6.21, 6) betray a fascination with the relationship between art and new technology. Particularly telling is a review of Friedrich Schnack's collection of legendary narratives, *Der Lichtbogen* (*DlW*, 8.7, 5–6), where Raschke takes the author to task for his narrow-mindedness in describing stars as '"Sternnägeln", die "Himmelsräume aneinander nieten"'. Instead, Raschke advocates employing a scientific explanation founded on gravitational fields, not out of a drive towards rationality and objectivity, but because of the entirely appropriate sense of wonder which this science is able to inspire. Raschke's is a highly aestheticised, almost mystical, view of science, and this view seems to have found wider expression in two special issues of *Die literarische Welt*, 'Am Rande der Wissenschaft' in August 1931 (*DlW*, 7.32) and 'Der neue Mensch und sein Bild' in October 1932 (*DlW*, 8.41/42).

1930–1932: crisis and tradition

In the same issue of the journal in which Lehmann was given such a prominent platform, Haas also sought to promote a young and as yet unpublished *Arbeiterdichter* named Karl Lechner. Despite the stark differences between the two, Haas saw one significant common factor between Lehmann and Lechner: 'daß sich unbedingt ein Verleger für sie finden muß, trotz der trostlosen Zeiten' (*DlW*, 8.3, 1). In part, this criticism of the publishing industry and in particular of the adverse effects wrought on it by a difficult economic climate seems to reproduce sentiments first expressed in the founding phase of the journal. And yet, from the autumn of 1930 onwards, the front page of *Die literarische Welt* is dominated by a profound cultural pessimism far in excess of that enunciated by Haas in 1925 and 1926. The trigger for this new mood seems to be growing political polarisation, exemplified by the September 1930 *Reichstag* elections (*DlW*, 6.39, 1). Taking as his starting-point the organised attempts by Communist writers to ban Döblin's *Berlin Alexanderplatz*, Haas's front page editorial on 24 October 1930 sums up the dominant mood in a single word, 'Angst...'. (*DlW*, 6.43, 1). By July 1931 Haas has been moved to devote a special issue to 'Die Krise' which includes a *Rundfrage* inviting figures such as Heinrich Mann and Stefan Zweig to offer their opinions on 'Die Krise des Buches, Wege zu ihrer Linderung' (*DlW*, 7.3, 5–6). In October of the same year Haas's editorial entitled 'Vertrauenskrise' proclaims a crisis of trust in all areas of society, from medicine to the law, from the government to capitalism itself (*DlW*, 7.44, 1). By Christmas 1931, the tone of Haas's *Rundfrage* has become decidedly desperate: 'Zu diesem traurigen Weihnachtsfest haben wir einige hervorragende Männer gebeten, unseren Lesern eine Hoffnung zu schenken. "Geben Sie uns eine Hoffnung!", haben wir ihnen geschrieben' (*DlW*, 7.51/52, 1). Throughout 1932, while Haas is championing the nature poetry of the young generation, the cultural climate improves little. A special issue in January/February tackles political radicalisation under the title 'Rechts und links' (*DlW*, 8.4/5), while the front page editorial on 8 January 1932 poses the stark question 'Ende des Theaters?' (*DlW*, 8.2, 1–2), a pessimistic inquiry which by October 1932 has been modified to 'Ende der Dichtkunst?' (*DlW*, 8.44, 1–2 and 8). As Haas writes on the front page in the very next issue: 'Wir stehen in einer jener tief tragischen Situationen, wie sie kein anderes Volk als das deutsche erleben kann' (*DlW*, 8.45, 1–2).

Amidst this worsening cultural climate, Haas's active promotion of tradition also re-emerged. Particularly striking in this regard is the juxtaposition in the summer of 1931 of special issues devoted to 'Die Krise' (*DlW*, 7.30) and 'Traditionen' (*DlW*, 7.35/36). In this latter *Sondernummer*, a lengthy editorial entitled 'Tradition' (*DlW*, 7.35, 1–2 and 8) sought to distinguish between literary 'experiment' and 'modernism'. While the former was characterised by a fruitful process in which 'man experimentiert mit Vorhandenem und gelangt zu Neuem', the latter encompassed all movements, 'die die These der radikalen Demolierung und des Aufbaus aus dem Nichts vertreten'. While the former was typified by the Surrealists, by Joyce, and by Brecht's reworking of oriental drama, the latter was typified by Expressionism and Dadaism. Significantly, Haas also drew a connection to Marxism and to Lenin's disregard for the latter type of creative process:

> Mit Spott und Hohn verfolgt [Lenin] als der Lenker des revolutionären Sowjet-rußlands jene kopf- und hirnlosen literarischen Radikalinskis, die aus dem Nichts eine 'neue proletarische Kultur' schaffen wollen. Wer meint, beim Aufbau einer neuen Kultur auf das Material der alten verzichten zu können, ist antirevolutionär und antimarxistisch.

Clearly, Haas's agenda and the literary phenomena which he held up were very different, but the reasoning he presented in his investigation of the psychological and intellectual appeal of traditionalist thought would not have been out of place in the final phase of *Die Linkskurve*. These ideas, recognisable already from 'Wege in die Vergangenheit', also appeared a month later in September 1931 in a front-page editorial, headed 'Programmatisches' (*DlW*, 7.39, 1–2 and 8), which makes clear that the proximity of the 'crisis' and 'traditions' special issues was not merely coincidental. As well as stressing two editorial elements which have already emerged strongly from the post-1930 phase of the journal – namely the significance of young writers and the deployment of special issues to reflect important contemporary tendencies – Haas made the clearest possible connection between social crisis and literary tradition:

> *Wenn wir eine einheitliche, im strengsten Sinn geschlossene programmatische Aufgabe der* L.W. *sehen, so ist es die, die alten Großen unserer Literatur als aktuelle Symbole, als Orientierungs- und Entscheidungsmöglichkeiten für die Gegenwart herzustellen, und durch diese etwas, was das deutsche Volk seit drei Jahrhunderten nicht mehr hat: eine wirkliche literarische Tradition.* An diesem mitgewirkt zu haben, wäre unser größter Stolz. [...] Der Mensch in der welt-historischen Brandung verlangt andere, sichere, lebenshaltigere Orientierungspunkte, als sie ihm das Geplätscher des politischen Alltags mit seinem Parteigezänk zu bieten vermag. [...] Eine ganz neue Macht der Aktualisierung geistiger und dichterischer Vergangenheit findet statt, im Bekenntnis wie in der Ablehnung. Eine solche Zeit steht uns offenbar bevor; und die *L.W.* sieht ihr – wenn sie die Krise überdauert, was heute kein Unternehmen von sich mit Sicherheit behaupten kann – mit Optimismus entgegen. Wir selbst werden vielleicht erst dann ganz genau verstehen, was es mit unserer – mehr als richtig empfundenen als programmatisch ausgedachten – Pflege der literarischen Traditionen, mit unseren Versuchen einer sinnbildlichen Aktualisierung und 'Vivifizierung' (wie Novalis sagt) der großen Alten unserer Vergangenheit eigentlich auf sich hatte – Versuche, die heute von dummen Menschen als 'reaktionär' getadelt werden.

Less programmatic, but no less significant in its representativity, is a short theatre review published by Haas the following month, entitled 'Sowjet-Biedermeier' (*DlW*, 7.43, 7). The revival of a little-known Russian play from 1817 at the *Lessingtheater* is clearly symptomatic of the cultural phenomenon outlined in

Haas's editorial above: 'Die ganze Aufführung war temperamentvoll, lustig, und das ganze Beidermeierpublikum von 1817, pardon, das ganze fortgeschrittene, revolutionäre und bekannt anspruchsvolle literarische Berliner Publikum von 1931 applaudierte begeistert.'

The central questions here concern just how far these ideas, expressed after 1930 amidst the crisis identified by Schäfer as the catalyst for his restorative cultural shift, differ from those expressed by Haas around the journal's foundation in 1925 and 1926 and to what extent any causal linkage can be established between the notions of crisis and tradition, so suggestively juxtaposed in *Die literarische Welt* in 1931. Certainly a comparison of 'Wege in die Vergangenheit' from 1926 and the explicitly programmatic editorial of September 1931 suggests that Haas's cultural values had not undergone significant change as a result of the social and economic crisis. Indeed, what is most noteworthy is the sheer consistency of Haas's views, at the heart of which lay belief in cultural innovation through an appreciation of the tradition and in literary quality. What had changed was the cultural climate in which Haas sought to promote his programme, as his front-page essay, 'Restauration?' (*DlW*, 6.20, 1–2), from May 1930 indicates:

> Man spricht überall in Literatenkreisen von der kulturellen und literarischen Reaktion in der letzten Saison. Die radikale Berliner Literatur fühlt den Boden unter den Füßen schwinden. Die Theater wollen weder von dem sich revolutionär gebärdenden Pubertätsgebrülle, noch von der forschen Sozialreportage in wilhelminischem Schnarrton weiterhin etwas wissen. Es ist vorbei. [...] Der Kredit ist einmal zu Ende.

Notably, however, Haas seems to attribute this restoration not to political or social factors but to discourse-internal factors:

> Man bringt das mit der politischen Reaktion in Verbindung. Mit Unrecht. [...] Die Symptome des Verfalls liegen in der verfallenden Sache selbst. [...] Die Frist ist vorbei: Mit der Revolution an sich hat das gar nichts zu tun. Es wird nur einfach kein Kredit mehr gegeben. Nach einer gewissen Zeit kehrt man eben automatisch in die letzte sichere zurückliegende Stellung zurück und verschanzt sich dort. Also in das Jahr 1914, das ist es, was geschehen ist und geschieht. [...] Eine bürgerliche Kunst-Restauration mußte unter solchen Zuständen wie den gegenwärtigen eintreten: als wichtige Korrektur.

Indeed, this diagnosis of the restorative cultural climate of 1930 precedes the journal's pre-occupation with economic, social, and political crisis. For Haas at least, the crisis seems not so much to cause a restorative shift as to provide fertile ground for its subsequent propagation. That crisis radicalised and crystallised pre-existing aesthetic tendencies.

Conclusion

Given the centrality of *Die Kolonne* in existing accounts of the 1930 paradigm, it is perhaps the least unexpected finding to emerge from this first section of the journal corpus that the editorial programme, both explicit and implicit, consistently promoted by Raschke in his journal fits very comfortably into our conceptualisation of a restorative cultural shift located at 1930. Initially reacting polemically against the threat posed to the conventional notion of literature by journalistic *Sachlichkeit*, *Die Kolonne* acts as forum for a young generation of writers to re-assert literary *Innerlichkeit*, deploying the conventional idiom of nature poetry and drawing on the perceived highpoints of the German lyric tradition. And yet, stated in these terms the *Kolonne* project remains something of a crudely sketched caricature. Notable in Raschke's editorial practice, for example, and expressed in the award of the journal's annual prize, are two potentially contradictory sources of stability and authenticity in poetry: on the one hand, the security provided by an elitist intellectual tradition itself disrupted at points by a lingering post-Expressionist sensibility (embodied by Peter Huchel); on the other, the cruder authenticity provided by peasant and folk lyrics (Guido Zernatto). Similarly, the often cited rejection of *Neue Sachlichkeit* at the journal's foundation should not be read as an outright rejection of a modern world predicated on the *sachlich*. Rather, Raschke's project is more accurately characterised as an attempt to integrate the poles of *Sachlichkeit* and *Innerlichkeit*, in his own terms, a fusion of *Sachlichkeit* and *Wunder*. In these respects, literary modernism and social modernisation continue to leave their impression on *Die Kolonne* irrespective of the 'conservative' shift which the journal represents, and this demonstrates the importance of not conceptualising this shift simply as a straightforward turn towards *Innerlichkeit*.

The analysis of *Die literarische Welt* confirms the value of deploying Haas's journal as an indicator of the broader literary climate around 1930, clearly demonstrating that the *Kolonne* programme reached beyond the narrow confines of its own contributors and readership. Raschke's use of the platform afforded to him by Haas to develop and promote his literary agenda is buttressed after 1930 by Haas's own advocacy of such figures as Huchel and Lehmann. As carriers of a tradition of high literature, the young generation of nature poets clearly struck a chord with Haas, pre-occupied as he was with the crisis of the institution of literature amidst a burgeoning modern popular culture. Equally, despite the overt antagonism of the journals as concerns the function and theme of literature, it is also possible to identify strong points of contact between *Die Kolonne* and *Die Linkskurve*. Above all, the tension between bourgeois intellectualism and a less sophisticated, less elitist mode of literature informs both journals. The authentic appeal of peasant poetry for Raschke finds a striking parallel in the function of artistically unpretentious *Arbeiterdichtung* for the Marxist intellectuals of the BPRS. In this way, the fault-line between populist and elitist conceptions of literature opened up before 1930 continues to run through *Die Kolonne* and *Die Linkskurve*, even if it is the latter which emerges as dominant, not least in the eventual ascendancy of Lukács's Marxist aesthetic in the final phase of *Die Linkskurve*. Here again, a point of contact emerges in the form of the literary criticism practised by Raschke and Lukács. The secure frame of reference for both is the bourgeois literary tradition: the writer functions as *Dichter*, writing is a creative process of *Gestaltung*, *Entwicklungsroman* narrative, rounded characterisation, and realistic dialogue act as stable benchmarks. Similarly, for all Haas's protestations of objectivity, his editorial programme and practice are underpinned by robust notions of literary quality and tradition which set him alongside Raschke and Lukács. More than any other factor, it is this elitist conception of high literature which unites the three journals under consideration; all are strongly shaped by a variety of the *Bildungsdialekt*, even if its specific manifestation differs for each editor. The restoration which these journals embody is above all a restoration of an institution of literature founded on quality and tradition.

As well as attesting to this restorative literary climate, the journal corpus around 1930 functions as a testament to rapidly deepening crisis. Not surprisingly given its apolitical programme, explicit reference to the social and political conditions of the times are rare in *Die Kolonne*. For contributors to *Die Linkskurve*, by contrast, the radicalising political climate accompanied by legal and physical repression is a constant pre-occupation. Similarly, the front page of Haas's journal from 1930 onwards offers a vivid record of the times, as growing concern about political extremism mixes with a palpable mood of fear and all-encompassing cultural crisis. It is significant in this context that Haas explicitly singles out the literary tradition as a source of orientation and security in uncertain times, thereby seeming to uphold Schäfer's thesis of a crisis-induced turn to the refuge of aesthetic conservatism. Very clearly, it is this profound sense of social and cultural crisis which informs the renewed emphasis on quality and tradition in Haas's journal in these years. At the same time, this programme is largely indistinguishable from that set out in 1925 and 1926 immediately after the journal's foundation, and this is valuable evidence of the importance of an aesthetic conservatism which has its origins not in the crisis of 1930, but already in the mid-1920s when Expressionism was widely perceived to have forfeited its own credibility. To the immediate trigger of crisis around 1930 must be added these longer-term processes of aesthetic development; to external social and politcal factors must be added discourse-internal elements.

The perspective which *Die literarische Welt* is able to offer from several years in advance of 1930 is invaluable in relativising somewhat the significance of 1930 as a cultural turning-point. In this sense, Schäfer's periodisation must be understood as a polemical substitution of the sudden political break of 1933 with an apparently equally abrupt cultural rupture located around 1930. In the empirical reality of literary practice, 1930 can surely no more constitute a moment of sudden change than can 1933. Instead, the journal corpus offers evidence of an incremental process of cultural change readily compatible with the methodology we have developed from Hüppauf. Haas's own observations, both at the time and in retrospect, seem to confirm the importance of the partial re-alignment of cultural values which was initiated around 1924 and for which the 'new sobriety' seems a particularly apt designation.[77] Conceived in these terms, the second half of the 1920s constitutes a kind of transitional phase between a 'modernist' and 'restorative' dominant. The stabilisation of meaning inherent in this new sobriety is a central feature of the post-1930 climate, but the continuing fascination with modernity and modernisation and the accompanying erosion of the pillars of the institution of high literature continue to set it apart from our restorative paradigm. In this respect, 1930 must be viewed not as a single, discrete turning-point in Weimar literary history, but as one of Hüppauf's multiple periods of accelerated cultural activity, during which existing cultural norms are put into question, cultural alternatives are debated, and individual figures adopt an enhanced determining capacity in the future direction of culture. In this, 1930 shares a status with 1918, 1924, and 1933. However, as the journal activity discussed in this chapter attests, shaped above all by the attempts of such key individuals as Raschke, Haas, and Lukács to adopt a role as agents for change in a literary climate in flux, the processes of cultural debate and development were particularly intense in this period. By 1930 the cultural alternatives at stake had clearly narrowed and intensified, and the prominence by 1932 in each of our journals of broadly comparable programmes and, above all, the emergence of a new generation of writers, for whom this restorative agenda constituted their own orthodoxy, is persuasive evidence that the process of incremental cultural change had taken an accelerated step forward and effected a change in the prevailing literary dominant.

---

77   See John Willett, *The New Sobriety: Art and Politics in the Weimar Period 1917–1933* (London: Thames and Hudson, 1978)

Literary Journals 1933–1945
Das innere Reich, Maß und Wert, Das Wort

Introduction

The methodology in this part of the journal corpus proceeds in the opposite direction to that of the previous section. Where our thesis invites literary journals around 1930 to be interrogated for a cultural discontinuity which has remained conventionally unacknowledged, for the period 1933–1945 the thesis demands investigation for continuity across a moment of the most profound political rupture, namely the Nazi seizure of power and subsequent *Gleichschaltung* of the cultural and literary spheres. Although not entirely removing all trace of 1933, Schäfer is clear that this moment of political change did not bring about cultural change:

> Es spricht vieles dafür, daß der Nationalsozialismus die traditionalistischen Tendenzen der deutschen Literatur verstärkt, das Weiterleben der demokratisch engagierten Traditionen unterbrochen und den Aufstieg der Modernen Klassik verzögert hatte, doch eine radikale Veränderung der Epoche ist von ihm nicht ausgegangen, zu sehr ist er selbst ein Produkt der Krise und weist in seiner Kunstauffassung mit den antithetischsten Richtungen auf einheitliche Grundlagen.[1]

The persistence of the mood of crisis and the restorative literary dominant is seen to bridge 1933, so that Schäfer asks us to disregard the institutional changes brought about by National Socialism and the changes in writers' mood and method necessitated by the experience of exile and/or dictatorship. As Hüppauf has suggested, Schäfer's over-reliance on a 'non-Nazi' strand of writing clearly poses problems here. After all, Schäfer's thesis would seem to suggest that 'der Faschismus [...]auch keinen Anteil an der Konstitution einer literarischen Epoche in Deutschland gehabt [hätte], die von ca. 1930 bis 1960 reicht, also die "klassische" Zeit des europäischen Faschismus einschließt.'[2]

Of course, literary journals are themselves particularly dependent on the institutional structures subject to change at moments of political rupture. While *Die Linkskurve* and *Die Kolonne* had already ceased publication for economic

---

1   Hans Dieter Schäfer, 'Zur Periodisierung der deutschen Literatur seit 1930', in Hans Dieter Schäfer, *Das gespaltene Bewußtsein: Über deutsche Kultur und Lebenswirklichkeit 1933–1945* (Munich: Hanser, 1981), pp. 55–71 (p. 62).
2   Bernd Hüppauf, 'Krise ohne Wandel: Die kulturelle Situation 1945–1949', in Bernd Hüppauf (ed.), *'Die Mühen der Ebenen': Kontinuität und Wandel in der deutschen Literatur und Gesellschaft 1945–1949* (Heidelberg: Winter, 1981), pp. 47–112 (p. 57).

reasons in 1932, it was the Nazi seizure of power which led directly to the end of *Die literarische Welt*, at least in the form conceived by Haas. By the same token, the foundation of each of the journals in this section of the corpus — *Das innere Reich: Zeitschrift für Dichtung, Kunst und deutsches Leben; Maß und Wert: Zweimonatsschrift für freie deutsche Kultur;* and *Das Wort* — is tied intimately to the changed circumstances after 1933. In April 1934, permission to found *Das innere Reich* was dependent on the institutions of Nazi cultural policy at a time when a ban on the publication of new journals had been introduced. The journal's publishers, Langen-Müller, fostered National Socialist literature in a number of book series, and the journal's editors, Paul Alverdes and Benno von Mechow, made clear the connection between the new journal and the National Socialist revolution in their opening editorial essay (*DiR*, 1, 1–8). Likewise it is impossible to disassociate *Maß und Wert* and *Das Wort* from the context of exile. First published in September 1937 by Emil Oprecht in Zurich, the aims and preoccupations of *Maß und Wert* and its editors Thomas Mann and Konrad Falke were consistently defined by the German political situation across the border. In his opening programmatic essay, for example, Thomas Mann explicitly sought to position the journal against the cultural barbarism of National Socialism (*MuW*, 1, 1–16). Similarly, *Das Wort* filled the gap left by the disappearance of the literary exile journals *Die Sammlung* and *Neue deutsche Blätter*. First published by the Soviet publishing house, Jourgaz, under Mikhail Koltsov, *Das Wort* was, in the words of Fritz Erpenbeck, 'ein Kind der Volksfront', its founding impetus arising out of the more inclusive anti-fascist stance adopted by the German political Left in exile in the mid-1930s.[3] The choice of editors — Willi Bredel, Bertolt Brecht, and Lion Feuchtwanger — reflected these founding goals. As well as shaping editorial aims, the restrictions of exile and the fragmentation of German cultural life necessarily placed limitations on the identity of contributors and the nature of contributions, not to mention the inherent financial difficulties associated with producing a German-language journal in the precarious circumstances of exile. Indeed, the short-lived publication span of many exile journals can be attributed to these difficulties, and in this both *Das Wort* and *Maß und Wert* are typical, each lasting only three years and being beset by financial and editorial difficulties. By the same token, the longevity of *Das innere Reich* was clearly dependent on its capacity to remain within the acceptable parameters of Nazi cultural policy, its fluctuating page volume a product of variations in material conditions inside the Third Reich. Needless to say, the journal did not survive the collapse of the Third Reich. As such, the search for continuities in this section across 1933 and 1945 proceeds within journals whose existence is firmly bounded by those political date-boundaries.

Existing research into these journals largely reflects the strength of those date-boundaries. Understandably, and necessarily, scholarly interest in *Maß und*

---

3   Fritz Erpenbeck, *Das Wort* (Berlin: Rütten & Loening, 1968), *Registerband*, p. 5.

Wert and *Das Wort* in the 1970s emphasised the function of the journals as a forum for German writers in exile from National Socialism. The detailed work carried out by Hans-Albert Walter, for instance, provides an important foundation and succeeds in establishing initial connections and contrasts between the two journals, albeit within the self-contained category of exile literature.[4] Otherwise, studies of these two journals have largely been dominated by a single-issue approach: in the case of *Maß und Wert*, as an episode in Thomas Mann's exile and part of his response to National Socialism;[5] and in the case of *Das Wort*, from the perspective of the Expressionism Debate and the development of Marxist aesthetics through figures such as Lukács, Brecht and Bloch.[6] Much more recently, Thomas Baltensweiler's monograph begins to set *Maß und Wert* in a longer-term intellectual context, identifying continuities in thought to positions adopted in the Weimar Republic, but the focus rests entirely on political, rather than literary, contributions.[7] Research conducted into *Das innere Reich* has almost exclusively concentrated on the ideological function of contributions and contributors in terms of their proximity or distance to National Socialism. Again, important detailed foundations exist here in the work of Denkler and Mallmann from the late 1970s and in the index and exhibition catalogue produced by the *Literaturarchiv* in Marbach.[8] Similar bibliographic apparatus exists for the two exile journals in the indexes compiled in the GDR in the early 1970s.[9] Nonetheless, there remains very little research which has investigated these journals from 1933 to 1945 across the constraining categories of exile and inner emigration, or National Socialist literature and resistance literature.

And yet, the landscape of Third Reich scholarship looks rather different now than it did 25 years ago when Schäfer first published his periodisation thesis. The social history of the Nazi dictatorship written in that time, given added impetus in

---

4   Hans-Albert Walter, *Deutsche Exilliteratur 1933–1950*, IV: *Exilpresse* (Stuttgart: Metzler, 1978). See also Liselotte Maas, *Handbuch der deutschen Exilpresse 1933–1945*, IV: *Die Zeitungen des deutschen Exils in Europa von 1933 bis 1939 in Einzeldarstellungen* (Munich: Hanser, 1981); Angela Huß-Michel, *Literarische und politische Zeitschriften des Exils 1933–1945* (Stuttgart: Metzler, 1987); and Angela Huß-Michel, *Die Moskauer Zeitschriften 'Internationale Literatur' und 'Das Wort' während der Exil-Volksfront (1936–1939)* (Frankfurt a.M.: Lang, 1987).

5   See Thomas Sprecher, *Thomas Mann in Zürich* (Zurich: Fink, 1992).

6   See Hans-Jürgen Schmitt (ed.), *Die Expressionismus-Debatte: Materialien zu einer marxistischen Realismuskonzeption* (Frankfurt a.M.: Suhrkamp, 1973); Fredric Jameson (ed.), *Aesthetics and Politics* (London: Verso, 1980).

7   Thomas Baltensweiler, *'Maß und Wert': Die Exilzeitschrift von Thomas Mann and Konrad Falke* (Bern: Lang, 1996).

8   Marion Mallmann, *'Das innere Reich': Analyse einer konservativen Kulturzeitschrift im Dritten Reich* (Bonn: Bouvier, 1978); Horst Denkler, 'Janusköpfig: Zur ideologischen Physiognomie der Zeitschrift *Das innere Reich* (1934–1944)', in Horst Denkler and Karl Prümm (eds), *Die deutsche Literatur im Dritten Reich* (Stuttgart: Metzler, 1976), pp. 383–405; Werner Volke, *'Das Innere Reich': 1934–1944: Eine 'Zeitschrift für Dichtung, Kunst und deutsches Leben'* (Marbach: Deutsche Schillergesellschaft, 1983).

9   Volker Riedel, *'Maß und Wert': Zurich 1937–1940: Bibliographie einer Zeitschrift* (Berlin: Aufbau, 1973); Gerhard Seidel, *'Das Wort': Moskau 1936–1939: Bibliographie einer Zeitschrift* (Berlin: Aufbau, 1975).

the last ten years by the application of comparable methodologies to the GDR, has done much to soften the perception of the date-boundaries of the dictatorships. The monumental otherness of totalitarianism has been relativised by an emphasis on the shortfall between regime claims and outcomes and on continuities with the more conventional types of society which bordered the Third Reich, both temporally and geographically. Not least Schäfer's work, with its methodological affinities with the Bavaria Project, has acted as a spur to such developments in the cultural-historical sphere, so that it is possible to find the following view expressed in an historical survey of the period:

> Entgegen dem Eindruck, den eine breit angelegte Kontroll- und Lenkungsbürokratie zu erwecken versuchte, entfaltete das Regime auf kulturellem Gebiet nur vehältnis- mäßig geringe Prägekraft. [...] Weder in der Literatur, noch in der Musik oder in den bildenden Künsten markiert das Jahr 1933 einen völligen Bruch der Entwicklung. Der politisch erzwungene mannigfache Abbruch personeller und institutioneller Kon- tinuität, der insoweit auch das Ende einer Epoche bedeutete, fällt nicht zusammen mit einer entsprechenden kunsthistorischen Periodisierung.[10]

All the same, the writing of German cultural and, above all, literary history remains relatively untouched by the seismic paradigm shift in the social historiography of the Third Reich. Annette Schmollinger's 1999 study of the parallels between the prose-writing of exile and inner emigration demonstrates the potential fruitfulness of an approach which challenges these boundaries, as does Jeanette Atkinson's 1978 doctoral dissertation comparing the poetry of, amongst others, the prominent Marxist exile Johannes R. Becher and Josef Weinheber, a frequent contributor to *Das innere Reich*.[11] In seeking to question ideologically determined categories of literary analysis and suggesting instead 'ways in which exile and inner German literature could be treated from a common frame of reference rather than under separate categories', Atkinson's work acts as an all too isolated methodological forerunner to the analysis presented in this chapter.

Already around 1930 we have sought to identify parallels, or horizontal continuities, within the same date bracket but across ideological boundaries. Notwithstanding ideological differences, we were able to identify significant similarities, both stylistic and thematic, between *Die Kolonne*, *Die Linkskurve*, and *Die literarische Welt*. In this section an additional dimension is added to the search for these common features, in that between 1933 and 1945, vertical continuities across date boundaries also come into play. Most obviously these can be sought within ideological boundaries, both in institutional continuities and in continuities in personnel. Clearly, such continuities are to be expected from *Die Linkskurve*

---

10 Norbert Frei, *Der Führerstaat: Nationalsozialistische Herrschaft 1933–1945* (Munich: dtv, 1987), p. 109.

11 Annette Schmollinger, *'Intra muros et extra': Deutsche Literatur im Exil und in der Inneren Emigration, ein exemplarischer Vergleich* (Heidelberg: Winter, 1999); Jeanette Atkinson, *Traditional Forms in German Poetry 1930–1945* (Ann Arbor: University Microfilms International, 1983). Subsequent reference, Atkinson, p. 3.

into *Das Wort* through the German and Soviet Communist parties and writers allied to them. Similarly, a trajectory may be expected to be traced from *Die Kolonne* into *Das innere Reich* through the broadly conservative tenor of the journals and their advocacy of *Innerlichkeit*. More challenging will be attempts to identify continuities which cut across ideological and institutional contexts, diagonal continuities, as it were. Such continuities must be a sought at a more general level in terms of what we have described as the search for stability of meaning and in terms of the strategic positioning of the journals in relation to the bourgeois cultural tradition.

Das innere Reich

Ideologiekritik

Clearly it would be perverse in any analysis of *Das innere Reich* not to grant considerable significance to the ideological and political context of the Third Reich, and it comes as little surprise that existing attempts to analyse the foundation of *Das innere Reich* in 1934 and the evolution of the journal over the following ten years share a common methodology grounded in the political or ideological paradigm of literary history. Indeed, the two principal works to treat the journal, namely Marion Mallmann's monograph and Horst Denkler's essay, appear to be examples of a scholarly *Zeitgeist*, the two authors more or less simultaneously rescuing the journal from academic neglect in the mid-1970s, so that neither author was able to take account of the work of the other.[12] This shared approach extends from their contextualisation of the research problem posed by the journal to their proposed solution to that problem. Both Mallmann and Denkler seek to locate their respective analyses within the context of the starkly contradictory, and often uninformed, assessments of the journal's function within the Third Reich which had been upheld by critics in the 1950s and 1960s. These range from Harry Pross's apparent equation of *Das innere Reich* with the Hitler Youth organ *Wille und Macht* to Hans Mayer's identification of the journal as 'den geheimen Sammelpunkt einer Gegenliteratur'.[13] Both authors also engage with the paradigm of 'inner emigration', within which the journal had already been positioned, if not entirely unproblematically, by scholars such as Herbert

---

12 See note 8 above.

13 Harry Pross, *Literatur und Politik: Geschichte und Programme der politisch-literarischen Zeitschriften im deutschen Sprachgebiet seit 1870* (Olten: Walter, 1963), p. 125; Hans Mayer, 'Konfrontation der inneren und äußeren Emigration: Erinnerung und Deutung', in Reinhold Grimm and Jost Hermand (eds), *Exil und Innere Emigration: Third Wisconsin Workshop* (Frankfurt a.M.: Athenäum, 1972), pp. 75–87 (p. 81).

Wiesner.[14] As an antidote to the contradictory picture of ideological compromise and distance which emerges from such non-specialist accounts of the history of *Das innere Reich*, both Mallmann and Denkler propose a detailed analysis of the contributions to the journal itself. Nonetheless, these analyses are not primarily literary or stylistic in nature, but remain concerned above all with the dominant 1970s paradigm of *Ideologiekritik*. Hence, Denkler's stated aim in the title of his essay to dissect the journal in order to reveal its 'ideologische Physiognomie' mirrors Mallmann's attempt to determine 'den Stellenwert der Zeitschrift innerhalb des ideologisch-politischen Rahmens im Dritten Reich'.[15]

For Denkler, the history of *Das innere Reich* is one of 'Tendenzen' and 'Gegentendenzen', that is, of elements supportive of National Socialist ideology and elements undermining that ideology. Similarly for Mallmann, consideration of individual contributors or of themes and genres represented in the journal is framed throughout in terms of conformity or opposition to the perceived norms of National Socialism. Thus in both analyses the focus rests either on strongly supportive contributions or on those contributions which led to conflict between the journal and the authorities. Under the former heading would fall the *Führergedichte* of Richard Billinger (*DiR*, 5, 1), Josef Weinheber (*DiR*, 6, 1) and Erna Blaas (*DiR*, 7, 1), which opened the first issues of 1938, 1939, and 1940 respectively, or the proliferation of *Heimatdichtung* and *Blut-und-Boden* literature by largely unknown *völkisch*-nationalist writers; under the latter, such contributions as Rudolf Thiel's essay on Frederick the Great in August 1936 (*DiR*, 3, 543–73) or Georg Britting's First World War poem 'Die freiwilligen Knaben' (*DiR*, 6, 742–43). Tellingly, Werner Volke's Marbach exhibition catalogue also devotes much space to the controversies surrounding these latter contributions, despite his explicit aim not to offer a structured ideological analysis of the journal.[16] Clearly, such analyses serve to re-inforce the significance of the specific Nazi context as a determining factor in the make-up of the journal and thereby the unique status of literary production inside Germany between 1933 and 1945, both in relation to the literature which preceded and followed that period and in relation to the literature produced outside Germany within the same date bracket. Indeed, for Denkler it is not only 1933 which shapes the contents of *Das innere Reich*, but his adherence to a politically determined paradigm extends to the identification of phases within the publication run of the journal. Hence, it is the stages in the expansion of the German state between 1938 and 1941 which are seen to bring about a change in the previously aestheticised approach of the

---

14 Herbert Wiesner, 'Innere Emigration', in Hermann Kunisch (ed.), *Handbuch der deutschen Gegenwartsliteratur*, 2 vols (Munich: Nymphenburger Verlag, 1970), II, pp. 383–408 (p. 391).
15 Mallmann, p. 3.
16 See Volke, pp. 31–49.

journal and the defeat at Stalingrad which ushers in a final phase of resignation allied to an assertion of the enduring values of literature and culture.[17]

The kind of contributions highlighted by Denkler and Mallmann signal the legitimacy of such an approach, as do institutional factors surrounding the journal's foundation and longevity. As head of the conservative Langen-Müller *Verlag*, the journal's founder Gustav Pezold was recognised as a publisher who had contributed actively to the National Socialist cause. Indeed, Pezold's 1933 essay 'Schrifttum und Buchhandel und ihre Bedeutung im Leben der Nation', quoted at length by Volke, helps to explain why a licence was granted for the foundation of *Das innere Reich* at a time when new periodicals had been prohibited by the National Socialist authorities. In his advocacy of 'volks*echter* Dichtung' at the expense of 'volks*fremdes* und lebensfeindliches Literatenwerk' and by promoting 'die konservative Volkskunst gegen jede Entartung', Pezold began to move beyond a conventional conservative-nationalist position towards more specifically National Socialist ideology and discourse.[18] Further, the relative success and longevity of the journal under the conditions of German totalitarianism also seem to point to the necessity of positioning the journal within an analytical framework which takes into account the specific political circumstances of publication under National Socialism. As Denkler indicates:

> Auflage, Verbreitung und Erscheinungsdauer [beweisen], daß *Das innere Reich* von den literatur- und pressepolitischen Lenkungsämtern des nationalsozialistischen Staates und der Staatspartei, die die 'öffentliche Wirksamkeit' der Zeitschriften 'hauptsächlich politisch' zu bewerten und zu beurteilen hatten, mehr als geduldet wurde.[19]

If we consider too the constituency of regular contributors on which the editors could draw, then such Langen-Müller authors as Hans Friedrich Blunck, Wilhelm Schäfer, and Erwin Guido Kolbenheyer can be seen to occupy a position at the more actively pro-Nazi end of a spectrum of conservative-nationalist writers which includes the so-called *Starnberger-Kreis* around Rudolf Binding (Alverdes, Georg Britting, Ludwig Friedrich Barthel, Heinrich Zillich, Edwin Erich Dwinger) and Hans Grimm's *Lippoldsberger Dichtertreffen* (Alverdes, Kolbenheyer, Friedrich Bischoff, Hermann Claudius, Rudolf Alexander Schröder). Also worthy of note in this context are the recruitment of the ideologically orthodox Benno Mascher as editor from the end of 1935 onwards, the special editions of the journal which included in March 1938 a 'Sonderheft zur Heimkehr Deutsch-Österreichs ins Reich' and in December 1938 an edition dedicated to 'der Heimkehr des Sudetenlands in das Reich', and the kind of political poetry exemplified by Weinheber's epic tribute to the annexation of Austria, 'Hymnus auf die Heimkehr' (*DiR*, 5, 113–17). In this light, it is manifestly impossible to

---

17 Denkler, pp. 386–87.
18 See Volke, p. 1.
19 Denkler, p. 384.

maintain a counter-factual scenario in which the journal's composition would have been in essence unaltered in the absence of the Nazi *Machtergreifung* in 1933.

Reading against the grain: the opening issue

And yet, it is precisely where the political paradigm is seemingly at its most persuasive that the aesthetic mode of analysis advocated in our study can be most illuminating. The opening issue of the journal, for example, does much to establish a direct connection to the National Socialist regime, in particular through its 'non-literary' pieces. The journal opens with Alverdes's and von Mechow's introductory essay, 'Inneres Reich' (*DiR*, 1, 1–8), which explores the meaning of the journal's title. Here, the principal rhetorical strategy is a call for national unity in the face of a perceived external threat which draws a direct parallel between the current political situation and that which faced Germany in 1914. As during World War One, so now the German people must recognise the threat 'in ihrem ganzen Sein: das meint eben die unzertrennbare Einheit des äußeren und des inneren Reiches der Deutschen auf dieser Erde'. Drawing on the common frame of reference provided by the experience of 1914–1918, and in the process on one of the core political myths of National Socialist ideology, the editors' opening explanation of the journal's metaphorical title demands to be read as a statement of ideological support for the new German Reich, at whose service the journal is to be put. This reading is buttressed by the publication in the same issue of Rudolf Binding's call for subjugation to order in 'Über die Freiheit' (*DiR*, 1, 8), Karl Alexander von Müller's tribute to Theodor von der Pfordten, a martyr of the abortive Munich Putsch of 1923 (*DiR*, 1, 47–50), and Friedrich Blunck's orthodox essay on 'Deutsche Kulturpolitik' (*DiR*, 1, 114–44) which rounds off the opening issue.

At the same time, the editors' opening statement has a strong aesthetic and cultural dimension, albeit one couched in strongly nationalistic and militaristic terms. Here, the journal's title offers two further readings. Firstly, the editors make an explicit contrast between their inner German concerns and those of the German literary culture of exile, so that some critics have seen the journal as a conscious rebuttal to the emigrés, as 'betont gegen die Emigration gegründet'.[20] This 'innere Reich' then is that inside, rather than outside, the geographical and political boundaries of Germany. Secondly, the 'inner realm' is that of traditional German literature and culture, that which opposes the crisis of the times. Hence, Alverdes and von Mechow highlight the value placed on the German bourgeois literary tradition (*Faust, Wilhelm Meister*, Hölderlin, Eichendorff, Mörike, Brentano) at times of profound crisis, in this case the outbreak of World War

---

20   Dietrich Bode, *Georg Britting: Geschichte seines Werkes* (Stuttgart: Metzler, 1962), p. 74.

One. In their capacity to reflect man's emotions the great works of the German tradition acquire a heroic, pseudo-mystical status on the battlefield:

> Und darum hatte der Kriegsfreiwillige des großen Krieges seinen *Faust* im Tornister und ein anderer die Gedichte von Hölderlin: als eine Essenz, als einen geistigen Auszug wenigstens alles dessen, was ihm nicht weniger teuer war als die Unantastbarkeit der vaterländischen Erde, und für das er ebensogut den Tod nicht verweigern wollte.

The nationalism of the editors' foreword is that which is expressed through art and as such, notwithstanding the particular political colouring provided by the context of National Socialism, Alverdes and von Mechow position themselves within the recognisable intellectual trajectory of the German *Bildungsbürgertum*, the same trajectory which carries Thomas Mann to a position in opposition to National Socialism in *Maß und Wert*. Indeed, if we look beneath the nationalistic and militaristic rhetoric, we can see that the central procedure underpinning this opening issue is that which lies at the heart of the 1930 paradigm, namely the search for stability and wholeness of meaning. Both the editors and Binding enunciate this search for order, unity, and wholeness in telling terms which are to be understood not only politically but also aesthetically: 'Mit immer mächtigerem Begehren trachtet die denkende Menschheit des Abendlandes wieder nach einer Ganzheit des Begreifens oder doch wenigstens der Anschauung' (*DiR*, 1, 1); 'Es gibt Dramen und Erzählungen [...], in denen sich auf eine wunderbare und eigentlich unerklärliche Weise unsere ganz besondere, eigentümliche, deutsche Wesensart mit einer beglückenden Vollkommenheit ausdrückt' (*DiR*, 1, 4); 'Die gewollte Einordnung ist die Grundlage der Freiheit – ebensowohl im Staate wie für Geist und Seele' (*DiR*, 1, 8). It is easy to see how in *Das innere Reich* the political solution to crisis offered by National Socialism coalesces with the aesthetic search for stability of meaning which has been the dominant cultural mood since 1930.

Aside from the non-literary contributions, the most striking feature of the opening issue of the journal is the editors' commitment to lyric poetry. As we have seen, one of the central manifestations of the re-assertion of the conventional bourgeois institution of literature around 1930 is the resurgence of lyric poetry in general, and nature poetry in particular, and this above all is where our study is able to position the content of *Das innere Reich* in a context which extends beyond that of the Third Reich. This opening issue includes more than twenty poems by ten different poets, and, in keeping with the programmatic *Innerlichkeit* of the journal, none of these poems in the first issue moves beyond the traditional frame of reference provided by personal experience and nature. Notably, the two contrasting strands of poetry which come to characterise the journal are already represented here: on the one hand, the work of poets with more elitist aspirations (represented in issue one by Georg Britting and Peter Huchel); on the other, the rather less sophisticated kind of poetic output for which the labels *Heimatdichtung* or *Blut und Boden* are more appropiate (represented in the opening issue by Paula Grogger and Hermann Claudius). Two factors in particular – the political context of National Socialism and the geographical identity of the journal as a South German publication – heighten the tendency towards *Heimatdichtung* in *Das innere Reich*, but this fundamental tension between poetry with bourgeois pretensions and that imbued with the authentic peasant experience is clearly recognisable from *Die Kolonne* and, albeit along a very different ideological parameter, also the proletarian-revolutionary writing of *Die Linkskurve*. In effect, this tension can be seen to have been institutionalised under National Socialism. On the one hand, the regime sought to promote an accessible, collective form of literature, figures such as Alfred Rosenberg rejecting elitist intellectualism in the arts. On the other, it appealed to a traditional notion of the inspired *Dichter* as a kind of *Führer*-figure and sought justification and legitimacy in the bourgeois literary tradition of Goethe and Schiller. In this way, *Das innere Reich* and its opening issue typify not only the self-contradictions in Nazi cultural policy but also a pre-existing tension which the re-assertion of traditional literary values at 1930 could not resolve.

Sources of continuity across 1933

In the light of the above discussion, Alverdes's subsequent claims that the journal's title was never intended to be read politically – 'gemeint war mit diesem Reich überhaupt kein politischer Begriff'[21] – and that that title and the planning for the foundation of the journal extended as far back as 1932 cannot be immediately dismissed simply as retrospective self-justification. The inner realm to which the title alludes also highlights the most readily discernible source of cultural continuity running into *Das innere Reich*, namely that which comes from *Die Kolonne* and which is signalled by the shared subtitle of the two journals, *Zeitschrift für Dichtung*. The enthusiasm towards the new regime in the opening issue, whether genuine or pragmatic, the explicit nationalism of its subtitle, and the presence of *Blut-und-Boden* writing do not obscure the commonality of purpose between these two journals dedicated to promoting the elitist category of *Dichtung*, founded on literature as the expression above all of *Innerlichkeit*. The privileging of a relatively elitist, aesthetic 'inner realm' in Alverdes's and von Mechow's opening statement clearly parallels the kind of pre-1933 developments represented by the *Kolonne* Circle and expressed, for instance, in Günter Eich's notion of 'innere Dialoge' (*Kolonne*, 1, 8). As we have seen, this continuity of literary concerns and personnel is already represented in the strong presence of lyric poetry, including that of Peter Huchel, in the opening issue. Indeed, this kind

---

21 Volke, p. 11.

of continuity in personnel between the two journals is considerable. Huchel, Eich, Horst Lange, and Oda Schaefer all had a number of poetry or prose pieces published in *Das innere Reich*, and, significantly, the nature of these contributions did not deviate substantially from the aesthetic position already adopted in *Die Kolonne*. In politically determined analyses of the journal the presence of these *Kolonne* figures serves two inter-related purposes, acting both as a guarantor of the literary quality of the journal and, in the process, as a strand of literary production untouched by, or even in opposition to, the National Socialist regime. However, as representatives of aesthetic continuity, the *Kolonne* poets necessitate a revision of one of Denkler's central theses concerning the development of *Das innere Reich*. Denkler sees initial enthusiasm for National Socialism being replaced from 1935 onwards by 'ästhetischer Zeitenferne, formalistischer Gediegenheit, anspruchs-voller Langeweile', primarily as 'Fluchtreaktionen' from the reality of the regime.[22] Yet, as we have seen, it is precisely these characteristics which constitute one of the paradigmatic manifestations of the 1930 shift, away from a socially engaged, more populist *Sachlichkeit*, and it is *Die Kolonne* which acts as a forum for such a shift. As such, these are not entirely new developments in the mid-1930s, replacing earlier expressions of enthusiasm for National Socialism. Rather, these tendencies may be seen as cultural continuities onto which that enthusiasm was applied as a political veneer in the immediate wake of 1933, only to subsequently evaporate.

Important as such an observation is, the identification of continuity between *Die Kolonne* and *Das innere Reich* is scarcely unexpected, having been widely acknowledged in the existing literature. Indeed, the two journals figure prominently in the research which feeds into Schäfer's periodisation essay. Furthermore, this continuity originating in such a small-scale, narrow-interest circle of writers could easily be dismissed as being of little broader empirical significance. It is here that the value of *Die literarische Welt* as a representative cross-section of literary life in the Weimar Republic is once again highlighted, since the presence of the *Kolonne* poets, and in particular of Peter Huchel, in the final years of Haas's journal lends a considerable new dimension to the continuities running from *Die Kolonne* into *Das innere Reich*. In this way, *Das innere Reich* can be shown to be the carrier of significant literary continuity across 1933. Above all, Martin Raschke again emerges as a key figure, since his 25 contributions to *Das innere Reich*, across the full publication run of the journal and across a range of genres, provide continuity not only to his role as editor and central spokesperson of *Die Kolonne*, but also to his role as reviewer and spokesperson for the young generation in *Die literarische Welt*. Ideologically more conservative than other *Kolonne* writers, Raschke's continued presence in *Das innere Reich* is not surprising. Indeed, Helmut Peitsch explicitly denies the validity

---

22 Denkler, p. 386.

of the kind of homogenous stylistic period posited by Trommler and Schäfer for this very reason: 'Martin Raschke jedenfalls war ein faschistischer Autor, vielleicht sogar "von Rang".'[23] However, what Peitsch sees in Raschke's Nazi-era prose as exemplary of fascist ideology, namely the heavy-handed celebration of marriage and the military as sources of discipline and order, can be viewed in the broader context provided by our study as a more generalised search for cultural stability, for which fascist ideology is able to provide one solution. Above all, Raschke's contributions to *Das innere Reich* are characterised by a predominance of diary-like forms, drawing both on childhood and wartime experiences. These functional and secure forms of literary representation offer a stable idiom for Raschke and many of his contemporaries.

In purely numerical terms two nature poets act, in addition to Raschke, as the principal interfaces between Haas's journal and *Das innere Reich*, namely Georg Britting and Georg von der Vring. Indeed, it is the somewhat unlikely figure of von der Vring who emerges from our study as one of the principal sources of literary continuity, not only across 1933 but also 1945. Largely neglected by scholarship after his death in 1968, von der Vring is one of the most frequently published poets in four of our journals: *Die Kolonne; Die literarische Welt; Das innere Reich;* and *Merkur.* As far as *Das innere Reich* is concerned, von der Vring makes some 43 contributions, all of them poems, distributed evenly across the ten years of its publication. Neither a friend of Alverdes nor a Langen-Müller author, his frequent presence in this journal is not readily explicable through direct institutional factors. Indeed, von der Vring is said to have been strongly critical of Alverdes and also of the National Socialist regime.[24] In fact, as the most conventional of bourgeois lyric poets, von der Vring's popularity seems rather to be indicative of the prevailing literary tastes of the times as we have sought to describe them. Britting, meanwhile, emerges as the single most frequent contributor to the journal with over 80 pieces of poetry and prose, largely as a result of his status as a Langen-Müller author who also had close ties to Alverdes and to the *Starnberger Kreis.* Notably too, Britting is the subject of six, overwhelmingly positive review articles in *Das innere Reich*, three of them by Kurt Hohoff (*DiR*, 2, 507–17; 3, 1370–72; 4, 1242–45), who would carry this reception forward to *Merkur* after 1945. The output which established this privileged status will be subjected to more detailed study below.

---

23 Helmut Peitsch, 'Ästhetische Introversion und Nationalsozialismus: Die Erzähler Martin Raschke, Ernst Schnabel und Alfred Andersch', in Jörg Thunecke (ed.), *Leid der Worte: Panorama des literarischen Nationalsozialismus* (Bonn: Bouvier, 1987), pp. 321–47 (p. 343).
24 Mallmann, p. 90.

Case study: Georg Britting

As a poet whose own aesthetic trajectory originated in the late German Expressionism of 1919–1920 and the Expressionist journal *Die Sichel* which he edited with the painter Josef Achmann, Britting offers a particularly fruitful line of inquiry within the context of the present study. In demonstrating a continuity of aesthetic development, Britting's case exposes the shortcomings of the kind of ideological paradigm outlined at the outset of this section. As far as Denkler is concerned, for example, Britting's most significant contributions are the poems 'Die freiwilligen Knaben' (*DiR*, 6, 742–43) and 'Wo sind, Achill...' (*DiR*, 7, 161), both of which are seen to contradict propagandistic notions of heroism, the latter in particular noteworthy for its sympathetic but unheroic treatment of the Langemarck veterans.[25] Not only does such an analysis narrow down the breadth of Britting's literary output in these years to two essentially unrepresentative poems, but it also highlights the inadeqacies of attempts to categorise individuals within a conventional conformism/opposition dichotomy. As Mallmann concedes, the label 'tendenziell oppositionell' is problematic when applied to a writer such as Britting who she otherwise categorises as 'volkhaft'.[26] It is here, given the extent of Britting's contributions, that a literary-stylistic analysis can bear substantial fruit in charting his aesthetic development over the period 1934–1944.

In the seven years between 1935 and 1942, Britting published nine short stories in *Das innere Reich*, of which three are worthy of particular attention, namely 'Das Fliederbäumchen' (*DiR*, 1, 425–38), 'Die Schwestern' (*DiR*, 3, 806–20) and 'Der Schneckenweg' (*DiR*, 6, 17–25). As Dietrich Bode has shown, in each of these stories Britting is moving towards a new sphere of expression, characterised above all by the depiction of relatively subtle internal and emotional realities and by a striving for harmony.[27] No sudden events or harsh reality intrude. Rather, the emphasis is on the gradual exposition of what Bode terms the 'seelische Landschaft'. In particular in 'Die Schwestern' a gentle humour has replaced anger as the underlying tone. Noticeable too is the conventionality of form and narration, a single, stable narrative voice presenting a linear, retrospective chronology of events. In these thematic and stylistic developments, Bode sees Britting moving much closer to the conservative style of *Das innere Reich* contemporaries such as Alverdes himself, Ina Seidel or even Emil Strauß. In terms of historical influences, Britting is now drawing on different stylistic ideals to those he followed in the 1920s:

> Deutsche Klassik und nachklassischer Realismus liefern die Maßstäbe. Diese mit den dreißiger Jahren vordringenden Tendenzen mag man mit zu der Wirkung des

---

25 Denkler, p. 396.
26 Mallmann, p. 92.
27 See Bode, pp. 86–89.

Konservativen nach der literarischen Revolution rechnen. In Kontakt mit den
repräsentativen Absichten im Dritten Reich kann hin und wieder auch von einem
Neoklassizismus gesprochen werden. Allgemein herrscht eine restaurative und
traditionalistische Orientierung, durch die sich – sekundär ob mit, neben oder
entgegen staatlichen Direktiven und oft quer durch die Lager – mitunter fast eine
gewisse Stileinheit abzeichnet.[28]

As Bode suggests, the stylistic development in Britting's work renders secondary
the issue of conformity to National Socialist norms. By side-stepping the
ideological paradigm, we are able to privilege Britting's own aesthetic trajectory. It
then becomes a question of the requirements of the regime being seen to coincide
with this existing trajectory, rather than necessarily the other way round.

Most significantly, Britting's stylistic and thematic choices in his prose in *Das
innere Reich* are far from unique to him. The subject-matter of 'Das Fliederbäumchen', for instance, which tells of the unrequited love of an inexperienced
seventeen year-old boy for an older, unknown woman is strongly reminiscent of
Günter Eich's semi-autobiographical story 'Katharina' (*DiR*, 2, 934–80) which
appeared in *Das innere Reich* in November 1935. With their melancholic endings
and explicit treatment of loss and suicide, both of these stories mark themselves
out as rather more problematic than much of the prose in the journal.
Nonetheless, both the clichéd portrayal of village and family life by writers of
trivial and entertainment literature who rose to prominence only in the Third
Reich and the more subtle writing of better-known writers such as Britting and
Eich have much in common with one another. None deals with the conflicts and
concerns of urban, industrial or intellectual life, so that the only conflicts depicted
arise from catastrophes of nature or personal, and in particular childhood,
experience. Stories are largely apolitical and in terms of form remain within the
confines of the kind of literary convention epitomised by Stifter. As such, the
narrative fiction represented in *Das innere Reich* clearly matches the kind of norms
implied in Raschke's reviews for *Die literarische Welt* and formally does not
contravene the programmatic line maintained by Lukács in *Die Linkskurve*.

While Britting's prose in *Das innere Reich* is characterised in the main by a
uniformity of style, his 73 individual poems bear witness to a stylistic
development from post-Expressionism to a form of neo-classicism. In 'Vorm
Wald', for instance, published in the opening issue of the journal (*DiR*, 1, 109), we
can identify traces of Trakl and Heym:

> Die Hitze blickt grünäugig aus dem Wald.
> Riesenfichten, urgewachsen, alt,
> Drehen ihre Äste rauchend. Kuckucksruf erschallt.
> Rote Kerzen,
> Blumen treiben übern Weg wie Kinderherzen.

---

28 Bode, p. 87.

Taken from Britting's 1935 collection *Der irdische Tag*, the poem seems to hover between the free and vivid imagery of Expressionism and the more concrete frame of reference provided by the tradition of nature poetry. Similarly, 'Der Morgen', taken from the same collection and published in March 1935 (*DiR*, 1, 1471), can be seen to retain Expressionistic elements of abstraction, while later poems – such as 'Abstieg vom Berg' (*DiR*, 3, 70); the Mörike-influenced 'Frühmorgens' (*DiR*, 4, 334); 'Mondnacht auf dem Turm' with its Biedermeier tone and scenery (*DiR*, 6, 679); and the Goethe-influenced 'Das Windlicht' (*DiR*, 6, 680) – demonstrate important staging points on Britting's move away from the post-Expressionism of *Der irdische Tag*.[29] Across the course of *Das innere Reich*, Britting's lyric output follows a trajectory towards a more conventional poetic idiom – characterised by the re-instatement of the poetic self ('Am Fluß', *DiR*, 8, 93), increasing use of symbolism ('Rabe, Roß und Hahn', *DiR*, 3, 1359–63), and increasing deployment of more epic and tightly restrictive poetic form ('Verwilderter Bauplatz', *DiR*, 4, 929–31) – until from 1942 onwards Britting publishes a series of sonnets dealing with Death and from 1943 a series of classical Greek odes (*DiR*, 9, 253; 9, 406–87; 9, 638–39; 10, 394–96; 11, 39–42).

Again, Britting's development in this respect is far from unique, but is rather part of a more general trend embodied by prominent contemporaries, such as Friedrich Georg Jünger, Rudolf Alexander Schröder and Josef Weinheber, the last of whom was also a frequent contributor to *Das innere Reich* with 56 pieces between 1936 and 1942. Again, these developments also match the norms of National Socialism. Thus, in Britting's poetic development in *Das innere Reich*, from more objective and concrete nature poetry, still imbued in the mid-1930s with traces of Expressionist imagery, to a severe form of classicism in the 1940s, we are faced with the familiar difficulties of weighing the significance of politics and aesthetics as causal factors which lie at the heart of our study. Certainly Jeanette Atkinson attributes Britting's restorative poetic shift both to the influence of his contemporaries and to practical, political considerations, asserting, for instance, that 'consciously or unconsciously [...] Britting adapted himself to the prevailing literary winds'.[30] And elsewhere: 'Practicality was, however, determined by politics in the Third Reich. The direction Britting would have followed under other circumstances remains moot.' Yet, as far as Weinheber is concerned, Atkinson is clear that he was engaged in an 'attempt to create meaning through form and language', while in her concluding comments on the shared features of Britting's, Weinheber's, and Becher's poetry, Atkinson points out, drawing on Heidegger's 'Haus des Seins', that 'strict poetic form as a source of existential and artistic security is another factor which must be considered'. Hence, politically determined explanations are 'not altogether satisfactory',

---

29 See Bode.
30 Atkinson, p. 181. Subsequent references, p. 204, p. 283, p. 288, p. 291.

assuming as they do 'that the entire literary production of a twelve-year period is anomalous, without historical roots and devoid of influence'.

In bracketing out narrow political determination, Atkinson presents a set of more general cultural concerns which match strikingly those of Alverdes and von Mechow in their opening programmatic statement:

> Moreover, a strong restorative, antiexperimental trend was already exerting consider-able influence in the twenties. A pervading sense of insecurity, uncertainty over the individual's relation to history and the 'mass', a feeling of pernicious fragmentation and relativism had reached crisis proportions by the end of the twenties. A move towards restoration in aesthetic, ethical, and political values was well under way before 1933.[31]

Of course, it is precisely this generalised classicist shift towards the sonnet and ode which Schäfer cites in his essays from the 1970s as evidence of the predominance of restorative aesthetics in the 1930s, 1940s and 1950s and precisely this underlying mood of uncertainty which Schäfer sees as the main causal factor. This classicist trend extends to pro-Nazi and non-Nazi writers both within Germany and within *Das innere Reich* itself, as exemplified by the odes composed by Franz Tumler and Johannes Bobrowski, and also to exiled authors, including Brecht and Becher. As Schäfer suggests, this evidence does seem to confirm the view of Walter Mönch that 'in Zeiten, die großen Erschütterungen unmittelbar folgen, das Sonett zu wuchern beginnt'.[32]

Modernism and restoration under National Socialism

However, for Schäfer this is not just a question of the simple re-instatement of classicism but also of an attempt to reconcile classicist norms with the insights of modernism. Britting again acts as a representative example here, both in terms of the persistence of Expressionism in his early poems in *Das innere Reich* and also in what Atkinson sees as a more experimental approach within the strictness of form found in his odes, such as 'Die Jäger', 'Der See', (*DiR*, 9, 638) and 'Der Kuckuck' (*DiR*, 9, 253).[33] It is this procedure – 'das Bemühen [...], den Expressionismus durch klassische Formen und eine Rückbindung auf die Natur-wirklichkeit zu bewahren' – which Schäfer sees above all as the enduring significance of the *Kolonne* Circle.[34] It is in this context that Schäfer sees Horst Lange's essay on Georg Heym (*DiR*, 2, 209–20) as 'ein zentrales Dokument für

31 Atkinson, p. 292.
32 See Hans Dieter Schäfer, 'Die nichtnationalsozialistische Literatur der jungen Generation im Dritten Reich', in Hans Dieter Schäfer, *Das gespaltene Bewußtsein: Über deutsche Kultur und Lebenswirklichkeit 1933–1945* (Munich: Hanser, 1981), pp. 7–54 (p. 43).
33 See Atkinson, pp. 196–200.
34 Schäfer, 'Periodisierung', p. 59.

die Poetologie der neuen Epoche'.[35] Here, Lange proposed Heym, and also Trakl, as models for contemporary lyric poetry. Alongside Lange's essay appeared Heym's fragment 'Atalanta' (*DiR*, 2, 221–29), while already in November 1934 Adolf Beiß (*DiR*, 1, 945) had commemorated the twentieth anniversary of Trakl's death. These explicit attempts to promote the legacy of Expressionist poetry were matched in the visual arts by Kurt Mathies's attempts to promote Rohlfs, Nolde, and Barlach (*DiR*, 3, 759–64) and by the striking inclusion of a series of reproductions of sculpture by Gerhard Marcks in the June 1936 edition of the journal. Work by Britting's Expressionist collaborator, Josef Achmann (*DiR*, 3, 575–76), was also featured prominently two months later.

In this promotion of an aesthetic strand which contrasts so strongly with *Blut-und-Boden* writing, *Das innere Reich* reflects the contradictions in National Socialist cultural policy embodied most clearly in the factional dispute between Goebbels and Rosenberg in the early years of the regime, the former advocating a Germanic form of Expressionism, the latter a *völkisch* aesthetic. In these contradictions there also exists a potential tension in the 1930 paradigm as it applies to cultural production in the Third Reich. While these lingering traces of Expressionism can be comfortably positioned within the kind of re-assertion of the conventional bourgeois institution of literature advocated by the *Kolonne* Circle, we might reasonably ask how an aesthetic aimed at propagandistic mass appeal, arising from and accessible to the *Volksgemeinschaft*, can be rendered compatible with the elitist notion of the *Dichter* promoted in *Die Kolonne*. Here, two principal points can be made. Firstly, as the analysis of Günter Eich's contributions to Nazi radio will make clear, the functional and propagandistic Nazi aesthetic rested paradoxically on a conventional notion of authorship. In *Das innere Reich* this can be seen most clearly in pieces of literary criticism such as Hermann Pongs's programmatic essay 'Zur Lyrik der Zeit' (*DiR*, 2, 1155–70 and 1566–86), where criticism of the individualism of Expressionism and calls for the integration of the writer with the *Volksgemeinschaft* co-exist with praise for the spontaneous creativity of the *Ich*-centred poet. Throughout, the writer is explicitly a *Dichter* and the *Bildungsdialekt* of Hölderlin, Goethe, and Rilke acts as the principal frame of reference. Secondly, it is the search for a stability of meaning which provides the common element in these two divergent aesthetic strands. The post-Expressionist/post-*Kolonne* strand embodied by Britting seeks this stability inside the conventional bourgeois institution of literature pursuing a trajectory which increasingly, although never entirely, eliminates openness and uncertainty of form, imagery, and meaning. The *völkisch* strand derives stability in functional, readerly texts where meaning remains secure.

---

35 Hans Dieter Schäfer, 'Horst Langes Tagebücher aus dem zweiten Weltkrieg', in Hans Dieter Schäfer, *Das gespaltene Bewußtsein: Über deutsche Kultur und Lebenswirklichkeit 1933–1945* (Munich: Hanser, 1981), pp. 72–90 (p. 75).

In this way, it is essential to recognise the dual nature of *Das innere Reich* which evades the caricature of an entirely backward-looking and *völkisch* outlook. As in *Die Kolonne*, traces of modernism survive within the idiom of nature poetry. More remarkably, a presence is also given in *Das innere Reich* to an overt brand of *Sachlichkeit* in the form of a series of photographs which appeared in April 1937 depicting some of the regime's new construction projects, including the *Reichssportfeld* and Ernst Sagebiel's *Reichsluftfahrtministerium* in Berlin, Albert Speer's *Zeppelinfeld* in Nuremberg, and even snapshots of new motorways. Once more, we are alerted to the danger of viewing these mid-decades as a straightforward retreat into *Innerlichkeit*, even in a literary journal where that stance is inscribed in its title. If this constitutes one of many lines of continuity from *Die Kolonne*, then the overt politicisation of the journal within the context of National Socialism represents a radical break. And yet here it is possible to identify strong parallels to *Die Linkskurve* in the way that an ideologised totality is perceived to offer a much-needed source of cultural stability. Here as there, a functional and readerly strand of literary production threatens to undermine the conventional bourgeois institution of literature but is ultimately absorbed within it.

Maß und Wert

Two figures dominate critical opinion on *Maß und Wert*: Thomas Mann who maintained overall editorial control; and Ferdinand Lion who was responsible for the day-to-day editorial management of the journal during its first two years. On two central issues relating to the editorial practice of Mann and Lion, this existing scholarship is all but unanimous. Firstly, the editorial tenure of Ferdinand Lion during these first two years is widely perceived to have been little short of disastrous, characterised above all by a capacity to alienate contributors and a failure to establish and pursue any consistent editorial agenda. Secondly, Thomas Mann is acknowledged to have been the dominant editorial presence, taking a keen, interventionist interest in the running of the journal from its foundation to its closure. In his account of Mann's exile in Zurich, for instance, Thomas Sprecher concedes that he can add nothing to the judgement made by Peter Stahlberger over twenty years previously in his biography of Emil Oprecht:

> Letztlich war *Maß und Wert* […] die Zeitschrift Thomas Manns. Er gab ihr mit seinen Vorworten […] das Gepräge; er stand am Anfang und bestimmte schließlich auch das Ende; er bewegte verschiedene Freunde zur Mitarbeit an der Zeitschrift und vermittelte bei Spannungen zwischen Redakteur und Mitarbeitern, Redakteur und Verleger; kurz er war 'der feste Punkt' (Ferdinand Lion), er war selber das Maß und bestimmte den Wert von *Maß und Wert*.[36]

---

36 Peter Stahlberger, 'Der Zürcher Verleger Emil Oprecht und die deutsche politische Emigration 1933–1945' (doctoral dissertation, Zurich, 1970), quoted by Sprecher, p. 186.

Not only behind the scenes, but also on the pages of *Maß und Wert*, Thomas Mann's is the most significant voice. Through his programmatic forewords to each of the three years of the journal's existence (*MuW*, 1, 1–16; 2, 3–7; 3, 5–6) and six instalments of *Lotte in Weimar* (*MuW*, 1, 17–34; 1, 209–72; 1, 667–97; 1, 827–56; 2, 453–503; 3, 28–46), and also through the publication of his speech to commemorate the opening of the Thomas Mann Library at Yale (*MuW*, 2, 137–45) and essays on Wagner (*MuW*, 1, 377–401), *Faust* (*MuW*, 2, 590–612) and *Anna Karenina* (*MuW*, 3, 458–73), Thomas Mann accounts for more than one tenth of the entire contents of the journal, or over 15% of its main section, a figure which rises to a remarkable 20% for the first two years of publication. Significantly, for Thomas Baltensweiler these two issues are not unrelated: 'Dass Thomas Mann allerdings oft mehr als einen "gewissen allgemeinen Einfluss" geltend machen musste, hing mit Lions [...] redaktioneller Glücklosigkeit und seinem menschlichen Ungeschick zusammen.'[37]

Maß and *Wert*: Thomas Mann's programme

This connection between Ferdinand Lion's shortcomings in his day-to-day editorial practice, on the one hand, and Thomas Mann's concerted efforts to impose his broader editorial interests, on the other, focuses attention on Mann's editorial forewords, which Stahlberger sees as the primary shaping influence on the journal. Of these three programmatic statements, it is the foreword to the very first edition of the journal in September 1937 (*MuW*, 1, 1–16), composed, as Thomas Mann's diaries indicate, with no little struggle over a period of two weeks, and more than twice the length of the other two forewords put together, which is of principal interest.[38] While the two later forewords, of September 1938 and November 1939 respectively, are relatively brief and concern themselves principally with the worsening political situation in Europe and the viability of the journal's existence, in the opening foreword Mann provides an involved exposition of the rationale behind the foundation of the journal, above all through a discussion of its chosen title. Having conceded the conservative and refined resonance of the terms of that title, Mann goes on to describe the kind of world to which the journal is to be opposed. That world is one of self-proclaimed, but now bankrupt, revolution, a counter-world 'zu der der Qualität, des Ranges, der Kunst, aus welcher die Wortsymbole stammen, mit denen wir unser Wollen, unseren Glauben bezeichnen'. Resolutely defending this alternative world of aesthetic quality, Mann specifies what he understands by the two symbolic terms 'Maß' and 'Wert', which Johannes R. Becher would later try to claim for the publishing enterprise which became *Sinn und Form*:

---

37 Baltensweiler, p. 125, quoting Thomas Mann, letter to Carl Seelig, 14 October 1937.
38 See Sprecher, pp. 187–88.

Maß, das ist Ordnung und Licht, die Musik der Schöpfung und dessen, was schöpferisch ist; es ist auch das Errungene, dem Chaos Abgewonnene, das Anti-Barbarische, der Sieg der Form, der Sieg des Menschen. [...] Es ist das Richtende, die kritische Waage, auf der gewogen zu werden gefährlich ist, denn gar bald ist sie mehr als nur eine Prüferin von Geschmacklichkeiten, sie entscheidet über [...] *den Wert* selbst in des Wortes substantiellster und fundamentalster Bedeutung: 'Heute', sagt Goethe, der Künstler, 'kommt es darauf an, was einer wiegt auf *der Waage der Menschheit*. Alles Übrige ist eitel'. Künstler wollen wir sein und Anti-Barbaren, das Maß verehren, den Wert verteidigen.

For Mann, quality is explicitly a defining feature of art: 'Kunst ist durchaus eine Sphäre der Kühnheit des Wagnisses [...]. Das Mittelmäßige perhorresziert sie, wie sie das Triviale, das Abgeschmackte und Niedrige, das ekle Klischee perhorresziert; denn sie ist Qualität selbst, der Anspruch, die Ungenügsamkeit.'

Typical of the foreword in the section quoted above is Thomas Mann's appeal to Goethe as a supporting authority for his statements. Indeed, as Liselotte Maas points out: 'Kein Gedanke im programmatischen Vorwort des Eröffnungsheftes von *Maß und Wert*, der nicht mit einem Goethe-Zitat abgesichert wäre!'[39] Appropriately through one of these many references to Goethe, Thomas Mann presents a further central plank in his programme for the journal, namely his approach to the literary tradition: 'Es gibt kein Vergangenes, das man zurücksehnen dürfte, es gibt nur ein ewig Neues, das sich aus den erweiterten Elementen des Vergangenen gestaltet, und die echte Sehnsucht muß stets produktiv sein, ein neues Bessres erschaffen.' Mann goes on to emphasise the importance of this productive relationship between old and new as a core feature of artistic quality. The programmatic search for 'Maß', lost in the contemporary world, is viewed by Mann as both a conservative and revolutionary undertaking:

Sie ist konservativ, insofern sie etwas bewahren will, was bisher die Würde des Menschen ausgemacht hat: die Idee eines überpersönlichen, überparteilichen, übervölkischen Maßes und Wertes [...]. Sie ist aber revolutionär, da sie dieses Maß selbst aus keinerlei Vergangenheit ungeprüft übernehmen will, sondern es an den heutigen Bedingungen und Erfahrungen mit größter Wahrhaftigkeit zu erproben, aus der gegenwärtigen Situation zu gewinnen unternimmt.

Denn Künstlertum ist gerade dies: Das Neue, das sich aus den erweiterten Elementen des Vergangenen gestaltet; es ist immer überlieferungsbewußt und zukunftswillig, aristokratisch und revolutionär in einem; es ist seinem Wesen nach das, womit es der Zeit und dem Leben ein Vorbild sein kann: konservative Revolution.

In appropriating and re-defining the term 'conservative revolution' in this way, Mann adds a notable dynamic element to the secure foundations with which the bourgeois literary tradition provides him.

That all the time in this undertaking Mann is explicitly offering an antidote to the chaos and confusion of the times, and that it is very clearly the political

---

39   Maas, p. 215.

context of exile and National Socialism which lends this programme its urgency and validity, is self-evident. Indeed, it is the perceived validity, or otherwise, of this primarily aesthetic position as an appropriate response to National Socialism which has dominated much critical discussion of the opening foreword.[40] Walter, for instance, describes Mann's justification of the aesthetic purity of the journal's title in the face of political reality as 'seltsam abseitig, weltfremd, ja unwirklich'. Similarly, he highlights the directly opposed stance maintained by Fritz Erpenbeck in response in *Das Wort*: 'Kein Mensch, auch der Künstler nicht, kann sich befreien von den unausweichlichen Forderungen seiner gesellschaftlichen Realität' (*Wort*, 2.11, 6). In this way, and valid response or not, it would clearly be misleading and inappropriate to disassociate Thomas Mann's conception of artistic 'measure' and 'value' from the barbarism of National Socialism against which it explicitly acts as a counterpoint. At the same time, we can identify strong continuities in Mann's position both back and forward across 1933 and 1945. Walter's diagnosis of the mood underlying Thomas Mann's composition of the foreword, for example, points to continuities with the predominant mood of 1930:

> Daß er schließlich die gesamte Argumentation in ein Plädoyer für die Existenz-berechtigung von Kunst in finstern Zeiten einmünden ließ – man kann daran nur ablesen, wie groß insgeheim seine Zweifel [...] am Sinn seiner ganzen Existenz gewesen sein müssen, wie tief die Beziehungslosigkeit seines literarisch-künstlerischen Tuns zur politischen Wirklichkeit ihn gequält haben muß, wie groß aber auch die Orientierungs- und Auswegslosigkeit gewesen ist, in der er sich befunden hat.

Implicitly, Walter seems to be ascribing to Mann's *Maß und Wert* programme what amounts to an 'inner emigration' position in exile, complete with the same condemnatory tone which was attached after 1945 to those who had maintained that position inside Nazi Germany, and this lends support to Schäfer's observations concerning the common mood between the two groups: 'Die wiederholt vertretene These, die Flüchtlingsliteratur stünde auf Grund ihrer konträren Erfahrungswelt in einem krassen Gegensatz zur Literatur der Daheim-gebliebenen, berücksichtigt zu wenig [...] das auch außerhalb Deutschlands aufgebrochene Angstgefühl.'[41] In terms of post-war continuities with Mann's programme, two journals in our corpus are of particular importance. Mann's resolute belief in the capacity of the German literary tradition to oppose the barbarism of National Socialism will find its echo in the prisoner-of-war version of *Der Ruf*, while his faith in 'measure' and 'value' as the cornerstones of a progressive tradition will find a remarkable echo in the founding programme and editorial practice of *Sinn und Form*.

In a similar vein, it is impossible within the context of our current study to ignore in Thomas Mann's explicitly elitist programme of artistic quality the strong

---

40 See Walter, pp. 512–14.
41 Schäfer, 'Periodisierung', p. 61.

echoes of the programmes advanced by Lukács, Raschke, and Haas around 1930, each buttressed by conventional literary tradition as the authoritative representative of that artistic quality: frequently, and above all of course in 1932, in the shape of Goethe. In particular, in the significance attached to 'Maß' and 'Wert' as timeless symbols of order amidst chaos and in the choice of language which again propagates a traditional discourse of high literature through terms such as 'Schöpfung' and 'Gestaltung', Thomas Mann's editorial programme fits almost seamlessly with the manifestations of the 1930 paradigm we have already identified in *Die Linkskurve*, *Die Kolonne*, and *Die literarische Welt*. Indeed, despite the otherwise unbridgeable ideological divide between them, and notwithstanding the fact that each sought to explicitly oppose what the other stood for, some commonality of approach is also discernible between Thomas Mann and Paul Alverdes in their advocacy of an inner aesthetic realm. Above all though, Thomas Mann's first programmatic foreword resonates with the editorial position explicitly promoted by Willy Haas in *Die literarische Welt*. Where Thomas Mann defines art as 'die Qualität selbst' and the role of his journal as 'die kritische Waage', Haas defends 'unseren Glauben, Qualitäten messen zu können; unseren Glauben an die Qualität selbst' (*DlW*, 4.43, 1). Where Thomas Mann, citing Goethe, defines art as 'das Neue, das sich aus den erweiterten Elementen des Vergangenen gestaltet', Haas defends 'ein höchst harmonisches und organisches Gebilde aus geistiger Vergangenheit und geistiger Zukunft, über dem der Goethesche Leitspruch stehen könnte: "Ältestes bewahrt mit Treue, freundlich aufgefaßtes Neue"' (*DlW*, 2.29, 5). In both cases too, these robust notions of quality and tradition are tied to an overt rejection of political extremes and an embrace of what one might term a very broadly defined liberal humanism, or what Walter refers to, in connection with *Maß und Wert*, as 'der Suche nach einem dritten Weg'.[42] At the same time, this rejection by Mann and Haas of extreme Left and Right does not obscure the aesthetic elements in their programmes which bridge the ideological divide to the trajectories of *Die Linkskurve* and *Das Wort* and of *Die Kolonne* and *Das innere Reich*.

Ferdinand Lion: editorial dilettante?

If Mann's first editorial foreword in *Maß und Wert* can be viewed in this way as a paradigmatic statement for any posited period of mid-century aesthetic retrenchment, what is less clear is the extent to which publication practice in *Maß und Wert* might have matched Thomas Mann's opening programme. The question of harmony between programme and practice is all the more important for *Maß und Wert* given critical opinion on Lion's competence as editor. Maas, for

---

42   Walter, p. 518.

instance, identifies already in the second editorial foreword evidence of Thomas Mann's dissatisfaction with the way Lion was putting his programme into practice: 'Der Weg zwischen den Unleidlichkeiten, zwischen den Müßigen, Abseitigen, Zeitflüchtigen, Ästhetisch-Verspielten und dem Polemisch-Verbissenen, zwischen allzuviel Freiheit und geistig herabsetzender Verstricktheit ist schwer [...] zu finden' (*MuW*, 2, 3).[43] Similarly, Walter points to correspondence between Thomas Mann and 'einigen der von der Redaktionspraxis Betroffenen – oder soll man besser sagen: Geschädigten?' in which Lion's editorial style is a matter of discussion.[44] As early as September 1937, Thomas Mann was prepared to concede to Martin Gumpert, whose poems had been rejected by Lion, that the latter was a 'häkelig-mäkelig Köpfchen'. Only three months later, in response to a letter from his son Klaus in which the latter had complained about the cuts demanded on his contribution to the journal – 'Niemals habe ich einen schwierigeren Redakteur wie Sie gekannt' – Thomas Mann wrote with dismay both of Lion's tendency to make cuts in all contributions apart from his own and of the quality of the review section – 'mit dem Oprecht nicht zufrieden ist' – and for which Albin Zollinger was now to be responsible, instead of Lion. These exchanges, in addition to those regarding an unpaid honorarium to Menno ter Braak and the treatment of Annette Kolb, the comments of Döblin and Hans Sahl, and Klaus Mann's withdrawal of his collaboration on the journal under Lion's editorship, demonstrate, in Walter's words, 'mit welcher Sprunghaftigkeit und Willkür Lion sein Redaktionsamt (zum Schaden der Mitarbeiter wie der Zeitschrift) verwaltet hat'.[45]

Lion's alienation of potential regular contributors seems to have only served to exacerbate the perceived inconsistency, if not arbitrariness, which characterised his selection of contributions. Apparently the choice of the journal's sponsor, the widow of a Luxemburg steel magnate, Aline Mayrisch de Saint Hubert, Ferdinand Lion seems to have possessed neither the appropriate background nor character for the role of editor. Above all, it is Lion's apparently natural inclination towards the esoteric which emerges from the pages of *Maß und Wert* and which is seen to have undermined Thomas Mann's editorial programme. Sprecher, for instance, is clear that, as 'Bohémien und Charmeur, Autodidakt, durchschlagloser Dilettant', as 'immer etwas unfassbar und unzuverlässig', Lion was responsible for the shortcomings in the journal alluded to by Thomas Mann in his diaries as early as December 1937: '[Die Mängel] lagen hauptsächlich in der Amtsführung des Redakteurs, mit der niemand so recht glücklich wurde. [...] Lion hatte den Redaktorenberuf sowenig gelernt wie einen anderen.'[46] Most swingeing in his criticism of Lion's editorial practice is Hans-Albert Walter. Having considered the

---

43 Maas, p. 218.
44 See Walter, pp. 505–06.
45 Walter, p. 506.
46 Sprecher, pp. 183–84 and p. 188.

relatively small number of strictly political essays to appear in *Maß und Wert* –
'zufällig und bunt zusammengewürfelt' – Walter turns his attention to cultural,
philosophical, and literary essays:

> Im kulturellen Teil von *Maß und Wert* hat es an redaktioneller Planung ebenso gefehlt
> wie in den bisher behandelten Sparten. [...] Überblickt man die Essays zu
> philosophischen, kultur- und geistesgeschichtlichen, literarischen, musikalischen, ja
> selbst naturwissenschaftlichen Fragen, die unter Lion veröffentlicht worden sind, so
> gewinnt man sehr schnell den Eindruck, der Zufall sei der eigentlich federführende
> Redakteur gewesen. [...] Verallgemeinernd kann man sagen, Lion habe mit sicherem
> Instinkt stets das Esoterische, das Beiläufige und Abseitige aufgegriffen, und er sei mit
> großem Erfolg bemüht gewesen, alle die Themenkreise zu umgehen, auf die sich die
> Aufmerksamkeit der exilierten Schriftsteller konzentrierte.[47]

The same analysis is applied also to the review section of the journal and to
literary contributions.[48] Amidst the broad spectrum of works reviewed 'ist ein
Auswahlprinzip gar nicht erkennbar'. As far as literary pieces are concerned: 'Im
Grunde könnte man das zu den kulturellen und literarischen Essays Gesagte hier
wiederholen und zum Refrain erheben. [...] Um Thomas Mann herum aber
gruppierten sich Werke unterschiedlichster Provenienz und Qualität.'

For Walter, it is not the esoteric nature of Lion's editorship in itself of which
he is so critical, but rather the way in which this undermined Thomas Mann's
editorial programme and failed to adequately represent the concerns of German
intellectuals in exile.[49] Writing of the overwhelming impression of the obscure
and esoteric given by the journal, Walter suggests: 'Vor allem aber gefährdete er
den Repräsentanzanspruch, den *Maß und Wert* mit seinem Untertitel erhob, und er
stellte schließlich auch die Gültigkeit der "musischen Symbole" des Titels selbst
in Frage.' Here Walter compares *Maß und Wert* unfavourably with *Das Wort*. While
the latter pre-occupied itself with the Expressionism Debate, Lion is seen to be
wasting thirty sides on Oskar Goldberg's essay, 'Die Götter der Griechen' (*MuW*,
1, 163–91), and a dozen on a review of obscure new titles treating themes
connected with mythology, such as I. I. Meyer's *Trilogie altindischer Mächte und Feste
der Vegetation* (*MuW*, 1, 498–511). Not only that, but the active engagement with
the German literary tradition which lay explicitly at the heart of Thomas Mann's
programme is seen to have been restricted in *Maß und Wert* to a few isolated
contributions, mostly stemming from Thomas Mann himself:

> Man muß aber mit einiger Verblüffung registrieren, daß sich kommunisitische Organe
> mit dieser Problematik unvergleichlich häufiger und intensiver auseinandergesetzt
> haben als die Zeitschrift, die von traditionsbewußten bürgerlichen Intellektuellen
> gerade zum Zweck der revolutionären Erneuerung des Überlieferten gegründet
> worden war. [...] Weder hat Georg Lukács in *Maß und Wert* einen kritischen
> Widerpart gefunden noch Walter Benjamin eine Heimatstatt für seine Arbeiten, und

---

47 Walter, p. 532 and pp. 535–36.
48 See Walter, pp. 538–39.
49 See Walter, pp. 537–39.

die 'Erbe'-Diskussionen der Exilliteratur blieben vollends ohne Ausstrahlung auf die Zeitschrift.

The same is seen to hold true for literary contributions: 'Thomas Manns Hoffnung, das Revolutionäre und Neue solle aus dem Traditionellen hervorgehen, hat sich auch im literarischen Teil von *Maß und Wert* nicht erfüllt.' As a summary of this critical opinion, Baltensweiler's judgement needs little elaboration: 'Die Hefte wirken nicht von ordnender Hand zusammengestellt, sondern kunterbunt zusammengewürfelt; den Ankündigungen des programmatischen Vorworts entsprechen sie nur teilweise.'[50]

The 'thick' literary journal: Lion's editorial practice

Certainly the first impression the reader gains from *Maß und Wert* is of a largely unstructured and thematically diverse selection of pieces. Apart from the regular headings 'Glossen' and 'Kritik', contributions are placed alongside one another without genre designation or, usually, editorial comment. In the very first edition, Thomas Mann's foreword is followed by an extract from *Lotte in Weimar* (*MuW*, 1, 17–34) which, together with another prose fiction extract (from Josef Breitbach's *Die Rückkehr* (*MuW*, 1, 75–99)), sits alongside three essays treating aspects of contemporary and historical German politics and society (Erich Kahler, 'Die preussische Ökonomie' (*MuW*, 1, 35–62); Herrmann Steinhausen, 'Die Zukunft der Freiheit' (*MuW*, 1, 63–74); and Karl Mannheim, 'Zur Diagnose unserer Zeit' (*MuW*, 1, 100–21)). The range of contributions is broadened in the second issue, so that here the second extract from *Lotte in Weimar* (*MuW*, 1, 209–72) is published alongside: poetry by Heinz Politzer (*MuW*, 1, 289–91); prose by Oskar Maria Graf (*MuW*, 1, 292–309); essays on Greek mythology (*MuW*, 1, 163–91), contemporary opera (*MuW*, 1, 273–88), and culture under National Socialism (*MuW*, 1, 310–18); reproductions of letters written by Nietzsche's mother (*MuW*, 1, 192–208); and a review article on new editions of Kafka's diaries and letters (*MuW*, 1, 319–25). If we consider that issues three and four include essays on topics ranging from Austrian political autonomy (*MuW*, 1, 352–65) to Mozart's humanism (*MuW*, 1, 545–55), from the purely aesthetic value of lyric poetry (*MuW*, 1, 424–56) to indeterminism in quantum physics (*MuW*, 1, 597–604), then charges of esotericism seem valid enough.

And yet, it is difficult to escape the feeling that the literature on Lion's editorship rests in a rather comfortable orthodoxy which is happy to take advantage of Lion as a convenient scapegoat to preserve Thomas Mann's reputation in what is perceived to be a flawed and failed literary venture. Here, a number of points might be made in relation to the perceived arbitrariness of

---

50 Baltensweiler, p. 125.

Lion's editorial practice. Firstly, it should be self-evident that what one individual perceives as obscure esotericism another might see as the valuable expression of a pluralist and polymath culture, and, further, that the political and historical context of exile and National Socialism scarcely encourages a generous view of what Maas refers to as Lion's 'Vorliebe für esoterische, zeitabgewandte Texte'.[51] Indeed, the criticism implicit in the repeated insistence on Lion's neglect of left-wing exile figures is revealing evidence of what is perceived to have been the more worthwhile response to National Socialism. It is worth noting that in this respect Lion's editorial practice in fact matches the founding conception of the journal, and this is a point which Maas's criticism of Lion acknowledges:

> Elitäre Spiele in einem freien und von der Wirklichkeit abgehobenen Reich der Kunst; das könnte eine Formel abgeben für den esoterischen Flair von *Maß und Wert* in seinen ersten beiden Jahrgängen. Dazu kam ein [...] weitgehender Verzicht auf jedwede Polemik. Vornehm-zurückhaltend und sozusagen aussschließlich dem Zeitlosen verpflichtet, verstand man sich ausdrücklich als eine 'der geistigen Kultur gewidmete Zweimonatszeitschrift' (*MuW*, 2, 104).[52]

In this respect at least, Lion's editorial practice does not diverge from Thomas Mann's opening foreword. Whatever the quality of the individual pieces concerned, his practice, through, for instance, his own essay 'Die Schönheit des Lyrischen' (*MuW*, 1, 424–56) which draws on examples from Trakl, Hofmannsthal, Rilke, Hebbel, and Klopstock among others and Einstein's essay on Mozart – 'Gemäss war ihm das Mass' (*MuW*, 1, 553) – seeks to present precisely the rich and diverse cultural world which Mann sought to oppose to National Socialism.

It is here that the typological distinction between the 'thick' and 'thin' literary journal is able to provide a useful conceptual framework for Lion's editorial practice, since the make-up of the journal must be considered against its programme, function, and structure, all of which are typical of the thick rather than the thin type of literary journal. Published bi-monthly and typically incorporating only six long pieces, the main section of *Maß und Wert* was not structured so as to be responsive to topical events in the manner of *Die literarische Welt* with its weekly, newspaper format, its short multi-column articles, and front-page headlines which permitted a high degree of immediacy and topicality. Without editorial and formatting gimmickry, the enduring principles of 'measure' and 'value' were inscribed into the layout and make-up of each issue which sought to uphold a notion of the high literary work in its sober and erudite contents. In keeping with the notion of the thick journal, these contents were not restricted to a narrow-interest agenda intent on effecting short-term action, but rather sought to cover a broad range of topics, extending far beyond the mere literary, achieving a degree of influence in a much longer-term context, primarily through quality

---

51   Maas, p. 217.
52   Maas, p. 218.

and prestige. What Maas dismisses as 'elitäre Spiele in einem freien und von der Wirklichkeit abgehobenen Reich der Kunst' are entirely in keeping with this thick-journal agenda, so that critics bemoaning the absence of interventions in the Expressionism Debate rather miss the point. Such criticism betrays the academic pre-occupations of the 1970s rather than the contemporary cultural function which *Maß und Wert* sought to achieve, the latter entirely appropriate to the cultural climate of the times.

At the same time, the structural constraints of the journal, which permitted the publication of only 30–40 main pieces each year, clearly hampered attempts to develop consistent thematic strands, and it is in this context that an individual piece such as Louis de Broglie's 'Betrachtungen über den Indeterminismus in der Quantenphysik' (*MuW*, 1, 597–604) can become an isolated piece of editorial esotericism. And yet, we have already noted Martin Raschke's pre-occupation with such themes as Heisenberg's Uncertainty Principle, and this kind of contemporary scientific theory makes a significant re-appearance in *Merkur* after 1945. De Broglie's essay is to be read then not on its own specialist terms, but in a broader intellectual climate in which such matters were part of more general philosophical and metaphysical debates. Awareness of this underlying preoccupation helps to explain why Alfred Döblin's sole contribution to *Maß und Wert* is the historical-philosophical essay, 'Prometheus und das Primitive' (*MuW*, 1, 331–51), and not his literary-historical essay, *Die deutsche Literatur (im Ausland seit 1933)*, a choice which Walter considers symptomatic of Lion's shortcomings.[53] The former essay, through its attempt to understand historical development in a broad, abstract sweep, is thematically and methodologically in keeping with much of the remainder of *Maß und Wert*.[54] Döblin's mythological frame of reference also highlights one of the most prominent strands to run throughout the journal. In this case, Goldberg's 'Die Götter der Griechen' (*MuW*, 1, 163–91) finds a consistent thematic context through a host of direct and indirect references to Greek mythology, ranging from his own review article, 'Mythologische Bücher' (*MuW*, 1, 498–511), and essay, 'Die griechische Tragödie' (*MuW*, 1, 729–52), to Brentano's 'Phädra' (*MuW*, 1, 556–79), from Friedrich Walter's prose set in Troy, 'Die stummen Götter '(*MuW*, 2, 146–66), to Helmut Kuhn's 'Der gefesselte Prometheus: Gedanken über den Zusammenhang von Tragödie und Kosmologie' (*MuW*, 3, 609–35). Through this classical *Bildungsdialekt*, *Maß und Wert* provides a source of intellectual security, and in a similar vein we might note the contributions which deal with themes of childhood experience, an alternative source of thematic stability. Notable in this context is not only the juxtaposition of Benjamin's 'Berliner Kindheit um Neunzehnhundert' (*MuW*, 1, 857–67) with Albin Zollinger's 'Kindheitsgeschichte' (*MuW*, 1, 868–71), but also Oskar Maria Graf's 'Menschen aus der Heimat' (*MuW*, 1, 292–309), a short story detailing the

---

53 Walter, p. 536.
54 See, for instance, Jan Romein, 'Dialektik des Fortschritts', *MuW*, 2, 305–22.

first person narrator's 'Erinnerung an den ersten Proletarier, der mir in meinem Leben begegnet ist', which would scarcely have been out of place in *Die Linkskurve*.

The characteristic lack of topicality is also carried into the review section which omits much that was being published in exile and seems to act principally as a platform for Oprecht's new titles. In this respect, scholarly criticism does seem justified. Still, a number of significant contemporary literary trends do emerge. In the very first issue, for instance, Lion reviews Döblin's *Die Fahrt ins Land ohne Tod*, noting a shared primitivism with Thomas Mann's *Joseph* and hinting at common preoccupations in the exile and inner-German experience: 'Die beiden mythischen Romane der Emigration, das Jakob-Josephwerk Thomas Manns und dieser Roman Döblins: beide geschaffen aus der gleichen Not und Bedrängnis wie die innere Politik Deutschlands' (*MuW*, 1, 145). Indeed, Döblin is a frequent presence in the review section of *Maß und Wert*, and these reviews seem to highlight the kind of shift in his output which Schäfer deploys as evidence in his periodisation essay. Thus Lion on Döblin's *Der blaue Tiger*: 'Vielleicht ist noch nie Döblin so Mildes gelungen. [...] Dieser Anti-Römer (der keine Ordnungen kennt) wird hier fast klassisch' (*MuW*, 2, 120). Elsewhere (*MuW*, 1, 967–71), Friedrich Georg Jünger's flight into antiquity, *Der Taurus*, is singled out as one of the very few worthwhile works of inner-German literature: 'Man erlebt in Jünger eine Wiederkehr des gelehrten Dichters.' What the review section does imply is a tangible sense of a cultural period which has moved beyond the threshold debates of 1930 and accepted the new status quo, a sense re-inforced by Lion's historicised references to Kaiser and Döblin as the great experimenters of Weimar literature and to Weimar in general as a period of theatrical experimentation which is no longer current (*MuW*, 2, 343–44; 2, 677–89). In a similar vein, Ernst Krenek's essay on contemporary opera (*MuW*, 1, 273–88) can be viewed not simply as an example of esoteric arbitrariness, but rather as a potentially significant attempt to engage with the legacy of modernist, atonal music and the implications of Brecht's dramatic theories for a genre reliant, principally through Wagner, on principles of empathy and *Genuss*. Einstein's review of Hindemith's *Unterweisung im Tonsatz* (*MuW*, 2, 120–32) adopts a similar position, praising this as a notable stage in the development of 'new music', away from the negative rejection of all that has gone before and towards a more considered attempt to develop a positive system. Hence, there is an engagement, albeit low-key, with manifestations of German modernism. The absence in *Maß und Wert* of any resonance of the Expressionism Debate seems to be attributable to the sense that this was something which had already passed, that the journal is located, in Hüppauf's terminology, beyond the immediate period of *Kulturkrise*.

Zeitdiagnose: the crisis of modernity

Amidst Lion's often frustrating intellectual diversity, one consistent set of concerns is addressed in the journal, and this is apparent already in the first issue in Herrmann Steinhausen's 'Die Zukunft der Freiheit' (*MuW*, 1, 63–74) and Karl Mannheim's 'Zur Diagnose unserer Zeit' (*MuW*, 1, 100–21). Writing as Steinhausen, Eugen Gürster sets out to explain what he sees as a turn amongst the young away from freedom and towards order, and what he identifies above all is a sense of fear, both, narrowly – 'Angst [...] vor einem Leben ohne Aufstiegs-chance [...] vor dem wirtschaftlichen Untergang' – and also, more broadly: 'die geistige Verzweiflung, einen individuellen Sinn der Existenz überhaupt noch zu finden.' The modern masses have come to believe in existence as a crisis, so that they perceive 'diese Welt nicht als ein von einer höheren Ordnungsidee bestrahltes Ganzes, sondern als ein unübersehbares Chaos'. In this way, Gürster identifies on a social level the mechanisms which Schäfer makes so much of on an aesthetic level: 'Wie das menschliche Denken mit Notwendigkeit nach der Wahrheit verlangt, so strebt das menschliche Zusammenstreben mitten im Chaos tastend nach einem Ordnungsprinzip hin.' For Gürster, as for Schäfer, National Socialism is as much a product of this chaos and accompanying search for order, as it is the source. In this first issue, Mannheim also takes up the problems of the individual in a technologically driven society. Locating the source above all in a chaotic industrialisation process, and in the unemployment and the breakdown of the family which accompanies it, Mannheim diagnoses a loss of faith in the progress which can be made through technology, a turn towards irrationalism, and a disintegration of any coherent means of understanding the world. Hence, the dominant pre-occupation of the journal which is signalled in this first issue is, perhaps not surprisingly, a sense of crisis, but this is not a crisis tied directly to National Socialism but rather one which is consistently framed in terms of longer term trends of modernisation, technology, and the mass society.

Baltensweiler also identifies these two essays, together with Gürster's 'Die Umformung des Menschen durch Propaganda' (*MuW*, 2, 111–19) and André Siegfried's 'Die industrielle Revolution und ihre Rückwirkungen auf die Probleme unserer Zeit' (*MuW*, 2, 437–52), as representative of a broader thread running through the journal, to which he gives the label 'Zeitdiagnose':

> Einigkeit herrscht darüber, dass die gegenwärtige Epoche als die der industriellen Massengesellschaft zu bezeichnen ist und dass sich in ihr aufgrund tiefgreifender ökonomischer Umwandlungen eine gesellschaftliche und moralische Krise artikuliere.[55]

Indeed, this tendency is more broadly represented than Baltensweiler suggests. So, for instance, Gürster's *Die Zukunft der Freiheit* is reviewed later in the first year

---

by Golo Mann, who tellingly positions it alongside Spengler's *Untergang des Abendlandes*, Jaspers's *Geistige Situation der Zeit* and Ernst Jünger's *Der Arbeiter* (*MuW*, 1, 654). The journal's regular engagement with such philosophical thought is a further indicator of the contemporary mood. Also of interest in the same issue as Gürster's 'Epoche des Massenstaates' is a contribution under the pseudonym Karl Otto, purporting to be written by a worker who has remained in Germany. Such is its tone and its defence of conservative dictatorship, that the piece has been suspected of originating in the Propaganda Ministry in Berlin and deployed as further evidence of Lion's lack of editorial judgement. However, of more interest in the current context are the opening lines which are entirely in keeping with the diagnosis of the times: 'Der Mensch lebt im Zeitalter der Technik und der Massen in der Massengesellschaft, […] in der der Einzelne sich als Atom in der unfaßbaren Masse verliert' (*MuW*, 2, 93). As Baltensweiler suggests, these discussions of crisis, above all within the framework of modernisation, provide a connection across the threshold of 1933:

> Ich habe den Bogen zurückgespannt zur Weimarer Republik. Möglich war dies, weil das Exil keine Abkehr von, sondern verstärkte Beschäftigung mit Deutschland bedeutete und für die Kontinuität des deutschen Geisteslebens einstand. Das modernistisch-bildungsbürgerliche Epochenverständnis überdauerte den politischen Einschnitt von 1933 im wesentlichen unverändert.[56]

Significantly, this preoccupation also spans the editorial switch from Lion to Golo Mann which separates years two and three of the journal. In the first edition of the third year, for instance, Alfred Zimmern presents in 'Um was es geht' (*MuW*, 3, 11–27) a diagnosis of the shift from optimism to pessimism which has taken place between 1919 and 1939, identifying three distinct sets of problems (the short-term/political; the longer-term/economic; and the eternal/moral), while Otto Braun's 'Letzte Kämpfe' (*MuW*, 3, 62–79) focuses above all on the political crisis of 1930–1932. Certainly under Golo Mann, a shift in emphasis is apparent, away from the more abstract-philosophical treatment of crisis and towards the kind of concrete political solutions advocated by Alfred Bingham ('Wesen und Aussichten des amerikanischen New Deal', *MuW*, 3, 50–61), Denis de Rougemont ('Gedanken über Föderalismus', *MuW*, 3, 291–99), and Hermann Görgen ('Was soll werden?', *MuW*, 3, 300–22). In particular, the dicussion of models of political federalism and also the American New Deal pre-empts the ground covered in early issues of *Der Ruf*. Nonetheless, the underlying preoccupation of philosophical crisis expressed by Hans Barth ('Die Krise des Wahrheitsbegriffs in den Staatswissenschaften', *MuW*, 3, 485–504) or Eugen Gürster in his review of Hans Zbinden's *Die Moralkrise des Abendlandes* and Walter Schubart's *Geistige Wandlung* (*MuW*, 3, 673–700) remains more or less constant.

---

56 Baltensweiler, p. 171.

Das Wort

The drastic changes in German literary life brought about by the experience of the Nazi seizure of power had a devastating effect on those who were trying to establish a tradition of German Marxist literary thought, to which *Die Linkskurve*, for all its limitations, had made an important contribution through articles by Wittfogel and Lukács. The continuity offered by the existence of the Soviet Union as the guarantor of the legitimacy of such a newly created tradition was an important factor in motivating writers and thinkers, and the developing line on Socialist Realism served for many as an inspiration, whether in a positive or negative sense. Nevertheless, the profound process of rethinking in the German communist movement, which led to the announcement of the Popular Front policy at the KPD's 'Brussels' conference in 1935, necessitated the creation of a forum where these questions could be debated in a specifically German context. The precarious financial situation of writers in exile, especially in the first few years after 1933, led to the failure of projects such as *Neue deutsche Blätter*, which had aspired to create just such a forum, although with a far broader range of contributors than had appeared in *Die Linkskurve*.

The new circumstances ensured that the isolationist stance of the BPRS was no longer tenable, and its members were obliged to find accommodations with writers whose work they had previously dismissed as worthless. The question of how far this fundamental change in personal and political circumstances actually affected the terms of aesthetic discourse is not an easy one to answer. The needs of the Popular Front, as well as practical considerations of collaboration and communication with fellow exiles, necessitated a softening of the KPD's tough anti-bourgeois line; however, as we have seen, Lukács's *Linkskurve* articles had already suggested a rapprochement with the 'bourgeois inheritance'. The Nazi seizure of power simply accelerated this process and gave it a new political urgency.

It is of course important not to lose sight of the fact that the changes in the line of the BPRS and the terms of the debate amongst left-wing exiles were determined by the changing political line in Moscow, which was tailored to the needs of internal Soviet politics rather than those of foreign communist parties. The creation of the Soviet Writers' Union as a body to enforce conformity amongst Soviet writers under the banner of Socialist Realism was seen by many as a means of putting an end to the years of bitter division in the Soviet literary world, and more importantly, to end the aggressive dominance of a single organisation, the Russian Association of Proletarian Writers (RAPP). Many of those who had suffered at the hands of RAPP were prepared to go along with the new conditions because, after all, the new literary dogma was flexible enough in its terms to offer a home to writers of 'bourgeois' origins whose work had found no echo in the cacophony of avant-gardist styles which held the limelight in the

Soviet 1920s. Socialist Realism also meant a defeat both for *Proletkult* theorists
and for those who argued that a truly socialist literature could only be created by
writers of unimpeachably proletarian origins. This may go some way towards
explaining the guarded welcome with which the pronouncements of the 1934
Writers' Congress were received by western writers such as Heinrich Mann, who
had suffered years of abuse from proletarian organisations such as the BPRS. The
emotional significance of a shift in cultural emphasis which chimed in with the
need to mend bridges with former opponents after the Nazi seizure of power is
an important factor in assessing the cultural mood in the mid-1930s.
Nevertheless, it would be a mistake to see this shift solely as a result of a general
political re-thinking after 1933, since, as we have shown, the theoretical
parameters for this shift were being set earlier. The Nazi seizure of power
brought an added urgency to the discussions, and perhaps we can say that it
provided the impetus for a shift from theory to practice. What had begun as a
reaction to the perceived demise of modernism rapidly became a political
necessity.

The situation is complicated by the fact that the impulse to rein in the
excesses of proletarianism in literature stemmed from internal political developments in the Soviet Union, and had little to do with the needs of German
antifascists. As we shall show in our discussion of the role of Lukács's essays in
Das Wort, the journal gains its particular colouring from the tension between the
Soviet context and the German cultural assumptions in which even the most
radical communist writers are rooted.

As in western countries where developments in literary style were less directly
dependent on political expediency, the problems of the modernist 'episode' were
seen to be solved by rehabilitating styles, genres and attitudes to language and
meaning which had not disappeared, but which the discourses of modernism had
pushed to the margins and labelled 'conservative'. However, the resulting cultural
atmosphere, for which we have used the term 'restorative', remained profoundly
troubled by the experience of modernism. In rejecting or modifying modernist
attitudes, writers and theorists were still obliged to take seriously the intensity of
the modernist critique of realism and mimesis, and to deal with issues connected
with *Sprachkritik*, utopianism and the rejection of the idea of an unbroken cultural
tradition.

The doctrine of Socialist Realism, as it was presented at the 1934 Writers'
Congress and worked through in detail in the following years, should not be seen
exclusively as the re-imposition of norms of aesthetic conservatism, but rather as
a sophisticated attempt to reject aspects of Soviet modernism which did not meet
the needs of the regime, while absorbing others into an uneasy synthesis with
traditions of Russian social realism and religious writing. For example, the idea
that the writer should become an 'engineer of human souls' is adopted directly
from the Soviet constructivist avant-gardism of the 1920s, and it sits

uncomfortably with the demand for the formal properties of realism. In essence, it is an attempt to put aspects of various Russian traditions to contemporary political use, and it was possible to read it as a rapprochement with parts of the intelligentsia who had felt excluded by avant-gardism and proletarianism. The fury of the Purges later destroyed any such illusions, but the ideological developments of 1934–1935 had immense psychological significance, not least for German antifascists.

Just as Soviet Socialist Realism needs to be seen in the context of the Russian literary tradition, so the German antifascists – whether they made their home in the Soviet Union or not – interpreted these developments in the light of a German tradition which was threatened by fascism. Thus, we should avoid the suggestion that even the most conspicuously loyal of theorists, such as Alfred Kurella, simply adopted Soviet Socialist Realism for German literature; instead, the task was to find ways of making the Soviet models fit the German tradition, as well as vice versa. Although writers central to the German tradition, in particular Goethe, are forcefully re-interpreted to give the impression that the desired new realism has grown organically out of the cultural inheritance, this means that the debate in a journal such as *Das Wort* is in fact conducted in a German, rather than a Soviet, context, and the issues which trouble the contributors – Expressionism, the *Volksstück*, the *Bildungsroman*, to name but three – have only minor relevance for Soviet cultural politics.

We therefore intend to read *Das Wort* as a continuation under changed circumstances of debates which had preoccupied those who worried about the future of German culture in the latter years of the Weimar Republic. Our discussion is intended to supplement, rather than replace, important work on the journal's character and history by Hans-Albert Walter and Angela Huß-Michel by considering it in the light of a periodisation that shifts the immediate emphasis away from day-to-day issues of political control.[57] In the following, we will concentrate on aspects of the journal's practice which illustrate how the changing cultural line of the journal, in its response to internal Soviet concerns and the demands of the Popular Front policy, is reflected in and shaped by responses to the German tradition. Specifically, we will examine the significance of Georg Lukács's programmatic essays and the role of the journal's *Vorwort* in setting an ideological line, moving on to discuss the journal's attitude to National Socialist literature, modernism and Expressionism.

---

57 See note 4 above.

Programmatic statements: the *Vorwort*

The first thing that strikes the reader on opening the journal is the clear and unequivocal reassertion of genre boundaries. The demarcation between drama, prose, poetry, essay, satire and reportage is taken for granted, with contributions grouped according to genre rather than any other consideration, such as theme. This clear separation on the contents page is occasionally abandoned for special issues, such as the number which aims to stand as a *Bestandsaufnahme* of antifascist literature (April–May 1937). The structure of the journal implies that the genre-crossing experiments of 'proletarian' writing, reportage literature and the experimental novel of the 1920s, against which Lukács had campaigned in later issues of *Die Linkskurve*, have been solved, and that genres have clear and objective functions. In this sense, *Das Wort* has inherited a theoretical position set out in *Die Linkskurve*, but which coincides with developments outside the KPD's cultural line. Lukács's interventions against proletarian and documentary styles are not taken up again, and the only discussion focussing specifically on genre is an exchange on the historical novel in the October 1936 number. We can therefore see the journal as representing literary preoccupations in a time when the questions and uncertainties of a transitional, or crisis, period are seen to have been more or less settled; the terms of debate have already shifted.

The influence of Lukács's thought and practice on the journal's editorial line is clear; one can identify his approach to questions of realism and Marxism as providing the fixed point around which the debates revolve. In the years which have passed since the demise of *Die Linkskurve*, an approach that stresses mimesis and the formal properties of realism has shifted from the periphery to the centre of literary discourse. It no longer needs to justify its presence within the pages of the journal or its legitimacy as the theory against which other approaches must define themselves. The tenor of the responses to the Expressionism Debate, for example, largely take the form of attempts to take up a position for or against Lukács. Even Ernst Bloch, the most sophisticated of the theorists who responded to the debate, is obliged to tailor his responses to the terms of a debate taking place within the newly established 'restorative' paradigm. Although Lukács's theoretical statements are sophisticated, he can allow himself the occasional dogmatic outburst secure in the knowledge that the terms of the debate endow his views with a legitimacy that need not be defended at every turn. The often crude polemics of Alfred Kurella (writing under the pseudonym Bernhard Ziegler) which, although they do not go unchallenged, nevertheless aspire to represent an 'official' line, demonstrate how far the discourse has shifted since 1930.

Throughout its existence, *Das Wort* existed in a state of tension between its aspiration to be a forum for exile literature and the desire to take a lead and set the terms of debate. The journal's editorial policy shifted markedly after the departure of Willi Bredel for Spain in early 1937, when Fritz Erpenbeck effectively took over the day-to-day running of the journal and brought it into line with the Soviet Union's hardening political line, yet this fundamental tension was not dispelled, but simply framed in new terms, with a particular type of discourse claiming a more authoritative function and pushing alternatives to the margins. In order to trace these shifts, we shall examine the function of the *Vorwort* and programmatic statements which set the journal's literary-political agenda. The *Vorwort* itself, where it is present, sets the political agenda for the current issue, though it rarely refers directly to the issue's contents; this may reflect the difficult circumstances of the journal's production, with its widely scattered editorial board, as well as the need to respond quickly to the developing political situation and to the changing Soviet line. Thus, the *Vorworte* sometimes give a misleading impression of the contents, emphasising an ideological unity of purpose which may not reflect the variety of the contributions.

The *Vorworte* have a tendency to portray problems of form and content as having been solved, implying that the last remaining problem in literary-political debate is the requirement of writers to make the necessary decision to commit themselves to antifascist realism. This is the implication of the statement in October 1937, in the context of the Second International Writers' Congress, that reality no longer poses problems, but demands action: '[...] Wirklichkeit, die kaum noch Probleme, sondern eine Aufgabe stellt' (*Wort*, 2.10, 4). This is scarcely surprising after the 1934 Soviet Writers' Congress, yet the journal (unlike *Internationale Literatur*) is not primarily concerned with propagating the doctrines of Socialist Realism, but is concerned with the theory and practice of realism within the German context. Part of the function of the *Vorworte*, as well as giving rallying-cries for the front against fascism, is to provide a certain amount of camouflage for Lukács and others to develop a theory of realism which, if not critical, at least diverges from aspects of Soviet literary practice.

An example may be found in the journal's first issue, in July 1936, whose *Vorwort* is, as one might expect, a statement of the journal's purpose and programme. The hagiographical tribute to Gorky is par for the course for the Soviet literary discourse of the period, since works such as *Mat'* (*The Mother*) and his autobiographical trilogy had been raised to the status of untouchable canonical precursors of Socialist Realism (*Wort*, 1.1, 7). However, Gorky's iconic status was not necessarily as a model for imitation, since the theory and practice of 1930s Socialist Realism diverged markedly from the procedures of bourgeois realism which characterise his work. Significantly, the work of other contemporary Soviet writers is largely absent from the pages of *Das Wort*, and the validation of the widely admired Gorky as a model representing the Soviet scene sets the journal's aesthetic centre of gravity firmly within a bourgeois context. This can be partly explained by the requirements of the Popular Front, many of whose supporters recoiled at the products of Soviet Socialist Realism, and yet a space is also created for the discussion of Marxist theories of realism which in fact owe very little to Stalin and Zhdanov.

The *Vorworte* perform the function of presenting the reader with a simple choice, for or against fascism, for or against realism (though not Socialist Realism). In order to show that the struggle against fascism permeates every area of political and cultural life, the editors quote in September 1936 Thomas Mann's statement in *Die literarische Welt* that the battle lines have been drawn up between the friends and enemies of *Geist* (*Wort*, 1.3, 5). The literature of National Socialism is contrasted with 'true' literature, though the emphasis in these programmatic statements is generally on content rather than form; the discussion of formal matters connected with realism is left to the more substantial contributions. Nevertheless, the rhetoric connected with the concept of the 'Word' – as a weapon, as a cultural resource, as the guarantor of truth and the connection with tradition – implies that the connection between language and world has been re-established, or rather rediscovered (*Wort*, 1.2, 3). The creation of a tradition which offers ways out of linguistic and aesthetic crisis is a fundamental gesture of the journal's practice, offering common ground to all those who sympathised with the Popular Front, and disguising, through a strategy of rhetorical polarisation, any shared aesthetic approach with those excluded from this circle.

In later issues, the *Vorwort* begins to hint that there is more to realism than a simple decision in favour of content over form. The October 1937 *Vorwort* (*Wort*, 2.10, 3–8) is the most explicit statement of the journal's line in the period after Willi Bredel left Moscow for Spain; the aesthetic and political stance is becoming narrower under the influence of the Soviet Union's hardening line over the Popular Front. Amongst a series of statements demanding that writers take up an unambiguous position towards the 'antifascist' struggle in Spain, we find an argument about the properties of realism. Realism is defined in terms dependent purely on content, so that it consists entirely in a decision in favour of content over form, allowing the writer to engage with events. Yet this is not quite the same thing as saying, as Lukács does, that the role that form has to play is in connecting the text with reality, bridging the gap, which had been opened by modernist practice, between language and world. No indication is given of the precise formal strategies necessary to achieve the desired end, thus rather glossing over, for expediency's sake, the incompatibility between the practices of nineteenth and twentieth-century realism and of Socialist Realism. As the unspoken problem, formal questions become the defining centre of the journal's discourse; barely veiled threats equating the rooting-out of Formalism with support for the Spanish Republic serve only to emphasise this point more clearly.

The stress here is on literature's ability to affect the world, rather than to portray it objectively (though the word 'objektiv' makes its regulation appearance in Socialist Realist theory, its significance is not the same as in Lukács's conception). The editors argue in the next issue that literature's task consists in the contructivist ambition to rebuild humanity: 'der neue, sozialistische Mensch ist zu gestalten' (*Wort*, 2.11, 6). It is perhaps here that we can detect the troubling legacy of modernism in the restorative aesthetic discourse of *Das Wort*. The doctrine of the 'neuer Mensch' provides a moment of connection and continuity between aspects of Russian modernism and Socialist Realist theory: in the German context, the doctrine, although imported from Soviet rhetoric, has inevitable echoes of Expressionism, and German supporters of Soviet literary theory are left with the dilemma of distancing their theoretical stance from a form of modernism which has influenced it, but which is now associated, through the example of Gottfried Benn, with fascism. Many of the responses to the 'Expressionism Debate' can be read in this way, as attempts to use a rhetoric of polar opposites to conceal the profound and continuing influence of Expressionism on their work.

Programmatic statements: Lukács

Lukács is rather more consistently conservative in his approach, since his own work is not troubled by the legacy of Expressionism in the same way as that of many of his allies and opponents. The consistency of his theoretical position, and its centrality within the discourse of post-1930 German aesthetic thinking on the Left, allows him to set the terms of the debate within the pages of *Das Wort*, even while his position within the Soviet Union is becoming precarious. Since the Soviet regime had raised to canonical status a doctrine which is marked by an ambivalent approach to the legacy of Russian modernism, Lukács's attempt to enshrine bourgeois realism as the one true Marxist literary form, while at the same time extrapolating, with the help of Hegel, a comprehensive, objectively valid literary theory from the fragmentary texts on the subject by Marx and Engels, places him firmly in the German, rather than the Soviet, tradition. Thus, in order to trace a 'restorative' discourse through the pages of *Das Wort*, we need to adopt a differentiated view of the role of programmatic statements in the journal's editorial practice: although both fall within the restorative paradigm of the period, sharing many assumptions about, say, the use of literary language as a means of knowing the world, the *Vorworte* attempt to site the journal within the Soviet aesthetic context, while programmatic contributions by Lukács tacitly locate it within a different tradition with often very different assumptions.

Lukács's first programmatic intervention in the journal comes in October 1936, with an important essay on formal questions of characterisation in the novel, 'Die intellektuelle Physiognomie der künstlerischen Gestalten' (*Wort*, 1.4, 72–82). Giving the lie to the editors' frequent statements in the *Vorworte* that formal questions are a secondary concern for the realist writer, Lukács sets out his stall for an aesthetic stance in which only an obsessive concern with form and structure can embed a literary text in the world. Taking Plato's *Symposium* as a model – a provocative choice in itself when one considers that orthodox Marxism-Leninism took the contrast between Plato and Aristotle as the beginning of the struggle between Idealism and Materialism in philosophy – Lukács criticises literary approaches which produce characters who are simply mouthpieces for a political standpoint, pleading instead for a more complex and mediated literary psychology, which he calls the 'intellektuelle Physiognomie' of the individual character. While this develops his concerns with realism and the theory of *Widerspiegelung* in the novel, and takes up in a more subtle way his arguments in the controversy over proletarian literature in *Die Linkskurve*, it is also directed at some of the practices of Socialist Realism: for example, he rejects the stipulation that the novel must be structured around a positive hero.

A context for this piece is provided by its juxtaposition with Alfred Döblin's essay on the historical novel. Döblin discusses the preoccupation with the genre as a product of the exile writer's isolation from German culture (*Wort*, 1.4, 56–71). Döblin's piece is a contribution to the ongoing discussion in German literary circles about the role of the historical novel in a crisis-ridden culture; as Annette Schmollinger has shown, this discussion was being carried forward simultaneously amongst writers both within and outwith Germany, and has its roots in the changing aesthetic climate in the late 1920s and early 1930s.[58] The editors' choice of this essay as a companion piece to Lukács's thus performs the function of connecting *Das Wort* with broader trends in the literature of the German-speaking world; not only does it place Döblin in the context of left-wing thinking on the novel, but it also places Lukács in a bourgeois context. There are various differences of emphasis between the two pieces, in that Döblin is still searching for a rationale for developing new forms in the service of realism, but both occupy substantial common ground in rejecting documentary literature and experiment for its own sake and stressing the boundary between literature and propaganda. The juxtaposition of the two pieces is designed to show in exemplary fashion the coming together of bourgeois and Marxist literary theory after the period of modernist literary experiment. The *Vorwort* to this issue (*Wort*, 1.4, 3–5), which discusses connections between the 1848 revolution and the present day, provides a political context for the articles, but its insistence that 1936 is an equivalent revolutionary situation sits uneasily with the stress on consolidation, exploration and the long haul which characterises the articles of Döblin and Lukács.

Two issues later, Lukács takes up a number of these issues in his essay 'Der Niedergang des bürgerlichen Realismus'. Here, he sets out his historical scheme whereby the failure of the 1848 revolutions leads to a split between bourgeois and proletarian literature, with bourgeois writers moving away from the achievements

---

58 Schmollinger, pp. 82–107.

of Balzac and Stendhal towards the superficial Naturalism of Zola and Flaubert. Always at his most dogmatic when writing from a historical perspective (compare this essay with the more subtle discussion of 'intellektuelle Physiognomie' in the previous issue), Lukács associates modernist styles from Naturalism onwards with decadence and authoritarian government, claiming that advanced capitalism produces a literary world split between 'abstrakte Scheinobjektivität' (for example in Naturalism or montage techniques) and 'irrationalistischer Subjektivismus' (as in Expressionism), both of which distract the writer from the task of realistic narration and political engagement (*Wort*, 1.6, 58).

Lukács also argues from nature in order to give his views substance, taking his cue from the classical humanist ideal of the harmonious personality as the goal of human development; in line with the restorative trends of the period, he contrasts modernist preoccupations with psychoanalysis, Nietzschean multi-perspectivity and the end of the unified, rational personality, with an ideal of individual harmony reflecting the desired harmony of the new society. In this, he argues from within the tradition of German idealism, rather than of the French realists whom he quotes to illustrate his argument. The gesture that underlies this work is one which is characteristic of writers across the German-speaking world, namely the aspiration to re-establish connections which have supposedly been disrupted by the nature of modernity and by the modernist assault on literary values: relocating oneself within the tradition is seen as going hand-in-hand with re-establishing the 'natural' connection between literary language and the world outside the text. For Lukács, the modernist emphasis on the problematic nature of literary communication is a symptom of the atomisation of social relations under capitalism, and thus has an identifiable cause and solution (*Wort*, 1.6, 63). Naturally, this marks him out from non-communist conservatives, since his work is concerned with finding ways of overcoming the dilemmas of modernity, rather than wishing to return to some putative pre-modern state, yet he shares many of the aesthetic preoccupations which link 'conservatives' and 'modernists' across the political spectrum, regardless of political orientation.

National Socialist literature in *Das Wort*

The journal's response to the literature of National Socialism is complex, although this complexity is often disguised by the editorial rhetoric of absolute rejection. The somewhat ambivalent response of some of the contributors can be explained first and foremost by the ideological assumptions that underpin the journal's editorial line. Since, as we have seen, questions of literary form are assumed to have been solved in favour of a certain form of realism, many contributors do not pay any substantial attention to formal matters in their discussions of Nazi literature. For example, in an essay from August 1936,

Ludwig Marcuse discusses Nazi war poetry in terms that suggest that content is
the key issue. In this view, the power of lyric poetry lies in the fact that it 'sich
unmittelbar an die Gefühle [wendet]', and so it is the ideological content which is
being transmitted that is the key issue (*Wort*, 1.2, 66). There are many unspoken
assumptions that lie behind Marcuse's view of lyric poetry, the most obvious of
which being that finding an appropriate form for a direct appeal to the emotions
is unproblematic, and that the ideological content is more or less interchangeable.
The form, which is the most effective way of conveying direct appeals to the
emotions, is detachable from the content, which must be judged using political
and moral categories. This view is confirmed by a review in the same issue of
works of Nazi political poetry, which describes in deeply affronted terms the way
in which Nazi writers 'perverted' the traditions of *Arbeiterdichtung* by stealing
forms and styles supposedly developed by the workers' movement (*Wort*, 1.2, 63).

Similarly, a discussion of Nazi drama in August 1936 in the section *An den
Rand geschrieben* bases its condemnation on the Nazis' attempts to pervert the
notion of *Volksnähe* and on the ideological content of Nazi plays, which is
supposedly being rejected by German audiences (*Wort*, 1.2, 106–08). Reviews of
Nazi literature tend to concentrate purely on content (see, for example, the review
by 'H.' of Sophie Rogge-Boerne's novel *Der Ahnengrund*, *Wort*, 2.3, 107–09) or on
personal criticisms of authors such as Dwinger (*Wort*, 2.10, 46–47) or Joseph
Ponten (*Wort*, 2.11, 138). There is a shift towards a concentration on authors'
personalities in the issues that follow the abusive campaign against André Gide.
For example, in the Dwinger review, the author is presented as an intellectual
seduced by a fantasy of violence. This is in itself a fairly accurate description of
Dwinger's work, but if we set the reviewer's comments in the context of the
'Gide controversy', then it becomes clear that the journal's response to Nazi
literature is aimed more at anti-Nazi intellectuals than at Nazi writers themselves.
Nazi writers are portrayed in terms of the intellectual journey they have
undertaken from positions of decadent aestheticism to acceptance of the regime;
so, for example, Kurt Kersten describes the career of Joseph Ponten as an
inevitable trajectory from the description of vague 'seelische Zustände' to fascism
(*Wort*, 2.11, 138), and the *Thingspiel* author Richard Euringer is taken as an
example of how Expressionist primitivism, combined with excessive *Bildung*, can
lead an author away from the ability to tell the truth in art.

Such reviews of Nazi literature seem to owe more to a need to structure the
journal's practice around the editorial line on modernism than to an attempt to
get to grips with the texts themselves. Nevertheless, the reviews reveal a
theoretical contradiction which is typical for the journal, in that writers working
with the aesthetic strategies of realism are criticised for the content of their texts,
while those whose work is, or has been, influenced by modernist styles are
condemned using aesthetic criteria. It is as if the aesthetic strategies of realism
cannot be investigated too closely for fear of exposing their constructedness;

Lukács alone is entrusted the task of putting forward an aesthetic of realism, since he has the intellectual stature to construct such a theory which posits an objective connection between the structures of realist art and the structures of society. As an example, the essay on the Nazi short story by Karl Obermann uses Lukácsian categories to emphasise those features of the short story genre that reflect structures in reality. The essay criticises the Nazi short story for evading the requirements of plot and narration, which require the author to engage with reality; Nazi stories are characterised by extensive use of dialogue between characters who are 'Träger von Ideologien' (*Wort*, 2.8, 55). The key point here is that the author considers that the 'true' nature of the short story genre is realistic, in other words, that a return to the centre of the generic tradition enables the writer to re-establish a genuine connection with the world. For *Das Wort*, we can say that versions of Lukács's aesthetics connect many of the journal's contributors with the restorative cultural atmosphere of the time, contrasting strongly with much of the rhetoric of Socialist Realism which finds its way into the journal's pages. In fact, one can see in the discussion of the Nazi short story an implicit critique of some of the practices of Socialist Realism.

Contributions on the culture of National Socialism which do not fit snugly in to this consensus, such as Ernst Bloch's important December 1937 essay, 'Die Originalgeschichte des Dritten Reiches', seem to occupy a place rather on the journal's ideological periphery (*Wort*, 2.12, 54–72). Bloch's essay questions the assumptions about the conflict between rational and irrational traditions in German cultural history that underlie Lukács's theories and many of the contributions to the Expressionism Debate. His work on the cultural and mythical longings which produced National Socialism seems profoundly radical in this context. However, as we shall see, his contributions to the Expressionism Debate are obliged to move within the context set by Lukács and Kurella, dealing with the same terminology and sharing certain assumptions.

The Expressionism Debate

The series of essays and commentaries which make up what is now known as the 'Expressionism Debate' have been subjected to exhaustive analysis, both as contributions to Marxist aesthetics and as a case study of the tactics of Stalinist literary politics in the Popular Front period. Rather than setting out a detailed account of the debate as a separate entity, which would be beyond the scope of a study of the journal as a whole, we intend instead to offer a re-reading of certain aspects of the discussion in the light of our exploration of broader trends in aesthetic discourse. To this end, we will reverse the usual procedure in discussions of the 'debate', concentrating less on what divided the contributors than on assumptions and concerns which they shared.

We have already considered the influence of Lukács on the contours of debate in *Das Wort*, and in a sense, the Expressionism Debate itself is simply an explicit attempt to demonstrate the authority of this particular discourse of realism within the antifascist camp. Reading the debate in this way seems to account for its nature in a more satisfactory way than describing it as an attempt simply to impose a particular aesthetic discourse upon a characteristically recalcitrant collection of individuals. Those contributions which line up behind the line established by Alfred Kurella in his first essay, and with the more complex aesthetic position set out by Lukács, have little need to set out the theoretical terms of their enquiry since they are working within the dominant discourse whose terms can be more or less taken for granted. Thus, the Lukácsian aesthetics of realism is established at the centre of the discourse of literary antifascism, with other approaches required to justify their existence with reference to it.

The debate itself is as much about realism as it is about Expressionism, especially when one considers the range of contributions provoked by the discussion, including Brecht's unpublished responses to Lukács and the correspondence between Lukács and Anna Seghers on questions of realism. However, any discussion of the aesthetics of realism is, first and foremost, a discussion about the nature of reality and of our perception of it, and of the potential of literature to either reflect reality (in the Lukácsian sense) or to describe it in some objective way. If one investigates the idea of reality which underlies the work of the contributors, then common concerns become apparent. Although Lukács's conception of social reality as a 'totality' which can be reflected in the structure of the realistic novel conflicts with, say, Bloch's notion of 'Ungleichzeitigkeit' and the fragmentary nature of perception, the two positions, although radically different, are not absolute opposites. Both begin from a position which assumes that social reality exists independently of its perception and is graspable through the application of sociological theory; both also criticise an overly deterministic view of the relationship of 'base' to 'superstructure'. The disagreement is, in essence, about the function of literature: should it, as Lukács maintains, reflect in its form the totality of social reality, or can it be used to disrupt the false totalities of ideology?

Clearly implicit in the latter view, that ideology creates false totalities which radical art can break down and expose, is a critique of the strains of the German Idealist tradition which have fed into Lukács's work, and thus of the Lukácsian approach to realism itself. Also implicit, at least in Bloch's work, though perhaps not in the more materialist thinking of Brecht and Eisler, is an attempt through a discussion of Expressionism to rehabilitate aspects of Romanticism, both in its aesthetic practice and its critique of the system-building of German Classicism. This alone puts Bloch's work well outside the realist consensus.

Yet Bloch's thought is radical first and foremost in relation to the 'restorative' consensus against which it operates, rather than in comparison to the practices of Expressionism or of his own earlier works, like *Geist der Utopie*. This is because he is engaged in a similar process to all the participants in the debate, namely the creation of traditions that establish the relationship of art to a social reality which exists independently of its perception. The argument is about the place of Expressionism and realism in a tradition that can be employed in the antifascist struggle; in other words, it is a struggle over the history of modernism.

The basic gestures of the debate are all concerned with this process of establishing a meaningful narrative to locate Expressionism in history; since the ideological purpose of the exercise seems to be to demonstrate the dangers inherent in a literary career which does not overcome the aesthetic practices of Expressionism, many of the contributions take the form of accounts of individuals' life stories, told in ways which illustrate ideological messages. Whereas Expressionists themselves, especially the highly politicised, 'activist' artists such as Becher, tended to think in apocalyptic, utopian terms, expecting the end of history and the beginning of a new era, the same artists are, in the 1930s, still coming to terms with the failure of this impossible aspiration. The Expressionists' emphasis on the personality of the artist is in a sense reversed here. Expressionist avant-gardism had tended to view the world in aesthetic terms, with the personality, viewpoint and will of the artist as the final arbiter; other discourses, of history or politics, are seen as subordinate to the discourse of aesthetics. The Expressionism Debate refers to this characteristic of Expressionism by reversing it: the personality of the artist, and the discourse of aesthetics, gain their legitimacy with reference to the discourses of politics and the historical narratives of Marxism-Leninism. Rather than reducing the significance of the artist in the face of political factors, as one might expect, this process in fact gives a considerable boost to the significance of the artist's life story, since the 'correctness' of the biography (with Becher's life story as the exemplary model) guarantees the correctness of the ideological narrative, as well as vice versa.

The debate is therefore, amongst other things, a struggle over ownership of the right to self-definition as an artist, and is fought out over the question of locating the individual's biography within literary history. Former Expressionists, who have reached a stage in their careers when they are assessing the role that the movement played in their own development, are offered a straightforward, ideological narrative (with the theoretical spadework already done by Lukács) into which they can write their biographies. The literary-historical narrative of Marxism-Leninism overlaps with the more general restorative literary discourses of the period in the work and example of Lukács; part of the attraction of the Lukácsian position for artists was that it involved a serious, and often sympathetic, view of valued aspects of a specifically German aesthetic tradition, which seemed to offer a way back to acceptability for bourgeois artists after the

excesses of Soviet proletarianism and Five-Year-Plan literature. Where this
coincided with an individual artist's reassessment of his/her career and youthful
avant-gardism, the combination of restorative literary discourse with the assertion
of a comforting, unbroken tradition and the offer of a genuine antifascist
community was powerfully attractive.

The aesthetic practices of Expressionist avant-gardism call into question the
assumptions about the tradition, the role of the artist and the relationship of text
to world which characterise the restorative discourse of the 1930s. Although the
Expressionism Debate itself takes place in the context of a journal whose editorial
line suggests that the challenges of this kind of avant-gardism have been met and
overcome, the contributions to the debate, whatever position they take up,
indicate that the legacy of Expressionism is still troubling for those who
experienced it. The re-assertion of tradition which the journal's editorial practice
strives for is, in fact, the forcible creation of tradition, and the points where
ideological assertion pushes out intellectual challenge demonstrate the strains and
contradictions in this effort.

Conclusion

The three journals we have considered in this section present particular challenges
to our restorative paradigm, since the circumstances of their publication have
such a defining influence on their character. Consideration of the contributions to
Maß und Wert, *Das Wort* and *Das innere Reich* without reference to the constraints
of Nazi cultural policy and exile would clearly be absurd. Nevertheless, Schäfer
chooses to found his thesis of continuity across the *Einschnitt* of 1933 at least in
part on an analysis of the content and editorial policy of *Das innere Reich*. There is
certainly an element of cheek in choosing a journal that had been at the centre of
heated discussion about 'inner emigration' and *Ideologiekritik* in the 1970s to
illustrate a thesis that stresses non-political factors in literary change; yet, as we
have shown, the journal represents an attempt to develop particular trends which
had already emerged in the late 1920s. Once we begin to consider all these
journals with this slight shift of emphasis, then common concerns become clear,
and we are able to establish the terms in which the contributors and editors view
the world, and which they use to support their very different ideological
perspectives. Our analysis of contributions and editorial policy suggests that there
are research questions to be asked of these journals which have been
overshadowed by the predominantly political paradigms which have dominated
discussion since the 1960s and 1970s. The predominance of approaches which
stress the journals' problematic positions within the context of Nazi cultural
policy and exile has tended to obscure the fact that both contributions and
editorial policy represent serious attempts to make sense of a changing world in

terms of a crisis-ridden tradition. All three, including *Das Wort*, need to be seen in a specifically German context and in a tradition of debate about the place of modernism and modernity (however it is imagined) within the German bourgeois cultural tradition.

Despite their contrasting approaches to these questions, the journals all bear the hallmarks of a period in which the transition from one cultural mood to another has been completed and certain fundamental precepts are taken for granted. A tradition is asserted, often by largely rhetorical, exhortatory means, which is held to preserve uncorrupted certain key German values. Whether they are imagined as the values of Romantic *Kultur* as opposed to foreign, Enlightenment-influenced *Zivilisation*, or as traditions of rational, humanist discourse, the emphasis is on specifically *German* values which have survived the crises of the modern world more or less intact. Differences then become apparent in the uses to which such traditions are to be put: the practice of *Das Wort*, and to some extent of *Maß und Wert*, suggests that a re-established tradition can be creatively re-assessed and put to use in progressive politics, whereas *Das innere Reich* hovers uncomfortably between a desire to establish traditions which the literary culture of the new state can draw on and an increasing feeling that the journal itself represents a threatened bastion of high culture.

In the light of the above considerations, we need to reconsider Schäfer's use of the term 'conservative' to describe the literary discourse of the era, since there are several problems connected with it here. The fact that it is a term used by some of the contributors to these journals to describe their own cultural and/or political attitudes should make us pause before using it as a literary-critical term from a contemporary perspective; secondly, it seems rather inadequate to describe as simply 'conservative' the idiosyncratic compexity of the attitude to tradition which arises in, say, *Maß und Wert*, or Georg Lukács's important essays in *Das Wort*. So, instead of simply employing the term 'conservative' as a catch-all for very different aesthetic programmes – a use which would certainly merit the charge that it ignores the salient ideological differences – we have instead examined the status of a re-imagined tradition in the three journals. What they all share, which differentiates them from the journals in the first chapter of this study, is the sense that the shape of the tradition can more or less be taken for granted. In other words, the struggle is over protecting the tradition and the values embodied in it from its ideological enemies, rather than establishing the necessity of the tradition in the face of a seemingly traditionless modernity.

With few exceptions, contributors to all three journals exhibit a confidence that literary language is a suitable means of gaining access to the 'eternal' values of the German tradition. The careful selection of specific styles, forms and metaphors from the tradition, say of nineteenth-century nature poetry or Weimar Classicism, gives the impression of seamless continuity stretching back beyond modernism. The language of German bourgeois humanism is also important here, with its emphasis on the harmonious development of the personality; despite the anti-Enlightenment stance of *Das innere Reich*, it too is profoundly marked by these essentially German bourgeois values. In this sense, setting *Das innere Reich* in a comparative context with the ideologically opposed *Wort* provides an important reminder of the complexity and contradictoriness of the nineteenth-century German bourgeois inheritance with which the journals struggle. The attempt to crystallise out of this complex mixture clearly separate traditions of Romantic and Enlightenment thought, in order to put one or other of them to use in the twentieth century is, at best, problematic. Contributors tend, with few exceptions, either to ignore this problem or attempt to sweep it away through politicised rhetoric.

For a generation of writers marked by the experience of modernism, this attempt to reconnect with the tradition – or, to put it a better way, to connect with a re-invented tradition – is a complex, uncertain business made urgent by the political needs of the hour. The concerns which we have identified as the fundamental gestures of much of the literary discourse of this period – authenticity of expression and truth-telling, the search for objective measures of quality which have stood the test of time, the re-establishment of genre boundaries and the status of the literary work – are all characteristic of a reaction against forms of modernist discourse which sets in well before 1933. However, the new political circumstances in which writers found themselves give these concerns a particular kind of life-and-death urgency where one's stance on the tradition is held to reflect an attitude to political questions.

The explicitness with which the editors and contributors to *Das Wort* deal with the political consequences, as they see it, of a writer's attitude to the tradition arises from an emotional need to distance themselves as far as possible from National Socialism, as well as, on the part of those living in Soviet exile, a need to comply with political demands to make their ideological position absolutely clear at all times. The language of German Classicism and the humanist emphasis on striving for the harmonious personality are linked with a discourse of truth and authenticity of expression which takes its legitimacy from the establishment of 'objective' theoretical criteria. A theoretical sleight-of-hand is performed by justifying the thoroughly bourgeois need to reconnect with the tradition of Goethe by presenting this tradition as the precursor of Marxist rationalism. Despite the occasional rhetorical gesture in the direction of Socialist Realism, many of the contributions to *Das Wort* are unaffected by Soviet literary practice, and, for all the political limitations of the Popular Front policy, the journal as a whole represents a remarkable forum for discussion of a specifically German tradition, even under the more narrowly partisan direction of Fritz Erpenbeck. The editorialising often seems to lack organic connection with the content of the journal, except perhaps in the committed editorial commentaries of Willi Bredel, and it is difficult to reconcile, say, the scandalous denunciation of André Gide with the depth and variety of much of the discussion. Appeals to the nation and to writers to concentrate on popular accessibility in their work are rather superficial, since the emphasis is clearly on the 'high culture' with which the writers and theorists of bourgeois origin grew up. Important essays by Lukács set the tone of the journal, and it is his theoretical stance which forms the aesthetic and ideological centre against which other contributors have to define themselves. It is notable that Lukács's categories are taken for granted by many other contributors, for example in essays by Alfred Kurella: the theoretical work has been done and those who follow this line can allow themselves the luxury of polemic. The absolute clarity over genre boundaries, the emphasis on the status of the writer as fully rounded, rational, humanist personality with the ability to achieve knowledge of the world in the literary work, and the insistence on the objective necessity of certain strict formal criteria, all stem from the Lukácsian attempt to banish the traces of modernism from literary discourse.

Whereas *Das Wort* deals with the issue of the troubling legacy of modernism head on, *Maß und Wert* filters such concerns through the idiosyncratic world views of Thomas Mann and his editors. As we have indicated, the approach to the tradition in the journal's pages, and in Mann's own work, is too complex to be characterised simply by a term such as 'conservative', since Mann himself was concerned to establish lines of rational continuity with the German and European past which could be used to tear the tradition from the hands of the Nazis and rebuild a civilised life after the coming catastrophe. With Mann, as with so many antifascist artists, there is an element of personal need about this project, since it involves finding ways of dealing with aspects of the artist's past which were influenced by intellectual currents now politicised and associated with fascism. To a certain extent, then, Mann interprets the world in the light of personal preoccupations, and his view of National Socialism is coloured by what he perceives to be the dangerous aspects of his own nature. *Maß und Wert* presents itself as a response to the threatening, irrational, chaotic side of modernity and modernism. The aesthetic project becomes identified with the political needs of the day in a way which parallels the responses in *Das Wort*; in both cases, National Socialism is identified with chaos, the unconscious, a breaking of objective values and forms and the preoccupations of German Romanticism and Expressionism. Mann's own approach to Romanticism is far more complex than that of Lukács, but the editorial practice of *Maß und Wert* makes it very clear what are the values that are still usable at a time when the world is threatened by Nazi barbarism. The journal is explicit in its defence of an elitist definition of artistic quality at a time when such values are seen to be threatened by an all-encompassing *Mittelmäßigkeit*; there is no political need to gesture towards popularity or to reach broader audiences. The association of fascism with petty-bourgeois hostility to culture completes the constellation of enemies against which the 'objective' standards of European high culture must be maintained. As with *Das Wort*, the political crisis of the 1930s and 1940s is interpreted through a system of values, concepts and attitudes which has its roots in the pre-1933 world.

The ideological precepts of National Socialism also imagine the modern world as a realm of chaos in which order needs to be restored: as Schäfer has pointed out, fascism in Germany arose from the same shared sense of crisis which motivated its opponents. Where *Das innere Reich* makes such an instructive comparison is in the way in which shared preoccupations can lead artists and thinkers to such radically opposed ideological conclusions. The fundamental aesthetic gestures which characterise many of the contributions to the journal bear comparison with the other elitist journals in this study, and are in sharp contrast to the narrow, iconoclastic viciousness of other Nazi publications. The restorative climate of the era is reflected in what one might term the pseudo-problem which preoccupied intellectuals who were attracted to Nazism, namely what aesthetic categories of form can and should be applied to the renewal of German culture. Is Nazism the long-awaited return of 'das uralte Barbarentum, das jahrhundertelang unter der Formenstrenge einer hohen Kultur verborgen und gefesselt lag', as Spengler saw it in 1933, or is its appeal more to the ultra-conservative desire for form and discipline, to be 'Wächter an der Schwelle der Werte'?[59] *Das innere Reich* tends clearly towards the latter, and, although the creation of a tradition to legitimise its practice concentrates explicitly on Romantic-influenced critiques of modernity, these too belong to the inheritance of nineteenth-century German bourgeois thinking. An emphasis on formal strictness, complexity, harmony and quality points to the continuing, though under the political circumstances unacknowledged, influence of the models of German Classicism.

Because of its unique position within the literary life of the Third Reich, *Das innere Reich* has, naturally enough, tended to be placed by scholars in the context of debates on questions of 'inner emigration', resistance and intellectual complicity. However, we have shown that, as with *Das Wort* and *Maß und Wert*, the journal can *also* be seen as a serious, if limited, attempt to come to terms with the problems of modernity from within the German bourgeois tradition. The editors' emphasis on setting their practice in longer cultural terms establishes connections with habits and attitudes from the pre-1933 period; it is clearly connected with the thinking about the tradition that was developing in Germany in the late 1920s. The continuity in some of the regular contributors reaching back to the *Kolonne* poets is striking, and has a significant influence on the style and atmosphere of the journal. The poetry of the *naturmagische Schule* represents a complex attempt to register mythical and magical impressions using precise, *sachlich* language; as such it is a re-invention of the tradition of German nature poetry after the shock of modernism. We find in these concerns a link with artists

---

59 Oswald Spengler, *Jahre der Entscheidung* (Munich: Beck, 1933), I, p. 12; Arthur Moeller van den Bruck, *Das dritte Reich* (Hamburg: Hanseatische Verlangsanstalt, 1931), p. 244.

across the German-speaking world who are attempting to assimilate the experience of modernism with a desire to re-establish (i.e., re-invent) disrupted traditions. Whereas this problem is fought over openly in the pages of *Das Wort*, it is a quiet, but insistent, presence in the literary contributions to *Das innere Reich*.

Where *Das innere Reich* differs markedly from its counterparts in this study is in its privileging of an inner realm beyond politics, the apolitical ideal of the Biedermeier and post-1848 liberalism so bitingly characterised by Thomas Mann as 'machtgeschützte Innerlichkeit'. The attempt in *Das innere Reich* to extend this bourgeois inheritance into a period of totalitarian rule exposes the apolitical ideal as a fiction, albeit one which is clung to with an emotional intensity as the state makes ever greater inroads into the individual's space. In this sense, the journal represents a consistently restorative attitude in its stance on the relationship of art to political life and to its own traditions. Although this attitude is rejected in theory by left-leaning writers, an examination of *Das Wort* and *Maß und Wert* shows in practice how profoundly influenced their contributors were by it. This results in complex, and often contradictory, theoretical attempts to reconcile the idea that objective values are preserved in the German literary tradition with the desire to save that tradition from its own apolitical tendencies; the emotional needs associated with the restorative attempt to 'reconnect' with a threatened tradition merge with the urgent political demands of the antifascist struggle. All three journals exhibit the related tendency to see political problems in aesthetic terms.

If we read slightly against the grain of interpretations which privilege political categories, we discover common concerns in the practice of these three journals which emerge from a shared bourgeois frame of reference. Taken together, the journals represent different sides of a single debate over the tradition and the threat of modernity, chaos and mass culture to objective standards of literary quality and to the role and self-image of the writer. The difference lies in the way in which modernity and the political and ideological questions of the day are interpreted. The terms of literary discourse have shifted markedly since the 'transitional' period which we examined in the first chapter of this study. There is no longer the need to struggle to place a 'restoratve' attitude to the tradition in the centre of the argument: this attitude now dominates the scene and forms the 'objective' standard against which all other attitudes must define themselves. Even the definition of 'crisis' has shifted: whereas before, it was the tradition itself which was seen to have splintered and collapsed under its own weight, it is now a restored (reinvented), natural national tradition which is under threat from political forces hostile to culture itself. The moral distinction between antifascist artists and those who made their accommodations with the regime is as clear as ever, but by shifting the terms of enquiry slightly, we are able to tease out a common frame of reference which links the contributors to our journals, and which a purely political or *ideologiekritisch* approach tends to overlook.

Post-1945 Literary Journals
Der Ruf, Merkur, Aufbau, Sinn und Form

Introduction

'Es hat auch für die deutsche Literatur keine "Stunde Null" gegeben.'[1] It is more than 30 years now since Heinrich Vormweg refuted the *tabula rasa* thesis of post-1945 German literary development, and in this respect our starting-point in this chapter is a contradictory one. On the one hand, such has been the demolition of the *Nullpunkt* theory that the denial of a new literary beginning after the Second World War is now a commonplace. On the other, the German catastrophe of 1945 subjects our thesis of literary continuity to the most profound of tests. Or, as Bernd Hüppauf puts it:

> Wie läßt sich die Behauptung verstehen, daß die literarische 'Epocheneinheit' über den Zusammenbruch des gesellschaftlichen Kommunikationssytems, der Medien, aller Institutionen der Kulturpolitik, des Erziehungsystems, des dominierenden Wertsystems hinweggreiche, da die Literatur doch Teil dieser Strukturen und Institutionen ist?[2]

In our previous section, we tested our periodisation thesis by exploring the common ground between journals that appeared under a wide range of different circumstances, both inside and outside Germany during the period of Nazi rule. At 1945 the applicability of our thesis boils down to the following slightly different questions. To what extent can a set of cultural assumptions survive such extremes of social collapse? Can using the same terms to conceptualise post-1945 German culture that we have used for the period from 1930 tell us anything of use about that culture? Given the flood of new publications founded immediately after 1945, which acts as such a powerful symbol of the institutional rupture referred to by Hüppauf, these questions pose a particular challenge in the context of our synchronic journal corpus.[3]

---

1   Heinrich Vormweg, 'Deutsche Literatur 1945–1960: Keine Stunde Null', in Manfred Durzak (ed.), *Die deutsche Literatur der Gegenwart: Aspekte und Tendenzen* (Stuttgart: Reclam, 1971), pp. 13–30 (p. 29).

2   Bernd Hüppauf, 'Krise ohne Wandel: Die kulturelle Situation 1945–1949', in Bernd Hüppauf (ed.), *'Die Mühen der Ebenen': Kontinuität und Wandel in der deutschen Literatur und Gesellschaft 1945–1949* (Heidelberg: Winter, 1981), pp. 47–112 (pp. 50–51).

3   On literary journals after 1945, see Janet King, *Literarische Zeitschriften 1945–1970* (Stuttgart: Metzler, 1970); Gerhard Hay (ed.), *Zur literarischen Situation 1945–1949* (Kronberg: Athenäum, 1977); Gerhard Hay (ed.), *'Als der Krieg zu Ende war': Literarisch-politische Publizistik 1945–1950*

Nowhere was this institutional rupture so profound as in the Soviet Occupied Zone and thereafter the GDR, where post-war reconstruction was predicated explicitly on the promise of a new political, and above all idelogical, beginning. Two of the journals under consideration in this chapter, *Aufbau: Kulturpolitische Monatsschrift* and *Sinn und Form: Beiträge zur Literatur*, take this as their founding institutional context, each the product of new East Berlin cultural institutions: the former the literary journal of the *Kulturbund zur demokratischen Erneuerung Deutschlands*; the latter of the *Deutsche Akademie der Künste*.[4] The key figure in the foundation of these institutions, Johannes R. Becher, establishes common ground both between these journals and between those discussed in previous chapters, but important differences exist too. While the *Kulturbund* was designed to have mass appeal and the notion of socialist (re)construction was inscribed into the title of its literary journal, the Academy of Arts was by its nature an elite cultural institution, the name of its literary journal intended to signal the preservation of enduring and universal cultural values. The developing ideological needs of the SED meant that the official language of culture in the Soviet Zone/GDR fluctuated between the restorative tones of *Bündnispolitik* and a modernising tendency that drew its inspiration from the type of literary proletarianism that the Party had rejected in the 1930s: restorative language was characteristic of individuals who were concerned to keep open channels of communication with the West. *Aufbau* survives in a state of tension between these conflicting forces, while *Sinn und Form* was founded with the explicit aim of preserving the unity of German literature in a European context. We will show how the notion of a restorative period can be used to contextualise and shed light on these conflicts.

These two journals, together with the two West German journals covered in this chapter – *Merkur: Deutsche Zeitschrift für europäisches Denken* and *Der Ruf: Unabhängige Blätter der jungen Generation* – represent a range of responses to the needs of the immediate post-war period, while demonstrating the substantial common ground that existed between individuals across the political divides. Not only does the restorative language of the period provide the context for a range of serious attempts to come to terms with National Socialism, but it could also develop a potential form of resistance to the political division of Germany. Journals on the western side of the divide, in particular *Merkur*, which was founded on similar aspirations to those which underpinned *Sinn und Form*, found it a much easier claim to sustain, since the legitimacy of the West German state

---

(Marbach: Deutsches Literaturarchiv, 1986); Doris von der Brelie-Lewien and Ingrid Laurien, *Politisch-kulturelle Zeitschriften in den Westzonen 1945-1949: Ein Beitrag zur politischen Kultur der Nachkriegszeit* (Frankfurt: Lang, 1991).

4 From the second issue of 1945 to the final issue of 1953, *Aufbau*'s sub-title was extended to *Kulturpolitische Monatsschrift mit literarischen Beiträgen*, before reverting in 1954 to simply *Kulturpolitische Monatsschrift*.

rested on a form of restorative cultural language. In this respect, *Der Ruf*, famously the platform of the 'young' generation headed by Alfred Andersch and Hans Werner Richter and their call for a new beginning, functions as a counter-example, demonstrating the difficulty of occupying a critical position that questioned the cultural assumptions of the time. Indeed, it is this reception of the journal which has come to dominate, not least because of the iconic status afforded to Andersch and Richter and the other founders of the *Gruppe 47*. The most recent treatment of the journal in English, for example, concentrates almost exclusively on Andersch's and Richter's editorship and on their radical agenda of political and cultural change.[5] However, as much as this 1946 version of *Der Ruf* stands for the rhetoric of a new beginning, so its direct predecessor, the prisoner-of-war version of *Der Ruf* published in the US between 1945 and 1946, acts as a forum for remarkably tradition-centred, inward-looking aesthetics. In this respect, our analysis of the literary and cultural contributions to *Der Ruf* in all its manifestations is able to re-situate the familiar narrative of a radical impetus frustrated by the broader restorative climate in a fruitful longer-term context which suggests that this impetus was undermined as much from within as from external forces.

Despite the fact that Germany seemed to be *tabula rasa* as far as the institutions of literary life were concerned, what is most striking about the four journals in this chapter is the continuity of contributors and editorial personnel: the names that set the tone in 1930 appear again in 1945, in a variety of different combinations. It is clear that the circumstances of war prevented a younger generation being able to assert their own values, so that the destruction of institutions did not lead to the destruction of institutionalised attitudes. However, what is remarkable is how effectively voices that questioned the foundations of the shared cultural values of the time were shut out of a literary culture that claimed to be rebuilding itself in the name of openness and tolerance. What will become clear in our sections on *Der Ruf, Merkur, Sinn und Form*, and *Aufbau* is the emotional necessity of a discourse that originated before 1933, but which seemed to offer a set of certainties that explained (and sometimes explained away) the disasters of the era. Since the restorative cultural discourse had arisen as a set of assumptions and forms of language that tried to comprehend and give meaning to a sense of crisis, and which therefore helped to create and formulate that sense of crisis, it could be applied without fundamental challenge to the national catastrophe of 1945. It offered a 'deep', and in some senses reassuring, long-term context for events that otherwise threatened meaninglessness. In extreme cases, those who had allowed restorative thinking to justify an acceptance of National Socialism could employ the same categories to justify their subsequent rejection of it.

---

5   Clare Flanagan, *A Study of German political-cultural Periodicals from the Years of allied Occupation 1945–1949* (Lampeter: Mellen, 2000), pp. 151–82.

In the case of all the journals in this section, our approach is designed to supplement the already extensive literature on institutional context and editorial practice by seeking common ground in the language used to interpret the post-war world. By placing this language in a longer-term context reaching back to the late 1920s, we are able to define the contours of a cultural discourse that survived the catastrophe of 1945 by helping to define intellectuals' understanding of that catastrophe. The idea of 'post-1945 German literature' is so ingrained in the theory and pedagogical practice of German literary studies that it is very difficult to disentangle its critical usefulness from its privileged institutionalised status, despite the discrediting of the *Nullpunkt* theory. The sections in this chapter are not intended to replace this periodisation with a different one, since it would be absurd to deny the profound break in the institutions of cultural life, but to show how a shift in emphasis away from institutional factors and away from a focus that stresses the conflicts between exile and non-exile writers can reveal the persistence of ways of understanding culture that had developed before the Nazi *Machtergreifung*. The real significance of 1945 can be seen in the way that a radically changed political situation was accompanied by a reassertion of a language that had been developed in response to an earlier situation.

Der Ruf

Der Ruf (US): a call to tradition

None of our journals is shaped quite as clearly by the circumstances of its foundation and publication, at least on the surface, as is *Der Ruf* in its initial incarnation as the *Zeitung der Deutschen Kriegsgefangenen in den USA*. At this point, the call of the journal's title is not the rhetorical appeal of the young generation for abrupt change in post-war Germany made in its Munich successor. Instead, as the opening editorial makes clear, it is a morale-boosting call for unity amongst German prisoners-of-war: 'Es ist der Ruf von Camp zu Camp [...]. Es ist der Ruf aller Deutschen hier, die ein schweres Schicksal tragen. Es ist der Ruf der Heimat, die, unerreichbar fern und von finsteren Wolken verhängt, doch in uns allen hier stark und lebendig bleiben soll' (*Ruf* (US), 1, 1). In keeping with this purpose and with the re-education purpose ascribed to the journal by the US authorities, regular columns are devoted to news from Germany ('Deutschland'), to extracts from other camp newspapers and readers' letters ('Lagerstimmen'), and to the political, economic, and social structures of the US ('Die vereinigten Staaten'). The attempts to promote democratic values in this last column are supported by a series of essays which appear on page three under the journal's emblem of torch and scales and its motto 'Für Vernunft und Recht'. In successive issues, this editorial position is occupied by essays entitled: 'Demokratie oder Despotie' (*Ruf* (US), 8, 3); 'Demokratische Tradition' (*Ruf* (US), 9, 3); 'Demokratische Aussen-politik' (*Ruf* (US), 9, 3); and 'Demokratie als erzieherische Aufgabe' (*Ruf* (US), 10, 3). In turn, this promotion of American values of constitutional freedom and prosperity finds a very obvious counterpoint in the reports on Germany. Characteristically, the tone is neutral, factual, and objective, but there is little doubt about the journal's opposition to National Socialism. This emerges most clearly in the illustrated supplement to the special issue devoted to the fall of the Third Reich where the disconsolate faces of German prisoners in the ruins of Berlin are juxtaposed with images from Buchenwald under the caption 'das wahre Gesicht des Nazismus' (*Ruf* (US), 6). Similarly, in December 1945 a front-page article is devoted to 'Todesfabrik Belsen' (*Ruf* (US), 18, 1).

In spite of the situation in Germany, or perhaps precisely because of the editors' escape from it, the tone of the journal is overwhelmingly optimistic. This optimistic tenor has three principal foundations. Firstly, as contributions to the regular column, 'Ideen zur Nachkriegswelt', make clear, the editors invest their faith in some form of supra-national, co-operative structure in Europe. In this respect, the message presented in 'Die Lehre der Niederlage' (*Ruf* (US), 7, 3) is typical: 'Wir können und müssen die entschiedenen Wortführer einer Welt-kooperation werden [...] um einer ehrlichen internationalen Zusammenarbeit willen. [...] Das ist die grosse Lehre aus der zweiten grossen Niederlage.' Secondly, the journal expresses a powerful faith in the enduring values of Western civilisation. In part this is a Christian standpoint, and as Vaillant indicates, there is a strong Christian presence in early issues.[6] However, more striking and more consistently applied by all editors is an optimism bound up in the perceived highpoints of Western, and often specifically German, humanist culture. In his essay 'Rettung des Abendlandes', for example, Hocke holds up Dante, Shakespeare, Calderon, Bach, Goethe and Dostoyevsky as 'abendländische Sinnbilder' (*Ruf* (US), 4, 1) whose legacy refutes Spenglerian theories of the decline of the West. Much is made in this context of the parallels between the chaos and hopelessness of the present situation and that of the aftermath to the Thirty Years War. So, although the material destruction of the war is acknowledged to bring with it 'Verzweiflung und Untergangsstimmung', 'es bleibt uns eine Grundlage [...]: Geist und Hände, Neues zu gestalten, der Wille zur Behauptung und die fast zweitausend Jahre alte christlich-abendländische Tradition, die uns verpflichtet' ('Die produktiven Kräfte', *Ruf* (US), 3, 1). Invoking also an eternal cycle of destruction and renewal, the author of 'Wandlungen der Geschichte' (*Ruf* (US), 5, 1) identifies this 'Untergangs-stimmung' as a parallel between 1648 and 1945, but the capacity of survivors of the former period to rebuild offers hope for the present:

---

6   Jerome Vaillant, *'Der Ruf: Unabhängige Blätter der jungen Generation' (1945–1949): Eine Zeitschrift zwischen Illusion und Anpassung* (Munich: Saur, 1978), p. 38.

Sie besannen sich allmählich auf die Werte ihrer Kultur, die ihnen die seelische Kraft für die Überwindung ihrer Alltagsnot gab. Und schon zwei Generationen später entwickelte sich ein Geistesleben, das mit Klopstock und Lessing die klassische Epoche der deutschen Dichtung einleitete, die ihren Höhepunkt mit Goethe und Schiller erreichte.

Finally, there is an unshakeable confidence in the capacity of the 'young' generation to take responsibility in shaping a free and democratic future for Germany. So, for example, in September 1945 (*Ruf* (US), 13), when the front page proclaims the end of the war, the back page is given over to the voice of youth as readers' letters unanimously reject Pastor Niemöller's notion of a generation 'lost' to democracy.

The literary and cultural contributions to this first version of *Der Ruf* match the central concerns imposed by the journal's context. Space is devoted to the cultural production of German prisoners-of-war in the USA, through short prose or selections of 'Kriegsgefangenenlyrik' (*Ruf* (US), 12, 8). Prominent also is American literature and culture, so that the series of articles on US politics and society features a strong literary and cultural element. Issue 1, for instance, reproduces an article from Stephen Benet's *Amerika* and includes a report on 'Amerikanisches Musikleben', while issue 7 publishes Andersch's essay, 'Die neuen Dichter Amerikas'. Prominent also in this context is the reception in the United States of German Expressionism in the visual arts (*Ruf* (US), 3, 6; 8, 6; 11, 4). Throughout the run of *Der Ruf* in the USA, the editors show an interest above all in the work of Ernst Barlach, Emil Nolde, and Käthe Kollwitz (*Ruf* (US), 12, 6; 2, 6). Set in the context of the central preoccupations of the journal, the selection of these three artists, each of whom remained in Germany after 1933 and was subject in varying forms to the strictures of Nazi cultural policy, serves an additional programmatic function. The work of these artists, juxtaposed with reports on the workings of the *Reichskulturkammer*, Nazi press censorship, the exhibitions at the *Haus der deutschen Kunst* and *Entartete Kunst* (*Ruf* (US), 12, 4; 17, 6), functions as an emblem of intellectual quality and purity amidst the prevailing cultural barbarism. As Manfred Hausmann makes clear in his essay 'Kunst und Not' (*Ruf* (US), 20, 1–2), 'der Widerstand kann mannigfacher Art sein', and, as the example of the Thirty Years War is again used to demonstrate, great art arises out of hopelessness and out of conflict with power. Accordingly, the journal employs a very broad definition of internal opposition to National Socialism. In July 1945 in answer to the question 'Gab es keinen Widerstand?', Hocke highlights 'einen heimlichen Widerstand der Anständigen aus allen Schichten' expressed in an ideological distance to National Socialism: 'Es soll nicht übersehen werden, dass viele einzelne [...] sich erfolgreich zumindest ein persönliches Denken und eine unabhängige Urteilskraft bewahrt haben' (*Ruf* (US), 8, 1–2). Further examples of these 'Inseln der Besonnenheit' include the rather ambiguous case of Hans Carossa and, in subsequent pieces, the journalism of the *Kölnische Zeitung*, to which Hocke himself had contributed (*Ruf* (US), 13, 5), Ernst Wiechert's speech to the

Munich students of April 1935 (*Ruf* (US), 9, 4; 25, 6), and Albrecht Haushofer's *Moabiter Sonette* (*Ruf* (US), 15, 1 and 6).

In its first incarnation, *Der Ruf* can thus be termed a journal of 'inner emigration', encompassing the full breadth and ambiguity of the term. Indeed, this extends to a continuing advocacy of a turn inwards, as in Hocke's programmatic essay 'Die inneren Mächte' which occupies the opening front page of the journal. Here, the crisis of the age is attributed not only to political and economic factors, but also to a failure to cultivate the inner values of religion or culture: 'Es ist aber so, dass der Mensch noch eine andere Macht in sich entfalten muss, diejenige nämlich der reifen Innerlichkeit' (*Ruf* (US), 1, 1). Elsewhere, the optimistic parallel drawn to cultural renewal after the Thirty Years War also acts as a justification for the advocacy of *Innerlichkeit*:

> Der dreissigjährige Krieg mit allen seinen Zerstörungen und Verlusten an Land und Leuten hatte eine Verinnerlichung zur Folge, aus der heraus geboren wurde, was wir und die Welt 'geistiges Deutschland' nennen. (*Ruf* (US), 3, 1)

The maintenance of such a position at a time when the war was still on-going is understandable, but it is noticeable that there is no recantation of the validity of this position even after the reality of Belsen and Buchenwald has appeared in the same pages. In the Christmas edition (*Ruf* (US), 19, 3), the space under the masthead is occupied by the essay 'Der Weg nach Innen' which defends the turn of the German book-reading public to the classics following the prohibition of modern works: 'Wo die Trümmer einer äusseren Welt sichtbar werden, wird der Weg nach Innen zur unsichtbaren Notwendigkeit.' Most clearly of all, the anniversary editorial of 1 March 1946 re-asserts the validity of Hocke's opening programmatic essay and the necessity of that inward turn: 'Die Wirkungsfähigkeit einer Gesinnungsstärke setzt heute unbedingte Verinnerlichung voraus. Solange diese Verinnerlichung der inneren Mächte, die der *Ruf* vor einem Jahr aufrief, fehlt, bleibt jedes protestierende Wort nichts anderes als der Ausdruck geistloser, chauvinistischer Verbitterung' (*Ruf* (US), 24, 1).

Hocke's opening essay (*Ruf* (US), 1, 1) is accompanied by an inset Goethe quotation, and from here onwards, despite only a small number of articles specifically addressing his works, it is Goethe's presence which is by far the dominant one in the journal. Much as in *Maß und Wert*, Goethe is invoked in *Der Ruf* as an authority in relation to a wide range of cultural and political issues, so that he is mentioned at least once in each of the first five issues of the journal in articles on literature, politics and language.[7] After Goethe come Beethoven, Schiller and Hölderlin, and from the twentieth century Thomas Mann and Rainer Maria Rilke. This cultural stance, where these acknowledged grandees of German bourgeois culture implicitly oppose the barbarism of National Socialism, is

---

7   See 'Das Janusgesicht der Sprache', *Ruf* (US), 2, 5; 'Um den Frieden', *Ruf* (US), 3, 1; 'Ein Pendelschlag', *Ruf* (US), 3, 4; [Hocke], 'Steine und Menschen', *Ruf* (US), 4, 1; 'Wandlungen der Geschichte', *Ruf* (US), 5, 1.

embodied in Hans Giselius's observations on the music of Beethoven, Mozart, and Schubert which had been chosen by US radio to accompany news of Roosevelt's death and which he desribes as 'Zeitlose Musik': 'Uns Deutschen aber mag es in Leid und Nacht ein besonderer Trost sein, dass das Beste, was wir der Welt gegeben haben, nicht verloren gehen kann. Die Dauerwerte unserer Kultur sind auch die Dauerwerte unseres Volkes' (*Ruf* (US), 6, 6). Thomas Mann – 'dieser grösste lebende Dichter und Humanist' (*Ruf* (US), 8, 1) to whom a double-page tribute is devoted (*Ruf* (US), 14, 4–5) – is only the modern embodiment of what one contribution to the 'Ideen zur Nachkriegswelt' series programmatically terms 'Das humanistische Erbe' (*Ruf* (US), 20, 2). Against this background, Walter Zibell's is a lone voice in calling for new works from young dramatists: 'Mit der blossen Nachäffung der Antike, in der sich die Jünger der Reichsschrifttumskammer so gern versuchten, ist nichts getan' ('Neue Masstäbe: Zur Lage des deutschen Theaters', *Ruf* (US), 15, 6). Indeed, as the celebration of the *Faust* production in Salzburg in 1937 makes clear (*Ruf* (US), 20, 6), the classical tradition is seen to be unsullied by National Socialism, and already in April the prevailing cultural direction to be followed in the journal has been signalled as 'Ein Pendelschlag' (*Ruf* (US), 3, 4). Here, the dominant literary direction is welcomed as a return to the 'Grundwerte menschlichen Lebens und die Hauptgegenstände aller klassischen Literaturen in Europa': 'Man erkennt von neuem, dass die wahre Schönheit und Grösse des Lebens in seinem inneren Wert besteht. Auch die Abgründe und Schrecken des Lebens können diesen Wert nicht beeinträchtigen.'

It is here that the cultural position adopted in the first, US version of *Der Ruf* can be seen to move beyond the circumstances of its publication, mirroring that expressed in other post-1930 journals. What all the manifestations of culture present in the journal share is a perceived intellectual depth which opposes and exposes the shallowness of National Socialist culture. As the anniversary editorial of 1 March 1946 makes clear, the aim of the journal was to distance itself from the 'massenfängerischen, niveaulosen Zeitungstyp der schreierisch aufgemachten Demagogenpublizistik der Despotie' and to achieve 'Erziehung zu kritischem, vertieftem und besonnenem Nachdenken' (*Ruf* (US), 24, 1). Or as the opening editorial had put it:

> Er ist ein anspruchsvolles Blatt. In Erfüllung seiner kulturellen Aufgabe wird er das Beste bringen, was zu haben ist: keine dilettantischen Versuche, sondern erlesene Beiträge der Fähigsten. [...] Er dient nicht der Befriedigung ehrgeiziger persönlicher Bestrebungen, sondern der Pflege der echten deutschen Kulturgüter. (*Ruf* (US), 1, 1)

As witnesses of the destruction of the German *Kulturnation*, now seeking a common voice for prisoners from a defeated army held on a foreign continent, the editors of *Der Ruf* in the United States consistently turn to the enduring values of German culture, to their shared *Bildungsdialekt*. Telling in this respect is the interest in the survival of cultural monuments amidst the allied bombing of Germany and the sabotage attempts of retreating Nazi officers. This repeated pre-occupation takes on a symbolic function so that the survival of the *Goethehaus*, or Beethoven's house or that of Thomas Mann, comes to stand for the survival of German culture itself ('Steine und Menschen', *Ruf* (US), 4, 1; 'Sprengstoff-anschlag auf Goethe und Schiller', *Ruf* (US), 6, 4). The 'book' too, as a cultural object, acquires this symbolic status. Where Leipzig once produced the finest books in the world (*Ruf* (US), 2, 6), National Socialism has now overseen, through book-burning and war, 'Das grosse Büchersterben' (*Ruf* (US), 25, 4). As such *Der Ruf* is concerned in this incarnation with re-asserting not only bourgeois literary culture, but also the value of the printed word itself. Central in this task are the new editions of the *Bücherreihe neuer Welt*, to which articles are devoted from the first issue to the last. To these short pieces, Curt Vinz's final discussion ('Das freie Buch', *Ruf* (US), 26, 5) offers an all too appropriate conclusion: 'Und der Sinn des Goethewortes wurde wieder in ihnen lebendig.'

Der Ruf (Munich): a call to the 'young' generation

In terms of editorial personnel, editorial principles, and not least its title, the version of *Der Ruf* which was published in Munich on 15 August 1946 clearly invites analysis as a continuation of the prisoner-of-war journal whose final edition appeared four months earlier on 1 April 1946. Paragraph 8 of the principles of the newly founded Munich journal, for instance, explicitly stresses these continuities: '*Der Ruf* wird so die besten Traditionen des hinter Stacheldraht entstandenen Blattes aufnehmen und unter den veränderten Verhältnissen in einem weiteren Wirkungsbereich fortführen.'[8] More specifically, paragraph 3 takes up Niemöller's notion of the lost generation which acted as a focal-point for its US predecessor. Such continuities extend beyond any tactical convenience they might have provided for the journal's licence application. Early numbers of the Munich journal, for example, continue to represent the interests of returning prisoners-of-war, both through political interventions and literary contributions.[9] Early numbers also share the underlying optimism of the American journal, although, as the opening editorial essay demonstrates ('Das junge Europa formt sein Gesicht', *Ruf* (Munich), 1.1, 1–2), this optimism has acquired a much more forceful, programmatic rhetoric. Again, this optimism is founded on European co-operation and carried by the young generation – 'das Gesetz, unter dem [die junge Generation] antritt, ist die Forderung nach europäischer Einheit' – but now the programme of 'socialist humanism' stresses not continuity with European

---

8   'Redaktionelle Prinzipien des *Ruf*', C. Vinz Archive, reproduced in Vaillant, pp. 194–95.
9   See for instance Alfred Andersch, 'Gespräche am Atlantik', *Ruf* (Munich), 1.1, 6–7; Hans Werner Richter, 'Lyrik der Kriegsgefangenen', *Ruf* (Munich), 1.3, 9–10; Alfred Andersch, 'Die Kriegsgefangenen: Licht und Schatten', *Ruf* (Munich), 1.5, 6–8; 'Gedichte der Kriegsgefangenen', *Ruf* (Munich), 1.14, 12.

tradition, but 'einen radikalen Neubeginn': 'Das Werkzeug, welches sie zu diesem Zweck anzusetzen gewillt ist, ist ein neuer, von aller Tradition abweichender Humanismus.' This programme, it is claimed, is to be shared by a range of other new cultural journals, including notably *Aufbau*, and by a new Europe-wide elite. As the founding principles of the journal make clear, *Der Ruf* is unashamed in this programmatic elitism: 'Der Weg, den *Der Ruf* dabei beschreiten wird, ist derjenige der Elitenarbeit. [...] *Der Ruf* erwartet seine Breitenwirkung auch nicht trotz, sondern wegen der höheren Ansprüche, die er stellt.' Decisive in its success will be the principles of 'Wert, Güte und Klarheit'. Already the rhetoric of new beginning presupposes certain elite cultural values which suggest continuity.[10]

The programme of new beginning is underlined in the editorial essay which occupies the front page of issue 2 ('Warum schweigt die junge Generation', *Ruf* (Munich), 1.2, 1–2). The silence of the young generation alluded to in the title of the essay stems from an unbridgeable gulf to the traditions of the older generation: '[Die junge Generation] weiß, daß jenes Bild des Menschen, das die ältere Generation von ihren Vorvätern ererbt hat, und das sie nun wieder errichten möchte, nicht mehr aufgebaut werden kann. Sie weiß, daß dieses Bild endgültig zerstört ist.' Out of the violence of their experiences 'erscheint ihr heute die einzige Ausgangsmöglichkeit einer geistigen Wiedergeburt in dem absoluten radikalen Beginn von vorn zu liegen'. This new beginning includes a break with social and political traditions, but also with cultural traditions, and it is here that the most striking discontinuity exists with the US version of *Der Ruf* and its strongly tradition-centred conception of culture. Hence, where Walter Zibell's was a lone voice calling for new work in the theatre in the US journal, Walter Heist is much more in keeping with the programme of the Munich journal in his essay 'Vom Theater in unserer Zeit' (*Ruf* (Munich), 1.16, 13–14). While the classics are acknowledged to have served a legitimate purpose during the Third Reich as a reminder of the real world, 'in der die ewigen menschlichen Werte gelten', the new circumstances demand a new approach: 'Flucht in eine isolierte Kulturwelt wäre heute nicht mehr Flucht zum menschlichen Wert, sondern Verrat an ihm.' In this spirit, a performance of Horst Lange's *Die Frau, die sich Helena währte* is reviewed as a welcome attempt to overcome the perceived stagnation of contemporary theatre – 'Es ist der Mut zum Experiment, den wir bewundern' (*Ruf* (Munich), 1.14, 13) – while Hans Armin Schrey adopts a similar position in 'Die Situation des Theaters in der Gegenwart', demanding 'ein zeitnahes Theater, das seine Möglichkeiten nicht nur in der Restaurierung alter Gebrauchsware sieht, sondern gebieterisch nach Neuem ruft' (*Ruf* (Munich), 1.8, 13). This rejection of tradition applies equally to Christian art – 'Es besteht kein Zweifel: Der Mensch der Gegenwart sucht nach einer neuen Form. Aus dem Bewußtsein des völligen Zusammenbruchs eines Gestrigen streben wir nach

10 See note 8 above.

neuen Formen unseres Lebens und unseres Lebensausdrucks' (*Ruf* (Munich),
1.15, 13) – to painting (*Ruf* (Munich), 1.11, 12), and to architecture:

> Natürlich meine ich [...] nicht, daß man zur Nachahmung früherer Stile zurückkehren
> sollte. Nichts Schlimmeres wäre denkbar. Zum Glück ist die Zeit der Stil-Imitationen
> ein und für allemal vorüber, wenn auch die Reaktionäre aller Länder das nicht
> wahrhaben wollen. Nein, Nachahmung hat noch niemals lebendige Architektur oder
> lebendige Dichtkunst zuwege gebracht! (*Ruf* (Munich), 1.4, 9–11)

While crisis very clearly persists in the physical ruins, food shortages, and black
market corruption which are documented in each issue, it is noteworthy that the
search for *Vorbilder* no longer finds an adequate answer in the traditions of
Goethe: 'Da nützt es nichts, mehr oder minder edelmütigen Humanismus zu
predigen' (*Ruf* (Munich), 1.1, 8). As Andersch writes in October 1946:
'Deutschland besitzt aus der unglaublichen Gunst einer totalen Niederlage heraus
die Kraft zur totalen Wandlung' (*Ruf* (Munich), 1.5, 3).

This new beginning promoted in the Munich incarnation of *Der Ruf* also
carries with it a rejection of *Innerlichkeit*, both as a valid response to National
Socialism before 1945 and, above all, as an appropriate gesture in the new post-
war circumstances. Already in the first issue, Ernst Kuby's attack on German
cultural provincialism contains a regretful, if not entirely condemnatory,
assessment of works of inner emigration as 'gleich den Mumien ohne Blut' (*Ruf*
(Munich), 1.1, 7). A similar tone is adopted by the former *Kolonne* member Horst
Lange (*Ruf* (Munich), 1.10, 9–10) who undertakes the kind of recantation so
characteristic of the 1945–1949 threshold. Lange describes 'inner emigration', or
as he also terms it 'das "innere Reich"', as 'einen beklagenswerten rückläufigen
Vorgang [...] viele Ausflüchte, ästhetische Winkelzüge und eine überzüchtete
Geistigkeit, die nichts als Eloquenz war'. Too often talented writers tended
towards 'Zeitferne und Traumverlorenheit', 'idyllische Seelenlandschaften von
geschmackvollem Klassizismus', or 'die edlen und wohlklingenden Perioden des
Goetheschen Altersstils oder der Stifterschen Klarheit'. In the final balance,
'solche Bücher waren überaus edel, feinsinnig und kunstvoll, – aber auch müde,
eklektisch und epigonenhaft'. This is also the tenor of two important editorial
pieces: Hocke's 'Deutsche Kalligraphie: Oder Glanz und Elend der modernen
Literatur' (*Ruf* (Munich), 1.7, 9–10); and Hans Werner Richter's 'Literatur im
Interregnum' (*Ruf* (Munich), 1.15, 10–11). Hocke concedes 'die moralisch und
praktisch bedingte Abwendung von der Wirklichkeit der Diktatur', and the notion
that the aestheticised prose of inner emigration elevated language 'aus dem
Sumpfbereich des Amts-, Zeitungs- und Rednerdeutschs der Diktatur' matches in
part the central impetus of the journal in the US. Yet in stark contrast to the
earlier version of the journal, Hocke is also clear that such a stance is no longer
tenable: 'Wird aus der einst berechtigten Introversion [...] nun nicht bald eher
Narzißmus?' Now is a time for the *Contenutisti* ('Inhaltler') rather than the
Calligrafisti ('Schönschreiber'). Scornful of the 'Hölderlin-Rilke-Epigonentum', it is

Richter's position too that the experiences of the new post-1945 generation cannot be reconciled with the stylistic methods of 1933–1945: 'Diese Erlebnisse sind nicht mehr faßbar mit den Stilmitteln von gestern. Sie verlangen nach neuen Formen der Gestaltung und des Ausdrucks. [...] Um diesen Menschen zu erfassen bedarf es neuer Methoden der Gestaltung, neuer Stilmittel, ja einer neuen Literatur.' Here, the distinction between the Munich and Fort Kearney journals could not be drawn any more clearly: 'Verinnerlichung – das ist die Restauration des Vergangenen. Doch weder eine neue deutsche Klassik noch eine neue deutsche Romantik wird aus den Ruinen unserer Zeit ihre Auferstehung feiern.'

Creeping restoration

Richter's essay in particular features prominently in Walter Veit's exposition of his central thesis concerning the shortfall between the editorial programme of *Der Ruf* and the reality of contemporary literary practice. As he summarises:

> Richters Abrechnung mit der gegenwärtigen Lage ist zugleich ein literarisches Manifest, das die Notwendigkeit des neuen Anfangs postuliert und damit gegen die Tendenzen der Kontinuität, die sich für den *Ruf* in den Spielplänen der Bühnen und der Produktion der Verlage nur allzu deutlich manifestieren, protestiert.[11]

In this respect, the earlier essay 'Warum schweigt die junge Generation?' (*Ruf* (Munich), 1.2, 1–2) can also be seen as initial evidence of the editors' suspicion of a creeping restoration of values. Rightly, Veit also highlights Heist's observations on contemporary theatre (*Ruf* (Munich), 1.16, 13–14) which are evidence not only of an editorial programme of new beginning but also of the difficulties of putting that programme into practice. More telling still is Lange's 'Bücher nach dem Kriege' (*Ruf* (Munich), 1.10, 9–10). Referring explicitly to 'dem geistigen Vakuum, das sich heute in Deutschland überall bemerkbar macht', Lange's view of post-1945 literary production is a depressing one for the advocates of a radical new beginning: 'Welche ideenmäßige Stagnation, welche gebildete Öde, welche konventionelle Langeweile zeichnen die meisten neuen Bücher aus, die bei uns letzthin erschienen sind!' Here, Lange also bears witness to the contemporary fascination with conventional literary form: 'Wie auffällig ist auch sonst in der gegenwärtigen deutschen Literatur die Rückwendung zu den Formen der strengsten Bindung.' If confirmation were needed of the absence of new literature from a new generation then it is provided by other articles in this same issue which opens 1947. Walter Kolbenhoff, for example, concerns himself with Toller, Tucholsky, and Arnold Zweig (*Ruf* (Munich), 1.10, 5–6), while in the *Kritische Umschau*, Andersch confesses to be baffled by the continuing attraction of

---

11 Walter Veit, 'Die Stunde Null im Spiegel einiger zeitgenössischer Zeitschriften', in Bernd Hüppauf (ed.), *'Die Mühen der Ebenen': Kontinuität und Wandel in der deutschen Literatur und Gesellschaft 1945–1949* (Heidelberg: Winter, 1981), pp. 195–232 (pp. 205–06).

Richard Wagner ('Richard Wagner redivivus?', 13). This short essay is accompanied by reviews of *Lotte in Weimar* (14–15) and of Nymphenburger's other new cultural journal, the overtly tradition-centred *Deutsche Beiträge*, which is described as 'in seiner edlen, schlichten Klassizität vorzüglich gestaltet' (15). It is this reality which informs Richter's still optimistic, but now rather more cautious, 'Blick in das Jahr 1947' (7). Subsequent editorials – 'Die versäumte Evolution' (*Ruf* (Munich), 1.11, 1–2) and 'Aktion oder Passivität' (*Ruf* (Munich), 1.12, 1–2) – continue a gradual shift towards pessimism, induced by a perceived restoration of liberal, bourgeois values.

Just how far Andersch and Richter had to fight against the restorative cultural climate of the times is further illustrated in the final number of the journal to appear under their editorship, that of 1 April 1947 (*Ruf* (Munich), 1.16). Alongside the Heist piece on contemporary theatre and another by Karl Wörner bemoaning the world-wide tendency to favour older forms of music – 'Die "klassizistische" Rückschau in der Kunstmusik der Gegenwart ist die allgemeine Tendenz geblieben' (10–11) – Wolfdietrich Schnurre delivers a damning verdict on the poetry being produced by the young generation in whom the editors had invested so much hope:

> Wer Gelegenheit hat, in den Gedichtmanuskripten heutiger junger Menschen zu blättern, dem wird, abgesehen von stilistischer Geschraubtheit, mangelndem Formgefühl und innerer Substanzlosigkeit, ein Gemeinsames auffallen, das sie alle verdunkelt: Der Schatten Rilkes. [...] Keinem merkt man die große Erschütterung an, keinem die Sehnsucht nach Neuland, den Mut zur Originalität, die Absage an die Tradition. ('Alte Brücken – Neue Ufer', 12)

Schnurre is clear that the new times demand new examples to follow, and in this there seems to be a partial echo of the 'democratising', anti-elitist impulses of the late 1920s:

> Wie dürfte uns, den taumelnden Überlebenden dieses Krieges, den verbissenen Suchern, den abgrundtief Gestürzten heute noch ein Rilke Vorbild sein? Kannte er die Nächte des Grauens? Kannte er das Heulen der Bomben? Kannte er das Chaos? [...] Rilke und Hölderlin sind Gipfel. Wir stehen jedoch am Fuß ihres Gebirges. [...] Wir haben die Aufgabe, neue Massen zu finden. Meiden wir daher die lockenden Gemeinplätze der Epigonen. Beginnen wir andere Wege zu suchen. Ein Gebirge hat viele Gipfel. Einer heißt Goethe, einer heißt Hölderlin, einer heißt Rilke. Hunderte aber sind namenlos. [...] Wie dürfte es auch sein, daß eine Zeitwende größten Ausmaßes angebrochen ist und wir [...] bedienen uns, unsere Freuden und Schmerzen, unsere Sehnsuchte und Zweifel auszudrücken, noch der gleichen Vokabeln, wie sie schon Generationen vor uns gebrauchten? Nein, das Alte ist abgetan. Vor uns liegt, wenn auch unter Trümmern verborgen, eine neue und morgendliche Welt.

And yet tellingly, a rebuff to Schnurre's iconoclasm is not long in coming. Two months later under Kuby's editorship, Egon Krauss's 'Um das Rilkesche Tintenfass' (*Ruf* (Munich), 2.12, 13) is published with an editorial note acknowledging strongly negative reactions to Schnurre's original article, above all from those who fear 'man wolle journalistische Ersatzstoffe an die Stelle zeitloser Werte stellen'. The new editors seek not to take sides, praising what they perceive as two valuable tendencies, 'den Elan, mit dem das Neue gesucht wird' and 'die Besorgnis um die echten überlieferten Werte'. Krauss himself is rather less equivocal, claiming that wherever Schnurre's article has been discussed it has been vehemently rejected. Rilke is praised in traditional terms – 'Das Wunderbare an den Werken eines Rilke liegt in ihrer Zeitlosigkeit' – and the values of tradition and quality forcefully re-asserted. Rilke's example provides 'eine gewisse Niveauverpflichtung' without which it would be impossible to protect oneself 'vor dem dann eintretenden Platzregen an Banalitäten, Geschmacklosigkeiten und Trivialität'.

Friedrich Schwank's essay, 'Die Inflation der deutschen Lyrik' (*Ruf* (Munich), 2.18, 13), offers a similar snapshot of the contemporary literary situation to that provided by Schnurre. Queues outside poetry recitals (Schiller, Rilke and Hölderlin are mentioned), enthusiastic audiences, and above all a flood of poetry publications all seem to be indicators of a renaissance of poetry:

> Die Sammlungen und Gedichtreihen, die Sonette und die Ansammlungen von Stimmungsgedichten, Zeugnisse von Naturbeobachtungen und anscheinend neu-entdeckter Naturliebe, immer wieder aber jene Gedichte, die man mit 'Ruinen-Lyrik' bezeichnen möchte, weisen auf ein Interesse am Vers, zum mindesten an der gebundenen Sprache hin, das inflationistisch anmutet.

Significant is Schwank's diagnosis of the causes of this trend, which seems to indicate continuity with the mood of 'inner emigration': 'Dieser Zustrom zur Lyrik ist eine Flucht der Menschen aus der Gegenwart, ist zu werten als ein seelischer Ausweg aus der Irre der Gegebenheiten [...]. Die Menschen, die heute in den Trümmerstätten leben, suchen Abkehr von den Erscheinungsformen des Alltags, die abstoßend und grotesk häßlich sind.' In noting 'die allgemeine Sehnsucht nach dem Buch, überhaupt nach dem Gedruckten in jeder Form', Schwank also echoes a central impetus of the US version of *Der Ruf*. The following year, Schwank himself confirms his diagnosis in a similar article describing 'Kunst-Inflation?' (*Ruf* (Munich), 3.9, 13). The interest in art exhibitions is seen as a turn towards lasting artistic values induced by a mood of crisis, 'als Hinwendung des ziellos gewordenen Gegenwartsmenschen zu den ewigen Maßen und Gesetzen der Kunst. Als Besinnung aus nihilistischem, chaotischem Denken zu bestimmten Denkformen'.

All this evidence seems to further confirm the thesis of an editorial agenda of radical change thwarted by cultural practice on the ground. While Andersch and Richter saw the crisis conditions of the immediate post-war period as reason to reject the culture of the past, many others clearly saw it as precisely the impetus for a renewed turn back towards it. If not promoting this backward turn, then these conditions of material shortage are seen to be hampering the emergence of new writers altogether. In either case, there is unanimity that little of quality is being produced. Both Schnurre and Schwank criticise the quality of new poetry, the latter estimating that only 20 percent of new publications are worthy of being published. For the publishers taking part in the journal's survey ('Zwei magere Jahre: Eine Umfrage bei deutschen Verlegern über die literarische Situation', *Ruf* (Munich), 2.20, 13), this figure is put at 1 percent and for Rowohlt as low as 1 in 1000. According to the *Deutche Verlags-Anstalt* in Stuttgart, there is simply a shortage of talented young writers: 'Es fehlt an der dichterischen Gestaltung. Man hat den Eindruck, daß sich vor allem die jüngeren das Schreiben zu leicht machen, es fehlt an der Vertiefung, am handwerklichen Können und am sprachlichen Ausdruck.' The end of the war has very clearly failed to dispel the mood of intellectual and literary crisis: 'Die Krise in der deutschen Gegenwarts-literatur kann aus der allgemeinen deutschen Geisteskrise, deren Höhepunkt noch keineswegs erreicht ist, nicht herausgelöst werden.' A response to this survey suggests that the public's tastes have remained largely unchanged (*Ruf* (Munich), 2.23, 13). Indeed, these tastes remain wedded to the conventional intellectual pre-occupations of the *Bildungsbürgertum*, namely history, philosophy, and cultural history, the same pre-occupations which shape so many exile and post-1945 literary journals.[12] In terms of literature, the most requested authors are said to be Goethe, Hölderlin, Lessing, Schiller, Mörike, Hofmannsthal, and Rilke. The *Bildungsdialekt* retains its currency.

1930 all over again? *Sachlichkeit* and *Innerlichkeit*

While on a broad social and political level Carl August Weber continues to rail against 'die deutsche Armut an neuen zukunftsgestaltenden Gedanken' and the 'gegenwärtigen Chaos bürgerlicher Restaurierungsbestrebungen' (*Ruf* (Munich), 2.18, 5–6), a gradual shift is perceptible in the journal's attitude through the editorship of Kuby and then von Cube. Indeed, through these editorial changes Vaillant sees *Der Ruf* undergoing a shift from opposition to support for restoration, a shift strongly influenced by a conservative publishing house disappointed in the new path taken by Andersch and Richter on their return to Germany: 'Sie träumte dem amerikanischen *Ruf* nach, während seine Redakteure anderen Träumen nachliefen.'[13] Certainly in the cultural sphere, the rhetoric of new beginning fades noticeably, and an increasing number of voices can be found supporting traditional tendencies. Writing in August 1947, for example, Hedwig Rhode is far more supportive of traditional theatre than Walter Heist had been six

---

12 See Christoph Kleßmann, '"Das Haus wurde gebaut aus den Steinen, die vorhanden waren": Zur kulturgeschichtlichen Kontinuität nach 1945', *Tel Aviver Jahrbuch für deutsche Zeitgeschichte*, 29 (1990), 159–77 (p. 165).

13 Veit, p. 191.

months earlier. Techniques which problematise the relationship between audience and drama are rejected, and ultimately it is classical material which is preferred:

> Einer der Grundfehler des heutigen Theaters ist der, daß es glaubt, den Abstand zwischen Bühne und Zuschauerraum verringern zu müssen. [...] Wir brauchen nicht unbedingt das zeitgenössische Drama. Die ewige Größe unserer Klassiker erweist sich gerade darin, daß aus ihren Werken [...] jeder Epoche ganz neue, ungeahnt 'aktuelle' Wahrheiten aufgehen. ('Das neue Theater und sein Publikum', *Ruf* (Munich), 2.15, 13)

Likewise, Rolf Robischon's preference for traditional architecture expressed in March 1948 contrasts starkly with the stance which we saw adopted towards modern styles by Donner in 1946: 'Die sogennante moderne Architektur [...] kann sich aber an Stärke der Anhängerschaft und auch an absoluter Qualität nicht mit der weitaus kräftigeren Gruppe der Traditionalisten messen' (*Ruf* (Munich), 3.5, 10–11). In these latter stages of the journal, Ernst Jünger acquires a prominence difficult to imagine in the initial rhetoric of new beginning.[14]

The number including Rhode's article also reproduces Artur Koestler's 1941 speech to the 17th PEN-club Congress (*Ruf* (Munich), 2.15, 9–10). Here, Koestler addresses notions of authorship and creativity, drawing a clear distinction between reportage and the novel. Criticism of the socially committed writers of the 1920s is made in terms reminiscent both of Eich in *Die Kolonne* and Lukács in *Die Linkskurve*:

> Er blieb nicht mehr Künstler, er wurde Reporter. Dies ist die Ursache für das Versagen vieler Prosaschriftsteller im roten Jahrzehnt. Damals wirkten Romane häufig nicht anders als Depeschen der Kriegskorrespondenten von den Fronten des Klassenkampfes. Die Romanfiguren schienen flache, zweidimensionierte Wesen.

The relevance of these observations to the post-1945 situation is made clear by Weber's piece 'Die Dichtung und die Zeit' (*Ruf* (Munich), 3.3, 13). The literature produced by the young generation over the past two years is rejected as a mere reflection of reality, lacking, in the familiar terms of post-1930 literary-critical discourse, 'die dichterische Schöpfung':

> Wir stehen nun vor einer literarischen Generation, die nichts anderes geben will als ein Dokument ihrer Zeit. Sie verzichtet auf Tradition. [...] Es fehlt ihnen demnach das wesentliche Merkmal aller literarischen Schöpfung. [...] Die Gegenwartsliteratur ist auch in der Form nicht schöpferisch. [...] [Sie] verharrt in der Form einer militanten Sachlichkeit, die aber unter ihrer Feder selbst des propagandistischen Tendenzzieles entkleidet ist. Sie pflegt diesen Stil einer Photographie mit Worten, und es wäre ungerecht, behaupten zu wollen sie habe keine Erfolge dabei erzielt. Die Jungen sind zu Technikern der Darstellung geworden. [...] Sie sind vorzügliche Journalisten. Aber sie sind keine Schriftsteller, geschweige denn Dichter.

---

14 See 'Die Audienz: Eine Erzählung von F. Panferow verbunden mit Zitaten aus E. Jüngers Vision *Auf den Marmorklippen*', *Ruf* (Munich), 2.22, 9–10; Alexander Parlach, 'Ernst Jünger', *Ruf* (Munich), 3.2, 9; Ernst Jünger, 'Atlantische Fahrt', *Ruf* (Munich), 3.4, 9–10. Kasack's *Die Stadt hinter dem Strom* is praised fulsomely for its stylistic similarities to Jünger. See 'Bericht aus dem Zwischenreich', *Ruf* (Munich), 3.1, 9.

At this stage, dissatisfaction with contemporary literary practice remains, but now this is measured not against the rhetoric of radical new beginning, but against much more conventional notions of literary production. What is being rejected is precisely the kind of journalistic prose – reportage and travel-writing – which so dominates *Der Ruf* under Andersch and Richter, much of it written by the editors themselves. Again, it is difficult not to be reminded of the concerns of those advocating restorative aesthetics around 1930: 'Wenn das deutsche Volk mit Recht über die mangelnde Qualität seiner Literatur klagt, so sollte es wenigstens die Gründe der scheinbaren geistigen Stagnation kennen. Dieser Fehlentwicklung zu grunde liegt die systematische Vermassung unseres gesamten Lebens' (*Ruf* (Munich), 3.8, 12).

And yet, it is not only a question of Andersch's and Richter's radical editorial programme being thwarted by external literary practice and eventually softened and abandoned through the editorial changes imposed by the publishers, Nymphenburger. Even leaving aside the generational issue of continuity represented by figures such as Günter Eich, Horst Lange, and Walter Bauer, prominent in *Die Kolonne, Das innere Reich* and *Der Ruf,* doubts must also be raised about the newness of what was actually being promoted by the advocates of radical change in the first year of the journal. Even if Andersch and Richter seem to stand for discontinuity both in the overt rejection of *Innerlichkeit* in their programme and in the active embrace of *Sachlichkeit* in the reportage and travel-writing which dominates the literary practice of the journal, it is clear that the notions of *Dichtung* and *Gestaltung* at the heart of the 1930 paradigm remain dominant in their approach to literature. Much as Hocke cannot entirely reject the *Calligrafisti,* so the new realism advocated by Richter in 'Die Literatur im Interregnum' – 'die unmittelbare Aussage und die lebendige Gestaltung' (*Ruf* (Munich), 1.15, 10) – seems to have a foot in two camps. The task of the new literature is described by Richter as follows:

> Hinter der Wirklichkeit das Unwirkliche, hinter der Realität das Irrationale, hinter dem großen gesellschaftlichen Umwandlungsprozess die Wandlung des Menschen sichtbar werden zu lassen. Das Leben unserer Zeit als Erlebnis des Menschen unserer Zeit in seinen Tiefen und Höhen, seiner Tragik und seiner Verworrenheit, als Ganzes zu erfassen und gestalten, das mag man vielleicht noch als Realismus oder als magischer Realismus oder als Objektivismus bezeichnen.

Also telling in this respect are the only two examples of recent literature approved of by Lange in his otherwise damning 'Bücher nach dem Kriege' (*Ruf* (Munich), 1.10, 9–10), namely Albrecht Haushofer's *Moabiter Sonette* and Theodor Plivier's *Stalingrad.* In his praise for the latter text, Lange adopts a position not altogether different from that of Koestler, but he seeks also to reconcile more conventional virtues of novel-writing with a newly relevant *Sachlichkeit*:

> Wir kannten Plievier [sic] als einen Autor, der sich im Bereich des politisch bestimmten, reportagehaften Romans einen Namen gemacht hatte, – hier aber stößt er weit in den Bereich der Dichtung vor. [...] Weit entfernt von der ethischen

Großartigkeit Tolstois [...] schlägt dieser Roman in der gegenwärtigen deutschen Epik einen ganz neuen Ton an: den einer überpointierten Sachlichkeit. [...] Wir brauchen solche Bücher, weil sie kühn, gerecht und entschieden sind.

In this way, the editorial programme of Andersch and Richter can be read as an attempt to integrate a newly topical *Sachlichkeit* into a resolutely conventional and elitist institution of literature. Although this *Sachlichkeit* opposes a conception of the 1930 paradigm founded purely on *Innerlichkeit*, we have seen through the course of this study that post-1930 'restorative' aesthetics are made up of multiple strands which do not necessarily express 'conservatism' along the same parameters. In some respects, *Sachlichkeit* as much as *Innerlichkeit* acts as a strand of continuity across 1933 and 1945. In its functionality, authenticity, and unproblematised relationship between text and reality, the literary style advocated by Andersch and Richter can be seen to represent continuity with other manifestations of the 1930 paradigm, such as workers' and peasant literature, war writing, and diary-forms.

Merkur

Editorial programme: 'Mittlertum im Strom der Zeit'

Less than one year after publication of the first issue of *Der Ruf* in Munich, the foundation of *Merkur* provides further evidence of the prevailing literary climate which had so frustrated the new beginning heralded by Andersch and Richter. Walter Veit, for example, is clear about the contrast between *Der Ruf* and *Merkur* in terms of the positions adopted by them in the immediate post-war debates concerning the future direction of German literature and culture:

> Die Vorstellung der Voraussetzungslosigkeit, [...] des originalen Schöpfungsaktes, der Konstruktion des Neuen auf einer tabula rasa werden vom *Merkur* und seinen Mitarbeitern entschieden abgelehnt. Denn wenn irgendeine Zeitschrift die Tradition als Basis akzeptierte, dann der *Merkur*.[15]

What strikes the reader of these two post-1945 journals is the extent to which this contrast in relation to tradition and new beginning is already manifested at the level of paratext, in layout and format. While *Der Ruf* was a large-format journal published fortnightly in 16-page issues, *Merkur* is a much more traditional small-format journal published bi-monthly, and then monthly, in issues of around 100–150 pages. While the front page of *Der Ruf* bore a newspaper-style headline and lead article, the front page of *Merkur* details only the contents of the current issue, the ten or so lengthy contributions in the main section of the journal being followed by shorter contributions to the long-standing *Chronik* and *Marginalien*

---

15 Veit, p. 223.

sections. While a substantial portion of the front page of *Der Ruf* was taken up by a topical photograph, typically in early issues returning German soldiers or ruined cityscapes, the sole image to appear on the front page of *Merkur* is the reproduction of a small, stylised relief showing the Roman god Mercury in profile. Allied to these strong visual differences are the associations of the journals' respective titles. The forward-looking 'call' for radical change made by Andersch and Richter on behalf of the young generation carries very different connotations to the title chosen by Paeschke and Moras which points explicitly backwards to Christoph Martin Wieland's *Der teutsche Merkur* (1773–1789) and *Der neue teutsche Merkur* (1791–1805). On the surface at least, the distinction between *Der Ruf*, as an innovative 'thin' journal, and *Merkur*, as a tradition-centred 'thick' journal, could scarcely be drawn more starkly.

The opening programmatic articles in the two journals serve to confirm this external contrast in approach. The opening edition of *Merkur* contains none of the radical editorial rhetoric of Andersch's and Richter's 'Europa formt sein Gesicht'. Indeed, in the tradition of a 'high' literary journal no contribution is explicitly marked as an editorial comment, Hans Paeschke's own essay being tucked away at the back of the main section and given equal status to the other contributions. Strikingly in the context of the *Trümmerzeit*, the journal opens not with a contemporary editorial but with a contribution made by Lessing 170 years earlier to the original *Teutscher Merkur* ('Über eine Aufgabe im *Teutschen Merkur*', *Merkur*, 1, 1–7). Much as *Nathan der Weise* was playing on Berlin stages in 1945, so *Merkur* opens with an overtly anachronistic article which thereby immediately signals a debt to, and continuity with, the journal's eighteenth-century literary antecedent. Although this editorial strategy goes uncommented at the time – itself a sign of Paeschke's much lighter editorial touch in comparison to Andersch and Richter – the tenth issue of the journal, which coincides with the currency reform and the move to the *Deutsche Verlags-Anstalt* in Stuttgart, is used as an opportunity to explain the programmatic significance of the Lessing piece. In their short editorial, 'An unsere Leser' (*Merkur*, 2, 481–84), Paeschke and Moras justify the inclusion of the Lessing essay as 'hohes Beispiel eines Geistes gewissenhafter Unterscheidung, als ein Muster kritischer Selbstbesinnung und Selbstbestimmung, der inneren Freiheit'. This is far from timeless aestheticism. Rather, the critical position adopted by Lessing, as a key figure of German Enlightenment debate, is seen to offer a contrast to the preceding 'Katastrophe der Kritiklosigkeit' as literary criticism was banned in the later years of the Third Reich. As such, Lessing represents one of the central tasks of the independent mind in the post-war climate, that is 'die Aufdeckung von Scheinproblemen, die Beseitigung falscher Gegensätze [...] wie [...] etwa derjenigen von Kritik und schöpferischem Geist'. In this way, and much as Willy Haas had done in the opening issues of *Die literarische Welt*, the editors make an explicit virtue out of the absence of editorial programme: 'Indem wir heute darauf verzichten, ein Programm zu verkünden, indem wir – statt eines solchen – erklären, daß wir keiner [...] "verschworenen Gemeinschaft" angehören, daß wir uns weigern, uns [...] zu "engagieren", müßten wir uns im gleichen Augenblick mit dem Vorwurf des "Eskapismus" [...] auseinandersetzen.' *Merkur* is to act as an independent, critical voice, representing not a particular ideology or dogma, but 'eine Haltung'.

Just as Haas's overt absence of programme concealed underlying editorial principles, so Paeschke clearly positions his literary journal against competing post-1945 voices. Two strands run through this programme. Firstly, Paeschke stresses the importance of the journal's sub-title, *Deutsche Zeitschrift für europäisches Denken*, hoping for a process of mutual German-European intellectual development in the post-war situation. Here, there are clear parallels to the pan-European intellectual voice which *Der Ruf* claimed to express. Secondly, it is clear that the enduring values of tradition are to play an explicit role in the editorial programme of *Merkur*, and this is seen to coincide with the agenda of the journal's new publishers, 'mit deren bewährter Tradition [die] eigenen Bestrebungen übereinstimmen'. Indeed, Hermann Leins and Hermann Maier add their own programmatic statement of continuity and tradition to issue 10 on behalf of the *Deutsche Verlags-Anstalt*:

> Dem freien Geiste Raum und Form zu geben, Wirkung und Echo zu schaffen, ist der Grundzug unserer Tradition, geprägt und gepflegt von alters her, durchgehalten selbst in den Zeiten der Diktatur und wieder aufgenommen unter den veränderten Verhältnissen des Nachkrieges. Von gleichem Wesen ist die Idee dieser Zeitschrift.
> (*Merkur*, 2, 484)

The definition of topicality underlying Paeschke's editorial programme clearly matches much more closely that of *Der Ruf* in its prisoner-of-war incarnation and the course steered by its later editors in Germany than that under Andersch and Richter: 'Das Aktuelle wird uns auch in Zukunft nicht um des Momentanen, das im Grunde das ewig Gestrige ist, sondern um des Dauernden willen beschäftigen, vor dem es sich auszuweisen hat.'

Eight years later in issue 100, as a guarantee of continuity in programme and approach, Paeschke's 'Geleitwort' (*Merkur*, 2, 501–04) reproduces extracts from the editorial article of issue 10 and re-affirms the programmatic significance of the Lessing piece. Again, Paeschke feels obliged to defend the journal from accusations of a lack of topical engagement, now given the label 'aestheticism' rather than 'escapism'. The importance of these perceived literary fashions and increasingly empty labels of critical discourse are seen to re-inforce the necessity of *Merkur*'s own critical task, now expressed in terms of bringing ideological and generational extremes into communication with one another. As with Haas, much responsibility is placed on the shoulders of the readers to choose between the alternatives placed in front of them. In this respect, Paeschke's 1956 editorial carries an echo of the 'Prinzip einer bewußten Widersprüchlichkeit' which Schoor sees as Huchel's fundamental editorial strategy in *Sinn und Form*:[16]

> Polarisierung der Kräfte – so hieß unser Leitprinzip bei der Wahl der Autoren wie der Themen. [...] Wir werden auch in der Zukunft die Probleme jeweils dort aufsuchen, wo Spannungen erzeugt und ausgehalten werden müssen: in den verschiedenen Schnittpunkten vor allem – den politischen von links und rechts, [...] den künstlerischen von Tradition und Experiment, den weltanschaulichen von Moral und Technik, Metaphysik und Psychologie, zeitlosem und zeitgebundenem Geist. Einen Beitrag zur Korrektur des Zeitgeistes zu geben – das sehen wir, wie gestern so morgen, als unsere Aufgabe an.

Karl Heinz Bohrer's retrospective tribute to Paeschke and his editorship of *Merkur* similarly stresses the importance of the journal as a site of *Diagnostik* rather than *Parteinahme*, as a forum for debate and discussion. As editor of the journal in the 1990s, Bohrer's thoughts on the longevity of *Merkur* and Paeschke's editorial principles are telling, since this longevity is seen to be a product of the journal's debt to Wieland's *Teutscher Merkur* and its relative lack of innovation: 'Paeschkes *Merkur* steht [...] in der Tradition des diskutierenden Forums im Sinne von Wielands *Teutschem Merkur*. [...] Friedrich Schlegels *Athenaeum* war sicherlich sehr viel origineller als Wielands *Teutscher Merkur*, aber es lebte nur in wenigen Nummern, während letzterer eine ganze Epoche mitprägte.'[17]

The precise substance of Paeschke's editorial agenda becomes clearer in his own essayistic contribution to the opening issue of the journal. As the title of his piece, 'Verantwortung des Geistes' (*Merkur*, 1, 100–10), suggests, this is no attempt to position the intellectual outside the sphere of social responsibility. Indeed, in considering explicitly the post-war German political context, the sharpening East/West polarisation, collective guilt and the legacy of National Socialism, Paeschke is clearly seeking to address many of the contemporary issues which concerned the editors of *Der Ruf*. In situating intellectual responsibility at a European level, there is a clear point of contact too with the solutions proposed by *Der Ruf* to these questions, and this position is strengthened through other contributions to this first issue which adopt a pan-European perspective.[18] Continuity in this respect exists also with *Maß und Wert*, not only in terms of the European federalist solutions proposed there, not least by De Rougement himself, but also in terms of the diagnosis of a longer-term crisis in modern European culture and society. The effects of National Socialism in Germany are explicitly set in a broader context: 'Der Nationalsozialismus hat mit seinem mörderischen Bildersturm auf die Ideen des Abendlandes für den deutschen

---

16   Uwe Schoor, *Das geheime Journal einer Nation: Die Zeitschrift 'Sinn und Form', Chefredakteur Peter Huchel 1949–1962* (Berlin: Lang, 1992), p. 138.

17   Karl Heinz Bohrer, 'Hans Paeschke und der *Merkur*: Erinnerung und Gegenwart', *Merkur*, 45, 991–96 (pp. 994–95).

18   Denis de Rougemont, 'Die Krankheiten Europas', *Merkur*, 1, 17–26; HP, 'Das europäische Gespräch', *Merkur*, 1, 118–26.

Geist liquidiert, was die Krise des modernen Geistes überall in der Welt seit langem in den Schmelztiegel geworfen hat' (*Merkur*, 1, 102). In response, Paeschke demands an engagement with the present, but this present must be informed by a notion of continuity and tradition:

> Aufgabe: eine möglichst erschöpfende und genaue Definition der Gegenwart zu finden, die nicht einfach Aktualität bedeutet, sondern Kontinuität, d.h. Mittlertum im Strom der Zeit. Es geht um eine schöpferische Polarisierung von Tradition und Gestaltendem. An unsere Vergangenheit kettet uns die Verantwortung für die Schuld. [...] Dies bringt uns in eine selbstverständliche Distanz gegenüber avantguardistischen Parolen. Wir sind in diesem Jahrhundert so oft und in so furchtbar falschem Sinne neu geworden, daß ein esprit de suite das erste ist, was nottut. [...] Was könnte uns an diesem Tiefpunkt unserer Geschichte auch anderes tragen als die Achtung vor den großen Weltgültigen unserer Vergangenheit? Wir sagen: tragen lassen – und nicht rückwärts schauen. [...] An diesem Punkt erweist sich der im Vergangenen Befangene als anderer Bruder des Avantguardisten: gebricht es ihnen auch nicht an Mut, der Forderung des Tages ins Gesicht zu schauen, so doch an Unbefangenheit der Wertung, wie sie echtes Kontinuitätsbewußtsein verleiht. Wir müssen weg von dem Zwang, uns immer wieder neu vor der Welt zu erklären und zu rechtfertigen. (*Merkur*, 2, 109–10)

In an echo of Haas and Thomas Mann, Paeschke proposes a dynamic and productive synthesis between tradition and the present, responding to a long-term sense of intellectual crisis with a call for continuity and tradition. But here, after 1945 and inside Germany, such a position is somewhat more problematic since it entails disregarding National Socialism as a profound rupture of that tradition. The necessity of the editorial task is explicitly re-stated by Paeschke four years later in a review article on European cultural journals: 'Gegen eine romantische Restauration wie gegen einen traditionslosen Aktivismus gleichermaßen das Verbindende herausstellen, nach vorn wie nach rückwärts blicken, an gestern und an morgen denken: das scheint mir das wichtigste Anliegen einer deutschen Kulturzeitschrift zu sein' (*Merkur*, 5, 775).

For Paeschke, a central category in this post-war undertaking is *Mittlertum*, defined both temporally and spatially. Understood in the former sense, *Mittlertum* implies the kind of continuity outlined above ('d.h. Mittlertum im Strom der Zeit'). In the latter, spatial sense the notion of *Mittlertum* entails an individual, micro-level response to the vast technological apparatus of modernity, an emphasis on a localised sphere of activity which seems to echo a socially conservative, almost Biedermeier, sensibility: 'Wir können [...] nur eines tun: nämlich immer wieder die natürlichen Bindungen, das Band von Mann zu Frau, von Freund zu Freund, das rechte Miteinanderreden und -Umgehen unserer Pflege anvertrauen' (*Merkur*, 1, 108). Telling are the intellectual points of reference which Paeschke draws on in his exposition of the notion of *Mittlertum*. In particular, in the capacity of the individual artist to influence events on a wider scale, an analogy is made with particle physics: 'Die Fernwirkung eines wahren oder falschen geistigen Aktes fordert in unserem Zeitalter der Mikrophysik den

Vergleich mit der Verstärkertheorie der Atome heraus: die Lageänderung eines kleinsten Teilchens vermag Riesenbrände zu entfachen' (*Merkur*, 1, 109). We have already noted the strong and consistent presence of this intellectual current in Martin Raschke's own review articles and in Ferdinand Lion's editorial practice in *Maß und Wert*. Of course, the subject-matter of atomic physics is lent a new and troubling dimension in the wake of Hiroshima, and this is reflected in the earliest editions of *Merkur*. At the same time, in his programmatic literary-historical essay, 'Die Bewußtseinslage der modernen Literatur' (*Merkur*, 3, 537–53; 680–89), Hans Egon Holthusen draws an explicit parallel between the development of modern physics and the much broader 'schwindelerregende Unsicherheit des modernen Menschen im Sein'. Quantum theory and the theory of relativity are seen to bring into question not only classical physics and the laws of causality but also 'das geistige Schicksal des menschlichen Geschlechts', to push back 'die Grenzen der Fassungskraft unseres Geistes'. The fascination of the discipline for intellectuals in our period of aesthetic restoration is clearly tied to its role in the propagation of the dominant consciousness of crisis and uncertainty.

Another important point of intellectual reference for Paeschke in his exposition of *Mittlertum* is provided by Goethe: 'Als Leitmotiv mag das Goethewort dienen, daß ein jeder die Dinge seiner eignen Welt ordnen möge, wenn er die Ordnungen des Universums bessern wolle' (*Merkur*, 1, 108). According to Veit, 'im *Merkur* wurde Goethe als der für das deutsche Geistesleben vorbildliche Dichter gefeiert', and certainly he is widely cited by contributors as a source of intellectual authority, as well as being the subject of a number of key-note essays.[19] The first of these is Ernst Robert Curtius's 'Goethe als Kritiker' (*Merkur*, 2, 333–55) which can be seen as an attempt to further the editorial aim of establishing a productive synthesis between literary criticism and production, already apparent in the selection of the Lessing piece. Curtius stresses the status of criticism as a form of literature, 'die Literatur der Literatur', and bemoans its current absence in German literary culture. By contrast, Goethe is held up 'in dem großen Zeitalter der deutschen Kritik [...] als Empfangender und Teilnehmender, als Mitwirkender und als Gegenwirkender'. As the final section of the essay makes clear, Curtius is also putting down a marker for the coming *Goethe-Jahr*, attempting to overcome what he sees as the prevailing 'Goetheferne'. Of course, this was a task which Curtius took up the following year in *Die Zeit* in his response to the much more sceptical approach which had been adopted by Karl Jaspers in his acceptance speech for the Frankfurt Goethe Prize eighteen months earlier:

> Wir stehen im Goethejahr. Wir beklagen im Namen aller, denen Goethe Höchstes bedeutet, daß ein Philosoph von internationaler Geltung das Ansehen des deutschen

---

19   Veit, p. 228.

Geistes und der deutschen Philosophie durch eine zugleich subalterne und arrogante Zurechtweisung Goethes kompromittiert.[20]

For all Paeschke's attempts to present a diversity of views, Curtius's role in the journal makes clear, together with other *Goethe-Jahr* contributions, that *Merkur* was positioned on the traditionalist side of the ensuing Jaspers-Curtius debate. Most directly of all, Holthusen's 'Goethe als Dichter der Schöpfung' (*Merkur*, 3, 1041–62) offers a rebuttal to Jaspers, re-asserting the importance of Goethe's writing in the chaos of the times, as the epitome of German *Dichtung* ('die Mitte, das Erstgeborene, die Sonne, die nach allen Seiten strahlt'). In his invocation of the literary 'word', Holthusen asserts the characteristic restorative gesture which connects so many of our journals, on this occasion tied intimately to Goethe's authority:

> Kann aber das Wort eines Dichters in der eisigen Luft unseres Zeitalters noch Wirkung tun? [...] Ich bekenne, daß mir eines Tages, mitten im reißendsten Strudel des Krieges, in einer angst- und schwindelerregender, gleichsam bodenlosen Situation, ein Dichterwort den Begriff der Wirklichkeit gerettet hat, genauer gesagt: den Glauben an Sinn und Zusammenhang meines Daseins. [...] Das dichterische Wort ist ähnlich wie das Bibelwort eine wirkende Kraft im Haushalt der Welt. [...] Goethe als der Dichter der Schöpfung oder, um es noch allgemeiner zu sagen, Goethe als der Dichter des Seins ist uns heute notwendiger als Goethe, der Dichter der Bildung, oder Goethe, der Dichter der Gesellschaft.

In its attitude to the German literary tradition in general, and Goethe in particular, *Merkur* is to be aligned through these contributions alongside the US version of *Der Ruf* under the influence of one of Curtius's pupils and defenders, Gustav René Hocke. In Veit's words: 'Der Jaspers-Curtius-Streit gewinnt damit programmatische Bedeutung.'[21]

A modernist tradition: Eliot, Rilke and 'das alte Wahre'

Yet there is rather more to the process of tradition-building undertaken in *Merkur* than a straightforward Goethe-cult. In keeping with Paeschke's editorial aims, the key contributors to *Merkur* also seek to construct a more modern tradition, and programmatic in this respect is Holthusen's 'Die Bewußtseinslage der modernen Literatur' (*Merkur*, 3, 537–53; 680–89). Applying his analysis to a modernist tradition which is seen to start around 1910 with Rilke, Kafka, and Heym and to extend through the Hemingway-led 'lost generation' of US writers to find its contemporary expression in French Existentialism, Holthusen views as a source of continuity the on-going political, social, and cultural upheavals which shape the modern consciousness and which are felt explicitly as a threat to the *Bürgertum*:

---

20 See Hay, '*Als der Krieg zu Ende war*', p. 498.
21 Veit, p. 224.

> Die sehr weitgehenden Veränderungen, Erweiterungen und Erschütterungen des epochalen Bewußtseins, die sich in den letzten vierzig Jahren ereignet haben, sind teils verursacht, teils begleitet von einem politischen, sozialen und kulturellen Erdrutsch von unabsehbarer Tragweite. Die beiden Weltkriege, die russische Revolution, Entstehung, Blüte und Untergang der faschistischen Systeme, die deutsche Tragödie, [...] die Entmächtigung des Bürgertums [...]: dies alles bildet den Hintergrund unseres geistigen und künstlerischen Lebens.

Against this background, Holthusen invokes *Sinn* as the central category which gives definition to a valuable work of art or literature: 'Sinn, verpflichtender Sinn ist in allen geistigen und künstlerischen Dokumenten von Rang, in denen unsere Zeit sich ausgedrückt findet.' While some responses to the modern intellectual consciousness are deemed to have been more successful than others, Holthusen, in language redolent of 1930, now reaches out for an 'intact' occidental tradition which might offer the necessary resolution to this modern crisis of bourgeois values:

> Es ist nun die Frage, ob [...] das geistige Muster, mit dem das Abendland beinah zwei Jahrtausende lang gelebt hat, wieder in Ordnung gedacht werden kann. [...] Für große Teile der zeitgenössischen Intelligenz in allen Ländern unseres Kulturkreises scheint das, was wir das alte Wahre nennen, also die ehrwürdige Welt der abendländischen Überlieferung völlig erledigt zu sein. [...] Nicht nur, daß sich der moderne Mensch von den alten geistigen Ordnungen losgemacht hat: er hat auch das System der bürgerlichen Gesellschaft zertrümmert und ihr Welt- und Lebensgefühl abgeschüttelt, ja er scheint das Kostüm des Kulturmenschen überhaupt abgeworfen zu haben.

> Die Zeit scheint reif zu sein, die aus allen Fugen geratene geistige Welt wieder in Ordnung zu denken, die Parodien auf das alte Wahre [...] zurückzunehmen. Einige der kühnsten und fortgeschrittensten Geister unserer Epoche sind am Werk, das alte Wahre in neuer Sprache wiederherzustellen.

For Holthusen, one modernist writer above all others, T. S. Eliot, offers a way out of this crisis. It is Eliot, in his Christian poetry of the late 1920s onwards, who is seen to provide the requisite synthesis between tradition and innovation: 'Indem der moderne Dichter zu [der Symbolsprache der Mystiker] zurückfindet, geschieht etwas sehr Denkwürdiges: der radikale Nicht-Klassiker findet den Anschluß an die klassische Poesie. Avantgardismus und Traditionalismus fallen zusammen.'

Accordingly, Eliot's presence is a prominent one in early issues of the journal. In issue 11, for example, Curtius traces Eliot's transition from anti-establishment avant-gardist to literary and critical authority (*Merkur*, 3, 1–23). The relationship between production and criticism is again central here, and it is noticeable that Eliot is presented as a writer who in his criticism has developed a sense of his own history. Holthusen too develops his analysis of Eliot in a review of a Munich production of *Murder in the Cathedral* (*Merkur*, 2, 930–37). Noting 'ein antikes Stilprinzip', 'eine Erneuerung der griechischen Tragödie', Holthusen again asserts: 'Eliot ist der literarische Fortschritt. Er ist "Traditionalist" und "Avant-gardist" zugleich.' In the following issue, Eliot himself is given space for his 1944 speech to the English Vergil Society, published as 'Was ist ein Klassiker?' (*Merkur*, 3, 1–21). In what amounts to a discussion of the process of canon-formation, Eliot considers conventional criteria such as 'Reife', 'Vollständigkeit', and 'Universalität', applied to the full range of Western European literature, in order to explain the status of Vergil and that of the writing of ancient Rome. In the context of our current analysis, the following comments emerge as paradigmatic for the post-1930 consciousness: 'Das Fortbestehen literarischer Schöpferkraft in einem jeden Volk besteht also in der Aufrechterhaltung eines unbewußten Gleichgewichts zwischen der Tradition in einem weiteren Sinne [...] und der Originalität der lebenden Generation.'

Alongside Eliot, the most prominent modernist figure to emerge at the centre of the *Merkur* agenda, again promoted primarily through Holthusen's contributions, is Rilke. Already in issue 8, the tone is set by Holthusen's 'Der späte Rilke' (*Merkur*, 2, 194–220). Rilke is lauded as the greatest German poet of the modern epoch, in the company of Holthusen's by now familiar modernist cast-list: Kafka, Proust, Eliot, Auden, and Joyce. Rilke's greatness is seen to lie in his poetic response to the on-going crisis of the modern world, in 'der gewissenhaften Subjektivität seines Denkens, in der wahrhaftigen Darstellung des ortslosen Menschen der Gegenwart'. In particular, Rilke is praised as a guarantor of an 'Einsamkeit' which re-instates the values which lie at the centre of the restorative paradigm: 'Es ist Einsamkeit in einer Welt ohne gesellschaftliche, politische und kulturelle Ordnung, einer Welt ohne Maß und Allgemeingültigkeit.' In a similar vein, Holthusen reviews in 1953 the latest material to be published posthumously by Insel: 'Die Gestalt Rilkes wird durch diese Veröffentlichung noch größer, die einzigartigen Errungenschaften seines sprachschöpferischen Genius kommen uns noch tiefer zum Bewußtsein' (*Merkur*, 7, 1089). Largely through his appreciation of Rilke, Holthusen is also moved to comment on contemporary trends in German poetry. In his first Rilke essay, attention had already been drawn to the renewed wave of 'Rilke- (und freilich auch Hölderlin-) Epigonen'. It was this tendency which had triggered debate in the pages of *Der Ruf* about the suitability of Rilke as an example for young poets to follow, and there is an echo of this discussion in Holthusen's 'Exkurs über schlechte Gedichte' (*Merkur*, 2, 604–08). Here, Holthusen makes a very pointed reference to the 'young generation' who are seeking to proclaim 'den Anbruch eines neuen Zeitalters' but are succeeding in producing only poor-quality poetry. Indeed, the official lies of National Socialism are perceived to have been replaced by 'die reine Maßstablosigkeit'. Particularly harshly dealt with is prisoner-of-war poetry. While these poets are able to draw on their war and home-coming experiences, Holthusen is clear that poetry is not made by experience but by 'Einbildungskraft'. The poetry of the young generation tends towards the empty vocabulary of journalism and politics ('Not', 'Elend', 'Grauen'), toward superficiality rather than depth: 'Anstatt es [ihr Erlebnis] zu gestalten, reden sie darüber'. Rilke's function is as an example of the subjective and original poet-genius, an example to be aspired to rather than cheaply imitated.

It should be clear enough that a very particular modernist tradition centred on Eliot and Rilke is readily compatible with the kind of restorative aesthetic discourse which runs through the journals under consideration in our study, and this is a brand of modernism founded on *Innerlichkeit* and on a conservation of the conventional institution of literature. Indeed, Rilke's *Malte* is acknowledged by Raschke to be a significant early influence, while Ferdinand Lion too draws on Rilke in *Maß und Wert*. In this context, two other figures stand out: Gottfried Benn as the intellectual authority of Raschke and the *Kolonne* Circle; and Hugo von Hofmannsthal who played a comparable role in Willy Haas's intellectual development. Benn's renewed post-war popularity is accurately reflected in the volume of contributions made by him to *Merkur,* that is, ten literary contributions in the first ten years of the journal's existence. To this must be added Max Rychner's two-part essay published in issues 18 and 19 (*Merkur*, 3, 781–93; 872–90). As such, Benn is a more frequent presence in the journal than Eliot, Auden, Rilke, or even Goethe, and this holds true for Hofmannsthal too. Hofmannsthal is also given a prominent role in the editorials which open issues 10 and 100, an extract from his 1920 'Zum Plan einer Zeitschrift' acting as a programmatic epigram: 'Im Sozialen und Geistigen schafft man durch das, was man voraussetzt' (*Merkur*, 2, 482). Both Benn and Hofmannsthal also feature in Holthusen's keynote essays, the latter in particular cited as an authority in the early Goethe essay. Beyond these thematic parallels, it is striking that both Haas and Lion themselves have a significant presence in *Merkur* in the 1950s. In 1952, for example, Haas offers his own 'Erinnerungen an Hofmannsthal' (*Merkur*, 6, 643–58), one of five contributions made by him in a brief period between 1951 and 1953. Perhaps more surprising, given critical opinion of his editorship of *Maß und Wert*, is the presence of seven typically esoteric contributions by Ferdinand Lion between 1952 and 1956 which serve to re-inforce the striking areas of continuity between *Maß und Wert* and *Merkur*. Indeed, a reader of the two journals is left with a strong impression that in terms of lay-out, the number and type of contributions, and even editorial programme, *Merkur* represents the kind of enterprise that *Maß und Wert* might have become under more favourable institutional conditions.

From *Das innere Reich* to *Merkur*

In this way, robust strands of continuity can be shown to run from Weimar and exile journals (*Die Kolonne, Die literarische Welt,* and *Maß und Wert*) into *Merkur*. Clearly, such continuities are part of Paeschke's programmatic response to the catastrophe of 1945, but striking too is that this programmatic continuity extends through the Third Reich. If we consider continuities in personnel between *Merkur* and *Das innere Reich*, then it becomes clear that the Third Reich does not constitute a rupture in the literary tradition pursued by Paeschke. In particular, Rudolf Alexander Schröder is one of the central figures charged with the critical task at the heart of the *Merkur* programme. Although only a short-lived contributor to *Das innere Reich*, making three contributions before 1937, Schröder was a member of the *Lippoldsberger Dichtertreffen*, attended in the 1930s by such nationalist writers as Grimm, Binding, Kolbenheyer and Paul Alverdes, and the strict classicism of his Third Reich poetry makes him an important figure for the restorative literary paradigm. As far as *Merkur* is concerned, Schröder features on average once per year in the first ten years of the journal's existence, including fulsome tributes to his 70th and 80th birthdays in 1948 and 1958 respectively and prominence for his translations from the English and French literary canons. Schröder's own views on the role of the writer – unequivocally a *Dichter* – emerge in two early essays. In both 'Vom Beruf des Dichters in der Zeit' (*Merkur*, 2, 863–76) and 'Eine neue Dichterin' (*Merkur*, 3, 703–11), Schröder makes it clear that writing is a vocation which endures beyond the transitory demands of the present. Indeed, in the former essay the transitory literary movements of the avant-garde are condemned in biological language reminiscent of German fascism: 'Einer der schlimmsten Schädlinge, die am kranken Leib der Zeit schmarotzen, ist der Bazillus, der auf den Namen "-Ismus" hört.' Citing Goethe as an authority and holding up values of *Ewigkeit* and *Dauer*, Schröder's restorative aesthetic position is evident enough. For another of the journal's most important critics, Walter Boehlich, Schröder's traditionalism is a direct and appropriate response to the modern(ist) crisis: 'Wenn eine Zeit dazu neigt, sich in chaotischen Gestaltungen wiederzuerkennen, wird doppelter Nachdruck darauf fallen müssen, daß in gleicher Zeit eine Reihe großer und edler Geister dem Chaos sich entgegengesetzt hat, mit Hoffnung auf Angst reagierte, mit Form auf Formzerbrechung' (*Merkur*, 8, 192).

Further continuity between *Das innere Reich* and *Merkur* is provided by Curt Hohoff. Prominent in *Das innere Reich* through fourteen contributions and also editorial involvement after 1935, Hohoff's first contribution to *Merkur* appears in January 1953. Thereafter, Hohoff is one of the most frequent contributors to the journal, appearing on average in every other issue from 1954 to 1956. Significantly, Hohoff continues his critical pre-occupation with Georg Britting which, as we have seen, first emerges in a series of reviews in *Das innere Reich*. One of Hohoff's *Merkur* pieces – 'Antike Strophen in der Dichtung Georg Brittings' (*Merkur*, 8, 777–84) – charts explicitly the traditionalist poetic trajectory which can be so clearly traced through Britting's contributions to *Das innere Reich*. Britting himself is well represented through literary contributions to *Merkur* in the 1950s. Two short stories and three selections of poetry appear before 1954, and his 1950 publications (*Merkur*, 4, 161–63) – 'Die Eulen', one of his 1930s *Tierbilder*, 'Der Fasan', a poem of strict classical form which appeared in *Das innere Reich* in 1942; and 'Im alten Haus', strongly influenced by Britting's renewed post-war study of Goethe – are symptomatic of the editorial preference for continuity over radical change. Also reviewed by Hohoff, and in the process establishing an explicit connection to R. A. Schröder, is Georg von der Vring's *Englisch Horn*, a collection of *Nachdichtungen* stretching from Shakespeare to Auden. Von der Vring too has a strong presence in *Merkur*, being granted a 65th birthday tribute and having a single prose piece and four selections of poetry published between 1954 and 1958. Given the volume of von der Vring's poetry which appears in *Die literarische Welt*, *Die Kolonne*, and *Das innere Reich*, this presence in *Merkur* has a much broader significance for the period 1930–1960, and in this respect W. E. Süskind's tribute to von der Vring after his death in March 1968 is very telling indeed.[22] As a *Dichter* rather than a *Schrifsteller* ('kein anderes Wort kann richtiger bezeichnen, was Georg von der Vring auf dieser Erde bedeutet hat'), as a writer whose own account of his poetic impetus could be mistaken for Brentano, Mörike, or the young Goethe, as 'den umittelbar dichterischsten und insofern unentbehrlichsten deutschen Lyriker der letzten vierzig Jahre', von der Vring is perceived by Süskind as a writer who maintained his attachment to conventional forms even when literary fashions had moved on: 'Einer Zeitströmung entgegen hat er an der romantischen-naturlyrischen Gedichtform und am Reimgedicht festgehalten.'

And yet, if Süskind's portrait of von der Vring as a poet out of step with the times held true at the time of his death in 1968, it is difficult not to see von der Vring's presence in our literary journals as paradigmatic for the dominant restorative mood of 1930–1960. As we observed in connection with *Das innere Reich*, his consistent and prolific presence in our corpus of literary journals is one of our more surprising discoveries, von der Vring neither having enjoyed anything like the post-war profile of, say, Günter Eich, nor having been acknowledged in existing accounts of the 1930 paradigm as a source of such continuity. Equally, Süskind's observations about von der Vring act as a useful barometer of the prevailing literary climate of the late 1960s, suggestive of a sense that the restorative literary mood had been passed by, and of course 1968 is symbolic here for rather more than von der Vring's death. Reading *Merkur*, it is difficult to identify a particular turning-point which signals this shift away from our restorative dominant. Indeed, given the function of *Merkur* within the public literary sphere – as a thick journal, a purveyor of continuity and tradition, apt to smooth out any jolts and starts in literary development – we would not expect to locate in its pages an immediate reflection of a changed mood. As Janet King points out, *Merkur* does not undertake the politicised shift perceptible in

---

22   W. E. Süskind, 'Georg von der Vring', *Jahresring*, 68–69 (1969), 305–12.

comparable journals at this time, and the maintenance of the journal's long-standing section-headings and of its principal body of contributors only strengthens this sense of continuity.[23] Rather, it is the foundation of new literary journals with an innovative function, such as *Das Argument* or *Kursbuch*, which bear the shift in mood and approach of the 1960s. At the same time, what does emerge from *Merkur* is a gradual expansion of personnel in the late 1950s and early 1960s, a palpable changing of the guard as the 1930 generation fade from view, and new figures such as Enzensberger and Handke gain in profile. The emergence of the kind of generational renewal which had been hampered and thwarted at 1945 and the dissipation of the mood of profound crisis which had persisted since 1930 seems to have begun to generate the conditions under which both textual meaning and the institution of literature could begin to be challenged. As the shift of 1930 must be viewed as an incremental process, rendered visible by certain key events and the public initiation of a new literary generation, so too is the shift of the 1960s a gradual one, rendered visible by such events as Handke's *Gruppe 47* debut at Princeton in 1966 or by the political and social upheavals of 1968 and all that they brought with them.

Sinn und Form

A product of Soviet policy for Germany

It might be expected that that calls for a radical new beginning in politics and culture after the defeat of Nazism would have been nowhere stronger than in the Soviet Zone, shaped as post-war reconstruction was there by the USSR's Marxist-Leninist ideology. Yet the rhetoric of an explicitly revolutionary anti-Nazism was tempered by two factors: one the political interests of the Soviet Union; the other the analysis of the Nazi phenomenon advanced by the leadership of Marxist Left. These two factors had a profound impact on cultural life in the Soviet Zone and the early GDR, arguably serving less to foster a revolutionary climate than to re-enforce existing restorative tendencies.

In the interest of preserving German political unity, without which Soviet security and economic interests could not be guaranteed, Stalin's German policy initially eschewed any revolutionary approach, favouring instead the establishment of a 'bourgeois democracy'. Political and cultural life in the Soviet Zone and the early GDR can consequently only be adequately grasped in the light of the gulf

---

23 See King, p. 27.

between revolutionary ideology and Stalin's extreme caution over the German Question.[24]

Philosophically, the opposition of the German Communist Party to Nazism was grounded in an understanding of socialism as the legitimate heir of a centuries-old humanist tradition, which Marx had re-defined in the light of modern urban-industrial life. As is well-known, a principal concern for a socialist anti-Nazism, as articulated by Lukács and others, was the re-affirmation of the continuity of a valid German humanist tradition, internationalist in character, embodied by the Enlightenment and Weimar Classicism. Party thinking followed a familiar, binary opposition: it contrasted that humanist tradition with the supposed irrationality and obfuscation of reactionary German Romanticism and its 'decadent' successors such as Wagner and certain elements of early 20th century modernism, among them Expressionism. These things – so the argument went – had paved the way for the victory of unreason. For those who subscribed to the official Marxist position, this opposition set the limits for any scrutiny of Nazism and the German tradition. Pursuit of a more radical critique in the manner of Adorno and Horkheimer's questioning of the Enlightenment tradition itself threatened the very legitimacy of the official stance. Prominent socialist artists such as Bertolt Brecht and Hanns Eisler would feel the force of this position, as it became fixed upon the recovery of values and the stylistic expression thereof. The much more demanding task of the critical re-appraisal in which they engaged in their texts often sat uneasily with the restorative mood.

The official Marxist appeal to tradition as the basis for the recovery of humane values, which had been obscured by twelve years of Nazism, clearly lent itself to support Stalin's policy of German political unity based on bourgeois democracy. However, a consequence was that the principal exponents of that 'bourgeois' tradition, Goethe, Schiller and Lessing, were held up, in often bizarrely caricatured fashion, as the precursors of German socialism, who would help the SED to win the hearts and minds of the educated middle classes in the early Cold War struggle for Germany between East and West.

Cultural policy in East Berlin was strongly coloured by the two factors outlined above. New institutions were created to promote the policy of German cultural unity. Prominent among them were the *Kulturbund zur demokratischen Erneuerung Deutschlands*, which was designed to have mass appeal, and the elite German Academy of Arts. As the leading SED cultural politician, Johannes R. Becher was the key figure in their creation. Both the *Kulturbund* and the Academy created journals, respectively *Aufbau* and *Sinn und Form*, which reflected the role of their parent organisations. Indeed, *Sinn und Form* is unthinkable without that institutional context, which was a source of strength as well as of predictable weakness. Crucially, *Sinn und Form*'s attachment to the elite Academy provided

---

24 See Winfried Loth, *Stalins ungeliebtes Kind: Oder warum Moskau die DDR nicht wollte* (Berlin: Rowohlt, 1994).

anchorage for editorial policy in the notion of aesthetic quality that cut across the simple binary oppositions of ideology. By contrast, *Aufbau* was required to appeal to a much wider range of interests, amongst which the call for partisanship was a common denominator.

The capacity of *Sinn und Form* to thrive in changing circumstances over several decades in the GDR is intimately linked to its appeal to quality.[25] This was readily understood by Academy members. In the early years, they included some of the journal's most prominent authors: Brecht, Eisler and Arnold Zweig, the first President of the Academy. On occasion, they and other figures challenged in *Sinn und Form* some of the crude certainties of Cold War cultural politics held by the SED, which generated fresh taboos at a time when informed exchange was necessary to promote a fresh cultural understanding in the immediate aftermath of Nazism. They supported the journal's founding editor, Peter Huchel, who pursued 'eine neue Verbreitung menschlicher Gesinnung' (PH, 2, 256). During his tenure (1948–62), Huchel placed his stamp on the journal, establishing it as the 'literarische Prestigeorgan der DDR'.[26] Not only could *Sinn und Form* avoid certain traps; it capitalised upon its potential in a manner unique in early Cold War Germany. By the mid-fifties, the journal had come to enjoy a 'besondere Bedeutung, ja einzigartige Stellung' in German literary life.[27] Its well-nigh legendary status was evoked by Walter Jens, who was moved to describe it as 'so etwas wie das geheime Journal der Nation'.[28]

Yet Huchel's tenure turned into a war of attrition, which ended extremely acrimoniously. Hitherto, research has concentrated on his resistance to the pressure exerted by the SED dogmatists, Alexander Abusch, Alfred Kurella and Kurt Hager, who sought to curtail the presence of western authors in the journal and to promote Socialist Realism. In keeping with that, there will be some emphasis on the journal as a forum for work otherwise banished from public discussion in a repressive climate that generally retarded cultural development in the GDR (though, of course, a similar retarding effect can be observed in the strident anti-communism in the early years of the Federal Republic). However, the parameters of the present study invite two further emphases: firstly, the founding programme of the journal which explicitly invoked tradition at a time when the prevailing rhetoric of journal foundation was heralding radical new beginnings; and secondly the extent to which, in the latter phase of his editorship, Huchel remained wedded to the success he had achieved by publishing

---

25 See Stephen Parker, 'Der Erkenntniswert von Dokumenten bei der Erforschung der Geschichte von *Sinn und Form* 1949–1989', in Helmut Kiesel and Corina Caduff (eds), *Akten des X. Internationalen Germanistenkongresses Wien 2000* (Frankfurt a.M.: Lang, 2002), pp. 33–38.

26 King, p. 83.

27 Hans-Jürgen Schmitt, 'Literaturbetrieb als Staatsmonopol', in Hans-Jürgen Schmitt (ed.), *Die Literatur der DDR* (Munich: Hanser, 1983), p. 74.

28 Walter Jens, 'Wo die Dunkelheit endet. Zu den Gedichten von Peter Huchel', *Die Zeit*, 6 December 1963.

established names with artistic assumptions not far removed from his own, whose horizons were not those of the post-war division. Huchel found no place for emerging GDR authors and essayists such as Heiner Müller, Volker Braun, Christa Wolf, Werner Mittenzwei and Robert Weimann. From the 1960s onwards, all would figure prominently in the journal, contributing to its international reputation and to that of GDR literature. Their early work bore the unmistakable influence of Socialist Realism, but they were creating significant critical perspectives upon it and upon the development of a socialist culture in the GDR. Those perspectives were being generated within a changing context of German division, in which the defining reality was the consolidation of the two German states within their respective power blocs. Stalin's overtures to the West were a thing of the past, and the politics of cultural unity was relegated to a longer-term agenda.

Strategic planning for a 'representative' undertaking

An undertaking as ambitious as *Sinn und Form* could only be conceived by someone with the strategic influence that Becher enjoyed. Becher, the erstwhile Expressionist, had adopted strikingly national and conservative cultural values in Moscow exile in the 1930s. He returned from Moscow to East Berlin obsessed with his historic mission to create out of the Nazi horror the German *Kulturnation* that had been invoked by Goethe and latterly Thomas Mann.[29] Like the Soviets, Becher was at pains to disarm western charges of communist sectarianism. He acted as co-founder of *Sinn und Form* with Paul Wiegler, a 'bourgeois' intellectual, who in 1945 was chosen for a senior editorial position at the *Aufbau-Verlag*, the publishing arm of the *Kulturbund*.[30] Already in August, at the first meeting of the Presidium of the *Kulturbund*, Wiegler outlined plans for a journal that bear striking similarities to *Sinn und Form*:

> Zu dem Verlagsprogramm gehören dann Zeitschriftenwerk, oder vielmehr Zeit-schriftenunternehmungen, und ich darf diesen Plural gebrauchen, da nunmehr der kulturpolitischen Monatsschrift *Aufbau* eine literarische Monatsschrift folgen soll, die für den Oktober vorbereitet wird und die gewidmet sein soll der Literatur in engerem Sinn, der Kritik, der Philosophie, und die ja in gleichem Maße zu berücksichtigen hat

---

29 For a discussion see Peter Davies, 'Johannes R. Becher and the *Kulturnation*', in Clare Flanagan and Stuart Taberner (eds), *1949/1989: Cultural perspectives on division and unity in East and West* (Amsterdam: Rodopi, 2000), pp. 27–42.

30 Widely respected as the author of a distinguished history of German literature and through his long association with the publishers Ullstein, Wiegler enjoyed, in Hans Mayer's words, 'einen angesehenen bürgerlichen Literaturnamen'. See Hans Mayer, 'Erinnerungen eines Mitarbeiters von *Sinn und Form*', in Hans Mayer (ed.), *Über Peter Huchel* (Frankfurt a.M.: Suhrkamp, 1973), pp. 173–80 (p. 174).

Bildende Kunst und Musik, um dieses Programm, das man von hier erwartet, ganz zu erfüllen.[31]

On and off, Becher pursued the grand design of what he consistently called a 'representative' literary journal, an organ to rank with established institutions of German literature such as *Die neue Rundschau*. On one occasion, he wrote to Wiegler of his intention 'gemeinsam mit Ihnen eine literarisch-repräsentative Zeitschrift herauszugeben unter dem Titel *Die Tradition*'.[32] Becher's list of proposed regular contributors, the conservative authors of inner emigration Ernst Wiechert, Ricarda Huch and Hans Carossa, underscores the values conveyed by the title.

By 1948, when he advanced the *Sinn und Form* project in the rapidly changing climate of the early Cold War, those values are placed within a much broader vision. Becher's choice of title, publisher, personnel and editorial seat all contribute to his aim to create a representative journal of high literary quality for the whole of the German-speaking world, an organ of cultural diplomacy to bridge the emerging Cold War division. His request to Thomas Mann for permission to use his title *Maß und Wert* for the new venture indicates a desired continuity with Mann's 'bourgeois', anti-Nazi humanism.[33] Mann did not release his title and Becher settled on *Sinn und Form*. Its classicistic balance nonetheless echoes *Maß und Wert*. The choice of *Beiträge zur Literatur* as the sub-title was a deliberate echo of Hofmannsthal's *Neue deutsche Beiträge*.[34] The long-established Potsdam publishing house Rütten und Loening, with its proud tradition of bibliophile editions, was an appropriate choice for *Sinn und Form*. To the annoyance of many Party figures but with the approval of the Soviets, Becher pointedly sought in Huchel another non-Marxist inner emigrant.[35] Indeed, Alfred Andersch, an early reviewer of *Sinn und Form*, characterised Huchel with telling acuity as 'eigentlich kein Marxist, sondern ein "bürgerlicher" Lyriker hohen Ranges, dem wohl am ehesten Absichten zuzutrauen sind, wie sie innerhalb des Nazi-Staates die sogenannte "innere Emigration" beherrscht haben'.[36] Subsequent events show that Andersch probably understood Huchel's motivation better than Becher. Becher's choice was significant not simply because Huchel, like Wiegler, provided literary continuity within Germany and re-assurance to western authors

---

31 The minutes are in the archive of the *Kulturbund*, 97/498. Before the foundation of the Academy in 1950, the journal was loosely under the aegis of the *Kulturbund*, though Becher owned the intellectual property in the title.

32 Letter to Wiegler, 3 May 1947, in Johannes R. Becher, *Briefwechsel 1909–1958*, ed. by Rolf Harder, 2 vols (Berlin: Aufbau, 1993), I: *Briefe 1909–1958*, p. 336.

33 Letter to Mann, 24 April 1948, quoted by Schoor, pp. 20–21.

34 See Schoor, pp. 31–34.

35 Huchel had collaborated successfully with Soviet cultural officers at Radio Berlin since the spring of 1945, proving to be a skilful exponent in the cultural sphere of Soviet policy for Germany. Huchel later commented: 'Die sowjetischen Kulturoffiziere legten Wert darauf, einen leitenden Mann zu haben, der nicht in der Partei war' (PH, 2, 374).

36 Alfred Andersch, 'Marxisten in der Igelstellung', *Frankfurter Hefte*, 6 (1951), 208–10 (p. 208).

and readers. Huchel was associated with Berlin literary life before 1933 in a particularly telling way. As we shall see in greater detail in the chapter devoted to him, between 1930 and 1933 he learned the editorial trade on Willy Haas's *Die literarische Welt*. Quite apart from the fact that he got to know virtually everyone who counted, including Becher, Huchel assimilated from Haas literary values that were well suited to an organ of cultural diplomacy like *Sinn und Form*, if less to the SED's domestic agenda. Haas played a key role in articulating the restorative turn of 1930, in re-asserting the primacy of literary quality, the traditional role of the *Dichter* and the institution of literature following its erosion in the 1920s. Although Haas took a stand against the politicisation of literature, his position was by no means unreconstructedly backward-looking: he insisted on the dynamic potential of the bourgeois tradition for cultural renewal, although he drew the line at what he regarded as gratuitous, avant-gardist experimentation.

If the presence of Huchel and Wiegler might instil confidence, Becher was aware that his own reputation and that of his political masters prompted quite different responses. His solution was to locate the editorial seat of *Sinn und Form* not in East Berlin but in Charlottenburg, explaining to a colleague that *Sinn und Form* was 'kulturpolitisch von grösster Wichtigkeit', and 'aus wohlüberlegten Gründen befindet sich die Redaktion in Westberlin'.[37] Quite simply, this organ of cultural diplomacy was aimed principally at a select, international elite of opinion formers, many of them in the West. Nearly 250 copies of an initial print run of only 2,500 were distributed free of charge to influential individuals and institutions.[38] The significance of *Sinn und Form*'s anomalous position was not lost on some western critics, who eagerly seized on the obvious analogy of the Trojan Horse.[39] Notably, Hans Paeschke, the editor of *Merkur*, which harboured similar 'representative' ambitions, scathingly described the first issue of *Sinn und Form* as 'ein recht schwacher Versuch, sowjetische Ideologie poetisch zu bemänteln'.[40]

Programme and early practice

But that charge never really stuck. Under Huchel's editorship, the journal achieved a breadth and depth that belied assumptions of an underlying sectarian agenda, although the publication of anti-communist material was, of course, unthinkable. The scale of 'representative' ambitions is conveyed in the publicity material accompanying the launch in January 1949. It is Huchel's only published

---

37 Letter to the head of Radio Berlin, 2 November 1949, *Stiftung Archiv der Akademie der Künste* (hereafter SAdA), Johannes R. Becher Archive, 10188.

38 For the distribution list, see SAdA, Johannes R. Becher Archive, 10614. The number doubled after *Sinn und Form* was adopted by the Academy in 1950.

39 See, for example, Wolfdietrich Schnurre, 'Das trojanische Panjepferd', *Berliner Montags-Echo*, 24 January 1949.

40 Letter to Hermann Kasack, 8 February 1949. See Hay, *'Als der Krieg zu Ende war'*, p. 517.

programme for the journal. It demonstrates that the founding principles for *Sinn und Form* were far removed from the Zhdanovite dogma of Socialist Realism that was adopted by the SED:

> Mit SINN UND FORM wird eine Literaturzeitschrift vorgelegt, deren Herausgabe nur gerechtfertigt ist, wenn sie – fern von jedem Ästhetizismus – dem Geist der Sprache und der Dichtung dient. Denn nur unter dieser Voraussetzung kann sie eine der wesentlichen und repräsentativen periodisch erscheinenden literarischen Veröffentlichungen in Deutschland werden. Die Auswahl der Beiträge erfolgt in erster Linie nach den Gesichtspunkten, die für eine derartige Umschau stets gegolten haben sollten: all den Stimmen Gehör zu verschaffen, die im Sinne menschlichen und gesellschaftlichen Fortschritts, des Humanismus und der geistigen Vertiefung mit künstlerischen Mitteln das Wort formen oder mit kritischen die literarischen Erscheinungen der deutschen und ausländischen Geisteswelt aus gründlichem Wissen bewerten.[41]

The journal's core commitment to literary quality signals the intention to occupy similar ground to *Die neue Rundschau* and *Merkur*. Like them, it is located in established literary value systems and, notwithstanding the common need felt after 1945 to defend itself against charges of aestheticism, like them it participates in the re-affirmation of a restorative mood. The references to human and social progress and to humanism are presented in the published version of the statement without explicit reference to socialism.[42] They could scarcely cause offence to anyone in the West who did not have a residual hankering after the Nazi dream. By the same token, the formulations hint at a humanism with a socialist dimension that was attractive to many intellectuals after 1945 in the West as well as the East, not least to Huchel himself. That set *Sinn und Form* apart from its main western competitors. *Merkur* and *Die neue Rundschau* contributed to the rehabilitation of figures such as Gottfried Benn and Ernst Jünger, who had scandalised progressive thinkers with their notorious proximity to Nazism. *Sinn und Form* drew the line at an aestheticism that in the German context had spawned the Nihilism that Benn and Jünger espoused.[43] That legacy was banished from the journal's re-negotiation of the canon, and something of the journal's ambitions in this direction is captured by Heinz-Winfried Sabais who wrote to Becher, reporting his conversation with Huchel about the project: 'Peter Huchel erläuterte mir letzthin noch sehr ausführlich den Plan der künftigen Zeitschrift *Sinn und Form*. Wir haben uns dabei aneinander ein wenig in Ekstase geredet. Ich glaube, daß diese Zeitschrift eine große und strenge Aufgabe erfüllen wird und

---

41 SAdA , Johannes R. Becher Archive, 10614.

42 Schoor (pp. 27–29) compares the published statement with an earlier draft, which contains the explicit reference to socialism.

43 Only from the mid-1980s would the journal begin to address that legacy. For an account of how the publications of Jünger's diaries nearly cost the editor, Sebastian Kleinschmidt, his job in the early 1990s, see Stephen Parker, 'Re-establishing an all-German Identity: *Sinn und Form* and German unification', in Osman Durrani et al (eds), *Literature and Society in Germany since 1989* (Sheffield: University of Sheffield Press, 1995), pp. 14–27.

denke dabei nicht an die Art, aber an die Funktion der *Blätter für die Kunst* Stefan
Georges, freilich ohne deren Seelenlosigkeit und reaktionäre Tendenz. Wenn ich
es richtig verstehe, hieß diese Funktion, die Dichtung über die Gartenlaube und
über die Orphile hinwegzuretten, Courts-Mahler und Rilke (zu einigen Strecken)
zu überwinden, Tradition und Fortschritt zu vereinen.'[44]

A principal task was the presentation of work by German authors suppressed
by the Nazis, as well as the publication of contemporary writing. The mediation
of international literature followed from the journal's remit in cultural diplomacy:
'Es soll bahnbrechende Arbeit geleistet werden in der Übermittlung auch all jener
ausländischen – gleichgültig in welcher Sprache geschriebenen – Dichtung, die
lebendige Wirkung ausübt und uns vorenthalten wurde oder, durch die
Nachkriegsverhältnisse bedingt, noch nicht in anderer Form bei uns publiziert
werden konnte.'[45] Huchel further outlined the project as follows: 'Es handelt sich
um eine Literaturzeitschrift, die ausländische Dichtung, also wertvolles Schrifttum
vermitteln soll. Alles, was zur leichteren Literatur oder zum Feuilleton gehört,
kommt nicht in Frage. Besonders interessiert uns die Literatur aus der
französischen Widerstandsbewegung.'[46]

Huchel, like his mentor Haas, believed in the importance of building upon
the established institution of literature, which a 'thick' journal like *Sinn und Form*
quintessentially represented. Again like Haas, he had a view of the tradition as
something dynamic and open to innovative, quality work, if not to gratuitous,
avant-gardist experimentation. Equally, Huchel had little time for the schematism
of a dogmatic and controlling Socialist Realism. His practice followed that of
other elite, 'thick' journals in juxtaposing material without editorial comment. The
editor remained an unobtrusive, background presence, encouraging readers to
make links between pieces for themselves in the interest of cultivating an
informed understanding and hence promoting cultural development. He sought
to maintain distance from the merely topical and from ideological pressures of the
moment by not putting into practice the intention to review new publications.

This approach added up to what Gustav Seibt has described as the journal's
'progressive Restauration', a phrase that captures something of the political and
aesthetic complexities of the journal under Huchel.[47] This proved attractive to
liberal and left-wing intellectuals in the West, who opposed the strident anti-
communism and the highly questionable assimilation of Nazis within the
prevailing climate of the Adenauer 'restoration'. In this way, *Sinn und Form* at the
very least held its own with its principal western competitors, *Merkur* and *Die neue
Rundschau*. The journal's mission also took it beyond the confines of official

44 Letter to Becher, 28 June 1948, SAdA, Johannes R. Becher Archive, 10172.
45 See note 41 above.
46 Letter to Henri Bergmiller, 14 June 1948, quoted in Schoor, p. 30. The journal's first issue
    contained a selection of French resistance poetry.
47 Gustav Seibt, 'Das Prinzip Abstand: Fünfzig Jahre *Sinn und Form*', *SuF*, 51, 205–18 (p. 208).

Socialist Realism, creating a space for writing with ambitions that frequently clashed with the enforcement of dogma. The task of recovering lost values and continuities necessarily took it back to the debates of the earlier decades of the century.

It could demonstrate its credentials in orthodox Marxist aesthetics forged in those years through regular contributions – at least until 1956 – from Georg Lukács, beginning with 'Heidegger redivivus' (*SuF*, 1.3, 37–62). For Lukács, despite attempts to present a new face, Heidegger remains the same anti-humanist thinker, who had prepared the ground for Nazism. Lukács broadens the attack to point out the suspect roots of Sartrean Existentialism, which 'alle Probleme der Gegenwart ausschließlich von ihren subjektiven Erlebnissen aus bewertet' (*SuF*, 1.3, 61). *Sinn und Form* would maintain its distance from Existentialism and from the subjectivity of the West German neo-avantgarde that accompanied the Existentialist fashion in the 1950s. Alfred Andersch, in his youth a Marxist who in the 1950s espoused Existentialism and promoted the avantgardist revival in his journal *Texte und Zeichen*, commented on Lukács's contributions: 'Die Kritik, die er vollzieht, ist zwar erregend wie eh und je, aber seine Trümpfe stechen nicht mehr.'[48] Lukács's method was, indeed, familiar, as he continued in *Sinn und Form* his interpretation of the German and European realist tradition in terms well-known from the 1930s. He produced substantial essays on Raabe and Fontane, the two-part 'Klassische Form des historischen Romans' and, on Thomas Mann's death, 'Der letzte große Vertreter des kritischen Realismus'.

The journal's essayistic re-interpretation of the European tradition from a Marxist perspective concentrated principally on the Enlightenment, Weimar Classicism and 19th-century Realism. The approach to the Marxist essay was, however, much broader than the Lukácsian position. The three Leipzig professors, Ernst Bloch, Hans Mayer and Werner Krauss, each had a rare gift that was placed at Huchel's disposal. The Romance philologist Krauss was a mainstay of Huchel's editorship. He introduces Lorca's work in the second issue in terms that closely match the concerns of the present study, relating the *Gypsy Ballads* of 1928 to a stylistic development in which Lorca broke out of the subjectivity of the 1898 generation and drew on popular traditions in order to create an 'authentic' Spanish modernism (*SuF*, 1.2, 32–48).[49] The eclectic Bloch remains the unpredictable, speculative counterpoint to Lukács that he had been in the 1930s. Mayer, meanwhile, not only writes about the German classical and the European realist tradition in essays on Lessing, Heine, Balzac and Flaubert, but also treats subjects from the nineteenth and early twentieth century that German Marxist

---

48 Andersch, 'Marxisten in der Igelstellung', p. 209.
49 Krauss's essay provides evidence for Schäfer's view that the 'turn' of 1930 was an international phenomenon. See Hans Dieter Schäfer, 'Zur Periodisierung der deutschen Literatur seit 1930', in Hans Dieter Schäfer, *Das gespaltene Bewußtsein: Über deutsche Kultur und Lebenswirklichkeit 1933–1945* (Munich: Hanser, 1981), pp. 55–71 (p. 57).

orthodoxy considered beyond the pale. His essay of 1953 on Wagner's intellectual development continues the journal's probing of this key figure in European Decadence that begins with the publication in the very first issue of Romain Rolland's memoirs, through which the journal also signalled its intention to examine the roots of Nazism and anti-semitism. Rolland writes of his love for Wagner and of his visit to Bayreuth after Wagner's death:

> Die ganze Familie huldigte einem ruhigen und überzeugten Antisemitismus [...] Was für mich aber in der Atmosphäre von Wahnfried am bedrückendsten war, das war ein unerträglicher germanischer Übernationalismus [...] Ich war später nicht überrascht, als ich sah, daß der Anstreicher von Berchtesgaden Bayreuth für sich beanspruchte, Es war wirklich eine der ersten Zellen des Hitlerismus. (*SuF*, 1.1, 38–39)

Mayer concludes his essay as follows:

> Die Aufgabe des deutschen und heutigen Beurteilers aber muß darin bestehen, die großen und unvergänglichen Leistungen Richard Wagners von den verfallenden und brüchigen Partien seiner Weltanschauung und seiner Werke kritisch zu scheiden. Das aber ist nur möglich, wenn Richard Wagners geistige Entwicklung in seiner Zeit in aller Klarheit und Konkretheit erkannt wurde. (*SuF*, 5.3/4, 161–62)

The contradictions that Mayer and Rolland outlined were too problematic for SED cultural politicians and their allies at a time when the GDR was participating in Eastern Bloc anti-semitism.[50] The crude binary oppositions adopted by the SED could be readily deployed in that campaign. For example, the journal's publication of verse by Gertrud Kolmar, the Jewish poet murdered by the Nazis, drew the charge of 'kranker Symbolismus' in the East Berlin press.[51]

Within the parameters of its programme, the journal sought to probe some of those contradictions. There was much to be presented for fresh consideration. At the outset, that included 'Odysseus oder Mythos und Aufklärung', an extract from Horkheimer and Adorno's *Dialektik der Aufklärung* (*SuF*, 1.4, 143–80), which, as we have seen, questioned the orthodox Marxist position. The same issue included Walter Benjamin's 'Über einige Motive bei Baudelaire' (*SuF*, 1.4, 5–47). The outstanding regular contributor to *Sinn und Form* was, however, Brecht, whose efforts to shift the terms of discussion led to repeated conflicts with the SED that are central to the journal's early history. They also contributed much to Brecht's standing as the epitome of the 'critically loyal' intellectual in the GDR. The launch of *Sinn und Form* with the Brecht special issue was the coup that, at a stroke, established *Sinn und Form* with a readership that was introduced to major work written in exile by Germany's most gifted and innovative socialist author:

---

50 Mayer's essay had in fact been removed from the issue at an earlier stage by Alexander Abusch, who was also instrumental in initiating Huchel's dismissal. See Stephen Parker, *Peter Huchel: A literary life in twentieth-century Germany* (Bern: Lang, 1998), p. 337. For a discussion of anti-semitism in the early GDR, see Jeffrey Herf, *Divided Memory: The Nazi Past in the Two Germanys* (Cambridge, Mass.: Harvard University Press, 1997).

51 Susanne Kerkhoff, 'Rausch und Tränen und Särge', *Berliner Zeitung*, 27 April 1949.

poems such as 'Die Maske des Bösen' and 'Die Rückkehr', the drama *Der kaukasische Kreidekreis* and his *Kleines Organon für das Theater*.

As has been shown in the chapter devoted to him, when Brecht returned to Berlin, he sought outlets for his work with prestige value that would cement his reputation. His interest and that of *Sinn und Form* met in a relationship in which the journal became his 'wichtigste literarische Plattform [...]. Seit 1950 erschienen in fast jedem zweiten Heft Beiträge von ihm'.[52] After his early death in 1956, the journal maintained the output by drawing on the Brecht archive. Among other things, Brecht's heirs released for first publication 'Volkstümlichkeit und Realismus' (*SuF*, 10, 495–502), which Brecht had written in response to Lukács in 1938 during the Expressionism Debate but had withheld from publication in *Das Wort*. Brecht's statements on cultural politics were published regularly in *Sinn und Form*, as he promoted his vision of a socialist culture that was being compromised by SED cultural politicians, who, in the Formalism Debate and later, showed that they understood only the simple binary oppositions of the Expressionism Debate. Brecht's statements include 'Notizen zur Barlach-Ausstellung' (*SuF*, 4.1, 182–86), his defence of Ernst Barlach following attacks on both Barlach and Brecht himself. Amidst a relentless campaign by the SED to discipline recalcitrant 'formalists' in the months before 17 June 1953, he defended his friend Hanns Eisler's artistic practice, as well as his own, in 'Thesen zur Faustus-Diskussion' (*SuF*, 5.3/4, 194–97). He was the leading light behind the publication of the 'Vorschläge der Deutschen Akademie der Künste', presented to the GDR government after 17 June (*SuF*, 5.3/4, 255–57). The principal issue was simply: 'Die Verantwortung des Künstlers vor der Öffentlichkeit muß wiederhergestellt werden' (*SuF*, 5.3/4, 256).

Through a balance of essays, prose, poetry and drama, Huchel placed the journal's centre of gravity within the first half of the twentieth century, tracing German and international currents of Classical Modernism, re-engaging with developments broken by the rise of Nazism, and reaching back into the tradition. Among the international figures that feature in early years are Rafael Alberti, Louis Aragon, Nazim Hikmet, Halldor Laxness, Vladimir Mayakovsky and Pablo Neruda. The established German 'inner' and 'outer' emigrants from the East and the West include: Hermann Broch, Alfred Döblin, Lion Feuchtwanger, Wieland Herzfelde, Hans Henny Jahnn, Georg Kaiser, Hermann Kasack, Oskar Loerke, Thomas Mann, Ernst Niekisch and Anna Seghers. Stephan Hermlin, who was born in 1915, was one of the few younger writers to feature as a regular contributor. Huchel's major discovery was Johannes Bobrowski, whose poetry had first appeared in *Das innere Reich* and who belonged to the same 'bourgeois' tradition of nature poetry as Huchel himself. Huchel chose Bobrowski's 'Kindheit' to introduce him to his readers (*SuF*, 7, 495–96). The vocabulary of

---

52 Werner Mittenzwei, *Das Leben des Bertolt Brecht: Oder Der Umgang mit den Welträtseln*, 2 vols (Berlin: Aufbau, 1986), II, pp. 379–80.

'Kindheit' echoes Huchel's 'Die Magd' (PH, 1, 52), while Bobrowski's looser formal structure and extensive use of enjambment are more in keeping with the later Huchel:

> Da sang die Alte in ihrer
> Duftenden Kammer. Die Lampe
> Summte. Es traten die Männer
> Herein, sie riefen den Hunden
> Über die Schulter zu.

A blend of idyll and elegy similar to that identified in the chapter on Huchel is established in the first verse of 'Nymphe' (*SuF*, 7, 496):

> Zeit der Zikaden, weiße
> Zeit, als der Junge am Wasser
> Saß, die runde Stirn
> Auf die Arme senkte. Wohin
> Ist er gegangen?

This recalls not only Huchel's 'Der Knabenteich' (PH, 1, 59) from the early 1930s but also his return to that voice in the mid-1950s in verse such as 'Widmung: Für Hans Henny Jahnn' (PH, 1, 134). Jahnn features, together with other prominent western authors like Thomas Mann and Döblin, in the double issue 5/6 in 1954, which Huchel heralded as the high point of his editorial work.[53] It also includes Becher, Brecht, Herbert Ihering, Bloch, Leonhard Frank and Mayer. Following its publication, Jahnn wrote of *Sinn und Form*: 'Eine Anzahl meiner Kollegen bezeichnen sie als die einzige würdige deutsche Literaturzeitschrift überhaupt.'[54]

More than any other, this issue embodied the all-German aspiration of *Sinn und Form*'s foundation and with that set the seal on the journal's legendary status that would endure throughout the Cold War.[55] Counting among its authors representative figures from the literature of the early to mid-twentieth century whose horizons were not principally those of the post-war division, *Sinn und Form* was also quite distinct from other literary journals in the GDR, not only *Aufbau* but also *Neue deutsche Literatur*. Indeed, the latter was established in 1953 as the organ of the GDR Writers' Union with a programme to promote new GDR literature alongside progressive new writing from the West. It was a move that was designed, among other things, to challenge the perceived aloofness of the Academy's journal and its remoteness from the new GDR reality.

---

53 For details, see Parker, *Peter Huchel*, pp. 348–49 and Schoor, p. 174.

54 See Huchel's letter to Jahnn of 11 February 1955 and Jahnn's letter to Huchel of 22 February 1955 in Bernd Goldmann (ed.), *Hans Henny Jahnn – Peter Huchel: Ein Briefwechsel 1951–1959* (Mainz: von Hase und Koehler, 1974), pp. 71–72.

55 It is, however, striking that Huchel did not succeed in attracting an appreciable number of authors associated with the *Gruppe 47*. For a discussion of the reasons why, see Stephen Parker, 'Peter Huchel und *Sinn und Form*', *SuF*, 44, 724–39 (pp. 732–33).

Towards the sea change of the 1960s

While Huchel's publication of figures such as Döblin and Mann drew many plaudits, the journal's strength also concealed a weakness, Huchel's reliance on those and other great names whose work was synonymous with German culture before 1933. This weakness was exposed by the simple, relentless march of time, combined with political shifts from the mid-1950s that set the seal on the German division for the foreseeable future. Brecht, Becher, Döblin, Mann and Jahnn all died within a few years of each other, while prominent essayists such as Bloch, Wolfgang Harich and Lukács were excluded from public life. Other prominent GDR figures such as Mayer, not to mention Huchel himself, were subjected to increasing pressure to address an agenda determined by the separate development of the GDR, which featured the demand for partisanship in the arts by means of Socialist Realism. That was anathema to Huchel, who had devoted his energies to what had been the official policy of cultural unity but which was increasingly his own personal mission. If the choice was, as he saw it, between partisanship or cultural unity, he could only choose the latter. The logic of his position was such that he was increasingly isolated from contemporary currents in GDR life.

He did not succeed in replacing those essayists whom he had lost with new figures from the East. In the early 1960s, the balance in the journal between East and West was tipped increasingly towards the West. It came to rely ever more heavily on the regular contributions of its two Marxist essayists from the West, Ernst Fischer and Konrad Farner. Western writers published for the first time included Paul Celan, Christoph Meckel and Klaus Wagenbach, while he reverted to his old friendship for poems by Eich and a story by Ilse Aichinger.

Fischer in particular played a significant role in Huchel's final years, when he repeatedly criticised the SED's dogmatic exclusion of work from the canon. Fischer attacked the sectarian attitude of Marxist theoreticians: 'Gibt es nur die einander ausschließenden Sprachen, Kunstformen, Ausdrucksmittel antagonist-ischer Klassen und Welten, der deformierten Bürgerwelt, der sich formierenden Welt des Sozialismus? Das ist die Auffassung vieler marxistischer Theoretiker; ich halte sie in dieser Schroffheit für anfechtbar' (*SuF*, 10, 465). In a magisterial essay written to commemorate the 150th anniversary of Kleist's suicide, Fischer points out the gross inadequacy of dismissing him as 'irrational' and concludes: 'Der große Träumer war ein großer Realist' (*SuF*, 13, 759–844). In similar vein, the final issues of *Sinn und Form* edited by Huchel contain Fischer's essay on Kafka (*SuF*, 14, 497–553) and his 'Entfremdung, Dekadenz, Realismus' (*SuF*, 14, 816–54). In the latter, Fischer criticises Marxists for, as he puts it, falling into the trap of viewing all non-Marxist writers as decadent. To do so simply follows the obfuscation prevalent in western criticism. In the former essay, he uses Kafka as a prime example of a writer alienated under prevailing conditions, whose work has its place in a progressive culture.

These publications were among the catalogue of Huchel's sins in the SED's reckoning with him. Fischer, of course, was a leading figure at the Kafka conference the following year in Czechoslovakia, when the SED maintained its position of dogmatic exclusion. And yet, while Huchel opposed dogmatic blindness to the importance of Kleist and Kafka, the choice that he made between cultural unity and Socialist Realism meant that he closed himself to the talents of some emerging GDR authors and essayists. Huchel became ever more attached to his mission of German cultural unity, promoted by authors of similar vintage to himself, who represented what we have called the 1930 paradigm. He equated calls for the publication of a greater number of young GDR authors with a sell-out to orthodox Socialist Realism. A cursory glance at the names introduced by his successor Bodo Uhse, such as Volker Braun, and then by Wilhelm Girnus, such as Christa Wolf and Heiner Müller, not to mention essayists such as Werner Mittenzwei and Robert Weimann, shows that *Sinn und Form* became closed to talent that no quality journal could afford to ignore.[56] They provided a fresh engagement with GDR reality from a perspective both Marxist and critical, in a searching dialogue with the exile generation of Becher, Brecht and Seghers. They would question the artistic assumptions of their role models of the 1950s as they evolved their stylistic practice in the 1960s, which would have an international impact in the West as well as the East, where it contributed to the erosion of official Socialist Realism and, in the process, to the erosion of the restorative mood of the mid-decades of the twentieth century.

Aufbau

As with other journals published through the influence of the KPD/SED, such as *Die Linkskurve* and *Das Wort*, discussion of *Aufbau* has tended to focus on the political role of the journal, or, more specifically, on the question of how the journal's contributions reflect political influence on the editorial process. Analyses of the content have naturally concentrated on tracing the developing line of the SED's policy towards the arts, the contradictions of its treatment of 'bourgeois' artists and intellectuals, and the rapid narrowing of opportunities for free expression which culminated in the campaign against the *Aufbau-Verlag* in 1956.[57] Particular attention has been paid to the circumstances of the journal's demise, and Simone Barck has demonstrated definitively that the SED undermined and

---

56 See Stephen Parker, '*Sinn und Form* unter Wilhelm Girnus', *SuF*, 51, 87–106.
57 See Flanagan, pp. 27–74; King, pp. 77–78; Harry Pross, *Literatur und Politik: Geschichte und Programme der politisch-literarischen Zeitschriften im deutschen Sprachgebiet seit 1870* (Olten: Walter, 1963), pp. 137–38.

finally closed the journal in late 1958 after it had come under attack for its supposedly 'bourgeois' cultural stance.[58]

This chapter is not intended as a contribution to this debate, but as a slight shift in focus that takes the journal and its contributions seriously in their own right, while not losing touch with the political realities of the period. In our analysis, *Aufbau* emerges as a case demonstrating the post-war re-establishment of the restorative aesthetic discourse that had dominated the preceding two decades, and which, by the early 1950s, had been reduced to a series of empty gestures and was coming under serious challenge.

Restoration and reconstruction

What is striking about the bulk of the contributions in the immediate post-war period is that the new situation is interpreted through old language. Instead of undertaking a radical reassessment of the assumptions of the cultural tradition, writers from all sides of the political spectrum attempt to fill the language of crisis and restoration with a new, positive political meaning. *Aufbau* provides a point of contact between bourgeois and communist writers, demonstrating the substantial common ground that existed between them. As with the discussion in *Das Wort*, however, it is clear that one side enjoys a certain institutional dominance, ensuring that the journal reflects a particular line while at the same time making space available for other voices. Thus, although the journal's first issues are dominated by bourgeois and religious voices, left-wing writers are able to speak with a confidence that their colleagues lack, since the debates which took place among the exile community have produced and defined a set of concepts and traditions which seem to have the weight of history behind them. One can therefore read the early volumes of *Aufbau* as a forum for bourgeois self-searching in a space defined by communists.

The linking of 'progressive' politics with 'restorative' aesthetic categories is one of the journal's characteristic gestures. The journal's first issue opens with programmatic statements which operate with the established cultural categories, while trying to put them to use in the new political situation. The opening statement, 'Zum Geleit', sets out a programme for 'geistige Neugeburt' based on the re-establishment of what it calls 'feste Maße und Werte' (*Aufbau*, 1, 1). In his 'Deutsches Bekenntnis' (*Aufbau*, 1, 2–12), Becher finds a virtuoso language which combines all these disparate themes, steering a path between communist, bourgeois and religious conceptions to establish a set of ideas which amount to a declaration that the values of German Classicism are the progressive opposite

---

58 See Simone Barck, Martina Langermann and Siegfried Lokatis, *Jedes Buch ein Abenteuer: Zensur-System und literarische Öffentlichkeiten in der DDR bis Ende der sechziger Jahre* (Berlin: Akademie-Verlag, 1998), pp. 348–57.

pole to National Socialism. The terms in which Becher, and the other contributors to the journal, set out their arguments, reflect a deeply ingrained way of understanding politics and culture; the catastrophe of 1945 served only to give this discourse a sense of political urgency.

The other contributions to the first issue take up Becher's themes and expand upon them; there is as yet no disagreement or debate in the journal's pages. Two contributions on religious themes stress the incompatibility of faith with Nazi doctrine and identify the *Bekennende Kirche* as the true voice of German Christianity (*Aufbau*, 1, 14–19 and 20–25). These essays share themes with the contributions on the nature of *Geist* and *Innerlichkeit* by Thomas Mann and Paul Valéry (*Aufbau*, 1, 25–31 and 32–35). Thus, the editors, a broad constituency of prominent *Kulturbund* figures, create by association a series of concepts which link democratic, antifascist politics with restorative cultural practices, playing on the strong emotional associations of the term *Geist* as a way of making disparate ideas seem irrevocably linked.

The tone of the journal remains very consistent in the first year of its existence, though the editors create space for more debate once the context has been set. A series of contributions attempt to define key concepts such as *Maß* and *Kultur*, applying them both to general issues and to specific art forms. Bernhard Kellermann's keynote essay, 'Gewogen und zu leicht befunden', sets the tone of the issue, arguing that National Socialism was the consequence of broken connections with the healthy roots of German culture (*Aufbau*, 1, 90–94). German culture is portrayed as an essentially healthy unity of art, religion, ethics, science and law, with which the German people (another unity) need to reconnect.

Prof. Henselmann's piece on the new tasks facing architects and city planners makes metaphorical connections between the physical form of a building and its place in its context, and the security of more abstract social structures: for him, 'Maß' and 'Form' equate to 'Sicherheit […] im Sinne der Standfestigkeit auf der Basis seines materiellen Untergrundes und Sicherheit in den Bezirken der umgebenden geistigen Welt' (*Aufbau*, 1, 129). Similar language is used in Herbert Ihering's discussion of the acting of Paul Wegener, who was able to preserve the values of Lessing's theatre against the depredations both of National Socialism and of Expressionist theatre. True acting is, for Ihering, a 'von Grund auf ordnender Geist' (*Aufbau*, 1, 147).

The result of this is that the atmosphere of the journal is almost exclusively bourgeois, with those communist writers who do appear, such as Becher, Lukács or Friedrich Wolf, sharing enough common ground with their bourgeois counterparts for the political tension to be submerged under the language of cultural restoration. Clare Flanagan identifies a shift in the journal's political rhetoric which occurs as soon as January 1946, with an essay by Becher which introduces a more aggressive, national note, accusing the Nazis of crimes first and foremost against the German people (*Aufbau*, 2, 9–18).[59] Yet the hardening political line is still imagined in terms of the restorative paradigm; the language of form and harmony has an emotional pull that allows the ideological content of statements to change while seeming to work with the same set of ideas. Although the journal's political line begins to shift fairly early in its run, the aesthetic line is remarkably stubborn, reflecting deep-seated longings for harmony and a 'return' to certain idealised traditions.

Essays such as Alfons Kauffeldt's 'Zurück zum deutschen Bildungsideal' (*Aufbau*, 2, 31–35), or Friedenberg's piece, 'Um die Einheit des Reiches' (*Aufbau*, 2, 23–31), are not first and foremost about education or political federalism, but are about attitudes to German culture and tradition, and about making a case for the centrality of cultural questions in the life of the nation. Language developed as a response to the aesthetic crisis of the late 1920s escapes the confines of discussion on art and is given legitimacy by being connected with the political reform of post-war Germany.

The pervasiveness of the language of cultural restoration across the political spectrum means that it comes as a shock when a voice is raised against it. Hans-Erich Haack's essay in May 1946, 'Tradition ist Schlendrian', is a polemic against the influence of an older generation whose passive stance during the Third Reich can be attributed to their traditionalism. Haack turns on its head the characteristic language of *Aufbau* contributors, for whom traditional cultural values were an active, antifascist force; he argues for the political urgency of educating German youth in the 'Notwendigkeit und Schönheit eines neuen Denkens und Formens', as a way of overcoming 'die Welt der vor jeder Neuerung Ängstlichen' (*Aufbau*, 2, 536). Despite this one exception, the journal's tone is remarkably uniform, with the political differences between bourgeois and left-wing writers being debated in shared cultural terms.

As we have seen, the basic editorial line of the journal on matters of the cultural inheritance follows the standard line on the conflict in German cultural history between rational, classical, humanist values and the forces of irrationalism and reaction. The extensive working-through of questions of the cultural inheritance in the communist exile press means that left-wing writers feel far more secure in their place within the tradition than their bourgeois counterparts, whose work in *Aufbau* registers the crisis of meaning brought about by the catastrophe of National Socialism. While bourgeois writers like Wolf Frank and Ernst Niekisch worry about the place of Fichte and Schopenhauer within the tradition (*Aufbau*, 2, 49–60 and 122–34), the Lukácsian canon no longer requires theoretical underpinning.

Thus, it is left to the bourgeois Herbert Burgmüller to discuss whether it is still possible to see Goethe as 'Maßstab für Größenvergleiche unter den

---

59 See Flanagan, pp. 36–37.

Erscheinungen des poetischen Geistes' (*Aufbau*, 2, 348). Naturally, he comes to the conclusion that Goethe must still be seen in this way, since personality and work stand in a harmonious unity with each other. Becher's assessment is, characteristically, far more confident, making connections between the harmonious unity of Goethe's work and the potential unity of Germany: Goethe is 'der Repräsentant der deutschen Möglichkeit, die wir verkörpern und zur Macht werden lassen wollen, der Seher und der Erzieher deutscher Nation' (*Aufbau*, 2, 681). The self-confident 'wir' contrasts strongly with the more cautious, searching tone of Burgmüller and other bourgeois contributors on the question of Goethe's importance and the supposed opposition between 'Klassik' and 'Romantik'.

An important debate in the April 1947 issue explores attitudes to the German tradition in some depth, under the title 'Gibt es eine besondere deutsche geistige Krise?'. At this stage, the participants are still in agreement that National Socialism arose from specifically German cultural conditions, and that the turn of the century saw the corruption of objective values, but there are telling differences. Where Alexander Abusch condemns the 'Auflösung der Begriffe, die einst den Stolz der deutschen Klassik ausmachten' (*Aufbau*, 3, 308), Günther Birkenfeld sets out a critique of the system-building of German Idealism which clearly draws on Frankfurt School thought (*Aufbau*, 3, 317).

There are signs that, as 1947 progresses, the journal's editors become increasingly anxious that the message about the cultural inheritance may be ambiguous or open to interpretations which work against the political needs of the present. Editorial comments on contributions become more common, ensuring that the reader makes the correct connection between the classical inheritance and progressive politics. The implication is that lack of critical clarity on such matters simply aids the forces of reaction. In the main, the journal still preserves a remarkable openness in the range of its contributions, but it is the interpretative context that narrows, closing down avenues of communication between conflicting approaches to the history of German culture.

The issue which commemorates the 30th anniversary of the October Revolution in November 1947 seems to point the way towards future priorities, though *Aufbau* rarely achieves again such absolute ideological unity. The contributions reflect the needs of *Tagespolitik* at a time of deepening divisions, with Becher's sonnet 'Dank an die Freunde in der Sowjetunion' (*Aufbau*, 3, 305) and Abusch's essay on the Soviet Five-Year Plans setting the tone (*Aufbau*, 3, 306–13). What is notable, however, is the prevalence of restorative categories in the discussion, reflecting the way in which Soviet traditions and influence are interpreted by the generation of writers who set the journal's tone. For example, an extract from Heinrich Mann's *Ein Zeitalter wird besichtigt* sets the context by placing the idea of revolution in longer, literary traditions: 'Die Oktoberrevolution ist, wie jede echte, tiefe Revolution, die Verwirklichung einer hundertjährigen Literatur' (*Aufbau*, 3, 303). Becher, in his speech 'Vom Willen zum Frieden', declares that the 'Geist des Wahrhaftigen' is inseparable from the 'Prinzip des Schönen', and it is the collapse of this certainty that led to the rise of fascism. The unity of the German nation is seen as a matter of conceptual clarity in literary language and of traditional aesthetic form – a conflation of radically different discourses which is typical of this kind of restorative thinking.

The banning of the *Kulturbund* in the British and American zones in November 1947 provokes aggressive self-defence from *Aufbau*, and marks the beginning of regular editorial opinion pieces from Klaus Gysi and others, with the ban being compared explicitly with Nazi acts of censorship. In January 1948, Gysi's defence of the *Kulturbund* sets the journal's editorial practice in long historical terms by accusing the Allies of preventing Germany from fulfilling the legacy of 1848 (*Aufbau*, 4, 1–4). The unambiguous historical lines that are drawn up here ensure that there is no misunderstanding of the journal's purpose, despite the presence in this issue of two essays that question some of the fundamentals of SED cultural dogma. Paul Lüth's piece on Thomas Mann emphasises the 'kalten, überlegenen Ironiker' in Mann, a view at odds with the standard interpretation of his work as standing in an unbroken tradition of German humanism (*Aufbau*, 4, 61), while C. F. W. Behl writes in extravagant praise of Georg Heym as a prophet of destruction, without setting either him or his work in any kind of comforting literary-historical narrative (*Aufbau*, 4, 68–70).

Despite this, 1948 sees the journal making efforts to fit its editorial practice into the template offered by the centenary of 1848; we can perhaps say that the urgency of the connection between the two dates meant that the context for pieces such as Lüth's was secure enough. The question of the 'cultural inheritance' is now seen to be closed, and essays on such questions proceed with a confidence that no longer requires lengthy discussion. Goethe is invoked as a friend of the proletariat by Walther Victor (*Aufbau*, 4, 796–98), Schiller is seen as being motivated by the longing for German unity (*Aufbau*, 4, 1048–52), and Herbert Ihering can state confidently that German *Klassik* 'unser Volk länger als ein Jahrhundert geistig genährt [und] die fortschrittlichen Geister gebildet [hat]' (*Aufbau*, 4, 780).

Challenges to restorative aesthetics

The journal receives a visual facelift at the beginning of 1949, when Bodo Uhse takes over the editorship: the cleaner, more sober appearance reflects the journal's assertion of a clearer editorial line and its status as an official publication. It also begins to take illustrations for the first time, breaking up the monotony of the text as well as providing exemplary demonstrations of realistic approaches to the visual arts and of the sound technique that artists are expected to master. If we sum up the tone and content of *Aufbau* in 1949, we can say that the year of the foundation of the GDR represents the high point of the restorative cultural discourse in the journal's pages. Questions have been answered and ambiguities smoothed out, and contributions and debates are more clearly linked to the needs of *Tagespolitik*. Uhse tends to work without editorial forewords, which under Gysi had often seemed rather inadequate in the face of the variety of material in the journal; instead, he begins each issue with a keynote essay that sets the ideological tone for the rest of the contributions. Similarly, each issue now closes with a section entitled 'Zu unseren Beiträgen', which explains the purpose behind each essay.

The January edition begins with Ernst Niekisch's essay 'Der Weg zur Souveränität', which is an attack on the western Allies for supposedly jeopardising the sovereignty of the German people and pushing for division (*Aufbau*, 5, 3–8). This is connected, inevitably, with an essay on Goethe by Paul Wiegler which stresses the poet's internationalism and longing for German unity (*Aufbau*, 5, 9–15). The Lukácsian view of realism and the cultural inheritance seems here to be in the ascendant, with an extract from Arnold Zweig's *Das Beil von Wandsbek* lined up alongside a piece by Lukács which presents Thomas Mann's work as the saviour of German literature from modernism, firmly rejecting the radical challenge to his view of Mann's work that Paul Lüth had proposed a year earlier (*Aufbau*, 5, 16–28 and 59–79).

The journal's approach to the cultural inheritance has hardened into a line that presents restorative cultural values as an unambiguous, militant weapon in the contemporary political struggle. Thomas Mann and Goethe are constantly invoked together as a way of purging cultural and historical discourse of ambiguity and modernist decadence: for example, the Goethe special issue in August 1949 opens with a quotation by Mann inveighing against an ironic interpretation of the conclusion of *Faust II* (*Aufbau*, 5, 675). This is followed by Ernst Fischer's essay, 'Goethe und die deutsche Misere', which presents Goethe as a precursor of the harmonious society which only communism can bring about (*Aufbau*, 5, 676–90).

However, at the very moment that Bodo Uhse has taken this narrow, politicised version of the restorative cultural discourse to its extreme conclusion, there are signs that the journal may be preparing for a move in a different direction. 1949 sees the introduction of reportage for the first time, with Hans-Jürgen Steinmann's piece on the Leuna chemical works (*Aufbau*, 5, 747–52). Although it is not yet clear, the Lukács-inspired cultural line is on the point of being challenged and revised; styles and attitudes which had been seen off in the pages of *Die Linkskurve* are about to re-emerge in *Aufbau*, and, significantly, will attract the label 'modern'.

The year 1950 begins with a statement of new intent. Klaus Gysi's programmatic statement to mark the New Year demonstrates a sharp change in cultural rhetoric. Only two months earlier, Max Schroeder had discussed the newly founded GDR in terms recognisable from the previous four years, asking:

> Was ist an den gegenwärtigen Vorgängen in Deutschland Echtes, Neues, Aufstrebendes, geeignet, die in unserer Vergangenheit beruhenden Werte fruchtbar zu machen? (*Aufbau*, 5, 980)

However, in January 1950, Gysi puts a very different spin on the new tasks ahead, adopting a rhetoric that echoes early Stalinism:

> Unsere Kultur, unsere kulturelle Arbeit in ihrer ganzen Vielfalt ist unlösbar verbunden mit dieser entscheidenden Aufgabe [...], einen neuen Menschen zu schaffen, den bewußten Lenker seiner Zeit. (*Aufbau*, 6, 5)

Although Gysi invokes Goethe as a defence against the American 'Schund-Überschwemming', his language makes it clear that it is Soviet models which point the way forward, and in particular those forms of writing which Lukács had criticised in *Das Wort*. Pieces which retain the old focus appear alongside such pronouncements, as a gesture towards the 'cultural inheritance', but the cultural wind has changed, and the 'inheritance' is now set in a new context, in which it appears as an era that has passed, rather than as a vital tradition that reaches into the present.

The political context of this shift is set by the SED's *Kulturverordnung* of March 1950, which guaranteed privileges for the *Intelligenz* while binding their work closely into the political needs of the regime. The practical political decision-making behind the *Kulturverordnung* is presented in an editorial by Gysi in terms with which its readers would have been familiar, namely as an act which overcomes the crises of the past: 'Zum erstenmal befinden sich staatliche Politik und kulturelle Entwicklung in fortschrittlicher Übereinstimmung' (*Aufbau*, 6, 390). Readers schooled on the deeply ingrained language of crisis, contradiction and 'Misere' are asked to consider the SED's policy as a solution to the longings for reconnection and purpose that had run through the cultural discourse of the previous decades. The implication is that Germany can now move forward.

The shift is visible in pieces by Stephan Hermlin on the 'Hennecke-Bewegung', raising the literary profile of reportage by presenting the writer as an observer who transforms himself as the new society is transformed (*Aufbau*, 6, 435–42), and Günter Caspar, who commits a cardinal sin against the Lukácsian canon by criticising bourgeois notions of literary quality, stating in September 1951 that the question of the 'Grenze zwischen dem Literarischen und dem Dokumentarischen' is 'müßig', since the writer can 'dokumentarisch gestalten' (*Aufbau*, 7, 806). Pieces like these begin to open up fields of conflict which had seemingly been resolved in the communist press by 1932

For the first time in May 1950, *Aufbau* sets aside a dedicated space for aspiring writers, the 'Forum junger Autoren'. Until this point, the journal had infrequently set aside space for writers of a younger generation, such as Franz Fühmann or Stephan Hermlin, but they had by no means set the tone of the journal, which had been concerned with notions of quality and continuity. Now, for the first time, writers such as Günter Kunert, Heinar Kipphardt, Uwe Berger and Christa Reinig are given space on the grounds of their youth and promise, rather than because of the polished quality of their work. The discussion of this policy in the December 1950 issue encapsulates the conflict between those who believe that the purpose of a literary journal is to demonstrate publicly the *process* of producing a finished work of literature in a journal, with its collaboration between writer, editor and reader and emphasis on trial and error (as in Stephan Hermlin's contribution, *Aufbau*, 6, 1176–77), and those who feel that a journal should only published finished works, conducting correspondence with authors in private (for example, Lothar Kusche, *Aufbau*, 6, 1177). An editorial reproduced from *Literaturnaya Gazeta* provides a significant afterthought to the discussion in February 1951, in a piece showing how all writers, including classical authors and those who worked with ideas of artistic genius, are in fact workers who collect raw materials, give and receive criticism, collaborate and rework: a thoroughly non-restorative conception of authorship (*Aufbau*, 7, 131–33).

Alexander Abusch addresses this theme in the August 1950 issue, in an essay that makes a clear distinction between the German bourgeois tradition and the modern, forward-looking Soviet example:

> Die literarischen Vorbilder und Maßstäbe des bürgerlichen Realismus und der Klassik in der Literatur, so unerläßlich sie sind, genügen beim neuen schöpferischen Tun nicht mehr (*Aufbau*, 6, 786).

Definitions of quality are changing towards an emphasis on experiment and openness, process rather than finished product. Anna Seghers makes a similar point in January 1951: 'Die Klassiker sind aber keine 'Quelle' wie das Leben und wie die 'ungehobelte' Literatur, die rauh und unverbrämt aus dem Arbeitsprozeß hervorgeht' (*Aufbau*, 7, 11).

Examples of an experimental attitude to aesthetics abound in the journal's pages, with an emphasis on operative forms and on the immediate, spontaneous registration of experience. The October 1950 issue is particularly rich in such ideas, with Karl Grünberg's reportage 'Sieben Musikstudenten fahren nach Masseberg' alongside Ingeborg Franck's drawings of workers. Grünberg's story of music students setting up a workers' choir stresses that their musical success is a result of their youth and commitment rather than of years of learning their handiwork (*Aufbau*, 7, 1011–15), while Franck emphasises in her commentary the immediacy of sketching from reality without forming the composition of a picture, as well as trusting the aesthetic judgement of unschooled workers (*Aufbau*, 7, 973–76). Amongst these enthusiastic voices, a piece by Becher which calls for young people to be schooled in the theory of genre and in the technical matters of literature seems like a voice from the past (*Aufbau*, 7, 697–703).

This sudden change inevitably raises questions connected with discourses of modernity and modernism, as well as with the nature of political control over literary discourse. The needs of the moment require a discourse of construction and transformation, and this means the resurrection of language and ideas which were current before the Lukács line triumphed in the early 1930s, and which are defined as 'modern', in opposition to what came before. A context in which Ernst Rademacher can suggest, in March 1951, that the 'Formensprache' of bourgeois literature is no longer appropriate (*Aufbau*, 7, 214), and Günter Caspar describes Socialist Realism as a 'Revolution der literarischen Form' (*Aufbau*, 6, 1125), is no longer a comfortable place for those who defined the previous terms of literary discourse. Even in the May 1951 issue, marking Becher's 60th birthday, the major essay by Lukács on his work suggests that the habit of 'Zurückgreifen auf die Traditionen gesünderer Zeiten und künstlerisch vollendeter Lebenswerke' is 'kein allgemeingültiges, abstraktes Vorbild', but instead represents a purely personal approach (*Aufbau*, 7, 401–02).

In the context of this burst of activity and redefinition of literary categories, the appearance in the journal of articles relating to the SED's March 1951 Plenum, at which the leadership railed against Formalism, seems to be as much about reigning in this exuberance as about condemning bourgeois modernism. Hans Lauter's speech to the Plenum, published in April 1951, in which he defines Formalism and demands the integration of literature into the Five-Year-Plan (*Aufbau*, 7, 345–48), sets the context for pieces by Soviet authors such as Konstantin Fedin, who re-establishes the importance of literary quality based on 'Meisterschaft' and 'Arbeit am Wort' (*Aufbau*, 7, 548). In its editorial practice, *Aufbau* has carried out a sustained critique of the restorative cultural values of the immediate post-war period, and yet the SED's cultural policy holds back a genuine renewal of literature.

The search for a role in the 1950s

With the founding of *Neue deutsche Literatur* in 1953, *Aufbau* takes on a different role, introducing international political reportage to complement the mainly literary preoccupations of the first period of Bodo Uhse's editorship. This outward-looking profile, which is also reflected in the breadth of the literary contributions, makes *Aufbau* a unique forum for the discussion and contextualisation of cultural-political matters in the GDR, though its aspiration to intervene directly in political life meant that it inevitably reflected the twists and turns of SED policy more directly than did *Sinn und Form* under Peter Huchel's editorship. Nevertheless, the breadth of Uhse's interests allowed at times the emergence of counterdiscourses that questioned SED dogma, as well as carrying forward, albeit in a more subdued way, the discussion of restorative cultural ideas that had begun in its early issues.

Simone Barck has provided a thorough examination of the political context of the final years of *Aufbau*'s existence, showing how Bodo Uhse struggled to keep the journal's horizons open during the crackdown on cultural life after the June 1953 uprising, as well as giving an account of particular instances such as the 'Rilke debate' and the campaign against Georg Lukács.[60] We intend to build on this work by tracing some of the strands that we have already followed in the journal's early years, and showing how they are developed and questioned in the mid-1950s as conceptions of culture interact in complex ways with the SED's need to legitimise its own rule.

Essays on aesthetics re-inforce the sense that the journal's workshop phase is well and truly over: pieces by Max Schroeder, Paul Wiens and Günter Caspar confirm that formal questions have been resolved in favour of the tradition (*Aufbau*, 9, 71–73; 73–75; and 173–76). The May issue re-inforces this turn with an open threat to GDR writers: a reprint of Stalin's letters to Soviet artists at a time (1929–1930) when the crackdown on experimental literature was beginning. Stalin criticises what he calls 'Komsomolzen-Avantgardismus', where young people correct the errors of the Party, and not vice versa (*Aufbau*, 9, 389). However, this re-imposition of discipline before the June uprisings is not a simple return to the journal's past: for example, Manfred Naumann takes Lukács to task for pessimism in his conservative preference for bourgeois realism over Socialist Realism (*Aufbau*, 9, 189–92), and Eduard Zak's praise of Becher seems to go through the motions before criticising Becher's restorative separation of the aesthetic and political aspects of his work (*Aufbau*, 9, 345–51). The publication a year later of extracts from his *Poetische Konfession*, in which he stresses the subjectivity and autonomy of literary production, simply emphasises how out of step Becher was with the changing political climate (*Aufbau*, 10, 1029–33).

There is much discussion of questions of form, with musicians like Ernst Hermann Meyer (*Aufbau*, 9, 312–22), and critics like Max Schroeder (*Aufbau*, 9, 327–32) and Peter Goldammer (*Aufbau*, 9, 369–72) using the language of tradition and objectivity in the Socialist Realist sense to justify a formal traditionalism. However, they key point here is what is missing from this rhetoric, namely a restorative emphasis on form as a means of preserving eternal values. It is as if the journal's original emphasis has been drained of its emotional content, leaving a series of political gestures that exploit the same language. There is a brief shift in the terms of the aesthetic discourse after the June 1953 uprising and the publication of the *Kulturbund*'s demands for freedom of expression and reform of the press (*Aufbau*, 9, 614–16). For example, Max Schroeder's important piece on contemporary theatre, 'Erfahrungen mit Zeitstücken', uses Heinar Kipphardt's *Shakespeare dringend gesucht* as a pretext for an attack on the GDR cultural bureaucracy (*Aufbau*, 9, 623–31).

---

60 Barck et al, pp. 348–57.

However, the rhetorical basis of the journal's approach to questions of cultural legitimacy has not shifted very far, and 1954 sees a series of attempts to re-interpret the language of cultural crisis in the wake of the restoration of the SED hard-liners' political authority. An essay by Abusch in March 1954, entitled 'Restauration oder Renaissance', makes this clear by re-interpreting the journal's history: the discussion of cultural crisis from the February/March 1947 issues of *Aufbau* is seen here as a sign of resignation, a 'Negierung der humanistischen Traditionen und geistigen Werte unserer Nation', rather than as an exemplary cultural exchange with bourgeois thinkers (*Aufbau*, 10, 227–28).

The June 1954 issue sets the rhetorical boundaries of the term 'crisis': it is no longer seen principally in a spiritual sense, but, in essays by GDR and left-wing US writers, as an economic term to describe the state of Western capitalism. Elli von Konschegg (*Aufbau*, 10, 501–7) extends this language of statistical analysis to the supposedly catastrophic situation of western intellectuals and artists: an intellectual or spiritual crisis is seen as a direct reflection of economic conditions that do not affect the East. 'Crisis' is no longer seen as an opportunity or obligation for critical self-reflection, but as a reason for adopting a more aggressive stance.

In this vein, discussion of aesthetics has narrowed to a stress on the agitational effect of art. References to the German literary tradition are now limited to political songs, fables or aphorisms that have a clear political punchline. For example, fables and 'Sinngedichte' by Lessing (*Aufbau*, 10, 29) and Gellert (*Aufbau*, 10, 555–58), and aphorisms by Lichtenberg (*Aufbau*, 10, 273–75) are set up as models for imitation for young poets: Uwe Berger's *Zweizeiler* in imitation of Lessing in the February 1954 issue (*Aufbau*, 10, 168) are intended to demonstrate this simplistic reception of the *Erbe*. Wieland Herzfelde's leading article in August 1954 makes clear that words are weapons rather than repositories of cultural values (*Aufbau*, 10, 673–77).

The journal continues broadly in the same vein, with nods back to the restorative attitudes of its early years only on occasions like Lukács's 70th birthday in 1955 or the death of Thomas Mann. Lukács's birthday gives an older generation of writers an opportunity to review the attitudes with which they are associated: without underplaying her conflicts with Lukács, Anna Seghers praises his efforts to preserve 'die große, die klassische Kunst der Völker' as 'Nahrung' during the period of exile (*Aufbau*, 11, 360). Thomas Mann sees in Lukács a paradigm of 'Bildung: eine Idee, welche heute vielerorts in beklagenswert geringen Ehren steht' (*Aufbau*, 11, 361).

Such references back to the journal's past – and to discussions in the pages of *Das Wort* – form a subtle counterdiscourse to the focus on Socialist Realism, represented by high-profile extracts from speeches to the 1954 Soviet Writers' Congress (*Aufbau*, 11, 108–14). These moments of retreat, in the context of the mid-1950s, in fact begin to open spaces for exploration of literary possibilities:

there is a subtle opening in the journal's stance, a tentative questioning of boundaries leading up to the publication of an extract from Il'ya Ehrenburg's *Ottepel'* (*The Thaw*) in August 1956 (*Aufbau*, 12, 681–96). Lukács takes the opportunity in June 1955 to revise his view of Thomas Mann in an essay entitled 'Das Spielerische und seine Hintergründe'. Although his view of formal matters as 'eine Wahrheit des Lebens' is unchanged, he begins to stress Mann's formal adventurousness, showing how Mann's style has been 'modernisiert' and how the formal properties of the *Joseph* novels show 'eine Annäherung an den Avantgardismus' as a way of approaching reality (*Aufbau*, 11, 501–24).

The journal's struggle to preserve notions of literary quality and openness is illustrated in the reproduction of a piece by Lenin in the November/December 1955 issue: Lenin's piece from the pre-revolutionary period on the journal *Svoboda* criticises 'Popularitätshascherei' in the press: 'Der populäre Schriftsteller setzt keinen nicht denkenden, nicht denken wollenden oder nicht denken könnenden Leser voraus' (*Aufbau*, 11, 1025). Bodo Uhse chooses his words carefully in a report on the 4th German Writers' Congress: 'Sozialistischer Realismus [erfordert] hohe literarische Qualität, [bietet] Raum für die verschiedensten Ausdrucks-formen aller literarischen Gattungen' (*Aufbau*, 12, 101). Max Schroeder is able to defend the German theatre, without irony, as 'ein Musentempel, eine moralische Anstalt', declaring its relevance through its aesthetic and moral qualities, and ignoring attempts to depict contemporary life (*Aufbau*, 11, 1086), while Ernst Schumacher rehearses some of the arguments against proletarian writing from *Die Linkskurve* (with reference to Lukács's article 'Reportage oder Gestaltung'), showing that some of the issues are being seen as a problem again (*Aufbau*, 12, 223–34). Georg Maurer, in an essay on 'Deutsche Literatur der Gegenwart', attempts to rescue the idea of aesthetic experiment for Socialist Realism, gently rejecting as models for young poets both the classicism of Becher and the simplistic imitation of folk styles (*Aufbau*, 12, 197–218).

In passing, Maurer classifies Expressionism as a necessary transitional stage for modern poetry, rather than as a precursor of fascism (211). This theme is taken up again in a series of early sonnets by Becher (*Aufbau*, 12, 399–407), which include avant-garde works like 'Sonett der Schlacht' (404), presented without the usual editorial commentary, as if they are no longer seen as too dangerous to print.

This marks the opening of a period of 3 or 4 months in which the journal opens its pages to a more adventurous and diverse range of material, with an eye clearly on the events unfolding in Hungary. Lukács's speech to the Political Academy of the Hungarian Workers' Party from June 1956 is reprinted in the September issue: his open critique of Stalinism goes hand in hand with a restatement of his notions of quality. Stalin is held to be responsible for the failure of the Popular Front policy, and by extension, in the Lukácsian view of the world, for proletarian literature and the rejection of established literary forms

(*Aufbau*, 12, 761–76). The same issue contains important essays by Bloch (*Aufbau* 12, 809–14) and Benjamin (*Aufbau*, 12, 815–30) that explore the modernism of Brecht's *Lehrstücke* and poetry respectively, introducing a form of Marxist aesthetic criticism for which the journal had previously had no space. The November issue continues this process with Ehrenburg's essay 'Einige Aspekte der Kultur in der Sowjetunion', in which he calls for the opening up of cultural contacts between East and West (*Aufbau*, 12, 947–57).

Aesthetic matters show a new openness, too: an extract from Wolfgang Koeppen's *Der Tod in Rom* (*Aufbau*, 12, 871–90) accompanies a notice on a competition run by Andersch's journal *Texte und Zeichen* for new socially critical, realistic writing which 'auf eine Erweiterung der Möglichkeiten deutscher Sprache abzielen soll' (*Aufbau*, 12, 933). However, the most radical moment comes in the November issue, with a playful collection of short texts on the theme 'Sandfloh' by Kafka, Benn, Ernst Jünger, Hemingway and Mac Lehmann-Düsseldorf, entitled 'Thema mit Variationen' (*Aufbau*, 12, 1036–39). This moment of playfulness and interpretative freedom is unique in the journal's output, questioning both its early restorative earnestness and the canons of Socialist Realism.

The December 1956 issue sees the journal in full retreat after the crushing of the Hungarian uprising, and order is restored politically with an editorial describing the government of Imre Nagy as a counter-revolutionary putsch (*Aufbau*, 12, 1041). In the next issue, Lenin's letters to Gorky describing the role of literature in preventing Party splits (*Aufbau*, 13, 7–24) and Ernst Engelberg's critique of socialist writers who keep their distance from the Party are sufficient warning to artists who may have overstepped the mark (*Aufbau*, 13, 120–28).

Despite this, the aesthetic stance of the journal continues its questioning of Socialist Realist norms. The new appearance of the journal in January 1957 also seems to be a step away from the earnestness of its origins: the sober Roman capitals of the title page are replaced by a more casual, italic style, and the dark brown cover is set off with a red or yellow central section designed to look as if it was torn away to reveal the contents page. However, although the cover is markedly less formal, regular humorous and satirical features, such as the 'Glossen' section, vanish leaving the tone entirely serious. The explicitly political editorials also disappear.

The journal now aims to provoke a 'kritische Auseinandersetzung' with previously unacceptable writers, such as Erich Mühsam (*Aufbau*, 13, 447–53) or Baudelaire (*Aufbau*, 13, 503–11). Such pieces no longer work with the Lukácsian method of highly selective quotation, but tend to leave the reader space to interpret the texts. Similarly, Fritz Cremer calls for greater trust in artists' ability to use Marxism-Leninism in their work, rather than forcing them to imitate certain models (*Aufbau*, 13, 575), and Kurt Liebmann implicitly criticises both Socialist Realist dogma and Lukácsian realism in rejecting Engels's 'Miss Harkness Letter' 'als Standard-Definition des Realismus für alle Zeiten und alle Künste' (*Aufbau*, 13, 325).

At times, 1957 seems to be a year in which *Aufbau* remembers its 'bourgeois' origins: Rolf Schneider's piece on Hermann Hesse's 'humanistisches Ideal' ('das Unvergänglich-Machen des Vergänglichen') mentions Hauptmann, Kafka, Hofmannsthal and Rilke as positive aspects of the German literary inheritance (*Aufbau*, 13, 10), while Richard Christ praises Döblin's 'Realismus' and 'religiöser Humanismus' in language echoing the early issues of the journal (*Aufbau*, 13, 201–02). The October issue contains pieces on Arnold Zweig (*Aufbau*, 13, 350–60), Eluard and Aragon (*Aufbau*, 13, 361–82), Alberto Moravia (*Aufbau*, 13, 392–404) and Mörike (*Aufbau*, 13, 406–22), that stress aesthetics over political commitment. A contrast is provided by Georg Maurer's poem 'Poetische Betrachtung über die Weltraumfahrt' (*Aufbau*, 13, 568), that returns to modernist enthusiasm in its depiction of space travel destroying traditional structures and hierarchies. It remains a lone example in the last year of the journal's existence, and the only other sign of aesthetic adventurousness is the inclusion in February 1958 of Peter Hacks's television play *Die unadelige Gräfin* (*Aufbau*, 14, 185–209). Hacks's play is presented as a theatrical text, ensuring that a work for a new mass medium is seen as an extension of familiar traditions.

The 1957 SED *Kulturkonferenz* forms the basis of the contributions to the November issue, which restores the idea of the Party's leading role in cultural matters with a vengeance. Essays and declarations on the 40th anniversary of the October Revolution provide the opportunity (*Aufbau*, 13, 452–55 and 521–22), and the journal retreats once again from its critical aesthetic stance. Essays by Alfred Kurella (*Aufbau*, 14, 453–73) and Peter Goldammer (*Aufbau* 14, 540–53) restate in stark terms the most dogmatic interpretation of the Marxist basis-superstructure theory, rejecting any idea of a relatively independent aesthetic sphere.

The most significant gestures in the final issues of *Aufbau* are its treatment of the two figures who did more than most to set the journal's early tone: Becher and Lukács. Jószef Szigeti's speech condemning Lukács for his role in the short-lived Nagy government is reproduced in the May-June 1958 issue, signalling the journal's final rejection of one of its principal theorists once association with him had become politically dangerous (*Aufbau*, 14, 597–618). A month later, an essay by the Soviet cultural officer Alexander Dymschitz, 'Johannes R. Becher und der Sozialistische Realismus', attempts to rescue Becher from any hint of disloyalty or taint of association with Lukács: Becher is presented, rather desperately and unconvincingly, as a writer whose entire work flows from his 'Parteilichkeit', and who had always set himself against the notion of 'überparteiliche Literatur' (*Aufbau*, 14, 779–80). This is a final irony for a writer who had helped to set the tone of the early years of the journal's existence: having emerged from an impulse to combine restorative cultural thinking with a progressive antifascist politics, *Aufbau* can only be an anachronism in the changing world of the late 1950s.

Conclusion

The four journals that we have discussed in this section demonstrate the extent of the common ground between writers and intellectuals that cut across the increasing political polarisation of the late 1940s and 1950s. Indeed, when one opens *Merkur* or *Aufbau* to be confronted with another essay on Goethe, it can often seem that these individuals form a social class of their own with more in common with each other than with the majority cultures in East or West. The importance of both *Aufbau* and *Sinn und Form* is that they aspire to, and often succeed in representing interests across the boundaries drawn by the victorious powers, and therefore represent important challenges to the basis of SED rule, as well as proving uncomfortable for western attempts to present the Federal Republic as the sole legitimate inheritor of German traditions.

The institutional position occupied by *Merkur* is less problematic, since it can occupy the status of a prestigious cultural forum that West German culture offers it without constantly having to look across the *Zonengrenze* for allies: for all its pluralism and critical potential, it exists comfortably within the *Kulturbetrieb* of the Adenauer years without questioning its fundamental assumptions. Indeed, this is a critical potential deployed in order to re-inforce, rather than undermine conventional assumptions. Paeschke's stated aspiration to reflect the contemporary 'Polarisierung der Kräfte' as a 'Beitrag zur Korrektur des Zeitgeistes' demonstrates a tension between liberal tolerance and social commitment that *Merkur* solves by setting itself up as a protected, privileged space for a liberalism that, in the context of the Cold War, becomes a political end in itself. The short-lived radical period of *Der Ruf* under Andersch and Richter demonstrates the limits of this restorative liberalism under western conditions: a conservative publishing house requiring a flagship cultural journal is not prepared to support an enterprise critical of the highly profitable mass-marketing of the German classics. At the same time, we have shown that the entire *Ruf* project is cut through by a dependence on cognate assumptions, manifested most clearly, but not exclusively, by the prisoner-of-war version of the journal. That even a short-lived, 'thin' journal calling for radical change was ultimately shaped by the restorative mood of the times is persuasive evidence of the force of these shared assumptions.

The institutional position of all the journals we have discussed in this chapter affects profoundly their character, as well as their implied, desired and actual readerships. Nevertheless, the journals' shared assumptions point to a set of cultural pre-occupations that cannot be reduced to institutional factors: a discourse that was persistent enough to link the scattered exile communities seemed to have been granted an opportunity to put theoretical principles into practice. It is this aspiration to concrete political intervention that reveals the contradictions inherent in the restorative faith in tradition and supposedly objective 'Maße und Werte': are such values timeless and universal, or are they subject to change and questioning under changing social circumstances? This question is never clearly answered in any of the journals, but, within the limits implied by the phrasing of the question, all the journals are able to discuss and debate the key problems of post-war German culture. We can say that the limits set by the restorative cultural paradigm provide a common language for framing debate about National Socialism and German cultural values across political boundaries, but also suffer from an inability to question their own fundamental assumptions: when challenges to the terms of discussion arise (as in the Jaspers-Curtius controversy on Goethe) the tendency is to retreat into shocked defence of classical values rather than explore a new language.

The emotional force of restorative aesthetic categories stems ultimately from a sense of the precariousness of German cultural values in the face of National Socialism; the more one insists on the objective and universal validity of an aesthetic standpoint, the more fragile it seems. This can help us explain why there were few calls for radical cultural change and questioning, as opposed to *Erneuerung*, a term that implies the revivification of old values rather than the creation of new ones: there was too much at stake in individuals' need to salvage a sense of self uncorrupted by the experiences of the Nazi period. More concrete institutional and personal factors played a role, too: the case of *Merkur* shows how easy it was despite the catastrophe of 1945 to re-establish connections with a number of previous journals, absorbing impulses and contributors from *Die literarische Welt, Die Kolonne, Maß und Wert* and *Das innere Reich*. *Aufbau* attempts to occupy some of the same territory, though it has a clear political sense of who is to be excluded from the cultural forum, while the combination of *Sinn und Form*'s institutional position in the GDR with Peter Huchel's personal history and connections allows the journal to demonstrate that a restorative aesthetic stance need not imply a conservative politics.

After the capitulation of May 1945, it is hardly surprising that the journals share a language of crisis and rebirth, yet this language is always framed in terms that were defined in the cultural controversies of the late 1920s and early 1930s: in some respects, it is remarkable how little has changed, rather than how much. The notion of crisis is not formed anew in the aftermath of defeat, but is rather adapted to the new conditions, drawing on well-established ways of thinking: restorative cultural thinking in the mid-century has created a tradition of talking about the end of tradition. The experience of National Socialism can be interpreted in the light of this tradition, producing a clear model according to which a set of 'objective', classical values have been catastrophically undermined in the crisis-ridden modern world. What is new amongst many of the writers is an explicit sense of the social significance of these values: rather than being seen as a means of preserving cultural values in the face of politics, they are re-interpreted as a means of guaranteeing that politics is conducted in a humane, responsible manner. For left-wing writers, this did not require any great shift of gear, since the exile journals had developed a self-confident language linking aspects of the German tradition with theories of social action. For other writers, the aftermath of National Socialism did involve a profound revaluation of cherished assumptions in line with the post-war de-ideologisation of German conservatism; however, rather than entailing a critique of restorative thinking, what emerges is an optimistic restatement of such thinking as a social good in itself.

With a few exceptions, the self-critical language of writers in our journals has been developed beforehand, and it does not fundamentally challenge the assumptions of the restorative period. Once the onset of Cold War hostilities has begun to make new demands on culture, the meaning of restorative categories in East and West begins to diverge, although the language remains fundamentally the same. *Merkur* is essentially in tune with cultural trends in the West German 1950s, providing a critical alternative to the materialism of the *Wirtschaftswunder* years but always operating within limits set by the culture and unable to provide the radical impetus to social and cultural change that emerged at the end of that decade. *Aufbau* and *Sinn und Form* are both able to use their attachment to restorative cultural categories to provide both explicit and implicit critiques of the SED cultural line. The tendency of *Aufbau* to aspire to make its standpoint explicit for the reader leaves it vulnerable to the twists and turns of the official line, and its critical potential lies in its preservation at all costs of the values that it espoused at its foundation. What makes *Sinn und Form* so unusual in this period is the trust it places in the reader and the fact that it is radical in both the East and West German contexts: its openness and challenging non-dialectical confrontation of the reader with problems and contradictions was too much for the SED, and its progressivism and openness to voices from across the political divides was uncomfortable in a West Germany forming its identity around non-critical Cold War values.

Part Two: Authors

Gottfried Benn

In order to explore the complexity of Benn's position within the developing aesthetic discourse of the mid-century, we will explore a number of related themes in this section, beginning with an exploration of continuities in the reception of Benn's work from the mid-1920s to the late 1950s. We will then move on to a discussion of Benn's place within the shifting cultural ground in the later 1920s, before exploring in detail aspects of his narrative prose and lyric poetry. It is beyond the scope of this study to provide a comprehensive account of Benn's work; instead, we intend to read aspects of his work and its reception against the theoretical considerations that have been developed in the previous chapters, in order to locate Benn as a writer working both within and against the cultural preoccupations of his time.

Benn in the eyes of his contemporaries

Augustinus Dierick, in his study of critical accounts of Benn's work, shows that Benn scholarship was for a long time influenced for the worse by the post-war 'glorification' of Benn and by a 'critical approach which itself may have been inspired by less than scientific considerations' and that tended to ignore anything that clashed with the view of the poet as a strict follower of Nietzschean *Artistenmetaphysik*.[1] Benn scholarship has long recovered from this post-war phase, and by reading the reception of Benn's work against the categories that we have developed in the course of this study, we are able to identify this reception as influenced by a 'restorative' view of Benn.[2] We need to qualify this by noting that,

---

1 Augustinus P. Dierick, *Gottfried Benn and his Critics: Major interpretations 1912–1992* (Columbia: Camden House, 1992), p. 2.

2 There are still remnants of the influence of the restorative paradigm in the editorial practice of the *Stuttgarter Ausgabe* of Benn's works, which is structured around the apolitical, ahistorical image of Benn that emerges from the 1956 *Gesammelte Gedichte*: Gottfried Benn, *Sämtliche Werke*, ed. by Gerhard Schuster (Stuttgart: Klett–Cotta 1986). Bruno Hillebrand's *Gesammelte Werke in der Fassung der Erstdrucke* is an edition that provides a corrective to this image long after it has been questioned and demolished by scholars from the 1960s onwards. As the edition that makes clear the chronological progression of Benn's work, as well as using textual versions that reflect the

at least at first glance, the reception of Benn's work in the late 1920s and early 1930s, in other words, in the period during which the restorative paradigm is developing, is quite different from that which developed after 1945. However, as we shall see, there are continuities in this reception that indicate the tenacity of ways of thinking about culture that bridge the catastrophe of 1945.

Since the publication of the *Morgue* poems in 1912, Benn was often referred to by commentators as the 'representative voice' of his generation.[3] He is seen as the writer who has taken to the furthest extreme the attitudes and preoccupations of Expressionism. Although Benn's work is referred to throughout his career as an example of quality in the face of a literary industry that produces 'Mache, Kunstgewerbe oder Gelall', a shift in the reception begins to set in the mid-1920s.[4] Whereas Benn had previously been positioned as a 'representative' writer, commentators begin to refer to Benn's 'Isoliertheit', stressing his distance from, or superiority to, the literary and political scene of the time.[5] The irony here is that the image of Benn as the isolated outsider begins to crystallise at the very moment that his work begins to exert an important influence on a new generation of writers: the more commentators insist on Benn's status as an outsider, the more he is transformed into the iconic figure who comes to stand for a whole complex of cultural-political ideas.

In the mid-1920s, reactions to Benn's work are still focused on his poetry. Oskar Loerke, whose name is mentioned in connection with Benn as a key influence on a new generation of poets, points to a reception of the poetry which is beginning to take on restorative categories. This is the way in which Benn would exert an influence on the *Kolonne* writers. In a review of the collection *Spaltung* in 1926, Loerke makes some criticisms of Benn's modernist eclecticism that point forward to the impending conservative turn, arguing that the broadening of poetic language to include 'antipoetische Gefühlskomplexe' may turn out to be a dead end: 'Kann die Verbreiterung nicht eines Tages als Verengerung erscheinen?'[6]

As we shall see in the section on Benn's poetry below, *Spaltung* did in fact represent a moment of change in Benn's approach to poetry, after which he begins to develop a style that we can identify as influencing the restorative

---

time of their composition, rather than the *Fassung letzter Hand,* we will be referring to Hillebrand's edition throughout this section: Gottfried Benn, *Gesammelte Werke in der Fassung der Erstdrucke,* ed. by Bruno Hillebrand, 4 vols (Frankfurt a.M.: Fischer, 1982).

3   For a full account of the reception of Benn's early work, see Dierick, pp. 3–28, and Hugh Ridley, *Gottfried Benn: Ein Schriftsteller zwischen Erneuerung und Reaktion* (Opladen: Westdeutscher Verlag, 1990), pp. 36–43.

4   Max Herrmann-Neiße, 'Gottfried Benn', *Der Kritiker,* 7 (1925), 70–72, in Bruno Hillebrand (ed.), *Über Gottfried Benn: Kritische Stimmen 1912–1956* (Frankfurt a.M.: Fischer, 1987), pp. 35–39 (p. 35).

5   Carl Einstein, review of Benn's *Gesammelte Gedichte, Die neue Rundschau,* 38 (1927), 446–48, in Hillebrand, pp. 41–45 (p. 41).

6   Oskar Loerke, review of *Spaltung, Berliner Börsen-Courier,* 21 February 1926, p. 4, in Hillebrand, pp. 39–41 (pp. 40–41).

aesthetic paradigm. Reviews of the poetry now tend to stress Benn's place within the tradition, as well as the purity of his language and attitude to form. Carl Einstein stresses Benn's inwardness, isolation and aestheticism, as well as the importance of form as a means of bonding together disparate 'Zeichen'.[7] Employing key restorative terms such as 'Gestaltung' and 'Reinheit' to describe a poetic attitude that overcomes the chaos of modernity, Hermann Kasack shows in exemplary fashion how Benn's change in direction was taken up and interpreted according to the needs of the day. Benn is seen (along with Loerke) as a model for a modern poetry that reconnects with the tradition of Goethe, Heine, Rilke and George, not through the imitation of discredited bourgeois models, but through the 'schöpferische[n] Geist deutscher Sprache'. His work is characterised by a totality that is the sign of the true 'Dichter', who is able to counter the 'Zerstreuungen der Welt' through 'Gestaltung'.[8] In an interpretation influenced by the structure of the 1927 Schmiede edition of the *Gesammelte Prosa* and *Gesammelte Gedichte*, which identifies new poems from 1926 as the culmination of his literary development, Benn's work is presented as a meaningful unity, in which contradictions and tensions are explained away with reference to a 'gleich-bleibende Mittelachse', around which his literary production revolves.[9]

This quieter, less ideological reception is soon overshadowed by the polarised and politicised debates that break out over the figure of Benn in the late 1920s; however, it is worth noting that this view of Benn had a significant influence on poetic practice (as opposed to *kulturkritisch* theory) in the period from the late 1920s. Equally importantly, the 'restorative' reception of Benn that we have just discussed sets the terms for the discussion of his work after 1945, once the highly politicised reception of his essays has been thoroughly discredited. Commentators have a pre-existing body of work on Benn, to which they can refer, enabling them to place him within a critical tradition that allows his political engagement to be dismissed as an aberration.

In the heated political atmosphere of the later Weimar years, Benn begins to take on a symbolic value as an authority representing an antidemocratic, radically conservative and *kulturkritisch* stance. This is partly his own doing (for example through the publication of cultural-political essays and participation in public controversies with left-wing writers) and partly an image that is built up through the desires of others. He is positioned as a figure who integrates a range of ideas that often seem contradictory: for example, the image of the apolitical artist is combined with an ideologised revolutionary conservatism that is often talked about in aesthetic terms, and a long view of culture stretching back to mythical origins is employed as a weapon in political debate. Erich Franzen uses Benn as

---

7   Einstein, in Hillebrand, p. 45.
8   Hermann Kasack, 'Gottfried Benns Lyrik', *Die Horen*, 4 (1928), 905–09, in Hillebrand, pp. 47–49.
9   Hermann Kasack, 'Notizen zu Gottfried Benns *Gesammelter Prosa*', *DAW*, 5.35, 5–6, in Hillebrand, pp. 62–65 (p. 63).

an authority for his own conservative *Kulturkritik* by discussing political matters in aesthetic terms recognisable as preoccupations of the restorative cultural turn. In this view, Benn stands for an aesthetic practice that overcomes the era of 'Sachlichkeit' in favour of 'mythische Verbundenheit' and rejects superficiality and irony for deeper connections.[10] Such statements function as barely concealed code for a rejection of the Republic and its institutions.

The controversy over Max Herrmann-Neiße's piece on Benn in *Die Neue Bücherschau* in July 1929 is a point at which the political polarisation of the later Weimar years intersects with the developing critical reception of Benn's work. It is worth here looking more closely at the essay that formed the pretext for the resignation of Becher and Kisch, in order to see how it situates itself in the 'restorative' reception of Benn that we have set out above. Far from being a call for writers to stay aloof from politics, the essay in fact proposes Benn as a superior model for a political writing that is closer to the essence of the age, allowing the writer to intervene more effectively. As had Hermann Kasack, Herrmann-Neiße is concerned to present Benn's work as a unity, but it is notable here that his focus on the prose writing leads inevitably to an emphasis on Benn as a committed writer rather than as an aesthete. The prose works, from the Rönne stories to the most recent essays, are seen as a 'vollkommene sinnvolle Einheit', a common rhetorical device in restorative interpretations of writers' work, referring back to the nineteenth-century tradition of Goethe scholarship and the notion of *Bildung*.[11] Yet this is no simple conservatism, and is very different from Max Rychner's view of Benn in 1932, as a writer who has returned to the tradition of Goethe after wandering in the nihilist wilderness, and has consequently overcome the ugliness of his earlier work in favour of the 'Gesetz der Form'.[12] Instead, Herrmann-Neiße employs the vocabulary of 'conservative revolutionary' thought, stressing that Benn is a political writer, though far above the parties, and that, far from being one of the herd of bourgeois 'Kultur-gläubigen', his work is 'durchweht von einem erfrischend kräftigen, kämpfer-ischen Winde' and is radically antisentimental, 'ein Naturereignis, vor dem Empfindsames wie Plunder fällt'.[13] Just as with the world-view of the communist Left, we can see such statements as an attempt to overcome aspects of the restorative response to cultural crisis, in other words, as an attempt to reject the era's conservative spirit.

The Nazi seizure of power and Benn's public defence of the regime brought about little that was new in interpretations of Benn's work; instead, there is a

---

10 Erich Franzen, review of Benn's *Gesammelte Prosa*, *Berliner Börsen-Kurier*, 18 April 1929, p. 7, in Hillebrand, pp. 59–61 (p. 59 and p. 61).

11 Max Herrmann-Neiße, 'Gottfried Benns Prosa', *Die neue Bücherschau*, 7 (1929), 376–80, in Hillebrand, pp. 67–74 (p. 68).

12 Max Rychner, 'Nach dem Nihilismus', *Kölnische Zeitung*, 29 November 1932, in Hillebrand, pp. 93–99.

13 Herrmann-Neiße, p. 73, p. 68 and p. 74.

hardening of certain positions and a shift in the political camps representing the common desire of bourgeois and socialist writers to defend the 'cultural inheritance' against the Nazis. Responses from the antifascist camp begin to stress the inevitable connection between the rejection of the inheritance and fascism, despite the fact that Benn's poetry and essays from the mid-1920s had attempted an idiosyncratic rapprochement with the tradition. Erich Heller and Klaus Mann both make the connection between bad style and bad thought: Heller reads Benn's 'Antwort an die literarischen Emigranten' as 'Unzucht gegen die Sprache', whereas Mann considers that Benn has begun to write badly now that he has put his pen at the service of the NSDAP.[14] Mann refers to the republication of Benn's 1932 essay 'Goethe und die Naturwissenschaften' in the 1933 collection *Der neue Staat und die Intellektuellen* to be a 'Niedertracht' against Goethe that perverts the essay's original significance.[15]

Criticism of Benn's 'perversion' of the tradition also characterises contributions to the 'Expressionism Debate' in the pages of *Das Wort*. We have discussed this debate in more detail in the section on the journal itself, but it is worth noting some of the terms in which Benn's work is discussed. Klaus Mann's contribution is characterised by his outraged humanism, and rests on the conviction that Benn is mistaken in assuming that National Socialism is driven by a will to form; it is 'Formlosigkeit' incarnate, whereas humanism and a concern for aesthetic form go hand-in-hand: 'Als ob ein ernsthafter Wille zur Form ohne den Willen zum Humanismus […] überhaupt vorstellbar wäre!' This conflation of questions of aesthetics with political questions is of course meat and drink for the protagonists of Socialist Realism, but it is also a characteristic of bourgeois and liberal thinking in this period, and is an attitude that crosses political boundaries. Mann is determined to rescue the notion of the 'purity' of lyric poetry in opposition to the political sphere, and he is able to state that fascist themes 'niemals in [Benns] eigentliches Werk eingedrungen sind'.[16] This critical strategy is necessary, since Benn's poetry does display a pronounced 'Wille zur Form' in this period, which Mann has explicitly associated with humanism; thus, a space is left for the poet that Mann admires to restore his tarnished reputation. The more dogmatic contributions to the debate, such as the essay by 'Bernhard Ziegler' (Alfred Kurella), ignore this aspect, assuming that literary production is inherently political, and being satisfied with literal readings of surface meaning rather than examining form, tone of voice and irony.[17]

14 Erich Heller, 'Gottfried Benns Hordenzauber', *Die neue Weltbühne*, 2 (1933), 688–91, in Hillebrand, pp. 101–04 (p. 104).

15 Klaus Mann, 'Gottfried Benn. Oder: Die Entwürdigung des Geistes', *Die Sammlung*, 1 (1933), 49–50, in Hillebrand, pp. 113–16 (p. 115).

16 Klaus Mann, 'Gottfried Benn: Die Geschichte einer Verirrung', *Wort*, 2.9, 35–42, in Hillebrand, pp. 142–52 (p. 147, p. 150 and p. 144).

17 Alfred Kurella, 'Nun ist dies Erbe zuende', *Wort*, 2.9, 42–49.

Mann's assumption that the formal properties of the poetry somehow resist appropriation by the 'formlessness' of National Socialism represents one of the strands of Benn reception that were to emerge again after 1945. Another is the argument that Benn has remained true to the spirit of Expressionism while his contemporaries have betrayed its legacy. Once again, Benn's shaping of his own image as the keeper of the Expressionist flame is important here, but we should note what an 'unmodernist' Expressionism his admirers praise him for. Oskar Schlemmer's letter to Benn from 1933, which was published after Benn's death, chimed in perfectly with the 1950s reception of Benn's work: Schlemmer sees the original energy of Expressionism as having been transformed through the political experiences of the 1920s into a preoccupation with 'Ordnung, Strenge und Gesetz' and an aestheticist attitude.[18]

There is no *Nullpunkt* in Benn reception: despite the long gap punctuated only by Benn's appearance in the 'Expressionism Debate', the terms in which Benn is seen are not transformed. Fundamental concepts remain the same, but they are rhetorically detached from the discourses of politics and history. In other words, what had been close to conservative revolutionary thought effortlessly becomes an attitude of abstract, formalist hermetic modernism. As we shall show in the section on Benn's poetry, this attitude does not in itself adequately represent Benn's literary practice after 1945.

There are few commentaries on Benn's work before the publication of *Statische Gedichte* in Switzerland in 1948, but those that do appear suggest that Benn was able to survive in his inner emigration through his truth to his own 'Wille zur Form'.[19] Frank Maraun gives a standard picture of Benn as a heroic Nietzschean nihilist, 'von Eiseskälte der Abstraktion umweht, auf der Zinne des Abendlandes'. Maraun claims that this attitude was, ultimately, what saved Benn from the Nazis, although he also attempts to save Benn's integrity by proposing that he defended the regime for positive reasons, connected with his 'künstlerische Vision': 'Ein starkes, kühnes Geschlecht, dem Hedonismus, der Gestaltlosigkeit, dem Mittelmaße des modernen Massendaseins entrissen, zum Opfer erzogen, zur Form gehärtet, zur Größe gewillt.' The Nazi leadership was simply 'geistig nicht auf der Höhe', and was unable to fulfil Benn's ambition.[20] Maraun's essay, dubious though it is, does illustrate how the *kulturkritisch* sentiments of the 1920s and 1930s are now simply transplanted into an implied critique of post-war Germany, and are pitched at an extraordinary level of abstraction. Benn is here used as an exemplary figure who is 'unerlaubt' both in

---

18   Oskar Schlemmer, letter to Benn, 22 October 1933, in Oskar Schlemmer, *Briefe und Tagebücher*, ed. by Tut Schlemmer (Munich: Langen-Müller, 1958), pp. 315–17.

19   Carl Werckshagen, 'Gottfried Benn 60 Jahre', *Schleswig-Holsteinische Volkszeitung*, 27 April 1946, p. 5, in Hillebrand, pp. 164–66.

20   Frank Maraun, 'Ein unerlaubter Autor', *Schwäbisches Tagblatt*, 28 October 1947, p. 3, in Hillebrand, pp. 166–70 (p. 166 and p. 168).

the Third Reich and post-war Germany, allowing the extremity of the Nazi period to be smoothed over in a general condemnation of a cultureless modernity.

The abstraction of this critical language continues to be a feature of the reception of Benn's literary 'comeback' after 1948, and his image in the 1950s is based almost exclusively on the reception of *Statische Gedichte*, even after the publication of later collections such as *Fragmente* (1951) and *Destillationen* (1953). *Statische Gedichte* is seen as the culmination of Benn's development as a writer from Expressionism to a form of classicism, and it is rare to find his new poetry from the 1950s discussed with anything like the same intensity: as we shall see in the section on Benn's poetry, much of the poetry that he produced in the 1950s was highly inconvenient for the image that Benn's admirers had created.

Statische Gedichte is referred to and received as 'neue Lyrik', a somewhat misleading term for a collection that contains poems written over the preceding two decades, and which smoothes over the breaks and discontinuities in Benn's development.[21] This is in a sense inevitable, since the collection is presented non-chronologically, and appears as a reassertion of Benn's presence in German literary life. The critical reception inevitably contrasts this most 'restorative' of Benn's collections with his earlier work, which is found wanting. Alfred Andersch sees in the poems a sign that Benn has overcome his earlier stylistic radicalism and has subsumed all the conflicting ingredients in perfect formal structures. On those few occasions where the form seems 'zersprungen', this is a sign that the content itself is 'fragwürdig'.[22] There is some disagreement over whether Benn should be seen as an 'Überwinder des Expressionismus' or as the 'Vollendung des Expressionismus'; in a sense, this is a distinction without a difference, since the critics tend to mean the same thing, namely that Benn's career has culminated in a static, classicistic approach to form as a timeless, Nietzschean defence against chaos and nihilism.[23]

Despite the emphasis on timelessness and similarity with the aesthetics of Abstract Expressionism – what Friedrich Sieburg calls a 'Kunst der Beziehungs-losigkeit', despite Benn's extraordinary sensitivity to the nuances of contemporary language – there is a general acceptance that the poems are defences against or rejections of the modern world.[24] Georg Rudolf Lind traces Benn's aestheticist abstraction back to the 'Zusammenbruch der Gesellschaftsordnung' before 1933, suggesting that Benn's turn to Nietzschean *Artistik* has been a consistent

---

21 Alfred Andersch, review of *Statische Gedichte*, *Die neue Woche*, 20 November 1948, p. 11, in Hillebrand, pp. 170–71 (p. 170).
22 Andersch, p. 171.
23 Kurt Leonhard, 'Der letzte Expressionist: Zu den Büchern Gottfried Benns', *Württembergische Abendzeitung*, 1 October 1949, p. 5, in Hillebrand, pp. 192–94 (p. 193); Frank Maraun, 'Mythische Welt: Neue Lyrik von Gottfried Benn', *Schwäbisches Tagblatt*, 12 January 1949, p. 4, in Hillebrand, pp. 200–02 (p. 202).
24 Friedrich Sieburg, 'Wer allein ist–', *Die Gegenwart*, 4.4 (1949), 22, in Hillebrand, pp. 205–07 (p. 206).

response to crisis ever since.[25] Other writers share this position, but try to rescue Benn for a traditional humanism that his poems and prose from the post-war years (such as *Der Ptolemäer*), resist strongly: Helmuth de Haas claims to spot in Benn's work 'die Horizonte einer späten, neuen Christlichkeit' that can overcome the 'zeitgenössische Aporie', while Frank Maraun uses the language of 'Geist' overcoming crisis: 'Der Geist wagt sich in die Mitte der Katastrophe, und er behauptet die menschliche Position.'[26]

The reverence shown towards *Statische Gedichte* is so pervasive that critics react harshly towards signs that this treasured image of Benn may not be adequate. Frank Thieß objects to the publication of Benn's *Frühe Lyrik und Dramen* in 1953, since these texts are 'literaturgeschichtliche Monstrositäten und Dokumente einer krisenhaften historischen Situation'.[27] Few critics are as harsh as this, since they tend to be of a generation that grew up with and admired Benn's earlier work, but as we have seen, their interpretations are not determined by responses to this work, but to the formal strictness of the poetry from the later 1920s and 1930s. It is rare for critics who base their case for Benn on *Statische Gedichte* to take note of the later collections in any consistent way: *Statische Gedichte* are seen as the pinnacle of Benn's achievement. Karl Krolow's piece on *Destillationen* (1953) shows how Benn's work from the 1950s could be a disturbing anomaly for the view of Benn that we have been discussing here: while praising some of the collection, Krolow identifies and criticises sharply Benn's montage techniques and his critique of the restorative cultural atmosphere of the 1950s, while interpreting Benn's irony as 'Fehlkonstruktionen'.[28]

The dominant view of Benn in the late 1940s and 1950s is countered by a few voices that acknowledge his later work as a development beyond *Statische Gedichte* and as an attempt to engage with the modern world. Karl Korn discusses Benn's later prose pieces as pure Expressionism: 'Stilistisch ist Benn der Alte geblieben, der Ekstatiker, der Expressionist.' As we shall see, this assessment does not do justice to the later prose, but it shows that Korn is attempting to construct a tradition for Benn that acknowledges and values his aesthetic radicalism at a time when critics were trying to downplay it. Korn also acknowledges Benn's sensitivity to the world around him (he is a 'Seismograph') and his engagement with the crisis-ridden post-war world: 'Benn macht mit der umfassenden Kulturkrise ernst, radikal ernst. Er deckt nichts mit billigen, restaurativen Phrasen

25 Georg Rudolf Lind, 'Gottfried Benn, der große Provokateur', *Europa-Kurier*, 1.51 (1949), 4, in Hillebrand, pp. 195–200 (p. 198).
26 Helmuth de Haas, 'Kommunikation oder Monologe?', *Rheinischer Merkur*, 18 June 1949, in Hillebrand, pp. 182–86 (pp. 184–85); Frank Maraun, 'Der Geist in der Katastrophe', *Schwäbisches Tagblatt*, 18 January 1950, p. 6, in Hillebrand, pp. 220–23 (p. 223).
27 Frank Thieß, 'Anatomielyrik', *Neue literarische Welt*, 25 April 1953, p. 12, in Hillebrand, pp. 246–48 (p. 247).
28 Karl Krolow, 'Subtilität und Plattitüde: Gottfried Benn, *Destillationen*', *Die neue Zeitung*, 27/28 June 1953, p. 19, in Hillebrand, pp. 244–46 (p. 246).

zu.'[29] Albrecht Fabri, writing in 1956, points forward to a new way of thinking about Benn that values aspects of his work that challenge the critical consensus: instead of seeking out texts that can be considered 'schön' and passing over others in silence, he acknowledges the formal modernity of Benn's style in the 1950s and the 'Schwierigkeit, das Gedicht rein als solches zu erkennen'. Fabri stresses the montage of registers in these poems ('halb tödlicher Ernst und halb sich selbst genießender Bluff') and a seemingly informal, *parlando* style ('Lyrik gewissermaßen mit den Händen in den Taschen').[30] In his polemical attack on 'restorative' critical attitudes to Benn, Gottfried Willems suggests that *Statische Gedichte* was in many ways a dead end, whereas Benn's later work exerted a largely unacknowledged influence on the 'Neue Lyrik' of the 1960s.[31]

However, such attitudes were rare in the 1950s, since the critical consensus was built almost exclusively on a particular interpretation of *Statische Gedichte* that saw Benn as representing a self-contained chapter in the history of modernism. Even at his death in January 1956, a critic like Kurt Pinthus could create a shape for Benn's career that proceeded from Expressionism to 'absolute Kunst'.[32] In the following sections we will explore the development of Benn's style in lyric poetry and prose narrative, in order to show how his work intersects with, influences and then distances itself from the restorative aesthetic discourse of the mid-century.

Benn's Poetry

The early poetry

The shocking brutality and detachment of the *Morgue* poems (1912) was what fixated Benn's contemporaries, who were stunned by the seemingly crude naturalism of the descriptions as well as by the absence of a voice which offered the humanist consolations of pity or outrage. This challenge, with its ultra-modern *Sachlichkeit*, to the horizon of expectations of a readership schooled on Aestheticism and Neo-Romantic styles was designed to signal 'reality' within the literary-aesthetic discourse of the time; yet a critical preoccupation with the poems' 'realism' does not completely do justice to their linguistic virtuosity. By

---

29 Karl Korn, review of *Der Ptolemäer*, *Allgemeine Zeitung*, 14/15 May 1949, in Hillebrand, pp. 186–89 (pp. 187–88).
30 Albrecht Fabri, 'Rede für Gottfried Benn', *Variationen: Essays* (Wiesbaden: Limes Verlag, 1959), pp. 119–33, in Hillebrand, pp. 256–67 (p. 259 and p. 261).
31 Gottfried Willems, *Großstadt- und Bewußtseinspoesie: Über Realismus in der modernen Lyrik, insbesondere im lyrischen Spätwerk Gottfried Benns und in der deutschen Lyrik seit 1965* (Tübingen: Niemeyer, 1981).
32 Kurt Pinthus, 'Von der *Morgue* zur "Trunkenen Flut": Zum Tode Gottfried Benns', *Aufbau* (New York), 22.29 (1956), 6–8, in Hillebrand, pp. 277–79 (p. 277).

assessing the problem which Benn poses in *Morgue*, we can go on to show how his poetic strategies in the 1920s develop from a layered, ironising montage towards an attempt to establish a voice which is internally consistent and suitable as a vehicle for 'truths'.

The extreme detachment of the voice that speaks in the famous opening poem, 'Kleine Aster', causes considerable problems of interpretation: it is not the voice of an individual existing in passive, detached contemplation, which would imply an aestheticist unity of voice, form and content, but is instead carrying out a series of practical, active techniques. The disjunction between an active, intervening physical activity and an almost casually observing instance produces a situation where the 'ich' in the text is fatally split. After the careful description of the opening up of the cadaver the speaker employs a casual modal verb in his account of how the flower ends up in the brain:

> Als ich von der Brust aus
> unter der Haut
> mit einem langen Messer
> Zunge und Gaumen herausschnitt,
> muß ich sie angestoßen haben, denn sie glitt
> in das nebenliegende Gehirn. (GB, 1, 21)

We can read this in several ways, either as an attempt on the part of the speaker to deny responsibility, or as an attempt to shrug it off, or as a sign of the absolute disconnection between hand and brain that such repetitive techniques bring about. However, the observing instance does not simply recount events in the text's carefully constructed conversational style, but shapes the text, giving it an inner formal coherence that is not apparent at first sight. After the matter-of-fact opening, which is closed off by the rhyming pair 'gestemmt/geklemmt', the description of the incision is a masterpiece of rhythmic balance, centring on the rhyme 'herausschnitt/glitt' which puts an irregular emphasis on the word 'muß'. The poem's form raises the question of why such a detached observer should be so careful to shape the description of an autopsy in such a way; it seems that pleasure is taken in imposing an aesthetic form on a prosaic subject. This reading suggests that Benn is not simply exploiting the subject-matter as a way of undermining traditional poetic modes, but is also suggesting that the observing instance – the alienated 'ich' of the poem – shapes its own response to its actions not according to patterns which are 'revealed' from within the material itself, but instead are determined by its own psychological needs. The poem's rhythmic and rhyming patterns throw a disruptive emphasis on the one verb which does not fit the matter-of-fact recounting of actions – 'muß ich sie angestoßen haben' – indicating its centrality to understanding the alienated consciousness of the observer. Yet, as we have seen, it is ambiguous and distanced, refusing definitive interpretation.

The mock-sentimental close simply emphasises the feeling of alienation: a traditional language which is used to establish a final, emotional connection with a loved one in the face of the unbearable reality of death is here employed for the opposite effect. Thus, 'Kleine Aster' demolishes at a stroke much of the poet's traditional linguistic armoury for making emotional, intuitive connections between poetic voice, reader and world; tracing Benn's later career involves exploring his attempts to deal with this problem, whether through an avant-gardist recreation of language or, as in the later 1920s, a tentative rapprochement with the tradition.

The second poem, 'Schöne Jugend', also works by defamiliarising the language of sentiment in its (literal and metaphorical) hollowing-out of the popular image of Ophelia. The word 'so' in the opening lines implies an emotional response that the rest of the poem denies:

Der Mund eines Mädchens, das lange im Schilf gelegen hatte,
sah so angeknabbert aus.
Als man die Brust aufbrach, war die Speiseröhre so löcherig. (GB, 1, 22)

However, the emotion seems to consist in admiration for the thorough work of the rats, and the delighted, childlike tone of voice satirises sentimental images of beauty in death. A traditional language of *Einfühlung* is hollowed out in the same way that the corpse is hollowed out by the rats.

We can perhaps say that the opening poems of *Morgue* represent – despite the sickening imagery of other poems such as 'Mann und Frau gehn durch die Krebsbaracke' – the last time that Benn presented so starkly the gulf between physical body and detached, observing instance. Later texts attempt to 'solve' this problem in some way, by locating the body and the personality within various kinds of cultural discourse, so that it becomes a linguistic construction.

'Nachtcafé' (1912) illustrates a tension between a desire to convey pre-linguistic, epiphanic experiences, and a concern with language as the medium of that experience and as the raw material of art. The observer's alienated consciousness has driven detailed, naturalistic observation to such an extreme that individuals are reduced to their skin complaints, or even further, to words representing skin complaints. The particular syndromes – goitres, conjunctivitis, barber's itch – suggest a world in which dirt lurks beneath the surface of civilised life. The consoling power of art is dismissed in a series of clichés: the power of the arch-Romantics Chopin and Schumann to bring about direct emotional connections between artist and audience is debunked. Thus, both close, 'realistic' observation and Romantic subjectivism are no longer able to bridge the gulf between alienated self and observable world.

Instead, the sudden flood of experience at the poem's close arises from a physiological process, in which layers of emotion are stripped away from the bare material of the brain. Traditional ways of expressing emotion have been exposed as fraudulent, and what is left is a series of fragmentary associations with distant, 'primitive' experience triggered by a physical process:

Die Tür fließt hin: Ein Weib:
Wüste. Ausgedörrt. Kanaanitisch braun.
Keusch. Höhlenreich. Ein Duft kommt mit. Kaum Duft.
Es ist nur eine süße Vorwölbung der Luft
gegen mein Gehirn. (GB, 1, 29)

Yet the attempt to convey a fundamental, pre-linguistic experience relies on language of the utmost sophistication: the construction of the last sentence mirrors in sound and rhythm the process it describes, the gentle but slightly disruptive forward impetus of the unusual word 'Vorwölbung' ending at the dull alliteration of the final words. Benn's early poetry gains its power from such paradoxes and from the awareness that the sophistication of human language has distanced Western humans from original, authentic experience, leaving only a vague longing for something lost.

Poems like 'D-Zug', 'Englisches Café', 'Das Plakat' or 'Kur-Konzert' expose the longings that echo in the debased language of bourgeois experience, particularly in inarticulate responses to art or in the commercialised language of tourism. The exhausted travellers in 'D-Zug', returning from the summer season on the Baltic, are tormented by intimations of experience that they are too far removed from. These poems juxtapose a variety of discourses, not only in order to undermine them satirically, but also to expose the inarticulate longings that they disguise.

Sometimes, Benn's early poetry implies that these longings are simply a function of modernity and of the deep associations with which certain words and ideas are laden at this late stage in European history. The important cycle *Alaska*, from 1913, seems at first glance to be a case of Expressionist primitivism, but Benn's linguistic ultra-sensitivity means that no word is stable and no meaning can be taken for granted. The poems in *Alaska* are games with the language of primitivism, *Rollengedichte* depicting Western voices in their imagined encounter with the primitive other. We therefore need to be careful when approaching the often-cited poems entitled 'Gesänge', which contain the lines:

Oh, dass wir unsre Ur-ur-ahnen wären.
Ein Klümpchen Schleim in einem warmen Moor.
Leben und Tod, Befruchten und Gebären
Glitte aus unseren stummen Säften vor. (GB, 1, 47)

Since voices in the cycle are often characterised as singing, these lines should be understood as operating within the structure of the cycle, rather than as an expression of an authorial voice. The language expresses the impossibility of return, rather than the potential fulfilment of a longing, and the poems, as with the complete cycle, are concerned with the secret longings hidden within the structures of a bourgeois modernity whose language is utterly alienated from the origins of human experience.

Benn explores a striking variety of methods in these works, discarding them when they seem to have failed. For example, the overripe sonority of 'Karyatide' (GB, 1, 81) sits alongside the disrupted stanza form of 'O, Nacht' (GB, 1, 85), both from 1916, or the attempt to revive the success of *Morgue* in the 1917 *Fleisch* cycle (GB, 1, 90–93). The overflowing assonance of the final lines of 'Karyatide' draws attention to its own constructedness, supporting an image which reflects the poem's theme of the tension in classical culture between self-conscious formal perfection and Dionysian dissolution. The poem is conceived as an instruction (clearly never to be fulfilled) to the caryatid to burst its boundaries and dissolve itself, and by implication, the culture that has been built upon it, all for the sake of a final moment of excess and fulfilment:

[…] tagen
Sieh' diese letzte Glück-Lügenstunde
Unserer Südlichkeit,
Hochgewölbt.

However, the absurd excess of these lines is a demonstration of their own artificiality, playing on the rich associations of the word 'südlich': for Benn, it is not the ideas that words 'stand for' that have associations, but the words themselves as physical, sensuous phenomena laden down with an unbearable weight of mythical association that modern culture denies at its peril.

The radical poetry of the early 1920s works with a hollowing out of traditional poetic forms and a montage technique which brings together a mass of mythical and historical references in a harsh, ironic tone. The montage is here less the political device of the Dadaists than a tool for analysing the state of modern consciousness, which consists in a jumble of mythical associations – what he calls 'Geröll im Traum' (GB, 1, 125) – which has lost the explanatory framework of nineteenth-century rationalism, and which is held together only by a meaningless formal structure and a contemporary, cold irony. The tone of poems like 'Schwer' (1922) or 'Prolog 1920' suggests a state of *posthistoire* in which there is no development, whether progressive or regressive:

Schädelstätten
Begriffsmanie
Kein Zeitwort zu retten
Noch Historie (GB, 1, 144).

The language of modern Western humanity is too ironic and distanced to do anything but gesture helplessly at inarticulate longings:

Wo ist das große Nichts der Tiere?
Giraffe, halkyonisch, Känguruh,
Du, du bist in Arkadien geboren,
Mein Beutelhase, grunz mir zu! (GB, 1, 131)

This vision of a language which has become the instrument by which modern Europeans have cut themselves off from their origins undergoes a development in Benn's work in the 1920s. His earlier attempts to access originary states through a radicalisation of language begin to give way to an approach to form and language which states the problem, rather than expressing or reflecting it, an admission of the limitations of aesthetic radicalism. The *sprachkritisch* radicalism of the earlier work is giving way to an ideological critique of the contemporary world, and Benn's posture of poetic isolation is rather belied by the fact that his work is sited within the developing radical conservative critique of Weimar modernity. The poem 'Wer bist du', from 1924, contains a key statement of the relationship of modernity to the past:

> Was ist, sind hohle Leichen,
> Die Wand aus Tang und Stein,
> Was scheint, ist ewiges Zeichen
> Und spielt die Tiefe rein. (GB, 1, 158)

The paradoxical interplay of ideas of depth and surface here illustrates Benn's developing conception of the tradition and of the emptiness of contemporary culture. More complex than ideas which contrast the 'shallowness' of modernity with the 'depth' of mythic experience, Benn's approach sees language as a series of signs which are laden with associations. This view implies two possible directions for further literary exploration, once the Expressionist impulse to re-establish the severed connections between word and past experience has receded: either he develops an approach to form and language which enables him to *talk about* modernity and its discontents, or he employs an appropriately modern montage technique as a way of *mirroring* modern consciousness. Benn's poetry, which had existed in a state of tension between these two possibilities, begins in the mid-1920s to move in the direction of the first, whereas his prose narratives re-attain in the 1930s some of the modernist radicalism that the second possibility implies.

The strict three stress line that becomes characteristic of Benn's poetry in the mid-1920s, for example in the short cycle *Betäubung* (1925), is in marked contrast to earlier poems, which showed either a virtuosic fluidity or the staccato rhythms of Benn's montage technique. Benn's formal scheme begins to tighten, giving a feeling of order, stillness and a declamatory 'objectivity' which strives to avoid development or ambiguity. However, the formal preoccupations are not first and foremost intended as a gesture of reconciliation with the reader or with the tradition; instead, the form acts as a straightjacket on the desire for dissolution and release:

> Spürt man nicht im Haupte
> manchmal Lücken feil,
> etwa als belaubte
> sich ein tiefer Teil,
> oder eine Wallung
> eine Woge weit
> von Systementballung

durch Unendlichkeit?

ist es Traum des Kranken:
ewig Grenzenlos,
sind es Zwangsgedanken,
ist der Zwang doch groß. ('Grenzenlos', GB, 1, 164).

Here, form is set against content in an icy stalemate that rules out all dialectic or development. The conflict is made clear in the dual meaning suggested by the capitalisation of 'Grenzenlos', i.e., the incompatibility of the idea 'grenzenlos' with 'Grenzen' as a 'Los', or destiny, imposed on the mind.

However, the voice of the *Betäubung* cycle is not the only one found in Benn's work in this period. Other poems, such as those that appeared in the 1925 collection *Spaltung*, begin to work with familiar tropes of human alienation from nature, prefiguring the 'restorative' attitude of poets from, say, the *Kolonne* Circle, whose attempted rapprochement with the language of nature poetry is undercut by an awareness of the gulf between language and world that had been opened up in modernism. For example, 'Schleierkraut' (GB, 1, 181) works with an alliterative lyricism mimicking in a very direct way the 'rauschen' of the gypsophila (chosen for the associations of its German name and its Mediterranean habitat) and the poem's theme of the distance ('Schleier') between speaker and nature.

The tension in these poems between the temptations of Romanticism and a distancing *Sachlichkeit* that emphasises the way in which such longings are constructed in language is perhaps best illustrated in 'Einzelheiten' (1925). The simplicity of the diction in the last stanza is in stark contrast with the avant-gardist complexity of Benn's earlier nature imagery, suggesting a desire to establish a stability of reference between language and object; the intrusive *Fremdwort* in the final line disrupts and estranges the mood, which is full of a sense of loss and intimation. However, while it dispels the mood it does not contradict the ideas implied in the imagery, but rather confirms them, stripping away the sense of Romantic ambiguity by giving it an explanatory, 'scientific' name:

der Abend kam mit Schatten,
er, der den Sommer verlor,
die Sträuße der Rosen hatten
einen Schleier von Tränen vor,
man trennte sich bei Zeiten,
als ahnte man Schweres schon:
es waren Einzelheiten,
nicht Totalisation. (GB, 1, 174)

The poems published after the *Spaltung* collection, especially those that appeared for the first time in the 1927 *Gesammelte Gedichte*, continue these developments in Benn's work, and help to establish part of what we have identified as the restorative mood in lyric poetry: they provide an authoritative set of references and techniques for a younger generation of writers trying to find ways of responding to the sense of impending cultural crisis.

This developing tone is exemplified in a poem like 'Stunden, Ströme' (1926), which achieves an elegiac tone with echoes of both Trakl and Hölderlin:

> dunkle Zeichen, alle voll Vergehn,
> einem Kusse, Augen, welche glänzen,
> fährt man eine Nacht nach, über Grenzen –
> fremde Sterne über fremde Höhn,
>
> doch dahinter stumm und aufgebrochen
> liegt das Reich, wo es zusammenrinnt,
> dunkle Meere, Sonnendiadochen,
> welche Himmel, die so tödlich sind. (GB, 1, 188)

This poem seems to be an attempt to rebuild a bridge to the tradition, while still acknowledging that that tradition has been disrupted in such a way that it can no longer offer absolute security of meaning. Whereas Benn's earlier poetry often suggested that longings for presumed past unities were simply a characteristic of the structure of European modernity, 'Stunden, Ströme' proposes that the fragmentariness of the modern world is a result of its alienation from an earlier state of grace, here described using imagery influenced by Hölderlin's similar concerns. The concern with the 'unreadability' of the world ('dunkle Zeichen'), providing a link between Trakl's nature lyrics and the poetry of the *naturmagische Schule*, suggests that language has lost its power, truth and ability to contain and communicate meaning now that it is cut off from its source. This idea represents a step back in the radicalism of Benn's thinking about language: the longing for origins ('das Reich, wo es zusammenrinnt') is now conceived as an intimation of a genuinely lost state. Benn's poems create a feeling that traditional forms have 'come alive' for him again after the icy stillness of *Betäubung*, that they have an ability to convey meaning through their connection with the tradition.

The sarcastic, cabaret-style montage technique of the 1927 poem 'Qui sait' (GB, 1, 201), that *reflects* in its form the fragmentary nature of modernity and its loss of direction, begins to give way to a style exemplified by, say, 'Sieh die Sterne, die Fänge' (GB, 1, 204), written in the same year, which uses a balanced stanza form to give stability to its poetic voice:

> wenn du die Mythen und Worte
> entleert hast, sollst du gehn,
> eine neue Götterkohorte
> wirst du nicht mehr sehn.

Even here, though, it is notable that the compound 'Götterkohorte' adds a slightly ironic edge to the tone of the poem, suggesting that, although Western humanity has exhausted the resources of its culture, none of this really matters.

Poems such as this, which present the development of European culture as a progressive emptying out of language as humanity moves further from its origins, contrast with others from the same year which suggest, as does 'Trunkene Flut' (GB, 1, 205–06), that original experiences can be recaptured through a ritualistic engagement with imagery that combines Christian and classical elements.

Formally speaking, 'Trunkene Flut' imitates its central image in its rhythm in a way which is unusually literal for Benn, suggesting a unity of form and content that is expressive rather than the form being a means of stabilising a statement. However, although there is a sense of tension between these two sets of ideas, Benn has purged his lyric style of almost all of the contradictions and linguistic destructiveness, as well as the social satire, of earlier works: we are, however, left with poetry that bears the marks of the extremity of Benn's early style, whether in the irony of the slightly misplaced word 'Kohorte' in 'Sieh die Sterne, die Fänge' or in the games with the language of myth and primitivism in 'Die hyperämischen Reiche', from 1928 (GB, 1, 213). The poems at this vital stage in Benn's career – just before the key essayistic statements of 1930 – hedge their bets in certain ways between declaring whether Benn's cultural preoccupations are simply a matter of a language which has come to its end, or whether the language of aesthetics does allow access to extra-linguistic truths.

'Die hyperämischen Reiche' suggests that there is an unchanging, eternal truth beyond individual existence and beyond the linguistic clichés that arise from an individual human perspective:

Dasein: die Küsse zerblättern,
Tränen: die Salze vergehn,
Leben, Sterben – Lettern,
die für alles stehn:
doch über Wahn und Weichen
steht das Immer und Nie
aus hyperämischen Reichen,
deren Verkünder Sie.

In contrast, 'Du mußt dir Alles geben' (GB, 1, 215–16), employing an identical stanza form and tone of voice, instructs the poet that all experience and association arises purely from inner processes:

Du mußt dir Alles geben,
Götter geben dir nicht,
gib dir das leise Verschweben
unter Rosen und Licht,
was je an Himmeln blaute,
gib dich in seinen Bann,
höre die letzten Laute
schweigend an.

Such tensions are submerged under a style which emphasises melody and formal harmony as a means of establishing unity and security. The poems have also gained a sense of history as process (in this case, a classic conservative attitude imagining a process of decline and loss) contrasting with Benn's earlier tendency to see history as a senseless jumble of image and association. In other words, the movement of history has been recreated as something meaningful: the poet reassembles the pieces into a new narrative.

A poem like 'Primäre Tage' (1930) works with these ideas, showing how the poet is able to recapture a sense of the echo of original unities resonating down the ages, occasionally overwhelming the alienated modern consciousness. Nevertheless, the poem shows that this is a tentative process, which is only offered in moments when the world is suffused with a particular quality of light, 'das rückwärts reicht und alte Dinge liebt' (GB, 1, 219). This emphasis on the rarity of such experiences, and the delicacy of the poet's task in reconstructing them, contrasts with the strident tone of some of the essays in this period and the political polemics in which Benn was engaged; yet they belong to the same ideological world, in which the raw material of history and language, which had been subjected to a radical critique, is reassembled into a cultural narrative of decline and loss. Such neo-conservative narratives, even as they lament the emptiness of contemporary experience, construct a set of meanings around the coordinates of their narrative that belie any claims to ideological neutrality.

We ought, however, to guard against a critical attitude which privileges *Ideologiekritik* when reading Benn's poetry in this period. Of course, we do not mean by this a return to that critical tradition which takes seriously Benn's stylisation of his own work in 1951 as 'absolut' and 'ohne Glauben und Lehre' (GB, 3, 529). By contrast, it is important to take as a starting point Hugh Ridley's statement that Benn's work 'nicht als Widerspruch – geschweige denn als Widerstand – gegen die Zeit verstanden werden darf'.[33] However, it would be wrong to assume that 'ideology' can be seen here as something pre-existing that is 'reflected' in Benn's writing, and that one can trace 'ideological' stances in his essays directly through to their more abstract expression in the poetry. We have already seen how contradictory Benn's poetry is in the late 1920s, and such a directly ideological reading would tend to explain away or ignore these contradictions.

The poetry of the late 1920s and early 1930s represents a series of attempts to solve aesthetic problems connected with the radicalism of Benn's earlier works, to reassemble a cultural narrative and set of formal principles that re-admit meaning and take back the extremity of Benn's avant-gardist *Sprachkritik*. In line with our comments on the nature of 'restorative' cultural discourse, we can read Benn's ideological preoccupations as attempts to solve deeply felt aesthetic problems, rather than as the expression of a momentary naivety in which aesthetics is 'put at the service' of ideology.

---

33 Ridley, p. 94.

The Nazi period and after

Benn's short-lived attempt to find solutions in some of the discourses associated with 'conservative revolutionary' thought and National Socialism had a profound effect on his poetry, even though he avoided any direct propaganda in his work. His claims that the poetry was above ideology are somewhat hollow, as we have seen, yet their response to contemporary intellectual currents is complex and ambiguous. Hugh Ridley has discussed Benn's 'massive Unempfindlichkeit gegenüber dem Jargon der Nationalsozialisten', and we can see the way that some of the Nazis' terminology creeps into the poetry as a way of grounding it.[34] It seems to us that if one can read the references to 'Sieg' and 'Reich' in 'Einsamer nie' (1936) (GB, 1, 281) as oblique criticism of Nazi nature mysticism, and therefore as an expression of an inner emigrant stance with analogies to that in the prose text *Weinhaus Wolf*, then it would be obtuse *not* to read poems from 1933 like 'Ein Land' (GB, 1, 241) or 'Dennoch die Schwerter halten' (GB, 1, 245) as reliant, at least in part, on a discourse of elitist intellectual fascism. The potential of the later poems as critiques gains strength precisely from the feeling of self-criticism that they exhibit. Nevertheless, the self-criticism, as in the prose works, remains oblique, and is expressed as a critique of the world around the poet rather than of the poet's own person.

Benn manages the transition from a supportive to a critical stance, by contrast to his prose works, seemingly without any upheaval in his lyrical production. This seems to be because he felt no need to question any of the fundamentals of the attitude to cultural history that he had developed by 1930: the sense that European culture has come to an end, having distanced itself so far from its origins that its supply of images has been drained dry. If we trace poems that express this view through the 1930s, we can see how Benn's position shifts depending on his political stance.

'Ein Land' expresses the view that the origins of human culture are irrecoverable:

Ein Land, ein dunkles Meer,
und dann ein Reich, das endet
so fern, daß nie sich wendet
ein Strahl hier her.

These lines echo 'Die hyperämischen Reiche', which had at least allowed the poet fragmentary moments of connection with the cultural past; here, though, the lifeline to the past has been cut. The extremity of this gesture serves only to prepare the ground for the rather casual gesture of renewal at the poem's end, namely the approach of the new powers:

---

34 Ridley, p. 94.

Auf Sänften und auf Truhn,
da lagern die Gestalten,
die Schweigenden, die Alten
und künden –: ruhn.

Die nur durch Tränen sahn
das tägliche Vernichten,
doch auch die Frei'n, die Lichten:
sie spähn, sie nahn.

The verb tense here suggests that this is happening now, in other words, that the old gods are about to depart. Similarly, the poet's attitude is striking: previously, Benn's poetic voice had identified itself strongly with the decaying European tradition, implying that he will go down with the sinking ship, since that is the tradition that formed his voice and the symbols through which he understands the world. Here, though, the voice stands above the departing gods, able to observe their fall and the arrival of the new powers.

This poem, published in the October 1933 issue of *Die Literatur*, contrasts strongly with poems exploring similar themes but composed only a year or so later. 'Träume, Träume' (GB, 1, 260–61) also explores time as a sense of increasing distance from origins:

Stunden, Stunden – die Gebilde weichen,
letzte Lösungen der Ursubstanz.

It is only in 'dreams' that the old images are summoned up again, but even then they eventually fade away:

Räume, Räume, Räume die verdammen,
Stunden, Stunden, da das Letzte weicht,
Träume, Träume rufen sie zusammen,
bis das Nichts auch diese Bilder bleicht.

Here, Benn has returned to his familiar attitude, presenting himself as the voice of a culture at the extremity of decay and decline. In political terms, it is clear that Benn is able to reject the attitudes of National Socialism by reinterpreting fascism as part of the modernity that he had always rejected. Yet Benn's poetry now takes on an austerity which seems to show a suspicion of the richness of the language he develops in the later 1920s, particularly where nature poetry is concerned. Where the avant-gardist Benn had begun to find his way back to aspects of the tradition in a search for a cultural narrative and a firmer foundation for his language, this connection has become problematic again. However, instead of returning to the radical *Sprachkritik* of his earlier work, he develops to an extreme his philosophy of *Statik*, setting up *Geist* and *Leben*, *Statik* and *Dynamik* as opposite poles: 'Die *Verwandlung* ist das Gesetz des Lebens, die *Erstarrung*, d.h. die Formwerdung das Gesetz des Geistes.'[35]

---

35 Letter to F.W. Oelze, 28 July 1936, in Gottfried Benn, *Briefe an F. W. Oelze 1932–1945*, ed. by Harald Steinhagen and Jürgen Schröder (Wiesbaden: Limes Verlag, 1977), p. 135.

A series of poems from 1936, which appeared for the first time in the *Ausgewählte Gedichte* of that year, deals with aspects of the literary tradition in a way that registers the shock of Benn's engagement with the language of National Socialism. 'Wer allein ist' (GB, 1, 277) portrays the poet as a figure standing apart from the dynamism of change:

> Ohne Rührung sieht er, wie die Erde
> eine andere wird, als ihm begann,
> nicht mehr Stirb und nicht mehr Werde:
> formstill sieht ihn die Vollendung an.

In setting his face against the Goethean 'Stirb und Werde', Benn rejects central concepts of the German cultural tradition, in which the individual is imagined as developing in a dynamic interrelationship with the changing environment in a perpetual process of self-reflection and rebirth. Similarly, as Mark Roche has indicated, the description of the poet as 'denkerisch erfüllt und aufgespart' subtracts one term from the Hegelian triad of *Aufhebung*, omitting the sense of forward movement that is the key to the dialectic.[36] This absolute rejection of the tenets of German philosophy and the bourgeois ideals of *Bildung* is part of a perverse attempt to conflate the Nazi emphasis on dynamism and evolution (which Benn had praised only a few years earlier) with all the aspects of German modernity that Benn rejected.

Other poems from this series reflect Benn's ambivalence towards the tradition in different ways, although the consistent tone and formal properties of the poems impose an illusory unity. 'Einsamer nie', with its suspicion of the language of nature poetry and its construction of an opposition between the realm of nature and the realm of *Geist*, occupies the same territory as the story *Weinhaus Wolf*:

> Die Seen hell, die Himmel weich,
> die Äcker rein und glänzen leise,
> doch wo sind Sieg und Siegsbeweise
> aus dem von dir vertretenen Reich?
>
> Wo alles sich durch Glück beweist
> und tauscht den Blick und tauscht die Ringe
> im Weingeruch, im Rausch der Dinge, –:
> dienst du dem Gegenglück, dem Geist. (GB, 1, 281)

The poem is about the language of nature as a discourse of fulfilment and presence, and the poem implicitly conflates this traditional language with the concerns of National Socialism; *Geist* is then in opposition to all this, the self-conscious, analytical attitude which defends itself through the abstract concerns of form above all else. National Socialism is here simply a part of that tradition that Benn rejects, and no distinction is made between a traditionalist attitude to

---

36 See Mark William Roche, *Gottfried Benn's Static Poetry* (Chapel Hill: University of North Carolina Press, 1991), p. 17.

culture and a fascist one. However, 'Anemone' (GB, 1, 275), although also clearly
a poem demonstrating a critical attitude, bases its critique of the contemporary
world on a form of Romantic nostalgia, with a nature image embodying a
connection to a lost paradise:

Erschütterer –: Anemone,
die Erde ist kalt, ist Nichts,
da murmelt deine Krone
ein Wort des Glaubens, des Lichts.

Der Erde ohne Güte,
der nur die Macht gerät,
ward leise deine Blüte
so schweigend hingesät.

Erschütterer –: Anemone,
du trägst den Glauben, das Licht,
den einst der Sommer als Krone
aus großen Blüten flicht.

The unexpected present tense of the verb in the last line even holds out the
possibility of return and renewal. 'Anemone' lacks the questioning attitude of
'Einsamer nie' towards the language of nature, and instead assumes a stability in
the relationship between the nature image and the thought that it stands for. A
nature image is here placed in opposition to 'Macht', whereas in 'Einsamer nie',
nature imagery was associated with it.

Thus, rather than being the purely monological, inward texts that they are
often seen as, Benn's poetry during the 1930s, whatever his attitude to the
prevailing political climate, places itself in dialogue with the tradition itself. It is in
this sense, rather than in any explicit attempt to communicate with the reader,
that the poetry is 'political', exploring and reflecting the points of connection and
conflict between Benn's practice, National Socialism and the restorative cultural
climate of the time.

The years between the publication of the *Ausgewählte Gedichte* in 1936 and the
collection of poems distributed privately in 1943 under the title *Zweiundzwanzig
Gedichte* do not mark a break in Benn's poetic activity (although he completed
only 3 texts in the bleak year 1937), but there is a marked shift in some of his
poetic concerns between these two dates. Although there are works in both
collections that we can consider as examples of an inner emigrant attitude, the
later poems point forward to Benn's post-war style in their gradual de-
ideologisation of the approach to myth, their rejection of an attitude that sees the
poet as achieving some deep connection with long-term cultural processes, and
their concentration on the poem as a place where the 'ich' encounters itself in
moments of painful truthfulness.

The poems of this period cannot be reduced to a single message on the role
of art, but instead examine the question from different angles, often contradicting
each other. Three poems from 1941 illustrate this approach: where 'Verse' (GB,

1, 299) proposes a form of collective function for the poem, 'Du trägst' (GB, 1, 303) reduces the function of language for the poet to a means of self-knowledge with no potential for communication:

> Du kannst dein Wesen keinem nennen,
> verschlossen jedem Bund und Brauch,
> du kannst dich nur im Wort erkennen
> und geben dich und trauern auch.

However, 'Gedichte' suggests that the poem is the only place in which the crises of the world can be confronted:

> die Dinge dringen kalt in die Gesichte
> und reißen sich der alten Bindung fort,
> es gibt nur ein Begegnen: im Gedichte
> die Dinge mystisch bannen durch das Wort. (GB, 1, 300)

This is a conception of the poem as a verbal artefact that registers and absorbs the phenomena of the world, the word 'bannen' revealing an ambiguity between 'enchant/fascinate' and 'ward off/exorcise'. Despite the use of the word 'mystisch' here, the poem no longer reveals a desire for 'redemption' of the fragmented world in a moment of connection between the poetic self and the movement of history, which was the key to Benn's ideologised avant-gardism in the early 1930s. Nevertheless, it seems to be an opposed conception to that expressed in 'Du trägst', suggesting that what 'Gedichte' defines as a 'Selbstgespräch des Leides und der Nacht' is in fact structured around images received from the external world. This had been the conception of the self that had arisen in many of the earlier montage poems, namely that inner life takes place within a cultural network of images and allusions, and is thus far removed from the traditional German concept of *Innerlichkeit*.

The contradictory, searching nature of these poems is summarised in lines from the 1943 poem 'Verlorenes Ich' (GB, 1, 309–10), a poem that laments the loss of a centre of faith that could give meaning and security: 'du möchtest dir ein Stichwort borgen –, | allein bei wem?' The post-war reception of Benn's work that orientated itself on the collection *Statische Gedichte* tended to overlook such contradictions, as well as ignoring the implication in poems like 'Gedichte' that the poet can, or even must, engage in an intensely personal way with the phenomena of the world. Written in 1943/44, the poem 'Statische Gedichte' itself, although seeming to summarise and give shape to the collection that bears its name, should thus not be seen as a final statement about Benn's work, or even as an adequate summary of the poetry of the 1930s and early 1940s.

The poem develops an aesthetic stance that suggests that the artist creates a reality in a way analogous to the rules of perspective, where a composition constructed carefully around a single point (in this case, the viewpoint of the artist) gives an illusion of space and fullness:

Perspektivismus
ist ein anderes Wort für seine Statik:
Linien anlegen,
sie weiterführen
nach Rankengesetz. (GB, 1, 323)

The notion that the artist's extreme subjectivity creates a world with its own laws, and that there is no other viewpoint from which to judge the world takes to an extreme a Nietzschean perspectivism, and this, combined with an attitude of quietism, helped create the post-war image of Benn the aesthetic purist that proved so convenient in the restorative atmosphere of the late 1940s and 1950s. But as we have seen, even as a summary of Benn's work during the 1940s, 'Statische Gedichte' is inadequate, despite the prominence it was given as title poem of the collection through which he reintroduced himself to the German public. Indeed, the attitude hinted at in 'Gedichte' is far more productive for Benn during the 1950s, in the renewed sense of poetic purpose that he demonstrated during these years.

Poems from 1943 and 1944, such as 'St. Petersburg – Mitte des Jahrhunderts' (GB, 1, 318–20) and '1886' (GB, 1, 324–26), which first appeared in *Roman des Phänotyp*, point to a desire to contextualise the poetic personality in a more concrete way than had been the case in the past. The poet is no longer seen as the prophet of the imminent downfall of a culture, but is simply located in time: the *kulturkritisch* and nostalgic sentiments are often still present, but they have lost some of the ideological urgency of Benn's work in the 1920s. Far from limiting Benn's poetic possibilities, however, this reigning in of ambition seems to liberate him, allowing him greater leeway to explore the nature of consciousness in the modern world and to critique the restorative cultural atmosphere of the time.

The 1950 poem 'Künstlermoral' (GB, 1, 378) has all the appearance of a poetic programme:

Nur in Worten darfst du dich zeigen,
die klar in Formen stehn,
sein Menschliches muss verschweigen,
wer so mit Qualen versehn.

Yet Benn's poetic practice in these years – particularly in the renewed formal freedom of his work – often belies such statements, as well as the image of the cold, formal modernist that proved so attractive in the 1950s. His re-engagement with the world in the poetry of the 1950s has been documented elsewhere, and so we will concentrate on those aspects of Benn's later work that deal with his attitude towards the restorative cultural climate of the time.[37]

Although Benn hints in 1946 that it is still – just – possible to 'diesmal noch das tiefe Wort erneu'n' ('Du liegst und schweigst und träumst der Stunde nach',

---

37 See, in particular, Willems.

GB, 1, 351), the post-war poems tend instead to deny the possibility of a 'depth' of experience through reconnection with the culture. All that is left are rare moments of clarity amongst the ruins, such as in 'Destille', from 1953:

> Ich will mich nicht erwähnen,
> doch fällt mir manchmal ein
> zwischen Fässern und Hähnen
> eine Art von Kunstverein.
>
> Die haben etwas errichtet,
> eine Aula mit Schalmei,
> da wird gespielt und gedichtet,
> was längst vorbei.
>
> Ich lasse mich zerfallen,
> ich bleibe dem Ende nah,
> dann steht zwischen Trümmern und Ballen
> eine tiefe Stunde da. (GB, 1, 430)

Clearly the term 'tief' here describes a very different kind of experience to the restorative emphasis on cultural depth: the verb 'dastehen' is strangely prosaic, and the poem seems in some ways to be an ironised response to much earlier works like 'O Nacht', substituting alcoholic dissolution for the cocaine-fuelled vision. The implication that alcohol offers a more authentic experience than the 'Kunstverein' and that the modern personality must accept and mirror the (real and metaphorical) ruins around it if it is to experience anything genuine, is a provocative commentary on contemporary culture, and on the reverence shown towards the classics.

In 'Fragmente', written in 1950 (GB, 1, 379), Benn demolishes the idea of *Persönlichkeit*, continuing his habit of attacking the fundamental concepts of the cultural discourse of the time:

> Ausdruckskrisen und Anfälle von Erotik:
> das ist der Mensch von heute,
> das Innere ein Vakuum,
> die Kontinuität der Persönlichkeit
> wird gewährt von den Anzügen,
> die bei gutem Stoff zehn Jahre halten.
>
> Der Rest Fragmente,
> halbe Laute,
> Melodienansätze aus Nachbarhäusern,
> Negerspirituals
> oder Ave Marias.

The idea that the personality is a combination of external influences and associations ('Melodienansätze aus Nachbarhäusern') is here combined with a standard contrast of the 'primitive' with the 'Western', though without the sense of impending disaster that often accompanied such images in defences of the *Abendland*. Instead, Benn quietly registers the clash of cultures in post-war

Germany, acknowledging without regret that the music brought by the American occupiers, with its distant connection to 'primitive' Africa, has become a constituent part of the modern personality.

If we place a well-known poem from 1950, 'Satzbau' (GB, 1, 370), in this context, we can see that it is more than just a defence of an aestheticist *Artistik* in the vein of 'Statische Gedichte', but is a direct rejection of the clichés of literary conservatism:

> Alle haben den Himmel, die Liebe und das Grab,
> damit wollen wir uns nicht befassen,
> das ist für den Kulturkreis besprochen und durchdacht.

An ironic pun deflates self-important notions of the Western *Kulturkreis* (a Spenglerian language that Benn himself had used) by conjuring up a bourgeois cultural circle where the classics are discussed and 'gepflegt' over coffee. The poem rejects such Romantic-religious notions as irrelevant in favour of the question of form as the problem of the moment: 'er wird vorübergehn, | aber heute ist der Satzbau | das Primäre'. However, the poem itself shows no sign of following its own prescription: 'auf Kosten des Inhalts ein formaler Priapismus.' Instead, it is written in Benn's deliberately casual, conversational style of the period, and conveys a message that is clear, though hedged with irony. The mock reference to Goethe as an authority at the end of the poem completes the picture of a provocative hollowing out of the literary preoccupations of the time.

In these later poems, there are unexpected echoes of the techniques Benn employed at the very beginning of his career, taking the literary discourse of the time and 'hollowing it out' from within by attacking the concepts and clichés upon which it is built. Whereas in the later 1920s and 1930s Benn looked to the tradition and to discourses beyond aesthetics in order to stabilise his language, from the mid-1940s onwards Benn's poetry regains its self-confidence, again becoming a space in which he can engage with and dissect the values of the culture in which he works.

Prose Narrative

Radicalism and restoration

A key text in Benn's prose output is the extraordinary piece *Weinhaus Wolf*, which he began in 1936 in a mood of increasing pessimism. Later, he was to talk of the text as an attempt, 'eine zweifellose Methode, Stil zu machen und Kunst d.h. Wirklichkeit (Kunst = Herstellung von Wirklichkeit) zu fabrizieren', using 'an

Gegenstände und Figuren herangeknetete Gedanken'.[38] His self-critical remarks are of great interest here, since the text does represent in some ways the culmination of a period in which Benn's prose narrative writing had moved away from the radicalism of the early novellas and had been searching for a more stable, essayistic voice. Characteristically, Benn refuses to return to the traditional narrative forms of realism, as so many others were doing, but instead attempts to construct within his texts a voice that can make authoritative statements and judgements about the various political and cultural discourses that he criticises. His narrator's criticism of Nazi nature mysticism is a case in point:

> Aus mir spricht die Zersetzung, wurde mir öfter erwidert. Nein, antwortete ich [...], aus mir spricht der abendländische Geist, der ist allerdings die Zersetzung des Lebens und der Natur, ihre Zersetzung und ihre Neusetzung aus menschlichem Gesetz [...] Wie denn, sagten meine Gegenüber, also doch. Sie wollen die Natur zersetzen, das ist die Höhe! Unser aller Blut und Boden? Ihre Natur, mußte ich erwidern, ist sie denn natürlich? Kann man von ihr ausgehen? (GB, 2, 141)

The narrator's sarcastic dismissal of his opponents' misunderstanding is indicative of the avant-gardist Benn's critique of what we have established as restorative attitudes to nature, namely, its re-establishment as an 'objective' foundation for literary and cultural discourse (an *a priori*, 'von dem man ausgehen kann'). Benn addresses his criticisms here explicitly towards Nazi thinking, but his words indicate a refusal to accept that the term 'Natur' has any meaning beyond discourse; in other words, the concept of 'nature' as a pre-linguistic realm is simply a discursive construct of what Benn terms the 'abendländischen Geist' itself.

Benn's stubborn negative radicalism in *Weinhaus Wolf* puts him at odds with much of the cultural thinking of the 1930s. However, he is forced to deal with these ideas in his work, and in doing so, he is influenced by them, most clearly in his approach to narrative form and the construction of a 'truth-telling' voice. If we compare the narrative situation of the text with scenes from his early novellas, we can see how much has changed and, most importantly, can assess the significance of late-1920s cultural shifts for Benn's prose narratives.

Weinhaus Wolf begins with the construction of a narrative voice through the re-telling of a personal history and the establishment of context and character, in order to provide a psychological motivation for the individual's radical ques-tioning of the values of the community. The 'Rönne novellas' from the mid-1910s provide the reader with no such comforting refuge in the generic markers of realism, but instead question radically the notions of character and motivation. Similarly, Rönne's experience of dissolution is often set side by side with attempts to join conversations in cafés, and to slip into the public role-playing which defines 'character' in bourgeois society, whereas the first-person narrator in *Weinhaus Wolf* is fully conscious of his self-imposed inner exile, and he sits

---

38 Letter to Oelze, 22 December 1943, in Benn, *Briefe an Oelze*, p. 349.

pointedly aside in that most bourgeois of institutions, the *Weinlokal*, composing mini-essays in reaction to what he hears around him. In each case, the narrative situation is at times comparable, but the voice that emerges is radically different.

To illustrate this changing attitude to narrative, we will trace Benn's developing approach from his early novellas to the mid-1930s, exploring the ways in which the shifting cultural atmosphere of the 1920s finds echoes in narrative technique.

The 'Rönne' stories explore the linguistic and narrative crisis of modernism, occupying in their narrative form an ambivalent space between the impossible, hollow conventions of realism and the sense of something new, but indescribable. Even the protagonist's name, as a subjunctive form of 'rinnen', suggests a personality perpetually at the point of dissolution. The stories depict a point where Western culture is seen as collapsing under the weight of its own history, where language is no longer able to function since rational discourse has produced nothing but a feeling of exhaustion; individual words have little positive content except as points where a vast and crippling series of cultural associations and references meet and conflict.

The narration allows the reader no illusion of objectivity: the distance between Rönne's subjectivity and the narrating voice is unstable, not as a form of modernist 'unreliable narrator', but as a way of illustrating the collapse of humanist notions of subjectivity themselves. As Rönne puts it in *Die Insel*: 'Die Konkurrenz zwischen den Associationen, das ist das letzte Ich' (GB, 2, 58). This is more than the Romantic procedure implied by Klaus-Dieter Bergner's interpretation of the nature imagery in these stories as 'Umschreibung des inneren Zustandes seiner Hauptfigur'.[39] In fact, it is in many ways an explicitly anti-Romantic notion. Benn's language illustrates the collapse of the illusion of 'personality' and the discourse of bourgeois cultural certainty in a series of epiphanies which Rönne undergoes, triggered not so much by the physical experience of nature (the stories deny such a direct, Romantic connection with the external world) but by the overwhelming associations which words and images bring with them, and which traditional language has tried to tame.

Unlike some of the Expressionists, attracted by the idea of primitivism, Benn is well aware that a return to pre-linguistic states is an impossibility for modern humans: his work documents an attempt to explore the point at which the language of Western culture begins to turn in on itself. Benn's linguistic ultra-sensitivity leaves him well aware of the paradox in the attempt to depict the collapse of language in language of the utmost aesthetic sophistication; his stories and poetry from this period revel in this paradox, and in the knowledge that the

---

39   Klaus-Dieter Bergner, *Natur und Technik in der Literatur des frühen Expressionismus: Dargestellt an ausgewählten Prosabeispielen von Alfred Döblin, Gottfried Benn und Carl Einstein* (Frankfurt a.M.: Lang, 1998), p. 154.

physical sensations which certain words produce are as much the product of centuries of acculturation as of the physiological processes which he documents.

The 'Rönne' stories do not advertise their historical context, although *Die Eroberung* explores in a somewhat tasteless way metaphors of conquest and colonisation as a means of talking about Rönne's attempt to find a role in the *Gemeinschaft* he finds himself in. However, the story *Diesterweg*, from 1918, announces itself as a commentary on the state of the personality after three years of war, seen through the eyes of a doctor whose vain attempts to occupy social spaces fail because of his awareness of the precarious nature of the 'personality'. The notions of 'character' which underlay bourgeois cultural and scientific practice are no longer tenable, reduced to the status of the grotesque linguistic or physical clichés that Diesterweg imitates in his comic attempts to count as a 'Persönlichkeit' (GB, 2, 69). Reason has brought humanity to the edge of nihilism, and its only consolation is the preservation of *form*. Playing on ideas of social form (as in the expression 'Form bewahren'), to which the clear contours of the humanist idea of personality have been reduced, Benn presents late bourgeois culture as a set of aesthetic gestures intended to preserve form in the face of chaos. Diesterweg himself has no personality, he has a function within this system. He represents the moment at which the system becomes self-aware and turns in on itself: 'Da war der Mensch, der sich zu schaffen trachtete, der sich in Formen trieb in Ängsten vor dem All, da war die Menschheit, die das Bewußtsein trug, doch nie erlitten hatte – und da war er, dem dies geschehn. Er hatte es erlitten, er erlebt' (GB, 2, 75). Yet despite his privileged position as recipient of this self-reflexive consciousness, Diesterweg is simply an individualised expression of a general principle, and he vanishes at the end of the story: 'Der Abend nahm ihn auf und verschlang das Diesterwegsche' (GB, 2, 76).

The texts which follow *Diesterweg* in the late 1910s and early 1920s consolidate Benn's essayistic narrative style and develop a voice which strives for the expression of certainty. If we compare the Rönne story from 1923, *Alexanderzüge mittels Wallungen*, with the earlier cycle, it becomes clear how the radicalism of Benn's style has developed into a series of politicised, and often rather empty gestures. The story's title picks up on images which go back to *Die Eroberung*, namely, the depiction of the individual's attempts to define his social space as a form of invasion, settlement or conquest. Yet instead of the delicacy, ambivalence and uncertainty which the earlier stories had displayed, the narrative of *Alexanderzüge* works with sarcastic commentary rather than disorientating irony.

This story represents a critical evaluation of Benn's earlier style, not without its moments of nostalgia, but characterised by an awareness that the changed political atmosphere excludes the forms of experience which the earlier stories had sought. The language of sociology, industry, progress and commerce – 'großes Schlafmotiv der Verbesserung, großes Beischlafmotiv von der Profilierung der Kultur' – has colonised the territory of human experience; there is no longer the delicate tension between form and dissolution, community and isolation, which had moved the younger Rönne. Other individuals are no longer objects of longing, but are 'Spurlosigkeiten, sogenannte Persönlichkeiten, Spasmen der Leere, Keuchhusten des Nichts' (GB, 2, 110). In attempting to preserve his avant-gardist stance in the face of what he sees as an unbearable world, he has reduced it to a series of rather empty, ideological gestures.

In this story, the narrative parameters are already set for the prose which Benn was to produce in the late 1920s and 1930s: he has developed a voice which employs a curious mixture of discourses as a way of commenting on the world while preserving the fiction of apolitical isolation. In the prose works from the late 1920s and early 1930s, Benn plays various types of discourse off against each other as a way of seeking deeper connections between the artistic personality and cultural developments than those represented by the fashionable first-night crowd in *Saison* (1930) or the doctor in the story *Urgesicht* (1928), whom the narrator observes as 'Herrn auf der Höhe seiner Zeit, den Führer weiter Schichten, den Träger der positiven Idee, den kausalgenetischen Denker' (GB, 2, 115). The doctor, a man who has made his fortune out of the pursuit of social improvement, is associated with the language of statistics and causality, as well as of humanism, which Benn's narrator dismisses as superficial and ahistorical. The narrative form reflects the way in which the intensity of Benn's neo-conservative critique has led him to take back some of the radical innovations of his earlier prose: here, the fronts are clearly set out in two figures that embody opposing principles. Benn's narrator employs a variety of discourses – biological, psychological, anthropological, aesthetic, political and cultural-historical – in his search for a unifying principle which establishes the place of the individual within the cultural and racial inheritance. However, instead of the radical questioning and irony which had characterised the montage of such discourses in the Rönne stories, Benn here employs them in support of each other, to create a voice with a claim to truth; aesthetics are here no longer their own justification, but are underpinned by Benn's creation of his own eccentric tradition.

It would of course be stretching the point to suggest that Benn's prose work in the late 1920s is in any way typical of the restorative attitude to aesthetics that we have identified: his case is rather that of an artist who has registered the crisis of modernism and is exploring ways of preserving as much as he can of the avant-gardist gestures of his early work. However, the climate in which he operates, and against which he defines his stance, necessarily brings about profound changes in his attitude to narrative: more, perhaps, than he would be willing to acknowledge.

The later prose narratives

The uncompromising statement of withdrawal from public life and the end of speech with which *Weinhaus Wolf* ends gives it an apocalyptic air and the feeling of a final reckoning with the culture around him: 'Man muß sehr viel sein, um nichts mehr auszudrücken. Schweige und gehe dahin' (GB, 2, 148). It is worth noting though that the figure who speaks these words is the narrator of a literary text, rather than it being the conclusion of a discursive essay. Benn frequently blurs the distinction, of course, but here he is at pains to create significant distance between author and narrator, thus neatly sidestepping the paradox of attempting to express the inexpressible. He never chose writers as narrators for his stories in any case, preferring to create figures embodying his own notions of cultural representativeness. However, whereas a figure such as Diesterweg emerges from the shifting contours of the text and is reabsorbed into it once his function has been fulfilled, the narrator of *Weinhaus Wolf* gives us a run-down of his background in the manner of a realist narrator establishing character and context. The underlying idea is remarkably similar, yet the manner in which it is given literary expression has changed radically since 1918.

As in *Diesterweg*, Benn has created a figure that is able to turn the founding concepts of the culture in on themselves. In this case, the narrator is concerned with the Western preoccupation with history as a demonstration of the culture's significance; as an individual who has represented this culture in other parts of the world, he is able to analyse it at a greater level of abstraction, and to historicise the idea of history itself. Benn's identification of a tradition of increasing intellectual abstraction as a defining characteristic of Western cultural develop-ment puts him at a distance from the restorative cultural longings of the time. There is no way out, since the culture develops according to its own laws, increasingly dissected and demolished by the ruthless abstraction of the nihilistic *Geist*.

If *Weinhaus Wolf* represents a reckoning with Benn's own past and with what he saw as the doomed Western cultural tradition, then his return to prose narrative in the final year of the war comes as something of a surprise. The 1944 text, *Roman des Phänotyp*, as with the poems of this period, represents something of a new beginning, coming at the unlikeliest of historical moments. The text is an exploration of the possibility of writing *in extremis*, and more specifically, of the question of literary genre and its usefulness in forming narratives which talk about the world.

The use of the term *Roman* in the piece's title seems at first sight to be a purely ironic gesture, since there is no trace of the procedures of plot or characterisation that the genre relies on, and which had enjoyed a renaissance in literary discourse in recent decades. The term *Roman* has been promoted from its usual status as a genre-defining subtitle, seeming to indicate that the text is above all a modernist dissection of genre conventions. Indeed, one of the text's narrating voices, siting the text within a contemporary intellectual context, makes the claim that the novel as traditionally understood is dead: 'Existentiell – das ist der Todesstoß für den Roman' (GB, 2, 150). The word 'existentiell' is taken up with an enthusiasm which indicates that contemporary philosophy has thrown up a word which finally acknowledges the truth of Benn's cultural attitudes, and which puts an end to humanism and to its literary standard-bearer, the novel:

> *Existentiell* – das neue Wort, das seit einigen Jahren da ist und entschieden der bemerkenswerteste Ausdruck einer inneren Verwandlung ist. Er zieht das Schwergewicht des Ich vom Psychologisch-Kasuistischen ins Arthafte, Dunkle, Geschlossene, in den Stamm. (GB, 2, 150)

Under such conditions, the novel is superfluous:

> Warum Gedanken in jemanden hineinkneten, in eine Figur, in Gestalten, wenn es Gestalten nicht mehr gibt? Personen, Namen, Beziehungen erfinden, wenn sie gerade unerheblich werden? (GB, 2, 150)

The echo of the self-critical letter to Oelze from December 1943, which we referred to at the beginning of our discussion of *Weinhaus Wolf*, indicates that Benn is no longer satisfied with his practice of creating individuals who are 'representative' of the state of the contemporary *Geist*. Instead, he attempts to find a way of allowing the 'phenotype' itself to speak, that is, the contemporary, representative expression of the unchanging essence of the culture, 'der Schnittpunkt von deszendentem Prozeß und schweigendem, aber immer gegenwärtigem Keim'. The 'phenotype' itself becomes the 'hero' of the novel, a protagonist who does not act, but whose nature 'findet Ausdrucksmittel' in the contrasting sections of the text (GB, 2, 149).

Benn's ironic demolition of the novel form leaves the text hovering between two approaches to the relationship of literary language and external reality. On the one hand, the text implies a reassertion of a pure aestheticism, with language referring only to itself, and with literary and non-literary discourses simply quoted and mounted into the text; on the other hand, the choice of biological metaphor and the claim to a form which arises inevitably from the state of contemporary culture tentatively re-establish the possibility of narrative. The avant-gardist Benn creates a world structured along the lines of language, and his political failure had resulted not from an abandonment of that stance, but from the attempt to interpret political realities through this language, in other words, through an ideological gesture which tries to make metaphor 'real'. The posture, characteristic of Benn's later work, of clinging to an avant-gardism against all the odds reflects an anxiety about this failure and an acknowledgement of the treacherousness of language; yet the need to re-engage with the world, through biological metaphor and cultural-political commentary, as well as through the text's autobiographical references, is too strong.

Roman des Phänotyp is thus simultaneously clear in its messages and frustratingly difficult to pin down, and is shot through with this anxiety. The narrative strategies are complex, and yet they seem designed to explore ways of making literary language and narrative form function again, rather than contradicting and undercutting each other. The text opens with Benn's familiar essayistic voice, which sets the intellectual context, establishing a narrative difference from a figure representing the 'phenotype', which is referred to as 'er', and whose thoughts are given in free indirect speech. He moves through situations which refer back to the earliest Rönne stories, such as the after-dinner conversation, though the narrator presents such events as generalised, linguistic abstractions shorn of psychological complexity: 'Er tritt in die Unterhaltungsbasis ein, ernst, aber gefestigt, vollzieht den Zusammenschluß in sprachlicher Gemeinschaft' (GB, 2, 151). Much of the text is then taken up with notes on contemporary cultural and intellectual issues, as well as reflective passages and memories, often introduced by an 'ich' whose status is at first uncertain.

Towards the end of the text, the initial essayistic voice reveals itself to be a fictional editor something like the anonymous editor in Goethe's *Werther*, and we discover that Benn has fictionalised some of his own wartime experience in an attempt to extract from it what is 'typical' of his time (GB, 2, 178). The phenotype is an individual expression of the culture's moment of self-analysis, where it turns in on itself and proceeds to another level of abstraction (a function which the figure of Diesterweg had fulfilled in the earlier story). The structure of the text reflects Benn's view of the European *Geist*, which, rather than penetrating ever deeper into the mysteries of the world, is simply an ever-accelerating process of abstraction and differentiation, a phenomenon that 'sich in immer neuen Ausdrücken, Ausbrüchen, neuen Auswegen seiner selbst [differenziert]' (GB, 2, 155).

The text itself is structured so as to reflect this differentiation, but the convoluted narrative folds it back on itself so that the parts all refer to and support each other: the authoritative, essayistic voice which introduces the words of the 'phenotype' can be nothing other than the phenotype reflecting on itself. Meaning is created only within the structure of the text itself:

> Alles trat in eine helle Beleuchtung, in feststehende Verhältnisse, in Beziehungen, die im Rahmen ihrer Lage gültig waren, – nur im Rahmen ihrer Lage: denn im Hintergrund stand die große Disharmonie als Gesetz des Alls. (GB, 2, 178)

This denial of meaning and reference outside the structures of the text cannot, however, be the end of the story, since the text as a whole makes claims to stand metaphorically for the structure of the culture in which it is produced, which is itself seen as endlessly self-referential and static. *Roman des Phänotyp* is built on this paradox: in order to make meaningful statements about the world, the text must operate at the extremes of self-referential aestheticism.

The text has a coda of sorts, in which Benn relaxes the intensity somewhat and, in doing so, gives us an indication of the text's purpose and its location within and against the restorative cultural atmosphere of the time. In an enjoyably sarcastic dismissal of the German obsession with the idea of 'depth' in cultural matters, Benn pours scorn over targets such as Spengler's *Preußentum und Sozialismus* and the work of myth-makers like Ludwig Klages. Benn distances his work from cultural conservatives who want to use myth to reach back beyond modernity to the instinctual origins of humanity. *Roman des Phänotyp* is a demonstration of the impossibility of this desire to reconnect to earlier ways of living or modes of thought: the text develops an aesthetics of surfaces and montage, in which the texture of images and ideas that characterise an era and its 'phenotype' are always nothing but contemporary, even when they consist of fragments of the culture's past.

After the crisis of narrative which is documented in *Roman des Phänotyp*, Benn's post-war narrative prose demonstrates a renewed confidence in the forms which he had developed during his career. The texts which make up *Der Ptolemäer* (1947) open with a reassertion of some of the contextualising techniques of realism, and they are more stable in their employment of these techniques than the texts of the 1920s, which tend to gesture in the direction of context as a way of marking an ideological territory. By contrast, these stories are unmistakeably set in the immediate post-war years, with references to harsh winters, the Nuremberg trials, the black market and other things setting a clear and familiar context for the reader. Benn's purpose in these stories is not to defamiliarise the context, but to critique contemporary ways of talking about that context.

The narrator, a beautician whose business seems absurd in the chaos of post-war Berlin, claims to be writing private notes for a friend, in which he responds to conversations with various customers (GB, 2, 206). He is a more traditional narrator in the sense that his character and situation are carefully constructed to allow him a distanced, observer role: he has adopted the correct intellectual posture to understand the 'phenotype', rather than embodying it himself. Whereas Benn's early texts collapsed the boundary between internal and external life, here the boundary is fixed and conscious, and the narrator of *Der Ptolemäer* is concerned with preserving freedom of thought against an overbearing state rather than with documenting the crisis of personality itself.

Having established this narrative situation, Benn uses his narrator to pass comment on the language of post-war reconstruction. Setting his face firmly against the cultural language of the time, he expresses nothing but contempt for the idea that culture and tradition can play a constitutive role in the re-construction of the nation: 'Die Bevölkerung sieht durch die Fenster gierig zu: die Kultur ist wieder im Vormarsch, wenig Mord, mehr Song und Klänge' (GB, 2, 208). He ridicules the cult of Goethe (GB, 2, 226) and maintains that the concept of 'Humanität', 'jene Vorstellung, die immer so ergriffen zitiert wurde und die heute mit angeblich ganz primären geschichtlichen Aufgaben bei uns ausstaffiert werden sollte', has been completely 'entzaubert' (GB, 2, 219). European culture is, in this view, a conspiracy against the analytical coldness of Benn's conception of *Geist*:

> Gegen den [Geist] rottete sich das moderne Lebenseuropa zusammen, suchte ihn zu zähmen, brachte ihn in Disziplinen und Methoden, desinfizierte ihn, machte ihn wissenschaftlich, das heißt unverdächtig und verdeckte seine letalen bionegativen Züge. (GB, 2, 202)

Der Ptolemäer represents a bitter reckoning with the restorative cultural discourse of the post-war period and an unflinching, and often compelling, view of the vague and contradictory notions that underpinned it. Its amorality and the extremity of its attacks on the occupying powers are shocking so soon after the collapse of the Third Reich, and we can certainly say that the moral inadequacy of Benn's long-term view of European cultural collapse is thoroughly exposed in his failure to deal with the causes of the catastrophe. Yet it is plain from the text that, in order to create a platform for his attacks on contemporary culture, Benn has had to adopt some of that culture's most treasured ideas, in particular that of individual freedom of thought and the defence of the inner life against the depredations of a hostile world. Although he states that the idea of *Innerlichkeit* is now 'verbraucht [...], leer, zusammengesackt' (GB, 2, 217) and that modern thought is nothing more than an attempt to avoid confronting this fact (GB, 2, 198), his construction of a sphere of inner freedom is part of the armoury of nineteenth-century humanism that his earlier work had dissected. The text's structure, with its narrator's unusual profession and his claim that these are personal jottings for some future reader, reflects and reinforces these ideas. Perhaps more than any of Benn's other texts, with the exception of *Weinhaus Wolf*, *Der Ptolemäer* demonstrates how dependent Benn was on the discourses that he criticised.

Benn's last piece of narrative prose, *Der Radardenker* (1949), is a text which shows less bitterness than *Der Ptolemäer*: the tone is lighter, even though it is designed to make final, conclusive statements about European culture. The criticisms of restorative cultural thinking are characterised by an amused resignation, even though the 'Radardenker' claims for himself a status as an individual persecuted because of his dangerous way of thinking. The narrative situation refers back to *Roman des Phänotyp*: an anonymous narrator has collected the thoughts of an individual whose personality is structured in a way which reflects the 'phenotype' of the time, and who bears certain autobiographical features.

The 'Radardenker' of the title is a technological metaphor which has replaced the biological metaphor of the 1944 text: he is an individual who collects, processes and assimilates impressions, ideas and images from across the world. His words are addressed to an unknown 'Sie', who is said to be a 'junger, bildungsfähiger Mensch' who is about to be exposed to the education system (GB, 2, 241). This situation affects the tone of the text, which has a didactic feel, as if the 'Radardenker' is providing a course of instruction in modes of thought and the use of *Geist* in the modern world. The view of *Geist* which emerges in the text is a familiar one in Benn's work: a cold, merciless dissection of ideas and concepts, rather than a spiritual comfort separate from the material of the brain.

Geist offers no false comfort, but drives mercilessly forward, exposing and destroying the object of its gaze, and allowing no return to the security of tradition:

> Sie wollen 'wieder' Boden unter den Füßen (als ob sie seit 500 Jahren irgendwo solchen gehabt hätten), 'Zurück zu den Klassikern, so kommen wir nicht weiter' (weiter, aber wohin denn, und was heißt 'so'?) – 'Humus' – also sie wollen ruhig Dreck an den Stiefeln, aber warmen Dreck – – ich persönlich glaube nicht an Restauration, die geistigen Dinge sind irreversibel, sie gehen weiter bis ans Ende, bis ans Ende der Nacht. (GB, 2, 243)

Benn's 'Radardenker' situates himself as a radical critic of the values of the post-war settlement, a figure able to assimilate the multiple discourses of contemporary culture and subject them to the processes of *Geist*: as with many of Benn's narrators, he does not view European culture from outside, but instead turns its own treasured modes of thought in on themselves. The reference in the last sentence to Céline's *Voyage au bout de la nuit* shows the company in which he sees himself, in opposition to the newly minted humanists of the post-1945 world.

The feeling of the downfall of a culture is topped off with a reference to the development of the atom bomb, and the portion of the text narrated by the 'Radardenker' ends on a note of finality. However, this mood, common in Benn's prose, is not the end of the story, since the fictional editor, much as in *Roman des Phänotyp*, takes up the thread. This voice, which we can assume is one of the younger addressees of the first part of the text, takes his teacher's ideas to a greater level of abstraction and shows them to be manifestations of a particular moment in history, which itself will pass as the operations of *Geist* act on it.

The doom-laden mood is dismissed as 'reine Stimmung, persönliches Gewoge' (GB, 2, 246) which is simply an expression of individual attitude. It seems to be too much humanism for the new narrator, for whom individuals are 'etwas allgemeine Gültigkeit mit Zeichen von Situationärem' (GB, 2, 248). For this new voice, it is not the mood that is modern, but the method employed by the 'Radardenker' which is the most appropriate for the time in which he writes:

> Dagegen ist sein Versuch, in jedem Satz alles zu sagen […] da es für den inneren Menschen Raum und Zeit und Übergänge nicht mehr gibt, sowie die einzelnen Sätze und Absätze ohne Motivbezeichnung hintereinander zu stellen (da es nebeneinander drucktechnisch nicht möglich ist), also blockartig zu verfahren, das ist modern. (GB, 2, 246–47)

In other words, the text is an attempt to rescue the avant-gardist procedures of montage for use in a cultural climate that is fundamentally hostile to them. It represents a stubborn adherence to a counter-tradition opposed to the dominant discourse of cultural restoration, using avant-gardist techniques to undermine the discourse from within.

Benn's response to the shifting cultural atmosphere of the mid-century in his prose works is complex, and at times different from the attitudes that emerge in his poetry. The ideas that are expressed in his prose works are almost always anti-restorative in their emphasis; Benn adopts a posture deliberately at odds with what he regards as the cultural mainstream of the time. This attitude becomes ideologised in the late 1920s, and his prose works begin to reflect some of the gestures of radical conservative responses to the sense of impending cultural crisis, climaxing in his attempt to interpret National Socialism in the light of his own cultural preoccupations. The works which he wrote from the mid-1930s onwards are characterised by an explicit rejection of a cultural discourse that he himself had helped to frame in the late 1920s. However, certain of his formal practices were inevitably affected by the paradigm against and within which he worked, and he took back some of the linguistic radicalism of his early work in order to explore ways of reconnecting text and world. Even where the solutions he found, as in *Roman des Phänotyp*, were stubbornly radical, they are still motivated by an attempt to find a set of formal practices that will bridge the gap between language and an external reality, however this is imagined.

Conclusion

Benn's prose narratives never became canonical in the same way as his poetry, and this has tended to obscure the fact that these works conduct a sustained and radical critique of the restorative cultural discourse of the 1930s and 1940s. It is notable, though, that Benn helped to frame aspects of this restorative literary climate through his poetry of the later 1920s, particularly in his influence on the *Kolonne* writers and in his immense symbolic significance in the cultural debates of the time. We should be careful, however, to separate the reception of his work, which was a defining feature of the literary climate in the late 1920s and early 1930s, and again in the 1950s, with the contradictory impulses that characterise the work itself. While his supporters were able to use Benn's example to establish their own cultural-political stance, his opponents, such as Becher, could define themselves in opposition to him and thus conceal the common ground that we have identified. The work itself, whatever its reception, engages in a continuous critical dialogue with the cultural tradition, the contradictions reflecting the complexity of Benn's developing reflection on his literary practice. A critical practice that overlooked these contradictions contributed to a 'restorative' view of Benn that could not do justice to the ambivalence of his position within mid-century German culture.

Johannes R. Becher

One of the key achievements of Schäfer's periodisation thesis, especially as presented in the context of the essays in *Das gespaltene Bewußtsein* in 1981, was to suggest a framework for explaining, rather than explaining away, the strikingly similar preoccupations of exile and non-exile writers during the years of Nazi rule. Presenting a piece on Oskar Loerke in the same context as one on Johannes R. Becher's exile poetry was a calculated challenge to the tendency to conceive of German literature as having divided into two absolutely incompatible strands.[1] A critical approach schooled in the methods of social history had rightly stressed the fundamentally different experiences of exile and non-exile writers, and had read their works as reflections of these experiences. This type of reading had neglected to consider that the ways in which these individuals experienced the world of the 1930s were affected by much longer term cultural developments in which they had all been intimately involved: their experience of exile and dictatorship was mediated in many cases through a set of shared cultural assumptions that Schäfer identifies as 'restorative'.

Schäfer's choice of Becher to illustrate his thesis works in the same way as his reading of *Die Linkskurve*: he takes a figure that stands as the personification of the totalitarian politicisation of literature and shows how a shift in the periodisation of literary history in the mid-century can open up new ways of reading:

> Bechers Exildichtungen wurden bislang immer isoliert gesehen und niemals in den innerdeutschen Kontext der dreißiger Jahre gestellt. Sie stehen der naturmagischen Dichtung der Daheimgebliebenen näher als der Sowjetlyrik, die damals [...] zum volkstümlichen Vers neigte.[2]

As we have shown in our earlier chapters, such an approach adds an extra level to our understanding of the journals' practice: it is not sufficient to say that political developments set a context for discussion of aesthetics, but also that long-term cultural changes set a context for discussion of political matters, and that the crises of the modern world are registered in literary practice in ways that show how dependent individuals across the political spectrum are on specifically German cultural assumptions. Nevertheless, Schäfer's claim that Becher's work

---

1   Hans Dieter Schäfer, 'Oskar Loerke, "Winterliches Vogelfüttern"' and 'Johannes R. Becher im Exil', in Hans Dieter Schäfer, *Das gespaltene Bewußtsein: Deutsche Kultur und Lebenswirklichkeit 1933– 1945* (Munich: Hanser, 1981), pp. 91–95 and pp. 96–106.
2   Schäfer, 'Johannes R. Becher im Exil', p. 101.

fits the literary-historical paradigm that he has constructed principally around the work of the *naturmagische Schule* requires testing, not least because Becher's personal and political development is so radically different from that of Loerke, Raschke, Eich, Huchel and Langgässer, with whom Schäfer compares him.[3] The fact that Becher produced a large amount of nature poetry in exile is not enough to demonstrate that the 'restorative' paradigm is helpful in discussing the career of a communist writer. Instead, it would be necessary to show that, despite his commitment to the Party's political and cultural line, Becher's work and thought emerge from the same concerns and context as that of writers whose work he dismissed out of hand in the late 1920s.

The problem with this notion is that, rather than being an ongoing development since the late 1920s, Becher's preoccupation with nature poetry is in fact a product of his Soviet exile, being one of the few permissible avenues of self-expression. It is not at all clear that Becher would inevitably have taken that path if he had lived under different circumstances. Therefore, a direct comparison with the non-emigrant nature poets may be misleading, since Schäfer's model is placed rather uncomfortably over two very different sets of experiences. If we are to test the usefulness of the model we have developed for understanding the career of a writer like Becher, we may need to approach the matter in a slightly different way.

As a starting point, we will look more closely at Schäfer's essay and its assumptions about Becher, before moving on to an assessment of Becher's career and his responses to the cultural crises of the mid-century.

Becher and the 1930 paradigm

Schäfer frames his essay on Becher with references to correspondence with Hans Carossa from 1947, emphasising the approval that Becher's exile work found among 'konservativen Erbauungsschriftstellern'.[4] The founding principles of the *Kulturbund* and the early volumes of *Aufbau* demonstrate this common ground very clearly, and bear the hallmarks of the language of German cultural unity that Becher had been developing since his Soviet exile. It is notable that Schäfer takes seriously Becher's language, attempting to find ways of understanding the longings expressed in the restorative discourse of tradition and humanism: as such, the essay provides an impetus for a deeper exploration of Becher's work than is offered by that strand of post-*Wende* criticism that sees in him little more

---

3   Schäfer, 'Johannes R. Becher im Exil', p. 100.
4   Schäfer, 'Johannes R. Becher im Exil', p. 96 and p. 106.

than his skill in 'couching doctrinal principles in language that appeared to be
ideologically non-committed'.[5]

The view that Becher's commitment to 'restorative' cultural principles is
more than just expediency relies on being able to demonstrate that the way he
understood culture and politics was shaped by influences beyond the Party's
Central Committee. Here, Schäfer offers some examples, but is not fully able to
explain them. He notes, for example, Becher's enthusiasm for the literary styles of
the first Soviet Five-Year Plan (1928–1932), which led to his own contribution,
the dramatic poem *Der große Plan*, and contrasts this with his silence in matters of
literary theory from 1932, when such experimentation was coming under attack.
This might seem to indicate a lack of engagement with the rapidly developing
doctrine of Socialist Realism, and a willingness to leave the theoretical work in *Die
Linkskurve* to Lukács, and there is certainly a case for saying that Becher's
commitment to formal conservatism is purely a product of the shock of exile and
the final necessity of following the developing Soviet line.

Yet, as Schäfer shows, this commitment cannot simply be seen as a matter of
expediency, since much of the poetry written in Soviet exile, as well as the
autobiographical novel *Abschied*, shows a commitment to making the new style
work as a vehicle for Becher's renewed preoccupation with nature poetry and the
German humanist tradition. Schäfer distinguishes between Becher's 'official'
poetry and what he calls 'höchst subjektive und formelitäre Arbeiten', which are
politically acceptable but are not shallowly affirmative.[6] He also suggests that the
poetry becomes 'glaubwürdig' when it is characterised by subjectivity and hidden
self-portraits, continuing a tradition of Becher scholarship that stresses his
'Gespaltenheit', and which employs various devices to try to identify Becher's
'true' voice in opposition to his 'official' poetry.[7] As we shall see, this is a
problematic notion that relies heavily on Becher's own self-stylisation throughout
his career, yet it has served the important purpose of keeping interest alive in
Becher as a writer, as opposed to simply as a political figure.

By stressing Becher's 'split' nature, Schäfer is able to locate those aspects of
his work that demonstrate his place within the totality of German literary activity
in the mid-century. He does this by showing how Becher's work still contains the
traces of Expressionist 'Wortrevolte', while at the same time sharing the
preoccupations of writers like Loerke, Raschke, Britting or Eich.[8] In this context,
he quotes Dietrich Bode's work on Georg Britting, putting Becher in the context
of a 'postrevolutionäre Mode' linking writers across the political spectrum. The

---

5   David Pike, *The Politics of Culture in Soviet-Occupied Germany 1945–1949* (Stanford: Stanford
     University Press, 1992), p. 75.
6   Schäfer, 'Johannes R. Becher im Exil', p. 98.
7   See for example Carsten Gansel (ed.), *Der Gespaltene Dichter: Johannes R. Becher: Gedichte, Briefe,
     Dokumente 1945–1958* (Berlin: Aufbau, 1991).
8   Schäfer, 'Johannes R. Becher im Exil', p. 96 and p. 100.

key term here is Bode's suggestion that they all share a longing for a return to 'Naivität', expressed in accounts of childhoods embedded in lovingly evoked descriptions of landscape and context.[9] The contemporary world is seen as a time of complexity and conflict, but the attitude of the writers whom Schäfer quotes is less a simple conservatism than a desire to use the emotional appeal of childhood and landscape as a way of exploring alternative modes of existence in the modern world. This attitude certainly links, as Schäfer suggests, writers as disparate as Ernst Bloch and Peter Huchel, although in other respects these two figures could not be more different: the complex dialectic of *Heimat* and of personal and universal histories in Bloch's work has its eyes firmly fixed on the future, while the texts of the *naturmagische Schule* struggle to create a language that can access authentic experience in the present.

Becher's work in exile seems to hover uneasily between a genuine conservatism and an attitude that seeks to project forwards into a possible future free of the fascist perversion of national sentiment. With rare exceptions, his texts seem to presuppose a lost unity, imagined variously as social, psychological or cultural at different stages in his career, that must be re-established through political action or cultural renewal. It is therefore not quite sufficient to talk, as Hans Mayer does, of Becher's 'subkutaner Konservatismus'.[10] Instead, we need to trace the notions of poetic form, political progress and the German cultural tradition as they develop through Becher's career. This requires us to take it seriously as a *literary* career, rather than as a purely political one, exploring moments of artistic and personal crisis, and setting them against the political crises through which he lived.

Scholarship on Becher has begun to move on from the atmosphere of the early 1990s, in which his career could be roundly denounced as a 'kanonisches Beispiel für Stalinismus in der Literatur' or defended in a rather undifferentiated way as 'ein Glücksfall für die Literatur'.[11] Jens-Fietje Dwars's 1998 biography, while characterised, and occasionally distorted, by post-1989 resentment, did a great service by demolishing Cold War perspectives on Becher, casting fresh light on neglected texts and opening new research perspectives.[12] This section does not intend to be a full account of Becher's career, but instead will concentrate on a number of key issues connected with literary form, the German cultural tradition and the relationship of literature to politics as Becher imagines them in his work.

---

9   Dietrich Bode, *Georg Britting: Geschichte seines Werkes* (Stuttgart: Metzler, 1962), p. 21.

10 Hans Mayer, 'Erinnerungen eines Mitarbeiters von *Sinn und Form*', in Hans Mayer (ed.), *Über Peter Huchel* (Frankfurt a.M.: Suhrkamp, 1973), pp. 173–80 (p. 174).

11 Fritz J. Raddatz, 'Die Selbstverstümmelung des Johannes R. Becher', *Die Zeit*, 1 November 1991, pp. 73–74; Hans Mayer, *Der Turm von Babel: Erinnerung an eine Deutsche Demokratische Republik* (Frankfurt a.M.: Suhrkamp, 1993), p. 111.

12 Jens-Fietje Dwars, *Abgrund des Widerspruchs: Das Leben des Johannes R. Becher* (Berlin: Aufbau, 1998).

Avant-gardism and self-overcoming

Although Becher's official reputation in the GDR was beginning to look a little
ragged in the latter years of the state's existence,[13] and developments in the
literary life of the GDR seemed to have left his work looking old-fashioned and
discredited (for which read 'pre-modernist' in the value-laden language of
Germanistik), the appearance in 1988 of his final, unpublished testament created
shock waves.[14] Becher's repudiation of the project of communism, which had lain
hidden in the archives for 40 years like a guilty secret, threw, for a time at least,
these opposing narratives of his life into disarray, providing graphic evidence that
the uncomplicated image of Becher as GDR *Staatsdichter* was in need of some
revision. Yet, after a brief flurry of interest after 1988 in questions of Becher's
'Stalinism', further fuelled by the collapse of the Berlin Wall, the problem of
Becher's allocation to the great literary-historical narratives which have been
constructed to explain the relationship of art and politics in the twentieth century
seemed to have been resolved. Becher could be assigned to that nether world of
German writers who had betrayed their calling by becoming involved in the last
century's totalitarian political movements. In a related way, many critics seem to
work with an aesthetic according to which the distance a work of art puts
between itself and ideological discourses becomes a factor in deciding its worth.
This is a common complaint raised against GDR writers, whose work is seen as
having failed to carry through what Bernd Hüppauf calls the 'Revolte der
Ästhetik' characteristic of modernism.[15]

Use of words like 'Revolte', and talk of modernist/post-modernist art
'liberating' itself from ideology and referential language, suggests an aesthetic
imagined, despite protestations to the contrary, in political terms. Thus, the
movement of writers like Becher in the middle decades of the twentieth century
away from styles associated with avant-gardist movements towards forms which
seemed to offer an appropriate medium for transmitting content is figured as a
betrayal of the true purpose of art. 'Conservative' styles are seen as being
'imposed' on art rather than emerging at least in part from developments within
the discourse of art itself. Thus, 'modernism' is identified with resistance to the
imposition of ideology, and art which does not pursue relentlessly the 'Revolte
der Ästhetik' is inevitably tainted with compromise.

Yet, even with a seemingly paradigmatic writer like Becher, the reality which
emerges from the bulk of the work and the patterns of the life is more complex.

---

13   See, for example the essays in *Das poetische Prinzip Johannes R. Bechers: Die sozialistische Gesellschaft und
     ihre Literatur. Ergebnisse des 5. Kolloquiums des Zentralen Arbeitskreises Johannes R. Becher am 5. und 6.
     Dezember 1980 in Berlin* (Berlin: Kulturbund der DDR, 1981).

14   Johannes R. Becher, 'Selbstzensur', *SuF*, 40, 543–51.

15   Bernd Hüppauf, 'Moral oder Sprache: DDR-Literatur vor der Moderne', in Heinz-Ludwig Arnold
     (ed.), *Literatur in der DDR: Rückblicke* (Munich: Edition Text + Kritik, 1991), pp. 220–31 (p. 225).

The grand narratives into which his life has been written are unable to do justice to the tense, conflicting selves which struggle to emerge in Becher's work. Our first obligation, then, is to demolish the notion that Becher's life, work and personality *represent* anything at all beyond themselves. Our reading goes against the grain of interpretations (including Becher's own) which read the works principally for their political content. Taking Becher's work as a whole, the message of each individual work is less important than the continuing process of renewal and revision to which Becher subjects his poetic self-understanding. The obsessive pursuit of self-transformation and self-overcoming, a flight from confronting his own psychological damage, coincides in various ways with the narratives of social and personal transformation offered by Marxism-Leninism. We will argue that, far from representing an abstract, totalitarian power imposed on a fragile artistic sensibility, Becher's acceptance of Party discipline, even after the KPD's 'Stalinisation' in the mid-1920s, was a logical continuation of the avant-gardist artistic methods through which Becher had been endeavouring to achieve an elusive psychological and artistic unity.

Looked at in this way, we can begin to see that the characteristic gesture in Becher's work is the attempt to merge the discourses of literary aesthetics, personal psychology and politics into a single utopian autobiographical narrative. This inner compulsion finds its expression first in Becher's desperate exploration of avant-gardist poetic forms, continues in his struggles with Party discipline, and reaches its peak in the ecstatic naming in works such as *Der große Plan* of the ultimate guarantor of utopian unities and realised metaphors: Stalin. Becher's later career, once disillusionment with Stalinism sets in, is characterised by tentative and doomed attempts to detach the history of his own subjectivity from the universal narratives into which it had been written.

So the changing terms of literary practice (Becher imagines this in avant-gardist terms, as progress or advancement) are one of the key discourses in whose margins Becher writes his life story. One can see this in his attitude to the literary greats whom he selects for his personal canon: in his earliest years Kleist, Dehmel, Rimbaud, Baudelaire and (inevitably) Nietzsche. Becher's letters to Dehmel (whom he was later to denounce as a 'Schmarotzer'[16]) between 1910 and 1912 illustrate the way in which the young Becher picked up the Wilhelmine cult of genius and tried to make it work for his personality. He addresses a genius figure, moving from 'Sie' to 'du' as a form of address, as the addressee becomes ever more abstract. Becher's language in these letters reflects that of much of his poetry: a 'du' is invoked as potential redeemer of the humiliated 'ich', as a perfect Other which promises healing and wholeness. Yet at the same time the 'ich' attempts, often in quite violent terms, to smash the barriers between 'du' and 'ich' and absorb the other. The Romantic fantasy of mystic union is intensified into a

---

16   Letter to Heinrich Bachmair, 25 January 1915, in Johannes R. Becher, *Briefwechsel 1909–1958*, ed. by Rolf Harder, 2 vols (Berlin: Aufbau, 1993), I: *Briefe 1909–1958*, p. 28.

brutal linguistic colonialism that erases the Other by aestheticising it. In this way, an expression of the individual's smallness, anguish or humiliation is simultaneously a megalomaniac desire to absorb (a part of) the world into the language and aesthetic procedures used to describe the self and its history. In his early work, Becher's aesthetic project has a universalist impulse to reach out and take hold of the whole world which later turns its attention to more manageable, if no less abstract entities: the working class, or later the nation.

The attempt to find a language which expressed adequately the shape of the self led to a radicalisation of this kind of technique, an avant-gardist attitude which tried to put 'an die Stelle des nur Mühelos-Verträumten das helle männliche Recht der bitter erkauften empirischen Erkenntnis' (JRB, 15, 15). A fear of 'das Mühelos-Verträumte' makes itself felt in Becher's work throughout his life, and it seems to have its roots in the desire to 'overcome' a trauma by rejecting the past and finding a language which admits no ambiguity. Becher was always prone to moods of brooding and despair, or detachment and disengagement, and creating a language which expressed a self with non-porous boundaries and excluded feelings of ambivalence and detachment, seemed to offer a solution. This is also an aesthetic problem, in that Becher's avant-gardism seems designed to overcome the ambiguity and irony of the modernist literature in which Becher was steeped. His attitude could not accept the consequences of modernist critique of language, but struggled instead to find ways of reuniting word and meaning, language and world.

With the publication of the 'Kleist-Hymne' *Der Ringende* (JRB, 1, 7–14) in Heinrich Bachmair's publishing house in November 1911, Becher began to make a name for himself in critical circles, yet he was still searching for a voice that reflected his inner tensions. The collection *Die Gnade eines Frühlings*, published by Bachmair in 1912, shows little of the extraordinary verbal violence which Becher began to employ under the impression of the war, yet it is already characterised by a desperate striving for self-overcoming and perhaps a feeling that conventional poetic language, the language of George or Dehmel which still exerts a profound influence on Becher's work at this stage, is not sufficient to express the extreme states which Becher experiences.

Nevertheless, Becher is on the point of producing some of the most significant poetry of the period, and it is this flight from the consequences of trauma which drives him to it. The language of *Die Gnade eines Frühlings*, which veers between inspiration and the overloading of very tired clichés, is on the very edge of something new. Yet Becher could never go the way of Expressionist poets like Trakl or Benn whose poetry, in the long run, had more radical implications for the development of literary modernism. As Dwars puts it:

> Noch ganz im (bildungsbürgerlich) tradierten Selbstverständnis von Dichtung als Bekenntnislyrik verankert, will Becher der große Dichter einer neuen Zeit sein, ohne

zu begreifen, dass die Moderne eben diesen Anspruch, das Ganze der multi-perspektivisch erscheinenden Welt in einem lyrischen Ich zu vereinen, aufgibt.[17]

Becher's radicalism lies in the development of an aesthetic which seeks to destroy and recreate the language of art for the sake of a glimpse of an ever-retreating absolute truth and unity. Perhaps we can think of this as an exploration of avant-gardist practice as a way of evading the consequences of modernism.

There are hints of this in *Die Gnade eines Frühlings*, where the speaker expresses his fear of alienation, distance and inauthenticity. There are times, even at this early stage, where Becher finds a modern, laconic diction which links him with later generations of GDR poets in a more profound way than his 'classic' Socialist Realist texts might suggest, as in the poem 'An einen Freund':

Seit ich dich vernommen,
Ist mir oft, als müsst ich
Weinen,
Ewig weinen
Um eine Stimme, die mein Eigen ist,
Um einen Schatten, der mein Eigen ist. (JRB, 1, 36)

The poems in *Die Gnade eines Frühlings* mark the beginning of a long process of searching for an authentic poetic voice. These lines are the most revealing in the whole cycle, as they encapsulate Becher's relationship with all the powerful Others in his life, culminating in the Party and, of course, Stalin.

The forms taken by the 'ich' presented to us in Becher's next significant statement, the 1914 collection *Verfall und Triumph*, are many-faceted, though Becher encloses the cycle within programmatic narratives of revenge, in which the poet's words unleash the powers of destruction. The teleology implied by the collection's title provides a way of reading the cycle as a journey from darkness to light, but it is never clear whether the triumph is an act of revenge or an act of breaking away and reaching new ground. The poems which frame the collection, entitled 'Eingang' and 'Ausgang', indicate an interpretation which presents the poet as an embodiment of a corrupt society which is due to collapse in an apocalyptic act of violence. Other poems in the collection suggest this, too; for example, 'Berlin' (JRB, 1, 129) presents a narrative of destruction and revenge which mingles imagery connected with social-critical city literature with a narrative in which civilisations rise and fall in catastrophic volcanic eruptions. The 'Dichter' summons up the eruption which engulfs his people: 'Einst kommen wird der Tag! ... Es rufet ihn der Dichter, | Dass er aus Ursprungs Schächten schneller her euch reise!'

The aesthetic of the word which is developed in poems like this is a magical one; in the face of a modernist aesthetic which questions assumptions about the relationship of text and world, Becher searched for ways of renewing language and of making words inherently meaningful again. The intensity with which he

---

17 Dwars, p. 69.

pursued this project indicates that it was more than simply a matter of aesthetics, but was connected with the desire to overcome a past life experienced in terms of ambivalence and suffering. Becher seems to be working towards a view of poetic language in which elements of time and space are bundled together in narratives of tension, catastrophe and release, with the Word achieving meaningfulness as a magical trigger. As the line from 'Berlin' quoted above suggests, the poet's language gains access to an 'Ursprung', a layer of originary meaning (here imagined as a primal violence beneath the 'milbige Kruste' of civilisation) which is repressed by the bourgeois world.

If we look closely at these poems, however, we find Becher working on two very different metaphorical levels. Although the collection's framing poems imply that there is no escape from the cycle of destruction, other poems propose a utopian alternative, which resolves images of conflict and dissolution through the promise of psychological and aesthetic unity. The penultimate poem, 'Triumph' (JRB, 1, 168), whose title suggests a programmatic purpose, is a vision of reconciliation reached once the tormented body has been overcome. The poem's final line, after the violence of the rest of the cycle, is a simple and, if one is aware of the circumstances under which it was written, quietly moving statement of Becher's longing:

> Einst wankten wir durch Gassen wirre Netze,
> Zerdacht die Stirnen und von Flucht bedrückt.
> Tod deckte auf die Herrlichkeiten=Schätze
> Wir voll erlebend, stumm und unzerstückt.

It is imagery such as this which seems to point a way out of Becher's predicament; perhaps we can read the term 'Herrlichkeiten=Schätze' as Becher's discovery of a set of metaphors which offer an end to suffering and to the cycle of violence and revenge. The word 'stumm' also implies an end to language, suggesting that Becher acknowledges that the violent energy of the language of his poetry, and the sheer bulk of his work, spring from unhealed wounds and internal conflicts. The power of much of *Verfall und Triumph*, as well as its exasperating length and its highly variable quality, seem to spring from Becher's tendency to take an aesthetic problem connected with modernism, the desire to restore to language an unambiguous presence and meaning which it is seen to have lost, and to invest it with life-or-death significance.

The self-disgust which underlies much of this poetry is reflected in images of decaying or dismembered bodies (the word 'Fetzen' acts as a leitmotiv for much of the collection). It is as if bodily decay and dissolution is the inevitable outcome of a failure to escape from internal conflicts, a graspable physical sensation which Becher recognised from his struggles with drug addiction used as a metaphorical resource for inner states. The sonnet cycle 'Herbst=Gesänge' within *Verfall und Triumph* (JRB, 1, 46–49) is a case in point, contrasting with a number of poems in the collection which present the collapse of the old order as a release from suffering. The speaker in 'Herbst=Gesänge' presents himself as the embodiment of humiliation, as an agent of decay – 'Ich made in dem flimmernden Totenkleide' – or as the representative of a collective, cowering in anticipation of punishment by a cruel, yet desired God, 'Der uns in Krankheit warf und Zuchthauszwang, … und den Kopf uns schor.' Once again, the emphasis is on the crippling effect of the individual's past: 'Wie Schnecken wir an schleimigen Straßen kleben … Vergangenheiten nach uns schleifen.' The ever-changing perspective of the sonnets, alternating between 'ich', 'du', 'wir' and 'ihr' with no clear indication of subject or object, suggests a personality fundamentally alienated from itself, without a centre:

> Ich bin nur Frage und Verkommenheit
> Fetzen im Wind, der um Balkone fährt.

The formal unity of the five-sonnet cycle might seem at first to speak against such a claim of disunity, with the strictness of the form providing a measure of control over the material. However, the nature of the sonnet does not provide the unifying narrative drive of the forms which Becher explores in other parts of the collection, and which allow him to present a series of often quite dissatisfying or distasteful triumphs and self-overcomings. Instead, he makes the sonnet work against itself, by refusing to construct it according to the principle of progress and unity of opposites built into the form, which becomes an empty gesture, deprived of meaning – perhaps a dim, mocking echo of German Classicism and its promise of harmony.

The competing inner voices take the roles of both victim and oppressor, and the 'Herbst=Gesänge' end with an accusing voice, which we can identify with the oppressive force of the cycle's beginning, commanding the decomposition and humiliation of the body:

> Verwickle dich ins Dunkele! Pack dich ein! …
> Dein Kopf ist Schorf. Verfrorene Ohren sind
> Papierene Schirme, dick verklebt mit Grind.
> Aus stinkichtem Maule wächst dir brauner Zahn.

The voice seems to announce itself here as God speaking to Job, allowing Becher to expand his own inner conflicts to mythical dimensions, gaining access to a reservoir of imagery and emotional connotation which serves to intensify his language, perhaps also offering a source of authority. Nevertheless, there is nowhere a hint that the many voices and figures referred to in the sonnets are anything other than manifestations of conflicting aspects of Becher's own self. He absorbs in his work an endless array of references to external narratives and imagery found in the world around him, and recreates them in bundles of extraordinary energy. In this sense, as we have already seen in the case of Richard Dehmel, individuals referred to in the work – other poets and role-models, God, Stalin – are literary amalgamations, created out of Becher's inner desires and fears using the linguistic resources available to him.

The hyperactivity of the collection as a whole can be read as a constant process of self-radicalisation in an attempt to overcome feelings of detachment and inauthenticity and to 'reconnect' poetic language, inner life and external world.

Becher's preoccupation in *Verfall und Triumph* with images of the body and landscape predates the beginning of the First World War, and reveals his affinity with Expressionist painters like Ludwig Meidner. However, under the impressions of reports from the front, Becher explores such imagery with an obsessive intensity, developing a symbolic language which will characterise his work through the 1920s. It is as if the war gave him access to a vast reservoir of emotionally charged imagery, using which he could give the intensely personal concerns of his previous work the form of social and political protest; the nightmarish imagery in which he had imagined his own psychological tensions seemed to have exploded into reality. Instead of developing a necessary distance to his stock of apocalyptic imagery, as many artists did who experienced the war at first hand, Becher found his self-image confirmed, as his fantasies about warfare seemed to connect his personality with events on a world scale. It is clear from his work during the war years that the feeling that he was somehow the representative artistic personality of his age was becoming a fixed idea, and so his aesthetic strategies took on a meaning for him beyond the purely artistic. In this sense, the imagery of violence and torture which pervades his work can be read as an attempt to overcome his sense of isolation and to reconnect his art and his personality with the world: an avant-gardism which invested everything in 'overcoming' a modernism that offered only the separation of language and world.

This attitude may help explain the huge claims Becher made for his wartime poetry, which he expected to burst upon an expectant world and end the fighting:

> So ist die Hoffnung noch größer geworden, so darf ich es täglich, ein noch Gesicherterer, es erfahren, wie meine Gesänge unwiderstehlich Völker zu sich heimwärts ziehen werden.[18]

Avant-gardist overestimation of the transformative power of art combines with (late) adolescent megalomania in an extraordinary dramatisation of the public personality; the self and its history are performed on a grand scale, but on a rather small stage. Nevertheless, we should avoid the kind of critical position which equates self-dramatisation with insincerity, an accusation which one finds levelled at Becher throughout his career. Becher's preoccupation with the power of his poetry to end the fighting is absolutely sincere because the great conflicts in Flanders or on the Eastern Front provide an interpretation for his own inner conflicts.

---

18   Letter to Alfred Wolfenstein, 19 September 1915, in Becher, *Briefwechsel*, I, p. 35.

Norbert Hopster has pointed out that Becher's preoccupation with an activist aesthetics of language in this period means that the term 'Expressionist', often used to describe his work, is inappropriate.[19] We have already noted how Becher is concerned to escape from the states of ambivalence and detachment evoked by other Expressionist writers, whose radicalism Becher is unable to see as artistic progress, and the Futurist activism proselytised in Germany in journals like *Der Sturm* seemed to offer a way of reconnecting art and life. Alongside writers like August Stramm and Alfred Döblin, Becher's work in the late 1910s and early 1920s can count as the most comprehensive German reception of the formal and stylistic preoccupations of Futurism. His association with the *Sturm-Kreis* during the war years, and, in particular, his relationship with Else Hadwiger, one of the first German translators of the work of the Italian Futurists Filippo Tommaso Marinetti and Paolo Buzzi, had brought him into contact with the small, but enthusiastic band of German disciples of Futurism. Herwarth Walden's journal *Der Sturm*, which had published a translation of Marinetti's *Manifesto tecnico della letteratura futurista* in 1912 had been spreading the gospel of Italian Futurism as an antidote to the mainstream of German Expressionism.[20]

A number of scholars, notably Norbert Hopster, Peter Demetz and Jens-Fietje Dwars, have acknowledged Becher's debt to Marinetti and have traced the influence of Futurism in his work.[21] Becher adopted and put to his own use Marinetti's theory of the *parole-in-libertà* with a vengeance, producing work in which the word, freed of the constraints of traditional syntax, takes on a magical quality, bursting open the bounds of time and space and of the isolated human individual, and overcoming the chaos and suffering of the war. In an essay written to introduce his verse collection *An Europa* of 1915, Becher sets out his Futurist programme:

> Ja –: unser neues Buch, *An Europa* betitelt, stellt sich nicht geringer die Aufgabe [...], heilige, schwerste, ruhmreichste Aufgabe, als Jüngster repräsentative Kraft aus dem gleichsam zu eiterigem Porphyr geronnenem knirschendem! Blut-Chaos endloser wirr über-, in- und durcheinander geschobener Schlacht-Flächen aufgebrochener Azure umwalltes Menschheits-Monument vereinter europäischer Völker mitzuerrichten. (JRB, 15, 20)

For Becher, the renewal of poetic language is a utopian project in which the redemption of the world is achieved through its transformation in an avant-gardist aesthetic project, illustrated in programmatic poems from *An Europa*, such as 'Die neue Syntax':

---

19 Norbert Hopster, *Das Frühwerk Johannes R. Bechers* (Bonn: Bouvier, 1969), p. 1. Hopster points out that Becher is often assigned to Expressionism in a purely chronological sense, through his association with Expressionist artists during the 'Expressionist decade'.

20 'Die futuristische Literatur – Technisches Manifest', trans by Jean-Jacques (=H. Jacob), *Der Sturm*, 4.29 (1912), 194–95.

21 See Dwars, pp. 83–86; Peter Demetz, 'The Futurist Johannes R. Becher', *Modernism/Modernity*, 1.3 (1994), 179–94; and Hopster, pp. 38–65.

Die Adjektiv=bengalischen=Schmetterlinge
Sie kreisen tönend um des Substantivs erhabenen Quaderbau.
Ein Brückenpartizip muß schwingen! schwingen!!
Derweil das kühne Verb sich klirrend Aeroplan in Höhen schraubt [...]

Ein junger Dichter sich Subjekte kittet.
Bohrt des Objektes Tunnel ... Imperativ

Schnellt steil empor. Phantastische Sätzelandschaft überzüngelnd.
Bläst sieben Hydratuben. Das Gewölke fällt.
Und Blaues fließt. Geharnischte Berge dringen.
So blühen auf wir in dem Glanz mailichter Überwelt. (JRB, 1, 228)

Futurism becomes for Becher a method for overcoming the crises of his past, an aesthetic of clarity and masculine hardness which overcomes the ambiguities of a decadent modernism. Becher pursues this project with messianic zeal, since the state of aesthetic decadence which he wants to overcome is associated in his mind with his own troubled mental state and with his own struggles with morphine addiction. The characteristic image in Becher's work which links these three concerns is that of apocalyptic bodily decay, for example, in the poem 'Krankenhaus', which describes in drastic terms the physical and psychological symptoms of drug addiction: 'Gott, den wir in uns faulen lassen, | Verfärbt die Ströme unseres Blutes trüb' (JRB, 1, 106). Becher's Futurist-influenced aspiration to purge language of ambiguity as a way of making it an effective weapon in the struggle against a corrupt society is, in fact, a fundamentally personal project: the new aesthetic will purge his own troubled psychology of the traumas and ambivalence of the past, and renew his personality in an act of creative will. Thus, ostensibly political statements in fact reflect intensely personal concerns, a link made clear in 'Gedichte für ein Volk' from 1917:

> Hinweg über alle Depressionistischen, Zwitterhaften, Ungreifbaren, Unplastischen, Beschaulichen, Dekadenten, Exzentrischen, Lyrischen, Egozentrischen, Literarischen, Künstlerischen, Anarchistischen, Passiven, Mimosenhaften, Pazifistischen, Privaten ... hinweg über sie alle und heran – hinauf – empor mit euch Imperativsten, Expressionisten, Hellstäugigen, Morgendlichen, immer Attackenhaften, Athleten, Ethischen, Repräsentativen, Organisatorischen, Sozialistischen, Unpersönlichen, Totalen, Eindeutigen, Weiblosen, Fabelhaften, den Männern! den Politikern! den Tätern. (JRB, 1, 408)

The radical unity of the discourses of aesthetics, psychology and politics which Becher strives for in this period clearly points forward to his later vulnerability to the attractions of totalitarian politics, for the new style will reflect the structure of a new state modelled on aesthetic lines: 'Stil: neue Grammatik, dem neuen Staat gleichgeordnet: Idealsyntax. Neuerungen in der Wort-, Melos-, oder Rhythmik-Technik, den sozialen Fortschritten des ersehnten Staat-Gebildes entsprechend.'[22] This potent mixture provides the basis for his fascination with political and

---

22   Letter to Bachmair, 13 October 1916, Becher, in *Briefwechsel*, I, p. 57.

cultural events in Russia; while he is languishing in enforced isolation in his hospital bed, registering from a distance the carnage of the First World War battlefields, or doing the rounds of Munich's bohemian café culture, he projects his utopian longings onto a country which, after 1917, seemed to embody everything that he missed in Germany.

Although a fascination with Russian culture and the great changes wrought by war and revolution was not confined to left-wing intellectuals in Germany, but affected figures across the political spectrum, Becher seems to have experienced this attraction with unusual intensity. Michael Rohrwasser has shown that Becher's fascination with the Russian Revolution was fed by a disgust at the failure of radical politics in Germany to produce the utopian resolution that he strove for in his work.[23] The Bolshevik Party, with its (seemingly) internally consistent and highly disciplined structure, is contrasted with the German revolutionaries who, according to Becher, suffered from just the problems of ambivalence and lack of structure against which he railed, and therefore could not offer him the perfect unity which he required. He had joined the newly founded KPD in late 1918, but Harry Graf Kessler reported in September 1919 that he had become disillusioned with its lack of internal discipline.[24] In a sense, with his stress on internal discipline and psychological unity, and with his progressive self-radicalization and periodic 'purging' of his past self, Becher is 'Bolshevizing' his inner life in advance of the KPD. However, the Party itself is not ready for him, and he turns his back on it.

When read in the context of Becher's work as a whole in this period, it is clear that he is talking about his own psychological needs and literary project as much as about the politics of revolution in Germany. His disillusion with revolutionary politics lasted precisely as long as it took the newly founded KPD to sign up to the principles of Comintern membership in 1920, which demanded that revolutionary parties adhere to the Leninist avant-garde principle and carry out regular shake-ups amongst Party cadres to promote discipline and loyalty. Although he did not finally commit himself again to KPD membership until 1923, after his period of disillusionment, his work and letters in 1921–1922 show a renewed interest and a growing realisation that the discipline which Party membership imposed on the individual seemed to offer a way to resolve his agonising psychological tensions.

A peculiarity of Becher's approach to the Party was his apparent ability to identify absolutely with any collective or tradition in which he placed himself, in order to find a structure for his thinking about his own mental health problems

---

23 Michael Rohrwasser, 'Das rettende Rußland: Erweckungserlebnisse des jungen Johannes R. Becher', in Gerd Koenen and Lew Kopelew (eds), *Deutschland und die Russische Revolution* (Munich: Fink, 1998), pp. 462–81.

24 Diary entry 4 September 1919, Harry Graf Kessler, *Tagebücher 1918–1937* (Frankfurt a.M.: Suhrkamp, 1961), p. 167.

238 Johannes R. Becher

which offered a potential resolution. The Party which Becher re-joined in 1923 was going through a period of internal reorganization following the failure of the armed revolts in 1918–1919 and March 1921, after which membership of the Party had halved. These experiences, as well as the memory of the collapse of the Second International at the outbreak of World War One, had shattered the blithe historical optimism of the workers' movement. The radical parties which came together to form the KPD saw the mainstream socialist movement as bourgeois traitors who had seduced the workers away from their 'true' selves; the dangers amongst their own ranks of becoming reconciled with a post-revolutionary situation, of putting ties to milieu, family or other forms of identification above Party loyalty, had to be combatted by the development of a priestly Party avant-garde on the Leninist model, which tried to create a sense of permanent crisis and mobilisation in the Party.

In a strangely parallel process, Becher had been portraying his own psychology as an avant-gardist, 'true' self which struggles constantly to discipline an unwilling, bourgeois side with a tendency to disengagement, depression and ambivalence. Constant, feverish Party work and radicalisation both of opinion and means of artistic expression were the result, and Becher identified the structure of the Party, with its internal tensions and perceived solutions, as a model for writing about his own personality. Michael Rohrwasser's account, according to which the Party plays the role of 'Ganzheitsmaschine', holding out the promise of totality in Becher's thinking, does not quite do justice to the dynamism of this relationship: Becher sees himself as engaged in a constant process of becoming and overcoming, the Party offering him a means to that end.[25] So what seems to be an eminently political process of submission to the will of the Party was seen by Becher in aesthetic terms, as a struggle to find a language which adequately expressed the shape of the self and which 'overcame' the crises and ambiguities connected with his Expressionist period. Whereas both Expressionism and individualism were associated for Becher with his traumatic past, the Soviet Union, and the literary practices associated with it, seemed to offer ways of writing life-stories into the broader story of history. They offer the legitimacy of a story bigger than the story of the individual self, as well as ways of telling that story which seem sanctioned by a vast political movement in a country where history is being made.

---

25 Michael Rohrwasser, *Der Weg nach oben: Johannes R. Becher: Politiken des Schreibens* (Frankfurt a.M.: Verlag Roter Stern, 1980), p. 238.

The Avant-garde Project in the Weimar Republic

Even in the years of relative stability in the mid-1920s, the KPD's ideological insistence that the Republic was on the point of crisis and civil war provided a range of aesthetic opportunities for Becher to drive his avant-garde project forward. This process can be traced through a series of poems that have often been neglected in studies of the poetry of the 1920s, but which Peter Demetz refers to as a key document of European avant-gardism.[26] In the space of three years, from 1920 to 1923, Becher's poetic language develops from a period of melancholy, religious-sentimental passivity to the extraordinary verbal violence of the collection *Maschinenrhythmen*. Demetz explores what he sees as language at the edge of its own self-destruction,[27] and the poems show that Becher has taken to an extreme the implications of an aesthetic theory that demands of his language that it reflects directly the processes that it describes:

Fabrik=Gevierte: fieberkurvige
Landschaft: Dämonen=Klumpen, eisen=
Gequadert, aufquollen, übergeworfen, wie
Ätzend umpanzert, von leuchtgasigen
Rauch=Mänteln; von Röhren=Geflechten
Umstellt; rissige Feuer=Gesichter;
Kraft=Wellen; schmelzende Erz=Fluten. ('Hymne an Lenin', JRB, 2, 284)

Becher's new engagement with the material conditions of the proletariat is, at this stage, less the product of direct experience and sympathy than a new resource of imagery and fantasised violence: what Dwars calls a 'neue Zeichenwelt'.[28] Even at this extreme of linguistic invention, we can observe a process through which Becher is trying to ground his language in seemingly objective discourses from outside aesthetics: where linguistic avant-gardism as an end in itself had failed to produce the desired transformation, the avant-garde project needs to be supported by grounding poetic language in another form of discourse. Becher's work shows this in various ways. For example, under the influence of the *Proletkult* theories of the 1920s, Becher begins to create a militant, essentialist view of the proletariat, employing a range of metaphor that anchors his language in 'nature': he endlessly repeats his range of body imagery, adapting it to the new circumstances, even resorting to images of blood and race. The poem 'Kaleidoskop 1923' from *Maschinenrhythmen* traces the conquest of a corrupt, fragmented world by 'Arbeiter=Völker! Muskel=harte Rassen!' (JRB, 2, 287). Such imagery is intimately connnected with Becher's membership of the *Roter*

---

26 Peter Demetz, *Worte in Freiheit: Der italienische Futurismus und die deutsche literarische Avantgarde, 1912–1934* (Munich: Piper, 1990), p. 108.
27 Demetz, *Worte in Freiheit*, p. 111.
28 Dwars, p. 228.

Frontkämpferbund, where he could live out the longings of the war years in a fantasy of civil war and insurgency.

Other developments served to provide Becher with a grounding or justification for his language and practice. Hectic Party work in the KPD cultural organisations (by 1924, he was head of the communist grouping within the *Schutzverband deutscher Schriftsteller* and worked in the KPD's *Abteilung Bildungswesen*) led to direct encounters with his desired audience, or at least with an ideologically constructed version of that audience.[29] We can identify a shift in his aesthetic stance arising from this experience with the publication of his tribute to Lenin, 'An der Bahre Lenins'. A letter to Eva Herrmann in January 1924 indicates his new thinking about aesthetics:

> Zur Lenin-Trauerfeier habe ich ein Gedicht verfaßt, das an fünf Orten zugleich in Berlin vor insgesamt 20 000 Menschen gesprochen wurde und das in einer Auflage von 10 000 Exemplaren gedruckt, verteilt und in der Stadt angeklebt wurde [...] Das Caféhaus ist vorbei, die lustige Künstlerei und Schwabingerei ist vorüber. Ich habe jede Minute zu tun. Ich zu funktionieren, so ist z.B. das Lenin-Gedicht im Auftrag innerhalb einer knappen halben Stunde geschrieben.[30]

The Lenin poem demonstrates a response to a situation in which Becher's work is expected to be performed in front of mass audiences: the poem requires a radically different set of aesthetic criteria in judging its success and quality. It no longer prioritises aesthetic values as an end in themselves, but relies on formal and linguistic features connected with the performance of the role of mouthpiece of the mass audience. The goal of breaking down the barriers between producer and consumer by stripping away the characteristic features of bourgeois tradition remains the same, but the focus of the text's aesthetic strategies has shifted away from internal factors to include the anticipated responses of a particular audience, who are imagined as co-creators of the 'event' at which the text is performed.

The 1925 collection *Der Leichnam auf dem Thron*, written in rapid reaction to the election of Hindenburg as President of the Republic in April of that year, develops these concerns further. The imagery is still drawn from Futurism, but Becher's style has lost the aesthetic complexity of his earlier Futurist poetry. Instead, the texts seek to intervene in the current political situation through their urgency of diction, so that their focus shifts away from text-internal factors: instead of trying to achieve transformation within the structures of the text, Becher assumes – in line with KPD doctrine – that German society is on the point of civil war, so that an ideologically constructed view of a society riven with internal tensions becomes a text in itself, within which the poet's words can act as triggers for destruction and transformation. The programmatic poem 'Warum schreibe ich "kommunistisch"?' (JRB, 2, 379–81) demonstrates this new clarity of

---

29 See Dwars, p. 232.
30 Becher, *Briefwechsel*, I, p. 122.

diction, alongside a continued stress on simultaneity and the 'liberated' word of Futurism employed as a weapon in the political struggle:

Warum schreibe ich 'kommunistisch'?
Was ist ein
'Kommunistisches Gedicht'?
Es ist das neue,
Das namenlose Heldentum,
Es ist die schöpferische Anonymität,
Gleichzeitigkeit alles Geschehens,
Es ist die Verkündigung
Der Ankunft einer neuen Menschenrasse,
Es ist Massenschritt,
Millionenmassenschritt,
Kampf und Gesang sind eins,
Es ist die Sichtbarwerdung
Einer neuen Menschenordnung,
Es ist die unerbittliche Wegbereitung
Kommender Geschlechter –
Erste Signale roter Völker...
Es schlägt eine Brücke
Von einem Ufer zum anderen,
Es ist ein Übergang,
Es erkämpft sich den Übergang.

Es ist Sender,

Antenne,
Turbine,
Streik,
Bajonett...
Roter Terror,
Tscheka,
Bombe.

The seemingly paradoxical combination of Nietzschean language with striving for anonymity within the proletarian masses reflects again Becher's reception of the *Proletkult* challenge to orthodox Marxist-Leninist determinism: the theories of Bogdanov and Lunacharsky had turned to Nietzsche for inspiration in the creation of the new proletarian *Übermensch* who could take up the challenge of the end of the era of bourgeois individualism. The desire to abandon the individual bourgeois self and to absorb a suffering subjectivity into a mass movement is a characteristic longing of the time, and for Becher it has the additional advantage of seeming to bridge the gap between language and world that had always troubled him.

Attempts in 1925 and 1926 by the *Staatsgerichtshof zum Schutz der Republik*, which had been founded in 1922 after the murder of Rathenau, to pin on Becher charges of high treason and incitement to civil war, and his brief internment in August 1925, served only to confirm his sense of his own significance and the truth of his social diagnoses. A major statement of this unity of psychological and social tensions is the extraordinary montage novel *(CH Cl = CH)₃ AS (Levisite) oder Der einzig gerechte Krieg* that was published in the KPD publishing house Agis in January 1926, and translated shortly afterwards into Russian. The text may well have been a response to the KPD's claims in September 1924 that the chemical industry was engaged in the secret production of poison gas, and, as Dwars indicates, it reflects clearly the Comintern policy of identifying Social Democracy and Fascism as two sides of the same coin.[31] Thorsten Bartz has also shown that the novel attempts to occupy similar semantic and rhetorical ground to the *völkisch*-militarist literature of the time, since the parties were struggling to attract the same working-class readership.[32] Becher transforms the language of national self-defence into the language of class conflict. In Jörg Vollmer's words: 'Becher [setzt] ganz auf die Selbstvernichtung des kapitalistischen Systems durch die Forcierung seiner autoaggressiven Tendenzen.'[33] In doing so, he provides another self-interpretation.

The novel is a generic hybrid, with features of the documentary-montage novel of the 1920s mingled with avant-gardist verbal violence, and held together by an ideologised structure working with binary opposites interpreted in class terms: a politicised transformation of the demonic Expressionist image of the city that is designed to portray the bourgeois individual's psychological conflicts as mirrors of social conflict. The novel integrates a mass of documentary material about gas production (collated by Becher's future wife Lotte Rotter from sources that are used as a foundation of 'objectivity' in the novel's structure), political pamphlets, wartime memoirs and brutal, ecstatic descriptions of violence into its narrative: a young bourgeois, Peter Friedjung, the great hope of his father's nationalistic circle, rejects his upbringing and finds his way to the Party against the background of a vast conspiracy to destroy the workers' movement in a civil war waged with poison gas. As it had been for Georg Kaiser, the poison gas is a complex symbol, in this case combining the notions of industrialised mass slaughter, capitalist abuse of technology turning back on itself and an invisible, almost metaphysical sense of corruption and violence directed against the body from inside. The bodies must be destroyed in order to be re-formed:

Unter konvulsivischen Zuckungen
Schaum ohnmächtiger Rache noch um den Mund wie ein Epileptiker
Aber

31 Dwars, p. 246.
32 Thorsten Bartz, *'Allgegenwärtige Fronten': Sozialistische und linke Kriegsromane in der Weimarer Republik 1918–1933: Motive, Funktionen und Positionen im Vergleich mit nationalistischen Romanen und Aufzeichnungen im Kontext einer kriegsliterarischen Debatte* (Frankfurt a.M.: Lang, 1997), pp. 27–76.
33 Jörg Vollmer, 'Gift/Gas oder das Phantasma der reinigenden Gewalt: Johannes R. Becher, *(CH Cl = CH)3 As (Levisite) oder Der einzig gerechte Krieg*', in Thomas Schneider and Hans Wagener (eds), *Von Richtofen bis Remarque: Deutschsprachige Prosa zum 1. Weltkrieg*, (Amsterdam: Rodopi, 2003), pp. 181–93 (pp. 191–92).

Es wird schon,
Es formt sich schon,
Hart, stahlhart gerinnen die Umrisse – [...]
Und die Revolution steht da. (JRB, 10, 290)

Having spent nearly a decade living and working in the artificial state of
emergency that the KPD imposed on its members, Becher's response to the
genuine crises of the Republic's final years is complex and contradictory,
reflecting the intersection of KPD policy with his own personal needs. In 1928,
the Comintern turned against the 'compromisers' in its ranks, reflecting Stalin's
campaign against Bukharin; the next year, the KPD's *Sozialfaschismus* theory
demanded a renewed emphasis on ideological purity in a Party that was just
recovering from a profound leadership crisis: in the light of these developments,
the crises that faced the Republic were seen more or less as a continuation of the
previous state. However, the Party's aesthetic programme began to go through a
series of profound debates, centring on the *Proletkult*, documentary literature and
the theatre of Brecht and Piscator. We have documented the twists and turns of
this debate in our section on *Die Linkskurve* and the politics of the *Bund
Proletarisch-Revolutionärer Schriftsteller*, but if we read Becher's own work in this
period in parallel with this, it becomes clear that his practice develops quite
independently.

A trip to the Soviet Union in 1928 made a profound impression: 'Zum ersten
Mal konnte ich zu der Umwelt aus vollem Herzen Ja sagen', he noted, accepting
at the same time the standard cliché for foreign communist visitors.[34] This
impression could only have been strengthened by the response to a new
indictment against him at home for treason and blasphemy: a large international
protest campaign was organised by the *Rote Hilfe*, with Gorky as its figurehead
and supported by German writers and artists including Toller, Kisch, Mühsam,
Döblin, Grosz, Brecht, Walter von Molo and Alfred Kerr, as well as voices from
abroad like Upton Sinclair, John Dos Passos, Romain Rolland and Henri
Barbusse. This, and the objection of public bodies like the *Deutsche Liga für
Menschenrechte*, ensured that the trial was put off for months and eventually
abandoned in August 1928 after the *Reichstag* declared an amnesty for some
politically motivated crimes.

Bearing this in mind, it is clear that the mood of crisis was not the all-
pervasive existential matter for Becher that it was for intellectuals who shared his
bourgeois background. The threat to the bourgeois tradition was an opportunity
rather than a disaster, since the Soviet Union, with the seeming economic miracle
of the Five-Year Plan, provided a basis for affirmation. Nevertheless, there are
signs that the urgency of his aesthetic avant-gardism is beginning to transform
into a need to find firm foundations for his work, not just in imagery connected
with a particular ideologised view of social conflict, but in tried and tested

34   See Dwars, p. 263.

aesthetic forms. The debate with Willy Haas, whose article 'Wir und die "Radikalen"', in *Die literarische Welt* in October 1928 (*DlW*, 4.43, 1) had attacked radical writers as fashion-chasing political parasites, illustrates the complex nature of this shift. In his response, Becher strikes a tone of reasoned tolerance, but makes it clear that proletarian writers must keep their distance until the new art has had a chance to develop: 'Trennen wir uns, grenzen wir ab, das ist die einzige Möglichkeit, um vielleicht einmal zusammenzukommen' (JRB, 15, 177). His statements are of a piece with BPRS policy, and still assume that a new, proletarian art will emerge that owes nothing to bourgeois styles, traditions and notions of individuality. Nevertheless, he uses an aesthetic language that is abstract enough to be put to different uses depending on the cultural climate of the time: he counters Haas's view that radical writers are destroying objective aesthetic values by stressing that quality consists in a synthesis of of form and content (JRB, 15, 178). Thus, although there is much that divides the opponents, they both use a language deriving from bourgeois aesthetic theory to discuss questions of literary quality: the distance between these two positions will diminish as the 1930s progress.

The years between the late 1920s and the beginning of Becher's residence in the Soviet Union are a transitional period in which he struggles to reconcile avantgardist longings with a need to reassess the progress of his life up to this point, while at the same time trying not to stray too far from a Party line that is beginning to reject the aesthetics that he had staked everything on in the 1920s. His 1928 collection, *Die hungrige Stadt*, displays some of these tensions. In some respects, it is an attempt to recapture the verbal virtuosity of *Maschinenrhythmen* in poems such as 'Die Fabrik' (JRB, 3, 55–57) or a programmatic Lenin poem:

Er rührte an den Schlaf der Welt
Mit Worten, die wurden Maschinen,
Wurden Traktoren, Häuser,
Bohrtürme und Minen –
Wurden Elektrizität,
Hämmern in den Betrieben,
Stehen, unauslöschbare Schrift,
In allen Herzen geschrieben. (JRB, 3, 147)

The programme here shows the same desire to transform the world through words, yet the language is used to talk about these ideas, rather than being regarded as a material which is itself to be transformed through acts of creative violence. Other poems move in a rather different direction, seeming to return to the styles and preoccupations of early Expressionism as a way of expressing states of hopelessness and disconnection:

Das Vieh brüllt in den Ställen. An dem Haus
Ist ein Gerüst. Die Maler streichen.
Ein Bettler kommt. Er lächelt blöd und grau.
Auf frischem Beet steht eine Vogelscheuche.

Ist's ein Erhängter? Hat man aus dem Fluß
Ihn, voll von Schlamm und Kraut, gezogen?
Dort steht er nun. Ein Kreuz sein Leib.
Ein armer Toter, der im Stehn vermodert.

Ein Hauch. Des Toten blechernes Gesicht
Klirrt laut. Ein Vogel fliegt davon.
Im Garten blühn Vergißmeinnicht.
Bald kommt der Kürbis wieder, grüner Mond… ('Frühling auf dem Dorf', JRB, 3, 62)

In poems like this Becher has rediscovered a different kind of radicalism from his Futurist word art, a way of looking hard at images of decay and corruption without trying to escape them. 'Meine Kindheit' (JRB, 3, 132–43) is a sarcastic dismissal of his upbringing and bourgeois family. The innocence of childhood is a bourgeois privilege maintained in this case through the father's brutal professional life:

'Vater', fragte die Mutter, 'wie war es denn?!'
'Na, wie Hinrichtungen eben sind -'
Der Vater nahm die Mutter beiseite:
'Pst. Ruhig. Nicht vor dem Kind.'

Der Vater hat den Braten zerteilt.
Der Braten schmeckte ihm gut.
Ich sah an seiner Hand ein Beil,
Seine Augen standen voll Blut.

The distancing irony of the narration ensures that the poem does not seem to get too close to Becher's past; no dangerous nostalgia or sympathy is displayed. However, this marks the beginning of a process in which Becher reconsiders his origins, at first ironically, but then more subtly as the need to rescue positive aspects of the bourgeois tradition becomes both an ideological and a personal necessity. Autobiographical material begins to appear in the verse collections alongside poems in simplified forms, such as 'Die Fahne' of 1932 from *Der Mann, der in der Reihe geht* (JRB, 3, 449):

Als er so dalag, nahmen die Genossen
Ein Tuch und deckten ihm zu das Gesicht,
Das Tuch war bald von Blut durchflossen
Von dem zerschossenen Gesicht.

So lag er da. Er hatte kein Gesicht.
Wo sein Gesicht war, lag die rote Fahne.
Genosse, lebe wohl! Als Fahne
Weht uns voraus von jetztab dein Gesicht.

A combination of such political religiosity with accounts of childhood and images from the past, bound together in stable, traditionalist forms, give a picture of a personality seeking its centre again, rather than fleeing from an inner emptiness. The desire for absorption into the mass movement is counterbalanced by a concentration on aspects of the poet's individual experience that have made him what he is. However, at the same time, he was producing one of the most strident works of modernist Five-Year Plan literature, the dramatic poem *Der große Plan,* which was premiered in October 1932.[35]

It is a sign of Becher's self-confidence, and his status as a Party writer, that he felt able to lecture delegates to a cultural conference in Kharkov in 1930 about the need for Soviet writers to produce works dealing appropriately with the great changes in their country, and then went on to produce such a piece himself. The text was conceived explicitly as a response to Brecht and Eisler's *Die Maßnahme,* and can with some justice be termed 'totalitarian' in its aesthetic and political claims. Whereas *Die Maßnahme* is a text concerned with communication and learning (and the consequences of their failure), Becher's work is ideologically centripetal, with a rhetorical structure designed to silence all opposition. *Die Maßnahme* cannot be considered a justification of show trials, whereas *Der große Plan* clearly is: in November 1930, Becher had attended the public trial in Moscow of the so-called 'Industry Party', bourgeois engineering specialists who were imprisoned on trumped-up charges of sabotage. The text reworks these events, even including speaking parts for 'conspirators', who are given the names of the real defendants, and are executed rather than imprisoned. Where Brecht puts his faith in the power of reasoned argument, and shows an extreme case in which it fails, Becher strives for a state of certainty in which language becomes unnecessary:

> Ohne ein Bild uns zu machen
> Und sprachlos –
>
> Die Grenze der Zeit
> Haben wir überschritten
> Und sind aufgebrochen
> Ins Zeitalter
> Des
> Kommunismus. (JRB, 8, 392)

In language drawn from the medieval mystics, Becher imagines a time when language, metaphor and the limiting concepts of space and time are overcome. Becher's avantgardism had always striven to overcome the limitations of language, and to achieve the state that he had already described in *Verfall und Triumph*: 'Wir voll erlebend, stumm und unzerstückt.' The naming of Stalin at the end of the text provides the moment of release and fulfilment

Der große Plan represents the end of a development in Becher's work, rather than the beginning: it is his last avantgardist text. Although his work had always been concerned with the shape of his personality, from this point on he reins in

---

35 For accounts of this work, see Dwars, pp. 338–48 and Peter Davies, 'Die Überwindung der Sprache: Johannes R. Bechers Weg in die Partei', in Stefan Neuhaus, Rolf Selbmann and Thorsten Unger (eds), *Engagierte Literatur zwischen den Weltkriegen,* Schriften der Ernst-Toller-Gesellschaft, (Würzburg: Königshausen & Neumann, 2002), pp. 277–85.

the impulse to encompass the world within it; instead, he acknowledges its limitations and boundaries, and in doing so, begins to return to the German humanist classics. Rather than a simple conservatism, Becher's rapprochement with the tradition stresses the humanist personality as a work-in-progress, a striving for harmony of inner life and external world. Links with the theoretical positions of Lukács are obvious here, and it is clear that Becher could see which way the wind was blowing in the debate in the BPRS. In 1929, he was still able to write, in a review of Hans Grünberg's *Brennende Ruhr*: 'Die Reportage ist die Avantgarde, der erste Vorstoß einer kommenden Dichtung in ein neues Diesseits' (JRB, 15, 197). Such comments were becoming inadvisable by 1932, and Becher begins to adapt his work to the prevailing line. However, as we shall see, this is not simply a case of knuckling under; Becher's response to ideological changes is to adapt them to his own psychological needs and to take them to a dangerous extreme.

Exile and Retrenchment

> Wenn ich in den merkwürdigen Jubelruf ausgebrochen bin anläßlich des [IV. sowjetischen] Schriftstellerkongresses, jetzt könne man endlich wieder dichten, so liegt darin allerdings nicht nur *keine* Abkehr von der Tendenz, sondern im Gegenteil die Befriedigung darüber bestätigt erhalten zu haben, daß man in der Dichtung die Tendenz *verarbeiten* müsse. In diesem Sinne ist dieser Jubelruf allerdings eine Abkehr von der *äußerlichen*, in die Dichtung von außen hereingetragenen Tendenz und ein Bekenntnis zu einer Dichtung, in der die Tendenz organisch aus der Dichtung selbst entspringt.[36]

Becher's letter to Willi Bredel from Paris in February 1935, referring to events at the 1934 Soviet Writers' Congress, reveals much about the change in Becher's aesthetic stance since the late 1920s. The disagreement with Bredel reflects the progress of the debate with the 'proletarian' writers in the BPRS in the years when the Popular Front policy had finally sealed the victory of the Lukács line. Becher's self-defence here is not entirely convincing, especially since the word 'dichten' implies precisely the kind of restorative attitude to authorship – raised above day-to-day political life – that he strove for in his work from this point onwards. In Dwars's words: 'Becher hat [den Sozialistischen Realismus] als Wendung zu wirklicher Literatur vorgestellt, die über politische Dichtung hinaus-reiche, indem sie das Erbe einbezieht.'[37] Far from seeming like the *imposition* of a totalitarian cultural policy, it was possible at this moment in history to see the new Soviet policy as an attempt to free antifascist literary production from the crippling conflicts of recent years, and to find common ground with bourgeois

---

36 Letter to Willi Bredel, 26 February 1935, in Becher, *Briefwechsel*, I, pp. 197–98.
37 Dwars, p. 381.

writers in a more stable concept of authorship and text. In our section on *Das Wort*, we showed how a restorative attitude to form and tradition became problematic for Lukács in his Soviet exile: Becher was to encounter similar difficulties.

Having arrived in Moscow in late 1933, Becher threw himself immediately into attempts to gather and organise the scattered and traumatised literary exiles, effectively offering himself as the KPD's 'enforcer' in establishing a consistent Party line. In doing this, he employs the Stalinist language of 'vigilance' as a way of persuading the leadership that this work cannot be done from Moscow. However, permission to leave was not granted until October 1934, and Becher set off via Czechoslovakia to Paris, where he began to lay the groundwork for the 1935 Conference for the Defence of Culture, and to 'win over' prominent authors like Lion Feuchtwanger and Heinrich Mann by persuading them that his attitude to their work and politics had changed.[38]

His work in this period is varied and contradictory, reflecting the activity and isolation of exile, as well as his own changing literary attitude. There are programmatic poems on the role of literature that suggest that a poem should be judged by operative effectiveness, and that quality lies in mastering simple forms:

Ich sage dir: in allen ihnen,
Den großen Formen und den kleinen,
Die dir vielleicht belanglos scheinen
Und grade darum mächtig sind,
Weil sie versteht auch jedes Kind,
Mußt du geübt sein. ('Vorspruch', JRB, 3, 522)

Alongside these are poems that continue the vein of autobiographical self-reflection that was to culminate in the novel *Abschied*. For example, the striking poem 'Mein Bruder Ernst' (JRB, 3, 513–14) explores feelings of guilt about his brother's early suicide with a clarity of diction stripped of the bitter sarcasm of earlier poems about his family.

The collections *Der Mann, der alles glaubte* and *Sonette* (1934) are the first comprehensive statement of the new style, containing verses that demonstrate how Becher was able to transform the language of ideological necessity into highly personal gestures, producing poems that hover between cliché and confession:

Was wär ich, ohne daß mich die Partei
In ihre Zucht genommen, ihre strenge?!
Ein wilder Spießer, der mit Wutgeschrei
Sich selbst zerfetzt, und dabei eine Menge

Von Alkohol vertilgt. ('Die Partei', JRB, 3, 715)

---

38 For fuller details of Becher's activities in France, see Dwars, pp. 378–409 and Pike, *German Writers in Soviet Exile*, pp. 92–94.

Becher does not simply adopt the KPD's cultural diction, but is actively involved
in creating it: this personal investment in ideological language ensures that he is
bound securely into the Party's linguistic structures, but also creates a language
that offers space for communication, exchange, and even opposition to the
norms of Socialist Realist practice. The collections are characterised by the first
signs of Becher's later sonnet style, in which he strives to employ the form in a
variety of ways: in this collection, the sonnet serves either to construct a clear,
consistent form to autobiographical accounts, as in 'Die Partei', above, or to
provide a strong rhetorical structure for defiant antifascist poems (e.g. 'Der Haß',
JRB, 3, 689) or satirical swipes at incompetent *Tendenzdichtung* ('Gegen das
Lärm=Gedicht', JRB, 3, 780). Heinrich Mann, in a review of *Der Mann, der alles
glaubte* in the *Pariser Tageblatt*, took up the implied offer of rapprochement in a
common reassessment of the tradition, and praised the collection as 'das erste
Schimmern [...] einer zweiten Renaissance' for its successful reclamation of
classical forms for a humanistic 'Volkstümlichkeit'.[39]

Other poems from the early years of exile continue the process of
readmitting the tradition for contemporary use; the long poem *Deutschland* (JRB,
7, 127–282) creates parallels in form and diction with Heine's *Deutschland: Ein
Wintermärchen*. Characteristically, though, Becher invests his energies in the forms
of German Classicism, since Heine's irony does not come naturally to him, and
the events in which he becomes embroiled on his return to Moscow serve only to
drive him further into an encounter with the tradition: what began as an offer of
communication in the light of the Popular Front policy becomes an attempt to
shore up a sense of self under unbearable pressure.

Becher and his future wife Lilly Korpus returned to the Soviet Union at a
dangerous moment in 1936: Zinoviev and Kamenev had been arrested for the
murder of Kirov in December 1934, and were tried in August 1936. The betrayal
and arrest of almost the entire membership of the illegal BPRS group in Berlin in
June 1935 (only Jan Petersen escaped, since he was in Paris for the cultural
conference) and the bankruptcy of the Prague-based journal *Neue deutsche Blätter*
meant that the potential for communist cultural institutions in Europe
independent of Moscow had shrunk at the very moment that the Purges were
about to break out. Becher and Lilly Korpus were in a dilemma: she was expelled
from France for political activities, while coming under suspicion for her
supposed former Trotskyist association with the Ruth Fischer group within the
KPD. In the end, Becher procured a Soviet visa for her, and they travelled to
Moscow so that Becher could continue with the process of setting up *Das Wort*.

In the follow-up to the Zinoviev and Kamenev trial, every Party organisation
was required to expose traitors in its ranks, and with the KPD this was intensified
by intense feelings of hopelessness about the situation at home. At a meeting in

---

39 Cited by Dwars, pp. 385–86.

September 1936, Becher came under intense pressure over a supposed slight to Stalin and over his relationship with Lilly. In August 1936, Becher and Hans Günther had left a meeting of the Writers' Union, called to acclaim the verdicts against Zinoviev and Kamenev, after the usual standing ovation for Stalin, without realising that the meeting was due to compose a telegram to the General Secretary afterwards.[40] Other accusations went closer to the heart of Becher's fragile self-image. Alexander Barta, and after him, in an act of desperate self-defence, Lukács, take Becher to task for a 'Theorie [...] von der besonderen Art des Schriftstellers', setting himself up as a 'Dichter' who needs to be judged according to different standards. In Lukács's words:

> Wenn wir jetzt die Genossen Gábor, Günther und Becher schlagen, und wir haben sie gewaltig geschlagen und müssen sie schlagen, so wollen wir einen Gen. Becher halten, nur seine dichterische Sensibilität soll sich nicht entwickeln, [um] als Kompensation dafür solche Fehler zu haben.[41]

Hugo Huppert attacks from another angle, criticising exile writers who fail to overcome their feelings of foreignness in the Soviet homeland.[42] Both of these accusations hit home, but Becher, to his credit and alone among his colleagues at the meeting, does not attempt to defend himself by denouncing others, and offers to make good the perceived insult to Stalin by composing an epic poem in his honour.[43] The poem was composed but refused publication in its original form, as were most of Becher's texts in this period; Becher then published part of it himself in *Internationale Literatur*.[44]

Somehow, Becher managed to escape arrest during the purge of the German exile community in which, according to David Pike, more than 70% of the Germans working in the cultural apparatus were arrested.[45] Although little was published in the late 1930s, Becher continued to work, producing the volume *Der Glücksucher und die sieben Lasten* in 1936, a collection that is a key document of German exile literature. The style that had caused Becher problems with publication – the avoidance of overt agitation and the stress on humanism as opposed to class conflict – were what met the approval of the exile authors who were Becher's lifeline to the living culture.

---

40 See the protocol of this meeting, published as *Die Säuberung: Moskau 1936: Stenogramm einer geschlossenen Parteiversammlung: Georg Lukács, Johannes R. Becher, Friedrich Wolf u.a.*, ed. by Reinhard Müller (Reinbek: Rowohlt, 1991).

41 Lukács's speech to meeting, *Die Säuberung*, pp. 195–97.

42 *Die Säuberung*, p. 197.

43 There is no written evidence to support Julius Hay's assertion that Becher 'verpetzte alles und jeden bei der Parteileitung': Gyula Háy (Julius Hay), *Geboren 1900: Erinnerungen* (Reinbek: Wegner, 1977), p. 169.

44 'Hymnen auf einen Namen', *Internationale Literatur*, 7.5 (1937), 5.

45 Pike, *German Writers in Soviet Exile*, p. 357. Dwars has provided a detailed assessment of Becher's actions during the purge, and concludes that the evidence is as yet insufficient to account for the reasons for his survival at a time where colleagues like Hans Günther and Ernst Ottwalt were arrested and died during their sentences.

The poems in *Der Glücksucher* explore the forms of German Classicism in a search for a tone of elegy and accusation, often schooled on the sound-world of Hölderlin:

> Weh dem, der liebt und will glücklich sein Volk und frei,
> Haßt den Verrat und haßt Lügen, irres Geschwätz:
>   Oh, sie lohnen mit Foltern
>   Reichlich den! ('Die Heimat', JRB, 4, 16)

The reception of Hölderlin, and of Romanticism in images of a humanity alienated from nature, form a clear connection with poetry written in Germany in the 1930s, as Schäfer has pointed out (the tone of 'Die Heimat' is reminiscent of Gertrud von le Fort's *Lyrisches Tagebuch 1933–1945*). However, Becher is always engaged in a movement away from the possible ambiguities of his style and of the traditions that he explores; as in his early work, the projection of a resolution to conflicts into a utopian future can sometimes lead to empty gestures and pastiche. However, the poems *Der Glücksucher* succeed more often than they fail, although they often require a sympathetic understanding of the circumstances of their composition. For example, 'Tübingen oder Die Harmonie' employs the sonnet form as the embodiment of a state of harmony between movement and stasis, of perfect correspondence and communication between part and whole (though the clear aspiration to the properties of the Rilkean sonnet does Becher's poem no favours):

> Könnt ich so dichten, wie hier alles klug
> Verteilt ist, jedes steht an seiner Stelle.
> Des Dunklen nicht zuviel, genügend Helle,
> Die Burg, die Brücke, und der Straße Zug
>
> Zur Burg hinauf: verborgen nicht zuviel
> Und sichtbar doch nicht alles. Auch die Wellen
> Des Neckars halten Maß: in ihrem Spiel
> Erscheint das Meer schon, und zugleich der Quellen
>
> Ursprung ist spürbar. So geordnet ist
> Dies alles, einfach, und doch reich gegliedert.
> Wie ewiges Gespräch. Darin vermißt
>
> Man keine Stimme. Alles wird erwidert.
> Zur Brücke spricht die Burg. Die Brücke spricht
> Hinab zum Fluß. Ins Dunkel spricht das Licht. (JRB, 4, 26)

The language of form and harmony as ends in themselves, the balance of opposites and the Enlightenment project of illumination link Becher more strongly to developments in German culture than they do to Soviet Socialist Realism. However, Becher's aspiration to overcome conflict rather than explore ambiguity leads him down the path of a rather abstract aestheticism. The sonnets of this period are very different from the radical early poems in the 'Herbst= Gesänge' cycle, for instance, that had employed the sonnet form as an empty shell gesturing at an Enlightenment project that had collapsed into fragments;

however, a poem like 'Tübingen' seems like an attempt to piece that project together again in formal devices that are an end in themselves.

Not all the poems reach such extremes of aestheticism: the important poem 'Das Holzhaus' (JRB, 4, 152–68) gains power from its successful employment of a formal, but flexible diction binding together an elegiac nostalgia for the South German landscape with self-criticism and defiance. The poem acknowledges the separation of the poet from his *Heimat*, but suggests that the language of art can preserve a deep connection if the writer takes his responsibilities seriously:

> Laß dich nicht ins Vergessen drängen, nicht
> Ins Abgetrenntsein! [...]

> Zu sehr verwachsen bist du, als daß dich
> Der Schnitt der Grenze trennen könnte, wenn
> Er auch tief geht.

The poem ends with a striking statement of defiance that deftly summarises that combination of restorative cultural values and antifascist commitment that characterises Becher's best work in this period:

> Nicht einen Klang geb ich euch ab, nicht eine
> Der Farben wird freiwillig überlassen,
> Das Sensendengeln nicht und nicht das Läuten
> Der Kühe von den Almen, nichts dergleichen
> Gehört euch. Auch die Abenrote nicht,
> Kein Stern, kein Sturm, kein Stillesein. Das Zirpen
> Der Grillen nicht, nicht eines bunten Falters
> Anblick, wenn er an Blüten säugt, den Feldweg
> Muß man euch streitig machen, jeden Halm
> Und jedes Käferchen, selbst den Geschmack
> Der Speisen. *Unser* Wein ist's, den ihr trinkt,
> Und *unser* Brot, das euch labt. Noch vorerst.
> Das alles fordern wir zurück und noch
> Viel mehr: die Luft, die euch beglückt beim Atmen.

In its self-consciousness as a linguistic artefact, the poem acknowledges that battles over culture take place within the language itself: ownership of the power of definition, and of the culture's reservoir of symbol and imagery, means the ability to make deep connections between language and world, and ultimately means ownership of the land itself.

The Hitler-Stalin Pact, the extreme pressure that the new cordial relations between Berlin and Moscow put on antifascist emigrants, and constant battles with the Soviet censors, served only to drive Becher further into his private life. An edition of his collected poems in Russian translation, due to appear for his 50th birthday in May 1941, was reworked constantly in order to purge it of any political or antifascist content. The worst moment must have come when his birthday celebrations were held in the presence of diplomats from the German embassy, and the speeches tiptoed around Becher's antifascism.[46]

The German invasion of the Soviet Union freed Becher from this state of tension and gave new impetus to his work, allowing him to put his energies again into political work. His extensive and committed reworking of the tradition in the 1930s is transformed into a form of intense wishful thinking about the coming victory over fascism and the liberation of the 'true' Germany. His involvement with the *National-Komitee Freies Deutschland* and the *Bund Deutscher Offiziere*, founded in July and September 1943, during which he interviewed dozens of former *Wehrmacht* soldiers and officers, must have strengthened this self-image, even though the reports he wrote tend to express disappointment.[47]

However, it is difficult to know what to make of the title of his 1944 collection, *Die hohe Warte*, that seems a deliberate echo of the lines from Freiligrath's 'Spanien': 'Der Dichter steht auf einer höheren Warte | Als auf den Zinnen der Partei.' Freiligrath counted as a model poet who had moved from aestheticism to committed *Vormärz* writing (a nineteenth-century Heinrich Mann, in other words). For Becher to take as his title a reference to his earlier rejection of political literature is an intriguing revaluation of the 'cultural inheritance', hinting that he continues to feel that the *Dichter* has a calling above and beyond *Parteilichkeit*.

A key poem in this collection underlines the sense that he regards poetic form and the tradition as a means of self-protection:

Wenn einer Dichtung droht Zusammenbruch
Und sich die Bilder nicht mehr ordnen lassen,
Wenn immer wieder fehlschlägt der Versuch,
Sich selbst in eine feste Form zu fassen,

Wenn vor dem Übermaße des Geschauten
Der Blick sich ins Unendliche verliert,
Und wenn in Schreien und in Sterbenslauten
Die Welt sich wandelt und sich umgebiert,

Wenn Form nur ist: damit sie sich zersprenge
Und Ungestalt wird, wenn die Totenwacht
Die Dichtung hält am eigenen Totenbett –

Alsdann erscheint, in seiner schweren Strenge
Und wie das Sinnbild einer Ordnungsmacht,
Als Rettung vor dem Chaos – das Sonett. ('Das Sonett', JRB, 5, 230)

On the surface, the poem works with Lukácsian categories of decadence and the overcoming of self-destructive modernism through a return to traditional formal principles. Becher clearly sees himself as an exemplary figure in this process, yet

---

46 See Dwars, p. 473.
47 See interviews with Hauptmann Adams, Oberstleutnant von Sass, Major Hoffmann, in Gansel, *Metamorphosen eines Dichters*, pp. 242–44.

the poem's abstraction removes it from Lukács's historical scheme, presenting on the one hand a 'timeless' statement in the tradition of German Classicism and an intensely personal response to an unbearable situation.

Becher's work certainly suggests that he was holding on in a state of tension waiting for the release and new beginning on his return to Germany. For example, the poem 'Anrufung des deutschen Geistes' of 1944 (JRB, 5, 193) resurrects some of his Futurist influences in a vision of an explosive fusion of *Geist* and *Macht*:

> Deutscher Geist, gleich welcher Arten von Gestalt:
> Geist in Stein gehauen und Geist in Orgellauten,
> Geistes Kraft, sich ballend in der Wort=Gewalt,
> Geistesglut in Farben und geformt in Bauten –
>
> Heimatlos bist du geworden und verwaist,
> Einsam ragst du über blutigen Niederungen –
> Du, in deinen hohen Fernen, deutscher Geist:
> Werde Macht! Dein sei das Reich! Dir sei's errungen!

In poems like this, the isolation of exile is compensated for by an echo of the avant-gardist gestures of his early poetry, which had tried to overcome isolation and sickness through an intensification of language. His style has moved on, though, and his more usual procedure is to seek a reconnection with the tradition as a way of holding up a model of 'true' nationhood for the Germans. The drama *Schlacht um Moskau*, written in Tashkent on hearing the news that the German offensive had been turned back, refers to Shakespearean dramatic forms in its story of German responses to the war. A proletarian character deserts at the front, while Johannes Hörder, whose father is a judge, struggles with his conscience and is eventually executed for refusing to execute prisoners. The character of Hörder embodies Becher's technique of thinking through German guilt by referring to his own inner conflicts. Thus, although David Pike dismisses it as farcical and unrealistic, it is not the 'realism' of the play that is the standard by which it should be judged.[48] After all, how could Becher have known anything about conditions in the German army? Instead, *Schlacht um Moskau* represents an impassioned self-portrait, a critique of Nazi crimes that goes beyond ideological cliché and a model for a new German nationhood that attempts to assimilate positive aspects of the tradition into a non-conservative worldview. It was this range of contradictory attitudes and aspirations that Becher brought back to Germany with him in 1945.

---

48 Pike, *German Writers in Soviet Exile*, p. 394.

Homecoming

The components that Becher combined in his creation of the tradition which he brought to Germany in 1945 are complex, and they form a private mythology which shaped his career from the moment of his return from exile. Intensely personal concerns intertwine with the ideological discourse of the KPD, part of which Becher had helped to formulate, and in the euphoria of 1945 there seemed to be no tension between the two. The connections which Becher makes between classical forms and the preservation during the period of exile of what he often refers to as 'objektive Maße und Werte' are a standard component of his 'Erbe' conception and of the KPD policy of forging alliances with non-communist intellectuals.[49] The reference to the journal *Maß und Wert* is no coincidence. However, Becher's personal investment in these ideas is immense, demonstrated by his request to Thomas Mann in April 1948 for permission to use the title *Maß und Wert* for the journal which eventually became *Sinn und Form*.[50] Therefore, establishing verifiable categories of literary quality was of prime importance for Becher, and it is at this point that his own conceptions part company with the expediencies of the official dogma, which he had himself helped to formulate. His response to the experience of two kinds of cultural barbarity – complicity in Soviet terror suppressed and/or justified through opposition to Nazism – was a fetishisation of language, an overloading of the capacity of the written word to carry moral force. The perceived defeat of German culture in 1933, and defensive mental habits ingrained in the Soviet Union, led to a turning-inward of this moral function of language, towards the preservation of cultural values which are somehow embodied in the uncorrupted 'Word'. Thus Becher can insist, in his speech to the First Writers' Congress in October 1947, that 'literature' resisted National Socialism:

> Unsere Literatur hat in ihren besten Vertretern, in ihrer eigentlichen schöpferischen Substanz, die härteste Prüfung deutscher Geschichte in Ehren bestanden. (JRB, 17, 167–68)

Becher's insistence that he is defending a 'true' literary tradition which embodies the humanist cultural values of the past binds him into the legitimising narrative of the KPD, which claimed to represent the culmination of these values, but this coincidence of Becher's private mythology with the expediency of the Party is highly problematic. When the hopes of 1945 begin to recede, differences and contradictions become increasingly clear, and the defensive reflex in Becher's attitude to form and language becomes more pronounced as he struggles with his

---

49 See, for example, his speech at the anniversary of the founding of the *Kulturbund*, 7 July 1946 (JRB, 17, 46).

50 See the letter to Mann requesting permission to use the title, 24 April 1948, in Becher, *Briefwechsel*, I, pp. 373–74, and Mann's polite refusal: 20 May 1948, in Johannes R. Becher, *Briefwechsel 1909–1958*, ed. by Rolf Harder (Berlin: Aufbau, 1993), II: *Briefe an Johannes R. Becher 1909–1958*, p. 345.

conscience over his role in the GDR. In a nutshell, he is emotionally dependent
on the categories of the *Erbe* theory, which helped him through the years of exile.

The remarkable poem, 'Turm von Babel', written after 1949, has been rightly
identified by Hans Mayer as an anti-Stalinist poem.[51] However, it is far more than
simply an allegory, especially if we recall the status of Stalinism in Becher's earlier
work: it documents the failure of a cultural, linguistic and psychological project
and the acceptance that his attempts to overcome the modernist crisis of language
have come to nothing:

> Das ist der Turm von Babel,
> Er spricht in allen Zungen.
> Und Kain erschlägt den Abel
> Und wird als Gott besungen.
>
> Er will mit seinem Turme
> Wohl in den Himmel steigen
> Und will vor keinem Sturme,
> Der ihn umstürmt, sich neigen.
>
> Gerüchte aber schwirren,
> Die Wahrheit wird verschwiegen.
> Die Herzen sich verwirren –
> So hoch sind wir gestiegen!
>
> Das Wort wird zur Vokabel,
> Um sinnlos zu verhallen.
> Es wird der Turm zu Babel
> Im Sturz zu nichts zerfallen. (JRB, 6, 40)

As Dwars puts it: 'Für seine Gedichte wäre es besser gewesen, Becher hätte diese
andauernden Widersprüche selbst zur Sprache gebracht, statt zuversichtlich von
ihrer Lösbarkeit zu sprechen.'[52] Unfortunately, a return to the kind of modernist
thinking about language from whose consequences he had fled all his life was
both psychologically and politically impossible. Instead, Becher works on other
solutions, gradually separating what he saw as his 'true' personality – the classicist
Dichter as inheritor of the cultural tradition – from the politician. The failure of
restorative cultural values to transform Germany does not lead him to question
these values, but to retreat into them as a renewed form of the 'inner emigration'
to which they are eminently suited.

On his return to Germany, Becher hoped to experience the resolution of the
conflict between state and nation, *Geist* and *Macht*, *Nationalautor* and *Staatsdichter*.
He consciously, and with all due public ceremony, takes over the baton of
Dichterfürsten like Gerhart Hauptmann or Heinrich Mann, and creates a tradition
for himself which supposedly leads directly back to Goethe, who becomes the

---

51   See Hans Mayer, *Der Turm von Babel: Erinnerungen an eine Deutsche Demokratische Republik* (Frankfurt
     a.M.: Suhrkamp, 1993), p. 12.
52   Dwars, p. 586.

archetype of a personality at ease with itself in its representation of all that is healthy in the nation: 'Goethe – ein schönes ungetrenntes Ganzes ... wer aber wünscht sich nicht als solches auch sein Volk, seine Heimat, sein Vaterland?' (JRB, 17, 262) This vision of Goethe personifies the attributes which Becher desires for himself, corresponding to the ideal of the 'neuer Mensch', which he describes in 1946 in thoroughly restorative terms as an: 'einheitliche, freiheitliche Persönlichkeit, in welcher Verheinheitlichung ... die Entfremdung des Menschen mit sich selbst aufgehoben ist und nicht das Herz dem Verstand widerspricht und Fühlen und Denken miteinander uneins sind und nicht das innere Sehnen im äußeren Handeln als Gegenteil und als verzerrt erscheint' (JRB, 17, 19).

Becher taps into traditions of the personalisation of complex social, political and cultural interactions, through which figures like Hauptmann, Mann or Goethe are stylised into representatives of German *Geist* standing in opposition to the misuse of power. Becher formulates it in this way at the inaugural meeting of the *Kulturbund* in July 1945: 'Unserer Klassik ist niemals eine klassische Politik gefolgt' (JRB, 16, 461). The resolution to this conflict is now at hand, and the old Expressionist idea of the unity of *Wort* and *Tat* is to be given a new set of clothes at this critical historical moment, where the opposites are united in a great synthesis which he calls 'die Machtwerdung des Geistes' (JRB, 13, 443). However, at the same time he is able to entrust his old supporter Katharina Kippenberg with the task of reissuing his 1940 volume of sonnets, *Wiedergeburt*, in such a way that 'das zu sehr politisch Zugespitzte wegfallen soll', and with making a selection of his early work concentrating on 'das Bleibende – Dichterische'.[53]

It was not long before the first signs of strain began to show in the delicate balancing act that Becher was trying to perform, and his tendency to identify absolutely with the roles he played made him an unreliable executor of political expediencies. With his passionate belief in the unity of the *Kulturnation*, he had the potential to become awkward when the emphasis of SED policy had to be shifted. In fact, there are indications that the Soviets considered replacing him as *Kulturbund* President in 1946 because he was too open to 'bourgeois' writers and politicians; archive material from the Soviet Military Administration records Becher's protests to the head of the Administration at the time, Semenov, that the Soviets 'have a false impression of those Germans working in the British or American Zones' and are 'alienating' the bourgeois parties.[54]

Becher's continuing preoccupation with questions of truth in art manifests itself in a peculiar mixture of elitism and openness in his relations with other

---

53 Letter to Katharina Kippenberg, 11 May 1946, in Becher, *Briefwechsel*, I, pp. 294–95. The volume of early poems appeared in 1950 in the Insel-Verlag Leipzig as *Vollendung träumend: Ausgewählte Gedichte aus dem frühen Werk*, although Kippenberg had died before she was able to complete the editorial work.

54 Norman Naimark, Bernd Bonwetsch and Gennady Bordyugov (eds), *SVAG: Upravlenie Propagandy (Informatsii) i S.I.Tyul'panov 1945–1949: Sbornik Dokumentov* (Moscow: Rossiya Molodaya, 1994), pp. 69 and 71. My translation.

artists. While he kept lines of communication open with bourgeois colleagues in the West, the concern for quality and strictness of form which was of such importance for him led to an attitude of exclusivity towards 'proletarian' writers, about whose work he was often dismissive and personally offensive, in ways reminiscent of the debates in *Die Linkskurve* more than two decades earlier. He polemicises in the *Kulturbund* against 'das "Wir"', das schädliche Verallgemeinern' in radically 'proletarian' writing in favour of quality and the individual voice.[55]

Differences of opinion with the *Schutzverband Deutscher Autoren* in the preparatory stages of the First Writers' Congress show that Becher was concerned that the representative organisations of German literature should rise above the role of *Berufsverband* and should be more concerned with *Weltanschauung*.[56] The *Kulturbund* was withdrawn from the organisation of the Congress in July 1947, because its status as a non-partisan organisation was seriously in doubt, and its banning in the American and British Zones in November 1947 demonstrated both the impossibility of the task which Becher had conceived for it and his contradictory conception of the political independence of culture.

These disappointments, and Becher's increasing bitterness at the tendency of his expected transformation in German culture to become submerged in bureaucratic work and the politics of the East-West confrontation, help to explain his pique that the *Kulturbund* was not represented at the first People's Congress (6/7 December 1947). This was just the kind of intervention that the *Kulturbund* had to make if it was to be effective according to Becher's conception, but tactical considerations only a month after the *Kulturbund*'s banning had led to its exclusion. Becher threatened to resign over this, and over accusations by Wilhelm Pieck that he had carried out 'keinerlei politische Arbeit'. His letter of resignation sets out in clear terms his dissatisfaction with the role he was being forced into, which contradicted his own self-image: as a writer, he is 'innerlich nicht in der Lage' to throw himself into day-to-day political work.[57]

Becher is brought back into the fold through the agreement to allow the *Kulturbund* to send a delegation to the second People's Congress (17/18 March 1948). Becher was trying to use the institutional framework of the Congresses to make an intervention in the cause of the unity of German culture; the fact that the Congresses were unequivocally a step on the road to the setting up of a separate East German state demonstrates the inadequacy of his conception of principled intervention and the shakiness of the representative role which he had created for himself.

The context for the shifting emphases in Becher's work is formed by the Two-Year Plan and the *Kulturverordnung* of the *Deutsche Wirtschaftskommission* of

---

55 Cited by Gansel, *Der gespaltene Dichter*, p. 18.
56 See Carsten Gansel, *Parlament des Geistes: Literatur zwischen Hoffnung und Repression, 1945–1961* (Berlin: BasisDruck Verlag, 1996), pp. 44–46.
57 Gansel, *Der gespaltene Dichter*, pp. 42–43.

March 1949. The attractiveness the privileged terms offered to artists, and the very fact that the state was going to promote and protect culture, enabled artists to combine their principles with healthy self-interest. Becher continued to protest against the 'monopolisierte Kritik' exercised by bodies such as the *Kulturelle Beirat*, claiming that this kind of practice was leading to the 'Abwanderung von Begabungen' to the West,[58] but he could not or would not see the connection between the administrative promotion of particular forms of literary activity and a strategy which was making inevitable the division of Germany. His more personal works in this period – such as the literary diary *Auf andere Art so große Hoffnung* (1950) and the aphoristic texts *Verteidigung der Poesie* (1952) and *Poetische Konfession* (1954) – are full of critical references to the direction of cultural policy in the GDR. In them principled criticisms of the Formalism Campaign mingle with personal resentments against critics whom he calls 'bürokratische Schnüffler' (JRB, 13, 586), but he still feels moved to appeal to the Central Committee of the SED as the highest arbiter if articles critical of his work appear in the press.[59]

Protests such as we have outlined above could record only temporary successes, if at all, and the form they take and Becher's inability to completely prise himself away from the terms of the official discourse of the SED reflect the influence of ideological categories on his inner biography. Becher is powerless to affect the official discourse of the SED in any meaningful way because he cannot dispense with the language in which he conceived his response to National Socialism, which is the same language used to legitimise the rule of the SED. However, the failure of his attempts to present himself as the personification of the unified *Kulturnation* manifests itself in a shift in the terms of his self-representation in his work. He adopts various strategies in order to deal with the contradictions in his public role. The personality which Becher works on in his writing no longer embodies an achieved unity of *Geist*, cultural tradition and political practice, but rather represents the unresolved contradiction between artist and functionary. This theme is the common thread running through his later work, particularly in the important prose publications, and unpublished poems such as 'Staatsmann und Dichter'.[60]

Becher turns out programmatic poems like 'Straße frei!' of 1950 (JRB, 6, 69), which celebrate the youth of the nation, who will bring about the changes which the older generation have prepared the way for, and he enjoys playing the high-handed role of father and protector to young poets such as Günter Kunert, who describes him as 'Heger und Pfleger im Dichtergarten'.[61] At the same time, a

---

58 At the *Tagung parteigenössischer Schriftsteller der Ostzone*, 8/9 April 1948, cited by Gansel, *Parlament des Geistes*, p. 128.

59 See his letter to the Central Committee of the SED, 25 March 1953, in Gansel, *Der gespaltene Dichter*, pp. 83–85.

60 First published in 1991, *SuF*, 43, 341, reprinted in Gansel, *Der gespaltene Dichter*, p. 188.

61 Günter Kunert, *Erwachsenenspiele: Erinnerungen* (Munich: Hanser, 1997), p. 143.

number of poems written in response to the various disappointments which he
experienced indicate that he is beginning to work at a version of his personality
which he hopes will survive beyond his death. For example, 'Das Nichts'
describes the survival of the poet's life and work beyond his death as 'Gestalt
werden' in the face of the 'Abgrund' (JRB, 5, 390). Works like *Verteidigung der
Poesie* and *Poetische Konfession* are full of pleas for understanding: a dark alter ego
figure from *Abschied*, 'der Andere' turns up again in the latter, this time as that
aspect of the poet-politician which gathers fame and praise through politics and
compromise, while suppressing the poet's true self, 'den Eigentlichen' (JRB, 13,
438). Editorial work on a Hölderlin edition and a collection of his beloved
Baroque poetry help to establish a personal canon that also challenges the
narrowness of the SED's official literary pantheon. At the same time, Becher
displays a concern with establishing measures for judging true literature that
sometimes descends into a helpless pedantry that clings to the increasingly
threatened values of Becher's poetic project. Nevertheless, what Dwars calls his
'Versuche, durch Selbstverständigung über die Eigengesetzte der Kunst wieder zu
den Quellen einer versiegenden Produktivität zurückzufinden' also demonstrate
the potential for a restorative attitude to aesthetics to challenge aspects of
Socialist Realist literary practice.

   What appears to be happening in his work is the adoption of a literary
quietism, in which the classical principles of harmony, which should govern the
state, can be applied without compromise in the literary sphere. As he says in the
Poetische Konfession: 'Im guten Gedicht kann es weder eine Diktatur des
Inhaltlichen noch eine solche des Formalen geben, aber wir meinen, daß im guten
Gedicht von einer Hegemonie die Rede sein kann, unter welcher man eine
Vorherrschaft versteht, der man sich freiwillig unterordnet' (JRB, 13, 466). Poetic
form is the last refuge for the utopia which Becher had brought back with him
from exile.

   The disappointments and pressures connected with the increasingly oppressive atmosphere of the GDR, as well as disgust at the compromises that were
necessary to push through cultural projects in which he passionately believed,
such as the Academy of Arts and, finally, the Ministry of Culture in 1954,[62] no
longer allowed him the option of projecting his cultural longings into a utopian
future. Becher is no longer able to sustain his customary level of poetic
production: at a time when poets are being encouraged to work quickly and
spontaneously in response to the construction of Socialism in the GDR, Becher is
no longer able or willing to keep up. After the short collection *Glück der Ferne –
leuchtend nah* and the *Neue deutsche Volkslieder*, his poetry seems to dry up. As a
writer committed to a progressive politics, he has closed off an avenue of retreat

---

62   See, for example, the speech he makes to the Central Committee meeting in July 1953, attempting
     to buy support for the creation of a Ministry of Culture by joining in the chorus of condemnation
     against Rudolf Herrnstadt after the June 1953 uprising: Gansel, *Der gespaltene Dichter*, pp. 95–108.

into a true conservatism that would at least have allowed him a further source of creativity: this dilemma is what differentiates him finally from the bourgeois writers with whom Schäfer compares him.

Conclusion

Schäfer's discussion of Becher's nature poetry as an illustration of his thesis was provocative, but it offered potential research perspectives that cut across the politicised categories of the Cold War. GDR *Germanistik* had long recognised the significance of Becher's nature poetry in exile, but it could not have accepted the connections that Schäfer makes with his 1930 paradigm and with the literature of inner emigration. On the other hand, western scholars still find it difficult to accept that Becher wrote anything of any quality after his Expressionist-Futurist years; works such as 'Das Holzhaus', the collection *Der Glücksucher und die sieben Lasten* or the novel *Abschied* have yet to achieve wide recognition as significant statements of German exile literature. The shift in perspective offered by the 1930–1960 periodisation allows us not only to view such works with new eyes, but also to place Becher's engagement with the tradition in a broader context, analysing the interaction of biographical and aesthetic factors without losing sight of the political imperatives of his career in the KPD. Far from denying political factors, a shift away from a political periodisation allows us to put such factors in a proper perspective: an understanding of Becher's literary career requires a complex combination of approaches that includes, but cannot be reduced to, political categories.

Bertolt Brecht

Introduction: Brecht and the 1930 paradigm

Amongst the five authors chosen to lend a diachronic dimension to our investigation of the dominant literary mood in Germany between 1930 and 1960, Bertolt Brecht appears, at least on the face of things, to constitute a strong counter-example. Neither a member of 1930 generation, like Eich and Huchel, who made their literary debuts at the onset of the cultural retrenchment which we have charted throughout this study, nor one of the early Expressionist generation, like Benn and Becher, whose output and/or reception underwent a shift in the late 1920s in tune with that retrenchment, Brecht's intellectual trajectory is not easily rendered compatible with what we have termed the 1930 paradigm. Indeed, Brecht's presence in the literary journals which form our corpus around 1930 is one which consistently challenges the establishment of the restorative dominant. As we have seen, despite acknowledgement of the influence of his early poetry, Brecht is frequently attacked by Raschke and Eich in *Die Kolonne*. His most widely known work of the time, the *Dreigroschenoper*, is written off for its perceived lack of serious literary merit (*Kolonne*, 2, 62), his work in general criticised for its nihilism and the suspect values of *Zivilisation* (*Kolonne*, 1, 65). Similarly, but more programmatically, it is Brecht's aesthetic position, or at least that which he is seen to represent, which acts as the principal counterpoint to the promotion of Georg Lukács's programme in the final phase of *Die Linkskurve*. In particular, the final issue of the journal sees Brecht and Ottwalt castigated for what Lukács views as their 'radikalen Bruch mit allem Alten' (*Lkv*, 4.11/12, 15–24) and Brecht's theoretical reflections on epic theatre explicitly rejected by Andor Gábor (*Lkv*, 4.11/12, 27–32). While in these two journals, as in *Das Wort* in the mid- to late 1930s, Brecht had this anti-restorative function largely imposed upon him by others without voicing his own position in public, in *Die literarische Welt* Brecht himself assumed a radical position at odds with the emerging restorative dominant. Through the damning verdict which he delivered on the poetry of the young generation in his judging of the journal's poetry prize in February 1927, 'Kurzer Bericht über 400 (vierhundert) junge Lyriker' (*DLW*, 3.5, 1), Brecht again became a counterpoint for proponents of a more conservative aesthetic discourse. Among the many outraged responses to Brecht's judgement, for example, was Klaus Mann's *Nachwort* to the 1927 *Anthologie jüngster Lyrik*, the publication of which gave Eich his first lyric platform and which has been seen as a symbolic document for the re-assertion of tradition-centred poetics.[1]

It is precisely this perception of Brecht from the Weimar Republic, as a political and aesthetic revolutionary, opposing both political and aesthetic reaction, which has informed Brecht's status in existing accounts of the 1930 paradigm. Brecht's verdict on the poems submitted to *Die literarische Welt* in 1927, for instance, is one of the pieces included by Anton Kaes in his documentation of Weimar literary manifestos, as is Klaus Mann's response.[2] Reproduced under the heading 'Zur Öffentlichkeitskrise der Lyrik', Brecht's polemic is cited as evidence of an 'epochengeschichtlich signifikanten Umbruch von einer ästhetisch-autonomen "Kunstliteratur" zu einer sachlich-kritischen "Gebrauchsliteratur"', that is, as evidence of the preceding literary mood against which the *Kolonne* shift towards *Innerlichkeit* is perceived to have taken place.[3] Elsewhere, in his introduction, Brecht is invoked by Kaes as a central member of the Weimar avant-garde, seeking to modernise and 'democratise' German literary culture in order to bring it into line with that of the United States, France, and Britain. Thus, emphasis is placed by Kaes on Brecht's radio work – both theoretical and practical – his positive engagement with the typically *sachlich* phenomena of boxing and jazz, and his proletarian-revolutionary writing.[4] Above all, of course, it is his role within the context of contested Marxist aesthetics, as the counterpoint to Lukács in *Die Linkskurve*, which establishes Brecht's anti-restorative credentials, and it is here that Brecht is deployed by Schäfer himself.[5] The status afforded to Brecht as an authority for this unorthodox aesthetic position is highlighted in Gallas's account of *Die Linkskurve* where the final issue of the journal tellingly becomes the 'Anti-Brecht Heft' and where Brecht's name comes to be used as a shorthand for the anti-restorative position in the BPRS: 'Die Entwicklung im Bund proletarisch-revolutionärer Schriftsteller und in der *Linkskurve* führte zur Konfrontation zweier sich marxistisch verstehender Theorien, für die die Namen Brecht und Lukács gesetzt werden können.'[6] In turn, Brecht's contributions to the Expressionism Debate, unpublished until the late 1960s, and his dissenting

---

1   See Leonard Olschner, 'Fractured Continuities: Pressures on lyrical tradition at mid-century', *German Studies Review*, 13 (1990), 417–40 (p. 425) and Hermann Korte, 'Lyrik am Ende der Weimarer Republik', in Rolf Grimminger (ed.), *Hansers Sozialgeschichte der deutschen Literatur vom 16. Jahrhundert bis zur Gegenwart*, 12 vols, VIII: *Literatur der Weimarer Republik 1918–1933*, ed. by Bernhard Weyergraf (Munich: Hanser, 1995), pp. 601–35 (p. 618).

2   Anton Kaes, *Weimarer Republik: Manifeste und Dokumente zur deutschen Literatur 1918–1933* (Stuttgart: Metzler, 1983), pp. 441–44 and pp. 446–48.

3   Kaes, p. xxxii.

4   See Kaes, pp. xxvi–xxx, p. xxxvi, and pp. 216–18.

5   Hans Dieter Schäfer, 'Zur Periodisierung der deutschen Literatur seit 1930', in Nicolas Born and Jürgen Manthey (eds), *Literaturmagazin 7: Nachkriegsliteratur* (Reinbek: Rowohlt, 1977), pp. 95–115 (pp. 97–98).

6   Helga Gallas, *Marxistische Literaturtheorie: Kontroversen im Bund proletarisch-revolutionärer Schriftsteller* (Neuwied: Luchterhand, 1971), p. 69.

interventions against the strictures of SED cultural policy in the GDR provide a trajectory for this same unorthodox position across both 1933 and 1945. It is no coincidence in this context that Frank Trommler cites Brecht's words in 1948 on re-entering German territory for the first time after his exile – 'Hier muß man ja wieder ganz von vorne anfangen'[7] – as a counter-example to West German restoration, nor that Trommler cites Brecht elsewhere as an exception amongst the exiled generation in the GDR, his non-conformity to official policy assuring an influence which lasted beyond the 1950s.[8]

Viewed in this way, through the lens of the radical positions adopted in the Weimar Republic, Brecht's career is scarcely compatible with our understanding of the 1930 paradigm, and it is this initial observation which informs the structure of this chapter. The programmatic position adopted by Brecht in 1927 in *Die literarische Welt* acts as the starting-point for a consideration of his lyric poetry, viewed through the lens of his attempts at this time to re-configure the status and function of poetry as an institution. In the second half, this perspective is reversed, insofar as we look back from the early 1950s at the changing nature of Brecht's institutional relationships and, in particular, at his publication practice. In both sections, we conclude by considering the restorative thesis where it seems to be at its strongest, namely in the relatively isolated literary existence of exile. As we shall see, Brecht's relationship to the 1930 paradigm is a complex one which remains to a substantial degree tied to the political history of the mid-twentieth century. Nonetheless, Brecht's literary career in these decades is susceptible to a 'restorative' reading which hinges on the dynamics of two key categories which define his writing, namely 'use-value' and 'prestige-value'. The former lends a consistent stability of meaning to his literary output throughout the period, albeit at the expense of the conventional institution of literature; the latter can be seen to gain ascendancy through exile and above all into the GDR where Brecht increasingly acquires a position at the centre of that conventional institution. It is in this latter development that Brecht manifests most clearly the prevailing restorative mood which we have sought to describe in this study.

---

7   Frank Trommler, 'Emigration und Nachkriegsliteratur: Zum Problem der geschichtlichen Kontinuität', in Reinhold Grimm and Jost Hermand (eds), *Exil und Innere Emigration: Third Wisconsin Workshop* (Frankfurt a. M.: Athenäum, 1972), pp. 173–97 (p. 173).
8   Frank Trommler, 'Nachkriegsliteratur: Eine neue deutsche Literatur?', in Nicolas Born and Jürgen Manthey (eds), *Literaturmagazin 7: Nachkriegsliteratur* (Reinbek: Rowohlt, 1977), pp. 167–86 (p. 182).

Brecht's Poetry

We have consistently noted the centrality of poetry, as the epitome of the conventional institution of literature, within the 1930 paradigm. One of the principal manifestations of the restorative shift around 1930, for example, is the revival of traditional forms of lyric poetry, at a time when their decline, or death, was otherwise being widely heralded. Similarly, a turn to the most personal and introspective of genres is all to easy to understand against the backdrop of dictatorship or exile, while the *Trümmerzeit* too brought with it a flood of new poetry publications. As existing accounts suggest, the notion of a restorative periodisation in the mid-decades of the twentieth century is at its most persuasive when applied to lyric poetry, and, as we have demonstrated in the second half of this study, this holds particularly true for the literary output of Benn, Becher, Huchel, and Eich. This highlights the importance of engaging with Brecht's practice as a lyric poet and with the theoretical programme which lay behind that practice, and in this respect significant points of contrast already begin to emerge with our four other authors. While Benn, Becher, Huchel, and Eich are each known predominantly as lyric poets, and were received as such during their lifetimes, Brecht's reception as a poet has only really gained momentum in the past three decades, increasingly escaping the shadows cast by his contributions as theatrical practitioner and theoretician. The lateness of this reception is all the more noteworthy given the sheer volume of Brecht's lyric output which encompasses some 2,500 poems.[9] Made up of an astonishing diversity – sonnets and ballads, epigrams and epics, love poems and political poems, nature poems and city poems, poems in strict form and poems in free form – and distributed across his entire literary career, this output invites comparison amongst German poets perhaps only with Goethe. At least this is the view maintained by Tom Kuhn in his introduction to the poetry volume of the latest *Brecht Handbuch*: 'In seinem Werk nimmt die Lyrik eine absolut zentrale Stellung ein.'[10]

Kuhn's reflections on Brecht's significance as a poet, and the barriers to his reception in this role, are particularly telling in the context of the present study in terms of what they reveal about the assumptions which inform judgements of poetic quality. If Brecht has only recently begun to be considered seriously for the crown of greatest German poet of the twentieth century, at the expense of Rilke and his heirs apparent Benn and Celan, then this is a function not only of lack of familiarity with Brecht's lyric output, but also of the persistence of a conventional evaluatively laden category of *Dichtung*. Two further examples of Brecht's reception may stand for many in illustrating the point. Writing in the Reclam

---

9   See Jan Knopf, *Gelegentlich: Poesie: Ein Essay über die Lyrik Bertolt Brechts* (Frankfurt a.M.: Suhrkamp, 1996), p. 8.

10 Tom Kuhn, 'Brecht als Lyriker', in Jan Knopf (ed.), *Brecht Handbuch*, 5 vols (Stuttgart: Metzler, 2001–2003), II: *Gedichte*, pp. 1–21 (pp. 1–3).

poetry edition *Deutsche Gedichte 1930–1960*, for example, Hans Bender highlights
in Brecht's late emergence as a poet precisely those qualities which contravene the
conventional category of the *Dichter* and which have therefore hindered reception
of his poetry: 'Brecht wurde zur Leitfigur anti-bürgerlicher, anti-akademischer,
sozial- und gesellschaftskritisch engagierter Lyrik; auch des subjektiven, unsen-
timentalen Erlebnisgedichts ohne poetische Stilisierung.'[11] Similarly, and
symptomatically, it is Brecht who is chosen by Karl Otto Conrady as the
antithesis of conventional *Dichtung*, where that term denotes an elevated poetic
realm entirely divorced from politically and socially engaged writing: 'Brecht hat
hier also wenig zu suchen, wenn man ihn ernst nimmt, wohl aber ein
Herbstgedicht von Nikolaus Lenau.'[12] Or, as Kuhn concludes: 'Der Abstand
zwischen [Brechts] Gedichten und [seiner] Poetik auf der einen und der von
Rilke, Benn oder Celan auf der anderen Seite ist immens.'[13] The more recent
acknowledgements of the quality of Brecht's poetry rest then to some extent on
the more open and inclusive definition of *Dichtung* which has developed since the
1960s, in itself a symptom of the erosion of the 1930–1960 paradigm as we have
described it. At the same time, Conrady's implication that we might not take
Brecht at his own word suggests that the door to the conventional category has
been left ajar. As he continues, 'so muß dann ein Interpret, der unter solchen
Vorzeichen Brecht "retten" will, aus seinen Texten "das Dichterische" heraus-
zufiltern suchen'. Of course, our aim is not to 'rescue' Brecht, but it is to establish
just how his poetic programme and practice measure up against this 'conventional' notion of *Dichtung*. As we shall see, Brecht's emphasis in his poetic
programme and the vast majority of his output on a functional and communicative approach results in a contradictory relationship to aesthetic restoration: on
the one hand, radical innovation of the institution of poetry; on the other, a
consistent stabilisation of meaning.

1926–1927: 'He! He! The Iron Man'

Brecht's 1927 polemic, 'Kurzer Bericht über 400 (vierhundert) junge Lyriker' (BB,
21, 191–93), offers an obvious point of departure for our consideration of
Brecht's poetic programme and practice. For all its deliberately exaggerated shock
value, Brecht's judgement on the poetry submitted to *Die literarische Welt*
enunciates a set of distinct poetological principles through a double strategy:
firstly, negatively, through the rejection of the poems submitted to the journal's

---

11   Hans Bender (ed.), *Deutsche Gedichte 1930–1960* (Stuttgart: Reclam, 1983), p. 12.
12   Karl Otto Conrady, 'Gegen die Mystifikation der Dichtung und des Dichters', in Karl Otto
     Conrady, *Literatur und Germanistik als Herausforderung* (Frankfurt a.M.: Suhrkamp, 1974), pp. 97–
     124 (p. 102).
13   Kuhn, 'Brecht als Lyriker', p. 4.

competition by young poets; and secondly, positively, through the selection of Hannes Küpper's 'He, He! The Iron Man!' – not submitted to the competition and found, according to Brecht, in a cycling magazine – as the winning poem. In this way, as a statement of Brecht's poetic principles in advance of the shocks of 1929–1932, the article bears fruitful comparison, or rather contrast, with the restorative poetological principles set out by Eich in 'Bemerkungen über Lyrik' (GE, 4, 458–61) in 1932. Above all, while Eich was steadfastly defending poetry as a natural and spontaneous phenomenon, free of intention and will, Brecht was seeking to measure poetry only in terms of its usefulness, and it is this measure which justifies Brecht's rejection of the poetry submitted to *Die literarische Welt*. The poems of Impressionism and Expressionism are criticised as '"rein" lyrische Produkte', formed out of 'hübschen Bildern und aromatischen Wörtern'. Rilke, George and Werfel are singled out as representatives 'einer verbrauchten Bourgeoisie', the young generation taken to task for following these literary models and for their failure to engage with reality, which has resulted in 'Sentimentalität, Unechtheit, und Weltfremdheit'. Notably for Brecht, this reality is a concrete, immediate and objective 'Wirklichkeit', far removed from Eich's subjective *Wahrhaftigkeit*. Poetry, writes Brecht accordingly, is 'etwas, [...] was man [...] auf den Gebrauchswert untersuchen muß. [...] Alle großen Gedichte haben den Wert von Dokumenten'.

It is for this reason that Brecht chooses Küpper's homage to the cycling champion, Reggie MacNamara, Küpper's poem having 'einen gewissen dokumentarischen Wert'. Here, Brecht goes on to contradict two further central principles outlined by Eich. The subject-matter of his chosen poem is clearly not the 'neutral' medium of nature poetry which allows for the expression of the subjective self. Rather, the sport of cycling is a typically *neusachlich* topos, and it is difficult not to be reminded here of the threat which mass spectator and participation sport was perceived by Willy Haas to pose to literary culture, particularly amongst the young. Further, Brecht's choice undermines the notion of poetry as an elitist genre, as the creation of a poet-genius not prone to making concessions to popular tastes. Küpper's poem has the virtue of being 'einfach' and 'singbar'. It is simply 'das Beste, was sein Verfasser zustande bringen konnte', for, after all, Brecht has long believed 'daß jeder halbwegs normale Deutsche ein Gedicht schreiben kann'. Clearly in his judgement for the poetry prize, Brecht's principal rhetorical strategy is a subversion of the institution of literature which has in the first place given him this prestigious office, and the tone and vocabulary deployed by Brecht throughout the article supports this iconoclastic procedure. The numeral '400' which appears in the title of the piece, the reference in the opening line to 'einen Haufen jüngster Lyrik' and later to 'ein ganzer Haufen sehr gerühmter Lyrik', the description of poets as 'Verfasser' and of the writing process as 'Herstellung' all work against the conventional values of *Dichtung*. Throughout, the emphasis is on poetry as something which is manufactured, a product of modern society in contrast to George's 'Druckkunst'. As Fähnders puts it, these are all 'Formulierungen, die [...] die in Deutschland mächtige Genie- und Schöpferästhetik konterkarieren'.[14]

The 'Bericht über 400 Lyriker' stands among a small number of related pieces in Brecht's writings from this period. 'Weder nützlich noch schön' (BB, 21, 193–94), for example, responds to the widespread criticism provoked by Brecht's judgement on the poetry competition and pursues many of the same themes using much of the same language. Again, poetry is to be judged from a 'Nützlichkeitsstandpunkt', and again Brecht refers to the poems submitted to Die literarische Welt in deliberately functional terms as a 'Haufen von [...] lyrischen Erzeugnissen'. Again, Rilke, George, and Werfel are singled out as the symbols of the 'Dichtung der ausgehenden Bourgeoisie', the isolationism of which is seen by Brecht to have given a common direction to the 400 poems submitted. 'Ich will Stefan George nicht für den Weltkrieg verantwortlich machen', Brecht concedes charitably, 'aber ich sehe keinen Grund dafür, daß er sich isolierte'. Similarly, in 'Bert Brechts Erwiderung' (BB, 21, 200–01), which appeared in the May/June edition of Die neue Zeit in Dresden as a direct response to a letter from one of the disgruntled poets who had submitted an entry to Die literarische Welt, Brecht re-affirmed 'Gebrauchswert' as the sole significant criterion for judging poetry. From around the same time, a note entitled 'Die Lyrik als Ausdruck' (BB, 21, 201–02) conceives of poetry as a two way process of exchange ('handeln'), criticising poets who view it only as a one-way process of expression: 'Von den Lyrikern meint man, sie gäben nur noch den reinen Ausdruck, so, daß ihr Handeln eben nur im Ausdrücken besteht und ihre Absicht nur sein kann, sich auszudrücken.' Again, the contrast to Eich's 1932 view of poetry, where reading and interpretation are incidental by-products of the process of poetic self-expression, is stark.

Brecht's less than reverential attitude in the 'Bericht über 400 Lyriker' towards those icons of bourgeois Dichtung, Rilke and George, was no isolated occurrence either. In a private note of 1926, for example, he observed mischievously that 'Rilkes Ausdruck, wenn er sich mit Gott befaßt, absolut schwul ist. Niemand, dem dies je auffiel, kann je wieder eine Zeile dieser Verse ohne ein einstellendes Grinsen lesen' (BB, 21, 158). Similarly, at the beginning of 1927 it was Brecht who spoke out most strongly within the Gruppe 1925 circle of writers against a proposed memorial ceremony in Rilke's honour. Comparable in this respect is Brecht's response to Haas's survey of writers to mark George's 60th birthday in July 1928 (BB, 21, 247). Asked about George's influence, Brecht again criticised him for his 'Isoliertheit' and expressed his hope that responses to the survey would reveal George's influence to be 'ganz unbedeutend'. With these interventions, Brecht was clearly positioning himself against the bourgeois literary

---

14   Walter Fähnders, 'Kurzer Bericht über 400 (vierhundert) junge Lyriker', in Jan Knopf (ed.), Brecht Handbuch, 5 vols (Stuttgart: Metzler, 2001–2003), IV: Schriften, Journale, Briefe, pp. 95–99 (p. 97).

establishment and in this respect contributions to the wider debate provoked by Brecht's 'Bericht über 400 Lyriker' prove instructive in mapping the prevailing literary mood. Foremost amongst these was that of Klaus Mann who, in the afterword to his unequivocally restorative *Anthologie jüngster Lyrik*, made a clear reference to Brecht's article, bemoaning the lot of the poet who was being made to feel that his writing was 'altmodische Liebhaberei', 'es sei denn, seine Verse handeln vom Sechs-Tage-Rennen und gefallen durch einen möglichst phantasie-losen amerikanischen Refrain'.[15] In stubborn hope, or with remarkable prescience, Klaus Mann also foresaw a shift in the balance of social and literary tastes.

> Wir verstehen, wenn die privat-lyrischen Ergüsse irgend eines suchenden, irrenden 'ich' manch einem nebensächlich, ja, verächtlich scheinen. – Haben wir keine Angst, es wird auch anders kommen, lassen wir uns nicht irre führen, glauben wir keinem Schwätzer, der sich 'auf dem Laufenden' glaubt, das Geistige könne jemals für eine Zeit bedeutungslos werden.

At least in these debates during the relative stability of 1927, Brecht was programmatically aligned with what Klaus Mann referred to as the 'Technischen und Sozialen' rather than the 'Geistig-Literarischen'. This programmatic position raises two principal issues which remain to be addressed. Firstly to what extent does Brecht's poetic practice match this programmatic stance? And secondly how did the growing crises of 1929–1932, and the accompanying shift in literary mood which Klaus Mann had hoped for, influence this position?

'Als heroische Landschaft habe ich die Stadt' (BB, 26, 282)

As far as Brecht's poetic practice in the late 1920s is concerned, two published collections stand out: the *Hauspostille* (BB, 11, 37–120) published by the *Propyläen-Verlag* in 1927; and *Aus dem Lesebuch für Städtebewohner* (BB, 11, 155–65) which appeared in the *Versuche* series in 1930. In part, both collections uphold the principles enunciated in the 'Bericht über 400 Lyriker', since both place an emphasis on use-value and reader-orientation. In the introduction to the *Hauspostille*, for example, Brecht explains to the reader: 'Diese *Hauspostille* ist für den Gebrauch der Leser bestimmt. Sie sollte nicht sinnlos hineingefressen werden' (BB, 11, 39). The form chosen by Brecht for the collection, that of the 'domestic breviary', reinforces this aim. As he wrote in an unused draft for the cover of the book (BB, 21, 202): '[Der Autor] hält diese Form, die uns aus frühester Jugend bekannt ist, für eine ausgezeichnete, da sie den Inhalt seinem Gebrauchswert nach, den verschiedenen Bedürfnissen der Leser entsprechend, anordnet und bestimmt.' Similarly, the designation of the 1930 collection as a

---

15   See Kaes, pp. 446–48.

'reader for city-dwellers' indicates an instructive, even educative, function relating to the changes in behaviour necessitated by the growth of the city. In Florian Vaßan's words, 'als Beschreibung und Reflexion von Haltungen zwecks Veränderung sind die Gedichte ein besonders anschauliches Beispiel für Brechts "Gebrauchslyrik"'.[16] Indeed, many critics have gone as far as to draw a parallel between the *Lesebuch für Städtebewohner* and the *Lehrstücke* which Brecht was developing at the same time, and the publication of the poems in the *Versuche* series helps to strengthen that connection.

Both the *Hauspostille* and *Lesebuch* were also delayed publications, the former composed predominantly of poems written between 1916 and 1925, the latter of poems written in 1926 and 1927, and the differences between the two collections mark the first significant turning-point in Brecht's lyric output. While the Munich and Augsburg ballads which make up the *Hauspostille* seek to subvert many of the conventions of bourgeois poetry, they do so largely from within the boundaries of that poetry. While the poetic self adopts a number of poses, none of which can be taken entirely seriously, these remain poems founded on an individual poetic subjectivity. In this respect, these early 'anti-ballads' could scarcely differ more starkly in tone from the colder and more detached observations of the Berlin *Lesebuch* poems where the poetic self has largely been replaced by the faceless voice of the city. Irregular in form and employing the everyday language of the city, these later poems clearly possess a stronger, more explicit 'documentary value'. This is not to say that the *Lesebuch* poems are straightforward documents of the urban landscape or expressions of the cult of modernity. The effect of the final line of the first of the *Lesebuch* poems – '[Das wurde mir gesagt]' (BB, 11, 155) – is to put into question the status of the remainder of the poem which otherwise reads as a straightforward set of instructions for city-living. As critical opinion testifies, this procedure, common to many of the poems, leaves sufficient interpretative room for diverse readings of the actual instructive function of the poems.[17] Nonetheless, there can be little doubt that these poems are much less conventionally poetic than the Villon and Rimbaud inspired lyrics of the *Hauspostille*, such as Brecht's anti-Ophelia ballad 'Vom ertrunkenen Mädchen' (BB, 11, 109).

These differences in Brecht's lyric output which made themselves felt in the mid- to late 1920s are those noted by Eich in his Villon review of 1930, in which he regretted Brecht's concessions to the 'Lockung der Zivilisation' (GE, 1, 547). Of course, this was the same Eich who maintained that 'Großstadtlyrik' was a contradiction in terms, and it is precisely 'Großstadtlyrik' which emerges as

16 Florian Vaßen, 'Aus dem Lesebuch für Städtebewohner', in Jan Knopf (ed.), *Brecht Handbuch*, 5 vols (Stuttgart: Metzler, 2001–2003), II: *Gedichte*, pp. 178–90 (p. 178).

17 See, for example, David Midgley, 'The poet in Berlin: Brecht's city poetry of the 1920s', in Tom Kuhn and Karen Leeder (eds), *Empodecles' Shoe: Essays on Brecht's poetry* (London: Methuen, 2002), pp. 89–106.

Brecht's central pre-occupation in these years. Poems such as '700 Intellektuelle beten einen Öltank an' (BB, 11, 174), 'Gedenktafel für 12 Weltmeister' (BB, 13, 379), or 'Sang der Maschinen' (BB, 13, 378) exemplify this tendency, the last of these from the 'Ruhrepos', the abortive musical review which Brecht planned with Kurt Weill in Essen in 1927. As Brecht recorded in a preparatory note headed 'Die Dichtung' (BB, 21, 205–06) from June 1927, the 'Ruhrepos' was to be 'ein zeitgeschichtliches Dokument' which demonstrated 'daß die Kunst in unserer Zeit es nicht verschmäht, der Wirklichkeit zu dienen'. His notes on the lyric elements of the work lay down a further set of poetological principles and make a direct connection to the innovations of the *Lesebuch*:

> Das 'Ruhrepos' wird also verschiedene Abteilungen haben [...] unter Umständen ein einfaches Lied an einen Kran sowie eine Reihe von primitiven lustigen Auftritten. Die Sprache wird zum größten Teil aus freien Rhythmen bestehen, in einer Form, die in meinen schon veröffentlichten Versen aus dem *Lesebuch für Städtebewohner* erstmalig angewendet wurde. Das 'Ruhrepos' ist für ein Publikum bestimmt, das sich aus allen Schichten der Bevölkerung zusammensetzt.

As Knopf suggests, Brecht's move to Berlin, physical and literary, represents a radical paradigm shift in his poetry. Instead of the guitar and the *Volkslied*, it is the gramophone and jazz music which set the rhythm.[18] Poetic imagery is replaced by technical vocabulary; the voice of the poetic self replaced by that of technical machinery. The popular entertainment of *Die Songs aus der Dreigroschenoper*, the internationalism of 'Surabaya-Johnny', and media experiments of the *Lesebuch* come to dominate.

1930 and beyond: re-functioning the institution and stabilising meaning

These observations are important because it is the attitude to lyric production established by Brecht in this shift in the mid-1920s which persists across 1930 and beyond. Above all, this attitude is radically divergent from that which underpins the conventional, elitist institution of bourgeois poetry, the re-assertion of which, through *Die Kolonne* for example, is such a characteristic feature of the 1930 paradigm. To summarise, Brecht's is a form of poetics which maintains a dialogic, communicative relationship between poet and reader, rather than a monologic act of poetic self-expression. This strong emphasis on use-value extends as far as an instructive or educative purpose. Form after *Hauspostille* is increasingly unconventional and irregular; vocabulary and theme, modern and often technical; tone and style stark, sober and detached. Brecht's lyricism is founded consistently in these years on *Sachlichkeit* rather than *Innerlichkeit*. The mid-1920s also mark the beginning of Brecht's collaborative writing process with

---

18 Jan Knopf, 'Gedichte 1924–1933', in Jan Knopf (ed.), *Brecht Handbuch*, 5 vols (Stuttgart: Metzler, 2001–2003), II: *Gedichte*, pp. 118–22 (p. 118).

Elisabeth Hauptmann and of Brecht's intensive attempts to distribute his poetry through unconventional modern media. His preferred outlets for his poetry around 1930 were the pamphlet and the flyer, the radio and the gramophone record, rather than the elitist 'Druckkunst' which he had criticised in the 'Bericht über 400 Lyriker'. As the notes on the 'Ruhrepos' indicate, these attempts are tied to a desire to broaden the accessibility of poetry. For these reasons, Kuhn is surely correct when he suggests that '[Brecht] was trying to re-function the institution of lyric poetry, to resituate it within the literary and wider social field'.[19]

And yet, at once a symptom and result of these attempts to radically reconfigure the institution of lyric poetry, particularly through new technological media, was the changed style and tone of Brecht's poetry in the late 1920s. In Knopf's words: 'Den neuen technischen Realitäten hat die Kunst mit einer entsprechenden Technifizierung im Wortsinn zu entsprechen. Die Sprache wird einfacher und karger, dafür aber auch deutlicher und für das Hören eingäng-licher.'[20] That is to say, Brecht's radical innovation brought with it a certain stylistic clarity and simplicity, a linguistic stabilisation of meaning. Brecht's poetic avant-gardism was not experimentation for its own sake, seeking to de-stabilise meaning or to problematise the relationships between text and reality or text and reader. Instead, and as the condemnation of Expressionism in the 'Bericht über 400 Lyriker' indicates, Brecht's project was defined through its post-Expressionist location, informed by a drive towards clarity and an attempt to imbue poetry with functionality and authenticity, stabilising the position of the text between reality and reader. It is here that we can locate commonality between Brecht's poetry and the 1930 paradigm. After all, 'Gebrauchsliteratur' and 'Leserorientierung' are two of the characteristic features of the period listed by Schäfer,[21] and it is here that Brecht demonstrates the strand of continuity which runs into the 'restorative' period from the 'new sobriety' of the 1920s. Innovative in terms of the institution of literature, Brecht's poetry must be judged to possess a conserving function in terms of the stability of meaning. In this respect, Brecht illustrates the importance of distinguishing between different parameters of avant-gardist innovation.

Significantly, Brecht's response to the crises of 1929–1932 serves to reinforce this process of stabilisation. Written at the end of 1929 in response to the Wall Street Crash, 'Verschollener Ruhm der Riesenstadt New York' (BB, 11, 243) has been seen to mark a turning-point in Brecht's enthusiasm for the US, his hope invested instead in the Soviet Union and revolutionary Marxism. Clearly, this constitutes the hardening of an on-going process, and personal and biographical factors have a role to play here too, but it is difficult not to see Brecht's 'turn' to Marxism as a search for an alternative source of order and stability amidst the

---

19 Tom Kuhn, 'Introduction', in Tom Kuhn and Karen Leeder (eds), *Empodecles' Shoe: Essays on Brecht's poetry* (London: Methuen, 2002), pp. 5–36 (p. 20).
20 Knopf, 'Gedichte 1924–1933', p. 121.
21 Schäfer, 'Periodisierung', p. 103.

political and economic turmoil which followed the relative stability of the mid- to late 1920s, as a means of bringing a system and method to his anti-bourgeois stance. Poetically, these are the years of the 'Solidaritätslied' (BB, 14, 119) with its simple but highly effective refrain, mass appeal, and overt political purpose, of the choral pieces from Brecht's *Lehrstücke* and of the *Geschichten aus der Revolution* (BB, 11, 177–82) which appeared in 1932. The extent to which Marxism imbued Brecht's poetry with stability is perhaps best seen in a piece such as 'Lob der Dialektik' (BB, 11, 237). Like the *Lesebuch für Städtebewohner*, the language and style is resolutely non-poetic, the everyday language of the city replaced by the slogans of revolutionary Marxism, but now there is no change of tone and perspective in the final line to cast doubt on what has gone before. Rather the poem is an exercise in certainty and closure, the optimistic inversions of the second half neatly matching the pessimistic formulations of the first half. Irregular in form and as far removed in theme and purpose as possible from the poetry of bourgeois *Innerlichkeit*, 'Lob der Dialektik' nonetheless provides a stability of meaning for which others can only continue to search.

1933 and 1945: continuity or change?

The notion of 'Gelegenheitsdichtung' is one which has become increasingly popular in recent years to describe Brecht's lyric output. Knopf, for example, applies the term to all of Brecht's writing, citing Goethe's original description of his own output as 'Gelegenheitsgedichte [...], das heißt, die Wirklichkeit muß die Veranlassung und den Stoff dazu hergeben'.[22] However, as Kuhn points out, Brecht's emphasis on concrete historical and social reality and on the potential for change in human behaviour rather contradicts Goethe's assumptions of a universality of human existence. Indeed, this is one of the unconventional characteristics of Brecht's poetry: 'Der Wirklichkeitsbezug ist bei Brecht so deutlich, dass es auch den geübten Leser von Gedichten zuerst erschreckt.'[23] Rather than seeking to derive a transcendental and timeless poetry from this stimulus in reality then, Brecht's poetry is much more directly and immediately the product of external happenings and circumstances, and this offers a considerable challenge to our attempt to position Brecht within a periodisation which seeks aesthetic continuity across historical and political rupture. It is manifestly absurd to claim that Brecht's poetry does not bear the marks of the Nazi seizure of power in 1933, of his peripatetic exile, or of the real existing socialism of the GDR. Indeed, as documents of the times Brecht's poems are surely shaped more strongly by these events than those of any other writer. Brecht's first post-1933 collection, *Lieder Gedichte Chöre*, for example, was

---

22 Knopf, *Gelegentlich: Poesie*, p. 10.
23 Kuhn, 'Brecht als Lyriker', p. 19.

conceived with Hanns Eisler and the publisher Willi Münzenberg specifically as
an 'anti-faschistisches Liederbuch' from which poems were to be distributed on
flyers and pamphlets within Nazi Germany. Similarly, later exile poems deal
specifically with the experience of exile ('Gedanken über die Dauer des Exils', BB,
12, 82), Brecht's negative experience of the United States ('Nachdenkend über die
Hölle', BB, 15, 46), the course of the war and the future of Germany ('Uber
Deutschland', BB, 14, 453), and specific events such as Walter Benjamin's death
('Zum Freitod des Flüchtlings W. B.', BB, 15, 48). In the GDR, Brecht wrote an
alternative national anthem ('Kinderhymne', BB, 12, 294), addressed poetry to the
new president ('An meine Landsleute', BB, 15, 205), engaged in propaganda
poetry against the West ('Herrnburger Bericht', BB, 15, 246), and intervened
against what he perceived to be mistakes in the development of cultural policy
('Das Amt für Literatur', BB, 12, 267; 'Die Lösung', BB, 12, 310).

Of course, this notion of *Gelegenheitsdichtung* in itself provides a strand of
continuity across these political boundaries. In particular, the concrete reference
of so many of Brecht's poems throughout the exile and GDR periods maintains
the secure relationship between reality, text, and reader noted around 1930.
Indeed, anti-fascism in exile and the construction of socialism in the GDR lend
the same kind of stabilising function provided by Marxism from 1929 onwards,
and important in this context are Brecht's 'Wahrheit' texts from the mid-1930s:
'Dichter sollen die Wahrheit schreiben' (BB, 22, 71–74) and 'Fünf Schwierigkeiten
beim Schreiben der Wahrheit' (BB, 22, 74–89). Initially in the former text, which
was published in the *Pariser Tageblatt* in December 1934, and then more fully in
the latter article, which first appeared in the exile journal *Unsere Zeit* in April 1935,
Brecht advocated 'truth' as the foundation for literary resistance against National
Socialism. Of course, Brecht's definition of truth was an historically specific one,
founded explicitly on dialectical materialism and in this sought to oppose any kind
of universal notion of truth. All the same, it is impossible not to be reminded here
of Eich's post-war faith in the truth of the literary word to oppose political power
or of the emphasis placed in the prisoner-of-war version of *Der Ruf* on culture as
a force which could oppose the barbarism of National Socialism. Indeed, despite
the grave misgivings about maintaining any form of cultural production which he
expressed in 1935 in a letter to Georg Grosz – 'Wir haben beschlossen, lieber
alles zu opfern, als die Kultur untergehen zu lassen. Nötigen Falles wollen wir 10–
20 Millionen Menschen dafür opfern' (BB, 28, 510) – Brecht continued to use
poetry as a medium of opposition to fascism. The contradictions of such a
position were expressed both in his journal in April 1942, where he both criticised
his continuing lyric output as a retreat into the ivory tower and at the same time
seemed to defend poetry in terms reminiscent of *Der Ruf*: 'Solche Lyrik ist
Flaschenpost. Die Schlacht um Smolensk geht auch um die Lyrik' (BB, 27, 79–
80). Most famously this position is expressed in the poetological reflections of his
1939 poem 'Schlechte Zeit für Lyrik': 'In mir streiten sich | Die Begeisterung

über den blühenden Apfelbaum | Und das Entsetzen über die Reden des Anstreichers. | Aber nur das zweite | Drängt mich zum Schreibtisch' (BB, 14, 432). Notwithstanding the contradictions generated by such a position, Brecht's exile poetry continued to be informed by the assumption that a secure and stable 'truth' could be expressed through it, an assumption which, conceived in whatever precise terms, is a typical gesture of the restorative post-1930 mood.

The mixture of institutional innovation and stabilising meaning is one which Brecht not only maintained across the political boundaries of 1933 and 1945, but even strengthened. The enforced loss of the societal context of Berlin clearly brought an end to much of his media experimentation, but the *Deutsche Satiren* broadcast on Spanish anti-fascist radio and the montage techniques of the *Kriegsfibel* demonstrate that Brecht was able to pursue unconventional means of composition and distribution in exile. In his journal in August 1940, meanwhile, Brecht re-affirmed the dialogic principles of poetry first set out in 1926 and 1927 in pieces such as 'Die Lyrik als Ausdruck':

> Lyrik ist niemals bloßer Ausdruck. Die lyrische Rezeption ist eine Operation so gut wie etwa das Sehen oder Hören, d.h. viel mehr aktiv. Das Dichten muß als menschliche Tätigkeit angesehen werden, als gesellschaftliche Praxis mit aller Widersprüchlichkeit, Veränderlichkeit, als geschichtsbedingt und geschichtemachend. (BB, 26, 418)

The process by which Brecht's poetic vocabulary was stripped down to its communicative essentials, and thereby meaning stabilised, also persisted into exile. As he himself acknowledged in his journal in August 1938, the exile collection *Svendborger Gedichte* constituted, in conventional bourgeois terms, a poetic 'impoverishment' in comparison to *Hauspostille*: 'Vom bürgerlichen Standpunkt aus ist eine erstaunliche Verarmung eingetreten. Ist nicht alles auch einseitiger, weniger "organisch", kühler, "bewußter"?' (BB, 26, 323) Indeed, for Günter Häntzschel this growing lyric simplicity and functionality is the defining characteristic of Brecht's exile poetry. 'Offenheit und Polyperspektive der Begriffe' have been replaced by 'Geschlossenheit und Eindeutigkeit der Begriffe'; 'Perspektivenwechsel, Zitatcharakter, Unstimmigkeiten und logische Brüche' by 'eine einzige Perspektive, kausal-logische Begründung des Dargestellten, Wirklichkeitsbezug oder empirische Grundlage, Realitätsnähe, das didaktische Moment'; 'Reim und gleichmäßige Rhythmen' by 'Reimlosigkeit und wechselnde Rhythmen'.[24] Of course, it is in this final shift to irregular rhythm and rhyme that we find the clearest manifestation of the trajectory of Brecht's poetic development, a trajectory expressed memorably in 'An die Nachgeborenen' (BB, 12, 85) and 'Schlechte Zeit für Lyrik' (BB, 14, 432) and formalised in the 1938 essay 'Über reimlose Lyrik mit unregelmäßigen Rhythmen' (BB, 22, 357–64). Not

---

24 Günter Häntzschel, 'Einfach kompliziert: Zu Bertolt Brechts Lyrik', in Hans-Jörg Knoblauch and Helmut Koopmann (eds), *Hundert Jahre Brecht: Brechts Jahrhundert?* (Tübingen: Stauffenberg, 1998), pp. 65–82 (p. 75).

only does that publication represent the fullest justification of the principles which had come to dominate Brecht's lyric practice since the late 1920s but the re-publication of the essay in *Sinn und Form* in 1951 indicates the continuing relevance of those principles for Brecht in the GDR.

Brecht's 'Inzwischenzeit': poetic retrenchment?

Clearly this notion of dialogic, communicative *Gelegenheitsdichtung* lies at the heart of Brecht's poetic programme and sets him against conventional notions of *Dichtung*. Or as Kuhn puts it: 'Diese Vision von Lyrik – die sich weit entfernt hat von dem Verständnis einer poetischen Lyrik, wie es im 19. und frühen 20. Jahrhundert vorherrschte – ist die überragende Leistung von Brechts lyrischem Werk.'[25] But this same central idea is also useful in putting the more conservative elements of Brecht's poetic output into an appropriate perspective. For all his protestations, albeit ambivalent, in 'An die Nachgeborenen' and 'Schlechte Zeit für Lyrik', Brecht continued to write nature poems after 1930, and he continued to write poems in strict and traditional form. During his exile, for example, Brecht wrote three cycles of sonnets: the *Sonette* and *Englische Sonette* of 1932–1935 and the *Studien* of 1938. Not only that, but in August 1940 Brecht made a direct connection between the isolation of exile and his apparent inability to write anything except epigrammatic four and eight line verses:

> Im Augenblick kann ich nur diese kleinen Epigramme schreiben, Achtzeiler und jetzt nur noch Vierzeiler. [...] Und es handelt sich nicht um Hitlers augenblickliche Siege, sondern ausschließlich um meine Isolierung, was die Produktion betrifft. [...] Das ist die Inzwischenzeit. (BB, 26, 413–14)

If Scandinavian exile was characterised for Brecht by an isolated impotence then this was only exacerbated in California – 'Die gesitige Isolierung hier ist ungeheuer, im Vergleich zu Hollywood war Svendborg ein Weltzentrum' (BB, 29, 254) – and it is for this reason that critics have increasingly come to apply the term *Inzwischenzeit* to Brecht's exile from National Socialist Germany. Significantly for our discussion in this section, this 'interlude' has been seen by some to be characterised by a turn to more conventional forms of poetic expression, that is, by increasing 'Privatisierung', 'Monologisierung' and 'Ich-Betontheit',[26] so that it is here, if anywhere, where we might find the strongest divergence between Brecht's poetic programme and practice. Conceivably, such an analysis might also be applied to some of the poems which make up Brecht's final GDR collection, the *Buckower Elegien*. Regular in form and apparently without direct political reference, 'Der Blumengarten' (BB, 12, 307) is one poem which might be read as

---

25 Kuhn, 'Brecht als Lyriker', p. 20.
26 See Hans Peter Neureuter, 'Gedichte 1933–1941', in Jan Knopf (ed.), *Brecht Handbuch*, 5 vols (Stuttgart: Metzler, 2001–2003), II: *Gedichte*, pp. 210–20 (p. 218).

a turn inwards in response to the shock of the events of 17 June 1953. Contemporary reception, at least in the GDR where the six published elegies were read 'als Rückzug des Dichters in die Natur' (BB, 12, 447), would lend weight to such a view.

Although superficially attractive, this thesis does not stand up in its entirety. As far as the exile period is concerned, for example, Hans Peter Neureuter is unequivocal in his refutation of a conventional turn in Brecht's lyric production. While the term *Inzwischenzeit* remains plausible to describe a temporary loss of productive energy located specifically in August 1940, 'alles andere sind haltlose Fiktionen. Es hat in Skandinavien keine menschliche Isolation Brechts gegeben und noch weniger etwas "Monologisches" in seinen Gedichten'.[27] Similarly, although Kuhn acknowledges a more private tone in some of the exile poems and even the presence of a recognisable lyric self, he firmly rebuts the suggestion that Brecht 'sich auf die monologische Stimme einer konventionellen Lyrik zurückgezogen hätte. [...] Das kam für ihn nie in Frage'.[28] The *Buckower Elegien* too are nothing if not *Gelegenheitsgedichte*, closely, if eliptically, connected to a concrete social and historical reality. In this way, it is not possible to use the conventional elements in Brecht's poetry to support, straightforwardly, a generalised thesis of aesthetic retrenchment in the 1930s, 1940s, and 1950s. Such is the diversity of Brecht's poetic output and such his consistent exploration of the potential offered by different lyric forms, that one can find traditional forms employed throughout his career to varying degrees. The sonnets of the mid-1930s, for example, can no more prove a thesis of aesthetic conservatism than can those which derived in the mid-1920s from Brecht's relationship with Elisabeth Hauptmann. Such conventional elements must always be seen as examples of *Gelegenheitsdichtung*, firmly tied to a dialogic function.

And yet, we might still make three significant points about this relatively 'conservative' poetic practice and its relationship to the 1930 paradigm. Firstly, Brecht's poetic practice demonstrates that he is never able to fully escape the bourgeois tradition, but rather remains in dialogue with it. As Frühwald writes of the codified *Bildungsdialekt* of the nineteenth century, so we might also write of Brecht's position in the mid-decades of the twentieth century: '[Der Bildungsdialekt] entwickelt sich zu einer bourgeoisen Zeitstimmung, der sich kein Mitglied der bürgerlichen Gesellschaft – und sei es nur in Kritik und Widerspruch – zu entziehen vermag.'[29] Secondly, within the context of an individual author's diachronic development aesthetic conservatism must be viewed as a relative,

---

27 Neureuter, p. 218.
28 Kuhn, 'Brecht als Lyriker', p. 11.
29 Wolfgang Frühwald, 'Büchmann und die Folgen: Zur sozialen Funktion des Bildungszitates in der deutschen Literatur des 19. Jahrhunderts', in Reinhart Koselleck (ed.), *Bildungsbürgertum im 19. Jahrhundert, Teil II: Bildungsgüter und Bildungswissen* (Stuttgart: Klett–Cotta, 1990), pp. 197–219 (p. 219).

rather than an absolute, phenomenon. While it is going too far to claim that Brecht ever returned to monologic poetic expression, or that his exile output was conventionally poetic compared, say, to Benn or Huchel, it should be clear that the balance of Brecht's later exile output can be viewed as relatively more monologic and relatively more conventionally poetic than the balance of his output around 1930. Finally, the notion of *Gelegenheitsdichtung* and the responsiveness of that poetry to external circumstances highlights the importance of political ruptures even within a periodisation which seeks continuities across those ruptures. If Brecht's exile output is relatively more conventional, then the circumstances of exile are a causal factor. Brecht's case, perhaps more than others, demonstrates that the turn at 1930 does not erase the significance of 1933. Rather 1933 combines to reinforce that development.

Brecht and the Institution(s) of Literature

If poetry is the principal area of focus of many existing accounts of the 1930 paradigm, then this has been supplemented in our study by a further key area, namely the capacity of individuals to shape the prevailing literary climate working within and through literary institutions. More specifically, our interest has focused on how literary journals as institutions have adopted a 'conservative' or 'innovative' function in relation to what we have termed the conventional bourgeois institution of literature, seeking either to preserve or to bring about change in prevailing notions of authorship and of the literary work itself. In this way, the institution of literature can be seen to be constituted of and by a series of literary institutions and by individuals and groupings working actively within and through these institutions. This apparently straightforward observation must inform our analysis of authors as it does our analysis of journals, since it is these institutions which act as the bridge between the writer as an individual and the writer as an active participant in, and constituent of, the broader literary sphere.

As far as Brecht is concerned, the preceding section has highlighted his attempts to re-configure the institution of poetry through a consistent program-matic approach initiated in the 1920s. In this section we invert that analysis, taking as our starting-point not the polemical 30-year-old Brecht who was working against existing institutions within the radical climate of Weimar, but rather the 50 year old who was seeking to find a place for himself and his new theatre company within the construction of socialism in the GDR. Here, we return to the particular manifestation of the 1930 paradigm amongst institutions of the Marxist Left, represented in our study in the trajectory of common ideas, and often personnel, which can be traced from the final years of the Weimar Republic in *Die Linkskurve,* into the exile Popular Front initiative of *Das Wort,* and finally to the GDR literary journal *Aufbau*. As we have seen, this orthodox strand of Marxist aesthetics is founded on the reflective literary theory of Georg Lukács where form constitutes an organic, representative totality and where the realism of the early nineteenth-century French novel acts as an aesthetic benchmark. In the early 1950s, the institutionalisation and codification of orthodox and unorthodox aesthetic positions under the 'total claim' of SED cultural policy extended far beyond Lukács's theoretical reflections on the novel, seeking to position cultural output across the arts in a binary framework of 'realism' (included as aesthetically orthodox) and 'formalism' (excluded as aesthetically unorthodox). Within this framework, Brecht has usually been positioned at the 'formalism' pole, both at the time by the SED regime itself and more recently by scholarship which since the late 1960s has looked to Brecht, along with such figures as Walter Benjamin, as the source of an alternative Marxist aesthetic. Reassessing this institutionalised polarity between formalism and realism, and Brecht's role within it, is the first step in an analysis which is able to recognise the fundamental shift in Brecht's institutional relationships towards a much more conventional position in relation to the institution of literature.

The anti-restorative icon: Brecht and 'Formalism'

No sooner had Brecht's production of *Mutter Courage* opened to rapturous acclaim on 11 January 1949, in what was then still the Soviet occupied sector of Berlin, than a debate had been initiated as to the formalist nature of Brecht's anti-Aristotelian theatre which sought to marginalise Brecht within the institutions of GDR culture. Less than a week after praising the opening performance as 'einen der "großen Theaterabende", wie sie die deutsche Hauptstadt vor 1933 kannte', Fritz Erpenbeck insisted on posing a fundamental question of Brecht's work which began to apply to it the negatively coded language of the nascent SED aesthetic discourse: 'Wo verliert sich, troz fortschrittlichen Wollens und höchsten, formalen Könnens, der Weg in eine volksfremde Dekadenz?'[30] These were the early skirmishes in a debate through which Brecht's theatrical practice in the GDR was to be increasingly threatened by the spectre of the Soviet dramatic model predicated on the work of Konstantin Stanislavsky. As early as 1945 Stanislavsky practitioners had begun to establish themselves in the Soviet Occupied Zone, but between 1947 and 1953 the Stanislavskian method moved from the cultural margins to the centre of official SED policy as the only appropriate medium for realising Socialist Realism on the stage. Under figures such as Maxim Vallentin and Armin-Gerd Kuckhoff, the *Deutsche Theater-Institut* schooled young actors and directors in a method which, through empathy and

---

30   See Werner Hecht, *Brecht-Chronik: 1898–1956* (Frankfurt a.M.: Suhrkamp, 1997), pp. 848–52.

identification, sought to oppose the perceived experimentalism and innovation of Brecht's epic theory, the principles of which he had set out publicly in his 'Kleines Organon für das Theater' in the first *Brecht-Sonderheft* of *Sinn und Form* in 1949. That publication had already, in Mittenzwei's words, 'den eklatanten Gegensatz der Methode Brechts zu der Stanislawskis sichtbar gemacht',[31] and as the Stanislavskian method gained the institutional centre, so Brecht and the Berliner Ensemble were pushed to the margins.

If the initial debate around *Mutter Courage* could be characterised as a constructive aesthetic discussion between literary critics, albeit with an unmistakeable political subtext, the same could scarcely be said of the critical response which the Berliner Ensemble's production of *Die Mutter* attracted two years later. While critics supportive of Brecht – notably Wolfgang Harich – had vigorously and successfully rebuffed Erpenbeck's attack in the press in early 1949, criticism of *Die Mutter* in March 1951, made within official GDR government circles, did not allow for the same freedom of response. In its discussions held on 15–17 March 1951, the Central Committee of the SED officially launched its campaign against 'Formalism' in the arts, and two delegates chose to single out Brecht's Gorky adaptation which he had first staged some twenty years earlier. For Hans Rodenberg, though willing to grant Brecht more time to relieve himself of his 'old baggage', a theatre where didacticism was an end in itself constituted *a priori* 'formalism'. Fred Oelßner was rather less forgiving in excluding Brecht from a category of 'realism' clearly predicated on a Lukácsian definition:

> Aber ich frage, ist das wirklich Realismus? Sind hier typische Gestalten in typischer Umgebung dargestellt? Ich will schon gar nicht reden von den Formen. Warum nicht? Entschuldigt, ich bin der Auffassung, das ist kein Theater; das ist irgendwie eine Kreuzung oder Synthese von Meyerhold und Proletkult.[32]

From this point on, and against the background of an increasingly dogmatic enforcement of the regime's aesthetic norms, Brecht found himself caught up in a series of intense cultural-political controversies in which he occupied a position of aesthetic non-conformity. Subject to accusations of formalism, particularly for Paul Dessau's music, Brecht's 1951 production of his *Lukullus* text at the *Deutsche Staatsoper* was initially banned and then revised in response to SED criticism. It is clear too that at this time SED cultural officials were concerned about the influence of a Brecht faction in the drama section of the Academy of Arts. In June 1951, for example, the cultural division of the SED reported that the 'Brecht-Kreis' were standing their ground, maintaining what it termed their 'einseitige Proletkulttendenzen'.[33] The following year Brecht made his first public

---

31 Werner Mittenzwei, *Das Leben des Brecht: Oder der Umgang mit den Welträtseln*, 2 vols (Berlin: Aufbau Taschenbuch, 1997), II, pp. 446–47. Subsequent reference, p. 218.

32 Hecht, *Brecht-Chronik*, p. 955.

33 Hecht, *Brecht-Chronik*, p. 968.

intervention in the Formalism Campaign, rejecting accusations made against an exhibition of Ernst Barlach's sculpture at the Academy of Arts (BB, 23, 198–202).

Through 1952 and 1953, it was his unorthodox position in relation to the German cultural tradition, for which Brecht attracted the ire of SED officials. Productions of *Urfaust* in Potsdam (April 1952) and Berlin (March 1953) received stinging criticism and were rapidly withdrawn, and by May 1953 a series of set-piece discussions at the Academy of Arts surrounding Hanns Eisler's libretto *Johann Faustus*, in whose composition Brecht had had a hand, were stage-managed with the express intention of extracting a recantation from Brecht of his unorthodox aesthetic position. These attempts 'Brecht zu isolieren und zur Zurücknahme einiger seiner theoretischen Marotten" zu bewegen',[34] coincided with the highpoint of the SED's 'Stanislavsky wave', the first German Stanislavsky Conference held at the Academy of Arts on 17–19 April 1953. Here, Brecht's principal opponent was again Fritz Erpenbeck who had also been able to use the forum provided by the journal *Theater der Zeit* to undermine Brecht's theatrical project in the GDR. That even the Berliner Ensemble's production in the spring of 1953 of Erwin Strittmatter's *Katzgraben* – a contemporary and partisan GDR play which Brecht subjected to a rigorous practical study of Stanislavskian methods – failed to satisfy these critics demonstrates just how marginal Brecht's aesthetic position had become. As Brecht wrote, dispiritedly, in his journal during the *Katzgraben* rehearsals: 'Unsere Aufführungen in Berlin haben fast kein Echo mehr' (BB, 27, 346).

In this way, SED cultural policy in the early 1950s can be characterised as an increasingly institutionalised conflict between a set of related, essentially conservative aesthetic positions, on the one hand, and the more experimental aesthetic position represented by Brecht, on the other. It is this conflict and Brecht's institutionalised status as 'formalist' which informs so many assessments of Brecht's activities in the GDR, so that this phase in his career is able to function as the endpoint in a consistent anti-restorative narrative. As such, the question poised by Werner Mittenzwei of Brecht's return to East Germany in 1949 seems to be purely rhetorical: 'Wie würde Brecht in eine Theaterlandschaft passen, die die faschistische Beeinträchtigung durch Besinnung auf die klassischen Traditionen und die sowjetische Stanislawski-Schule zu überwinden suchte?'[35]

34 Manfred Jäger, *Kultur und Politik in der DDR: 1945–1990* (Cologne: Edition Deutschland Archiv, 1995), p. 62.
35 Mittenzwei, *Das Leben des Brecht*, II, p. 218.

Brecht and the Berliner Ensemble: Stanislavsky, Realism and the tradition

And yet, if Brecht's position as a representative of aesthetic non-conformity in
the Formalism Campaign in the GDR reminds us of the *Linkskurve* debates of
1932, then we would do well too to remember the extent to which aesthetic
positions in those earlier debates were subsumed and obscured by factional and
political factors. As far as the Formalism Campaign in the GDR is concerned,
two such elements are of importance: Brecht's status, perceived or otherwise, as a
political outsider; and the particular political circumstances which shaped SED
cultural policy in the early 1950s. Although resolutely partisan in the developing
ideological rifts of the Cold War, institutionally Brecht succeeded in retaining a
certain distance from the SED. It is well-known, for example, that Brecht never
joined the ruling party of the GDR, that he acquired Austrian citizenship, and
that he lodged his copyright with Peter Suhrkamp in the West. Made by a figure
who had already acquired a reputation for an unorthodox aesthetic standpoint in
the *Linkskurve* and *Wort* debates and who had resisted the lure of Soviet exile for
California, such decisions were hardly likely to inspire confidence amongst SED
officials, for whom paranoia was, to borrow from Mary Fulbrook, a key
'mentality of power'.[36] More importantly, this peculiar paranoia which
characterised the GDR regime was exacerbated in the early 1950s by the
precarious position of the GDR within a Soviet foreign policy which sought to
jettison the East German state.[37] It was against this background that culture
became swept up into attempts by the hard-line integrationist factions of the SED
to purge those who favoured an all-German approach. Signalled above all by the
official declaration of the 'Aufbau der Grundlagen des Sozialismus' at the 2nd
Party Congress in July 1952, the Formalism Campaign received a new and
qualitatively different impetus as SED hardliners sought to seize control of
institutions such as the Academy of Arts, and it was in this atmosphere that loyal
comrades such as Brecht and Eisler became public targets of Party discipline and
that complex aesthetic positions became subsumed under factional polarisations.
It is very difficult, therefore, to see the reception of Brecht's East Berlin
productions, and in particular his growing isolation between 1949 and 1953, as
the product of the aesthetic nature of the productions themselves. Rather, this
must be seen as a function of the SED's more vigorous imposition of their total
claim on culture, that is, as a political development. Crucially within the context
of our study, this opens the way to an analysis of Brecht's theatrical practice with
the Berliner Ensemble which looks beneath the political label of 'formalism',

---

36   Mary Fulbrook, *Anatomy of a Dictatorship: Inside the GDR 1949–1989* (Oxford: Oxford University
     Press, 1995).
37   See Winfried Loth, *Stalins ungeliebtes Kind: Oder warum Moskau die DDR nicht wollte* (Berlin: Rowohlt,
     1994).

revealing a surprising proximity to the official 'realist' aesthetics of the GDR, and thereby to the 1930 paradigm.

Indeed, if we actually read Erpenbeck's reviews of the Berliner Ensemble's premieres, it becomes more difficult to sustain the thesis that it was Brecht's radical theatrical practice which set him at odds with GDR officials. Referring to the realism of the Ensemble's opening production of *Puntila* (12 November 1949), for example, Erpenbeck is moved to question his understanding of the distinction between conventional theatre and 'epic theatre': 'Episches Theater? Nun gut, wenn das "episches" Theater ist [...], dann mögen wir uns gelegentlich einmal über Terminologie weiterstreiten.'[38] Similar enthusiasm for Brecht's production of Lenz's *Hofmeister* (15 April 1950) – 'entgegen bestimmter Theorien Brechts [...] ein [...] ganz und gar nicht "verfremdetes", an Höhepunkten zu heißen Gefühlsausbrüchen gesteigertes, realistisches Theaterspiel!' – is even repeated two and a half years later for the premiere of *Die Gewehre der Frau Carrar*, by which time Brecht and the Ensemble were coming under increasing pressure:

> Bestes Theater. Bertolt Brecht möge verzeihen: bestes Illusionstheater. – Und der Darstellungsstil? Wenn das, was wir von Erwin Geschonneck als Pedro, von Ekkehard Schall als José [...] und nicht zuletzt von Helene Weigel als Frau Carrar sahen und tief erlebten, die von Bertolt Brecht *gewollte* Art der Menschendarstellung ist, dann sind unsere kunsttheoretischen Meinungsverschiedenheiten auf diesem Gebiet in der Praxis sehr gering.

Of course, such reviews demonstrate the dominance in the early GDR of a very traditional form of theatre criticism founded on conventional notions of 'good' Aristotelian drama, regardless of the actual nature of the productions being reviewed. At the same time, we are encouraged to consider the extent to which the Berliner Ensemble's theatrical practice occupied a position rather closer to official aesthetic prescriptions than we might at first assume, particularly when the most severe criticism attracted by Brecht was not for his formal experimentation but for thematic negativity, as he explored the politically volatile theme of *deutsche Misere* at a time when the SED hierarchy was at its most sensitive.

Clearly, Brecht's long-term attitude to formal innovation set him against the simple deployment and preservation of traditional forms in GDR theatre: 'Wir bauen unsere Häuser anders wie die Elisabethaner, und wir bauen unsere Stücke anders' (BB, 23, 145). Indeed, 'es ist ebenso formalistisch, alte Formen einem Stoff aufzuzwingen, wie neue' (BB, 23, 145). As such, it would be all too easy to ascribe to Brecht the status of iconoclast of the classical tradition, the status which was ascribed to him in the controversies surrounding the Berliner Ensemble's production of *Urfaust* and Eisler's *Johann Faustus*. Nonetheless, the productions staged by the Berliner Ensemble in the early 1950s – Goethe's *Urfaust*, Lenz's *Hofmeister*, Shakespeare's *Coriolanus*, Molière's *Don Juan*, Kleist's *Der zerbrochene Krug*, and Hauptmann's *Biberpelz und roter Hahn* – clearly point to a

---

38   Hecht, *Brecht-Chronik*, p. 896. Subsequent references, p. 918 and p. 1036.

consistent engagement with tradition, albeit a tradition conceived in rather broader terms than that promoted by official SED policy. In terms of Brecht's attitude to tradition, two points might usefully be made. Firstly, Brecht's engagement with diverse literary traditions was no new development of the 1950s. The literary and theatrical traditions of antiquity and the Orient, of Elizabethan England and the French Enlightenment, and of course of the German classics all exerted a strong influence on Brecht from his earliest literary projects. From this perspective, Brecht's active, eclectic, and productive engagement with tradition positions his literary practice not so very far from the kind of progressive traditionalism advanced by Willy Haas in *Die literarische Welt*, and it can be no coincidence that Haas subsequently picked out the *Dreigroschenoper* as the archetypal instance of the productivity of what he termed the Alexandrine phase of German literature in the mid-to-late 1920s.[39] Secondly, the post-1945 phase in Brecht's career witnesses a very real shift in his attitude specifically to the German classical tradition. As Mittenzwei summarises:

> In welchem Maße Brecht seine Haltung zum weltliterarischen Erbe änderte, erfährt der Leser sehr einprägsam, wenn er Äußerungen Brechts aus der frühen Phase mit denen aus der späteren vergleicht. Da ist eine neugewonnene Hochachtung zu spüren. Der schnoddrige, provokante Ton der Frühphase ist verschwunden, obwohl Brecht eher kritischer als unkritischer geworden ist. Größe wird auch als groß beschrieben. Nunmehr ist von der Würde klassischer Kunstwerke die Rede, eine Kennzeichnung, die dem jungen, aggressiven Brecht schwerlich eingefallen wäre.[40]

Of course, Brecht's definition of respect for the classical heritage did not match that of the Party dogmatists and his interest in using that tradition actively as a starting-point for new insights failed to match official prescriptions. Nonetheless, Brecht's own attitude to the tradition clearly evades the binary framework imposed upon it in the factional and cultural-political disputes of the early 1950s.

Similarly, the relationship between Brecht and Stanislavsky, where a radical disjunction between Brecht's position and the more conservative official position can be constructed from the 1930s all the way through to the Stanislavsky Conference of April 1953, is susceptible to some revision. As we have seen, Erpenbeck's reviews of the Berliner Ensemble's productions already suggest that the brand of epic theatre practised by Brecht in the GDR was perhaps not as radical as we might expect, and the SED's promotion of a Stanislavskian method prompted Brecht to a renewed study of the Russian dramatist (BB, 23, 224–36) which some critics have seen as the impetus for a synthesis between the two apparently opposing methods. Central to this process are the Ensemble's rehearsals for Strittmatter's *Katzgraben* which coincided with the Stanislavsky Conference and which were recorded in detail in the *Katzgraben-Notate*. Werner

39 Willy Haas, 'Nachwort', in Willy Haas (ed.), *Zeitgemäßes aus 'Der literarischen Welt'* (Stuttgart: Cotta, 1963), pp. 477–90 (p. 483).
40 Werner Mittenzwei, *Brechts Verhältnis zur Tradition* (Berlin: Akademie-Verlag, 1974), p. 186.

Hecht, for example, points to the use of fictional dialogues in the *Katzgraben* rehearsal notes and compares them to Stanislavsky's writings. 'Die Ähnlichkeit', he concludes, 'ist verblüffend'.[41] Indeed, Hecht concedes that the discovery of a new version of the *Katzgraben-Notate* necessitates something of a change of view: 'So kann vielleicht erst jetzt mit der ersten Veröffentlichung des ursprünglichen Textkonvoluts das wirkliche Ausmaß des echten Interesses an dem System Stanislawski erkannt werden.' Most directly of all, Meg Mumford not only highlights a range of Stanislavskian influences in the *Katzgraben* production – such as the high level of naturalistic detail, an increased use of empathy, and more individualised characterisation – but she also views these methods as a conscious, artistically motivated choice on Brecht's part.[42]

Admittedly, much Brecht scholarship has been dismissive of any claimed rapprochement between Brecht and Stanislavsky. Knopf, for example, described such claims in no uncertain terms as 'eine Erfindung der DDR-Brecht-Forschung',[43] and the very real pressure being exerted on Brecht and the Ensemble at the time of his Stanislavsky study makes it impossible to deny any place for tactical political motivations. At the same time, some of Brecht's public statements about the *Katzgraben* production, made crucially after the easing of the pressure on him which came after the popular uprising of 17 June 1953, maintain a surprisingly orthodox theoretical line: 'Die Gestalten des Stücks sind voller Individualität, mit köstlichen Einzelzügen' (BB, 24, 437); 'Völlig neu für die deutsche Bühne sind die realistisch und großzügig gezeichneten Bauern, welche die Merkmale ihrer Klasse tragen und zugleich sehr lebendige und widerspruchs-volle Einzelpersönlichkeiten sind' (BB, 23, 256). In particular, Brecht's advocacy of this orthodox play in *Sinn und Form* in the late summer of 1953 makes plain the fiction of presenting Brecht's position in the GDR as merely that of the marginalised 'formalist'.[44] Indeed, in one important respect the debate between tactical and non-tactical interpretations of Brecht's Stanislavsky study is irrelevant. Regardless whether we view this move as a tactical concession to the official SED line or as an expression of a genuine aesthetic position, it is clear that Brecht's practice in this instance was shaped by the prevailing, restorative climate of early GDR cultural policy.

41 Werner Hecht, 'Grund der Empörung über eine "ganz unerträgliche Behandlung": Brechts Stanislawski-Studium 1953', *Maske und Kothurn*, 33.3/4 (1987), 75–87 (p. 83). Subsequent reference, p. 87.

42 Meg Mumford, 'Brecht Studies Stanislavsky: Just a Tactical Move?', *New Theatre Quarterly*, 11 (1995), 241–58.

43 Jan Knopf, *Brecht Handbuch: Eine Widersprüchliche Ästhetik*, 2 vols (Stuttgart: Metzler, 1980), I: *Theater*, p. 466.

44 See Matthew Philpotts, '"Aus so prosaischen Dingen wie Kartoffeln, Straßen, Traktoren, werden poetische Dinge!": Brecht, Strittmatter, and *Sinn und Form*', *German Life and Letters*, 56 (2003), 56–71.

Finally, if we look more closely at the terms of the cultural-political controversies in which Brecht became involved, it is clear that the formalism-realism dichotomy as it was constructed in SED cultural policy does not accurately describe the position which Brecht himself sought to occupy. Central here are the collection of short texts written by Brecht in response to the initiation of the Formalism Campaign in 1951 and his involvement in it through the *Lukullus* project. In these private notes, Brecht sets out a consistent position which locates him somewhere between the artificially constructed poles of formalism and realism. On the one hand, Brecht defends the significant role played by 'form' in art – 'sie ist nicht alles, aber sie ist doch so viel, daß Vernachlässigung ein Werk zunichte macht' (BB, 23, 144) – and resolutely maintains the necessity of formal innovation: 'Ohne Neuerungen formaler Art einzuführen, kann die Dichtung die neuen Stoffe und neuen Blickpunkte nicht bei den neuen Publikumsschichten einführen' (BB, 23, 145). On the other, this is an emphasis on form which is intimately connected to, indeed derived from, content: 'Nur die neuen Inhalte vertragen neue Formen' (BB, 23, 147). Thus, Brecht's interest in formal innovation in the GDR stems from a need to represent the new subject-matter of post-war German socialism, and as such it is in Brecht's terms a realist undertaking. Only when form becomes divorced from content, when it becomes an end in itself, does formalism ensue, and for Brecht this is a feature of late capitalist, bourgeois art against which it is entirely legitimate, and necessary, to campaign in the new historical circumstances of the GDR:

> Situation:
> Eine soziale Umwälzung findet statt. Die neue Klasse im historischen Prozeß bemächtigt sich des Theaters.
> Sie eröffnet den Kampf gegen den Formalismus.
> Sie findet einmal auf dem Theater eine ihr verdächtige Vorherrschaft bestimmter Formen über den sozialen Inhalt vor, durch welche die Abbilder der Wirklichkeit, die sie vom Theater verlangt, verzerrt und die sozialen Impulse, die das Theater geben soll, in falsche Richtung gelenkt werden. (BB, 23, 148)

It is this more complex position, rather than that of the unreconstructed formalist, which informs Brecht's interventions in the Formalism Campaign, both in relation to *Lukullus* and Barlach. Dessau's music is not defended, for example, in terms of the legitimacy of formal innovation, but because its form is appropriate to the new social situation and acts a source of stability of meaning, rather than of its disruption: 'Der Sinn der Oper kommt in jeder Szene heraus dadurch, daß der Gesang sehr vereinfacht ist und hauptsächlich den Sinn herausbringt [...]. Ihre Schönheit ist mit verhältnismäßig wenig Studium erfaßbar' (BB, 23, 137). By the same token, Brecht defends Barlach's sculpture by emphasising its realism. So, Barlach's 'Buchleser' is, when compared to Rodin's 'Thinker', 'realistischer, konkreter, unsymbolisch' (BB, 23, 200). Likewise, those pieces which Brecht dislikes are rejected, in terms strikingly reminiscent of SED art criticism, as 'eine Deformierung der Wirklichkeit' (BB, 23, 202).

From use-value to prestige-value

Having re-considered Brecht's status as the archetypal anti-restorative figure in the artificially constructed framework of formalism and realism, it requires only a small shift in perspective to recognise a fundamental change in the nature of Brecht's institutional relationships in the 1950s. Above all through his activities in key cultural institutions, such as the German Academy of Arts, the 'use-value' which for so long and so consistently had underpinned his cultural activities was increasingly accompanied by a key new dynamic, the growth in what we might term the 'prestige-value' of those same activities. Brecht was one of the 23 artists called by the GDR president Otto Grotewohl to serve at the foundation of the Academy in March 1950, and before that he had served on the committee charged with drawing up its statutes. After its foundation he played an active role in discussions and decision-making in two sections, the *Sektion für Dichtkunst und Sprachpflege* and, at his own request, the *Sektion für Darstellende Kunst*, and he was appointed vice-president in September 1954. In this capacity, Brecht's institutional relationships were now cut through by a fundamental tension which is perhaps best illustrated through the somewhat curious poetic reflection, 'Ich benötige keinen Grabstein', which Brecht composed as early as 1933:

Ich benötige keinen Grabstein, aber
Wenn ihr einen für mich benötigt
Wünschte ich, es stünde darauf:
Er hat Vorschläge gemacht. Wir
Haben sie angenommen. (BB, 14, 191)

Here, the initial rejection of the need for a headstone and the understated provisionality of the inscription – recording suggestions rather than achievements – clashes with the ultimate need for permanent recognition and remembrance. It is this contrast between the typical desire to effect change through constructive critique and suggestion, on the one hand, and the need for the kind of recognition and status which would help to achieve that influence, on the other, that the poem mirrors the contradictions in Brecht's institutional relationships in the Academy.

After all, Brecht viewed the Academy as an institution through which he could intervene in both cultural and political matters, prompting, making suggestions, seeking, as he did through his writing, to effect changes in behaviour. Indeed, this was the platform from which he made his interventions in the Formalism Campaign, from which he presented the regime with ten suggestions for the reform of cultural policy in the wake of 17 June 1953 (BB, 23, 253–55), and which he used as a source of authority in a remarkable newspaper attack on SED cultural policy which he entitled 'Kulturpolitik und Akademie der Künste' (BB, 23, 256–60). As Mittenzwei has pointed out, Brecht saw the Academy as 'ein Gremium, das gegen Mißstände und Fehlentwicklungen auf künstlerischem Gebiet aufzutreten habe', as 'ein Forum, das Einfluß auf die Geschmacksbildung des Publikums gewinnen mußte. Zu ihren wesentlichen Aufgaben zählte Brecht, darüber zu wachen, daß die neuen politischen Aufgaben nicht dazu führten, das Künstlerische links liegenzulassen'.[45] At the same time, it was the institutional status and credibility provided by the Academy which lent Brecht's interventions their authority, so that Brecht's attempts to further the development of a genuinely socialist culture on German soil rested paradoxically on his membership of what was in its founding principles a highly elite artistic institution.

Although the foundation of the Academy in East Berlin functioned superficially as a symbol of an institutional new beginning and a fundamental break with the past, the underlying purpose and rhetoric of this foundation rested on the 250-year tradition of its Prussian predecessor.[46] For all Brecht's own warnings against repeating past mistakes (BB, 23, 118), the purpose of the Academy was bound up inherently with cultural prestige and the conventional notions of bourgeois literary quality which supported that prestige. The choice of Heinrich Mann as its first president and, even more so, the award of honorary membership to Thomas Mann at the Goethe celebrations in Weimar in 1949 reflected this purpose. As much as Brecht used the Academy as a site in which to contest orthodox cultural policy, he was deriving status from, and contributing status to, an institution inscribed with elite, traditionalist values which were only exacerbated by official SED prescriptions. In the words of the guidelines for members of the literary section: 'Die im Goethejahr 1949 sichtbar gewordene Pflege der fortschrittlichen Tradition unserer Nationalkultur auf dem Gebiete der Literatur [...] ist wirksam weiterzuführen.'[47]

Although largely neglected by Brecht scholarship, his activities in the elite Academy begin to establish a paradigm applicable to other areas of activity. This same tension between use-value and prestige-value, for example, can also be seen to characterise Brecht's relationship with Peter Huchel's journal *Sinn und Form*. On the one hand, Brecht exploited the use-value of *Sinn und Form* as an extension of the Academy and as a publishing outlet for his cultural and political interventions. These ranged from dissenting interventions against GDR cultural policy to more partisan interventions in Cold War political developments such as his open letter of September 1951 (BB, 23, 155–56). Indeed, Brecht went further,

---

45   Mittenzwei, *Das Leben des Brecht*, II, p. 378 and p. 379.

46   See Petra Uhlmann and Sabine Wolf (eds), *'Die Regierung ruft die Künstler': Dokumente zur Gründung der Deutschen Akademie der Künste* (Berlin: Akademie der Künste, 1993).

47   Uhlmann and Wolf, p. 111.

consistently agitating within the Academy for more topical contributions to the journal which would reflect the achievements of the GDR.[48] On the other, Brecht's function within the journal for Peter Huchel was as a source of literary authority and prestige. Brecht enjoyed an unrivalled volume and frequency of publication in *Sinn und Form*, including a host of first publications and two special issues. Deployed strategically in this way, at the heart of Huchel's programme of 'progressive restoration', Brecht's institutional position was not that of the disruptive outsider, but increasingly that of the respected *Dichter* within the archetypal 'thick' literary journal which was promoting enduring bourgeois literary values in a conscious echo of Thomas Mann's *Maß und Wert*. Particularly telling in this respect are the two Brecht special issues, the first a keynote accompaniment to the journal's foundation and Brecht's return to East Berlin in early 1949 – a striking parallel to the Thomas Mann special issue of *Die neue Rundschau* which signalled the re-establishment of German literary traditions in June 1945 – the second published in 1957 shortly after Brecht's death. What emerges from a comparison of the two special issues is the shift in Brecht's institutional position across the course of his seven years in the GDR, manifested most clearly in the bibliographic apparatus which concludes each issue. Where Gerhard Nellhaus's 1949 bibliography stretches only to six pages and the secondary bibliography to little over two, Walter Nubel's 1957 bibliography encompasses 144 pages, 60 of them devoted to critical writing about Brecht. In this way, *Sinn und Form* played a central role in the 1950s in beginning to integrate Brecht into the apparatus of the conventional institution of literature.

Weimar *Versuche*

The true significance of these institutional relationships in the GDR only becomes apparent when contrasted with Brecht's institutional position in the late 1920s and early 1930s. Here Brecht tended to work not within the boundaries of existing institutions but sought to re-configure those boundaries or to create his own innovative institutions. Perhaps the best example of these is the *Versuche* series, Brecht's principal publication outlet between 1930 and 1933 which he founded with Kiepenheuer and which he was to re-establish twenty years later after his exile. As the title of the series makes clear, this publishing institution was for Brecht characterised by experimentation and provisionality, and in the foreword to the first issue Brecht made it clear that this experiment extended to re-defining the function of the literary work:

> Die Publikation der *Versuche* erfolgt zu einem Zeitpunkt, wo gewisse Arbeiten nicht mehr so sehr individuelle Erlebnisse (Werkcharakter haben) sollen, sondern mehr auf

---

48   See Uwe Schoor, *Das geheime Journal einer Nation: Die Zeitschrift 'Sinn und Form': Chefredakteur Peter Huchel 1949–1962* (Berlin: Lang, 1992), p. 133.

die Benutzung (Umgestaltung) bestimmte Institute und Institutionen gerichtet sind (Experimentcharakter haben).[49]

As Lucchesi comments: 'Gleichzeitig opponierte Brechts Experimentbegriff auch dem herrschenden Werkbegriff als dem eines autonomen, in sich geschlossenen, singulären wie "endgültigen" Kunstwerks.'[50] In this innovative function, the *Versuche* series was supported by a number of paratextual factors. Issues were initially paginated consecutively to emphasise the periodical nature of the series, and works within each issue numbered so as to establish 'ein zuordnendes Verweissystem, um übergreifende Zusammenhänge zwischen scheinbar divergierenden Texten (und Heften) herzustellen'. In contrast to the conventional literary edition, type size and format varied between works, disrupting the sense of continuity and homogeneity, while cheap paper and card replaced durable cloth and hardbound volumes. A conscious choice on Brecht's part, the material nature of the *Versuche* embodied the immediate and temporary status of the literary work, to be read and thrown away, to work actively in the mind, rather than to be preserved for posterity in a classic edition.

In terms of content too, the *Versuche* series sought to work against the conventional institution of literature. Programmatically, Brecht opened the first issue with his 'Radiolehrstück', *Der Ozeanflug*, described in the foreword as 'ein pädagogisches Unternehmen' and as 'eine bisher nicht erprobte Verwendungsart des Rundfunks'. It was in the *Versuche* that Brecht first published the *Lehrstücke* and the theoretical observations which accompanied them, both of which sought to transform the institution of the theatre. It was here that Brecht published the *Lesebuch für Städtebewohner* which re-defined the function and nature of poetry, and it was here that Brecht published the *Dreigroschen*-complex culminating in his 'sociological experiment', the *Dreigroschenprozeß*. Not only did the arrangement of texts within the series break down conventional boundaries of literary genre, but literary pieces were intermingled with photographs and illustrations, musical scores and theoretical theses. In Knopf's words:

> Es ist sicher kein Zufall, daß die *Versuche*-Hefte mit der Publikation der Lehrstücke einsetzen und von vornherein alle Gattungen mischen. [...] Mit seinen Lehrstücken wollte der Dichter den Medien [...] alternative Kommunikationsformen gegenüberstellen. Die Gattungsmischung mit Bildbeigaben gibt den *Versuchen* den Charakter von Zeitschriften und damit von 'Wegwerfware'.[51]

In this way, the *Versuche* series did not simply acquire the periodical character which Knopf notes. Rather, the *Versuche* seemed to acquire the kind of immediacy, diversity, and temporality of an innovative, 'thin' literary periodical. In effect, Brecht was taking the institution of the author's edition, a literary series

---

49   Bertolt Brecht, *Versuche 1–12: Hefte 1–4* (Berlin: Suhrkamp, 1959), p. 6.
50   Joachim Lucchesi, '*Versuche*', in Jan Knopf (ed.), *Brecht Handbuch*, 5 vols (Stuttgart: Metzler, 2001–2003), IV: *Schriften, Journale, Briefe*, pp. 406–16 (p. 408). Subsequent reference, p. 407.
51   Knopf, *Gelegentlich: Poesie*, p. 9.

with a typically conservative function, and re-shaping it to serve the challenging and educative purpose which he ascribed to his writing.

As for the literary journal itself, in 1929 Brecht sketched out plans for his own periodical to be entitled *Kritische Blätter* and co-edited by Walter Benjamin (BB, 21, 330–31). Through this journal project Brecht again sought to erode conventional notions of the literary work as a discrete and completed entity uniquely tied to its author. Texts are referred to programmatically as products and were to be published 'nicht als Fertigprodukt' in order to ensure that the journal maintained its characteristic as 'das Bild einer Fabrik in Tätigkeit'. At the heart of this project lay a new form of literary criticism:

> Diese Kritik löst also fertige Werke in unfertige auf, geht also analytisch vor, jeweils das Werk als persönliches Dokument des Verfassers außer acht lassend, aber die Punkte sammelnd, die in ihm für weitere Werke nützlich sind, also geeignet für unpersönliche Anwendung.

This theoretical and analytical mode of criticism was to replace 'die "schildernde, auswählend anempfehlende" Haltung der Kritik', that is, the mode of criticism which serves a stabilising, reinforcing and canonising function within the institution of literature, such as that practised in *Merkur*. Significantly, the challenging and unsettling mode of criticism advanced by Brecht in this and a number of other short texts around 1930 is presented explicitly as a response, and even a contribution, to crisis. The journal, originally to be called *Krisis und Kritik*, was to see this period 'als in zweifacher Bedeutung "kritische Zeit"', seeking 'das ganze Stoffgebiet in eine permanente Krisis [umzudenken]'. While so many other writers responded to the crisis by retreating into the conventional institution of literature, the solidity of Brecht's dialectical Marxism allowed him to question and undermine the central pillars of that institution.

Equally, Brecht did not limit himself to the institution of literature. As much as anything the *Versuche* can be characterised as multimedia experiments, at a time when Brecht was expanding literary production to encompass gramophone records (*Lesebuch für Städtebewohner*), film (*Kühle Wampe*), and radio (*Lindberghflug*). In this respect, Lucchesi's observations are particularly telling:

> Die Etablierung der *Versuche*-Reihe setzte 1930 in jenem Moment ein, in dem Brecht [...] auf ganz unterschiedliche Weise (und für ganz unterschiedliches Publikum) sowohl gegen die vorherrschende Praxis kultureller Institutionen als auch gegen den kanonisierten Werkbegriff zu opponieren begonnen hatte. [...] Nicht 'endgültige' Texte in ihrem 'Ewigkeitsanspruch' waren das Ziel seiner publizistischen Arbeit, sondern Unabgeschlossenes sollte in den neuen technischen Medien zur Diskussion, zur kritischen Verwertung und vor allem in schneller Edition aktueller Texte öffentlich zugänglich gemacht werden.[52]

As we shall see in our discussion of Günter Eich, the pioneering attempts of Brecht and Benjamin to exploit the innovatory potential of such new media as the

---

52 Lucchesi, 'Versuche', p. 408.

radio as the basis for a new conception of literature, its production and reception, would themselves fall victim to the restorative literary climate of the 1930s, 1940s and 1950s, as a radio theory founded on much more conventional notions of *Dichtung* came to dominate. Only in the 1960s with the erosion of that prevailing climate was this innovative strand rediscovered and re-evaluated.

'Ich beobachte, daß ich anfange, ein Klassiker zu werden.' (BB, 26, 229)

Viewed against the innovation of the late 1920s and early 1930s, Brecht's publication practice in the GDR begins to look distinctly restorative in its function within the institution of literature. Indeed, far from being a marginalised outsider, Brecht's status in these years was increasingly developing into that of the 'Klassiker' which he had observed with such dismay some thirty years earlier in his diaries. Now though, increasingly secure with his own theatre after 1954 and increasingly aware of the need to make provisions for his cultural legacy, Brecht did not fight this status but rather contributed towards it. It is no coincidence, for example, that Brecht's principal statement of dramatic theory from this time, the 'Kleines Organon für das Theater', itself an attempt to draw together diverse pre-existing strands rather than to innovate, was first published in the restorative context of *Sinn und Form*, not in the kind of innovative institutional contexts he had been developing around 1930. Symptomatic too is Brecht's re-instituting of the *Versuche* series with Suhrkamp in 1949 and with Aufbau in 1951. By proposing to simply re-continue the series 'möglichst ähnlich in der Form der ersten Hefte' (BB, 29, 470) Brecht was re-establishing his own publishing outlet for what he perceived to be work in progress, but at the same time he was also establishing and preserving his own tradition. Twenty years after their foundation the *Versuche* were themselves now part of the canonisation of Brecht's modernism, Brecht himself now deploying a fusion of the principal publishing procedures – those of the *Werke* and of the *Hauszeitschrift* – by which publishing houses mediated and institutionalised the *klassische Moderne*.[53] When Brecht persisted in negotiating with Suhrkamp for a limited reprint edition of the pre-1933 *Versuche* in their original format, he even acknowledged the status of that edition as a collector's item, 'für Liebhaber sozusagen' (BB, 30, 222). Clearly a fundamental shift had taken place in the nature of Brecht's publication practice, for this was the Brecht who after 1953 undertook international tours as the figurehead of a renowned and prestigious theatrical institution and who from 1955 undertook the publication of the *Modellbücher des Berliner Ensembles* in a high quality edition under the auspices of the Academy of Arts. In Klaus Völker's words: 'Zwar hatte Brecht in den 50er-Jahren eine wesentlich positivere und

---

53   See Helmut Schanze, 'S. Fischer: Verlagsgeschichte als Kulturgeschichte', *Neue Rundschau*, 97.4 (1986), 187–202.

produktivere Einstellung zu "Klassischem" und zur Tradition; er maß sich jetzt unbedenklich an den klassischen Meistern Shakespeare, Diderot, Lessing, Goethe, Schiller und Kleist'.[54]

As befitted a classic author Brecht now pursued the realisation of a collected edition of his works, what Völker terms Brecht's 'Klassikernachweis'.[55] Two volumes entitled *Erste Stücke* began this process in parallel Suhrkamp and Aufbau editions in 1953 and 1955 respectively, the latter in red clothbound volumes. By 1957 the Suhrkamp *Stücke* edition had reached volume five and already a second edition of volume one had been produced. No longer the reluctant *Klassiker*, Brecht wrote to both publishers expressing thanks for the editions which he described simply, but perhaps all too tellingly, as 'schön' (BB, 30, 221; BB, 30, 365). Indeed, the nature of Brecht's pre-occupations and priorities at this time emerges clearly from his letter to Suhrkamp:

> So schön [ist die Ausgabe], daß ich mir sehr wünschte, wir könnten die Reihe schnell fortsetzen – nicht nur weil bei uns die Bedeutung eines Schriftstellers mit dem Zentimetermaß gemessen wird. Warum eigentlich nicht – anstatt der *Versuche* 1–8 – einfach die Dramen daraus drucken? Mit einem theoretischen Band dazu? (BB, 30, 221)

The young man who in the 1920s had berated George for his elitist *Druckkunst*, who had decried *Schönheit* in literature, and had explicitly advocated that poetry be 'auf Zeitungspapier groß gedruckt, fett gedruckt, auf Makulaturpapier, das zerfällt in drei, vier Jahren, daß die Bände auf den Mist wandern',[56] was now ensuring that his published work acquire this same status and permanence. In February 1956, for example, he insisted to Suhrkamp that the *Bibliothek* series was not appropriate for a collection of his *Gedichte und Lieder*. 'Die erste Ausgabe meiner Gedichte in Westdeutschland sollte nicht wie die eines Ausländers aussehen. Wenn es nicht möglich ist, die Gedichte repräsentativ – also in einem einzelnen Band, im Format der *Ersten Stücke* – herauszubringen, sollten wir [...] sie eben nicht herausbringen' (BB, 30, 427). The shift to prestige-value was complete.

Exile revisited

This stark contrast between Brecht's institutional relationships in the 1950s and those he was developing in the late 1920s and very early 1930s again shifts attention onto the exile period, this time as a transitional phase between the two. More so than for any other area of activity, the realities of exile and its accompanying isolation from the German speaking literary sphere could not help

---

54   Klaus Völker, 'Druckgeschichte', in Jan Knopf (ed.), *Brecht Handbuch*, 5 vols (Stuttgart: Metzler, 2001–2003), IV: *Schriften, Journale, Briefe*, pp. 479–98 (p. 496).
55   Völker, p. 496.
56   Knopf, *Gelegentlich: Poesie*, p. 9.

but have a profound influence on the development of Brecht's institutional relationships. The Nazi seizure of power led, for example, directly to the interruption of the *Versuche* series in 1933, as Brecht was forced to pursue, often fruitlessly, alternative publication routes. Above all, the central procedures of Brecht's cultural practice became untenable without the immediate human and technological infrastructure which he enjoyed within Germany in the early 1930s. As we have seen in the preceding section, this is not to overstate the degree of Brecht's isolation nor understate the extent to which he was still able to pursue innovative literary projects, particularly through the medium of poetry. All the same, Knopf's comments on the effect of exile on Brecht's cultural production have far-reaching implications for our study:

> Es ist viel zu wenig beachtet worden, was es für Brecht hieß, keine (oder nur beschränkt und dann traditionelle) 'Apparate' mehr zur Verfügung zu haben. Experimente waren nicht mehr möglich, und die Stücke [...] mussten [...] zwangsläufig wieder in relativ konventionelle Bahnen zurückkehren, da die geeigneten Theater fehlten.[57]

Knopf is clear that, in comparison to the late 1920s and early 1930s, the epic theatre of exile must be viewed as 'konservativ, insofern als es [...] auf die traditionelle Bühne rekurriert', and this tallies with Trommler's assessment of Brecht's exile plays:

> Auch in Brechts Werk lassen sich Ende der dreißiger Jahre Spuren der Rückbesinnung auf menschliche Grundhaltungen erkennen. Die Stücke dieser Jahre entfernten sich vom Lehrtheater um 1930, waren, wie Brecht selbst sagte, traditioneller in der Form. Gewiß waren auch die verstehende Schilderung des Opportunismus von Schweyk oder die Erhöhung der Güte in der Grusche im *Kaukasischen Kreidekreis* 'traditioneller'.[58]

A broad consensus exists that all the essentials of Brecht's dramatic theory were already in place in the early 1930s, so that the theoretical reflections of exile constitute only a 'Vervollkommnung' of a pre-existing body of thought. For Knopf, the exile prose too is characterised by a remarkable retreat to 'traditionellen, figurengebundenen Erzählweisen'. Only lyric poetry is seen to have been re-invigorated by the exile experience and that, as we have often observed in our study, 'galt doch (in der bürgerlichen Literatur) als "subjektiv" und verinnerlichend und deshalb als die Gattung, die am wenigsten "realistisch" war'. Consolidation and retrenchment are the watchwords here.

In this way, exile may be seen to provide the missing link between the contrasting institutional relationships of the 1920s and 1950s, and nowhere is this better expressed than in Brecht's publication practice, where the shift towards

---

57 Jan Knopf, 'Zu Literatur und Kunst', in Jan Knopf (ed.), *Brecht Handbuch*, 5 vols (Stuttgart: Metzler, 2001–2003), IV: *Schriften, Journale, Briefe*, pp. 220–31 (p. 224). Subsequent references, also p. 224.

58 Trommler, 'Nachkriegsliteratur: Eine neue deutsche Literatur?', p. 176.

prestige-value seems to have been an exile development. As early as 1934 Brecht entered into negotiations with Wieland Herzfelde regarding the publication of an edition of *Gesammelte Werke*, a project which was only partially realised with the publication of two volumes of plays by Malik in 1938. Under the conditions of exile, the notion of a collected edition served a familiar dual purpose, not only securing and gathering together existing work but also providing use-value as a much-needed outlet for new work. Brecht wrote in letters to Herzfelde of his despair in being able to write only for the desk drawer or wastepaper basket (BB, 29, 122) and sought to stress continuity with the *Versuche* series by referring to the project in 1934 as his 'gesammelte Versuche' (BB, 28, 439). At the same time, Brecht was also acutely aware of the prestige which the edition would give him, anxiously asking Johannes R. Becher, for example, whether he had received 'die ersten beiden Bände meiner *Gesammelten*' (BB, 29, 103) and making clear to Herzfelde that the edition could 'die entscheidende Position verschaffen, die ich in der Emigrantenliteratur bisher nicht habe' (BB, 29, 96). Precisely because of the restorative function of such an edition, Brecht expressed his desire in this same letter of May 1938 for a volume of contemporary essays to follow immediately as an intervention in the Expressionism Debate:

> Auf die *Gesammelten Werke*, die einen immensen Geländegewinn bedeuten, muß jetzt etwas absolut Aktuelles, Eingreifendes folgen, sonst sieht es aus, als hätte ich, wie gewisse Generale nach der Niederlage, meine Memoiren veröffentlicht, um gewisse in der Vergangenheit geleistete Dienste den geschätzten Zeitgenossen flehend ins Gedächtnis zu rufen.

As in the GDR debates through the Academy of Arts and *Sinn und Form*, Brecht seems to have realised in exile the connection between prestige-value and use-value, the former providing an institutional platform for the latter. At the same time, it is difficult not to see the former also as an end in itself as, faced with isolation and a peripatetic existence, Brecht sought to secure and preserve his literary work to date.

Conclusion

As such, Brecht's position in relation to the 1930 paradigm is complex and on the surface not easily generalisable. Exceptionally amongst our authors, it is 1933, rather than 1930, which constitutes the principal turning-point in his literary and cultural practice, the material and intellectual conditions of exile functioning as the principal causal mechanism in a move towards the promotion through that practice of a more conventional notion of authorship and of the literary work. This tendency can then be seen to have been strengthened by his privileged institutional circumstances in the GDR and, it is to be assumed, by the perception that he was entering the final stage of his career beset by failing health. The years around 1930, by contrast, saw the intensification of two existing tendencies bound up with the notion of use-value, one in keeping with the prevailing restorative climate, one radically opposed to it. The unshakeable value placed by Brecht on the political and social functionality of his writing could only be strengthened by the crises around 1930 and by his embrace of revolutionary Marxism, and this entailed at once a stabilising of meaning within his texts and a de-stabilising of the conventional institution of literature. The persistence of these principles throughout his subsequent career argues against an over-statement of the changes brought about by exile and his career in the GDR. All the time we are dealing in Brecht's case with a relative shift towards restorative aesthetic practice, rather than an absolute embrace of such practice. It is a question, for example, of use-value being supplemented, rather than supplanted, by prestige value in later years. In two key respects, however, this dynamic between use-value and prestige-value highlights issues of broader applicability in terms of the 1930 paradigm. Firstly, Brecht's unique starting-point at 1930 brings out the continuing importance of political turning-points and periods within the mid-decades of the century. For Brecht, 1933 can be seen to have effected a relative turn towards restorative practice, where for other authors it acted to maintain that pre-existing practice, or perhaps better, retard development away from that practice. Secondly, Brecht's absorption into the conventional institution of literature in the 1950s is clearly not in itself necessarily tied to the prevailing literary climate of these middle decades, but in large measure to the particular stage which his career and life had reached, and it is here that the absence of renewal through a new literary generation at 1945 makes its presence felt. The German literary sphere in the early 1950s was shaped by an earlier generation who carried with them a sense of their own history and who exerted influence largely through pre-existing work and achievements. Again, change in the literary sphere in these years was restricted by the dominance of a generation initiated into that public sphere in advance of, or at the latest around, 1930 itself.

Günter Eich

Introduction: Eich and the 1930 paradigm

Eine Entscheidung für die Zeit, d. h. also für eine Teilerscheinung der Zeit, interessiert den Lyriker als Lyriker überhaupt nicht. [...] Ja, ich meine, der Lyriker muß 'alte' Vokabeln gebrauchen, die [...] ihre Bedeutung erst durch das Ich gewinnen. An Vokabeln wie 'Dynamo' oder 'Telefonkabel' hängen soviele zeitlich bedingte Assoziationen, daß sie die reine Ichproblematik zumeist verfälschen. [...] Es gibt wirklich 'prosaische' Worte.
'Bemerkungen über Lyrik', 1932 (GE, 4, 459)

Man muß den Gegnern des Gedichts in weitem Maße recht geben, wenn man sieht, wie das Vokabular der Lyrik heute noch zu einem großen Teil einer Art Naturschutzpark zu entstammen scheint und gekennzeichnet ist etwa durch Wörter wie: Wald, Wiese, Mond, Stern, Frühling und Herbst. Man hat den Eindruck, die Lyrik sei im vorigen Jahrhundert geblieben und die Wirklichkeit der Maschine, des Flugzeugs und der Atombombe existiere für sie nicht. [...] Die Vorstellung, es gäbe prosaische und poetische Wörter, ist allgemein, aber deswegen nicht weniger irrig.
'Die heutige Situation der Lyrik', 1947 (GE, 4, 476)

In the literature advocating some form of 1930–1960 periodisation, Eich's role is paradigmatic in two principal respects: firstly his poetological statements in *Die Kolonne* around 1930 act as evidence of the cultural shift which ushers in the new period; and secondly his rise to prominence after 1945 functions as a central thread of continuity, not only back into the Third Reich across the political break of 1945, but also across 1933 and back into the final years of the Weimar Republic. As we have seen, Eich was the most frequent contributor to *Die Kolonne*, after Martin Raschke, and those contributions often adopted a position very close to Raschke's programme. As Cuomo has observed: 'Eich wrote numerous essays and reviews as a *Kolonne* member. [...] His views are consistent with the editorial thrust of *Die Kolonne* on all major issues, and at times he even appears in the role of a spokesman for the journal's policy.'[1] It is for this reason that the prominence of *Die Kolonne* and its contributors in Schäfer's periodisation thesis can be equated in large measure with prominence for Eich himself. When Schäfer makes specific reference to Eich in the exposition of his periodisation thesis, it is significant that he chooses to quote an assertion from the 1932 essay

---

1   Glenn R. Cuomo, *Career at the Cost of Compromise: Günter Eich's life and work in the years 1933–1945* (Amsterdam: Rodopi, 1989), p. 14.

'Bemerkungen über Lyrik' (GE, 4, 458–61) – 'Gedichte haben keinen beabsichtigten Nutzwert' – for it is this essay which establishes Eich's pivotal role at 1930.[2] Frank Trommler, for example, quotes a sizeable extract from this essay and also one from the shorter 1930 statement 'Innere Dialoge' (GE, 4, 457) in an attempt to demonstrate Eich's proximity to Loerke and Lehmann as a representative of a form of poetics, 'bei der der Dichter in einem sehr subjektiven Raum das Aktuelle auslöscht, um das Universale to beschwören'.[3] Anton Kaes too quotes 'Bemerkungen über Lyrik' in the introduction to his documentation of Weimar literary manifestos (under the heading 'Rückzug in die Innerlichkeit'), also reproducing it in full, along with three Raschke essays, in the section 'Auf dem Weg in die innere Emigration'.[4] For Kaes, Eich's aesthetic stance, as laid out in 'Bemerkungen über Lyrik' and 'Innere Dialoge', is representative of the dominant literary mood of the times, what he terms the 'im Formalen wie Thematischen rückwärtsgewandte[n] Traditionalismus'.[5] In very similar terms, Helmut Kreuzer cites these same Eich essays as evidence in the final years of Weimar of an 'Anwachsen des Traditionalismus im kulturellen Leben'.[6] As such, Eich emerges as not merely a peripheral practitioner of the attitude of 'lyric inwardness' advocated by the *Kolonne* Circle,[7] but as the prime proponent of that programme alongside Martin Raschke himself.

As important as his role at the initiation of the post-1930 period of aesthetic traditionalism is Eich's role as a perceived guarantor of post-war literary continuity and restoration. After all, it was the debates about the 1945 *Nullpunkt* or *Kahlschlag* and the publishing activities of prominent West German literary figures during the Third Reich which helped to instigate the re-appraisal of 1933 as a cultural turning-point. Eich was one of the literary figures, for example, whom Schäfer had in mind when he wrote the following: 'Das Jahr 1945 bedeutet nicht – wie lange Zeit behauptet wurde – einen Neuansatz der deutschen Literatur. Man versuchte vielmehr, die Strukturen der Moderne weiter-

---

2 See Hans Dieter Schäfer, 'Zur Periodisierung der deutschen Literatur seit 1930', in Nicolas Born and Jürgen Manthey (eds), *Literaturmagazin 7: Nachkriegsliteratur* (Reinbek: Rowohlt, 1977), pp. 95–115 (p. 103).
3 Frank Trommler, 'Emigration und Nachkriegsliteratur: Zum Problem der geschichtlichen Kontinuität', in Reinhold Grimm and Jost Hermand (eds), *Exil und innere Emigration: Third Wisconsin Workshop* (Frankfurt a.M.: Athenäum, 1972), pp. 173–97 (pp. 178–79).
4 Anton Kaes, *Weimarer Republik: Manifeste und Dokumente zur deutschen Literatur 1918–1933* (Stuttgart: Metzler, 1983).
5 Kaes, *Manifeste und Dokumente*, p. xlv.
6 Helmut Kreuzer, 'Kultur und Gesellschaft in der Weimarer Republik: Ein Vortrag', in Helmut Kreuzer, *Aufklärung über Literatur: Ausgewählte Aufsätze*, 2 vols, I: *Epochen, Probleme, Tendenzen*, ed. by Peter Siebert, Rolf Bäumer, and Georg Bollenbeck (Heidelberg: Winter, 1992), pp. 100–17 (pp. 115–16).
7 See Joseph P. Dolan, 'The Theory and Practice of Apolitical Literature: *Die Kolonne* 1929–1932', *Studies in Twentieth-Century Literature*, 1 (1977), 157–71.

zuentwickeln, wie sie sich vor 1933 herausgebildet hatten.'[8] In a similar vein, Dolan traces the significance of the *Kolonne* Circle through from the Weimar Republic into the Federal Republic – 'what is pertinent is that, after 1945, Eich and Langgässer and many others as well clung to their pre-war attitudes for considerable periods of time'[9] – while Wilhelm Kröll is more explicit still about Eich's role as a literary authority in the post-1945 restoration:

> Eich steht für Kontinuitätsbogen, die zurückreichen bis zur Sammlungsbewegung des *Kolonne*-Kreises von 1929/30, ein Kreis, der sich als 'antimoderne Bewegung' formierte und wesentlich mit zum 'Siegeszug metaphysischer Wertvorstellungen' beitrug; eine Saat, die nach 1945 so recht erst aufging. Die Autoren aus der *Kolonne*-Tradition und ihrer weiteren ideologischen Umsphäre bildeten recht eigentlich das Reservoir der Presiträger des restaurativen 'literarischen Wiederaufbaus', allen voran Günter Eich.[10]

For Olschner and Korte too, the continuity constituted by Eich and his *Kolonne* contemporaries across 1945 is a central factor in their attempts to establish the existence of a discrete period in German lyric poetry which spans the 1930s, 1940s, and 1950s.[11]

It is in this light that we might usefully consider the two statements made by Eich and quoted at the beginning of this chapter. Made 15 years apart and located, tellingly, either side of the Third Reich, these poetological statements could scarcely adopt more contrasting positions as regards the relationship between poetry and the modern world. As the editorial apparatus to the 1991 Eich edition makes clear, the 1947 essay on the state of contemporary German poetry stands 'in einem bemerkenswerten Gegensatz zu Eichs früheren "Bemerkungen über Lyrik": das dort abgelehnte ist nun Postulat geworden' (GE, 4, 650). The young *Kolonne* nature poet resolutely defending that position of lyric inwardness seems to have been replaced – after the experience of National Socialism, war, surrender, capture and occupation – by an engaged post-war writer demanding a rejection of that same, now untenable, aesthetic position. Given the paradigmatic status afforded to Eich's 1932 statement in the literature advocating a form of 1930–1960 periodisation and also the presumed continuity embodied by his post-1945 success, there is rather more at stake here than the

---

8   Hans Dieter Schäfer, 'Zur Spätphase des hermetischen Gedichts', in Manfred Durzak (ed.), *Die deutsche Literatur der Gegenwart: Aspekte und Tendenzen* (Stuttgart: Reclam, 1971), pp. 148–69 (p. 163).

9   Dolan, p. 158.

10 Wilhelm Kröll, 'Literaturpreise nach 1945: Wegweiser in die Restauration' in Jost Hermand, Helmut Peitsch, Klaus R. Scherpe (eds), *Nachkriegsliteratur in Westdeutschland 1945–49: Schreibweisen, Gattungen, Institutionen* (Berlin: Argument, 1983), pp. 143–64 (p. 151), quoting Schäfer, 'Periodisierung', p. 95.

11 Leonard Olschner, 'Fractured Continuities: Pressures on lyrical tradition at mid-century', *German Studies Review*, 13 (1990), 417–40; Hermann Korte, 'Lyrik am Ende der Weimarer Republik', in Rolf Grimminger (ed.), *Hansers Sozialgeschichte der deutschen Literatur vom 16. Jahrhundert bis zur Gegenwart*, 12 vols, VIII: *Literatur der Weimarer Republik 1918–1933*, ed. by Bernhard Weyergraf (Munich: Hanser, 1995), pp. 601–35.

issue of continuity or discontinuity in Eich's own literary career. Any radical discontinuity in Eich's aesthetic trajectory at 1945 would clearly raise searching questions about the viability of any such periodisation as a whole. In this sense, the repeated prominence of 'Bemerkungen über Lyrik' in accounts of the 1930 paradigm is liable to have a distorting influence. Only in the most recent Eich edition was 'Die heutige Situation der Lyrik' first included, together with a series of reviews published in the years 1947–1949 which, in Vieregg's words, 'werfen ein bezeichnendes Licht auf Eichs eigenes Literatur- und insbesondere Lyrik-verständnis' (GE, 4, 634).

Central again with respect to Eich's position in the posited periodisation is the distinction between programme and practice which has informed our analysis of literary journals. It is particularly noteworthy, for example, that Eich's poetological essays and reviews are clustered around the two potential cultural turning-points, 1930 and 1945, so that these can be examined as programmatic interventions in the key periods of accelerated cultural activity, seeking to shape a fluid literary climate. The first half of this chapter will be devoted to a detailed consideration of Eich's aesthetic programme as it is set out in these reviews and statements. Necessarily focus will rest on the position adopted by Eich at the two potential turning points: Eich's essayistic contributions to *Die Kolonne* between 1930 and 1932 allow us to identify the precise nature of the cultural shift as it was expressed by Eich; his reviews and essays between 1946 and 1949 raise fundamental questions about the existence, or otherwise, of a shift in the immediate post-war period. It is against these programmatic positions that Eich's literary practice throughout his career must then be tested, for on the surface this practice also seems to contradict the *Kolonne* position adopted at 1930. The elitist *Kolonne* poet seems scarcely compatible, for example, with the National Socialist radio author who Eich became after 1933, nor with the famous concluding words of his post-war radio play, 'Träume', seized upon in the 1960s as part of the iconic status afforded to Eich as an anarchic non-conformist, warning against conservative political restoration: 'Seid unbequem, seid Sand, nicht das Öl im Getriebe der Welt!' (GE, 2, 384). Central to the investigation of Eich's literary practice in the second half of this chapter will be, above all, the notions of literature and authorship established and maintained through his poetry and radio output. As we shall see, Eich's literary self-image was shaped throughout by the restorative category of *Dichtung* dominant at 1930. The story of Eich's literary career is in large measure the story of his struggle to reconcile that self-image with the more pragmatic reality of the professional writer in the mid-twentieth century.

Literary Programmatics

Poetological principles: *Die Kolonne* 1930

The obvious starting-points here are the two oft-cited poetological statements made by Eich in *Die Kolonne*, namely 'Innere Dialoge' (GE, 4, 457) from 1930 and 'Bemerkungen über Lyrik' (GE, 4, 458–61) from 1932, for which our earlier discussion of the journal as a whole serves a useful contextualising purpose. Both pieces are polemical interventions in contemporary debates about the nature and purpose of poetry: the former responding to the *Kolonne* editors' request for writers 'in möglichst aphoristischer Form über die Tendenz ihres Schaffens Auskunft zu geben'; the latter responding to the critic Bernhard Diebold's attack on the young generation of nature poets, 'An die jungen Lyriker'.[12] In this sense, the pieces themselves attest to the kind of accelerated activity perceptible at moments of potential change, to the particular determining role adopted by individuals at such times, and to the accompanying intolerance which exists towards existing and rival cultural positions. The arrogance of tone adopted in 'Innere Dialoge' is particularly striking, a product perhaps too of youthful exuberance and even insecurity in the 23-year-old Eich, as he positions himself squarely against the political commitment of the BPRS and *Die Linkskurve*:

> Ich finde es gänzlich unter meiner Würde, mich für meine Gedichte zu entschuldigen und mich vor Leitartikeln zu verbeugen, und werde immer darauf verzichten, auf mein 'soziales Empfinden' hinzuweisen, selbst auf die Gefahr hin, die Sympathie von Linksblättern nicht zu erringen und selbst auf die noch furchtbarere Gefahr hin, nicht für 'heutig' gehalten zu werden.

As 'inner dialogues' Eich's lyrics are utterly divorced from *Tendenz*. Indeed, poetry is seen to be incompatible with any explicit intention – political, social, or otherwise – and this is an idea picked up in the response to Diebold where the great value of poetry is explicitly said to lie in its 'Absichtslosigkeit'. This acts as one of four central, inter-related poetic principles which are outlined in 'Bemerkungen über Lyrik' and which constitute Eich's poetological position at 1930. Firstly then, poems are free of will and intention on the poet's part, and in this respect, poems are to be compared to natural phenomena: rain falls and causes plants to grow but we do not claim that that is the intention of rain; similarly poetry may generate effects and interpretations but that is not to say that poetry has these intentions. Secondly, it is the subjective poetic self, rather than contemporary political or social concerns, which stands at the centre of all true *Dichtung*: 'Der Lyriker entscheidet sich für nichts, ihn interessiert nur sein Ich [...] für ihn existiert nur das gemeinschaftslose vereinzelte Ich.' Eich rejects outright

---

12 For contextual details, see GE, 4, 648.

Diebold's call for the integration of modern, technological society into the realm of poetry, justifying instead the avowedly anti-modern frame of reference embodied by nature poetry and the use of 'old' vocabulary (*Mond, Stern*) rather than the vocabulary of modernisation (*Dynamo, Telefonkabel*). Thirdly, this poet who creates spontaneously out of the self makes no concessions to the reader – the meaning of poems cannot be read directly, as from a newspaper, 'aber wer Gedichte zu lesen versteht (was kaum zu erlernen ist), der wird auch das in ihnen spüren'. Finally, it is clear that Eich is searching for order and wholeness through his *Ich*-centred poetic discourse which expresses 'das Wesentliche einer Zeit' and 'die Gesamtheit der Zeit': '[Der Lyriker] fängt die Zeit als Ganzes in sich auf und läßt sie im ungetrübten Spiegel seines Ichs wieder sichtbar werden.'

To draw these observations together, it is clear that these poetic principles are of a piece with our restorative thesis, above all in terms of the status and institutions of literature and its thematic content. The privileged form of writing is *Lyrik*, the writer an individual poet-genius who spontaneously expresses the inner self without the slightest thought of his intended audience. The privileged themes are nature and a world untouched by social and technological modernisation. As such, Eich's programme clearly seeks to turn back the processes of massification and democratisation which had transformed the status and nature of the book, the author, and the poem in the 1920s. Eich is less explicit here about the specifics of poetic form, but the approving references to Eichendorff and Mörike, allied to the disapproval of a generalised 'Verfall der schöpferischen Kräfte' (GE, 4, 460), make it clear that it is a turn back to the German poetic tradition which is understood by Eich to offer a solution to an on-going cultural crisis.

Striking throughout this period is the sheer consistency with which Eich applies these poetological principles in his literary reviews for *Die Kolonne*, often published under the pseudonym Georg Winter. Clearly intended programmatically, for example, and published under his own name, is Eich's 1931 review of Becher's epic poem, *Der große Plan* (GE, 4, 551–52). Becher's greatest sin is to seek to reconcile propagandistic function with the medium of poetry which by definition lacks overt, or even covert, purpose. The fundamental mutual exclusivity of *Tendenz* and *Dichtung* is the central theme of this review: 'Die Forderung der Einheit von Dichtung und politischer Propaganda ist auch hier nicht Wirklichkeit geworden, und sie wird es auch anderswo nie werden.' Where propaganda is direct and its intention specific and overt, poetry is indirect and without intention. *Tendenzdichtung* thus contravenes the first of the unshakeable poetic principles set out in 'Bemerkungen über Lyrik'. As Eich writes of Becher: 'Wer glaubt, daß nur das auf der Welt Wert habe, was als Waffe im Kampf für eine Idee gebraucht werden kann, der sei konsequenterweise ein Gegner der Kunst überhaupt und überlasse das Verseschreiben denen, für die es kein Wollen ist.'

Unmistakeable too is the connection between 'Bemerkungen über Lyrik' and the review in the same year of a collection of *Großstadtdichtung* entitled *Um uns die Stadt* (GE, 4, 555). Eich's criticism centres on three related points: the superficiality of the poetic representation of the city; the mediocrity of the vast majority of the poems in the collection, described in no uncertain terms as a 'Wust von Mittelmäßigkeit'; and above all the use of modern vocabulary. This last point in particular is stressed by Eich and establishes an important point of connection to his response to Diebold: 'Der Begriff Großstadtlyrik umfaßt eben ein Vokabular, und deshalb nicht alle Gestaltungen.' Indeed the problem with the collection is seen to lie not in the poor choice of poems but in the very idea of an anthology of *Großstadtlyrik*. The explicit and willed focus on the city inevitably distracts attention from, and therefore rules out, the appropriate depiction of the inner self. In a similar vein, Eich's first *Kolonne* review (GE, 4, 545–46) uses Villon's poetry as the impetus to launch a polemical and increasingly familiar diagnosis of the faults of contemporary literature. On this occasion the blame rests on the modern reader whose monotonous existence, entirely determined by the ticking of his watch, has nurtured an insatiable thirst for real experience: 'Es ist die Zeit der dokumentarischen Romane und der Biographien, man will Wirklichkeit.' This in turn has spawned a mediocre and ubiquitous style founded on 'real', but ultimately superficial, experience. This style, the documentary style of *Neue Sachlichkeit*, has undermined the quality of literary output. Above all, it mistakes actual experience for 'true' experience. Only an exceptional few have the fundamental experiences on which to draw in their poetry. These experiences are founded on 'das Triebhafte' and 'das Asoziale' and find their natural expression in the poetry of such figures as Villon, Rimbaud, and, in his earlier work, Brecht.

That Eich is advocating a position of aesthetic, rather than political and/or ideological, 'conservatism' and that this aesthetic 'conservatism' is to be placed at a distance from a peasant, or even *völkisch*, attitude is indicated by two further reviews, both published in *Die Kolonne* in early 1931. First of all, in his criticism of the Austrian *volkstümlich* poet Guido Zernatto (GE, 4, 547), Eich diverges from his *Kolonne* editor Martin Raschke. From Eich's faint praise for Zernatto – 'kein so begrenztes Talent, wie es zunächst scheint' – which extends only to those of his poems 'die aus der ländlichen Begrenzung in die Weite des eigenen Ichs vorstoßen', comes the realisation that Eich sees the same dangers in rural, peasant poetry as he does in urban, proletarian writing. Zernatto's mistake is to focus on the superficial outward manifestations of rural life in a *sachlich* style, rather than shaping that external reality through the internal lens of the self. The rural context can then be as constraining as the urban, the rural poet as capable of allowing non-poetic vocabulary into his verse, and just as capable of writing poetry which is 'gewollt'. Just how far Eich's polemical position at 1930 is a poetological one applied across the ideological spectrum is indicated by his review of Benn's *Fazit der Perspektiven* (GE, 4, 549–50), for here he applies almost exactly the same critique to Benn, the intellectual authority for the *Kolonne* Circle, as he does to Becher, spokesperson of the proletarian Left. Eich's objections to Becher are not then, as Cuomo mistakenly claims, ideological in nature.[13] Benn's book is attacked for its fundamental formal shortcomings, that is, as a 'Vermischung der Formen von Aufsatz und Dichtung'. As such, Benn has produced a work of *Tendenzdichtung* which seeks to persuade the reader through the poetic medium. In a strong echo of Lukács's programmatic dichotomy between *Reportage* and *Gestaltung*, Eich denies any possibility of compatibility between the essay and the poem, maintaining his central poetological belief: 'Dichtung muß absichtslos scheinen.' It is the blurring of the boundaries of genre and form to which Eich also objects. Even for Benn, a poet who is 'ichbetont', the attempt to replace trusted old forms with more 'effective' new forms only lowers the quality of the artistic product:

> Es ist typisch für die Neigung der Zeit, alle Formen zu vermischen, für den Glauben, die Addition der Formen erziele eine größere Wirkung [...]. Ich glaube, daß die Wirksamkeit aller Kunst am größten ist innerhalb der Grenzen ihrer Form und daß die Versuche zu neuen Formen, wenn sie den Kreis aller Möglichkeiten durchlaufen haben, wieder münden in die reine ursprüngliche Beschränkung.

Here, then, Eich is also explicit about his attitude to form. Good art can only exist within the boundaries of conventional, restrictive form. Eich promotes a purity and wholeness of form.

Significantly, Eich does not restrict this literary-theoretical position to the sacred territory of lyric poetry. Rather, his reviews indicate that it can also apply to drama and prose. In the Benn review, for example, Eich denies the effectiveness of didactic drama, claiming that only those already convinced of the dramatist's viewpoint would welcome such a play. Irrespective of genre, any true literary work avoids a self-conscious, willed attitude, and central here is Eich's notion that literary form should be 'selbstverständlich'. This emerges particularly clearly in his review of Emil Belzner's novel *Marschieren – nicht träumen* (GE, 4, 553–54), the overwhelming shortcoming of which lies in the novelty of its form and plot:

> Man spürt zu sehr, daß die Fabel neuartig ist, daß die Form neuartig ist, und man sollte beides nicht spüren. Leicht übertrieben gesprochen: Alles, was in einem Roman auffällt, ist nicht richtig. Jeder endgültig gestaltete Roman hat die Eigenschaft, daß seine Form selbstverständlich ist, und daß seine Fabel nicht anders ausdrückbar ist als durch den ganzen Ablauf der Handlung.

The demand for a naturalness of form entails a lack of authorial visibility. Musil's *Mann ohne Eigenschaften* is criticised for its irony, for irony constitutes a value judgement on the characters on the part of the author: 'Das ist eine Einmischung des Autors in Dinge, die ihn sozusagen nichts angehen.' Belzner's mistake is to intervene in his own novel, placing himself between the reader and the book and

---

13   See Cuomo, *Career at the Cost of Compromise*, p. 15.

contravening the conventional boundaries of reading and writing. Here there is an unmistakeable echo of Raschke's literary criticism, taking to task modern novelists, 'die zwischen ihren Fingern wie in einem Wachsfigurenkabinett als Erklärer herumgehen, ängstlich, die Figuren könnten sich durch ihr Handeln nicht genügend verdeutlichen' (*DLW*, 7.35/36, 11). Belzner also, mistakenly, underestimates his reader: 'Es ist nicht nur Belzners Fehler, daß er seine Leser für dümmer hält als sie sind [...] Das tun heute fast alle Romanschriftsteller.' If Belzner encapsulates all that is wrong with modern novels, Eich offers a counter-example in the shape of Flaubert. In the Belzner review, *Madame Bovary* is held up as an example to follow while in a rare Third Reich review – of Stifter's *Witiko* (GE, 4, 565–56), published in the *Neue Leipziger Zeitung* in 1935 – it is *Éducation Sentimentale* which offers the ideal to aspire to. Sandwiched in between these references to Flaubert is Eich's final *Kolonne* review (GE, 4, 562–63), appropriately of *Éducation Sentimentale* itself. Flaubert's autobiographical experience, much like the experiences of Villon, Rimbaud and Brecht which inform their poetry, is real in a sense which differs fundamentally from the reality of *Neue Sachlichkeit*. *Wahrhaft*, rather than *wirklich*, the literature advocated by Eich is natural, real, and whole in a way that can only remind us of the Lukácsian doctrine developed in *Die Linkskurve* and perpetuated in *Das Wort*.

Noteworthy in Eich's *Kolonne* reviews is not only the consistency of poetological position, but also the tone and style of the reviews which again attest to the contested cultural situation around 1930. These reviews are to be understood as contributions to an increasingly polemicised debate, rather than pieces of genuine literary criticism. Just what the alternatives were which were being fought over in this debate can be read from Anton Kaes's account of Weimar culture where he refers explicitly to 'einer Spaltung der deutschen Literatur in zwei sich antagonistische gegenüberstehende Literaturen [...]: eine programmatisch moderne, avantgardistisch-intellektuelle Großstadtliteratur und eine bewußt antimoderne, thematisch wie formal rückwärtsgewandte, volks-tümlich-populäre Blut-und-Boden Literatur'.[14] The 1930 shift has been widely conceptualised as a shift in dominant from the former to the latter, so that in effect Kaes provides four parameters along which the 1930 shift towards conservatism is perceived to be taking place: attitude to modernity (from pro-modern to anti-modern); formal experimentation (from avant-gardist to traditionalist); status and appeal of literature (from elitist to populist); and, perhaps more implicitly, political orientation (from left/liberal to right).

In a sense, Kaes accurately reflects the narrowing and over-simplification of alternatives typical of the threshold moments of potential cultural change, but it

---

14 Anton Kaes, 'Schreiben und Lesen in der Weimarer Republik', in Rolf Grimminger (ed.), *Hansers Sozialgeschichte der deutschen Literatur vom 16. Jahrhundert bis zur Gegenwart*, 12 vols, VIII: *Literatur der Weimarer Republik 1918–1933*, ed. by Bernhard Weyergraf (Munich: Hanser 1995), pp. 38–65 (p. 63).

should be clear that Eich's aesthetic position consistently presented in *Die Kolonne* evades a binarism which seeks to oppose pro-modern, avant-gardist, intellectual *Großstadtdichtung* (pre-1930) with anti-modern, formally and thematically backward-looking, folksy-populist *Blut-und-Boden* literature (post-1930). Kaes's description of the literary situation at 1930 entails a conflation of divergent literary trends, both those before 1930 (anti-modern, elitist Expressionism and pro-modern, populist *Neue Sachlichkeit*) and after (populist *völkstümlich* writing and the more elitist bourgeois position represented by Eich and *Die Kolonne*). To take each of the parameters in turn, Eich was certainly programmatic in his rejection of literature which embraced modernity and the city and which sought to experiment with form and genre. Equally, he himself embraced forms of literary representation which favoured nature and a much more tradition-centred approach to form and genre. But Eich was equally programmatic in his advocacy of a conception of literature founded on elitism and the intellectual challenge offered to the reader and in the rejection of the ideologised use of literature, be it by Left or Right. Indeed, even the shift along the first parameter hides a more complex reality, for Eich's reviews and statements clearly indicate that the principle he is upholding is not the anti-modern against the pro-modern, the countryside against the city. Rather, Eich's interest is in the capacity of different themes to act as the medium for the representation of the inner truth of the self, the feelings and experiences of the subjective poetic voice. For this to be achieved the medium needs to be neutral – in Eich's terminology, *unauffällig*, *problemlos*, *selbstverständlich* – and, at least at 1930, it is the idiom of nature poetry with its conventional vocabulary, and indeed form, which Eich perceives to offer that neutral medium. Central then is the shift from the willed and purposeful depiction of outward, immediate reality and experience (*Wirklichkeit*) to the spontaneous and natural depiction of inner, true reality and experience (*Wahrhaftigkeit*). In Eich's poetics, the specifics of form and theme are subordinate or incidental to this central guiding principle.

1947–1949: principles reconsidered

It is now, with these poetological principles clearly established, that we are in a position to consider Eich's programmatic aesthetic stance in the years after 1945. After *Die Kolonne* ceased publication in 1932, Eich seems to have remained noticeably silent on matters of poetological and asesthetic principle. Indeed, it is only at the renewed threshold of 1945, that Eich's voice is heard again, seeking to intervene through a series of essays and reviews in the on-going debates concerning the future direction of German literature in the wake of National Socialism. The nature of these debates is familiar from our consideration of *Der Ruf*, both in its US and Munich incarnations, and Eich's short essays in these years are strikingly reminiscent of the contributions made to that journal which sought to diagnose and shape the contemporary condition of German literary culture. Particularly contested were positions in the debate between *innerlich* and *sachlich* approaches to writing, the former maintaining the viability of inner emigration as an aesthetic response in the Third Reich and of Rilke as a model in the post-war years, the latter championing an engaged *Sachlichkeit* as an antidote to the aesthetically and, not least, morally discredited stance of inwardness. What is noteworthy about Eich's contributions at this further moment of accelerated cultural activity and potential change is his apparent adoption of the *sachlich*, *Kahlschlag* position in direct contravention of the stance so consistently set out at 1930.

As we have already seen, this contravention finds its clearest expression in Eich's views on poetic language and above all the appropriateness of modern vocabulary in poetic discourse. The steadfast rejection of prosaic, modern vocabulary was one of the most striking constants in Eich's *Kolonne* statements and reviews, providing a link, for example, between 'Bemerkungen über Lyrik' (GE, 4, 458–61) and the review of *Um uns die Stadt* (GE, 4, 555). Yet in 'Die heutige Situation der Lyrik' (GE, 4, 471–75), published in June 1947, Eich seems to have turned this lyric principle on its head: 'Die Meinung, gewisse Vokabeln gehörten nicht in Gedichten, ist sehr charakteristisch für eine verflossene Art von Lyrik.' Droste-Hülshoff is praised as a poet who broke convention by using 'prosaic' vocabulary in her poetry. The artefacts of the modern world – the electric light, the car, railway station, and factory – are all said to have a place in contemporary poetry. Indeed, Eich sees the completion of its transition into *Zivilisation* as the central task of that poetry:

> Das Gedicht hat das ihm von der Konvention zugewiesene Gebiet, das einem Naturschutzpark ähnlich war, verlassen und ist im Begriff, sich im gesamten Bereich der uns bekannten Wirklichkeit anzusiedeln. [...] Der Schritt in die Bereiche der Zivilisatorischen [...] ist bisher noch nicht entschlossen getan. [...] Hier hinkt in der Tat die Lyrik bedenklich hinter der Wirklichkeit der Zeit nach. Es wird indessen für ihre Legitimation im kulturellen Bereich wichtig werden, daß dieser Abstand aufgeholt wird. [...] Der letzte entscheidende Schritt in den Bereich des Zivilisatorischen muß bald getan werden.

The continuing focus of the reading public on George and Rilke is seen to have obscured the true breadth of lyric output over recent decades. As in the Andersch and Richter phase of *Der Ruf*, criticism is directed at the 'Rilke-Nachahmer' and the 'George-Epigonen'. As proof, Eich reproduces a typical example of contemporary nature poetry, making clear that it is the experience of war and on-going social crisis which has robbed this kind of poetic stance of its validity: 'Man kann sich nicht vorstellen, daß ihr Verfasser in einer Welt lebt, die von Kriegen, Hunger, Verwüstung und Unsicherheit gepeinigt ist, in einer Welt tiefster sozialer, wirtschaftlicher und politischer Umschichtungen, in der Welt der Maschine des

Flugzeugs und der Atombombe.' Unacceptable in this context are 'Poesie' and 'Schönheit', 'zeit- und lebensferne Gebilde'.

Other essays from this time pick up on the new-found poetic validity of modern vocabulary. In his 1948 assessment of the state of German literature, 'Wo bleibt die deutsche Literatur?' (GE, 4, 478–80), Eich highlights poetry which is gaining strength 'mehr und mehr und allgemein des zivilisatorischen Bereichs' and refers above all to the 'Kraft, die dem Gedicht aus der Wirklichkeit zuströmt, und die vor dem Vokabular einer umgestalteten Welt so wenig zurückschreckt wie vor dem der Botanik oder der Biologie'. Similarly, Eich's own sketched 'Lebenslauf' from 1946 (GE, 4, 464–65) suggests a changed approach to poetry. Of his poems written as a prisoner of war, Eich claims: 'Sie haben nicht die Absicht, den Leser oder Hörer in eine schönere Welt zu versetzen, sie bemühen sich um Objektivität.' Most striking with regard to this apparent poetological shift is the short piece written by Eich in 1947 on the contemporary role of the writer ('Der Schriftsteller 1947', GE, 4, 468–70) which was included by Richter in first draft edition of *Skorpion* in 1948. Here the writer is no longer a *Dichter* but a *Schriftsteller*. Not only that, but Eich names this generic writer Rönne, 'mit ironischem Ernst nach einem verschollenen Vorbild'. Given the portrait of the writer which follows, the knowing reference to Gottfried Benn's alter-ego signals a radical departure from the *Kolonne* poets who proclaimed identity with Benn at 1930. Eich's Rönne is not a poet-genius elevated above the masses. The conditions of material hardship affect him as others, for 'seine Situation ist auch die Situation aller'. Production is a necessity for the writer as for the baker, a job of work, rather than a purely spontaneous creative act. But Rönne carries greater responsibility than other workers, for his material is language which has influence on others. When in weak moments he looks to the moon or turns to Stifter and Eichendorff, 'er belügt sich und andere, als gäbe es noch Inseln der Schönheit'. Significantly the change wrought on Rönne is not just a product of war, but rather of a process of change which Eich considers to have preceded the war, and the tempo of which has now accelerated. The effects of this process on the writer are profound:

> Das bedeutet vor allem, daß die Möglichkeit der Isolation schwindet. Die Verkapselung in die private Sphäre wird undicht. Die Atomkraft zertrümmert die starken Mauern, die sich die Seele errichtet hat; durch die Breschen pfeift der schneidend kalte Wind der unentrinnbaren Wirklichkeit. [...] Im Treiben der Welt kann [der Schriftsteller] sich der immer stärkeren Aktivierung nicht entziehen. Seine Aufgabe hat sich vom Ästhetischen zum Politischen gewandelt.

This position seems impossible to reconcile with the Eich who had attacked in *Die Kolonne* any element of *Tendenz* in literature or any conscious intention on the part of the writer and who had steadfastly defended the right of the poet to remain aloof from the times: 'Und Verantwortung vor der Zeit? Nicht im geringsten. Nur vor mir selber' (GE, 4, 457). Indeed, the explicit reference to Stifter and Eichendorff and to the defunct idiom of nature poetry seems to render the portrait of Rönne an astonishing recantation of everything Eich himself had represented at 1930.

Continuities 1930 vs 1945

It is here that the importance of identifying Eich's underlying poetological principles lies, because at this level a close reading of Eich's statements at 1930 and 1945 reveals strong compatibility in those fundamental principles. To take the notion of *Schönheit*, for example, Eich's rejection of poetic beauty is not a new phenomenon at 1945. In his Becher review of 1931, Eich was already rejecting the view that the aim of poetry was 'schöne Worte machen' (GE, 4, 551). The critical reference in that review to the thousands of 'Mondscheingedichte' produced by that approach to poetry is clearly reminiscent of the poetry rejected by Eich after 1945, and this was a theme expanded upon in his 1932 review of Fritz Dietrich's *Stern überm Haus: Gedichte und Legenden* (GE, 4, 557–58). Here, Dietrich's poetry is dismissed as sub-Rilkean cliché, the central misconception identified by Eich familiar from his 1947 position: 'Es ist ein Irrtum zu denken, etwas sei schon gültig, wenn es schön gesagt ist, und Dichtung sei das Gebiet des Schönen. Wenn es so wäre, dann allerdings hätten die Gegner der Dichtung recht, wenn sie ihr den Tod wünschen.' In this sense, the kind of poetry attacked in 1947 – 'So werden denn zeit- und lebensferne Gebilde geboren und gut-geheißen, ja das Blasse und Konventionelle erscheint geradezu erstrebenswert und als Zeichen der Qualität' (GE, 4, 473) – was already being attacked by Eich at 1930. By the same token, already at 1930 Eich did not see his aesthetic position as entirely divorced from the times. In his response to Diebold, for instance, Eich explicitly rejected the charge that his poetry was *zeitfremd* (GE, 4, 458). Where Eich and Diebold differed was in their definition of what they considered to be representative of the times. Rather than the superficial manifestations of the modern world, Eich sought to represent the essential truth of the times through a medium and vocabulary which he considered to be *selbstverständlich*. In the statements made after 1945, that fundamental principle has not changed. As Eich makes clear in 'Die heutige Situation der Lyrik', railway stations and cars are legitimate elements in poetic discourse, precisely because they have now become *selbstverständlich* (GE, 4, 475). For Eich, it is the world around him which has changed not the nature of his poetic principles, and one of the central principles enunciated in the Rönne piece is one which also underpins the *Kolonne* statements and reviews: 'Ich will nicht sagen, daß es keine Schönheit gibt, aber sie setzt Wahrheit voraus. Der Zwang zur Wahrheit, das ist die Situation des Schrift-stellers' (GE, 4, 470).

Here, it is again worth mentioning the centrality of *Sachlichkeit* in the *Kolonne* programme. Eich, even at 1930, was not by his very nature a neo-Romantic aesthete. As a private individual he was fully engaged with the modern urban world, and this engagement did find its expression in his *Kolonne* reviews. When considering the notion of *Großstadtdichtung*, for example, Eich acknowledges that humanity has been changed by the city. The modern city even has a positive, facilitating effect on the poet: 'Alle Dichtung unserer Zeit is soweit Großstadtdichtung, als die Großstadt das Leben und Denken des Schreibenden bestimmt. Vielleicht spricht jemand in einem Gedicht von der Insel Palau, und doch konnte dieses Gedicht niemals als heute und nirgends anders als in Berlin geschrieben werden' (GE, 4, 555). Similarly, in his Benn and Becher reviews (GE, 4, 549–50; 551–52), Eich advocates the power of persuasion through 'Statistiken und kühle Überlegungen'. Indeed, particularly striking in his review of Benn's *Fazit der Perspektiven* is his own explanation and justification of the indirect nature of poetry by recourse to arithmetic series. In this sense, Eich's welcome after 1945 for poetic vocabulary drawn from the modern world and more specifically from the sciences (botany, medicine, biology) is not without roots in the *Kolonne* programme, and it significant that in 'Die heutige Situation der Lyrik' Eich regrets the subsequent neglect of Benn's early attempts to integrate poetry with *Zivilisation* (GE, 4, 475). Also noteworthy in this context is Eich's fascination in the post-1945 essays with physics and the atom bomb. It is telling, for example, that Eich asserts in his 1949 essay 'Schlafpulver oder Explosivstoff?' (GE, 4, 481–82) that all books are informed now by the findings of physics and psychology. Indeed, whether in the novel or poem, the appropriate style advocated by Eich in this essay is one founded on *Genauigkeit*, 'genau und unverständlich, ähnlich wie ein Lehrbuch der Atomphysik'. Not only does the post-Hiroshima nuclear age constitute a source of renewed crisis and therefore continuity in the dominant post-1930 mood, but particle physics has been shown in our analysis of literary journals to be one of the defining pre-occupations of German intellectuals in this period, seeking to identify meaning in a world where it seems lost.

The notion of exactitude and incomprehensibility invoked by Eich in relation to the physics textbook highlights the most important thread of continuity running through Eich's poetics from 1930 to 1949, namely the challenge he continued to seek to pose to the reader. Conceived in his 1949 essay as a choice between sleeping powder and explosive, the function of writing for Eich persisted in being the latter: 'Der Schriftsteller [...] muß den Mut aufbringen auch gegen den Leser zu schreiben. Stil ist kein Schlafpulver, sondern ein Explosivstoff' (GE, 4, 481). Or as he in wrote in 'Die heutige Situation der Lyrik': 'Echte Dichtung besitzt nicht nicht die wünschenswerte Eigenschaft, den Leser in seiner Ruhe zu bestärken, sie stört ihn daraus auf' (GE, 4, 473). As such, even in his post-1945 call for political and *sachlich* writing and in his substitution of the *Schriftsteller* for the *Dichter*, Eich was resolutely defending an elitist conception of literature (*echte Dichtung*) which was not accessible to all readers. In 'Schlafpulver oder Explosivstoff?' Eich acknowledges that a journalistic background is no disadvantage for a writer, but at the same time he goes out of his way to explain that the American generation of Wolfe, Faulkner, and Hemingway – so often claimed by advocates of a new literary beginning at 1945 – are 'keineswegs jedem zugänglich'. As well as journalism, Hemingway has studied literary models, so that 'sein kunstvoller, ja raffinierter Stil ist nicht aus dem Journalismus ableitbar'. This matches a passage from the Rönne essay where Eich explicitly states that he is not advocating that the post-war writer should 'die deutsche Romantik zugunsten des amerikanischen Romans in Fetzen reißen, er muß nicht von Dichter zum Journalisten werden' (GE, 4, 469). As far as the institution of literature is concerned Eich is resolutely maintaining the conventional elitist position which he first set out in *Die Kolonne* against the perceived threat of *Neue Sachlichkeit*. Now, in 'Schlafpulver oder Explosivstoff?' Eich explicitly connects this position to the crisis of the book which he perceives to be a symptom of an on-going crisis in 'Bildung' (GE, 4, 481). Despite, or rather precisely because of, this crisis, Eich refuses to capitulate in his defence of elitist literature, so that here he expresses a position closer to that of the prisoner-of-war version of *Der Ruf* where a concept of high culture was maintained in the face of the crisis of bourgeois culture and the book, a crisis exacerbated not least by National Socialism.

Thus, in at least four respects, Eich's programme of abrupt discontinuity at 1945 can in fact be seen to possess significant points of continuity with his 1930 position: (i) in the search for truth, rather than beauty, through a poetic medium which is *selbstverständlich*; (ii) in the strands of *Sachlichkeit* which run back to the *Kolonne* programme; (iii) in the perceptible mood of on-going crisis; (iv) in the elitist conception of literature and the challenge offered by it to the reader. In this way, room can be found for Eich's programmatic post-1945 position within a 1930 paradigm, albeit one conceived in slightly different terms from Kaes or Trommler. At the same time, we must also consider the extent to which this post-1945 programme constitutes a largely rhetorical position undermined by Eich's actual practice. In effect, to what extent does Eich allow himself to give in to those weak moments which continue to afflict Rönne, when he looks up to the moon and sinks into self-indulgence, when he walks through the forest and feels lured toward Stifter and Eichendorff? Central here will be the subsequent examination of Eich's literary practice, but his reviews in these early post-1945 years, many of them published for the first time in 1991, already suggest that the old Rönne may be stubbornly persistent alongside the new Eich.

Reviews 1945–1949: 'Das neue Naturgedicht'

Significant in this respect are not only Eich's reviews, but also the 1948 essay 'Wo bleibt die deutsche Literatur?' (GE, 4, 478–80). Here, Eich sets out to refute the view, widely held and in this case represented by the Swiss journalist Manuel

Gasser and the publisher Bermann Fischer, that nothing of note has been published in the three years since the end of the war, that there is in effect no contemporary German literature. Eich's own position could not be any clearer – 'kurzum: es gibt eine deutsche Literatur!' – but what is worthy of note in the context of Eich's 1930 and post-1945 programme is the nature of the German literature which Eich heralds. Above all, that literature, which has been neglected by Gasser and Bermann Fischer, consists almost entirely of poetry: 'Die wichtigsten Veröffentlichungen im Nachkriegsdeutschland sind lyricher Art.' Even amidst the widely acknowledged flood of poetry publications in the immediate post-war years, such a common source of complaint of course in *Der Ruf*, Eich feels obliged to mount a vigorous defence of the poem against the commercial interests of the press and larger publishing houses: 'Ein Gedicht ist kein Erfolgsschlager. Es führt in der Zeitung wie im Verlagswesen ein aschenbrödelhaftes Dasein.' Defence of the poem itself was one manifestation of the 1930 shift, and here at 1945 Eich's reviews indicate a comparable intention. Of the nine review articles written by Eich between 1946 and 1949, for example, four are summary reviews which cover in total more than 30 newly published poetry volumes, while three deal with the output of individual poets. Very clearly, it is poetry which remains for Eich the privileged genre of writing, notwithstanding the upheavals of the immediate post-war period.

If we consider in more detail precisely what kind of poetry Eich was advocating and rejecting at this time, his reviews do seem to uphold to some degree the thesis that Eich's poetological position advocates a new beginning at 1945. In particular, two central aspects are consistently criticised in those volumes which Eich reviews negatively: firstly the attempt to retreat into a realm divorced from reality; and secondly a strictness or conventionality of form. So, for example, an anthology entitled *Junges Berlin* is attacked in one review for not reflecting the destroyed city and its uncertain present (GE, 4, 590), while in another Annemarie Herleth's central shortcoming in her collection *Auf einer Insel* is said to be the failure to leave the sanctuary of that island and engage with reality (GE, 4, 581). In the same review, 'Neue Gedichtbücher', Eich can find little enthusiasm for Gottfried Hasenkamp's *Carmina in nocte*, 'eine Welle aus der Flut der über uns hereinbrechenden Sonette' (GE, 4, 580), and this disquiet at the contemporary preference for strict classical form is also applied in the 1948 'Neue Versbücher' (GE, 4, 587–88) to Herbert Hinterleithner's *Südliche Terzinen* and Günter Rudorf's *Schwarz schreit die Sonne*. In between these two reviews, Eich gives the clearest indication of his views on form in the first of his 'Neue Versbücher' reviews when he considers Hans Erich Nossack's *Gedichte* (GE, 4, 586). Despite fulsome praise for Nossack's poetry, Eich strongly regrets his preference for the sonnet. This poetic form 'verwandelt, in Jahrhunderten zu einem festen Panzer geworden, auch hier die Beweglichkeit der Sprache und des Gedankens in Steifheit; Natürliches wird gespreizt, Eigenart unversehens zur Konvention'. In rejecting these two particular poetic tendencies, Eich is clearly rejecting two of the features which emerge from the analysis of our journal corpus as typical of the restorative post-1930 paradigm.

And yet, the kind of poetry advocated in 'Wo bleibt die deutsche Literatur?' (GE, 4, 478–80) is still readily compatible with what, by 1945, might be termed the developing *Kolonne* tradition and to some extent with that advocated in *Merkur*. In that essay, Eich is clear that the breadth and richness of contemporary German poetry can be traced back to German Expressionism. In this context, the familiar 'conservative' triumvirate of Rilke, George, and Hofmannsthal is mentioned, but more important for Eich are Heym, Loerke, Benn, and Lehmann who represent the increased subtlety and sophistication lent to language by Expressionism. Amongst young poets, Eich picks out Hermlin, Holthusen, König, Krolow, Nossack, and Podszus; among the older, but still active, generation of poets, von der Vring, Britting, F. G. Jünger, and Langgässer. Against the general perception of a lack of important post-war publications, Eich tellingly cites not the literature of a new generation, but rather the publication bans on Benn and Ernst Jünger, together with the work of his *Kolonne* contemporary Langgässer (*Das unauslöschliche Siegel*) and his long-standing associate Hermann Kasack (*Die Stadt hinter dem Strom*). Perhaps most important as literary authorities for Eich who span the Third Reich and reach back to 1930 are Loerke and Lehmann, paradigmatic figures in Trommler's version of the 1930 shift.[15] The on-going significance of these poets for Eich, and of the kind of writing they represent, can be read most strikingly from his response to the criticism which his apparent rejection of traditional poetry in 'Die heutige Situation der Lyrik' attracted from readers. The latest Eich edition reproduces a draft of a letter to Hans Bütow, feuilleton editor of the *Allgemeine Zeitung* which acted as Eich's main publishing outlet in these years:

> Daß ich nur Gedichte gelten ließe, die sich des Vokabulars der Zivilisation bedienen, ist eine Unterstellung die mir nicht verständlich ist, wenn ich ausdrücklich die naturversponne Lyrik Wilhelm Lehmanns rühme, den Namen Loerke erwähne und die lyrische Produktion der letzten Jahre ungewöhnlich reich und bedeutend nenne [...]. Wenn ich meinte, daß Körner und Schenkendorf ihre Zeit gültiger ausgedrückt hätten als Goethe, so hätte ich für die Gegenwart statt Lehmann und Loerke Rudolf Hagelstange genannt. (GE, 4, 649)

As these comments make clear, just as important as the emphasis on a new kind of poetry in 'Die heutige Situation der Lyrik' was Eich's on-going advocacy of a kind of nature poetry which continued to bear the traces of Expressionism: 'Noch ist es vor allem die Natur, die den Dichter ergreift und die nach zwei Jahrhunderten Naturlyrik ebenso unerschöpflich geblieben ist wie vorher. Liest man in Wilhelm Lehmanns Versen, so ist man versucht zu glauben, sie sei überhaupt in ihrer Fülle vordem nicht gesehen worden' (GE, 4, 474).

---

15 Trommler, 'Emigration und Nachkriegsliteratur', pp. 178–79.

This line of high-culture, bourgeois literary continuity which runs through *Die Kolonne* and *Das innere Reich* finds strong expression in Eich's post-1945 reviews. Langgässer and Carossa both attract fulsome praise in the summary review articles of 1948 (GE, 4, 587–88), while Kasack (GE, 4, 571–75) and Horst Lange (GE, 4, 595–96) are each the subject of individual essays or reviews. Particularly striking is the thread of continuity provided by Eich's reviews of Georg von der Vring. From his 1932 *Kolonne* review (GE, 4, 556) to the review of *Oktoberrose* and *Verse für Minette* in 'Neue Versbücher [II]' in 1948 (GE, 4, 587–89), from the tribute on von der Vring's 60th birthday which appeared in *Die Welt* in December 1949 under the heading 'Apfel, Mohn und Rose' (GE, 4, 592–94) to his appreciation of 'Der Bogenpfeil' which appeared in *Die Zeit* ten years later (GE, 4, 602–03), Eich's praise for von der Vring's own brand of apparently conventional poetic vocabulary and form remains a constant. In particular, in both of these latter pieces Eich describes his own enduring affection for von der Vring's poetry which has acted as a 'tröstende Kraft' in what Eich describes as 'Stunden der Not' (GE, 4, 592). The precise descriptions of nature and childhood experience, the indelible mark of the North German coast where von der Vring was raised, the *Volkslied* form, and playful use of sounds have all combined with von der Vring's poetic gifts to provide Eich with a stable point of reference across three decades: 'Seine Fähigkeit, das magische Wort zu finden, die öffnende Zauberformel, ist von bewundernswerter Sicherheit' (GE, 4, 586). Central to Eich's appreciation of von der Vring, and what sets him apart from the sentimental nature poetry criticised by Eich, is the latter's capacity to express himself with precision: 'Der Freude am Sichtbaren entspricht die Genauigkeit der Aussage. Nie werden die vagen Benennungen gewählt, die im deutschen Gedicht einer mißverstandenen "Allgemeingültigkeit" zuliebe bevorzugt sind. Die Natur wird bis in ihre kleinen und feinsten Züge gesehen' (GE, 4, 592). Thus, Eich's appreciation of von der Vring is not simply backward-looking sentimentality but rather part of what he perceives to be a new poetological agenda – in Eich's words 'das neue Naturgedicht', a synthesis of the nature idiom with a *sachlich* gaze, 'genau' and 'unverständlich' like a physics textbook, or, as he wrote in a review of Hermlin's poetry (GE, 4, 581) and repeated in a 1949 radio interview with Karl Schwedhelm (GE, 4, 483–84), the poem as hieroglyph. It is this single poetic principle which underpins Eich's aesthetic programme throughout the post-war years.

In this way, it might be possible to resolve the apparent paradox at the centre of the programmatic position maintained by Eich in these immediate post-war years: on the one hand the rhetorical adoption of a position fundamentally and seemingly deliberately at odds with that set out at 1930; on the other the continuing advocacy of poets and forms of poetry which represent unmistakeable continuity with that 1930 *Kolonne* position. In this, Eich's own response to 1945 is representative of the broader tendency in German literary development perceptible also in *Der Ruf*. Clearly these early post-war years must be regarded as a period of profound reappraisal and reassessment for the German literary community in which new approaches were considered and put forward. The significance for Eich and his contemporaries of the political rupture at 1945 and the on-going uncertainties of the immediate post-war years cannot be underestimated, and the evidence from Eich's programmatic essays in these years clearly suggests Dolan's view – that Eich 'clung to [his] pre-war attitudes for considerable periods of time'[16] – to be something of an over-simplification. At the same time, very strong continuities exist in Eich's underlying poetological principles, even if the acceptable outward manifestations of those principles highlighted by Eich had changed. Here again, we need to understand the circumstances which pertain at moments of accelerated cultural activity and the extreme rhetorical positions which are adopted at those moments: the emphasis on timeless nature poetry at 1930 was a function of the intolerance towards the perceived cultural orthodoxy of the Weimar Republic; the emphasis on a new engagement with reality after 1945 a response to National Socialism. Perhaps Eich's new position after 1945 is best conceived not as a rejection of his position at 1930, but as an admission to it of new possibilities. After 1945 his consistent poetic principles – the aim to represent the universal truth of the times through a *selbstverständlich* medium, in a way which offered a challenge the reader and which operated unashamedly within, and in support of, the institution of high literature – could now be applied to the modern world where previously they were restricted to the conventional medium of nature poetry. As a synthesis of the institution of poetry with a post-Expressionist, *sachlich* even, sensibility, Eich's post-1945 aesthetic programme has its origins at 1930.

Literary Practice

Ich fühle, hier beginnt Gott. Er offenbart sich im Strahlenden. [...] Dies ist jetzt die Aufgabe des Dichters. [...] Denn es ist die Stunde, da du, Dichter Julien Chabanais, und du, Reklamemann Julien Chabanais, endlich zu einer Person euch vereinigt, die Stunde, wo Propaganda zur Religion wird. ('Radium', GE, 2, 183)

The notion of a creative crisis in Eich's literary practice has dominated accounts of his writing during the 1930s. Much research over the past 25 years, for example, has concerned itself with dismantling theories of a self-imposed lyric silence under National Socialism, identifying numerous individual publications in a range of periodicals, including *Das innere Reich*, as well as lyrics composed for radio plays and many written during military service but only published after

---

16   Dolan, p. 158.

1945.[17] In the most recent research, the notion of a lyric crisis in Eich's work has
re-emerged, centred above all on the figure of Julien Chabanais, Eich's thinly
veiled alter-ego in his 1937 radio play 'Radium' (GE, 2, 157–94). A nature poet
forced by lack of public interest in his verse and the illness of his wife, Elisa, to
write advertising slogans for an unscrupulous industrialist, Chabanais was first
interpreted by Cuomo as 'Eich's cynical commentary about his own professional
activity during the Third Reich'.[18] Eich's reference in June 1936 to 'Chabanais', a
Parisian bordello, in his private correspondence with Artur Kuhnert confirms the
currency of the prostitute-poet theme in Eich's own reflections on his literary
practice under National Socialism.[19] Drawing on Cuomo's analysis, Axel Vieregg
views Chabanais as the expression of a profound moral and artistic crisis triggered
in Eich by the realisation of the compromises he had entered into with the Nazi
regime. Documented also in the deeply pessimistic tone of his 1938 poem, 'Der
Tag im März' (GE, 1, 199–200), this crisis represents, according to the title of
Vieregg's essay, Eich's confrontation with his own fallibility. Hardly surprisingly
given Eich's post-war reputation and his own obfuscation about his activities in
the Third Reich, the primary emphasis has rested in recent years on the extent of
this fallibility in direct relation to the Nazi regime, on the extent of assent and
dissent expressed by Eich towards German totalitarianism, all too often in a
binary framework of condemnation and approbation.[20] As far as Eich's crisis in
the mid-to-late 1930s is concerned, the shadow cast on scholarship by the Third
Reich is all the more regrettable, for it is precisely issues outside the politicised
interpretative framework of dictatorship – concerning above all the nature of
authorship and the viability of the traditional *Dichter* in modern society – which
are highlighted by this phase in Eich's career and which continue to have a
substantial bearing on our understanding of the remainder of Eich's literary
practice.

Expressed by Eich tellingly in the two genres which dominate his literary
practice – the poem and the radio play – this crisis is at the same time a product
of the conflict between these genres or, better, of the conflict between the

17 See Hans Dieter Schäfer, 'Die nichtnationalsozialistische Literatur der jungen Generation im
    Dritten Reich', in Hans Dieter Schäfer, *Das gespaltene Bewußtsein: Über deutsche Kultur und
    Lebenswirklichkeit 1933–1945* (Munich: Hanser, 1981), pp. 7–54; Glenn R. Cuomo, 'A Study of
    Günter Eich's Life and Work between 1933 and 1945' (doctoral dissertation, Ohio State
    University, 1982), revised and published as *Career at the Cost of Compromise* (see note 1 above);
    Glenn R. Cuomo, 'Günter Eichs Rundfunkbeiträge in den Jahren 1933–1940: Eine kommentierte
    Neuaufstellung', *Rundfunk und Fernsehen*, 32 (1984), 83–96; Wolfram Wessels, *Hörspiele im Dritten
    Reich: Zur Institutionen-, Theorie- und Literaturgeschichte* (Bonn: Bouvier, 1985); Axel Vieregg, *Der
    eigenen Fehlbarkeit begegnet: Günter Eichs Realitäten 1933–1945* (Eggingen: Edition Isele, 1991).
18 Cuomo, *Career at the Cost of Compromise*, p. 113.
19 See Vieregg, *Der eigenen Fehlbarkeit begegnet*, p. 25.
20 For an attempt to consider these issues in a more measured framework, see Matthew Philpotts,
    The Margins of Dictatorship: Assent and dissent in the work of Günter Eich and Bertolt Brecht (Oxford:
    Lang, 2003).

notions of literature and authorship which underlie these two genres. It can be no coincidence that Chabanais's epiphany, triggered by his realisation of the inhumanity of the radium industry, in whose service he has been writing, is expressed by Eich as an attempt to reconcile a split literary persona – Chabanais as *Dichter* and Chabanais as *Reklamemann* – and as an attempt to re-assert the prophet poet over the compromised copy-writer Chabanais has become. As we have seen, the new literary dominant established at 1930, and that which functions as Eich's own point of initiation into the public institution of literature, is predicated not least on the conventional notion of the *Dichter*, and Eich's defence of this position in his literary programme is consistent and resolute. After all, this is the same Eich who, in an echo of Chabanais, claimed 'daß alles Geschriebene sich der Theologie nähert' (GE, 4, 611). And yet, substantial tensions arise from the attempt to maintain this position in practice, and it is the examination of these tensions in Eich's literary practice which will provide the central thread to this section. Above all, this will involve the investigation of the relationship between the dominant genres of the poem and the radio play: firstly how the difference in status between the two genres generated the crisis enunciated through Chabanais in the 1930s, the former genre being betrayed by the latter; and secondly how this difference in status was largely overcome in the 1950s, the latter being raised to the privileged status of the former.

The radio writer under National Socialism

Eich's membership questionnaire for the *Reichsschrifttumskammer*, dated 20 May 1936 and retained at the Berlin Document Centre, provides details of his public literary output since 15 December 1933. At first glance, this output seems to be broadly based: examples of poetry publications, short stories, book reviews, theatre productions and radio work are all listed; as his area of 'Haupttätigkeit' Eich specifies 'Lyrik, Funk, Bühne, Erzählung'. However, Eich's remark in the section provided for detailing radio work leaves little room for doubt as to where his professional energies had been deployed under the Nazi regime: 'Es wären an die hundert Sendungen aufzuführen, wofür der Platz nicht ausreicht.' Or, as he put it in the concluding line of his accompanying biographical sketch: 'Meine schriftstellerische Tätigkeit dient seit Anfang 1933 fast ausschließlich dem Rundfunk.' This tallies much more closely with Eich's application form for membership of *Reichsverband deutscher Schriftsteller*, where less than six months after the Nazi seizure of power he had selected *Rundfunk* for his primary membership, *Lyriker* only for *Gastmitgliedschaft*. As such, it is difficult not to see 1933 as marking a decisive turning-point in Eich's literary practice, away from his pre-1933 *Kolonne* programme where the lyric poet was dominant. Eich's private correspondence with Martin Raschke also attests to the significance of the change in regime for his own career, as he actively sought to court important figures in the Nazi radio industry, aided by the cultural vacuum left by political exclusion and exile. As Vieregg points out, 'die Anfänge von Eichs Rundfunkkarriere und die Anfänge des Dritten Reiches [fallen] auf fatale Weise zusammen'.[21]

Given the paucity and/or inaccuracy of Eich's own statements on the matter and the fact that some 95% of the material is non-extant, judgements as to the precise nature of the radio work which Eich started to undertake from 1933 remain necessarily speculative. However, following detailed analysis of radio programme listings from the Third Reich, Cuomo has estimated Eich's contribution to the Nazi radio industry at 160 individually or jointly authored broadcast texts.[22] This compares to only 33 published poems in the same period, of which 15 derived in any case directly from radio work. Unsurprisingly given his sheer level of productivity, the majority of Eich's radio texts were adaptations rather than original compositions, often drawing on historical and biographical documents as well as literary material. Many of these texts were also aimed predominantly at children, including treatments of traditional German folk and fairy-tale themes such as *Till Eulenspiegel* and the von Münchhausen stories.[23] Such adaptations were stylistically straightforward and artistically unpretentious, not the original and creative output of the *Dichter* whose persona Eich had promoted in *Die Kolonne*. Indeed, Cuomo is able to cite contemporary evidence of the reception of Eich's adaptation of the Grimm fairy tale, 'Der Fischer und seine Frau', which indicates that it was successfully pitched at an uneducated peasant audience.[24] As such, Eich was clearly fulfilling what Cuomo identifies as the primary goal of the radio play under National Socialism:

> When it came to broadcast material of a less universal appeal than music, such as the radio play, writers were expected to cater to the tastes of the largest listener group, the unsophisticated masses, for whom the radio played a prominent role in leisure-time activities. That is, the new trend was characterized by anti-intellectualism and anti-elitism. Plebeian entertainment and popular 'enlightenment' were given priority over the more cultured interests of the middle and upper classes.[25]

Above all, it is the long-running radio serial which Eich co-wrote with his *Kolonne* colleague Martin Raschke, 'Deutsche Kalender: Monatsbilder des Königswuster-häuser Landboten' ('KWL'), which attests to the popular appeal of Eich's radio output during the Third Reich. In this respect, the remarkable longevity of the serial − it ran on the *Deutschlandsender* from October 1933 to May 1940 − is supported by positive reviews in the Nazi press, the appearance of a published anthology, *Das festliche Jahr*, and by the existence of Eich's own spin-off serial,

---

21 Vieregg, *Der eigenen Fehlbarkeit begegnet*, p. 18.
22 See Cuomo, *Career at the Cost of Compromise*, pp. 29–46.
23 See, for example, 'Eine Geburtstagsfeier bei Herrn von Münchhausen', GE, 2, 27–49.
24 Kurt Willimczik, 'Rundfunk in der Dorfwirtschaft', *Rufer und Hörer*, 3 (1935), 443–44, quoted by Cuomo, *Career at the Cost of Compromise*, p. 68.
25 Cuomo, *Career at the Cost of Compromise*, p. 55.

'Der märkische Kalendermann'. Similar in style and content to Matthias Claudius's *Der Wandsbeker Bote*, these folksy and anachronistic depictions of the postman's resolutely good-natured travels through a rural idyll long disappeared clearly fall a long way short of the 'Explosivstoff' with which Eich hoped to challenge his readers after 1945 (GE, 4, 481–82). Eich's own potent brand of sleeping powder, the 'KWL' serial and the majority of his other radio output under National Socialism betray the *Kolonne* poet who believed, in Dolan's words, 'that poetry is a matter only for the select few and that the genius [...] is not doing his job if he strives for popular success'.[26]

More recent evidence from Eich's letters concerning his work on the 'KWL' serial and the circumstances of composition surrounding his final Third Reich radio play, 'Rebellion in der Goldstadt', sheds further light on Eich's literary practice in this period and above all the process by which Eich produced work which conformed to National Socialist radio policy. Through Eich's correspondence with Raschke, for example, Vieregg demonstrates persuasively that the content of the 'KWL' was often specifically determined by interventions from party officials such as the series director and voice of the postman, Helmut Hansen, or by the originator of the series, Werner Pleister. Hence, in a letter of 17 April 1935: 'Pleister ist sehr angetan vom April-Kalender, nur bittet er uns, den Landboten nicht mehr schlafen und im Bett liegen zu lassen. [...] Hansen wiederholte den alten Plan "der Landbote reist durch Deutschland" mit je einer Landschaft im Monat.'[27] Similarly, the composition of 'Rebellion in der Goldstadt' can be connected directly to an anti-British propaganda campaign, launched at a meeting of radio authors with officials of the Propaganda Ministry in Berlin in January 1940, at which an official list of suitable radio play themes and titles was drawn up. Eich's correspondence from this period with A. Artur Kuhnert charts his entirely pragmatic motivations for undertaking the commission – financial considerations and much-needed leave from military service – together with his frustrated attempts to work with the prescribed anti-British themes before settling on the 1922 miners' uprising in Johannesburg. A letter of 20 April 1940, for example, reveals Eich's lack of creative engagement with the project: 'Mein Hörspiel ['Rebellion in der Goldstadt'] ist mit Ach und Krach fertig geworden und ist ein jammervolles Werk. Dennoch hoffe ich auf eine baldige Sendung, honoraris causa.'[28]

Of significance here is not the extent of assent or dissent expressed by Eich towards the Nazi regime nor the extent of his ideological and moral compromise, but rather the implications of this evidence for the nature of authorship which

---

26 Dolan, p. 163.
27 See Vieregg, *Der eigenen Fehlbarkeit begegnet*, pp. 26–27.
28 See Karl Karst, '"Honoraris causa": Materialien zur Entstehungsgeschichte des Hörspiels "Rebellion in der Goldstadt"', in Günter Eich, *Rebellion in der Goldstadt: Tonkassette, Text und Materialien* (Frankfurt a.M.: Suhrkamp, 1997), pp. 51–79 (p. 61).

underlie Eich's radio work at this time. Self-evidently, the existence of this direct interventionist mechanism from above, determining literary output with an overt propagandistic function, entirely contradicts the aesthetic position maintained by Eich, for example, in the review of Becher's *Der große Plan* where he demanded that poetry be left to those 'für die es kein Wollen ist' (GE, 4, 552). Also of importance in this respect is the critical debate which has surrounded the authorship of scene 1a of 'Rebellion in der Goldstadt', maintained by Eich apologists to have been added to Eich's original composition, without his knowledge and after his return to the army.[29] Largely fruitless in determing the extent of Eich's 'guilt', such debate is far more instructive in illustrating the co-operative process of radio authorship, 'in dem der Autor nur *eine* Rolle, die nicht unbedingt die wichtigste sein mußte, spielte. Der Dramaturg, der Spielleiter und die Produktion im engeren Sinne beeinflußten das Endprodukt in erheblichem Maße und konnten es in Extremfall dem Entwurf des Autors völlig entfremden'.[30] Allied to this dimunition in the role played by the author in writing the broadcast text is the lack of public recognition which Eich received for his radio broadcasts, in particular the 'KWL' serial. It was the actors voicing the parts who became the names associated with the broadcasts, a product in large measure of the transience of the broadcast text which normally lacked a concrete published form for which the writer could act as author. Even in the published anthology of the 'KWL' serial, Eich and Raschke are denied a conventional author function, their names appearing not as authors on the cover or title page but as 'Verfasser' in a short paragraph at the back of the volume.[31] It was this much denuded author function, rather than the privileged status of *Dichter*, which the vast majority of Eich's literary output afforded him during the Third Reich.

The *Kolonne* poet

The effective anonymity of many of Eich's radio texts is shared by his first lyric publications which appeared in the late 1920s under the somewhat unimaginative pseudonym Erich Günther. But in this instance, the anonymity derives not from the dehumanising and collective apparatus of modernised cultural production which strips the author of status and function, but rather from the process of mystification by which the lyric poet divorces the creative lyric self from the prosaic everyday self, establishing in Eich's terms the distinction between the poet 'als Lyriker' and the poet 'als Privatmann' (GE, 4, 459). In this respect and others,

---

29 For contributions to the debate, see Axel Vieregg (ed.), *'Unsere Sünden sind Maulwürfe': Die Günter-Eich-Debatte* (Amsterdam: Rodopi, 1996).

30 Wessels, p. 201.

31 *Das festliche Jahr: Ein Lesebüchlein vom Königswusterhäuser Landboten* (Oldenburg: Stalling, 1936), p. 109.

Eich's literary practice before 1933 – dominated by his poetry publications in *Anthologie jüngster Lyrik* (1927), in *Die neue Rundschau* (1928) and *Die Kolonne* (1929–1932), and his own volume of *Gedichte* (1930) – conforms much more closely to the notion of literature and authorship so vigorously defended in his *Kolonne* statements and reviews. None of the poems deals with contemporary social or political themes. The language is the timeless vocabulary of nature poetry, of autumn, the wind, and the night sky; the dominant theme the possibility of man's re-integration into nature through death: 'Du mußt dorthin zurückkehren. | [...] Du mußt wieder stumm werden, unbeschwert, | eine Mücke, ein Windstoß, eine Lilie sein' (GE, 1, 10). These are 'inner dialogues' (GE, 4, 457), drawing on the poetics of Benn, Trakl, and Loerke, and seeking to express spontaneously the truth of the poetic self's inner experiences through the unwilled medium of nature poetry. Perhaps most striking of all in Eich's early literary practice is his consistent proximity to the revival of the poem, not only through his role in *Die Kolonne*, but also in his literary debut in 1927 in the *Anthologie jüngster Lyrik*, edited by Klaus Mann and Willi Fehse. Leonard Olschner, for example, draws attention to Stefan Zweig's foreword to the anthology as an important testament to the changing attitude to lyric poetry which, it is worth noting, precedes the crisis period 1929–1932.[32] Similarly, for Hermann Korte this collection of poems acts as a central document in the generalised shift towards traditional poetry located in the second half of the Weimar Republic. The anthology constitutes 'eine erste Bestätigung der traditionalistischen Wende. Das sprachliche Repertoire der Gedichte stammt fast durchweg aus dem 19. Jahrhundert'.[33]

Although Eich's poetic practice before 1933 largely confirms his programmatic definition of the role of the *Dichter* set out in *Die Kolonne*, and in this contradicts the notion of authorship embodied in his post-1933 radio work, the Nazi seizure of power does not constitute a break in the nature of Eich's lyric output. If anything, it is 1930 which emerges as the stronger turning-point in the style and form of Eich's poetry, since many of the pre-1930 poems tend towards a more abstract philosophical and prosaic style, despite the conventionality of their subject-matter and of much of their vocabulary. Indeed, Eich's relatively strict adherence to more regular, folk-stanza forms after 1930 contrasts with the freer verse forms of poems, such as 'Verse an vielen Abenden' from 1926 (GE, 1, 9–10), which have attracted the label 'rhythmisierte Prosa'.[34] The aesthetic conservatism – thematic, formal, and stylistic – of poems published in the mid-to-late 1930s, such as 'Tag im Herbst' (GE, 1, 193), 'Kindheit' (GE, 1, 196), 'Wind über die Stadt' (GE, 1, 196–97), 'Rübenernte' (GE, 1, 198), and

---

32 See Olschner, p. 425.
33 Korte, p. 618.
34 See Larry L. Richardson, *Committed Aestheticism: The poetic theory and practice of Günter Eich* (New York: Lang, 1983), p. 42.

'Wiederkehr' (GE, 1, 62–63), is readily apparent. Indeed, irrespective whether critics' views are informed by an awareness of, or interest in, Eich's productivity in the Third Reich, unanimity exists that his poems from the mid-1930s constitute the outcome of a gradual and consistent development in his capacity to operate within the conventional idiom of nature poetry, unchecked by the political break of 1933.[35] In this respect, 1945 also fails to impose an abrupt rupture on Eich's public poetic output, in that a very substantial proportion of the poems included in the 1948 collection *Abgelegene Gehöfte* were written in the 1930s, some even before 1933. The *Kahlschlag* poems drawing on Eich's immediate experience as a prisoner of war and of the *Trümmerzeit*, 'Camp 16' (GE, 1, 33–34), 'Inventur' (GE, 1, 35–36), and 'Latrine' (GE, 1, 37), are then unrepresentative of Eich's first post-war collection. Much as in Eich's post-1945 statements, the rhetoric of new beginning represented by these poems and by the short prose pieces 'Züge im Nebel' (GE, 4, 297–305) or 'Zwischen zwei Stationen' (GE, 4, 293–94) is overcome by continuities in practice back to the conventional style and thematics of his 1930s nature poetry. The title of his 1955 anthology, *Botschaften des Regens*, for example, establishes a striking connection back to 'Bemerkungen über Lyrik' and the comparison drawn by Eich between poetry and rainfall in terms of their capacity to generate non-intentional effects (GE, 4, 461).

This kind of continuity in Eich's literary practice across 1933 can be identified in other genres too. Cuomo, for example, identifies strong thematic parallels between the 1934 poem 'Weg durch die Dünen' (GE, 1, 60), picked out by many critics as the epitome of Eich's pre-1945 poetic programme and practice, and one of Eich's original radio plays, 'Schritte zu Andreas' (GE, 2, 103–13), broadcast on 5 February 1935.[36] Resonant of the final stanza of 'Weg durch die Dünen', the mystical re-integration of the wood-cutter Andreas into nature through his death also picks up the central pre-occupation of Eich's pre-1930 poems. Such continuities highlight the dangers of reading Eich's Third Reich output only against the aesthetic and ideological norms of the Nazi regime, and the productive engagement with the literary tradition found in Eich's most successful prose work, the semi-autobiographical 'Katharina' (GE, 4, 226–74), is instructive in this respect. Cuomo analyses the story in terms of *Blut-und-Boden* motifs, which it is seen to share with the country postman serial, but although the depiction of rural life is again anachronistic and at times idyllic, the absence of a chauvinistic and nationalistic edge puts significant distance between the text and the official aesthetics of National Socialism.[37] Instead, the text can be more productively analysed in relation to the programmatic stance adopted in Eich's

---

35   See, for example, Cuomo, *Career at the Cost of Compromise*, pp. 115–35; Richardson, pp. 34–44; Egbert Krispyn, 'Günter Eichs Lyrik bis 1964', in Susanne Müller-Hanpft (ed.), *Über Günter Eich* (Frankfurt a. M.: Suhrkamp, 1972), pp. 69–89.

36   Cuomo, *Career at the Cost of Compromise*, p. 124.

37   See Cuomo, *Career at the Cost of Compromise*, pp. 87–88.

Kolonne reviews and in particular to his advocacy of Flaubert's depiction of inner experience in works such as *Éducation sentimentale*.[38] Viewed as an attempt to emulate Flaubert's representation of a powerful individual fate grown out of the poet's own experience – or according to Eich in his 1932 Flaubert review, 'die Gestaltung und Deutung des großen und in seiner Strenge beispielhaften Lebens ihres Schöpfers selbst' (GE, 4, 562) – 'Katharina' forms part of a constellation of texts from 1935 which demonstrate that Eich was able to pursue his *Kolonne* programme in his writing in the Third Reich across a range of genres. Indicative of the persistence of this programme in his writing – alongside 'Weg durch die Dünen', 'Schritte zu Andreas', and 'Katharina' – is Eich's sole extant review from the period, that of Stifter's *Witiko*, to which tellingly he gave the title 'Erziehung des Herzens' (GE, 4, 566), his own preferred translation of the title of Flaubert's *Éducation sentimentale*.

Both 'Katharina' and 'Weg durch die Dünen' are amongst those of Eich's works picked out by Schäfer in his essay on the young non-Nazi generation of writers who were active in the Third Reich. For Schäfer, both texts are undercut by a mood of melancholy which evades the confirmatory function of Third Reich literature. Striking in the latter poem is the pre-occupation with transitory and elusive signs: 'die Spuren [...] im Sande, | die bald vergehn'; 'Die Spuren, die im Grau verschwinden'; 'Die Vogelschrift im Sand verrinnt' (GE, 1, 60). The attempts by the poetic self to read such signs are frustrated. They are both 'fremde Zeichen' and, paradoxically, 'meine auch'. It is the final stanza and the troubling presence of 'eine fremde Nähe', 'eine Last von vieler Zeit', and 'die tödliche Unendlichkeit', to which Schäfer attributes particular significance. For Cuomo, this is an unconvincing attempt by Schäfer to read into the poem a dissenting response to National Socialism.[39] As Schäfer's own words indicate, Cuomo is surely mistaken here, for the tone of negativity is attributed by Schäfer not to the specific trigger of the Third Reich but to a longer-term mood of crisis:

> Das Gedicht zeigt, daß nicht das Kriegserlebnis, sondern vielmehr die Krisen-philosophie für die Umwertung der Naturzeichen zur negativen Signatur verantwortlich zu machen ist. In den Kreisen des Strandhafens und den Spuren der Vögel im Sand entziffert das Ich die 'tödliche Unendlichkeit'.[40]

In this way, 'Weg durch die Dünen' emerges as an archetypal post-1930 poem in which, firmly within the secure confines of conventional poetic discourse and

---

38 See Philpotts, pp. 203–05.

39 Cuomo, *Career at the Cost of Compromise*, pp. 123–24.

40 Hans Dieter Schäfer, 'Die nichtfaschistische Literatur der jungen Generation im national-sozialistischen Deutschland', in Horst Denkler and Karl Prümm (eds), *Die deutsche Literatur in Dritten Reich: Themen, Traditionen, Wirkungen* (Stuttgart: Reclam, 1976), pp. 459–503 (p. 486). In the later version of the essay published in the collection *Das gespaltene Bewußtsein*, Schäfer substitutes 'ein nicht näher bestimmbares Angstgefühl' for 'die Krisenphilosophie'. See Schäfer, 'Die nichtnationalsozialistische Literatur der jungen Generation', p. 47.

informed by a tangible sense of crisis, the lyric *Ich* performs the elusive search for stability in meaning characteristic of the period.

Hörspiel versus *Dichtung*

Four years after 'Weg durch die Dünen', the disrupted nature signs can be found again in 'Der Tag im März' (GE, 1, 199–200). Strong continuities exist between the two poems, but a notable shift in tone is perceptible too. For Eich, the magic of the poetic act – 'der große Traum der Erde, | der Traum von Vogelflug und Pflanzensein' – now seems to have been lost. Darkness and cold predominate, and in the final stanza comes a startling echo of Peter Huchel's 1935 'November Endlied', the expression of a poetic idiom robbed of all power and meaning:

> So geht der Tag im März zu seinem Ende.
> Ein Rinnsal Glück reicht für ein ganzes Leben aus.
> Das Wasser dunkelt, dunkeln Aug und Hände.
> Ist es genug? Es führt kein Wort hinaus.

A key document in Eich's posited crisis, 'Der Tag im März' is for Vieregg one of Eich's most pessimistic verses of the 1930s, 'ein dunkler Abgesang auf das, was für ihn einmal die Lyrik und die Existenz als Lyriker bedeutet hatte'.[41] In this, Vieregg goes beyond Cuomo's identification of the theme of prostitution in the characters of Chabanais and Patt, the resigned composer of the 'whore's lament' in the 1936 radio play 'Fährten in der Prärie'.[42] Instead of the mere recognition of compromise, Vieregg identifies a double crisis: 'eine *moralische*, das Bewußtsein, sich des Gelderwerbs wegen an eine Macht verkauft zu haben, die das Böse war'; and 'eine *künstlerische Krise*, das verlorene "Glück des Schöpferischen"'.[43] Here, guilt at moral compromise is compounded by the message of 'Der Tag im März', that the inner realm of nature poetry has been robbed of its validity, not least by the demands of the Nazi radio industry.

It is here that the contradictory notions of authorship underlying Eich's radio work and poetry are able to illuminate the nature of the crisis which Eich's output demonstrates in the mid-to-late 1930s, in the process moving beyong a narrow political explanation of that crisis. Consideration of Eich's correspondence reveals that his repeated complaints about his Nazi radio work relate almost exclusively to artistic and professional concerns, rather than moral and political matters. More specifically, both in early statements to Raschke from 1933–1934 and in those made to Kuhnert around the time of the crisis in 1936–1938, Eich's pre-occupation is the betrayal of the *Dichter* by the more prosaic and populist radio author. To Raschke on 1 May 1934, for instance, Eich stresses the contrast

---

41 Vieregg, *Der eigenen Fehlbarkeit begegnet*, p. 48.
42 See Cuomo, *Career at the Cost of Compromise*, pp. 107–10.
43 Vieregg, *Der eigenen Fehlbarkeit begegnet*, p. 49, emphasis in the original.

between his radio commissions and the poetry he would prefer to write: 'Das ist der dümmste Auftrag, den ich je bekommen habe. [...] Wenn man doch von Gedichten leben könnte! Dieser elende Funk, bis hierher verfolgt er einen. Meine Sendung am Sonnabend habe ich nicht gehört, da glücklicherweise das Radio kaputt war.'[44] Similarly, to Kuhnert on 18 June 1936:

> Ich sehe ein, daß meine Bemühungen ein Schriftsteller zu sein [...] vergeblich sind. [...] Ich werde nie und nimmer glücklich sein in dieser Rolle, das Verbogene in diesem Lebenszustand hält mich ewig in schlechtem Gewissen, jegliche undichterische Betätigung nehme ich mehr oder weniger nicht ernst. Also werde ich mit blauem Augenaufschlag und leicht flatterndem Haar auf den Parnaß meiner Jugend zurückkehren.[45]

The terminology employed by Eich here is all too revealing. The constructed opposition between the neo-Romantic self-image of an almost Byronesque figure inhabiting his youthful Parnassus and the contrasting '*undichterische* Betätigung' of the radio writer matches the opposition of the *Dichter* and *Reklamemann* in the characterisation of Chabanais. Above all, it is the contravention of the principles of *Dichtung*, set out so clearly by Eich in *Die Kolonne* and embodied so strongly in Eich's self-image, which is the root cause of Eich's creative crisis, not a recognition of moral compromise with a barbaric regime. This contravention also supplies an additional motivational background for Eich's repeated denial of the value, importance, or even existence, of his Third Reich output. In effect, this output did not constitute true literary output; it was not the output of a *Dichter*.

Clearly, the peculiar demands placed on writers by the 'total claim' of the Nazi regime have a role to play here too, and, as we have seen, 1933 does act as a significant turning-point in Eich's literary practice in terms of his move towards the radio. Nonetheless, the decisive date in Eich's betrayal of the *Dichter* is not 30 January 1933 but rather March 1932 when he made the decision to become a professional writer. It was this decision which brought the *Lyriker* and *Privatmann*, maintained as distinct entities in 'Bemerkungen über Lyrik' (GE, 4, 459), into collision with one another, so that Eich the writer was now in a relationship of co-dependency with the private individual whose car, flat in Berlin, and holiday home in Poberow carried a heavy financial burden, a burden only increased in the late 1930s by the morphine addiction of his future wife, Elsa Burke. It was this decision which brought with it the necessity of writing for commission, and it is worth noting here the extent of Eich's involvement with the radio which pre-dated 1933. Eich's practice in his *Kolonne* period was not devoted solely to poetry. His first radio play, 'Das Leben und Sterben des großen Sängers Enrico Caruso', jointly authored with Raschke, dates from 1929 and was first broadcast on 9 April 1931, while another, 'Ein Traum am Edsin-Gol' (GE, 2, 7–25), was published in the final issue of *Die Kolonne* in 1932. Indeed, several of Eich's broadcasts in 1933

---

44 See Vieregg, *Der eigenen Fehlbarkeit begegnet*, p. 45.
45 See Vieregg, *Der eigenen Fehlbarkeit begegnet*, p. 46.

included pre-1933 material and must have been arranged in the previous year. In December 1932, for example, Eich already felt sufficiently confident to be able to declare to the Kuhnerts: 'Wenn alles klappt, saniert mich die Funkstunde für das ganze Jahr 33.'[46] In this respect, the direction which Eich's career took after 1933 and the artistic crisis which this generated are conceivable outside the political context of dictatorship. Eich's high radio productivity in the late 1940s and 1950s, for example, including work aimed at children, helps to confirm this softening in the assumed determining force of National Socialism in Eich's literary choices of the mid-1930s. Indeed, this crisis may be viewed as the enunciation of the general dilemma of the professional writer in our post-1930 period. At a time when the traditional notion of *Dichtung* was dominant, it was increasingly difficult to reconcile that notion of authorship with the demands of the modern literary market and the necessity of writing to order, and in part this is a continuation of the fault-line between elitism and populism which we have shown to run through both *Die Kolonne* and *Die Linkskurve*. The conflict between the *Schriftsteller* and *Dichter* in Eich's career is testament to the cultural dominance of the restorative 1930 paradigm and the notion of authorship which it carries with it.

For Eich, three factors ensured that this conflict was particularly acutely felt. Firstly, as his *Kolonne* statements and private correspondence from the 1930s attest, Eich's self-image as a writer was intimately bound up with the values of *Dichtung*. His initiation into the public literary sphere as the traditional *Dichter*, through *Die Kolonne*, remained the standard against which the rest of his career was measured. At the same time, this literary self-image diverged strongly from the everyday reality of the private individual whose particular personal circumstances – not least his surprisingly strong consumerism – forced him to pursue a writing career which could not always match the high literary pretensions and aspirations of the neo-Romantic *Dichter*. For Eich, the gap between *Lyriker* and *Privatmann* was a particularly wide one, as his reasons for continuing work on the 'KWL' serial, explained in a letter of 21 April 1937, indicate:

> Mein alter Wunsch, eine eigene Wohnung, ließ sich bei der Gelegenheit auch verwirklichen und ich bin sehr froh darüber. [...] Leider Gottes hat mich die ganze Sache völlig bankrott gemacht und obwohl ich schon horrende Schulden habe, fehlen mir immer noch einige Möbel, die Vorhänge und viele Kleinigkeiten, die zusammen eine Menge Geld kosten. So werde ich mich die nächsten Monate intensiv dem Rundfunk widmen müssen.[47]

Secondly, the particular medium of the radio, which offered Eich his invaluable production outlet, also imposed on him a version of authorship which drew him further from that of the *Dichter*. Not only did the denuded author function affront Eich's self-image, but the relatively low fees necessitated a high level of productivity which in turn further reduced the degree of creativity and originality

---

46 See Vieregg, *Der eigenen Fehlbarkeit begegnet*, p. 18.
47 See Vieregg, *Der eigenen Fehlbarkeit begegnet*, pp. 24–25.

which could be devoted to the radio texts. Finally, both of these factors were radicalised by the rapacious total claim of the National Socialist regime. Above all, the ideological demands of the *Volksgemeinschaft* and the accompanying drive for populist entertainment and propaganda could only further exacerbate these tensions in Eich's literary self-image. It was these specific pressures which, for Eich, cracked open the fault-line that originated in a restorative turn to *Dichtung* not always compatible with the rapidly modernising society around it.

Radio and restoration

As we have seen, this fault-line was particularly acute for those writers working in the modern aparatus of the radio industry, but any assumed dichotomy between *Rundfunk* and *Dichtung* inevitably disguises a more complex reality. On the one hand, around 1930 the privileged medium of poetry could scarcely seem to contrast more starkly with the nascent medium of the radio, famously subject to the innovative theoretical reflections of such figures as Bertolt Brecht and Walter Benjamin. As a product and purveyor of the process of social modernisation and massification, the development of the radio from the 1920s onwards promised to create a technologically modern and genuinely democratised culture which re-drew the roles of cultural producer and recipient and thereby threatened to erode the conventional pillars of book, author, and poem. More ideologically conservative figures, such as Hermann Pongs, also saw in the radio a means of moving beyond conventional literary genres, stressing the potential for collective cultural experience, and this was one of the strands picked up by radio theoreticians and practitioners in the Third Reich, where the radio was instrumentalised as a tool in the attempted imposition of the regime's total claim on society.[48] On the other hand, as Wolfram Wessels outlines, the theoretical notion of radio authorship maintained under National Socialism remained paradoxically that of the conventional *Dichter*. Hence, although in practice institutional restrictions imposed on writers the role of *Schriftsteller* – 'deren Tun zweckgebunden, unfrei und auf bloßen Broterwerb ausgerichtet schien, im Gegensatz zur künstlerisch inspirativen Tätigkeit des Dichters'[49] – the radio was at the same time perceived as the ideal means to connect the *Volk* through a process which was conceived in terms of an organic, metaphysical wholeness. This process necessitated the writer to function, at least in theory, as a kind of *Führer*-prophet, oriented towards inner experience rather than agitation or propaganda: 'Wie der Rundfunk gleichzeitig Ausdruck des Volkes und seines Führers sein sollte, so galt gleiches vom Dichter und der Dichtung. Die

---

48   See Stefan Bodo Würffel, *Das deutsche Hörspiel* (Stuttgart: Metzler, 1978), pp. 47–48.
49   Wessels, p. 196. Subsequent reference, p. 200.

Forderung nach dem Dichter als dem geeigneten Hörspielautor scheint dann nicht weiter erstaunlich.'

In this way, Eich's literary practice embodies a fundamental tension between the theory and practice of radio authorship in the Third Reich, but this tension has its origins not in specifically National Socialist policy, but in the theoretical approaches to the radio play which began to be developed in the final two or three years of the Weimar Republic. Indeed, the history of the *Hörspiel* as a specific genre demonstrates remarkable congruence with a 1930–1960 period-isation, as an aesthetically conservative radio play theory gained primacy in the final years of the Weimar Republic and continued to exert a dominant influence not only in the Third Reich but also after 1945. In Wessels's words, the radio play functioned for many after 1930 'als Restaurator "wahrer Dichtung"'.[50] Embodied in Richard Kolb's *Das Horoskop des Hörspiels*, first published in 1932, this more conservative approach to the production and reception of the radio play placed at the centre of these processes a 'Verinnerlichung des Wortes'.[51] As a literary genre, the radio play was perceived to guarantee through the singularly aural medium of the radio a purity of word and language, in Wessels's terms, a 'Verabsolutierung des Wortes'. Founded on the primacy of the word and on processes of *Identifikation* and *Verinnerlichung*, this more conservative approach represented a decisive shift away from the kind of theoretical approaches to the radio play – experimental, socially-engaged, and mass-oriented – developed by Brecht and Benjamin. Only in the 1960s did the emergence of the *neue Hörspiel* bring with it a renewed interest in Brecht's radio theory and a turn away from the conception of the radio play which had in essence remained dominant since 1930. The award of the *Hörspielpreis der Kriegsblinden* to Ernst Jandl and Friederike Mayröcker in 1968 and the publication of his Klaus Schöning's anthology *Neues Hörspiel* in September of the following year formalised a process which can be traced back to the early 1960s.[52]

Hörspiel and *Dichtung*

The shift in status of the radio play identifiable around 1930 renders Eich's earliest incursions into the radio during his *Kolonne* phase rather easier to understand. The apparent contradiction between the timeless lyric poet and the modern mass medium of the radio is resolved, albeit at the expense of a persistent and underlying tension. Much as Eich stands at the centre of the revival and defence of the poem, so his literary practice from 1930 onwards is intimately connected with the elevation of the *Hörspiel* to the status of high literary genre.

---

50   Wessels, pp. 366–71.
51   See Würffel, p. 49 and p. 51.
52   Würffel, pp. 147–48

This procedure is particularly noticable in those Third Reich radio plays which constituted for Eich more than just routine commissions. 'Schritte zu Andreas' (GE, 2, 103–13) is important in this regard, as are the three radio dramas which have attracted most critical attention, 'Weizenkantate' (GE, 2, 121–26), 'Fährten in der Prärie' (GE, 2, 127–56), and 'Radium' (GE, 2, 157–94). Each of these three latter plays deals with the negative and de-humanising effects of social modernisation, perceived as such a central factor in the on-going German crisis as it was diagnosed, for example, by intellectuals in *Maß und Wert*. We have already noted the significance of 'Fährten in der Prärie' and 'Radium' for Eich in terms of the self-inscription of the prostituted poet figures, Patt and Chabanais. As far as 'Weizenkantate' is concerned, contextual factors indicate that Eich's treatment of source material derived from Benn – the 1932 essay 'Gebührt Carleton ein Denkmal?' – was attributed a high status both by Eich and his radio producers. The draft contract for the play recommends the unusually high fee of 900 RM, identifying the play as 'eine der bedeutendsten Dichtungen [...], die bisher im Rundfunk vorgelegt wurden',[53] while Eich's own intellectual investment in the play can be read from a letter addressed by Eich to Ursula Kuhnert on 18 April 1935: 'Damit will ich meinen Ruhm als Dichter endlich befestigen' (GE, 2, 790).

If these attempts in the 1930s were largely frustrated, then it was precisely Eich's radio output which, after 1945, finally cemented the literary renown as *Dichter* which he so coveted in the Third Reich. The broadcast of 'Träume', for example, in April 1951 is widely acknowledged as the 'Geburtsstunde des poetischen Hörspiels', its publication in 1953 the moment when the radio play became a genuine literary genre.[54] Through the radio plays which he had broadcast in the 1950s – among them several works from the Third Reich, such as 'Radium' or 'Fährten in der Prärie', and even 'Ein Traum in Edsin-Gol' from the *Kolonne* era – Eich became the measure of quality against which radio play authorship was measured. According to Würffel: 'Das "Eich Maß" [ist] bei der Beurteilung der Qualität eines Hörspiels normsetzend.'[55] Significantly, this was in the 1950s not a measure of quality defined innovatively for the specific requirements of the medium of radio, but rather a measure of conventional literary quality. The *Hörspielpreis der Kriegsblinden*, for example, the foundation of which in 1951 is itself a measure of the integration of the radio play into the institution of high literature, was to be awarded to the play 'das uns noch lange nach der Sendung am tiefsten bewegt und das uns innerlich bereichert, das uns vom Menschlichen her anredet'.[56] It was also through Eich that the *Hörspiel*

---

53 See Cuomo, *Career at the Cost of Compromise*, p. 160, note 2.
54 See Heinz Schwitzke, 'Günter Eichs "Träume"', in Susanne Müller-Hanpft (ed.), *Über Günter Eich* (Frankfurt a.M.: Suhrkamp, 1972), pp. 105–11 (p. 105).
55 Würffel, p. 85.
56 See Irmela Schneider, '"Fast alle haben vom Rundfunk gelebt": Hörspiele der 50er Jahre als literarische Formen', in Justus Fetscher et al (eds), *Die Gruppe 47 in der Geschichte der Bundesrepublik* (Würzburg: Königshausen & Neumann, 1991), pp. 203–17 (p. 205).

achieved a conventional author function. The publication of Eich's 1950s radio texts in book-form constituted a fundamental shift in status which allowed the radio play to be received and interpreted for the first time as a conventional artefact of high literature, not as a transient piece of mass entertainment. Symptomatic in this respect is Walter Jens's 1958 *Nachwort* to 'Die Mädchen aus Viterbo' in which he applies to the radio text interpretative tools taken from Eich's lyric production.[57] More striking still are the contemporary reviews of 'Träume' collected by Marlies Goß, not of the broadcast but of the subsequent book edition.[58] The emphasis in these reviews rests almost entirely on the inner realm alluded to by the play's title, so that the radio play is interpreted in essence as a work of conventional poetry – 'Traumdeutung ist Günter Eichs Gedicht, und man kann zu seinem Ruhme wohl nicht mehr sagen, als daß er unser aller Träume dichtet' – and Eich is viewed as 'ein Dichter, einer der wenigen, die das hohe Wort zu Recht tragen'.[59] As Goß summarises: 'Die Kritiker [leisteten] einer Etikettierung des Autors Vorschub, die ihn als Dichter, Fabulierer, Märchenerzähler und des "reinen Wortes kundigen Magier" ausweist.'[60]

Here, Eich succeeded in elevating the radio play to the status of *Dichtung*, in the process acquiring for himself in the literary public sphere the image of the *Dichter* which he had set out in *Die Kolonne* more than twenty years earlier. This public image was established and reinforced in the 1950s and 1960s not least by the raft of prizes which signal Eich's priviliged status in the institutions of West German literature. Indeed, if literary prizes can legitimately be viewed as, in Friedhelm Kröll's words, 'Wegweiser in die Restauration', then Eich's career emerges as paradigmatic for the West German literary restoration.[61] The award to Eich of the inaugural *Gruppe 47* prize in 1950 was followed in the two subsequent years by the literature prize of the Bavarian Academy of Fine Arts and the *Hörspielpreis der Kriegsblinden*, and in 1954 by the literature prize of the *Bundesverband der deutschen Industrie*. The *Georg-Büchner-Preis* and the *Schleußner-Schueller-Preis des Hessischen Rundfunks* followed in 1959, the *Förderungspreis der Stadt München für Literatur* and the *Schiller-Gedächtnispreis* in 1965 and 1968 respectively. Clearly, Eich's involvement with the *Gruppe 47* is of particular significance here, and, even if Kröll's characterisation of the group 'als Testamentsvollstrecker des *Kolonne-Kreises*' is born of an ideologically coloured polemic, the reality of the grouping as standard-bearers for the restorative re-assertion of the bourgeois institution of literature undercuts the rhetoric of radical new beginning first voiced in *Der Ruf*.

---

57 Walter Jens, 'Nachwort zu Günter Eichs *Die Mädchen aus Viterbo*', in Susanne Müller-Hanpft (ed.), *Über Günter Eich* (Frankfurt a.M.: Suhrkamp, 1972), pp. 123–28.

58 See Marlies Goß, *Günter Eich und das Hörspiel der fünfziger Jahre* (Frankfurt a. M.: Lang, 1998), pp. 160–63.

59 Karl Korn, 'Günter Eichs Traumspiele', *Frankfurter Allgemeine Zeitung*, 13 March 1954, cited by Goß, p. 162.

60 Goß, p. 160.

61 See note 10. Subsequent reference, p. 158.

As the evidence available in Susanne Müller-Hanpft's anthology of Eich's post-war reception makes clear, it is the persistence of the category of *Dichter* which marks this restoration. Made ten years apart, in 1949 and 1959, the comments of Alfred Andersch and Walter Höllerer demonstrate that this was the category which Eich was perceived to represent and uphold: 'Es kommt ganz von selbst, daß man sich lautlos und bezaubert sagt: "Seht an, ein Dichter!"'; 'Er hat bewiesen, daß es sinnlos ist, das Wort "Dichter" abschaffen zu wollen.'[62] Here, the restorative reception of 'Träume' functions as a guarantor of a conservative continuity in Eich's practice, the rhetorical new beginning signalled in the Rönne essay of 1947 (GE, 4, 468–70) and 'Inventur' (GE, 1, 35–36) largely an illusion.

Conclusion

By way of conclusion to this chapter, it is worth giving consideration to the alternative strand of Eich reception which stresses the unsettling and disruptive nature of Eich's literary practice. The immediate response of listeners to the original broadcast of 'Träume', for example, diverged radically from the literary-critical reception of the published edition, as the flood of protest phonecalls to the broadcasters attests. Similarly, reception of the broadcast text beyond the 1950s stressed not the inward-looking poetic elements, but its contemporary, socially critical frame of reference, its apparent call for a confrontation with the past and for non-conformism or even opposition to political and social restoration. Eich's acceptance speech for the Büchner prize in 1959 – 'Wenn unsere Arbeit nicht als Kritik verstanden werden kann, als Gegnerschaft und Widerstand, als unbequeme Frage und als Herausforderung der Macht, dann schreiben wir umsonst' (GE, 4, 627) – acts as another marker for this strand of reception which has been shaped above all by the other of Eich's works to dominate public literary conciousness, the *Maulwürfe*, published as a collection in the symbolic year of 1968. As critics have pointed out, these texts seem to contain a self-referential rejection both of the category of *Dichter* and of the viability of nature poetry.[63] The final sentence of 'Ein Nachwort von König Midas' (GE, 1, 355–56), for example, appears to signal Eich's break with the former notion of authorship:

> Da kommen sie an, die neuen Musen des Stumpfsinns, – laßt mich meinen ohnmächtigen Zorn ausschreien – die Dichter und Dichterinnen mit ihren

---

62 See Susanne Müller-Hanpft, 'Vorbemerkung: Überlegungen zur Aufnahme und Interpretation der Werke Günter Eichs', in Susanne Müller-Hanpft (ed.), *Über Günter Eich* (Frankfurt a.M.: Suhrkamp, 1972), pp. 7–18.
63 See, for example, Heinrich Vormweg, 'Dichtung als Maul-Wurf', in Susanne Müller-Hanpft (ed.), *Über Günter Eich* (Frankfurt a.M.: Suhrkamp, 1972), pp. 129–33.

wohlriechendem Strophen, das ganze mit Namen und Ländereien belohnte Gezücht
– ja wenn man Messer und Strick genug hat, ist alles Harmonie.

Similarly, in the piece entitled 'In eigener Sache' (GE, 1, 364) Eich apparently
distances himself from nature poetry through his knowing reference to the
Goethe quotation used by Lehmann as the motto to his first published collection
of poetry: 'Das ewig nachgestammelte Naturgeheimnis [...] Einmal genügt.
Nachtigallen kann auf die Dauer nur ertragen, wer schwerhörig ist.' Clearly, the
unique, genre-breaking style of the texts and the elusive nature of reference and
meaning with which they tantalise the reader seem to defy any classification
within a traditional, restorative category of literature, and this explains the
polarised responses which the *Maulwürfe* attracted at the time of publication. For
progressive critics, the texts were symbolic of a new literary period connected to
social and political revolution; for conservative critics a regrettable compromise
by an esteemed author to short-term literary fashions. In either case, the
Maulwürfe and their reception seem to provide powerful evidence of the shift away
from the literary dominant which had held since 1930. Vormweg, for example,
sees in these 53 short 'prose' pieces an abrupt break in Eich's literary practice,
describing the distance between the Eich of 1968 and the Eich of *Abgelegene
Gehöfte* as 'so groß wie etwa die zwischen den Wörtern "Dichter" und "Träume"
und den Wörtern "Maulwurf" und "Anarchie"'.[64] The *Maulwürfe*, 'von allen längst
durchsichtigen Ansprüchen der Poesie befreite Prosa, offen für das subjektiv-
menschlich und gesellschaftlich Wirkliche, gerieten zu Bestätigungen dafür, daß
die Literatur in eine neue Phase gelangt ist'.

And yet, in their apparent iconoclasm the *Maulwürfe* remain an isolated
eruption in Eich's literary practice as a whole. Indeed, as Peter Horst Neumann
suggests, it may well be as much the particular cultural circumstances of the late
1960s – when the term *Dichter* tellingly became a term of abuse hurled by students
at the final meeting of the *Gruppe 47* in 1967 – as the actual properties of the texts
themselves, which lend the *Maulwürfe* their status as markers of a radical break in
Eich's literary practice.[65] In this respect Eich's career, or perhaps better, the
perceptions and reception of Eich's career, seem to mirror the threshold
moments of cultural activity in the mid-twentieth century – through *Die Kolonne* at
1930; in the re-assessment of aesthetic principles between 1947 and 1949; and in
the radical rupture of the late 1960s – but any change in this career must be
viewed as a developmental process marked above all by continuity. Eich's own
comments, for example, point to important affinities between the *Maulwürfe* and
his poetic practice and also to a developmental process from the one to the other:
'Meine Möglichkeit, Gedichte zu schreiben, schwand mehr und mehr dahin –
meine Gedichte wurden mehr und mehr Prosa [...]. Die ersten dieser *Maulwürfe*

---

64 Vormweg, p. 129. Subsequent reference, p. 133.
65 Peter Horst Neumann, *Die Rettung der Poesie im Unsinn: Der Anarchist Günter Eich* (Stuttgart: Klett–
    Cotta, 1981), pp. 13–16.

waren also in gewisser Weise eine Fortsetzung meiner Lyrik' (GE, 4, 515). It is
here that it is worth returning to Eich's theoretical conception of the poem as
hieroglyph, Chinese character, or physics text book – 'genau und unverständlich'
(GE, 4, 481). It is the consistent realisation of this principle in Eich's poetic
practice which has enabled Schäfer to position this practice within a post-war
tradition of hermetic poetry, albeit one opened up towards social engagement.[66]
Indeed, this extends as far as the title poem of Eich's final collection, *Nach Seumes
Papieren*, published as late as 1972, which Schäfer acknowledges as an
anachronism in the era of the documentary poem.[67] Concise, precise, and
incomprehensible, Eich's own definition of the poem applies equally to his
Maulwürfe. For all the mood of free and automatic writing which seems to pervade
the texts, they are in a sense as much the careful expression of Eich's self-image
as *Dichter* as are the 'innere Dialoge' of his *Kolonne* phase.

In this sense, it is possible to see the *Maulwürfe* as the culmination of the
process signalled in Eich's literary programme after 1945, that is, the opening-up
of his literary practice to new possibilities, both in terms of form/genre and in
terms of the relationship to politics and society. Against this twin process of
change, the strong *Dichter* function in the institution of high literature remains a
constant. Part of this process was the admission in the 1950s of the radio play to
the sphere of high poetic language which was so fundamental to Eich's literary
practice. As he made clear in his acceptance speech for the 1953 *Hörspielpreis der
Kriegsblinden*, for example, the notion of a literary language set apart from everyday
language, a set of precise signs which translate reality, applied equally to his radio
practice, and this acts as a fundamental strand of continuity:

> Wir bedienen uns des Wortes, des Satzes, der Sprache. Jedes Wort bewahrt einen
> Abglanz des magischen Zustandes, wo es mit dem gemeinten Gegenstand eins ist, wo
> es mit der Schöpfung identisch ist. Aus dieser Sprache, dieser nie gehörten und
> unhörbaren, können wir gleichsam immer nur übersetzen, recht und schlecht und
> jedenfalls nie vollkommen. (GE, 4, 612)

It was this 'poetic' language, by the 1960s to be found not only in conventional
nature poetry, but also radio plays and the *Maulwürfe*, which Eich sought to deploy
against the threat posed by modernisation and, increasingly after 1945, by
restorative political power. This is not to say that the *Maulwürfe* are of a kind with
Eich's output from the 1930s, 1940s, and 1950s, nor that they inhabit the
restorative paradigm characterised by stable genre boundaries and by a search for
the stability of meaning which they so put into question. As crisis encourages a
search for stability, so the growing post-war stability may have encouraged an
urge to destabilise which finds its expression in the *Maulwürfe* and which helps to
explain the resonance which they achieved at the end of the 1960s. All the same,

---

66 Schäfer, 'Zur Spätphase des hermetischen Gedichtes'.
67 Hans Dieter Schäfer, '"Nach Seumes Papieren': Über ein spätes Gedicht von Günter Eich', *Neue
   deutsche Hefte*, 137 (1973), 45–55 (p. 45).

these radical prose pieces can be positioned within a developmental process in Eich's career, the constant thread of which is the self-image of the elitist *Dichter* who makes no concessions to his reader and who believes in the lasting power of the literary word.

Peter Huchel

Introduction: Huchel in 20th-century German Literature

Essentially, two stories are told about Peter Huchel's place in German literary life. The first follows the political reading of twentieth-century German literature. It traces the development of a figure who was born in 1903 into the Prussia of the Wilhelmine Empire, emerged in the final years of the Weimar Republic, remained in the Germany of the Third Reich and achieved prominence in the GDR, before spending his final years in the Federal Republic until his death in 1981. The political reading charts Huchel's sympathies with the Left, which included friendships with prominent communists such as Ernst Bloch and Alfred Kantorowicz, and resistance first to the totalitarianism of the Nazis, then to that of the SED, when as editor of *Sinn und Form* Huchel created a forum for German cultural unity in the face of German political division. Readings of his poetry, at times encouraged by him, were generated that supported this view of a consistent opposition to the evils of dictatorship. In keeping with that reading, he emerged after his death as an integrative symbol in German unification, untainted by the perceived collusion with the SED that damaged the reputation of prominent anti-Nazis such as Brecht. The political reading has generally overshadowed the literary-historical approach pursued by Schäfer, Trommler and others. This approach has brought to the surface broad contours of aesthetic and stylistic development, within which Huchel has affinities with the *Kolonne* Circle and with his friend from the 1930s, Günter Eich. Both are cited as exemplifying the restorative trend that set in around 1930 and remained dominant in German literature until the 1960s, particularly in lyric poetry.

Huchel found his voice with publications of nature poetry in the early 1930s in *Die Kolonne* and *Die literarische Welt*, where he also learnt the editorial trade with Willy Haas. By the turn of the 1960s, he had come to occupy a pre-eminent position in German literary life with *Sinn und Form* and as the author of verse such as the collection *Chausseen Chausseen*. Published in 1963, *Chausseen Chausseen* was hailed in many quarters as a consummate stylistic achievement by a poet who was held to embody the best of genuine lyrical qualities. He was hailed as a *Dichter* through and through, whose work represented a post-Expressionist re-engagement with the tradition that the mere *Schriftsteller* of *Neue Sachlichkeit* had lost. As we have seen in the examination of *Sinn und Form*, as an editor he was regarded not just as the major creative force behind that new, 'thick' journal of the Academy of Arts but as an institution in his own right, who in the inimical

Cold War climate had successfully mediated the re-establishment of a post-Nazi, progressive canon across the German-German divide.

Huchel's literary activities and the values which he professed at the start and at the end point of our study display a striking consistency. Yet that consistency belies the underlying tensions, both political and aesthetic, in the progression of a figure whose career reflects the dilemmas of the professional writer after 1930 within Germany. For many of the years between, Huchel struggled to maintain the 'pure' literary values that he espoused. During the Third Reich and the early post-war years, Huchel could maintain his artistic existence only at the expense of involvement in new mass media such as radio and film, the technological and financial workings of which had little regard for traditional notions of the poet and of artistic autonomy. Like Eich and other friends, in the Third Reich Huchel was sucked into the 'Tumult aller Stile' that was all the more pronounced in those media with their demands for serial production drawing on a variety of 'Gebrauchsformen'.[1] Yet Huchel differs somewhat from Eich in that he was less attached to their material blandishments and he had political reservations that lend his work a dimension beyond Eich's sense of a prostitution of his talent in an inferior medium.

In keeping with the approach of the present study, the aim of this chapter is to foreground Huchel's aesthetic and stylistic development with due regard for political contexts. In doing so, it seeks to lend substance to the view that criticism of early to mid-twentieth-century German literature, produced from the perspective of the political caesura in 1933, has not always appreciated that broadly progressive political sympathies – if not orthodox Marxist positions – do not always translate into progressive modernist and avant-gardist positions. Huchel's career within Germany from 1930 to 1960 provides an opportunity to explore a development more complex than familiar binary oppositions generally allow. In particular, as a nature poet Huchel occupied a position in literary life that enjoyed renewed prestige following the restorative turn of the final years of the Weimar Republic, a prestige that was boosted by ideological considerations in the Third Reich and the early GDR.

1930: Willy Haas's Protégé

Huchel was never given to the formulation of elaborate aesthetic programmes. Yet he placed himself within what we have called the 1930 paradigm to a much greater extent than the other authors whom we have examined, even Eich. Willy

---

1   For the use of these terms, see Hans Dieter Schäfer, 'Zur Periodisierung der deutschen Literatur seit 1930' and 'Nationalsozialistische Gebrauchsformen', in Hans Dieter Schäfer, *Das gespaltene Bewußtsein: Über deutsche Kultur und Lebenswirklichkeit 1933–1945* (Munich: Hanser, 1981), pp. 55–71 (pp. 58–60) and pp. 107–13.

Haas's influence upon him was crucial, as Huchel would later acknowledge when he reflected upon his debt to him for his entry into Berlin literary life: 'Alles, was mit Willy Haas zusammenhängt, ist mehr für mich als eine Erinnerung an wichtige Jahre [...] Nichts ist mit dieser Zeit zu vergleichen.'[2] Their friendship was based not simply on an editor-author relationship, but also on close collaboration as Haas initiated his protégé into the institution of literature through teaching him the editorial trade.[3] Those incomparable years of the early 1930s attained something akin to an ideal status for Huchel, a point of reference throughout the later stages of his career, especially when his literary values were under threat.

In the examination of *Die literarische Welt*, we have determined the key role that Haas played in articulating the restorative turn, in re-asserting the traditional role of the *Dichter* and of the institution of literature. We have seen, too, that Haas's position was by no means unreconstructedly backward-looking: he insisted on the dynamic potential of the bourgeois tradition for cultural renewal, and he saw Huchel's poetry as a contribution to the fulfilment of his agenda. Haas was captivated by the 'vollkommene[n] Durchdringung von Geist und Materie' in the verse that the unknown Huchel sent him.[4] In the 1932 special issue of *Die literarische Welt* devoted to 'Junge Dichtung', Haas promoted Huchel as a representative of the new generation, singling him out as a 'Figur von Rang' among the young poets whom he published (*DlW*, 8.15/16, 1). He characterised their work as a return to traditional diction, forms and themes, going so far as to advance the large, though as things turned out, very serious claim: 'es ist der erste Ansatz zu einer mittleren Traditionsgebundenheit über Generationen hinweg, den wir in der deutschen Literatur seit Jahrzehnten erlebt haben.' Haas had been searching for precisely that in order to promote cultural renewal through literature. For Haas, as for his revered friend Hofmannsthal, good taste in the arts translated into an ethical humanism for the benefit of civilisation. Set against this, the politicisation and massification of culture that had become well-nigh axiomatic in many quarters was a crude caricature of true art.

Huchel fashioned the distinctive voice that captivated Haas after earlier experimentation with contemporary or near-contemporary styles that was imitative of work by poets such as Dehmel, Rilke and Trakl and of voices that had emerged in Expressionism and *Neue Sachlichkeit*.[5] What Haas describes as the 'vollkommene Durchdringung von Geist und Materie' in Huchel's verse is

---

2 Letter to Rolf Italiaander of 5 November 1956 in Rolf Italiaander, *Gedanken-Austausch*, ed. by Harald Kohtz et al (Düsseldorf: Droste, 1988), p. 55.

3 Haas would later suggest that as editor of *Sinn und Form* Huchel had far outstripped his mentor. See Willy Haas, 'Ansprache', in Hans Mayer (ed.), *Über Peter Huchel* (Frankfurt a.M.: Suhrkamp, 1973), p. 160.

4 Willy Haas, 'Ein Mann namens Peter Huchel', in Otto F. Best (ed.), *Hommage für Peter Huchel* (Munich: Piper, 1968), p. 55.

5 For detailed analysis of Huchel's juvenilia see the early chapters of Stephen Parker, *Peter Huchel: A literary life in twentieth-century Germany* (Bern: Lang, 1998).

attested to in a very striking way by Haas's secretary, Rolf Italiaander, who describes his first encounter with Huchel as follows: 'Huchel überraschte durch seine Erscheinung. Er trug an nackten Füßen Ledersandalen, war rustikal angezogen wie ein Waldarbeiter – eine absolut unliterarische Erscheinung. Was er sagte, gefiel auch mir. Er sprach über Naturerlebnisse und Mythologisches.'[6] For the Berlin *literati* Italiaander and Haas, Huchel embodied something exotically different, fascinating and attractive, which contrasted with artistic horizons located in urban experience that had been at best indifferent to tradition and to a rural world whose 'organic' assumptions had been dismissed as hopelessly passé.

In the watershed years of the early 1930s, Huchel's turn against prevailing fashions itself quickly became the new fashion. In her memoirs, Oda Schaefer recalls how Huchel was 'von Berlin W hofiert [...] Huchel war schlagartig bekannt geworden' for his poetry of a rural childhood.[7] As Hans Dieter Schäfer notes, around 1930 this theme became 'eine zeittypische Erscheining'.[8] Huchel's verse typically drew on the form of the *Volkslied* and on the language of its principal practitioners in the early to mid-nineteenth century such as Mörike and Eichendorff. Huchel's attractiveness was by no means diminished by the apparently seamless unity between self and poetic voice evoked in an autobiographical piece for *Die literarische Welt*, 'Europa neunzehnhunderttraurig' (*DLW* 7.1, 3–4), in which he described childhood experiences on his grandfather's farm in Alt-Langerwisch near Potsdam, which he would later stylise as the 'Urgrund des Schaffens'.[9] That stylisation set the seal on the authenticity of his work for readers, yet his recourse to such stylisation underscores the poet's search for stability so characteristic of that time, which is evident, too, in stylistic choices from the tradition.

Huchel further underlined that authenticity through his reference to a phrase from St Augustine's *Confessions*, 'im großen Hof meines Gedächtnisses. Daselbst sind mir Himmel, Erde und Meer gegenwärtig', which he employed as a motif for his verse in 1932 (PH, 2, 250) and on a number of occasions thereafter, most notably in order to introduce *Chausseeen Chausseen* (PH, 1, 112). He linked St Augustine's 'Hof' quite explicitly with the Alt-Langerwisch 'Hof' of his childhood memories.[10] The unity between autobiographical and poetic self yielded a linguistic and thematic core to Huchel's poetry, upon which he would never cease to draw. For example, as late as 1977 he reflected:

6   Italiaander, p. 54.
7   Oda Schaefer, *Auch wenn du träumst, gehen die Uhren* (Munich: Piper, 1970), p. 260.
8   Hans Dieter Schäfer, 'Die nichtnationalsozialistische Literatur der jungen Generation im Dritten Reich', in Hans Dieter Schäfer, *Das gespaltene Bewußtsein: Über deutsche Kultur und Lebenswirklichkeit 1933–1945* (Munich: Hanser, 1981), pp. 7–54 (p. 30).
9   Peter Huchel, 'Der Preisträger dankt', in Axel Vieregg (ed.), *Peter Huchel: Materialien* (Frankfurt a.M.: Suhrkamp, 1986), p. 17. For a discussion of Huchel's stylisation of his childhood, see Parker, *Peter Huchel*, especially pp. 19–55.
10   Peter Huchel, 'Der Preisträger dankt', p. 17.

Gerade die Erlebnisse der Kindheit, etwa vom fünften bis zum zehnten Lebensjahr sind es, die später einmal einen entscheidenden Einfluß nehmen. Damals sammelte ich, ganz unbewußt, einen großen Vorrat an ländlichen Bildern, Vokabeln, Begriffen und Metaphern, von denen meine Dichtung noch heute zehrt. (PH, 2, 330)

Here as elsewhere, Huchel foregrounds an attention to detail born of experience that suggests a continuity with the *sachlich* trend of the 1920s. For all the play upon authenticity, Huchel's poetry of the early 1930s acknowledges that there could be no reversion to the stability of a childhood world that was forever gone. This was well understood by Martin Raschke in his address following Huchel's award of the *Kolonne* prize for poetry in 1932:

Doch diese 'Einheit des Lebens', von der die Gedichte wie von einem Traume zu sprechen scheinen, wird nicht vom Dichter in einem naturburschenhaften Sinne erlebt, auch nicht umweglos empfunden, sondern sie kann nur als Illusion durch Beschwörung jener Zeit erreicht werden, in der noch alles Seiende dem schauenden Auge und dem scheuen Herzen eins schien, ruhend in dem großen Mutterleibe der Jahreszeiten: durch Beschwörung der Kindheit. (*Kolonne*, 3, 4)

Verse such as 'Der glückliche Garten' (PH, 1, 74) exemplifies the conscious artistry. It is poised between idyll and elegy, between a re-affirmation of that stable unity and the knowledge that it is irretrievably lost:

Einst waren wir alle im glücklichen Garten,
Ich weiß nicht mehr, vor welchem Haus,
Wo wir die kindliche Stimme sparten
Für Gras und Amsel, Kamille und Strauß.

The elegiac tone is struck in the awareness of the transience of the childhood idyll. Throughout his life, Huchel's verse would exploit such a blend of idyll and elegy, however their configuration would change with the passage of time.

Huchel's sophisticated illusion of a rural childhood, however, acquired much of the lyrical charge that won over readers in *Die literarische Welt* and *Die Kolonne* through its use of the language of mysticism and mythology within a metaphysical conception of the rural world.[11] Huchel frequently observed that his poetry was unthinkable without the mystics.[12] 'Der Herbst', for instance, contains lines in which the seasonal change of nature is depicted quite explicitly in terms of an alchemical transformation, viewed by the mystics as an allegory for the spiritual metamorphosis of the world:

Herbst, dunkler Herbst, voller Gerüche,
Wo Wind dein Feuer groß beschrie,

---

11 For a discussion of Huchel's appropriation of mythological thinking, in particular the work of Oskar Goldberg, see Parker, *Peter Huchel*, especially pp. 82–95. Goldberg was published in Thomas Mann's journal *Maß und Wert*.

12 See, for example, Huchel's conversations with Ludvik Kundera, 'Fragmentarische Gespräche', in Peter Walther (ed.), *Am Tage meines Fortgehns: Peter Huchel 1903–1981* (Frankfurt a.M.: Insel, 1996), pp.53–59 (p. 58).

Wo Laub zu Gold kocht, dunkle Küche
Der erddurchflammten Alchimie. (PH, 1, 80)

To take another example, 'Kindheit in Alt-Langerwisch' combines precise descriptions of nature with superstition and popular mythology:

Hörten den Knecht beschwören die Kuh,
Kranke von Schierling und Klee:
Milch, blaue Milch, Satansmilch du,
Im Namen des Vaters vergeh! (PH, 1, 51)

In 'Die Magd', the maidservant's knitting links her with the Three Fates of the classical tradition, which – as frequently occurs in Huchel's poetry – is integrated within folkloric Brandenburg:

Sie wärmt mein Hemd, küßt mein Gesicht
Und strickt weiß im Petroleumlicht.
Ihr Strickzeug klirrt und blitzt dabei,
Sie murmelt leis Wahrsagerei. (PH, 1, 52)

In this way, the rural world experienced by the child is imbued with a numinous dimension, underscored by the musical quality of the verse, which leaves behind mundane reality, transporting the child into a magical realm of prophesy evoked by the maidservant. Alt-Langerwisch is transformed into the mythically heightened site of 'Naturerlebnisse' and 'Mythologisches', about which Huchel talked to Haas and Italiaander. As was acknowledged in the award of the *Kolonne* prize, Huchel's *Naturmagie* made a distinctive contribution to the new mood of the early 1930s with its subjective, visionary quality, upon which he himself commented:

Niemals wird die Landschaft fotografisch gesehen, niemals wird sie naiv – als Lied zur Laute – besungen; mit Horizonten und Bäumen von innen her will sie über die bloße Idylle hinaus; und meist erscheint sie nur, wenn der Mensch in ihr auftaucht. Oft trägt dann der Mensch die Züge der Natur, und die Natur nimmt das Gesicht des Menschen an [...] Aber nicht so sehr das Hinfinden des Menschen zur Natur, nicht so sehr das Einfühlen oder die Rückkehr in die Natur will in den Gedichten zum Ausdruck kommen, mehr noch ist es die Natur als Handelnde, die auf den Menschen eindringt und ihn in sich hineinzieht. (PH, 2, 248–49)

In the early post-war period, Huchel produced a quite different gloss on his authentic linkage with the rural world, which would become a truism in criticism. He played down his exploration of the magical, transcendent possibilities in nature and conveyed the impression that his principal concern in the early 1930s had been with social justice for the downtrodden rural poor: 'Um was ging es mir damals? Ich wollte eine bewußt übersehene, unterdrückte Klasse im Gedicht sichtbar machen, die Volksschicht, Mägde und Kutscher.'[13] Neither earlier nor later would Huchel reduce the relationship between author, world and work to such a straightforward, political equation. In 1931, for example, he concluded an

---

13   Eduard Zak, *Der Dichter Peter Huchel* (Berlin: Neues Leben, 1953), p. 32.

autobiographical piece for *Die literarische Welt* with words that place him as a private individual at a clear distance from contemporaries in the Communist Party such as Kantorowicz, for whom the social question had a clear priority:

> *Nachwort.* Dieses wird nicht das beste sein. Denn er hat sich nicht an dem Start nach Unterschlupf beteiligt. Seine Altersgenossen sitzen im Parteibüro, und manchmal geben sie sogar zu, daß es aus irgendeiner Ecke her nicht gut riecht. Immerhin, sie haben ihr Dach über dem Kopf. Aber da ihm selbst die marxistische Würde nicht zu Gesicht steht, wird er sich unter aussichtslosem Himmel weiterhin einregnen lassen. Sie winken aus der Arche der Partei, und er versteht ihren Zuruf. Der lautet: 'Wir können dir an Hand des Unterbaues nachweisen, daß du absacken wirst, ohne eine Lücke zu hinterlassen'. Aber er hat nicht viel einzuwenden, nichts zu erwidern. Sie müssen es wissen; denn sie haben die Wissenschaft. Doch unterdessen schlägt sein Herz privat weiter. Und er lebt ohne Entschuldigiung. (PH, 2, 218)

At certain points, these words recall Haas's sarcastic dismissal of Marxism in *Die literarische Welt* (*DLW* 5.35, 7–8 and 4.43, 1). Indeed, the work that Huchel submitted in the *Kolonne* competition contained no hint of his early post-war agenda. Nor was there, for that matter, any hint of that agenda in Raschke's address. After 1945, Huchel distanced himself from *Die Kolonne* in general and the conservative nationalist Raschke in particular.[14] Huchel's aesthetic and stylistic assumptions were much more in tune with the restorative mood promoted in *Die Kolonne* and in *Die literarische Welt* than he would later care to acknowledge. It is true that traces of Expressionism remained in neologisms such as 'nachtanbrausend' (PH, 1, 89), through which he heightened the visionary quality of his *Naturmagie*. Yet the extreme disruption of language and meaning in experimental work of the 1910s and 1920s has no place in Huchel's style of the early 1930s. He sought to re-ground meaning through exact description of nature, thereby continuing the 'empirical' trend of *Neue Sachlichkeit*. In doing so, he drew on the diction and forms of the tradition, shot through with a visionary, metaphysical dimension that employed concepts from mysticism and mythology.

To make such points is not to dismiss the poems of the early 1930s on the grounds of a remote *Innerlichkeit*, which, as we shall see, Huchel himself came close to doing just after the war. Rather, Huchel's poetry contributed to Haas's project of cultural renewal through the exploitation of the artistic potential in the tradition. Following the publication of the poems of childhood, Huchel enriches his poetic voice in the early 1930s through his immersion in the German tradition. He was attracted in particular to the poets of the *Biedermeierzeit*, perhaps through a sense of a artistic affinity in an increasingly repressive, post-revolutionary age. This bore fruit in 'Oktoberlicht' (PH, 1, 60), which was immediately anthologised by Ludwig Goldscheider in *Die schönsten deutschen*

---

14 For a discussion see Parker, *Peter Huchel*, pp. 150–54.

Gedichte and in Raschke's *Neue lyrische Anthologie*.[15] 'Octoberlicht' responds to Hebbel's famous 'Herbstbild'. The latter reads:

> Dies ist ein Herbsttag, wie ich keinen sah!
> Die Luft ist still, als atmete man kaum,
> Und dennoch fallen raschelnd, fern und nah,
> Die schönsten Früchte ab von jedem Baum.
>
> O stört sie nicht, die Feier der Natur!
> Dies ist die Lese, die sie selber hält,
> Denn heute löst sich von den Zweigen nur,
> Was vor dem milden Strahl der Sonne fällt.

Huchel's responded by elaborating upon the autumnal scene with a richness of nature imagery and an eye for detail, nuance and inter-connections in a tableau 'frozen' in the last glorious sunlight of the autumn:

> Oktober, und die letzte Honigbirne
> Hat nun zum Fallen ihr Gewicht,
> Die Mücke im Altweiberzwirne
> Schmeckt noch wie Blut das letzte Licht,
> Das langsam saugt das Grün des Ahorns aus,
> Als ob der Baum von Spinnen stürbe,
> Mit Blättern, zackig wie die Fledermaus,
> Gesiedet von der Sonne mürbe.

In what is surely one of Huchel's lasting contributions to the German lyric in its blend of the idyllic and the elegiac, he transforms Hebbel's imagery of the fruit harvest, re-casting it within his own rich and intricate vision of the final light and life of the autumn scene, underscored by a pattern of sounds gently falling away. In doing these thingss, 'Oktoberlicht' reveals a lyrical subjectivity quite subdued and controlled, in keeping with the tone of his lyrical antecedents in the *Biedermeierzeit*.

A Nature Poet in the Third Reich

With Haas's support, from 1930 Huchel developed literary values in conscious opposition to the politicisation and the relentless massification of culture, both of which were eroding the traditional image of the poet and the institution of literature. When on the eve of the Third Reich, in late December 1932, Huchel presented his verse on the radio, issues of the moment had no part to play. He maintained, instead, the perspective of 1930 that he had brought to bear in his statements in *Die literarische Welt* and in his published poetry. He emphasised the experiential background to his work and distanced it from any *Tendenz*, arguing –

---

15 Ludwig Goldscheider (ed.), *Die schönsten deutschen Gedichte* (Vienna: Phaidon, 1932), p. 441 and Martin Raschke (ed.), *Neue lyrische Anthologie* (Dresden: Jess, 1932), p. 38.

with an echo of Eich – for its indifference towards contemporary events: 'Die erste Bedingung zum Verständnis dieser Verse wird darin bestehen, sich diesem Buch ohne jede Programmforderung zu nähern. Denn *zeitnah* sind diese Gedichte nur zum Teil, nämlich insofern es ihnen gelungen ist, die *vergangene Zeit wieder gegenwärtig zu machen*' (PH, 2, 243). Looking back in 1959, he affirmed that his aim had been, 'eine Poesie zu schreiben, die kein anderes Thema haben sollte als sich selbst', however questionable the 'dichterische Existenz' itself had become in the crisis that set in around 1930 'da der Boden zu schwanken begann' (PH, 2, 300). The re-affirmation of aesthetic autonomy and of a poetic voice grounded in the tradition had been his response to the crisis of 1930. From that perspective, the Nazi assumption of power in January 1933 was merely the latest stage in an on-going crisis, from which it was necessary to protect fundamental values. It cannot be said that the onset of the dictatorship triggered at once in Huchel any radical re-appraisal of his artistic precepts and practice. The depth of the negative and destructive radicalism of Nazism in power was another matter, with which Huchel, like so many others who found the dictatorship repugnant, would struggle throughout its twelve years.

Huchel's poems published in the early phase of the Third Reich display much continuity with the richness of the vision established immediately before 1933. His dialogue with Hebbel continues in 'Das Haus' (PH, 2, 380), a response to 'Das alte Haus' that was published in *Vossische Zeitung* in May 1933. The night-time boat-ride evoked in 'Havelnacht' (PH, 1, 88) with its echoes of Goethe's 'Auf dem See' stands together with 'Oktoberlicht' as arguably Huchel's finest achievement after the publication of the poems of the rural childhood. 'Havelnacht' opens, 'Hinter den ergrauten Schleusen, | nur vom Sprung der Fische laut, | schwimmen Sterne in die Reusen, | lebt der Algen Dämmerkraut'. Contemplation of the stars' reflection on the water's surface yields a sense of cosmic plenitude. Within the vision of the heavens and the waters meeting, the poet evokes 'das sanfte Sein im Wasser', the principle of life that resides in this magical place. It is home to a dynamic 'Geist' that will presently reveal itself with the particular potency of its creativity. The poem ends with the affirmation, underscored by a gentle, even rhythm and by assonance, that the powers of nature sustain our lives: 'Und der Wind wiegt unser Leben, | wie er Weide wiegt und Rohr.'

However, as a nature poet Huchel was left in a wholly uncomfortable position in the Third Reich. Nature poetry and the traditional image of the poet cultivated by Huchel were held in high esteem by the Nazis within their cult of *Blut und Boden*. While Haas fled into exile, Huchel's name appeared on an official Nazi list of writers whose work merited promotion.[16] There is no evidence that Huchel sought to take advantage of this. Nor, by the same token, did he withdraw

---

16 Wilfrid Bade, *Kulturpolitische Aufgaben der deutschen Presse* (Berlin: Junker und Dünnhaupt, 1933), p. 22.

from literary life, as was often maintained in the early post-war decades. Without
the protection that Haas had provided, Huchel was exposed to the vagaries of the
Nazi culture industry. He came to occupy the typically schizophrenic position of
the artist in the dictatorship, giving voice to his opposition in private, while
maintaining a public presence with material that in some ways fitted the regime's
aims, in others expressed dissent. Huchel experienced a reality of niches and
compromises, expressions of dissent and conformity. Increasingly, he found
himself wedded to the mass production of the radio industry with its demands for
the *Gebrauchsformen* that the lyric poet of 1930 had set himself against.

This made for a reality much less clear cut than is suggested in many
accounts, one, too, that was clearly inimical to the concerted development of the
lyric poet. In verse written during the dictatorship without the prospect of
publication, 'Geist' appears not as magical spirit but as the autonomous intellect
under extreme duress. Consider, for example, 'Deutschland I':

> Späteste Söhne, rühmet euch nicht.
> Einsame Söhne, hütet das Licht.
> Daß es von euch in Zeiten noch heißt,
> Daß nicht klirret die Kette, die gleißt,
> Leise umschmiedet, Söhne, den Geist. (PH, 1, 98)

The language of these lines, culminating in the call to protect the 'Geist' now
under threat, maintains the understanding of the autonomous intellect that is
found in other statements examined above. By the same token, the recovery of
the values of 'Geist' would be a major concern for the poet after 1945.

The onset of the dictatorship saw a marked deterioration in the conditions
for a professional writer like Huchel. With Haas gone, he had no guaranteed
outlet for his verse at a time when in any case options were increasingly limited.
During a long stay with his wife's family in Kronstadt, Transylvania, Huchel
placed a number of poems with *Klingsor*, a magazine with serious artistic
aspirations that was edited by the Nazi Heinrich Zillich. Back in Germany,
Huchel joined with friends from the *Kolonne* Circle such as Eich, Horst Lange,
Eberhard Meckel and Schaefer in placing his verse in outlets such as *Der weiße
Rabe*, *Almanach der Dame* and *Das innere Reich*. These titles illustrate something of
the range of options open to Huchel in Germany after 1933. *Der weiße Rabe* was
the creation of V. O. Stomps's *Rabenpresse*, a niche publishing house for new
poetry, while the *Almanach der Dame* was a showcase for the fashion magazine *Die
Dame*, which was edited by Huchel's friend, Sebastian Haffner. As we have seen,
Das innere Reich was one of the few new foundations permitted after 1933. It was
of considerable significance for Nazi cultural politics, designed as it was to project
the quality of contemporary German literature internationally, as well as within,
and in doing so to counter the view that all German culture worthy of the name
had been forced into exile or had been suppressed within.

Stylistically, the work in these outlets until the mid-1930s shows a consistent development upon the *Naturmagie* fashioned around 1930. 'Winter' (PH, 1, 384) was placed in the *Almanach der Dame*. A much altered version of 'Winter' was published as 'Dezember' (PH, 1, 69) in the 1948 collection *Gedichte*. The changes between a poem published in the Third Reich and one published in East Berlin shortly after the war are striking, since they shed light on Huchel's concerns, not least the issue of his social engagement at those two dates, about which, as we have seen, there have been misconceptions. In 'Winter', the poet adopts the persona of the farmer in a narrative poem of ten four-line stanzas, following the form of the *Volkslied*. The poem charts the farmer's pre-occupation with the dead, culminating with his response to the sounds that he hears outside in the night, 'wer drämmert hat an meinem Tor?':

Ich hör am Tor den Balken knarren,
Im Nebel läuten ein Gespann.
Ich hör die Schattenhufe scharren
Und weiß, ein grober Knecht spannt an.

Bang halt ich mich im Haus verborgen.
Er aber weiß, wie nah ich bin.
Und klirrend hinter Nacht und Morgen
Fährt er durch kalten Winter hin.

The farm servant remains a mysterious figure here, the tensions between him and the farmer unspoken, whilst the poem maintains the farmer's perspective in an atmosphere of heightened realism. There is no social message in any class sense: Huchel's sympathies embrace the property owner as well as the labourer in his depiction of eerie Brandenburg winter night.

The 1948 publication, 'Dezember', is a much more pointed social statement. The persona of the farmer is abandoned and the lyrical voice becomes an observer of the rural community. Three new stanzas are introduced in the middle of the poem, which depict the forces of nature directed against the church and an unjust social order, which has, however, been overcome:

Das Licht der Tenne ist erloschen.
Schnee drückt der kleinen Kirche Walm,
Im Klingelbeutel friert der Groschen
Und beizend schwelt der Kerzen Qualm.

Der Wind umheult die Kirchhofsmauer
Des Todes karges Deputat
Ist ein vereister Blätterschauer
Der Eichen auf den letzten Pfad.

Hier ruhn, die für das Gut einst mähten,
Die sich mit Weib und Kind geplagt,
Landlose Schnitter und Kossäten.
Im öden Schatten hockt die Magd.

These lines enjoyed a particular resonance following the first stage of the Land Reform in the Soviet Zone after the war, when landowners were expropriated and peasants handed their land. As we shall see, it is of a piece with other compositions from that time. Yet, in the mid-1930s it was the mysterious tensions in rural life rather than social justice to which Huchel drew attention.

Huchel's depictions of the rural world continued to interest the custodians of the new Nazi culture, whose concern was quite explicitly with community, not class. Two poems were, for example, included in the anthology *Das Lied der Arbeit*, published by Leopold Klotz in collaboration with the *Deutsche Arbeitsfront*, including an introduction by Robert Ley.[17] However sophisticated Huchel's writing was in comparison with other poets represented in the anthology such as Heinrich Anacker and however sensitive in contrast to Anacker's aggressive chauvinism, Huchel's treatment of rural life in poems such as 'Die Magd' could be – and was on occasions such as this – accommodated within the official *Blut und Boden* cult, which, like Huchel's work, typically drew on traditional forms and diction.

The publications in *Das innere Reich* range from the visionary celebration of the dawn in 'Frühe' (PH, 1, 63), to the commemoration of the mysterious figure of the 'Ziegelstreicher' in 'Nachtlied' (PH, 1, 64), and on to the play of the imagination in 'Nächtliches Eisfenster' (PH, 1, 85). 'Letzte Fahrt' (PH, 1, 62) strikes a more sombre note, especially when read in conjunction with the slightly later publication of the cycle 'Strophen aus einem Herbst' in the same journal. In 'Letzte Fahrt', the elegiac mode comes to dominate the idyllic. The son depicts himself following the path through life chosen by his angler father. The poem describes a death, which is a death in life, as the dreams that the father had cherished ebb away: 'er sah die toten Träume ziehn | als Fische auf dem Grund'; and in the stanza that follows: 'sein Traum und auch sein Leben fuhr | durch Binsen hin und Sand.' The son comes to the fore in the final lines: 'in meiner Kanne springt der Fisch. | Ich geh den Binsenweg.' This publication from 1935 foreshadows the end for the poet who had emerged in 1930.

The Radio and Film Author: The Poet's Struggle with the 'Tumult aller Stile'

Like the other young authors in the *Kolonne* Circle, Huchel gravitated to work as a radio author after 1933. After 1945, he drew a veil over this aspect of his career, even though from 1945 to 1948 he actually worked for the Soviets in the same building on the Masurenallee in Charlottenburg from which much of his radio

---

17   Hans Mühle, *Das Lied der Arbeit: Selbstzeugnisse der Schaffenden* (Gotha: Klotz, 1935).

work had been broadcast during the Third Reich.[18] Had certain details become known, they would have been an obstacle to his rise in East Berlin.

Between 1934 and 1940, Huchel wrote as many as 35 radio plays, of which more than 20 were broadcast.[19] On the grounds of literary quality, just 3 of the 16 extant manuscripts were included in the 1984 edition. The selection indicates the limited opportunities in radio for work that fulfilled the poetic self-image and notions of authorship that Huchel had assumed, despite the fact that at the time the radio play was held up as a 'Restaurator "wahrer Dichtung"'.[20] The remaining manuscripts demonstrate how Huchel was drawn into the popular entertainment industry of the Third Reich, in which the position of the author was downgraded by the demands for serial production. As we shall see, Huchel turned his hand with some success to a whole range of genres that met the needs of an ever more tighly contolled medium. What might at first have looked like a niche for the production of harmless entertainment with the occasional prospect of more accomplished work to salve the artistic conscience, revealed itself in time to be the naked propaganda vehicle that it truly was. Huchel's work in these years in radio and in film in the early 1940s bears detailed examination.

Huchel's first radio play was a piece for the Berlin *Jugendfunk* in December 1934, 'Doktor Faustens Teufelspakt und Höllenfahrt', an adaptation of a traditional piece that remained very close to the original. The association between the Faust legend and the radio author's role in the medium presided over by Goebbels scarcely needs to be laboured:

Hört, ihr Leut, ich muß euch warnen,
Laßt euch nicht vom Teufel umgarnen.
Er hält nicht, was er euch verspricht,
Bis er euch gar den Hals zerbricht.
Zwölf ist die Glock ... Zwölf ist die Glock.[21]

After that debut, in the next two years Huchel established himself through the broadcast of four plays in the light entertainment slot of the *Reichssender* Berlin, 'Ein Fahrstuhl ist nicht mehr zu halten', 'Ballade im Eisfenster', 'Katzen auf allen Dächern' and 'Der Fesselballon'. All exploit perennially popular themes of love and adventure through a blend of humorous dialogue, music and popular verse, showing for the first time a side of Huchel that is not apparent in the serious project that was his poetry. However, the more substantial 'Die Magd und das Kind' and 'Die Herbstkantate', two of the three works that figure in the 1984

---

18 For a discussion, including critics' acquiescence, see Parker, *Peter Huchel*, pp. 180–84 and p. 227–67.
19 For details of those radio plays known at the time of the compilation of the 1984 Huchel edition, see PH, 2, 409–20.
20 Wolfram Wessels, *Hörspiele im Dritten Reich: Zur Institutionen-, Theorie- und Literaturgeschichte* (Bonn: Bouvier, 1985), pp. 366–71.
21 The lines are quoted by Wolfram Wessels, in '"Die tauben Ohren der Geschlechter": Peter Huchel und der Rundfunk', broadcast by *Südwestfunk* on 16 January 1994.

edition, are both constructed around verse published in the early to mid-1930s. In 'Die Magd und das Kind' the verse is interpolated within dialogue, while 'Die Herbstkantate', as the title suggests, is a sequence of poems set to music. Huchel signalled the more sophisticated nature of both pieces in the sub-title 'Eine Dichtung für den Rundfunk'.

'Die Magd und das Kind' develops Huchel's major poetic theme of the early 1930s, the Alt-Langerwisch world of childhood. The dialogue, in four sections representing the seasons, is woven around the poetry. As we have seen in the anthologisation of 'Die Magd', however, by the mid-1930s the treatment of regional themes and folkloric traditions had been consolidated within the *Blut-und-Boden* cult that was central to the official view of literature. Huchel's work could be understood in terms that were compatible with that cult, even though there was no trace of the aggressive chauvinism typical of 'hard-line' Nazi writing. Involvement by a non-Nazi author in what was inescapably the official literature made such ambiguities inevitable.

At the same time, the treatment of nature in 'Die Herbstkantate' can be read as an expression of Huchel's keen awareness of his doubly compromised situation as a sophisticated artist in the Third Reich who was working in radio. The first production of 'Die Herbstkantate' was praised by Gerd Eckert in the following terms:

> Für den Nebenbeihörenden ein Durcheinander von schwer verständlichen, zuweilen wiederholten Versen und Kammermusik. Dem lauschenden Hörer dagegen erschloß sich aus der Verbindung der klangreichen und lautmalenden Sprache Huchels mit der von Paul Hoeffer verständnisvoll geschriebenen Musik eine aus der Naturbeobachtung und der Tiefe des Gefühls eindringlich gestaltete Deutung des Herbsterlebnisses. (PH, 2, 412–13)

Huchel's cantata – a frequently used form in the official literature of the Third Reich – contains a depth of feeling that is not fully conveyed in Eckert's appreciation. The piece includes some of Huchel's finest elegiac, autumnal verse born of his immersion in the tradition, including 'Oktoberlicht'. It is structured around the cycle, 'Strophen aus einem Herbst', which appeared virtually simultaneously in *Das innere Reich*. Through their common structure, both works give voice to a progressively darkening vision of anguish and despair, as light yields to darkness, dream turns into nightmare, creativity gives way to barrenness, and life is overtaken by death. The starting point evokes the magical plenitude of a delicate, dynamic nature captured in the style of the early 1930s:

FRAUENSTIMME:
Die Sonne springt, ein weißes Geißlein,
Von Ahornschatten schön gefleckt,
Durch das Gewirre grüner Zweige,
Wo sie sich scheu ins Goldne streckt.

Wie eine schnelle Töpferscheibe
Dreht sich am Boden flach der Wind,

Auf dem ein Blätterwirbel steht:

Ein Napf aus Laub; und andere Zeichen,
Als liefen geisterhafte Füße
Hell übers heiße Blumenbeet. (PH, 2, 29)

As in other poems from the early 1930s, nature yields up its secrets to the poet, who enjoys the power to read the signs in the book of nature. By the final section, entitled 'November-Endlied' in the cycle, the vision has been blighted:

MÄNNERSTIMME singt:
Im Nebel nistet nun mein Traum.
Ich pflanze ein den Totenbaum.
Auf roten Wolken fuhr die Nacht.
Sie fuhr durch seine Zweige sacht.

FRAUENSTIMME singt:
Da rief ein Vogel – schlief ich schon?
Wie dunkel stieg der Vogelton.
O grauer Herbst, ich wünsch nichts mehr.
Ach käme doch der Schatten her.

MÄNNERSTIMME singt:
Die Nacht auf roten Wolken zieht.
Im Nebel nistet nun mein Lied.

FRAUENSTIMME singt:
Was rief der Vogel mich von fern?
Ich läg im steingen Acker gern. (PH, 2, 39)

The piece charts the defeat of a compromised voice, which utters a profound sense of melancholy and inner conflict in a work whose complexity would, as Eckert acknowledges, have eluded all but the sharpest listeners. Few would have picked up the associations with an earlier *Melancholiker* from the *Biedermeierzeit*, Nikolaus Lenau. Huchel's copy of Lenau's *Gedichte* in the 1857 Cotta edition contains evidence of his indebtedness to Lenau.[22] The imagery and tone of Lenau's autumnal elegies such as 'Herbstentschluß' can be traced to 'November-Endlied'. Huchel uses not only the form and style but also the allusive technique of the elitist poetic tradition to convey the impossibility of its continuation within the medium and the world in which he operates. 'Die Herbstkantate' struck a chord with Eich, who requested a copy from his friend.[23]

The publication of 'Strophen aus einem Herbst', if not the broadcast of 'Die Herbstkantate', signalled an end for Huchel: he virtually ceased to publish new poetry in the Third Reich. After the breakthrough of the early 1930s with the

---

22 The volume is in the Peter Huchel Collection in the John Rylands University Library of Manchester.

23 Eich requested the piece in a letter of 21 October 1935. See Peter Huchel, *Wie soll man da Gedichte schreiben: Briefe 1925–1977*, ed. by Hub Nijssen (Frankfurt a.M.: Suhrkamp, 2000), p. 38. Eich included 'November-Endlied' in the November broadcast of 'Der Königswusterhäuser Landbote'. For further details, see Stephen Parker, *Peter Huchel*, pp. 194–95.

publication of the Alt-Langerwisch material, which was followed by the dialogue with the poets of the *Biedermeierzeit*, Huchel's poetic development stalled in the conditions of the dictatorship. His repugnance at the Third Reich is conveyed in verse that maintains the traditional humanist values of 'Deutschland I' during years when Huchel had close links with conservative figures of inner emigration such as Werner Bergengruen:

> Göttlich bleibt der Mensch und versöhnt.
> Und sein Atem wird frei wieder wehen.
> Wenn auch die heulende Rotte höhnt,
> Sie wird vergehen. (PH, 1, 166)

After Auschwitz, many would question the worth of allusions to works such as Goethe's 'Das Göttliche' to provide re-assurance that the dictatorship would pass and established values would be restored. Yet the position that Huchel shared with Bergengruen and others within Germany was quite consistent with his trajectory from 1930. Nor would that trajectory be abandoned when the poet bore witness to the horrific destruction of the final stages of the war, which informs his early post-war verse.

That said, the crisis signalled in 'Die Herbstkantate' did not lead to any break with official Nazi culture in radio, a culture which became more firmly established as the years of the dictatorship passed. Huchel's shift from elitist nature poetry to serial radio production clearly involved a severe disruption of his artistic self-image, against which he contiued to struggle. Yet like his poetry, his work in the *Gebrauchsformen* required in radio production was grounded in the stabilisation of meaning that is such a feature of literary life around 1930. Huchel's work in the Third Reich can thus be seen to represent the tensions between the dual strands of elite nature poetry cultivated by the *Kolonne* Circle and the 'Tumult aller Stile' of the Nazi cultural industry, both of which partake of the stabilisation of meaning in the 1930 paradigm.

Huchel now gave himself up fully to the serial production of a sequence of plays, few of which have survived. Titles and programming information indicate that in some he maintained the rural Brandenburg theme (e.g. 'Der letzte Knecht'), in others he continued with children's radio (e.g. 'Putt, putt, putt, mein Hühnchen') and in others still he provided more popular entertainment for adults (e.g. 'Der Bernsteinwald'). 'Gott im Ährenlicht' appears to have been a more ambitious piece of work. It was characterised by a contemporary as follows: 'Immer wieder tritt die starke lyrische Begabung aus Liedern zutage, die in die Handlung verwoben sind, z.B. in der farbig bewegten, klangvollen Kantate über die Erntezeit und den Herbst "Gott im Ährenlicht" (1936), die den Duft und die Stimmung einer großen Ernte einfängt.'[24] One can read, too, that the cantata 'wurde unmittelbar vor der Übertragung der "Morgenfeier" aus der Potsdamer Garnisonskirche anläßlich des Erntedankfestes gesendet' (PH, 2, 415). Huchel's

---

24   Franz Lennartz, *Die Dichter unserer Zeit* (Stuttgart: Kröner, 1938), p. 138.

lyrical gift was deployed on a special occasion in the Nazi calendar, celebrated in an equally special place in Nazi image-building. The Nazis' efforts to extract maximum propaganda effect from harvest thanksgiving have been well documented. If little else can be established regarding Huchel's involvement in this piece of Nazi cultish practice, it is clear that his lyrical treatment of the autumnal theme struck a chord.

As the Nazis embarked on their expansionist plans, greater emphasis was placed on overt political propaganda, as listeners were encouraged to identify with the *Volksgemeinschaft*. Two of Huchel's plays, 'Brigg Santa Fé' and 'Die Freundschaft von Port Said', both realistic adventure stories and as such a fresh departure for him, reflect this new orientation, though in each case Huchel's treatment did not quite deliver what policy makers might have hoped for. Whilst both plays depict Germans abroad overcoming adversity, neither deliver the ideological points that the stories might have produced. In the latter play, for example, the emphasis is on friendship, not a growing awareness of Germanness. These plays add to a picture in which the talented Huchel proved himself adept in adjusting to the needs of various genres. He became sought after as an author who could deliver quality work and could, it seems, as a result afford to withhold ideological assent, even on occasion to express dissent through work whose complexity was beyond the Nazi officials who approved its rootedness in tradition.

Huchel's final play broadcast before the outbreak of war, 'Margarethe Minde', adds a further element to the understanding of his output as the dissenting collaborator that he became. He again turned to the German tradition for his sources, yet the play is much more than a simple adaptation of Fontane's story. Huchel evidently took great trouble over its creation. It is written in blank verse and the opening scene includes sections of a magical and prophetic quality. The play also includes speeches by two sympathetic characters, Morten and Helmreich, which can be interpreted as critical of the regime. They occur near the beginning and the end of the play and thus suggest a framework for interpretation. Morten, for example, evokes a doom-laden atmosphere of evil in the opening scene, which can also be found in some of Huchel's poems from the late 1930s such as 'Zwölf Nächte', which were published only after the war:

Die dumpfe Erde brütet Unheil nur,
Seit der Saturn dem Mars sich nähert –
Ja, was für Zeiten! Mensch und Tier zittern,
Bricht über sie die Nacht herein! (PH, 2, 44–45)

When near the end Helmreich assumes the role of the judge, he exclaims:

Ungern, ihr Bürger, walt' ich des Amts!
Wer möchte hier noch Richter sein? – Die Stadt,
Sie war voll Rechts, nun ist sie eine Mördergrube! –
Zornhaus der Hölle, öffne dich!! Verschling

> Doch diese Brut, die über Tangermünde kam!
> Im Blutdunst des Verbrechens lebt hier alles! (PH, 2, 97)

The first half of the speech can certainly be construed as a critique of the regime. Yet, as Wessels points out, the second half of the speech contains terms that were deployed by the Nazis in their attacks on the Weimar Republic.[25] Many readers would have made that link. Wessels also suggests that in general listeners would have understood the piece as an historical play, whatever Huchel's intentions might have been. And Huchel's use of the German tradition was in itself attractive to the regime.

As in 'Die Herbstkantate', in 'Margarethe Minde' Huchel re-stated his credentials as the *Dichter* of the 1930 paradigm, yet once more he was drawn further into serial production. The onset of war exacerbated the situation. Anti-British propaganda occupied a significant slice of air time for radio plays. The adaptation of quality literature as a vehicle for veiled expressions of dissent could no longer be sustained. Instead, literary sources were deployed in 'soft' propagandistic broadcasts that at times took place in sensitive border areas or occupied territory. Huchel's 'Die Greuel von Denshawai', an adaptation of George Bernard Shaw's 'Denshawai Horror' – a story of British colonial atrocities in Egypt – was broadcast from Danzig on 23 January 1940 and from Breslau on 5 April the same year.[26] In between those two broadcasts came an adaptation of Goethe's *Hermann und Dorothea*, to which Huchel appended a prologue with the following lines:

> Dort an der Grenze im Westen,
> Wo immer ein Schicksal wohnt,
> Lebten vor Zeiten sie auch,
> Hermann und Dorothea.
> Deiner gedenken wir heut,
> Du herrliches Paar,
> Das sich im Feuer des Krieges
> Suchte und fand. Seid ihr nicht
> Näher dem Herzen der Lebenden heute? –
>
> [...]
>
> Schicksal, es treibt uns hinauf
> Und stürzt uns hinab!
> Aber was klagend begann,
> Nicht immer endets in Tränen;
> Denn Leiden gehn unter
> Im Herzen des ewigen Volks.[27]

---

25 See Wessels, '"Die tauben Ohren der Geschlechter"'.

26 For further details, see Stephen Parker, 'Peter Huchel als Propagandist: Huchels 1940 entstandene Adaption von George Bernard Shaws "Die Greuel von Denshawai"', *Rundfunk und Fernsehen*, 39 (1991), 343–53 and 'On Peter Huchel's adaptation of George Bernard Shaw's "Denshawai Horror" and related matters', *Neophilologus*, 79 (1995), 295–306.

27 See Wessels, '"Die tauben Ohren der Geschlechter"'.

The 'Volk', not 'das Göttliche', comes now to feature as the repository for eternal values. The old enemy on the Western Front is, of course, France, now in union with Britain. Goethe's text is used to forge a link with the present conflict in a manner which assures listeners that the outcome will be favourable despite suffering, which is deemed both necessary and justified, subsumed as it is within the collective 'Herzen des ewigen Volks'. In the final lines, Hermann declares his readiness to fight the enemy in order to secure peace, a peace won, according to the logic of Huchel's adaptation, on Germany's terms against the powers ranged against it in the West. Whatever Huchel's personal views, in 'Hermann und Dorothea' he delivered the required propaganda message through the vehicle of Weimar Classicism.

Huchel turned to European art history for 'Peter Paul Rubens', his final radio play before the genre disappeared from the airwaves in June 1940, which was broadcast in Dutch on 30 May 1940 from the Berlin short wave station to the Dutch colony of Indonesia (PH, 2, 420). Any puzzlement over these arrangements is resolved if one recalls that German troops overran Belgium and Holland between 10 and 14 May 1940. As is appropriate in a situation in which the Germans were seeking to win over the population of newly conquered territories, Huchel's slight text is by no means agitatory. Just as Germany was placing itself at the forefront of the new Europe, so too could the 300th anniversary of Rubens's death be celebrated on the basis of the status that he had achieved as a pan-European artist born in Germany.

Like others, Huchel now turned to the film industry as a remaining outlet for his material. His letters to his first wife, Dora, show his intermittent collaboration with film companies for virtually the duration of the war.[28] It is unclear whether one of Huchel's radio plays, the comedy 'Zille Martha', formed the basis for Helmut Käutner's 1944 film 'Unter den Brücken'.[29] Two *Filmnovellen* are extant, 'Der Nobiskrug' and 'Das Fräulein von Soor'. Though neither were turned into films, both were undoubtedly acceptable material during wartime. The latter treats a popular patriotic theme from Prussian history, the struggle against Napoleon's army of occupation, though as always with Huchel there is no recourse to crude chauvinism typical of hard-line Nazi propagandists. 'Der Nobiskrug', meanwhile, tells a story of rural life which underlines the primacy of the citizen's responsibility towards the community over individual wishes. In both texts we witness Huchel as the skilful wordsmith that he had become. His letters to his wife show that he continued his relationship with the film industry after he was called up in August 1941 to a signals unit. He was spared the Eastern Front, but

---

28 The letters are in the Peter Huchel Collection in the John Rylands University Library of Manchester. For details see my essay, 'Recent additions to the Peter Huchel Collection in the John Rylands University Library of Manchester', *Bulletin of the John Rylands University Library of Manchester*, 74.2 (1992), 85–125. A small number are published in Huchel, *Briefe 1925–1977*.

29 For a discussion see Parker, *Peter Huchel*, p. 206

he witnessed the destruction that Nazi Germany brought upon itself in the latter stages of the war.

Undoubtedly, Huchel, like others in the *Kolonne* Circle, was filled with dismay at the course his career had taken. Huchel's friend Horst Lange surely spoke for him and others in their circle when he wrote wistfully to Ernst Kreuder that friends 'mit denen man vor 7, 8 Jahren eine kleine Front jugendlicher Begabungen gebildet hat' had in the meantime 'einträgliche und weniger anstrengende Beschäftigungen'.[30] The aspirations of that generation of 1930 to re-ground literature within the tradition, protecting it from the ephemera of mass urban culture had proved unsustainable.

1945: 'Eine neue Verbreitung menschlicher Gesinnung'

Huchel delivered occasional readings of his poetry on the radio during the later war years but there was only one new publication of verse, 'Späte Zeit', which appeared in late 1941 in *Die Dame* under the title 'Im nassen Sand' (PH, 1, 94). The poem had been submitted in a competition for war poetry and Huchel's title changed by the editors, who evidently regarded it as too pessimistic.[31] His wartime activity of spotting allied planes finds its way into his diction. The poem displays a subtle blend of imagery drawn from nature, mythology and warfare ('Über allen Jägern jagt | hoch im Wind ein fremder Hund') within a composition informed by a sombre mood of impending death ('Herbst schoß seine Schüsse ab | leise Schüsse übers Grab'). This elegiac treatment of war is far from the heroism officially fostered, not to mention Huchel's prologue to 'Hermann und Dorothea'. However, the context of publication in the 1941 competition places some distance between it and the 1933 date of composition which Huchel gave it in *Gedichte*, which encouraged an anti-fascist reading.

Other war poetry, most notably the cycle 'Der Rückzug' (PH, 1, 100), would be collected in the third section of *Gedichte*. In this, actually Huchel's first book publication, he presented his verse since the composition of the childhood poems. The wretched years of the serial production of *Gebrauchsformen* for radio and film were set to one side, seemingly an aberration. For all the scenes of destruction in the war poetry, the collection has little in common with the language of the *Kahlschlag* or of a *Nullpunkt* of 1945, nor does it reflect the view that art had been changed irrevocably by Nazism and the Holocaust. Huchel's aesthetic understanding remains within the contours of established literary values. That is not to say that Huchel's war poetry and other early post-war verse

---

30 Horst Lange's letter to Ernst Kreuder of 27 February 1939 is deposited in the *Deutsches Literaturarchiv*, Marbach.
31 Huchel expresses his anger regarding the change in a letter to his wife of 23 October 1941, an extract of which appears in Huchel, *Briefe 1925–1977*, p. 477.

represent a simple reversion to the position of 1930. Rather they show a development, the consistency of which can be traced back to that point.

It is striking that, speaking in East Berlin in 1947, at that threshold moment of potential cultural change, Huchel maintained the consistency of the discourse that we have traced from the early 1930s and the late 1950s. He spoke of radio play authorship in the Nazi dictatorship as follows:

> Und wie auf allen Kunstgebieten, so erntete auch auf dem Gebiet des Hörspiels ein rein künstlerisches Formstreben keinen Dank und keine Anerkennung mehr. Die alles vergiftende politische Tendenzlüge bemächtigte sich auch des Funks und des Hörspiels, so daß der wertvollere Teil der Hörerschaft, der nach menschlicher und künstlerischer Erhebung verlangte, sehr bald das Interesse am Hören verlor. (PH, 2, 256)

He went on to link the situation in 1947 quite explicitly with that in the early 1930s, again using the language of the restorative turn:

> Heute, wo eine neue Verbreitung menschlicher Gesinnung mit einer neuen Pflege des künstlerischen Geschmackes wieder Hand in Hand zu gehen beginnt, stehen wir wiederum vor der gleichen Aufgabe, wie sie andeutungsweise die Kritik bereits vor anderthalb Jahrzehnten zum Ausdruck gebracht hat. (PH, 2, 256)

Huchel's experience in radio after 1933 could have yielded much more telling observations concerning art in the dictatorship. More pertinent at this point, however, is that Huchel's language remains rooted within the aesthetic parameters of 1930 in order to promote a recovery of values in opposition to 'politische Tendenzlüge'. Artistic autonomy is the pre-condition for good taste and for the 'Verbreitung menschlicher Gesinnung' in cultural renewal.[32]

In another statement from the same year, using language that echoes contemporaneous statements by his friends from the *Kolonne* Circle, Elisabeth Langgässer, Eich and Lange, Huchel again reflects on the experience of 1930, before emphasising the public responsibility of the artist for the recovery of an ethical humanism that had been destroyed by the Nazis.[33] While praising the moral stance of those few writers who stayed in Germany and who 'sich geistig nicht gleichschalten ließen' (PH, 2, 263), he nonetheless criticises their writing (and implicitly much of his own work) because of its metaphysical remoteness:

> Unsere besten Dichter – und ich meine jetzt die wieder, die ideologisch keineswegs mit den Nazis paktierten – auch dann noch ins Gebirge der dichterischen Schau stiegen und auf den höchsten Eisfirnen, losgelöst von jeder Realität in methaphysischer [sic] Einsamkeit mit dem Unendlichen Zwiesprache hielten, als am

---

32 These statements also match the aesthetically conservative discourse surrounding the radio play, which is identified by Wessels as dominant within Germany from 1930 to 1960, when the genre was conceived 'als Restaurator "wahrer Dichtung"'. See note 20 above. It goes without saying that Huchel's discussion of the genre is far removed from Brecht and Benjamin's theoretical statements from the 1920s concerning the exploitation of the new medium for new listeners from the working class.

33 Elisabeth Langgässer, 'Schriftsteller unter der Hitlerdiktatur', *Ost und West*, 1 (1947), 36–41.

Fuße des Gebirges schon längst Städte und Dörfer in Flammen aufgingen und Menschen erschlagen wurden. Es war eine Flucht vor der Verantwortung. (PH, 2, 264)

The moral intensity of Huchel's language reflects Langgässer's criticism of the abdication of responsibility by the practitioners of German *Innerlichkeit*. These sentiments translate in Huchel's early post-war verse into a more deliberately public voice, deployed with the rhetorical confidence of a figure embarked on such a mission. Those whose understanding of Huchel's post-war verse is formed by the hesitant, elliptical voice found in *Chausseen Chausseen* and later collections will be surprised by such a emphasis, which can, however, be justified by reference to Huchel's compositions until the mid-1950s.[34]

In the early post-war compositions, the interplay of idyll and elegy remains of central importance. The elegiac mode comes to the fore in the scenes of destruction that predominate in 'Der Rückzug'. The cycle opens with the well-known lines redolent of Baroque verse: 'Ich sah des Krieges Ruhm. | Als wärs des Todes Säbelkorb, | durchklirrt von Schnee, am Straßenrand | lag eines Pferdes Gerippe.' Employing a striking, graphic realism, Huchel testifies to the horror of the final, bloody stages of the war: 'Zwischen den beiden | Sicheln des Mondes wurde ich alt | wie der blutdurchtränkte Fluß voll treibender Leichen, | wie der aschig trauernde Wald.' Nature poetry composed within the formal parameters of the *Volkslied* is swept away in the shock of the final collapse. The elegiac tone is left to run on and on: long and short lines alternate without any set pattern, and they are no longer bound by rhyme in the unfolding scene of destruction, which is echoed in the harsh dissonance of many of the cycle's consonant sounds. As already in 'Späte Zeit', he extends his range to take in the vocabulary of modern, mechanised warfare, in which machines are deployed to cause death and destruction to humans and nature, and where the burnt-out shells of tanks are abandoned amidst the debris and decaying flesh.

Yet elemental nature remains a source for an idyllic counterpoint, for what Walter Jens has called Huchel's 'zarte Gegenbilder' to the scenes of destruction.[35] The scenes of war are contrasted with the finely drawn swallow: 'Weißbrustige Schwalbe, | dein Schnabel ritzt | das grau sich kräuselnde Wasser | an Schilf und Toten vorbei | im gleitenden Flug.' The survival of the swallow points to the regenerative capacity of nature, thematised in the final stanza of the cycle: 'Und es wächst im Nebel das Korn, | noch überwölbt von Finsternis, | hinter dem Hang vergorener Herbste, | Wasser und Schlamm, leuchtet die Sichel | im Widderhorn.' At this end point, the crescent comes together with Huchel's personal sign, the 'Widderhorn', which signifies both his birth sign and the gift of

---

34 As I have argued elsewhere, the Huchel of the 1950s has generally been sought and found in *Chausseen Chausseen* of 1963. Yet that collection is not a suitable guide to the Huchel of the early to mid-1950s. See Parker, *Peter Huchel*, p. 272.
35 Walter Jens, 'Wo die Dunkelheit endet', in Mayer (ed.), pp. 22–27 (p. 24).

song. In the face of the appalling destruction, the poet asserts through his song the primacy of elemental nature, which possesses regenerative properties beyond the capacity of man to destroy the planet. Here, Huchel still draws on the view of nature that he articulated in 1932: 'Mehr noch ist es die Natur als Handelnde, die auf den Menschen eindringt und ihn in sich hineinzieht' (PH, 2, 249). The poem moves from the elegiac to the idyllic, from the graphic depiction of destruction to the reassurance of the final lines, which are certainly far removed from the idea that Auschwitz signalled a radical break in civilisation. Rather, the poem offers the prospect that the regenerative powers of nature can usher in the recovery of civilised values.

The rhetorical manner and the concluding note of 'Der Rückzug' are characteristic of Huchel's other poetry of the late 1940s and early 1950s, which a reviewer of *Gedichte* described as containing 'ein[en] neue[n] lebenszugewandte[n] Klang [...] einer Freudigkeit des Beginnens'.[36] Huchel was one of the few poets in the foundation years of the GDR to respond with a degree of success to the many calls from cultural politicians for the depiction of the revolutionary changes occurring in the countryside. As a nature poet of some distinction, he was at the time well-nigh unique in the early GDR. Following Marx's scathing comments about the idiocy of the countryside, poets of the Left had generally shunned the countryside as hopelessly backward. The Nazis' appropriation of blood and soil had served to confirm established attitudes. However, Soviet policy identified the German peasantry as an important part of the population to be won over through its Land Reform.

Huchel responded with his major new piece from the start of the 1950s, the cycle 'Das Gesetz' (PH, 1, 283). The title refers to the law passed to introduce the first stage of the Land Reform. That first stage involved expropriation of large landowners and the re-distribution of the land to the peasantry. Huchel, the man with political sympathies for the Left, saw the reform as the means to imbue the life of ordinary people in the countryside with a dignity that had previously been denied them. For a while, the poet's humanist mission and the socialisation of the rural world came together in a ready acceptance of the politicisation of art. This rests uneasily with the reservations that he expressed at other times and with a metaphorical practice drawing heavily on nature imagery that is more suited to allusive than direct statement. His support for the Land Reform is developed in other poems published in the early 1950s such as 'In der Heimat' (PH, 1, 408), which was dedicated to Johannes R. Becher. However, as the 1950s progressed, this early enthusiasm turned to disillusion. Just as the rhetorical confidence gives

---

36 Ltz., 'Peter Huchel, *Gedichte*', *Tägliche Rundschau*, 6 May 1949.

way to a predominantly hesitant, elliptical voice, so too the political affirmation of the early 1950s is removed from poems collected in *Chausseen Chausseen*.[37]

Huchel produced a series of notes on the production of 'Das Gesetz' (PH, 2, 293–95), in which he announced his intention to forge an idiom more realistic than magic. The notes describe a linkage between the poet's language and his intimate knowledge of the language and practices of rural workers:

> Wenn sich der Dichter mit der Sprache der Arbeit, der Arbeitsgeräte, d.h. mit der Sprache des Volks beschäftigt, wenn er diese nicht poetisch verbrämt, *wohl aber zu seiner eigenen Sprache werden läßt*, so wird er im Gedicht ganz neue Wege gehen können. Schreiben aus dem Lebensgefühl des arbeitenden Menschen heraus heißt nicht, die auf den Hund gekommene Sprache der Kleinbürger benutzen, um sich 'verständlich' zu machen, was von einigen 'Kritikern', die nicht die Volkssprache kennen, geschweige deren Reichtum, immer wieder gefordert haben. Diese platte Forderung ist eine Beleidigung für das Volk! (PH, 2, 294–5)

Huchel places himself here in the camp of the politically engaged writers that he had rejected in *Die literarische Welt* in 1931. Equally, he foregrounds for his verse not subjective experience yielding visionary *Naturmagie*, but the appropriation of the authentic language of the toiling peasantry. In its own way, this shift appears as drastic as the mid-1930s shift from poetry to serial radio production. Yet, as we have seen, Huchel's discourse of authenticity is a constant feature of his self-understanding. It is a feature of his *Sachlichkeit* that is integrated within the 1930 paradigm. Aesthetically, Huchel's fresh emphasis can be understood in similar fashion to Raschke's attraction to the work of Zernatto and Billinger that he published in *Die Kolonne*.

Huchel's confidence that he could give expression to the working people's 'Lebensgefühl' feeds into the affirmative message of 'Das Gesetz'. Yet even a cursory glance at the cycle demonstrates the extent to which his poetic practice remains wedded to a visionary *Naturmagie*.[38] 'Das Gesetz' opens with the majestic topos of an elemental nature grander and more powerful than the deeds and misdeeds of humans: 'Aber noch dreht sich, | Sterne und Steine schleudernd | das alte Schöpfrad der Nacht.' This also provides continuity with 'Der Rückzug' and with other poems in the final section of *Gedichte*. Despite the destruction of war, elemental nature remains intact and order can therefore be created out of chaos. This message is transferred to the depiction of the German people: 'O des Volkes vergessenes Leben! | Hielt es nicht immer bereit | die Schlüssel zum Tor der Tiefe?' More than fifty years on, this rather sanguine view of the people would surely not go unchallenged, nor, one might argue, should it have in 1950. 'Das Gesetz' and other compositions from the time consistently represent the

---

37 'In der Heimat' is collected in *Chausseen Chausseen* as 'Die Pappeln' (PH, 1, 145). See, too, the title poem of *Chausseen Chausseen*, which reads very differently in the context of its first publication in 'Das Gesetz'.

38 Huchel later acknowledged the problem, explaining, 'ich kann nicht dafür, diese Naturmetaphern drängen sich mir immer wieder auf' (PH, 2, 393).

orthodox communist position that Nazism was the responsibility of the property-owning classes, not the people, who were the receptacle of a sound national consciousness.

Huchel depicts the people in their successful struggle against a pernicious capitalism, contrasting their wisdom with the problems of egotistical individual endeavour. The latter is dismissed as follows: 'und hadernd geht | das Vergangene um | auf modernden Füßen.' The people's lot under Nazism is described as a 'durstige Schicksal', which culminates in the hardship and suffering of the German people at the war's end, especially refugees from the East. They are taken up within a narrative that takes shape as a founding myth for the GDR, charting the revolutionary changes that take place at the war's end. Yet, of course, the focus on German suffering does little to foster a critical attitude as to why that suffering came about in the first place.

A 'Greisin' symbolising an unreconstructed consciousness is, it is true, contrasted with the figure of a child who stands for regeneration. Through the refrain 'Aber das Kind war nahe dem Tag', the child's unsullied innocence stands out against all the darkness, death and suffering, as the advancing 'Heer' breaks through the 'Mörder'. The promulgation of the Land Reform is celebrated in a rhetorical flourish:

O Gesetz,
Mit dem Pflug in den Acker geschrieben,
Mit dem Beil in die Bäume gekerbt!
Gesetz, das das Siegel der Herren zerbrochen,
Zerrissen ihr Testament!

At this time of a new beginning, the people can take full possession of the world: 'Zwischen Acker und Stern, | o Volk, die ganze Tiefe ist dein!' The people must, however, rise to the challenge through the labour in which the poet, the master of their language, exhorts them to engage:

So legt den neuen Grund!
Volk der Chausseen,
Zertrümmerter Trecks!
Reißt um den Grenzstein des Guts!

The poem concludes on the confident note that the work has been done and that the 'Volk' has been redeemed though hard work: 'Dezemberrissiger Acker, | auftauende Erde im März, | Mühsal und Gnade trägt der Mensch.'

Here and elsewhere, Huchel grants to the Soviets and the SED the cultural legitimation that he had sought to withhold from the Nazis. 'Das Gesetz' affirms that the balance between nature and the rural community has been established on a fresh and just basis due to the revolutionary changes in the ownership of the land. For a while, the stance of the independent artist was abandoned for a voice more confidently affirmative of social developments. Huchel sought to adjust his style to introduce a much more popular appeal, exchanging something of the esoteric for the accessible and, with that, a degree of subtlety for rhetorical effect. Yet, while subtlety was compromised, the rhetorical effect was not always convincing.

Other poems from the period follow the founding myth of 'Das Gesetz' in charting the establishment of the new rural order and concluding in the manner of a socialist pastoral. 'Dezembergang' (PH, 1, 295), for example, celebrates the end of a successful year on the land: 'Das Jahr, es gab uns Brot, nicht Steine. | Es gab dem Volk das ganze Korn.' 'In der Heimat' (PH, 1, 408) contains a similar scene of harmony between nature and rural activity:

> Schön ist die Heimat,
> Wenn über der grünen Messingscheibe
> Des Teichs der Kranich schreit
> Und das Gold sich häuft
> Im blauen Oktobergewölbe;
> Wenn Korn und Milch in der Kammer schlafen,
> Die rußige Schmiede des Alls
> Beginnt ihr Feuer zu schüren.

The magnificence of renewal is conveyed in the richness of colour, underpinned as in 'Das Gesetz' by a familiar metaphysic of elemental nature. It goes without saying that there is no sense that German culture has experienced a profound and irreversible fracture. Nature, aided by wise human action, acts as the fundamental source for regeneration.

Towards 1960: Protecting the Values of 1930

Yet the optimism that spawned the rhetorical confidence of the socialist pastoral was short-lived. The first stage of the Land Reform was a mere prelude to collectivisation. And the early phase of the GDR culminated in 17 June 1953, when Huchel survived as editor of *Sinn und Form* only thanks to Brecht's intervention.[39] Later that year, at the mid-point of the fifth issue Huchel published 'Eine Herbstnacht', a poem with quite different associations from the socialist pastoral. It signalled the poet's withdrawal from an affirmative position and his reversion to the voice of the 1930s, its blend of idyll and elegy responding to the poets of the *Biedermeierzeit*, here perhaps Mörike's 'Im Frühling':

> Wo bist du, damals sinkender Tag?
> Septemberhügel, auf dem ich lag
> Im jähen blätterstürzenden Wind,
> Doch ganz von der Ruhe der Bäume umschlungen. (PH, 1, 138)

'Eine Herbstnacht' forms a small group of publications from the mid-1950s, including 'Damals', 'Widmung: Für Hans Henny Jahnn' and 'Caputher Heuweg',

---

39 For a detailed discussion see Parker, *Peter Huchel*, pp. 321–39.

in which Huchel resumes his treatment of the rural childhood in the manner of 1930. In these poems, he imbues the theme of childhood with a richness and plenitude all the greater for the distance in time. With its line 'Wann war dieser Sommer? Ich weiß es nicht mehr', 'Caputher Heuweg' (PH, 1, 138) echoes 'Der glückliche Garten'. The ending of 'Damals' (PH, 1, 137) recalls 'Die Magd':

Der Hund schlug an, ich lauschte lange
Den Stimmen im Sturm und lehnte am Knie
Der schweigsam hockenden Klettenmarie,
Die in der Küche Wolle knäuelte.
Und wenn ihr grauer schläfernder Blick mich traf,
Durchwehte die Mauer des Hauses der Schlaf.

While these poems do not, of course, provide a comprehensive account of Huchel's stylistic development from the mid-1950s, they strikingly demonstrate the extent to which his trajectory of 1930 remains a significant factor. Other work from the mid-1950s includes not only the socialist pastoral, some of which continued to appear for a while, but also the most significant advance of these years, the publication in 1955 of 'Widmung: Für Ernst Bloch' (PH, 1, 134), which signals the direction that Huchel's verse would take for the rest of his life. Its opening lines read:

Herbst und die dämmernden Sonnen im Nebel
Und nachts am Himmel ein Feuerbild.
Es stürzt und weht. Du mußt es bewahren.

The opening of Trakl's nightmarish 'Grodek' is not far away. Gone is the affirmative tone of the early 1950s and the confident expectation of productive exchange and renewal. Gone, too, is the recall of the richness of experience in the poems of childhood. 'Widmung: Für Ernst Bloch' represents a first step by Huchel in the articulation of a more difficult stylistic orientation, resistant to ideological affirmation, that characterises much of *Chausseen Chausseen* and later collections. The poem draws a clear line between the realm of the thinker and the hunter in order to signal the need to escape the trap of collusion with power into which the poet had fallen in the Third Reich and the early GDR. Huchel draws upon imagery from his poetry from the 1930s and early 1940s such as 'Späte Zeit' in order to convey his sense of a world inhabited by dark forces preying upon the vulnerable:

Am Hohlweg wechselt schnell das Wild.
Und wie ein Hall aus fernen Jahren
Dröhnt über Wälder weit ein Schuß.
Es schweifen wieder die Unsichtbaren.

The poem contrasts the rapacious activity of the hunter with that of the thinker, whose path brings him close to the 'goldne[n] Rauch' that recalls Hölderlin's verse. The thinker is granted privileged insight into the deeper workings of the world: 'Er ahnt, was noch die Nacht verschweigt.' Huchel explained that the words 'Du mußt es bewahren' referred to the thinker's role in protecting eternal values at a time of great turmoil and threat.[40] The thinker takes his place with the 'späteste Söhne' of the 1930s in protecting humanist values under threat. If the message is not very different from the poems of the late 1930s, its articulation is now much sparer, much more allusive, making demands on the reader beyond earlier publications, as the nature poet abandons elements of stylistic facility that, in the context of the dictatorships, had bred compromise and disillusion.

While *Gedichte* culminates in hope rekindled after fascism, *Chausseen Chausseen* conveys the painful articulation of the illusory nature of that hope. As we have seen, the collection is introduced by the words from St Augustine that Huchel had first used in 1932. When in 1959 Huchel was honoured by Haas, he reflected: 'Der "große Hof des Gedächtnisses, daselbst Himmel, Erde und Meer gegenwärtig sind", kann nicht nur verfinstert werden – er kann ausgelöscht werden' (PH, 2, 300). That possibility is rehearsed again and again in *Chausseen Chausseen*. Until the mid-1950s, the regenerative powers of a magically conceived nature remained a cornerstone in Huchel's poetics. The collection contains remnants of *Naturmagie*, as moments of visionary energy are captured, as in the beautifully understated imagist poem 'Unter der Kiefer' (PH, 1, 139):

> Nadeln ohne Öhr,
> Der Nebel zieht
> Die weißen Fäden ein.
> Fischgräten,
> In den Sand gescharrt.
> Mit Katzenpfoten
> Klettert der Efeu
> Den Stamm hinauf.

On occasion, the visionary quality is somewhat forced, as in 'Auffliegende Schwäne' (PH, 1, 139), which breach the early-morning darkness of the Brandenburg lake:

> Ein jähes Weiß,
> Mit Füßen und Flügeln das Wasser peitschend,
> Facht an den Wind. Sie fliegen auf,
> Die winterbösen Majestäten.
> Es pfeift metallen.
> Duck dich ins Röhricht.
> Schneidende Degen sind ihre Federn.

The first two sections of the collection include verse treating landscapes and people that act as a counterpoint to Brandenburg, particularly the ancient and contemporary Mediterranean world, as Huchel re-immerses himself in mythology and mysticism. From this point on, Greek and Roman mythology figure prominently in his verse, as does the Bible. Poems such as 'Chiesa de Soccorso'

---

40   See Parker, *Peter Huchel*, p. 356.

(PH, 1, 121) leave behind secular socialism in a spiritual search pre-occupied with the problem of death. The poem explores the fate of souls within the Saviour's sphere of influence: 'Odem der salzigen Brandung | Erquicke die Seelen.' Yet here, as in other poems such as 'Monterosso' ,orthodox religion yields no answers. Increasingly, the topos of silence comes to the fore.

Huchel quite pointedly opens the collection with a new type of Brandenburg poem, 'Das Zeichen' (PH, 1, 113). The title signals a resumption of Huchel's dialogue with Eich from the 1930s and provides a telling counterpoint to the dazzling play of 'Zeichen' that we saw in the opening section of 'Die Herbstkantate'. 'Das Zeichen' evokes a hostile, frozen world without any trace of the magical, creative potential found in the poet's earlier reading of the book of nature. The poem begins:

Baumkahler Hügel,
Noch einmal flog
Am Abend die Wildentenkette
Durch wäßrige Herbstluft.

War es das Zeichen?

It ends:

Wer schrieb
Die warnende Schrift,
Kaum zu entziffern?
Ich fand sie am Pfahl,
Dicht hinter dem See.
War es das Zeichen?

Erstarrt
Im Schweigen des Schnees,
Schlief blind
Das Kreuzotterndickicht.

This frozen landscape contains an enigmatic, yet deadly potential which the poetic voice records, as he surveys the scene, an alien in a world emptied of meaning that he had previously claimed as his own.

The rhetorical confidence of the early 1950s is present only when the poet slips into the masks of figures from classical literature or employs allusions to biblical, historical or mythological sources in order to project a seemingly timeless voice prophetic of doom. The ominous potential for destruction hangs over the whole collection. It concludes with these famous lines from 'Psalm' (PH, 1, 157):

Die Öde wird Geschichte.
Termiten schreiben sie
Mit ihren Zangen
In den Sand.

Und nicht erforscht wird werden
Ein Geschlecht,

Eifrig bemüht,
Sich zu vernichten.

'Psalm' and 'Das Zeichen' provide a framework for the collection, while at its very centre Huchel placed the four poems of childhood from the mid-1950s, 'Caputher Heuweg', 'Damals', 'Eine Herbstnacht' and 'Widmung: Für Hans Henny Jahnn'. Their position demands that they are read in relation to other poems in the collection, thereby pointing up the contrast between the idyllic richness of the style of 1930 with its dazzling metaphors and the lament over an icy, impoverished world emptied of meaning, to which a slow-moving, warning voice bears witness. This work sees the nature poet of 1930 approaching an end point in his development that would be reached with *Gezählte Tage* and *Die neunte Stunde*. The contrast between these collections of the 1970s and the publications of writers who had come to the fore in East and West since 1960 was stark: they were read as belonging to a different age from the new radicalism of the 1960s and early 1970s, when nature poetry was viewed in many quarters simply as an anachronism. Equally, this work highlights the divergent trajectory taken by Huchel in the 1960s in comparison to Eich who, after 1945, supplemented his own brand of hermetic poetry with a form of social engagement and, in the late 1960s, with the remarkable linguistic innovation of the *Maulwürfe*. While Huchel responded to the post-war decades with a return to the idiom of 1930 and a relatively straightforward re-establishment of the *Dichter*, Eich responded to this period of re-appraisal rather differently, managing to extend that idiom and to reconcile the role of *Dichter* with the social and cultural realities of the 1960s.

In addition to 'Psalm', the final section of *Chausseen Chausseen* contains in 'Winterpsalm', 'An taube Ohren der Geschlechter' and 'Traum im Tellereisen' some of Huchel's finest, late verse. In 'Der Garten des Theophrast' (PH, 1, 155), Huchel draws on the figure of the Greek philosopher Theophrastus in order to lament the mindless destruction of a fragile culture nurtured with dedication and creative intelligence. As in 'Widmung: Für Ernst Bloch', the imperative remains the defence of the intellect against forces hostile to the cultivation of civilised exchange. This time, the poem is dedicated to Huchel's son, who is similarly encouraged, 'Bewahre die Stunde'. Yet the struggle has become hopeless: 'Sie gaben Befehl, die Wurzel zu roden. Es sinkt dein Licht, schutzloses Laub.'

Conclusion

In the successive crises that mark the early to mid-decades of the last century, Huchel did not attempt any fundamental break with his artistic values and their stylistic expression. He shared a common starting-point around 1930 with other young poets in a search for stability in the new, restorative mood, which led them to turn to the potential of the tradition. Huchel's development is shaped by his abiding attachment to Haas's strong promotion of the tradition within the established bourgeois institution of literature. Huchel followed Haas in distinguishing the realm of the *Dichter* with his civilising mission from a politicised understanding of art and from the massification of culture. The richness of Huchel's vision of a magical nature is conveyed by a distinctive blend of idyll and elegy. Yet Huchel could not maintain the purity of his practice. His response to his compromises with politics and mass culture in the Third Reich and the GDR was to re-affirm his commitment to the values of 1930. The imperilled status of those values is reflected in his creation from the mid-1950s of a more difficult, allusive poetic voice in which the elegy is barely interrupted. In the 1960s, when Huchel's trajectory was nearing completion, new writers in the East and the West pursued a fresh radicalism, showing only limited interest in the thematic and stylistic path followed by Huchel in the light of his watershed experiences around 1930.

Conclusion

Using as our starting-point the thesis of Schäfer, Trommler and others that the years 1930–1960 represent a stylistically distinct period in German literary history, we set out in our study to test our own thesis that the middle decades of the twentieth century are characterised by a prevailing literary mood which we have the labelled the 'modern restoration'. We conceptualised this restorative literary climate in terms of three key elements: the re-assertion of the conventional institution of literature; the search for stability of meaning; and the on-going mood of crisis. The procedure that we have followed permitted us first to examine synchronically a cross-section of journals from those years, which we divided into three phases: at and around 1930; 1933–1945; and 1945–1960. We can now bring together the findings from those three phases, before we consider the second element in our procedure, the diachronic examination of five authors active in literary life during the years 1930–1960.

The chapter devoted to journals from 1930–1933 reveals the paradigm shift from a residual experimental modernism towards a restorative dominant, in which the bourgeois institution of literature founded on quality and tradition is re-asserted by editors and embraced by a new generation of writers. Prominent among them are the poets who engaged in the renewal of nature poetry. The journals from 1933–1945 all bear the hallmark of a period in which the transition from one cultural mood to another has been completed: the tradition is accepted as a given rather than being regarded as something that must be established in the face of a seemingly traditionless modernity. It has become a matter of protecting the tradition and the values that it is seen to embody from ideological enemies. The journals from 1945–1960 continue to privilege a language that was forged in the upheavals of the late 1920s and early 1930s. The notion of crisis is not formed anew in the aftermath of the defeat of National Socialist Germany, but is rather adapted to the new conditions, drawing on well-established ways of thinking. What is new is that in the immediate post-war years writers across the political spectrum have a sense of the social significance of those values as a means of guaranteeing that politics is conducted in a humane, responsible manner. Yet that attitude, frequently couched in terms of the kind of moral fervour characteristic of the *Gruppe 47*, does not fundamentally challenge the assumptions of the restorative period. Indeed, these rhetorical gestures of the immediate post-war years are shown in a very different light within the trajectory which we have traced back to 1930. Taken together, the three chapters chart the establishment of the restorative mood, its general acceptance and its enduring ascendancy until the 1960s.

The diachronic study of our five authors was designed to explore their engagement with this restorative mood, how they contributed to it – be it through their programme, practice, or reception – and how they negotiated their divergence from it. The perspective that they bring to bear is intimately connected to the particular trajectory of their artistic development. In the case of Benn and Becher, that trajectory was traced to their background in, respectively, Expressionism and Futurism, which remains a factor throughout their careers. Both are drawn towards the restorative mood, but despite its attractions, and in Benn's case a reception that portrayed him as its champion, neither fully commits to it artistically. In many respects, Brecht's reception is the antithesis of Benn's. Brecht lives up in large measure to his portrayal as the radical iconoclast of the conventional bourgeois institution of literature, particularly through his resolute insistence on the dialogic use-value of poetry. Yet, Brecht's development is more complex. Not only does his literary practice defy the label of avant-gardist modernism where that is understood in terms of the disruption and problematisation of meaning, but Brecht's aesthetic development also reveals a gradual and relative shift towards prestige-value through and after his exile years. By contrast, Eich and Huchel are much more the creatures of 1930 in their programmatic statements and their artistic practice, even if they each undertake a re-appraisal of that practice after 1945. The values they proclaim at the outset are consistent with the turn towards an elitist view of literature and the poet. Huchel's stylistic choices until the 1960s continue to locate him within the 1930 paradigm to an extent that surpasses even Eich. Equally, while Huchel's stylistic development is essentially complete by the end of our period, Eich goes on, paradoxically, to embody the shift away from the restorative mood undertaken in the mid- to late 1960s. Critical reception emerges as often a more powerful force in maintaining or re-assessing the prevailing literary climate than does the practice of individual writers.

One of the most striking findings to emerge from our approach is the enduring centrality throughout our period of the *Bildungsdialekt* of the educated middle classes. Bourgeois cultural values inform thinking in the literary world across political viewpoints to an extent that *Germanistik* has hitherto not acknowledged. However problematic their legacy, it is clearly no longer adequate to dismiss the contribution of middle-class cultural values as at best reactionary, decadent and nationalist.[1] Our findings will be less surprising for some students of German social and cultural history, which has been pre-occupied by a re-evaluation of the role of the *Bürgertum*, recently described by Matthew Jefferies as 'that much-maligned section of German society whose failings have been

---

1   See, for example, Georg Bollenbeck, *Tradition, Avantgarde, Reaktion: Deutsche Kontroversen um die kulturelle Moderne 1880–1945* (Frankfurt a.M.: Fischer, 1999).

castigated by generations of historians'.[2] If, as Jefferies claims, studies of high culture in Wilhelmine Germany remain disappointingly wedded to the tired caricatures of a retreat into inwardness and of the 'cultural pessimism' of the educated middle class, they ignore the immense energy expended by the *Bildungsbürgertum* in the realm of aesthetic culture, an appreciation of which is essential to the analysis of the *Kaiserreich*. That evaluation holds good, too, for the years 1930–1960, when an essentially middle-class system of aesthetic values was deployed in publications as politically diverse as *Das Wort* and *Das innere Reich*. Nor, for that matter, have those values disappeared from view in post-unification Germany. For example, in negotiating the transition from the GDR to the new Federal Republic as 'eine dynamische Mitte im Geistesleben', *Sinn und Form* deployed a vocabulary which fits not only with the journal's own tradition but with that of other 'thick' journals which reflect the dominant mood of the mid-decades of the twentieth century.[3]

We are aware that the tightly drawn parameters of our study leave many questions open. Clearly, more work needs to be done on journals and writers from our period in order to test the validity of our findings. In particular, our choice of five canonical male authors leaves open the question of women authors who were active during the period, among them Anna Seghers, Marieluise Fleißer, Marie Luise Kaschnitz and Elisabeth Langgässer. The typological potential of the thesis could be explored in a number of ways, most obviously with regard to other arts in Germany or to literary developments viewed internationally. To re-consider the years 1930–1960 implies scope for re-evaluation of what came before and after in twentieth-century German literary historiography. To do so, we would argue, requires a methodology which takes account of a number of hitherto somewhat neglected literary-historical factors which have occupied the foreground of our own study: firstly, the empirical analysis of the multiple processes of cultural change conceived in terms of continuity rather then abrupt rupture; secondly, an appreciation of the constitutive role of literary journals in these processes at the expense of the traditional sequencing of book publications; and finally, the importance of the positive and dynamic contribution made to cultural developments by a middle-class value system which has too often been written off in existing accounts of twentieth-century German literary history.

2   Matthew Jefferies, *Imperial Culture in Germany 1871–1918* (Basingstoke: Palgrave, 2003), p. 4.
3   The words are those of Sebastian Kleinschmidt. See Stephen Parker, 'Re-establishing an all-German Identity: *Sinn und Form* and German unification', in Osman Durrani et al (eds), *Literature and Society in Germany since 1989* (Sheffield: University of Sheffield Press, 1995), pp. 14–27 (p. 27).

Select Bibliography

Primary corpus material

Journals

Die literarische Welt: Unabhängiges Organ für das deutsche Schrifttum
    1 (1925) – 9 (1933)
    Reprint edition. Nendeln: Kraus Reprint, 1973
Die Linkskurve
    1 (1929) – 4 (1932)
    Reprint edition. Frankfurt a.M.: Materialismus, 1976-1980
Die Kolonne: Zeitschrift für Dichtung
    1 (1929–30) – 3 (1932)
Das innere Reich: Zeitschrift für Dichtung, Kunst und deutsches Leben
    1 (1934–35) – 11 (1944–45)
    Microfiche edition. Erlangen: Fischer, 1998
Maß und Wert: Zweimonatsschrift für freie deutsche Kultur
    1 (1937) – 4 (1940)
Das Wort: Literarische Monatsschrift
    1 (1936) – 4 (1939)
    Reprint edition. Berlin: Rütten & Loening, 1968
Der Ruf: Zeitung der Deutschen Kriegsgefangenen in den USA
    1 (1 March 1945) – 26 (1 April 1946)
    Reprint edition. Munich: Saur, 1986
Der Ruf: Unabhängige Blätter der jungen Generation
    1 (1946) – 3 (1948)
Aufbau: Kulturpolitische Monatsschrift
    1 (1945) – 14 (1958)
Merkur: Deutsche Zeitschrift für europäisches Denken
    1 (1947) –
Sinn und Form: Beiträge zur Literatur
    1 (1948) –

Authors

Benn, Gottfried, *Gesammelte Werke in der Fassung der Erstdrucke*, ed. by Bruno Hillebrand, 4 vols (Frankfurt a.M.: Fischer, 1982)

Benn, Gottfried, *Briefe an F. W. Oelze 1932–1945*, ed. by Harald Steinhagen and Jürgen Schröder (Wiesbaden and Munich: Limes Verlag, 1977)

Becher, Johannes R., *Gesammelte Werke*, 18 vols (Berlin and Weimar: Johannes-R.-Becher-Archiv der Akademie der Künste, 1966–1981)

Becher, Johannes R., *Briefwechsel 1909–1958*, ed. by Rolf Harder, 2 vols (Berlin and Weimar: Aufbau, 1993)

Brecht, Bertolt, *Werke. Große kommentierte Berliner und Frankfurter Ausgabe*, ed. by Werner Hecht, Jan Knopf, Werner Mittenzwei, and Klaus-Detlef Müller, 30 vols (Berlin and Weimar: Aufbau; Frankfurt a.M: Suhrkamp, 1988–1998)

Eich, Günter, *Gesammelte Werke in vier Bänden*, ed. by Karl Karst and Axel Vieregg, 4 vols (Frankfurt a.M.: Suhrkamp, 1991)

Eich, Günter, *Rebellion in der Goldstadt: Tonkassette, Text und Materialien* (Frankfurt a.M.: Suhrkamp, 1997)

Huchel, Peter, *Gesammelte Werke*, ed. by Axel Vieregg, 2 vols (Frankfurt a.M.: Suhrkamp, 1984)

Huchel, Peter, *Wie soll man da Gedichte schreiben: Briefe 1925–1977*, ed. by Hub Nijssen (Frankfurt a.M.: Suhrkamp, 2000)

Secondary Sources

General

Atkinson, Jeanette, *Traditional Forms in German Poetry 1930–1945* (Ann Arbor: University Microfilms International, 1983)

Dolan, Joseph P., *Die Rolle der 'Kolonne' in der Entwicklung der modernen deutschen Naturlyrik* (Ann Arbor: Xerox University Microfilms, 1976)

Dolan, Joseph P., 'The Theory and Practice of Apolitical Literature: *Die Kolonne* 1929–1932', *Studies in Twentieth-Century Literature*, 1 (1977), 157–71

Frühwald, Wolfgang, 'Büchmann und die Folgen: Zur sozialen Funktion des Bildungszitates in der deutschen Literatur des 19. Jahrhunderts', in Reinhart Koselleck (ed.), *Bildungsbürgertum im 19. Jahrhundert, Teil II: Bildungsgüter und Bildungswissen* (Stuttgart: Klett–Cotta, 1990), pp. 197–219

Hüppauf, Bernd, 'Krise ohne Wandel: Die kulturelle Situation 1945–1949', in Bernd Hüppauf (ed.), *'Die Mühen der Ebenen': Kontinuität und Wandel in der deutschen Literatur und Gesellschaft 1945–1949* (Heidelberg: Winter, 1981), pp. 47–112

Hüppauf, Bernd, 'Einleitung: Schwierigkeiten mit der Nachkriegszeit', in Bernd Hüppauf (ed.) *'Die Mühen der Ebenen': Kontinuität und Wandel in der deutschen Literatur und Gesellschaft 1945–1949* (Heidelberg: Winter, 1981), pp. 7–20

Kaes, Anton, *Weimarer Republik: Manifeste und Dokumente zur deutschen Literatur 1918–1933* (Stuttgart: Metzler, 1983)

Korte, Hermann, 'Lyrik am Ende der Weimarer Republik', in Rolf Grimminger (ed.), *Hansers Sozialgeschichte der deutschen Literatur vom 16. Jahrhundert bis zur Gegenwart*, 12 vols, VIII: *Literatur der Weimarer Republik 1918–1933*, ed. by Bernhard Weyergraf (Munich: Hanser, 1995), pp. 601–35

Olschner, Leonard, 'Fractured Continuities: Pressures on lyrical tradition at mid-century', *German Studies Review*, 13 (1990), 417–40

Schäfer, Hans Dieter, 'Stilgeschichtlicher Ort und historische Zeit in Johannes R. Bechers Exildichtungen', in Manfred Durzak (ed.), *Die deutsche Exilliteratur 1933–1945* (Stuttgart: Reclam, 1973), pp. 358–72

Schäfer, Hans Dieter, 'Naturdichtung und Neue Sachlichkeit', in Wolfgang Rothe (ed.), *Die deutsche Literatur in der Weimarer Republik* (Stuttgart: Reclam, 1974), pp. 359–81

Schäfer, Hans Dieter, 'Die nichtfaschistische Literatur der jungen Generation im nationalsozialistischen Deutschland', in Horst Denkler and Karl Prümm (eds), *Die deutsche Literatur in Dritten Reich: Themen, Traditionen, Wirkungen* (Stuttgart: Reclam, 1976), pp. 459–503

Schäfer, Hans Dieter, 'Zur Periodisierung der deutschen Literatur seit 1930', in Nicolas Born and Jürgen Manthey (eds), *Literaturmagazin 7: Nachkriegsliteratur* (Reinbek: Rowohlt, 1977), pp. 95–115

Schäfer, Hans Dieter, *Das gespaltene Bewußtsein: Über deutsche Kultur und Lebens-wirklichkeit 1933–1945* (Munich: Hanser, 1981)

Sengle, Friedrich, *Biedermeierzeit: Deutsche Literatur im Spannungsfeld von Restauration und Revolution 1815–1848*, 3 vols (Stuttgart: Metzler, 1971–1980)

Trommler, Frank, 'Der "Nullpunkt 1945" und seine Verbindlichkeit für die Literaturgeschichte, *Basis: Jahrbuch für deutsche Gegenwartsliteratur*, 1 (1970), 9–25

Trommler, Frank, 'Emigration und Nachkriegsliteratur: Zum Problem der geschichtlichen Kontinuität', in Reinhold Grimm and Jost Hermand (eds), *Exil und innere Emigration: Third Wisconsin Workshop* (Frankfurt a.M.: Athenäum, 1972), pp. 173–97

Trommler, Frank, 'Nachkriegsliteratur: Eine neue deutsche Literatur?' in Nicolas Born and Jürgen Manthey (eds), *Literaturmagazin 7: Nachkriegsliteratur* (Reinbek: Rowohlt, 1977), pp. 67–86

Vormweg, Heinrich, 'Deutsche Literatur 1945–1960: Keine Stunde Null', in Manfred Durzak (ed.), *Die deutsche Literatur der Gegenwart: Aspekte und Tendenzen* (Stuttgart: Reclam, 1971), pp. 13–30

Literary journals at 1930

Barck, Simone, 'Achtung vor dem Material: Zur dokumentarischen Schreibweise bei Ernst Ottwalt', in Silvia Schlenstedt (ed.), *Wer schreibt, handelt: Strategien und Verfahren literarischer Arbeit vor und nach 1933* (Aufbau: Berlin, 1986), pp. 84–118

Berman, Russell, 'Lukács' Critique of Bredel and Ottwalt: A political account of an aesthetic debate of 1931–32', *New German Critique*, 10 (1977), 155–78

Burschka, Manfred H., *Indices zu 'Die literarische Welt': 1925–1933*, 2 vols (Nendeln: Kraus-Thomson, 1976)

Cohen, Robert, 'Die gefährliche Ästhetik Ernst Ottwalts', *The German Quarterly*, 61 (1988), 229–48

Deutsche Akademie der Künste (ed.), *Zur Tradition der sozialistischen Literatur in Deutschland: Eine Auswahl von Dokumenten* (Aufbau: Berlin, 1967)

Gallas, Helga, *Marxistische Literaturtheorie: Kontroversen im Bund proletarisch-revolutionärer Schriftsteller* (Neuwied: Luchterhand, 1971)

Haas, Willy, *Gestalten* (Frankfurt a.M.: Ullstein, 1963)

Haas, Willy (ed.), *Zeitgemäßes aus 'Der literarischen Welt'* (Stuttgart: Cotta, 1963), pp. 477–90

Kliche, Dieter and Gerhard Seidel (eds), *'Die Linkskurve': Berlin 1929–1932: Bibliographie einer Zeitschrift* (Berlin: Aufbau, 1972)

Schiller, Dieter, 'Goethe in den geistigen Kämpfen um 1932: Über die Goethe-Nummern der Zeitschriften *Die neue Rundschau* und *Die Linkskurve* im April 1932', *Goethe Jahrbuch*, 103 (1986), 54–72

Schlawe, Fritz, *Literarische Zeitschriften 1910–1933* (Stuttgart: Metzler, 1962)

Schlenstedt, Silvia, 'Schnittpunkt 1930: Standort und Funktion des Schriftstellers in der großen Krise', in Silvia Schlenstedt (ed.), *Wer schreibt, handelt: Strategien und Verfahren literarischer Arbeit vor und nach 1933* (Aufbau: Berlin, 1986), pp. 11–52

Valentini, Luisa, *Willy Haas: Der Zeuge einer Epoche* (Frankfurt a.M.: Lang, 1986), pp. 102–03

Literary journals 1933–1945

Baltensweiler, Thomas, *'Maß und Wert': Die Exilzeitschrift von Thomas Mann and Konrad Falke* (Bern: Lang, 1996)

Denkler, Horst, 'Janusköpfig: Zur ideologischen Physiognomie der Zeitschrift *Das innere Reich* (1934–1944)', in Horst Denkler and Karl Prümm (eds), *Die deutsche Literatur im Dritten Reich* (Stuttgart: Metzler, 1976), pp. 383–405

Huß-Michel, Angela, *Literarische und politische Zeitschriften des Exils 1933–1945* (Stuttgart: Metzler, 1987)

Huß-Michel, Angela, *Die Moskauer Zeitschriften 'Internationale Literatur' und 'Das Wort' während der Exil-Volksfront (1936–1939)* (Frankfurt a.M.: Lang, 1987)

Jameson, Fredric (ed.), *Aesthetics and Politics* (London: Verso, 1980)

Maas, Liselotte, *Handbuch der deutschen Exilpresse 1933–1945*, IV: *Die Zeitungen des deutschen Exils in Europa von 1933 bis 1939 in Einzeldarstellungen* (Munich: Hanser, 1981)

Mallmann, Marion, *'Das innere Reich': Analyse einer konservativen Kulturzeitschrift im Dritten Reich* (Bonn: Bouvier, 1978)

Riedel, Volker, *'Maß und Wert': Zurich 1937–1940: Bibliographie einer Zeitschrift* (Berlin: Aufbau, 1973)

Schmitt, Hans-Jürgen (ed.), *Die Expressionismus-Debatte: Materialien zu einer marxist-ischen Realismuskonzeption* (Frankfurt a.M.: Suhrkamp, 1973)

Schmollinger, Annette, *'Intra muros et extra': Deutsche Literatur im Exil und in der Inneren Emigration, ein exemplarischer Vergleich* (Heidelberg: Winter, 1999)

Seidel, Gerhard, *'Das Wort': Moskau 1936–1939: Bibliographie einer Zeitschrift* (Berlin: Aufbau, 1975)

Sprecher, Thomas, *Thomas Mann in Zürich* (Zurich: Fink, 1992)

Volke, Werner, *'Das Innere Reich': 1934–1944: Eine 'Zeitschrift fur Dichtung, Kunst und deutsches Leben'* (Marbach: Deutsche Schillergesellschaft, 1983)

Walter, Hans-Albert, *Deutsche Exilliteratur 1933–1950*, IV: *Exilpresse* (Stuttgart: Metzler, 1978)

Westhoff, Adelheid (ed.), *'Das Innere Reich' 1934–1944: Eine 'Zeitschrift fur Dichtung, Kunst und deutsches Leben': Verzeichnis der Beiträge* (Marbach: Deutsche Schiller-gesellschaft, 1983)

Post-1945 literary journals

Barck, Simone, Martina Langermann and Siegfried Lokatis, *Jedes Buch ein Abenteuer: Zensur-System und literarische Öffentlichkeiten in der DDR bis Ende der sechziger Jahre* (Berlin: Akademie-Verlag, 1998)

Bohrer, Karl Heinz, 'Hans Paeschke und der *Merkur*. Erinnerung und Gegenwart', *Merkur*, 45 (1991), 991–96

Brelie-Lewien, Doris von der and Ingrid Laurien, *Politisch-kulturelle Zeitschriften in den Westzonen 1945-1949: Ein Beitrag zur politischen Kultur der Nachkriegszeit* (Frankfurt: Lang, 1991)

Flanagan, Clare, *A Study of German political-cultural Periodicals from the Years of allied Occupation 1945–1949* (Lampeter: Mellen, 2000)

Hay, Gerhard (ed.), *Zur literarischen Situation 1945–1949* (Kronberg: Athenäum, 1977)

Hay, Gerhard (ed.), '*Als der Krieg zu Ende war*': *Literarisch-politische Publizistik 1945–1950* (Marbach: Deutsches Literaturarchiv, 1986)

Hermand, Jost, Helmut Peitsch, Klaus R. Scherpe (eds), *Nachkriegsliteratur in Westdeutschland 1945–49: Schreibweisen, Gattungen, Institutionen* (Berlin: Argument, 1983), pp. 6–35

King, Janet, *Literarische Zeitschriften 1945–1970* (Stuttgart: Metzler, 1970)

Kleßmann, Christoph, '"Das Haus wurde gebaut aus den Steinen, die vorhanden waren": Zur kulturgeschichtlichen Kontinuität nach 1945', *Tel Aviver Jahrbuch für deutsche Zeitgeschichte*, 29 (1990), 159–77

Mayer, Hans, 'Erinnerungen eines Mitarbeiters von *Sinn und Form*', in Hans Mayer (ed.), *Über Peter Huchel* (Frankfurt a.M.: Suhrkamp, 1973), pp. 173–80

Parker, Stephen, 'Peter Huchel und *Sinn und Form*', *Sinn und Form*, 44 (1992), 724–39

Parker, Stephen, '*Sinn und Form* unter Wilhelm Girnus', *Sinn und Form*, 51 (1999), 87–106

Parker, Stephen, 'Der Erkenntniswert von Dokumenten bei der Erforschung der Geschichte von *Sinn und Form* 1949–1989', in Helmut Kiesel and Corina Caduff (eds), *Akten des X. Internationalen Germanistenkongresses Wien 2000* (Frankfurt a.M.: Lang, 2002), pp. 33–38

Scheibe, Siegfried (ed.), '*Aufbau*': *Berlin 1945-1958: Bibliographie einer Zeitschrift* (Berlin: Aufbau, 1978)

Schmitt, Hans-Jürgen, 'Literaturbetrieb als Staatsmonopol', in Hans-Jürgen Schmitt (ed.), *Die Literatur der DDR* (Munich: Hanser, 1983)

Schoor, Uwe, *Das geheime Journal einer Nation: Die Zeitschrift 'Sinn und Form': Chefredakteur Peter Huchel 1949–1962* (Berlin: Lang, 1992)

Seibt, Gustav, 'Das Prinzip Abstand: Fünfzig Jahre *Sinn und Form*', *Sinn und Form*, 51 (1999), 205–18

Vaillant, Jerome, '*Der Ruf: Unabhängige Blätter der jungen Generation*' *(1945–1949): Eine Zeitschrift zwischen Illusion und Anpassung* (Munich: Saur, 1978)

Veit, Walter, 'Die Stunde Null im Spiegel einiger zeitgenössischer Zeitschriften', in Bernd Hüppauf (ed.), '*Die Mühen der Ebenen*': *Kontinuität und Wandel in der deutschen Literatur und Gesellschaft 1945–1949* (Heidelberg: Winter, 1981), pp. 195–232

Gottfried Benn

Bergner, Klaus-Dieter, *Natur und Technik in der Literatur des frühen Expressionismus: Dargestellt an ausgewählten Prosabeispielen von Alfred Döblin, Gottfried Benn und Carl Einstein* (Frankfurt a.M.: Lang, 1998)

Dierick, Augustinus P., *Gottfried Benn and his Critics: Major Interpretations 1912–1992* (Columbia: Camden House, 1992)

Hillebrand, Bruno (ed.), *Über Gottfried Benn: Kritische Stimmen 1912–1956* (Frankfurt a.M.: Fischer, 1987)

Ridley, Hugh, *Gottfried Benn: Ein Schriftsteller zwischen Erneuerung und Reaktion* (Opladen: Westdeutscher Verlag, 1990)

Roche, Mark William, *Gottfried Benn's Static Poetry* (Chapel Hill: University of North Carolina Press, 1991)

Schlemmer, Oskar, *Briefe und Tagebücher*, ed. by Tut Schlemmer (Munich: Langen-Müller, 1958)

Willems, Gottfried, *Großstadt- und Bewußtseinspoesie: Über Realismus in der modernen Lyrik, insbesondere im lyrischen Spätwerk Gottfried Benns und in der deutschen Lyrik seit 1965* (Tübingen : Niemeyer, 1981)

Johannes R. Becher

Davies, Peter, 'Johannes R. Becher and the *Kulturnation*', in Clare Flanagan and Stuart Taberner (eds), *1949/1989: Cultural perspectives on division and unity in East and West* (Amsterdam: Rodopi, 2000), pp. 27–42

Davies, Peter, 'Die Überwindung der Sprache: Johannes R. Bechers Weg in die Partei', in Stefan Neuhaus, Rolf Selbmann and Thorsten Unger (eds), *Engagierte Literatur zwischen den Weltkriegen*, Schriften der Ernst-Toller-Gesellschaft (Würzburg: Königshausen & Neumann, 2002), pp. 277–85

Demetz, Peter, *Worte in Freiheit: Der italienische Futurismus und die deutsche literarische Avantgarde, 1912–1934* (Munich: Piper, 1990)

Demetz, Peter, 'The Futurist Johannes R. Becher', *Modernism/Modernity*, 1.3 (1994), 179–94

Dwars, Jens-Fietje, *Abgrund des Widerspruchs: Das Leben des Johannes R. Becher* (Berlin: Aufbau, 1998)

Gansel, Carsten (ed.), *Metamorphosen eines Dichters: Johannes R. Becher: Gedichte, Briefe, Dokumente 1909–1945* (Berlin: Aufbau, 1991)

Gansel, Carsten (ed.), *Der Gespaltene Dichter: Johannes R. Becher: Gedichte, Briefe, Dokumente 1945–1958* (Berlin: Aufbau, 1991)

Gansel, Carsten, *Parlament des Geistes: Literatur zwischen Hoffnung und Repression, 1945–1961* (Berlin: BasisDruck Verlag, 1996)

Hopster, Norbert, *Das Frühwerk Johannes R. Bechers* (Bonn: Bouvier, 1969)

Kulturbund der DDR, *Das poetische Prinzip Johannes R. Bechers: die sozialistische Gesellschaft und ihre Literatur: Ergebnisse des 5. Kolloquiums des Zentralen Arbeitskreises Johannes R. Becher am 5. und 6. Dezember 1980 in Berlin* (Berlin: Kulturbund der DDR, 1981)

Müller, Reinhard (ed.), *Die Säuberung: Moskau 1936: Stenogramm einer geschlossenen Parteiversammlung: Georg Lukács, Johannes R. Becher, Friedrich Wolf u.a.* (Reinbek: Rowohlt, 1991)

Pike, David, *The Politics of Culture in Soviet-Occupied Germany 1945–1949* (Stanford: Stanford University Press, 1992)

Rohrwasser, Michael, *Der Weg nach oben: Johannes R. Becher: Politiken des Schreibens* (Basel: Stroemfeld; Frankfurt a.M.: Verlag Roter Stern, 1980)

Rohrwasser, Michael, 'Das rettende Rußland: Erweckungserlebnisse des jungen Johannes R. Becher', in Gerd Koenen and Lew Kopelew (eds), *Deutschland und die Russische Revolution* (Munich: Fink, 1998), pp. 462–81

Vollmer, Jörg, 'Gift/Gas oder das Phantasma der reinigenden Gewalt: Johannes R. Becher, *(CH Cl = CH)₃ As (Levisite) oder Der einzig gerechte Krieg*', in Thomas Schneider and Hans Wagener (eds), *Von Richtofen bis Remarque: Deutschsprachige Prosa zum 1. Weltkrieg*, (Amsterdam and New York: Rodopi, 2003), pp. 181–93

Bertolt Brecht

Häntzschel, Günter, 'Einfach kompliziert: Zu Bertolt Brechts Lyrik', in Hans-Jörg Knoblauch and Helmut Koopmann (eds), *Hundert Jahre Brecht: Brechts Jahrhundert?* (Tübingen: Stauffenberg, 1998), pp. 65–82

Hecht, Werner, 'Grund der Empörung über eine "ganz unerträgliche Behandlung": Brechts Stanislawski-Studium 1953', *Maske und Kothurn*, 33.3/4 (1987), 75–87

Hecht, Werner, *Brecht-Chronik: 1898–1956* (Frankfurt a.M.: Suhrkamp, 1997)

Jäger, Manfred, *Kultur und Politik in der DDR: 1945–1990* (Cologne: Edition Deutschland Archiv, 1995)

Knopf, Jan, *Gelegentlich: Poesie: Ein Essay über die Lyrik Bertolt Brechts* (Frankfurt a.M.: Suhrkamp, 1996)

Knopf, Jan (ed.), *Brecht Handbuch*, 5 vols (Stuttgart: Metzler, 2001–2003)

Knopf, Jan, *Brecht Handbuch: Eine Widersprüchliche Ästhetik*, 2 vols (Stuttgart: Metzler, 1980)

Kuhn, Tom and Karen Leeder (eds), *Empodecles' Shoe: Essays on Brecht's poetry* (London: Methuen, 2002)

Mittenzwei, Werner, *Brechts Verhältnis zur Tradition* (Berlin: Akademie-Verlag, 1974)

Mittenzwei, Werner, *Das Leben des Brecht: Oder der Umgang mit den Welträtseln*, 2 vols (Berlin: Aufbau Taschenbuch, 1997)

Mumford, Meg, 'Brecht Studies Stanislavsky: Just a Tactical Move?', *New Theatre Quarterly*, 11 (1995), 241–58

Philpotts, Matthew, '"Aus so prosaischen Dingen wie Kartoffeln, Straßen, Traktoren, werden poetische Dinge!"': Brecht, Strittmatter, and *Sinn und Form*', *German Life and Letters*, 56 (2003), 56–71.

Günter Eich

Cuomo, Glenn R., *Career at the Cost of Compromise: Günter Eich's life and work in the years 1933–1945* (Amsterdam: Rodopi, 1989)

Cuomo, Glenn R., 'Günter Eichs Rundfunkbeiträge in den Jahren 1933–1940: Eine kommentierte Neuaufstellung', *Rundfunk und Fernsehen*, 32 (1984), 83–96

Goß, Marlies, *Günter Eich und das Hörspiel der fünfziger Jahre* (Frankfurt a. M.: Lang, 1998)

Müller-Hanpft, Susanne (ed.), *Über Günter Eich* (Frankfurt a.M.: Suhrkamp, 1972)

Neumann, Peter Horst, *Die Rettung der Poesie im Unsinn: Der Anarchist Günter Eich* (Stuttgart: Klett–Cotta, 1981)

Philpotts, Matthew, *The Margins of Dictatorship: Assent and dissent in the work of Günter Eich and Bertolt Brecht* (Oxford: Lang, 2003)

Richardson, Larry L., *Committed Aestheticism: The poetic theory and practice of Günter Eich* (New York: Lang, 1983)

Schäfer, Hans Dieter, 'Zur Spätphase des hermetischen Gedichts', in Manfred Durzak (ed.), *Die deutsche Literatur der Gegenwart: Aspekte und Tendenzen* (Stuttgart: Reclam, 1971), pp. 148–69

Schäfer, Hans Dieter '"Nach Seumes Papieren': Über ein spätes Gedicht von Günter Eich', *Neue deutsche Hefte*, 137 (1973), 45–55

Schneider, Irmela, '"Fast alle haben vom Rundfunk gelebt": Hörspiele der 50er Jahre als literarische Formen', in Justus Fetscher et al (eds), *Die Gruppe 47 in der Geschichte der Bundesrepublik* (Würzburg: Königshausen & Neumann, 1991), pp. 203–17

Vieregg, Axel, *Der eigenen Fehlbarkeit begegnet: Günter Eichs Realitäten 1933–1945* (Eggingen: Edition Isele, 1991)

Vieregg, Axel (ed.), *'Unsere Sünden sind Maulwürfe': Die Günter-Eich-Debatte* (Amsterdam: Rodopi, 1996)

Peter Huchel

Bade, Wilfrid, *Kulturpolitische Aufgaben der deutschen Presse* (Berlin: Junker und Dünnhaupt, 1933)

Goldscheider, Ludwig (ed.), *Die schönsten deutschen Gedichte* (Vienna: Phaidon, 1932)

Haas, Willy, 'Ein Mann namens Peter Huchel', in Otto F. Best (ed.), *Hommage für Peter Huchel* (Munich: Piper, 1968)

Italiaander, Rolf, *Gedanken-Austausch*, ed. by Harald Kohtz et al (Düsseldorf: Droste, 1988)

Mayer, Hans (ed.), *Über Peter Huchel* (Frankfurt a.M.: Suhrkamp, 1973)

Parker, Stephen, 'Peter Huchel als Propagandist: Huchels 1940 entstandene Adaption von George Bernard Shaws "Die Greuel von Denshawai"', *Rundfunk und Fernsehen*, 39 (1991), 343–53

Parker, Stephen, 'Recent additions to the Peter Huchel Collection in the John Rylands University Library of Manchester', *Bulletin of the John Rylands University Library of Manchester*, 74.2 (1992), 85–125

Parker, Stephen, 'On Peter Huchel's adaptation of George Bernard Shaw's "Denshawai Horror" and related matters', *Neophilologus*, 79 (1995), 295–306

Parker, Stephen, *Peter Huchel: A literary life in twentieth-century Germany* (Bern: Lang, 1998)

Schaefer, Oda, *Auch wenn du träumst, gehen die Uhren* (Munich: Piper, 1970)

Vieregg, Axel (ed.), *Peter Huchel: Materialien* (Frankfurt a.M.: Suhrkamp, 1986)

Walther, Peter (ed.), *Am Tage meines Fortgehns: Peter Huchel 1903–1981* (Frankfurt a.M.: Insel, 1996)

Zak, Eduard, *Der Dichter Peter Huchel* (Berlin: Neues Leben, 1953)

Index